Readings in the Theory of Economic

**Blackwell Readings for Contemporary Economics**

This series presents collections of writings by some of the world's foremost economists on core issues in the discipline. Each volume dovetails with a variety of existing economics courses at the advanced undergraduate, graduate, and MBA levels. The readings, gleaned from a wide variety of classic and contemporary sources, are placed in context by a comprehensive introduction from the editor. In addition, a thorough index facilitates research.

*Readings in Urban Economics: Issues and Public Policy* edited by Robert W. Wassmer
*Readings in Industrial Organization* edited by Luís M. B. Cabral
*Readings in Applied Microeconomic Theory: Market Forces and Solutions* edited by Robert E. Kuenne
*Readings in Social Welfare: Theory and Policy* edited by Robert E. Kuenne
*Readings in the Theory of Economic Development* edited by Dilip Mookherjee and Debraj Ray
*Readings in Games and Information* edited by Eric Rasmusen

# Readings in the Theory of Economic Development

Edited by

**Dilip Mookherjee,** *Boston University*

and

**Debraj Ray,** *New York University*

Copyright © Blackwell Publishers Ltd 2001
Editorial matter and organization copyright © Dilip Mookherjee and Debraj Ray 2001

First published 2001

2 4 6 8 10 9 7 5 3 1

Blackwell Publishers Inc.
350 Main Street
Malden, Massachusetts 02148
USA

Blackwell Publishers Ltd
108 Cowley Road
Oxford OX4 1JF
UK

*Library of Congress Cataloging-in-Publication Data*

Readings in the theory of economic development/edited by Dilip Mookherjee and Debraj Ray.
     p. cm.—(Blackwell readings for contemporary economics)
    Includes bibliographical references and index.
    ISBN 0–631–22005–4 (hc : alk. paper)—ISBN 0–631–22006–2 (pb : alk. paper)
    1. Economic development.   I. Mookherjee, Dilip.   II. Ray, Debraj.   III. Series.
HD75   .R423 2000
338.9—dc21
                                      00–030468

*British Library Cataloguing in Publication Data*
A CIP catalogue record for this book is available from the British Library.

Typeset in 10/11.5 pt Ehrhardt
by Kolam Information Services Pvt Ltd., Pondicherry, India
Printed in Great Britain by TJ International, Padstow, Cornwall
This book is printed on acid-free paper.

# Contents

# Acknowledgments

Acemoglu, D. and Zilibotti, F. (1997): "Was Prometheus Unbound by Chance? Risk, Diversification, and Growth," *Journal of Political Economy*, 105 (4), 709–51.

Adserà, A., and Ray, D. (1998): "History and Coordination Failure," *Journal of Economic Growth*, 3, 267–76.

Banerjee, A. and Newman, A. (1993): "Occupational Choice and the Process of Development," *Journal of Political Economy*, 101 (2), 274–98.

Besley, T., Coate, S. and Loury, G. (1993): "The Economics of Rotating Savings and Credit Associations," *American Economic Review*, 83, 792–810.

Braverman, A. and Stiglitz, J. (1982): "Sharecropping and the Interlinking of Agrarian Markets," *American Economic Review*, 72, 695–715.

Coate, S. and Ravallion, M. (1993): "Reciprocity without Commitment: Characterization and Performance of Informal Insurance Arrangements," *Journal of Development Economics*, 40, 1–24.

Dasgupta, P. and Ray, D. (1986): "Inequality as a Determinant of Malnutrition and Unemployment: Policy," *Economic Journal*, 96, December, 1011–34.

Dasgupta, P. and Ray, D. (1987): "Inequality as a Determinant of Malnutrition and Unemployment: Theory," *Economic Journal*, 97, March, 177–88.

Eswaran, M. and Kotwal, A. (1985): "A Theory of Two-Tier Labour Markets in Agrarian Economies," *American Economic Review*, 75, 162–77.

Eswaran, M. and Kotwal, A. (1986): "Access to Capital and Agrarian Production Organisation," *Economic Journal*, 96, 482–98.

Foster, A. and Rosenzweig, M. (1995): "Learning by Doing and Learning from Others: Human Capital and Technical Change in Agriculture," *Journal of Political Economy*, 103 (6), 1176–209.

Galor, O. and Zeira, J. (1993): "Income Distribution and Macroeconomics," *Review of Economic Studies*, 60, 35–52.

Ghatak, M. and Guinnane, T. (1999): "The Economics of Lending with Joint Liability: Theory and Practice," *Journal of Development Economics*, 60, 1–34.

Ljungqvist, L. (1993): "Economic Underdevelopment: The Case of a Missing Market for Human Capital," *Journal of Development Economics*, 40, 219–39

Mookherjee, D. (1997): "Informational Rents and Property Rights in Land," in J. Roemer (ed.), *Property Relations, Incentives and Welfare*, London: Macmillan Press and St Martin's Press, 3–42.

Murphy, K., Shleifer, A. and Vishny, R. (1989): "Industrialization and the Big Push," *Journal of Political Economy*, 97, 1003–26.

Romer, P. (1986): "Increasing Returns and Long-Run Growth," *Journal of Political Economy*, 92, 1002–37.

# Introduction

## 1. Introduction

The purpose of this reader is to provide an introduction to new ways of thinking about the problem of economic development. The emphasis throughout is on economic *theory*, a selective sort of theory which we feel will define and shape the conceptual landscape of development research for some years to come.

While the readings speak for themselves, we felt the need to knit them together and thereby expound a consistent thread of research themes, hoping this will benefit both the interested scholar seeking an entry into development economics, as well as the teacher planning a course outline in the subject.

The volume is divided into two parts. The first is devoted to broader conceptual themes in development economics, and economy-wide perspectives on the nature of the development "problem." The second part deals with a variety of market imperfections pervasive in the developing world, and informal institutions that arise to fill the resulting gaps. The readings selected represent only a small sample from a burgeoning literature. They have been chosen primarily for their theoretical completeness, accessibility and clarity. While many of these papers address policy implications, they have not been selected primarily for their usefulness in policy design. This is based on our conviction that policy analysis must be preceded by an adequate understanding of the way in which an economy functions. Moreover, a satisfactory treatment of policy issues would have to give equal attention to institutional problems faced by the state or activist agencies with respect to information and incentives, a topic which deserves a separate volume in its own right.

## 2. The Development Problem: A Macro Perspective

There is one central, simple question in the study of economic development: why are some countries developed, and others less so? In other words, what accounts for the phenomenal disparities in living standards around the world? In a related vein, will developing countries eventually catch up? If not, why not? If yes, how long will it take? Does policy have an important role in the process, or can development be left to the market?

Beginning with the work of Robert Solow (1956), the dominant paradigm for several decades in the neoclassical tradition has been one of inter-country (or inter-personal) *convergence*. This fundamental model has led to an explosion of literature – largely empirical – on the subject. The basic idea is described as follows. By the law of diminishing returns to inputs, poor capital-scarce countries should exhibit higher rates of return to capital. Consequently, *assuming* that savings and fertility rates are the same across countries, per capita incomes in poor countries should grow faster, and eventually living standards in all countries must converge. Reversing the argument: if disparities between rich and poor countries persist over time, it must be because other things, such as savings and population growth rates, are not equal.

This hypothesis, it should be noted, does not postulate the refutable – and empirically refuted? – view that per capita incomes *do* converge. It allows for persistent differences, but then the cause of such differences are laid at the door of "fundamental" or "exogenous" variation across countries. In these respects, the neoclassical approach is similar to the more classical view of W. Arthur Lewis (1954). Both stress factors promoting convergence, as well as the role of key parameters in affecting the speed of development. These parameters range from variables that no one would question are endogenous in some deeper analysis, such as fertility and savings rates, through variables that some genuinely believe are exogenous to economic discourse, such as corruption, traditions, and incompetent government, and finally to less disputed (but, alas, a small number of) fundamental variables, such as geography or climate. In short, by truncating our willingness to go further, this sort of analysis has two important implications:

First, it appears to suggest that societies are somehow basically different, for instance with regard to underlying attitudes, preferences or culture, and these account for their differences in economic development. For instance, some may believe that Confucianism or the Protestant ethic breeds economic success. Or it may be argued that the feudal *zamindari* system in West Bengal was inimical to the development of entrepreneurship. Other more naive approaches may blandly assert that overpopulation and endemic corruption are at the heart of the development problem. These views may or may not be correct in some sense, but the way in which they are phrased suggests a comfortable distinction between our notions of what is exogenous and what is endogenous, a distinction that the papers in this volume are less willing to make.

Second, this approach also generates a particular set of attitudes towards economic *policy*. By stressing the role of factors such as savings, population growth or levels of corruption that might actually be symptoms rather than causes of underdevelopment, they direct policy concerns in superficial and often wrong directions, missing deeper sources of the problem. If these factors are truly endogenous variables – the *result* of underdevelopment rather than its cause – they are unlikely to be prone to manipulation by simpleminded policy tinkering. And even if the policies are effective, such approaches can lead to misjudgment on the required duration of necessary interventions. For instance, if it is truly Hindu fatalism that keeps Indian savings rates low, a policy of encouraging savings (say, through tax breaks) will certainly have an effect on growth rates. But the tax breaks would have to be offered indefinitely to preserve their effect. In contrast, an interactive approach to the savings–growth problem may suggest permanent effects of one-time interventions, an issue we shall return to below in more detail.

The papers included in the first part of this reader take a different approach. Briefly, one might interpret this literature as implicitly arguing – or at least taking as its working basis – that there are *no* fundamental differences across people of different societies. One can draw a line arbitrarily down through the middle of some country and endow the two parts with different initial conditions, captured perhaps by the initial state of their economic systems. The convergence hypothesis would predict that disparities in living standards in the two parts would shrink over time and eventually disappear. Alternative theories in contrast predict that the disparities would persist, absent suitable shocks or policy interventions: the very same fundamental society can be subsequently locked into very different, self-reinforcing modes of behavior. Initial historical legacies – by pinning down expectations or some other, more concrete variable, such as the distribution of assets – can precipitate one or more of these self-reinforcing outcomes. Yet, happily, the bifurcation process can be reversed: the gaps in standard of living between the two parts of the formerly same country might eventually vanish if the disparities in the economic systems are removed, perhaps by means of a one-time policy. A variety of such theories emphasizing the role of history are included in this section.

It will be useful to distinguish between two forms of *self-reinforcing equilibria*. The first is based on the existence of a particular type of externality known as a *complementarity*. That is, it is possible to order the actions spaces of all the agents in a way so that a movement up the "action order" for some agents induces other agents to move up *their* action orders. Complementarities frequently (though not always) manifest themselves in coordination failure: situations in which the interactions across agents may lock them into inefficient action configurations, while at the same time there are other action configurations that are also self-justifying, but do better for all concerned. Put another way, there are multiple equilibria (associated with differing levels of development) that are driven by alternative degrees of optimism or pessimism. The equilibria, in turn "justify" these beliefs. Beliefs that a "bad" outcome will occur do come true, in the sense that such beliefs precipitate the bad outcome. Such beliefs may exhibit enormous inertia; hence we use the term *inertial self-reinforcement* to describe this outcome.

The second form of self-reinforcement arises from the possibility that historically given initial conditions can persistently influence current outcomes, thereby reinforcing historical legacies. Notice that given a particular past experience, the subsequent evolution of the economy may be uniquely defined; hence this approach is not necessarily based on the phenomenon of multiple equilibria. We use the term *historical self-reinforcement* to describe this phenomenon.[1]

The papers in the first part of this reader fit conveniently under these two categories.

## 2.1. Inertial self-reinforcement

Writing in 1943, Paul Rosenstein-Rodan argued that economic development could be thought of as a massive *coordination failure*, in which several investments do not occur simply because other complementary investments are not made, and these latter investments are not forthcoming simply because the former are missing. Thus one might conceive of two equilibria *under the very same fundamental conditions*, one in which active investment is taking place, with each industry's efforts motivated and justified by the expansion of other industries, and another equilibrium involving persistent stagnation, in which the inactivity of one industry seeps into another. This serves as a potential explanation of why similar economies may behave very differently, depending on the nature of beliefs held by agents in different sectors concerning the actions of each other.

It should be obvious that, for this sort of situation to arise, there must be interactive effects or *externalities* across industries. Broadly speaking, these externalities can take two forms. First, two industries could be *linked*, in the sense that the expansion of one may provoke a greater demand for the product of the other (a demand link), or facilititate the production of the second industry (a supply link). These links receive particular emphasis in the work of Albert Hirschman (1958), in an old debate on "balanced" versus "unbalanced" growth, and in the related concept of leading sectors. Unfortunately, there has been little serious formalization of this all-important theme.

The second form that externalities might take is more indirect. Industries generate income, and income generates demand for other industries. Because no individual firm internalizes these effects, a coordination failure, reinforced by pessimistic expectations, may generate a low level of economic activity. As Henry Ford wrote in his autobiography, higher wages paid by firms will actually be good for those firms in the long run, because the income returns in the form of greater demand. (But that does not mean, of course, that a *particular* firm will unilaterally raise its wages to please Henry Ford and the other firms in the economy.)

The argument, then, is that an enhanced level of economic activity generates greater national income, and the generation of national income may create additional demand to justify that activity. As Scitovsky (1954) later clarified, these externalities are "pecuniary" rather than "technological" and are inconsistent with the traditional Arrow–Debreu paradigm of a complete set of perfectly competitive markets. A full set of forward, contingent markets would enable these interdependencies to be mediated through the price mechanism, eliminating the possibility of multiple Pareto-ordered equilibria. So these pecuniary externalities are particularly pervasive in early stages of development, when well-developed financial markets are yet to emerge. This phenemomenon is formalized in the reading by Acemoglu and Zilibotti (chapter 7, this volume) discussed further below.

These broad pecuniary externalities need not work through demand alone. Suppose that the expansion of some sectors contributes to the generation of a skilled, reliable, educated workforce. Then the supply of a labor pool of high quality will stimulate the development of other industries. Alternatively, they may stimulate the development of infrastructure such as transport, power and communication which foster the development of other industries previously stymied by the absence of such infrastructure. These are general externalities that work by facilitating production, not by raising the demand for products. Since they involve the development of a range of nontraded services, they cannot be circumvented via international trade.

Our first reading (Murphy, Shleifer and Vishny, chapter 1, this volume) presents a simple, coherent formalization of this broader externality in a general equilibrium setting. In this paper, the authors go through a succession of models that attempt to capture "indirect externalities" across firms and industries. There are two aspects of this paper that governed its choice for inclusion in this volume, both of which merit explicit attention. First, the paper is noteworthy for its systematic theoretical exploration of the Rosenstein-Rodan hypothesis. The pecuniary externalities arise from the lack of perfect competition inherent in the economies of scale and indivisibilities associated with infrastructural service. While the models are highly stylized and simplistic, they are consciously so, and allow us to see the coordination failure in particularly stark form.

Second, the paper shows that not all forms of income generation lead to the possibility of a coordination failure. For instance, income generation in the form of additional *profits* means higher demand for the products of other firms. Moreover, this is an externality that the profit-creating firm cares nothing about. Nevertheless, this externality cannot precipitate a coordination failure. The reason is that the externality does not distort a firm's *actions* away from the socially desirable level – as long as marginal profits are positive, output will indeed be expanded, and that is all that is needed to avoid the coordination failure. But this is not true of other forms of income, such as additional wage income. Not only does this create an externality, it also distorts actions away from the social optimum – a firm will not take actions to maximize the wage income it generates.

The Murphy–Shleifer–Vishny formulation is echoed in several other papers of independent interest. Notable among them are Rodríguez-Clare (1996) and Ciccone and Matsuyama (1996) (see also the special issue of the *Journal of Development Economics* in which these last two papers appear).

Inertial self-reinforcement can appear even in dynamic models of economic growth, as our next reading illustrates. To be sure, the concept must now be restated in terms of *growth paths*. It is the multiplicity of such paths that signal the possibility of self-reinforcement driven by pessimistic expectations. The reading we chose to illustrate this, Romer (chapter 2, this volume), is a classic in its own right. The source of the externality in Romer's model is the assumption that all the social benefits of economic knowhow cannot, in general, be expropriated by the creator(s) of that knowhow. The circle is completed by observing that one possible impact of expanded knowledge is a greater incentive to invest in knowledge-creation. This leads to the possibility of multiple equilibrium. As Romer writes, " . . . the private response to an aggregate increase in the stock of knowledge will be to reinforce its effects rather than to dampen them. Since the rate of growth of the stock of knowledge is increasing in the level, this kind of disturbance causes the stock of knowledge to be larger at all future dates. Thus small current or anticipated future differences can potentially have large, permanent, aggregate effects."

Simple exercises based on the Romer paper allow us to take the idea of self-reinforcement beyond one just based on expectational inertia. For instance, while it is true that there may be multiple equilibria from some initial stocks in the Romer model, it is also true that that the *set* of possible equilibria also vary from stock to stock, and that this variation may persist into the indefinite future. For instance, it is possible to check (under some conditions) that "high enough" initial stocks of knowledge *must* be associated with subsequent growth (though a variety of such paths may coexist, as already discussed). But the same is not true of "low enough" initial stocks – there may be some paths emanating from these that grow, and others that stagnate. For even lower stocks, it is possible that growth paths do not exist at all. There is an interplay here between history and expectations, a theme that we now turn to.

## 2.2. What creates the inertia of expectations?

A fundamental issue associated with inertial self-reinforcement concerns the use of the word "inertia". This has to do with the fact that at any given moment of time, a *particular* equilibrium is in force, and has possibly been in force in that society in the medium- or long-run past. What causes the past to stick? How is a particular equilibrium pinned down by the force of historical inertia and what will it take to unpin it?

Unfortunately, the multiple equilibrium or coordination-game paradigm is not of much use in this regard beyond the demonstration that multiplicities may exist. In some sense, it avoids altogether any answer to the question: why is one society less developed than another, and what can be done about it? For this would require a theory of where the pessimistic beliefs originally came from, or how they could be manipulated by policy interventions. The paradigm is also at a loss for *explaining* historical inertia: repeat a multiple equilibrium story and numerous dynamic equilibria emerge, including those in which the society jumps between the bad and good equilibria in all sorts of deftly coordinated ways. We lack good economic theory that actually identifies the "stickiness" of equilibria. Rosenstein-Rodan and Hirschman were certainly concerned with this issue in a very central way though they did not make much serious progress on it.

A small literature – too small, in our opinion – exists on this topic (see, for instance, Krugman (1991), Matsuyama (1991), and Adserà and Ray (chapter 3, this volume)). There is also a corresponding smattering of literature among macroeconomists studying business-cycle models based on coordination failure (see, e.g., Chamley and Gale (1994) and Cooper (1999)). We have chosen the Adserà-Ray paper for its clear exposition of the basic problem. The paper embeds a coordination game into a real-time model of "intersectoral choice" (the choices corresponding to the actions of the static coordination game). Now agents may switch sectors (more than once, if they so desire), and their returns are added over time, by applying a discount factor. The objective of the paper is to give meaning to the notion of inertia, to the idea that historical predominance of a "sector" might impede the development of a Pareto-superior "sector." The main result is that, if externalities manifest themselves with a lag (which may be arbitrarily small), and if there are no congestion costs in intersectoral migration, then initial conditions *do* pin down equilibria – there is inertia. The paper suggests a research program in which the study of lagged externalities may be fruitful, as also the study of moving costs (a topic given more emphasis in the Krugman and Matsuyama papers).

## 2.3. Historical self-reinforcement: The inequality-development interaction

Inertial self-reinforcement is a story of *multiple equilibrium*, and therefore directs our attention to the beliefs or expectations of the economic agents which shore up one or another of the equilibria. In particular, one might ask – and we do ask this above – how the formation of such expectations may be significantly conditioned by history.

This view of underdevelopment may be usefully complemented by a related, though distinct approach. This is the observation that historical legacies may actually select among *different sets* of equilibria (quite apart from the possible multiplicities in each set). In short, past history may echo persistently into the future, and not just via the determination of expectations.

We have already seen how this works in the Romer model. The same sort of historical pressure may be exerted by factors as diverse as legal structure, traditions, or group reputations; see, for example, the review in Ray (1998) or Hoff and Stiglitz (1999). But of all these, perhaps the darkest shadow is cast by initial inequalities in the distribution of asset ownership. With imperfect capital markets, the poor are limited in their access to credit necessary for production and investment. Hence, increased inequality can exert negative effects on both levels and growth rates of per capita income. High initial inequalities may also create conditions for self-perpetuation, generating a lock-in effect with economic stagnation. The very same fundamental economy would perform differently were initial inequality to be altered.

The three readings that we have chosen emphasize various aspects of this connection between inequality and development. These are the papers by Galor and Zeira (chapter 4, this volume), Banerjee and Newman (chapter 5, this volume), and Ljungqvist (chapter 6, this volume). For related literature, see, for example Aghion and Bolton (1997), Banerjee and Newman (1991), Bowles and Gintis (1994, 1995), Dasgupta and Ray (1986, 1987, reprinted as chapter 9, in this volume), Hoff (1994), Hoff and Lyon (1995), Legros and Newman (1996), Mookherjee (chapter 13, this volume), Piketty (1997), and Ray and Streufert (1993).

The Galor–Zeira model shows how the convergence prediction of the neoclassical growth model can be overturned by dropping the assumptions of a convex technology and perfect capital markets. With setup costs in the acquisition of certain occupations or skills, and borrowing constraints for poor agents, the initial distribution of wealth will influence the aggregate skill composition of the economy and total output, resulting in self-reinforcement. Poor families will not find it worthwhile to invest in the education of their children, locking their descendants into a poverty trap. High initial inequalities thus tend to perpetuate themselves. Moreover, countries with a historically higher poverty rate will have a persistently lower per capita income.

Capital market imperfections alone would not generate this result. The question of the interconnection between credit market imperfections and the dynamics of inequality was earlier explored by Loury (1981) in a pioneering paper. He assumed that the technology was convex, and showed that the convergence occurs nonetheless, despite the complete absence of capital markets. The nonconvex technology in the Galor–Zeira model is therefore essential to their result concerning the persistence of inequality and under-development. If, for instance, skills could be upgraded gradually and continuously across successive generations, the poverty traps would disappear in the long run, even if capital markets were entirely missing.

The simple demonstration of possible lock-ins to underdevelopment and poverty in the simple version of the Galor–Zeira model can be subjected to further criticism. Even in the presence of indivisibilities in investment, substantial stochastic perturbations might restore ergodicity, by simply permitting different wealth levels to communicate (though possibly with very small probability). For instance, in the presence of random elements reflecting luck, a poor family may tip over the required threshold and join the ranks of the prosperous, just as wealthy families may encounter a string of failures and temporarily drift into poverty.

A rebuttal to this criticism would argue that under the conditions of the Galor–Zeira model, those in poverty would remain locked there for a long period of time; the problem would be manifested instead by a low degree of wealth mobility. In part, this is a signal that ergodicity (and convergence, more generally) is itself a problematic concept, a topic that we return to below. But in part, it points to a second inadequacy of these simple models, which is that they are not interactive across agents. The economy is just several copies of isolated agents (or families) running in parallel. Then, inequality has no aggregate effects that are not simply trivial sums of individual effects. The model misses the interdependence in the evolution of fortunes of different families in a given society, which may strengthen the tendency towards lock-in.

More specifically, the "isolationist" model has an important implication. Historical self-reinforcement in such a model can only be the outcome of a lack of *individual* mobility (as might be the case with individual nonconvexities). If individual mobility is present (as it is, for instance in the convex case or even in the nonconvex case with sufficient stochastic variation), the final outcome is ergodic in a macroeconomic sense as well.

In contrast, the more complicated interactive models – such as those in the later part of the Galor–Zeira paper, and more fully explored in chapters 5 and 6 by Banerjee and Newman, and Ljungqvist respectively – shows that there need be no contradiction between individual mobility and aggregate hysteresis. With interdependent evolution of the wealth of different families, there are numerous additional sources of historical lock-in.

The wide range of forms of interdependence can be illustrated in the following simple overlapping generations model, which also serves to explain the connection between the seemingly different models analysed in the three readings.[2] Let $H$ be some list of *occupations*, over which a population of unit size is distributed at any date $t$. The date $t$ is to be interpreted as the lifetime of the generation alive at $t$.

For each $\lambda$, $\lambda'$, to be interpreted as occupational distributions (of successive generations), a wage function $w = \{w(h)\}_{h \in H}$ is defined on $H$. These define the incomes earned by different occupations.

A wage function $w$ on $H$ in turn helps to determine a cost function $x = \{x(h)\}_{h \in H}$ defined on $H$. This can be interpreted as the cost, payable in the current date, of acquiring skills necessary for occupation $h$ for members of the next generation.

Thus given a sequence $\{\lambda_t\}_{t=0}^{\infty}$ of occupational distributions on $H$, we obtain a sequence $\{w_t, x_t\}_{t=0}^{\infty}$ of wage and cost functions defined on $H$, where each wage function $w_t$ depends on the neighboring occupational distributions $(\lambda_t, \lambda_{t+1})$, and each cost function $x_t$ is determined in turn by this wage function. We can then say that $\{w_t, x_t\}_{t=0}^{\infty}$ is *generated* by $\{\lambda_t\}_{t=0}^{\infty}$.

Individuals only foresee the wage-cost sequence (the actual generation of this sequence is of little import to them). They care about their own income, and those of their descendants. For an individual $i$ (or current representative of family $i$) with $h_0(i)$ given, the problem is to maximize

$$\sum_{t=0}^{\infty} \beta^t u(c_t)$$

subject to the constraints

$$y_t = w_t(h_t)$$

and

$$y_t = c_t + x_t(h_{t+1})$$

for all $t$. Similar to Loury (1981), this formulation presumes that parents care about the utility (rather than just the consumption or income levels) of their descendants in a consistent fashion, so bequests or educational investments in children will be nonpaternalistic, thus removing one potential source of market imperfection. However, capital markets are missing: investments must be financed entirely from current income. The maximization problem above will result in a sequence of occupational choices made by successive generations, which we may denote by $\{h_t(i)\}_{t=0}^{\infty}$ for each family $i$.

Aggregate these occupational choices across families by defining, for each $t$ (where $\mu$ denotes the corresponding fraction of the population)

$$\lambda_t(h) \equiv \mu\{i : h_t(i) = h\}$$

(Of course, the distribution $\lambda_0$ is exogenously given.) This generates a sequence of occupational distributions: say that $\{\lambda_t\}_{t=0}^{\infty}$ is an *aggregate response* to $\{w_t, x_t\}_{t=0}^{\infty}$ (for given $\lambda_0$).

An *equilibrium* (given the historical distribution $\lambda_0$) is a sequence of succeeding occupational distributions, income and cost profiles $\{\lambda_t, w_t, x_t\}_{t=0}^{\infty}$ such that

(a) $\{w_t, x_t\}_{t=0}^{\infty}$ is generated by $\{\lambda_t\}_{t=0}^{\infty}$, and
(b) $\{\lambda_t\}_{t=0}^{\infty}$ is an aggregate response to $\{w_t, x_t\}_{t=0}^{\infty}$.

In such an equilibrium, all families have perfect foresight concerning the future evolution of the economy and the returns to different occupations; their optimal responses in turn justify their beliefs.

It is possible to embed several well-known models – as well as the readings included in this volume – within this framework. Consider four examples: models of noninteracting agents, entrepreneurship, demand effects and labor skills.

MODELS OF NONINTERACTING AGENTS  $H$ is the set of all capital stocks, $w(h)$ is *independent* of the occupational distribution, and equals some production function $f(h)$ while $x(h) = h$. This is the framework (with uncertainty added) studied in Loury (1981), under the assumption that $f$ is a "standard" concave production function. Alternatively, one might interpret $H$ as some discrete set of skills. This is the first model studied by Galor–Zeira (chapter 4, this volume) (they also use a simpler paternalistic "warm-glow" formulation of the bequest motive).

ENTREPRENEURSHIP  $H = \{1, 2\}$ where 1 stands for worker and 2 stands for employer. $x(h)$, the cost function, is independent of the wage function: it is 0 if $h = 1$, and is $S$, a setup cost for entrepreneurship, if $h = 2$. To determine the wage function, suppose that there is a production function $F$ defined on the amount of employed labor. Each entrepreneur chooses $L$ to maximize

$$F(L) - w(1)L$$

where $w(1)$ is the wage rate for labor. In equilibrium, $L$ is just the employment per capitalist, which is $\lambda(2)/\lambda(1)$. So $w(1)$ is given by

$$F'\left(\frac{\lambda(2)}{\lambda(1)}\right) = w(1)$$

while $w(2)$ is the resulting profit:

$$w(2) = F\left(\frac{\lambda(2)}{\lambda(1)}\right) - F'\left(\frac{\lambda(2)}{\lambda(1)}\right)\frac{\lambda(2)}{\lambda(1)}$$

This is essentially the Banerjee and Newman (chapter 5) model. Like Galor and Zeira, they employ a warm-glow model of bequests, and assume a fundamental indivisibility in the occupational structure (i.e., there are two discretely different occupations). The evolution of wealth and of occupational decisions is, however, fundamentally interdependent across different families. The resulting dynamics are complicated. Banerjee and Newman manage to describe the nature of this dynamic in a number of special cases, and show how distinct occupational structures and related production systems (such as the factory system rather than independent cottage production) may evolve in the long run, depending on historical conditions.

Further developments of a related model with a divisible investment technology and random shocks were subsequently explored by Piketty (1997), who showed that the interactive nature of the wealth dynamic may still result in multiple long-run steady states from different historical conditions. In this sense, historical lock-in can persist even in the presence of wealth mobility at the level of individual families, and the presence of a convex technology.

DEMAND EFFECTS   $H$ is a finite set of commodities. A person with occupation $h$ can produce one unit of the specialized commodity $h$. Again, take $x(h)$ as independent of other variables.

Let $\mathbf{p} = \{p(h)\}_{h\in H}$ be a *price vector* on $H$. Given income $y$, a consumer generates a demand vector $c(\mathbf{p}, y)$ on $H$.

An equilibrium price vector will equate supply and demand. But the demand by occupants of occupation $h$ is just $c(\mathbf{p}, p(h))\lambda(h)$, so that equilibrium prices must be given by the solution to the system

$$\sum_{h\in H} c(\mathbf{p}, p(h))\lambda(h) = \lambda$$

By constant returns to scale, $p(h) = w(h)$ for all $h$. A model of this kind is studied by Mani (1998).

LABOR SKILLS This is the approach followed in chapter 6 by Ljungqvist. $H = \{1, 2\}$ where 1 stands for unskilled worker and 2 stands for skilled worker. The production function $F(a_1, a_2)$ defines output produced by $a_1$ and $a_2$ units of unskilled and skilled labor respectively. This determines the wage pattern:

$$w(h) = F_h(a(1), a(2))$$

for $h = 1, 2$. The function $x(h)$ defining the cost of training for different occupations in turn depends on the wage function: it is 0 if $h = 1$, and is $\alpha w(2)$ if $h = 2$. The idea is that, to acquire skill, a worker needs to be trained by $\alpha$ units of currently skilled workers, who need to be paid their opportunity cost of not working in the production sector and earning the wage $w(2)$. Skilled workers in the economy thus divide themselves between the production and training sectors, depending on the demand in the two sectors. Unskilled workers work only in the production sector. In equilibrium, the occupational distributions at successive dates will determine the allocation of skilled workers in the following manner. Let $\lambda$ and $\lambda'$ denote the occupational distributions for succeeding generations. Then, notice that

$$a(1) = \lambda(1)$$

while

$$a(2) = \lambda(2) - \alpha\lambda'(2)$$

so that the wage function is ultimately related to the successive occupational distributions:

$$w(h) = F_h(\lambda(1), \lambda(2) - \alpha\lambda'(2))$$

for $h = 1, 2$.

It is precisely the dependence of the wage and training cost functions on the occupational distribution that generates new insights. For instance, even if there is *perfect equality* to start with, the subsequent evolution of inequality is inevitable. To illustrate this, suppose all individuals in a particular generation have equal wealth. Is it possible for all of them to make the same *choices*? The answer is, in general, no. If all of them choose to leave their descendants unskilled, then the return to skilled labor will become enormously high, encouraging some fraction of the population to educate their children. Similarly, it is not possible for all parents to educate their children, if unskilled labor is also necessary in production. Thus identical agents are forced to take nonidentical actions, precisely because of the interpendence of decisions made by different families. This means, of course, that, in the *next* generation, some inequality must emerge. This is why all steady states in the Ljungqvist model involve inequality.

This inequality, in turn, leads to a lack of efficiency. Individuals cannot simply compensate for their unequal positions by taking recourse to a credit market. In the models studied here, there is no credit market; or if there is one, it is imperfect. It is this imperfection that underlies the inefficiency of inequality. Individuals with low wealth may be unable to take advantage of profitable opportunities open to them, be these in the form of skill acquisition, certain occupational advantages, or remunerative investment opportunities.

Moreover, as we have already noted, inequality fundamentally affects the working of equilibrium prices – broadly defined – and, in so doing, it affects the dynamic fate of individuals in a way that cannot be disentangled by simple stochastic perturbations of individual outcomes. Banerjee–Newman (chapter 5, this volume) make it clear that a multiplicity of unequal distributions may all be self-reinforcing. One must be careful not to interpret these as "multiple equilibria" – *given* the historical circumstances each economy follows a unique path. And the seeming quibble is important: with multiple equilibria, economic policy must overcome expectational inertia. The policy implications here are quite different: the intervention will require, in general, a change in the distribution of asset ownership, and a one-time intervention can have effects that last into the indefinite future.

## *2.4. Self-reinforcement as slow convergence*

There is a third view on convergence that we have referred to so far only in passing. It is a viewpoint that has not received as much attention in the literature as it deserves. Consider, again, the stochastic version of the neoclassical growth model. It predicts convergence, to be sure, but how "soon" is the long-run? Why do ergodic distributions receive so much attention, if they do not matter to the relevant future of current generations?

One answer to this question is based on considerations of tractability: we don't know how to usefully analyze "non-steady state" behavior. It should be noted that this is even more true of the new generation of models discussed above than of the neoclassical growth models, where some form of nonsteady state analysis, such as turnpike theory, has traditionally been carried out. But, even in the earlier literature, the analysis raises a relatively limited set of questions, concerning eventual convergence to a steady state, and the speed of such convergence.

The Acemoglu–Zilibotti paper (chapter 7) has been chosen because it does not display this preoccupied focus on the steady state or on eventual convergence to it. The appropriate stochastic process governing economic evolution *is* ergodic in their model. They describe, instead, the arduous and difficult period that an economy can go through in the process of transition to this ergodic distribution. The example they use is the development of financial depth. An added attraction of their model is the endogenous explanation for incompleteness of the market structure of an economy, and of how this evolves in the process of development, formalizing the ideas of Scitovsky (1954) concerning the role of pecuniary externalities in the development process.

Consider a society in which there are several *potential* sectors that can be opened, though to open any one of them a scale requirement for minimum investment in that sector must be met. The Acemoglu–Zilibotti model is crafted so that the opening of an additional sector does nothing to expected returns (all sectors have the same mean return), but permits additional diversification of financial assets (because sectoral returns are only imperfectly correlated).

Now, suppose that individual savings are divided among the (risky) securities floated on the basis of investment in the productive sectors, and some safe sector (such as storage). The supply of savings to the risky financial sector depends, then, on two factors: the income of the savers, which raises savings, and the allocation of savings between the safe and risky sectors.

Begin with the very short run, in which income is given. Then, it is easy to see that savings will be low, so that the economy will only be able to sustain a relatively small number of open financial sectors. This limitation comes from the minimum scale requirements for each sector. Consequently, diversification is limited, so that a poor economy is capable of enormous variability in its income process.

Two factors might exacerbate this situation. First, *given* the number of open sectors, an individual investor will be interested in spreading his risky portfolio evenly over these sectors. But this evenness, in the aggregate, may prevent some sectors from opening up if different sectors have different scale requirements. No individual – indeed, no financial subcoalition – internalizes the externality created from opening a new sector. Second – and somewhat less interesting in the sense that we have already discussed several examples earlier – the depth of the risky financial sectors may be a self-reinforcing variable in the following sense. A larger number of open sectors creates greater diversification and pulls savings away from the safe asset. The greater supply of savings may then "justify" the larger number of open sectors. These pecuniary externalities can conceivably provide a rationale for interventionist policies.

What Acemoglu–Zilibotti (chapter 7, this volume) bring out with particular power, however, is the observation that poor societies may languish in their state of poverty for an inordinately long period of time before finally receiving a series of lucky draws that pulls them into the limiting distribution. This is because poor societies generate low levels of savings, and low levels of savings make for limited diversification. It is therefore possible – perhaps even likely – that poor societies will be often faced with calamitous outcomes in which very low incomes are generated, while these outcomes reinforce, in turn, the likelihood of a similar calamity being repeated in the next period. To be sure, sooner or later, there will be a string of lucky successes, which will create high incomes. The resulting high savings will then create a self-reinforcing move towards greater diversification, insulating the society from low income shocks in the future.

Notice that *ultimately*, all societies converge. But that convergence may be a long time coming, and is not half as interesting as the lingering, self-reinforcing phase that precedes the diversification-based jump to maturity. This is why we find chapter 7 an excellent example of "self-reinforcement as slow convergence," and offer it to our readers in the hope of provoking greater interest in the subject.

## 3. Market Incompleteness and Informal Institutions: A Micro Perspective

We turn now to a more fine-grained analysis of market imperfections in developing countries, and the nature of informal institutions that arise to fill the resulting gaps. While many of the macroeconomic models described in the preceding section rely on some of these imperfections, particularly in the credit market, they do not adequately address where these imperfections stem from. The literature in this area has witnessed a remarkable explosion in the last two decades, drawing on advances in game theory and the economics of information. The chief contribution of this literature is to explain the source of distinctive institutional characteristics of the informal economy in developing countries extensively documented by empirical economists, sociologists and anthropologists:

(a)   Fragmented labor and credit markets, e.g., large variations in wages and interest rates within a narrow geographic region, despite the presence of competition

(b)   Persistent lack of market clearing, such as unemployment or credit rationing, despite absence of any regulations that prevent prices from adjusting flexibly

(c)   Pervasiveness of long-term contracts between borrowers and lenders, employers and employees, or farmers and traders

(d)   Coexistence of diverse contractual forms, e.g., tenancy contracts, some of which involve fixed rents and others sharecropping

(e)   Unequal treatment of observationally similar workers or borrowers, e.g., dual labor markets in which some workers enter into long-term contracts while others are employed to carry out similar tasks on a casual basis at substantially lower wages

(f)   Interlinked transactions and exclusive dealing between specific agent pairs across multiple markets, such as bundling of credit with tenancy, employment or marketing contracts

(g)   Importance of asset ownership in access to credit, tenancy or employment markets, e.g., limited access of the poor to credit owing to lack of collateral, to tenancy owing to higher risks of rent default, and to employment owing to malnutrition and absence of human capital

(h)   Higher yields achieved by small farms *vis-à-vis* large farms, despite superior access of the latter to credit and technology

(i)   Thinness of certain markets, such as the market for land sales, causing persistence of tenancy and unequal landownership distributions despite the superior productivity of small family farms

(j)   Importance of informal cooperatives and kinship networks in determining access to essential productive inputs such as credit, insurance, technological information, water and common lands

These phenomena are typically difficult to explain within the traditional neoclassical theory of a complete set of Arrow–Debreu markets. Neither are most of them consistent with textbook versions of monopoly or oligopoly. Accordingly many traditional scholars have inferred the irrelevance of neoclassical economics to the context of developing countries, and the need for alternative paradigms. The new economics of information does, however, provide a cogent explanation of many of these institutional characteristics, within the context of an analytical framework grounded on the same methodology as the traditional approach. Apart from intellectual coherence, the grounding in explicit microfoundations allows assessment of counterfactuals; of the implications of these phenomena for efficiency, equality and growth; and of the effects of policy interventions. The models also serve as a useful basis for empirical testing and measurement.

## 3.1. Implications for agrarian organization

Eswaran and Kotwal (chapter 8, this volume) discuss the implications of imperfections in credit and labor markets for the nature of agrarian organization. The principal focus is on the emergence of different "classes" within a given agrarian economy, as conventionally defined by sociologists or Marxist scholars in terms of ownership of assets such as land (the "means of production"). Chapter 8 also highlights the importance of class structure for the performance of the economy (e.g., levels of farm productivity). Specifically, the model can explain some empirical regularities (such as the inverse farm size–productivity relationship), why the poor may be restricted in their productive choices, and how inequality in landholding affects class structure and agricultural productivity.

To focus on the principal implications, Eswaran and Kotwal assume empirically plausible forms of credit and labor market imperfections. The credit market imperfection is represented by a constraint on the amount that can be borrowed by any given household to finance working capital needs, which depends on the amount of land owned by the household. The labor market imperfection is represented by the need to supervise hired workers. Households are assumed similar in all respects apart from their endowment of land: this assumption permits the effects of differences in landownership *per se* to be isolated. Competitive markets for fixed rent tenancy and of labor are also assumed, and farm cultivation is assumed to involve a (possibly small) fixed cost.

When there is an imperfection in only one market, credit or labor, all cultivating households select the same efficient farm size and land–labor ratio. The resulting allocation is efficient from the point of view of production. Poor households lease in land from richer households, and the market for hired labor is thin, as all farms are cultivated entirely by family labor. All households select the same labor effort. In this world, therefore, unequal landownership patterns have no productive implications, affecting only the distribution of income.

In the more realistic scenario with imperfections in both credit and labor markets, poor households are unable to borrow sufficiently to meet their rental payments, thus forcing inefficiently small scales of cultivation. Those with little or no land derive their livelihood from hiring out their labor services, and constitute a class of *workers*. Those owning more land can viably enter cultivation, but small landowners face a credit crunch in meeting their working capital needs. To alleviate these problems, they supplement cash inflows by hiring out their labor to other farms, and avoid hiring in any non-family labor from the market. This corresponds to a second class of *worker-cultivators*. Within this class, the richer households cultivate larger farms and hire out less labor. After a further landowner-ship threshold is reached, they cease hiring out any labor at all, devoting themselves entirely to working on their own farms. This generates the next class of *owner-cultivators*. With further increases in landownership in this class, the credit constraint is progressively eased. Labor shortage is now the overriding constraint. Families supplement family labor with hired labor, resulting in the emergence of a fourth class of *small capitalists*. Further increases in wealth will result in the household hiring in more workers and diverting its own labor away from cultivation to supervision. Eventually, a wealth level is reached when the household cultivates the farm entirely on the basis of hired workers, and devotes all its time to supervision, creating the fifth class of *large capitalists*.

Different classes are characterized by differing farm sizes, technology and productivity. Poorer households cultivate smaller farms and cultivate their lands more intensively using their own labor, resulting in high levels of productivity per acre. As households become wealthier, the stringency of credit constraints is eased, while labor shortages become endemic. The result is a progressive substitution of land for labor and adoption of less intensive methods of production, resulting in lower farm yields. A more equal distribution of land will, *ceteris paribus*, increase the average productivity in the economy, and alter the class structure: there will be fewer landless workers, more family farms, and fewer capitalist farms. To confirm these predictions, Eswaran and Kotwal carry out a number of illustrative numerical simulations of the model to illustrate the effects of land redistribution and credit interventions, incorporating attendant general equilibrium effects. In sum, the model explains the observed differences between agrarian structure of the Latin American *latifundias* based on large inequality in landholdings and large capitalist farms, with the more equal ownership patterns in Asian agriculture dominated by small family-farms.

## 3.2. *Labor market imperfections*

The readings in this section focus on imperfections in the labor market, such as involuntary unemployment and dual labor markets.

MALNUTRITION AND EFFICIENCY WAGES   Dasgupta and Ray (chapter 9, this volume) consider the phenomenon of nutrition-based *efficiency wages*, and its resulting implications for the labor market, a topic which goes back to earlier work by Leibenstein (1957), Prasad (1970), Mirrlees (1976), Stiglitz (1976) and Bliss and Stern (1978).

The phenomenon of involuntary unemployment poses a challenge for conventional economic theory. If wages are flexible in the downward direction, any excess supply ought to be eliminated by corresponding wage cuts. For instance, unemployed workers could undercut the going wage by offering to do the same work for less pay, an offer that should be accepted by profit-maximizing employers. What prevents such arbitrage? The efficiency wage theory provides one answer to this conundrum: if the productive efficiency of the worker depends on the wage, a wage cut will be accompanied by a drop in the worker's efficiency, thus rendering the arbitrage worthless to the employer.

Dasgupta and Ray embed this story into a general equilibrium setting, permitting analysis of the effects of land endowment patterns on unemployment and productivity. Assuming the existence of a mass of landless individuals, they show that the supply curve of productive "tasks" is subject to a discontinuity at the threshold piece rate at which it is just feasible for the landless to enter the labor market. Below this rate, the poor are excluded because the incomes they would earn at any given level of productive effort would be insufficient to finance the nutritional intake required to sustain that level of effort. The nature and position of the supply curve depends on the landholding distribution, while the position of the demand curve depends on the total endowment of land, the product price and the nature of the technology.

If the equilibrium involves a piece rate at or below the threshold, some or all of the landless cannot participate in the labor market, though there are others very similar who do get employed, and are strictly better off. Hence, if the demand for labor is low – owing either to a low endowment of land, or absence of technological innovations – involuntary unemployment and malnutrition results, despite the operation of perfectly competitive markets. *Laissez faire* cannot then be relied on to "solve" problems of unemployment and poverty.

Indeed, competitive markets tend to amplify the effects of unequal asset ownership: at a common piece rate a wealthier worker will be able to perform more tasks and thus earn a higher wage income. Alternatively, employers may only employ workers above a certain wealth threshold, while poorer individuals are excluded from the market. This suggests that the market mechanism can be the source of increasing disparity between *ex ante* identical workers. For instance, of two landless workers starting their working careers, one may be employed and the other unemployed while young, causing the former to accumulate greater wealth and thus be favored by employers in middle age as well, while the latter drifts into destitution.

What are the policy implications? This question is addressed by Dasgupta and Ray in the sequel to the first paper, where they show that the competitive equilibrium is Pareto efficient. So there is no scope for external interventions to improve the welfare of the poor and malnourished, without making the non-poor better off. However, if the government were to redistribute land from those that are rich enough to not want to work, to the landless or to the landed working force, the effect would be to increase total output. There are three effects of this land redistribution: a larger range of workers can now participate in the labor market; those that do participate are more productive owing to improved nutrition, and some of the "landed gentry" who were previously voluntarily unemployed may now join the labor force. The total effect is to shift the labor supply function rightward. Hence, output must increase, whereas unemployment may or may not increase. Dasgupta and Ray, however, do show that there exist economies where complete equalization of landownership must eliminate involutary unemployment and malnutrition. In such cases, inequality of landownership can be said to be the real cause of these problems. Differing asset distributions can therefore serve to explain differences in agricultural output and productivity across time or across regions.

INCENTIVE-BASED EFFICIENCY WAGES   The next reading by Eswaran and Kotwal (chapter 10, this volume) analyzes an alternative source of efficiency wages, stemming from the problem of eliciting trustworthy behavior from employees. Certain tasks in agriculture require the application of effort which is difficult to monitor. This is especially true of ploughing, planting seeds, weeding, and many household needs. Certain other tasks that are seasonal, such as harvesting, are less subject to worker moral hazard, since the product of the worker's effort (e.g., fruit plucked or crop harvested) is easily monitored. Piece rates may suffice for harvesting labor, but not for labor hired for the first category of tasks. The performance of the worker on these tasks can be ascertained by the employer only much later, perhaps at the end of the year or in future years, whereas wages have to be paid upfront. Moreover workers' performance may not be verifiable by third-party contract enforcers. For either of these reasons, wages for the first category of tasks will be independent of performance levels; accordingly trust plays a significant role.

The employer will therefore seek to employ family members or other kin for these tasks. If hired hands are employed for these tasks, they have to be induced to behave in a trustworthy fashion. This is made possible by an implicit long-term contract, which is renewed in future years only if the employer verified the employee's performance to have been satisfactory. To give the employee a stake in the continuation of the employment relationship, long-term workers have to be treated better than short-term workers hired for harvesting tasks. This implies in turn that the market for long-term contracts will be characterized by involuntary unemployment: all workers will queue up for long-term contracts but employers will typically be willing to employ a fraction of the entire labor force in long-term contracts, the remaining workers being forced into the residual short-term sector. The unemployment will not be eliminated despite wage flexibility, since wage cuts will reduce the stake of long-term workers in the subsequent continuation of the relationship, inducing them to abuse their employers' trust.

This explanation for long-term contracts is similar to earlier theories advanced by Simon (1951), Klein and Leffler (1981), Shapiro (1983) and Shapiro and Stiglitz (1984). What is of particular interest here is the explanation of coexistence of long-term and short-term workers, and how the composition of the work force shifts in response to demand and technology changes. The number of workers on long-term contracts is determined by the demand for such workers. A principal result of the model is that, under reasonable assumptions on parameter values, an increase in the supply of labor (relative to derived demand) lowers the relative wage of short-term workers, thus inducing employers to substitute long-term workers by short-term workers. Long-term workers will therefore form a minority in overpopulated countries. On the other hand, an expansion in the scale of output (resulting from growth in market demand or technological innovations) will increase the demand for labor and the relative pay of short-term workers, inducing employers to switch to permanent workers. Hence, the process of development will be accompanied by an expansion in the proportion of workers on long-term contracts. Eswaran and Kotwal cite historical accounts of such processes in Chile, Germany and Russia in the nineteenth century. As development continues, short-term workers will form a minority, though dualism can never entirely vanish in order to preserve effort incentives.[3]

## 3.3. Credit and land

The readings in this section study credit markets, interlinked contracts and land markets.

THE CREDIT MARKET    Eswaran and Kotwal (chapter 8, this volume) clarify the central role of credit market imperfections in determining the nature of agrarian organization. Yet it does not explain why such imperfections arise in the first place. Empirical studies of credit markets in developing countries frequently describe numerous institutional characteristics such as the existence of credit rationing; wide variations in access to credit and in interest rates within narrow geographical regions and between formal and informal sectors; the importance of collateral and interlinkage with transactions in tenancy, employment or marketing contracts; the prevalence of long-term exclusive credit relationships of borrowers with single lenders; the significance of screening and enforcement costs in the costs incurred by lenders; and the importance of ethnic and kinship networks in determining credit access.[4]

Many of these features can be explained by problems of asymmetric information and contract enforcement. The informational problems are typically either of two kinds: *adverse selection* – borrowers are better informed about their default risks – and *moral hazard*, wherein borrowers have to be induced to take adequate precautions to avoid defaults. Owing to these problems, access to credit may have to be limited. For instance, the credit rationing theory of Stiglitz and Weiss (1981) is based on adverse selection: higher interest rates cause low-risk borrowers to drop out of the applicant pool. Competitive equilibrium can then be consistent with credit rationing: only a fraction of loan applicants actually receive loans. Lenders do not react to the excess demand for loans by raising the interest rate because of the adverse selection effect.

This theory has been subjected to numerous criticisms; see, for instance, Bester (1985) and Riley (1987). It can be argued (as Bester does) that the rationing stems from restrictions on the instruments available to lenders to screen borrowers of differing risks. One such instrument is collateral: with interest rates conditioned on collateral posted by borrowers, high-risk borrowers would self-select into high-interest-rate–low-collateral loans, while low-risk borrowers would opt for low-interest-rate–high-collateral loans. This separation would free up interest rates to clear the market and eliminate credit rationing. The adverse selection theory has also been frequently criticized as implausible in the context of traditional close-knit agrarian societies where lenders are well informed about the characteristics of potential borrowers.

Several recent studies have relied instead on the moral hazard of credit markets. As far as informal credit markets are concerned, one might distinguish between two aspects of the moral hazard problem. First – because of limited liability on the part of the borrower – loan repayment may be conditional on the realization of particular outcomes, such as the success of the project or (more generally) the solvency of the borrower. Moreover, the probability of occurrence of such outcomes may be influenced by borrower effort. This creates the well-known problem of debt overhang; see, for example, Aghion and Bolton (1997), Piketty (1997), and Mookherjee (chapter 13, this volume).

Second, the contract itself may not be honored: the borrower may default irrespective of his ability to repay. This is the problem of *enforcement* rather than *information*. This sort of model appears (in different ways) in Eaton and Gersovitz (1981), Banerjee and Newman (chapter 5) and Ghosh and Ray (1996, 1999). As the research of Udry (1994) for rural credit in Northern Nigeria demonstrated, credit imperfections can arise entirely from this source, rather than any form of imperfect information.

Because no one paper adequately summarizes the moral hazard view, we include a paper especially written by Ghosh, Mookherjee and Ray (chapter 11) for this reader. This paper studies the two aspects of the moral hazard problem described above. As in the adverse selection model, this approach gives rise to quantity restrictions of various kinds and, moreover, such restrictions may occur both at the level of the individual and at an aggregative, economy-wide level. The former may take the form of (individualistic) *credit rationing*, in the sense an individual is offered terms under which he would have liked to have taken a bigger loan than the one he is offered. Or it may involve *loan pushing*, in the sense that an individual wants to take a smaller loan under the terms offered to him. Ghosh *et al.* explore both these cases.

The latter – economy-wide – mode of credit rationing is quite different. As chapter 11 reveals, such rationing stems mainly from macroeconomic considerations that keep the credit market functional in environments where information flows are limited. This sort of aggregative rationing serves to lower the outside option available to borrowers contemplating wilful default, thus maintaining incentives for an ongoing credit relationship.

INTERLINKED CREDIT CONTRACTS    Another institution commonly observed in many developing countries is the interlinking of credit transactions with tenancy, employment or marketing contracts. Poor farmers (resp. workers) are frequently observed to borrow exclusively from their landlords (resp. employers). Conversely, tenancy contracts are bundled with credit: the landlord leases land, provides credit to cover working capital and consumption needs in the lean season, contributes to certain farm inputs, and receives a share of the resulting farm output in lieu of rent, besides repayment of loans. In some cases, the landlord may also act as marketing agent for the farmer's share of the crop. With the farmers dependent on the same landlord for so many diverse transactions, many scholars have viewed these patterns of interlinkage as symptomatic of *semi-feudalism* or implicit bondage.[5]

In chapter 12, Braverman and Stiglitz provide a canonical example of the interlinked-contracts literature. They study sharecropping tenancy and demonstrate why such contracts may be linked to credit relationships. In the Braverman–Stiglitz model (as in many others), sharecropping is viewed as the outcome of two countervailing forces: the need to attentuate the risks faced by a risk-averse tenant, and the need to provide incentives to the same tenant. As extreme examples: fixed-rent contracts would impose too much risk on the tenant, while fixed-wage contracts would provide him with insufficient incentive to work hard. Accordingly, an optimal tenancy contract must strike an appropriate balance between these two considerations. Sharecropping may be viewed as one such contract.

Once this view is adopted, it is hard to escape the observation that a tenant's effort incentive will *also* depend on the loans that fall due at the time of harvest. The direction this pushes effort is *a priori* unclear. If there is limited liability, a higher debt burden will reduce effort because of the debt overhang. On the other hand, if debts are repaid in all states of nature, the extra burden increases the *marginal* (utility) gain from higher income. This will encourage the farmer to work harder, with consequent benefits that accrue partly to the landlord.

Interlinkage arises as a way of internalizing this externality between the credit contract and the tenancy contract. For instance, in the second scenario described above, the landlord can provide the tenant with subsidized credit, encouraging the latter to borrow more, and subsequently work harder to make the larger repayments. In fact, Braverman and Stiglitz show that interlinkage is a property of *all* Pareto efficient contracts; it allows an outward shift of the entire utility possibility frontier. In particular, it has no necessary connection with the exercise of monopoly power by the landlord: one would expect it to observe it just as much in contexts where markets are competitive and tenants have considerable bargaining power. Likewise, in the first scenario highlighted above, landlords would wish to restrict loans to their tenants, or at least impose credit exclusivity as a precondition for a tenancy contract.

LAND MARKETS   A related issue associated with sharecropping tenancy is its alleged inefficiency, an observation that goes back to classical economists such as Adam Smith and Alfred Marshall. Since the tenant receives only a fraction of the output produced, the sharecropping arrangement operates in a manner similar to that of a distortionary tax which dulls his incentive to work hard. In contrast, fixed-rent tenancy or owner cultivation awards the entire residual claimancy to the farmer, encouraging effort. This observation has received substantial empirical support in careful econometric analyses; see for example Shaban (1987) or Laffont and Matoussi (1995). It has been at the basis of recommendations for land reform, since the redistribution of the land from landlord to the tenant would convert sharecropping to owner cultivation, with resulting benefits in both higher productivity and reduced inequality.

Yet, as the reading by Mookherjee (chapter 13, this volume) discusses, this case for land redistribution leaves a number of questions unanswered. First, if sharecropping arose in the first place as a mechanism for tenants to receive partial insurance against crop risk, the same need for insurance would be faced by the farmers once they received possession of the land. Presumably, credit relationships would then replace tenancy contracts as the suppliers of such insurance. But the possibility of default, limited liability and the consequent debt overhang would dampen effort (just as sharecropping did). It is not *a priori* clear why this effort incentive problem would be any less serious than under sharecropping.

Moreover, there is the task of explaining why landlords do not *sell* the land to their tenants if the subsequent transition to owner-cultivation results in superior productivity. Land markets would then automatically "solve" the inefficiency inherent in sharecropping by causing the institution to disappear. What prevents these markets from performing this role, and why can state intervention lead to superior outcomes? This sort of question provokes a related exercise: to identify the precise welfare effects of (nonmarket) land redistribution. If farmers have higher effort incentives, this may be the expense of higher risks borne by them. Are they necessarily better off?

The answer to these questions lies in the nature of informational rents inherent in moral hazard with limited liability. As explained in the simple example above, these rents arise from the need to provide adequate effort incentives. A transfer of ownership of land to tenants will augment their bargaining power. This causes a larger weight to be accorded to the interests of the farmer *vis-à-vis* their contracting partners, which increases informational rents and effort incentives. This explains the superior productivity of owner-cultivation, which leads to a welfare improvement owing to the more successful internalization of the externality between landlord and farmer of the latter's informational rents. Despite this potential welfare improvement, Mookherjee's paper shows that land-lords would never voluntarily sell their land to their tenants, as the latter would lack the credit necessary to finance the purchase.

This sort of argument is symptomatic of a wider problem concerning the applicability of the Coase Theorem, which asserts the irrelevance of the allocation of ownership rights for efficient incentives. The Coase Theorem does not apply because of the presence of credit constraints that prevent the use of side transfers to internalize the relevant externalities. For the same reason, land markets would not serve to "solve" the problem; coercive state intervention is necessary to empower farmers at the expense of landlords, which the latter would tend to politically resist. Coercive land redistribution programs cannot generate a Pareto improvement. But they can lead to an increased total surplus or efficiency in the Kaldor–Hicks sense: the gainers could potentially compensate the losers and still remain better off.

## 3.4. Cooperatives and informal institutions

We have seen that the formal sector may leave large gaps in the efficiency of resource allocation. It is natural to expect that the local informal sector will step in to fill these gaps. This is particularly true when the failure of the formal sector stems from its paucity of information about the characteristics and activities of local agents, and its inability to enforce contractual agreements. In contrast, civil society and the rich web of social networks that such society comprises is frequently better informed and more able to enforce obligations through social sanctions. Local villagers have access to a large amount of information regarding each other from informal sources. This information base may be "soft" and "unverifiable" and sometimes unreliable – being based often on local gossip rather than on hard facts. But it is typically far richer than can be represented by the statistics and formal documentation to which external agents in the formal sector will have recourse. Local villagers will also interact on a frequent basis in a variety of social and economic dimensions, allowing deviant behavior to be punished via social sanctions of diverse forms and degree.

Individual behavior can be influenced by community pressure in traditional societies in extreme ways – going as far as inducing deviants to the point of suicide and self-immolation. The pressures that can be brought upon citizens by a distant state often pales in comparison. Thus, repayments on even small informal loans and leases will be scrupulously observed by the very same people that routinely default on larger payments due to the government or commercial banks. It is no surprise then that the informal economy will be better placed to discipline opportunistic behavior, especially in credit and insurance transactions, where problems of trust play such an important role.

MUTUAL INSURANCE    A leading example of these general considerations is the provision of insurance. Anthropologists and sociologists have frequently described and extolled the ability of traditional communities to provide mutual credit and insurance. Coate and Ravallion (chapter 14, this volume) cite relevant evidence in the context of mutual insurance, where villagers help each other in times of sickness or crop failures. Yet, as they note, it is important to avoid an over-romanticized view of the "moral economy": the anthropological evidence and several case studies – see, for instance, Attwood and Baviskar (1993) – describe numerous instances when this form of mutual insurance tends to break down. Understanding the relative strengths and weaknesses of informal insurance is important not only for its own sake, but also as a guide to circumstances where external intervention by the formal sector may be warranted.

Coate and Ravallion develop a theory of self-enforcing mutual insurance, where a pair of *ex ante* identical agents face a stationary but random income process. Insurance from the formal sector is assumed absent, as also the possibility of self-insurance via savings (e.g., because of costs of storage). They focus on mutual insurance arrangements, which prescribes transfers from the individual obtaining a higher income realization at any given date to the other individual who is poorer at that date. The chief simplifying assumption is that these transfers are conditioned only on the *current* income realizations, rather than the past history of their incomes or transfers. Extensions of the model to incorporate credit-like elements via history-dependence have since been developed in the work of Fafchamps (1994), Kletzer and Wright (1995), Ligon, Thomas and Worrall (forthcoming) and others.

In the absence of any enforcement problem, complete sharing is the optimal (symmetric) insurance arrangement, in which the individual with the better income draw gives away half the difference between the two income realizations, resulting in perfect *ex post* equality in consumption. However, when the income differences are large, equal sharing may not be viable as the richer individual may balk at the thought of making large donations, even if the deviation may result in the breakdown of the sharing norm in the future. In other words, equal sharing may not be a self-enforcing norm.

Drawing on some results in the theory of repeated games, Coate and Ravallion are able to provide a simple and elegant description of all self-enforcing sharing norms, and thereafter describe the characteristics of the "best" self-enforcing norm. The results provide insight into the strengths and failures of informal insurance. For instance, it can provide reasonable insurance with respect to moderate idiosyncratic income shocks, but limited insurance against more extreme shocks. The extent of insurance also tends to fall when times are collectively bad for both parties, or when they face risks that are less idiosyncratic. Hence, the scope for mutual insurance is limited in times of drought or famine, and in regions more prone to common weather or market shocks.

Numerical simulations also reveal that the insurance arrangement may be unstable with respect to small perturbations in the parameters of the economy. For instance, a substantive insurance arrangement may entirely disappear with small changes in discount rates, owing to a "bootstrapping" character of such schemes. As the scope for such transfers are narrowed by small parametric changes that cause the enforcement constraints to bind more sharply, the mutual benefit to participants in future continuation of the scheme is lessened. This further reduces the level of enforceable transfers, leading to a cumulative unraveling of the entire mechanism.

MUTUAL CREDIT    Credit represents a different context where informal cooperatives play an important role, in the form of *rotating savings and credit associations* (ROSCAs). Such cooperatives are pervasive throughout the developing world; indeed, many modern commercial banks in the developed world derive their historical origins from them. This is the topic of chapter 15 by Besley, Coate and Loury. In a ROSCA, a group of individuals get together at different dates and jointly contribute money to a common pool; at any date, the entire pool is allocated to one of the members. The winner at any date may be picked randomly, or may be decided on the basis of bidding. Besley, Coate and Loury develop a theory of the role and nature of ROSCAs based on the existence of indivisibilities in desired purchases that make it useful to pool savings. For instance, suppose that a bicycle costs 100, and each member can only save 10 every month. In isolation, each of them would have to wait ten months to buy the bicycle from their own savings. If ten of them form a ROSCA and contribute 10 every month to the pool, one of them can purchase the first month, another the second month, and so on. This enables earlier purchases for all but one member, resulting in a Pareto improvement. To be sure, this is not necessarily an *optimal* ROSCA, which might prescribe lower individual savings rates as a result of the greater pooling now made possible.

Less obvious is the question of how the ROSCA should be constituted. Besley–Coate – Loury compare the performance of random and bidding ROSCAs, and establish a general result: random ROSCAs always outperform bidding ROSCAs if the individuals are all alike *ex ante*, but the opposite will be true if they are sufficiently heterogeneous (e.g., with respect to time preference). The simpler version of their theory does not incorporate enforcement constraints, arising from possible opportunistic behavior by early winners who stop contributing thereafter. Clearly, social sanctions play an important role in reining in such forms of opportunism. They show how enforcement constraints may also explain why the size of the group may be limited, and why random ROSCAs rather than bidding ROSCAs are so commonly observed.

MICROCREDIT AND JOINT LIABILITY LOANS   Microcredit programs represent yet another context where the advantages of peer monitoring and social sanctions within close-knit traditional societies play an important role. The success of group loans made by the Grameen Bank in Bangladesh to the rural poor have become well-known throughout the world. Ghatak and Guinnane (chapter 16, this volume) survey the experience with these programs as well as the theories explaining their success. As they argue, these practices have their origins almost a century ago in the practices of German credit cooperatives, and have been used in more recent times in numerous developing countries. Joint liability loans have typically succeeded in allocating credit in the form of small loans to poor borrowers lacking the assets to post collateral required typically by commercial and government banks. They rely instead on a form of social collateral: different members of the group are jointly liable for each other's loans.

Different authors have stressed a number of possible advantages of joint liability. Different members of a given social group typically know more about each other's creditworthiness than does the bank. By encouraging groups to self-form and making members jointly liable for each other's loans, safe borrowers are provided incentives to form groups with others like themselves, thus weeding out high-risk borrowers. Joint liability can also relax the implications of limits to individual liability, lowering default risk faced by lenders. Moreover, to the extent that a default imposes costs on others in the same group that the borrower has social relationships with, it results in the borrower internalizing the social costs of default, alleviating moral hazard problems. These effects are illustrated by a sequence of simple examples in the theoretical section of Ghatak and Guinnane's paper.

They subsequently discuss problems experienced by attempts to transplant joint liability schemes to different countries and social contexts. In some countries, the problem is that the group sizes are too large for the scheme to work effectively. In urban settings and in more developed countries, the social bonds between participants are not particularly strong, with individualistic behaviour more prominent in local culture. In yet other settings (such as nineteenth century Ireland) where community involvement played an important part, the schemes failed because members were loathe to impose social sanctions on defaulters. The schemes also require the threat of sanctions applied to the group to be credible and actually applied by lenders to all group members following the default of a single member. In addition, they require the prospect of being cut off from the program to exercise a strong punitive role, which would not be the case if they have access to alternate credit sources.

SOCIAL LEARNING   Learning from others about the effectiveness and appropriate use of new technologies represents another avenue by which social structure affects the process of development. Foster and Rosenzweig (chapter 17, this volume) present a model of learning about new cultivation practices from past experience. Farmers learn about appropriate fertilizer application levels in connection with new high yielding varieties (HYV) of seeds, both from their own past experience, and the experience of their neighbors. The learning process is modeled as the outcome of an optimal Bayesian updating of priors over the correct fertilizer level, in the light of past experience. It is assumed that the farmer learns the correct fertilizer dosage appropriate to any particular parcel of land at any given date from observing *ex post* the experienced yield on that parcel. This is a noisy signal of the optimal fertilizer level for any given parcel at any future date. Accordingly, one's own past experience with plantings of HYV seeds, as well as those of one's neighbors, allow the farmer to obtain a more precise estimate of the optimal fertilizer application over time. The model allows a precise expression of these experience effects: in general, they are positive and diminishing over time, and there is a constant ratio between the extent of learning from one's own experience and neighbors' experience over time.

In this setting, farmers are presumed to strategically select the number of parcels in which they will plant an HYV seed at any given date, as a function of the experience they have accumulated so far, and the corresponding planting strategies of their neighbors. The resulting dynamic equilibrium is difficult to characterize in closed form. But the model does indicate the complex interdependence among farmers that results from the presence of learning spillovers. Increased levels of adoption by one's neighbors allows a farmer to learn more about the HYV cultivation process, raising profitability of the new technology; this induces greater adoption. In this sense, the social learning process encourages the diffusion of the technology. On the other hand, the higher level of experience can cause the returns to additional future experience to diminish; this free-riding effect implies that the increased adoption by neighbors will reduce own-adoption incentives. The overall effect of the learning spillovers on the average speed of adoption will then depend on the trade-off between the profitability and free-riding effects, which cannot be determined at the level of theory.

Foster and Rosenzweig thereafter use data from HYV adoption decisions of farmers in north India in the late 1960s during the Green Revolution to empirically identify the relevant learning effects, as well as to test some of the restrictions imposed by the theory (e.g., the constancy of the own-learning effect relative to the social-learning effect over time). These restrictions are upheld in the data, providing support to the theory. Both forms of learning turn out to have significantly affected profitability of the HYV seeds. They also have roughly similar positive effects on adoption decisions, though the adoption effect of social learning is not statistically significant. Hence, the social learning process had a positive but weak effect on the adoption process on average. Simulations of adoption dynamics predicted by the model yield the familiar S-shaped diffusion curve, the exact position of which for any given farmer depends on the nature of interaction with neighbors. In particular, Foster and Rosenzweig find evidence for a significant free-riding effect among farmers with respect to adoption decisions. This suggests a possible role of enhanced coordination among farmers in the village, as well as public subsidies that allow the externalities associated with learning spillovers to be internalized. In common with the previous reading by Ghatak and Guinnane, this paper exemplifies how a proper understanding of the functioning of the informal economy can enable the design of enlightened interventionist policies that fruitfully complement the relative strengths of formal and informal sectors of the economy.

### Notes

1 As Karla Hoff has pointed out to us, the distinction between inertial and historical self-reinforcement may need to be more carefully explored. For instance, part of the historical legacy may be a set of "pessimistic" beliefs that perpetuate a state of underdevelopment. The key issue

is whether there is some state variable that affects the feasible set of payoffs at any date, and such state variables may well include beliefs regarding, say, agent types. Nevertheless, we feel the distinction *is* useful precisely because historical legacies may include observable and tangible factors such as unequal wealth distributions that are amenable to policy tinkering.

2  What follows is based on Mookherjee and Ray (1999).

3  Mukherjee and Ray (1995) temper this view by analyzing another class of long-term labor contracts that actually decline with development. These are contracts which are long-term, not because of the nature of the tasks that are entailed, but as a way of offering security against seasonal fluctuations.

4  For an overview, see, for example, Hoff and Stiglitz (1993).

5  For instance, Bhaduri (1973) suggested that such forms of interlinkage may result in technological stagnation: landlords may prevent the adoption of new innovations by the farmer for fear of reducing the latter's credit needs, and hence the landlord's income from usury.

## References

Aghion, P. and Bolton, P. (1997): "A Theory of Trickle-down Growth and Development," *Review of Economic Studies*, 64, 151–72.

Attwood, D. and Baviskar, B. (1993): *Raising Cane: The Political Economy of Sugar in Western India*. New Delhi: Oxford University Press.

Banerjee, A. and Newman, A. (1991): "Risk-bearing and the Theory of Income Distribution," *Review of Economic Studies*, 58, 211–35.

Bester, H. (1985): "Screening vs. Rationing in Credit Markets with Imperfect Information," *American Economic Review*, 75, 850–5.

Bhaduri, A. (1973): "A Study in Agrarian Backwardness Under Semifeudalism," *Economic Journal*, 83, 120–37.

Bliss, C. and Stern, N. (1978): "Productivity, Wages and Nutrition, Part I: The Theory," *Journal of Development Economics* 5, 331–62.

Bowles, S. and Gintis, H. (1994): "Credit Market Imperfections and the Incidence of Worker Owned Firms," *Metroeconomica*, 45, 209–23.

——(1995): "The Distribution of Wealth and the Assignment of Control Rights," mimeo, Department of Economics, University of Massachusetts, Amherst.

Chamley, C. and Gale, D. (1994): "Information Revelation and Strategic Delay in a Model of Investment," *Econometrica*, 62, 1065–85.

Ciccone, A. and Matsuyama, K. (1996): "Start-up Costs and Pecuniary Externalities as Barriers to Economic Development," *Journal of Development Economics*, 49, 33–59.

Cooper, R. (1999): *Coordination Games: Complementarities and Macroeconomics*, Cambridge University Press.

Eaton, J. and Gersovitz, M. (1981): "Debt with Potential Repudiation: Theoretical and Empirical Analysis," *Review of Economic Studies*, 48, 289–309.

Fafchamps, M. (1994): "Risk Sharing, Quasi-Credit, and the Enforcement of Informal Contracts" mimeograph, Department of Economics, Stanford University.

Ghosh, P. and Ray, D. (1996): "Cooperation in Community Interaction without Information Flows," *Review of Economic Studies*, 63, 491–519.

——(1999): "Information and Repeated Interaction: Application to Informal Credit Markets," mimeograph, Department of Economics, Texas A&M University.

Hirschman, A. O. (1958): *The Strategy of Economic Development*. New Haven, CT: Yale University Press.

Hoff, K. (1994): "The Second Theorem of the Second Best," *Journal of Public Economics*, 45, 223–42.

——and Lyon, A. (1995): "Non-leaky Buckets: Optimal Redistributive Taxation and Agency Costs," *Journal of Public Economics*, 58, 365–90.

——and Stiglitz, J. (1993): "Imperfect Information in Rural Credit Markets: Puzzles and Policy Perspectives," in K. Hoff, A. Braverman and J. Stiglitz (eds), *The Economics of Rural Organization: Theory, Practice and Policy*, London: Oxford University Press (for the World Bank).

——and—— (1999): "Modern Economic Theory and Development," in G. Meier and J. Stiglitz (eds), *Pioneers in Development*, Oxford University Press.

Klein, B. and Leffler, K. (1981): "The Role of Market Forces in Assuring Contractual Performance," *Journal of Political Economy*, 89, 615–41.

Kletzer, K. and Wright, B. (1995): "Sovereign Debt as Intertemporal Barter," mimeograph, University of California, Santa Cruz.

Krugman, P. (1991): "History versus Expectations," *Quarterly Journal of Economics*, 106, 651–67.

Laffont, J.-J. and Matoussi, M. (1995): "Moral Hazard, Financial Constraints and Sharecropping in El Ouja," *Review of Economic Studies*, 62, 381–400.

Legros, P. and Newman, A. (1996): "Wealth Effects, Distribution and the Theory of Organization," *Journal of Economic Theory*, 70, 312–41.

Leibenstein, H. (1957): *Economic Backwardness and Economic Growth*. New York: Wiley.

Lewis, W. A. (1954): "Economic Development with Unlimited Supplies of Labor," *The Manchester School of Economic and Social Studies*, 22, 139–91.

Ligon, E., Thomas, J. and Worrall, T. (forthcoming). "Informal Insurance Arrangements in Village Economics," *Review of Economic Dynamics*.

Loury, G. C. (1981): "Intergenerational Transfers and the Distribution of Earnings," *Econometrica*, 49, 843–67.

Mani, A. (1998): "Income Distribution and the Demand Constraint," mimeograph, Department of Economics, Vanderbilt University.

Matsuyama, K. (1991): "Increasing Returns, Industrialization, and Indeterminacy of Equilibrium," *Quarterly Journal of Economics*, 106, 617–50.

Mirrlees, J. (1976): "A Pure Theory of Underdeveloped Economies," in L. Reynolds (ed.), *Agriculture in Development Theory*, New Haven, CT: Yale University Press.

Mookherjee, D. and Ray, D. (1999): "Persistent Inequality and Endogenous Investment Thresholds," mimeograph, Department of Economics, Boston University.

Mukherjee, A. and Ray, D. (1995): "Labor Tying," *Journal of Development Economics*, 47, 207–39.

Piketty, T. (1997): "The Dynamics of the Wealth Distribution and the Interest Rate with Credit Rationing," *Review of Economic Studies*, 64, 173–89.

Prasad, P. H. (1970): *Growth with Full Employment*. Bombay: Allied Publishers.

Ray, D. (1998): *Development Economics*. Princeton: Princeton University Press.

——and Streufert, P. (1993): "Dynamic Equilibria with Unemployment due to Undernourishment," *Economic Theory*, 3, 61–85.

Riley, J. (1987): "Credit Rationing: A Further Remark," *American Economic Review*, 77, 224–7.

Rodríguez-Clare, A. (1996): "The Division of Labor and Economic Development," *Journal of Development Economics*, 49, 3–32.

Scitovsky, T. (1954). "Two Concepts of External Economies," *Journal of Political Economy*, 62, 143–51.

Shaban, R. A. (1987): "Testing between Competing Models of Sharecropping," *Journal of Political Economy*, 95, 893–920.

Shapiro, C. (1983): "Premiums for High Quality Products as Returns on Reputation," *Quarterly Journal of Economics*, 98, 659–80.

——and Stiglitz, J. (1984): "Equilibrium Unemployment as a Worker Discipline Device," *American Economic Review*, 74, 433–44.

Simon, H. (1951): "A Formal Theory of the Employment Relationship," *Econometrica*, 19, 293–305.

Solow, R. M. (1956): "A Contribution to the Theory of Economic Growth," *Quarterly Journal of Economics*, 70, 65–94.

Stiglitz, J. (1976): "The Efficiency Wage Hypothesis, Surplus Labour and the Distribution of Income in L.D.C.'s," *Oxford Economic Papers*, 28, 185–207.

——and Weiss, A. (1981): "Credit Rationing in Markets with Imperfect Information," *American Economic Review*, 71, 393–410.

Udry, C. (1994): "Risk and Insurance in a Rural Credit Market: An Empirical Investigation in Northern Nigeria," *Review of Economic Studies*, 61, 495–526.

# PART I:

# Underdevelopment As Market Incompleteness: Economy-wide Implications

# A: Coordination Failures and Underdevelopment

# CHAPTER 1

# Industrialization and the Big Push

KEVIN M. MURPHY, ANDREI SHLEIFER AND
ROBERT W. VISHNY

This paper explores Rosenstein-Rodan's idea that simultaneous industrialization of many sectors of the economy can be profitable for them all even when no sector can break even industrializing alone. We analyze this idea in the context of an imperfectly competitive economy with aggregate demand spillovers and interpret the big push into industrialization as a move from a bad to a good equilibrium. We present three mechanisms for generating a big push and discuss their relevance for less developed countries.

## 1. Introduction

Virtually every country that experienced rapid growth of productivity and living standards over the last 200 years has done so by industrializing. Countries that have successfully industrialized – turned to production of manufactures taking advantage of scale economies – are the ones that grew rich, be they eighteenth-century Britain or twentieth-century Korea and Japan. Yet despite the evident gains from industrialization and the success of many countries in achieving it, numerous other countries remain unindustrialized and poor. What is it that allows some but not other countries to industrialize? And can government intervention accelerate the process?

Of the many causes of lack of growth of underdeveloped countries, a particularly important and frequently discussed constraint on industrialization is the small size of the domestic market. When domestic markets are small and world trade is not free and costless, firms may not be able to generate enough sales to make adoption of increasing returns technologies profitable, and hence industrialization is stalled. In this paper, we present some models of economies with small domestic markets and discuss how these markets can expand so that a country can get out of the no-industrialization trap. In particular, we focus on the contribution of industrialization of one sector to enlarging the size of the market in other sectors. Such spillovers give rise to the possibility that coordination of investments across sectors – which the government can promote – is essential for industrialization. This idea of coordinated investment is the basis of the concept of the "big push," introduced by Rosenstein-Rodan (1943) and discussed by many others.

According to Rosenstein-Rodan, if various sectors of the economy adopted increasing returns technologies simultaneously, they could each create income that becomes a source of demand for goods in other sectors, and so enlarge their markets and make industrialization profitable. In fact, simultaneous industrialization of many sectors can be self-sustaining even if *no* sector could break even industrializing alone. This insight has been developed by Nurkse (1953), Scitovsky (1954), and Fleming (1955) into a doctrine of balanced growth or the big push, with two important elements. First, the same economy must be capable of both the backward preindustrial and the modern industrialized state. No exogenous improvement in endowments or technological opportunities is needed to move to industrialization, only the simultaneous investment by all the sectors using the available technology. Second, industrialization is associated with a better state of affairs. The population of a country benefits from its leap into the industrial state.

In this paper, we attempt to understand the importance of demand spillovers between sectors by looking at simple stylized models of a less developed economy in which these spillovers are strong enough to generate a big push. In doing so, we chiefly associate the big push with multiple equilibria of the economy and interpret it as a switch from the cottage production equilibrium to industrial equilibrium. The main question we address is, What does it take for such multiple equilibria to exist? In addition, we ask when the equilibrium in which various sectors of the economy "industrialize" is Pareto-preferred to the equilibrium in which they do not. We thus make precise the sense in which industrialization benefits an economy with fixed preferences, endowments, and technological opportunities.

In all the models described in this paper, the source of multiplicity of equilibria is pecuniary externalities generated by imperfect competition with large fixed costs.[1] Yet such multiplicity is not automatic: in section 3 we show that even where pecuniary externalities are important, equilibrium can be unique. The idea behind the uniqueness result is that if a firm contributes to the demand for other firms' goods *only* by distributing its profits and raising aggregate income, then unprofitable investments must *reduce* income and therefore the size of other firms' markets. Starting from the equilibrium in which no firm wants to adopt increasing returns, each investing firm would then lose money and therefore make it even less attractive for other firms to invest. As a result, the second equilibrium with a higher level of industrialization cannot exist. When profits are the only channel of spillovers, the industrialized equilibrium cannot coexist with the unindustrialized one.

In contrast, multiple equilibria arise naturally if an industrializing firm *raises* the size of other firms' markets even when it itself loses money. This occurs when firms raise the profit of other industrial firms through channels other than their own profits. In the models we present, industrialization in one sector can increase spending in other manufacturing sectors by altering the composition of demand. In the model of section 4, industrialization raises the demand for manufactures because workers are paid higher wages to entice them to work in industrial plants. Hence, even a firm losing money can benefit firms in other sectors because it raises labor income and hence demand for their products.

The model of section 5 focuses on the intertemporal aspect of industrialization. In that model, industrialization has the effect of giving up current income for future income because the benefits of current investment in cost reduction are realized over a long period of time. The more sectors industrialize, the higher is the level of future spending. But this means that the profitability of investment depends on there being enough other sectors to industrialize so that high future spending justifies putting down a large-scale plant today. Since an investing firm generates a positive cash flow in the future, it raises the demand for the output in other sectors even if its own investment has a negative net present value. In the models of both sections 4 and 5, coordinated investment across sectors leads to the expansion of markets for all industrial goods and can thus be self-sustaining even when no firm can break even investing alone.

The effect of a firm's investment on the size of the markets for output in other sectors is not the only relevant pecuniary externality. An important component of industrialization for which pecuniary externalities can be crucial is investment in jointly used intermediate goods, for example, infrastructure such as railroads and training facilities. To the extent that the cost of an infrastructure is largely fixed, each industrializing firm that uses it helps defray this fixed cost and so brings the building of the infrastructure closer to profitability. In this way, each user indirectly helps other users and hence makes their industrialization more likely. As a result, infrastructure develops only when many sectors industrialize and become its users. In section 6 we associate the big push with the economy making large investments in a shared infrastructure. This approach has the advantage of being important even in a completely open economy.

The emphasis of this paper on the efficiency of industrialization warrants some explanation. All the deviations from the first-best are ultimately driven by imperfect competition and the resulting divergence of the price of output from marginal cost. But inefficiency manifests itself in two distinct ways. First, at any positive level of industrialization, there is a static monopoly pricing inefficiency in that industrial goods are overpriced relative to cottage-produced goods. Second, given monopoly pricing in industrial sectors, the level of industrialization can be too low from a second-best welfare point of view. In particular, welfare is lower in the nonindustrialized equilibrium than in the fully industrialized equilibrium. In our discussion of government policy, we take monopoly pricing in industrial sectors as given and always focus on second-best policies that bring about a Pareto-preferred, higher level of industrialization. We stress, however, that because all our models are highly stylized and capture what we can only hope to be one aspect of reality, policies suggested by these models should be interpreted with caution.[2]

## 2. The Importance of Domestic Markets

Except for the example of infrastructure (section 6), our analysis relies crucially on the importance of domestic markets for industrialization. Such analysis runs into an obvious objection. If world trade is free and costless, then an industry faces a world market, the size of which cannot plausibly constrain adoption of increasing returns technologies. Yet despite this theoretical objection, there is now considerable empirical evidence pointing to the importance of the domestic market as an outlet for sales of domestic industry.

The best evidence comes from the work of Chenery and Syrquin (1975) and Chenery, Robinson, and Syrquin (1986). Using a sample of rapidly growing economies over the period from the early 1950s to the early 1970s, Chenery et al. look at a change in domestic industrial output over that period in each country and divide it between a change in domestic demand and a change in exports. Because some outputs are also used as intermediate goods and the structure of production as measured by the input-output matrix is changing, Chenery et al. correct their results for changes in technology. By far the most important sources of growth in output, however, are growth in domestic demand and growth in exports.

The findings of Chenery et al. point to a dominant share of domestic demand in growth of domestic industrial output. In countries with populations over 20 million, expansion of domestic demand accounts for 72–74 percent of the increase in domestic industrial output (1986, p. 156).[3] In such countries, when per capita income is between 200 and 800 1964 U.S. dollars, the share of industry in gross national product is five to six percentage points higher than in countries with populations under 20 million, with the difference concentrated in industries with important economies of scale, such as basic metals, paper, chemicals, and rubber products (Chenery and Syrquin, 1975, p. 78). In small primary goods-oriented countries with populations under 20 million, a rise in domestic sales accounts for 70–72 percent of the increase in the domestic industrial output (Chenery et al., 1986, p. 156). Even in small manufacturing-oriented countries with populations under 20 million, expansion of domestic demand accounts for about 50–60 percent of industrial output expansion (p. 156). In Korea – the paragon of an open, export-oriented economy – domestic demand expansion accounted for 53 percent of growth of industrial output between 1955 and 1973 (p. 158) and a much larger fraction if one abstracts from export-intensive sectors such as textiles. Moreover, the intensive export of manufactures began only after the industry became established in the domestic market (Chenery and Syrquin, 1975, p. 101). Whether the causes of limited trade are natural, such as transport costs or taste differences across countries, or man-made, such as tariffs, the bottom line is the overwhelming importance of domestic demand for most of domestic industry.

## 3. A Simple Aggregate Demand Spillovers Model with a Unique Equilibrium

The existence of multiple, Pareto-ranked equilibria of the type envisioned in the big push literature requires that the economy be capable of sustaining two alternative levels of industrialization. This means that industrialization must be individually unprofitable at a low aggregate level of industrialization but individually profitable as long as a sufficient number of other sectors industrialize. Put another way, even individually unprofitable industrialization must have spillover effects on other sectors that make industrialization in other sectors more profitable.

In this section, we discuss a simple model in which profit spillovers across sectors are present, but they are still not sufficient to generate the conditions for the big push. The firm in this model has a positive spillover on the demands (profits) of other sectors if and only if it makes a positive profit itself. Hence, even though the firm does not internalize the effect of its dividends on the profits in other sectors, it still makes a (second-best) efficient investment decision and has a positive spillover on other firms only to the extent that its own industrialization decision is individually profitable. We start with this model in order to illustrate the fact that the conditions for individually unprofitable investments to raise the profitability of investment in other sectors are more stringent than those loosely expressed in much of the big push literature of the 1940s and 1950s (see, e.g., Rosenstein-Rodan 1943).

Consider a one-period economy with a representative consumer, with Cobb–Douglas utility function $\int_0^1 \ln x(q)\mathrm{d}q$ defined over a unit interval of goods indexed by $q$.[4] All goods have the same expenditure shares. Thus when his income is $y$, the consumer can be thought of as spending $y$ on every good $x(q)$. The consumer is endowed with $L$ units of labor, which he supplies inelastically, and he owns all the profits of this economy. If his wage is taken as numeraire, his budget constraint is given by

$$y = \Pi + L \tag{1}$$

where $\Pi$ is aggregate profits.

Each good is produced in its own sector, and each sector consists of two types of firms. First, each sector has a competitive fringe of firms that convert one unit of labor input into one unit of output with a constant returns to scale (cottage production) technology. Second, each sector has a unique firm with access to an increasing returns (mass production) technology. This firm is alone in having access to that technology in its sector and hence will be referred to as a monopolist (even though, as we specify below, it does not always operate). Industrialization requires the input of $F$ units of labor and allows each additional unit of labor to produce $\alpha > 1$ units of output.

The monopolist in each sector decides whether to industrialize or to abstain from production altogether. We assume that the monopolist maximizes his profit taking the demand curve as given.[5] He industrializes ("invests") only if he can earn a profit at the price he charges. That price equals one since the monopolist loses all his sales to the fringe if he charges more, and he would not want to charge less when facing a unit elastic demand curve. When income is $y$, the profit of a monopolist who spends $F$ to industrialize is

$$\pi = \frac{\alpha - 1}{\alpha} y - F \equiv ay - F \tag{2}$$

where $a$ is the difference between price and marginal cost, or markup.

When a fraction $n$ of the sectors in the economy industrialize, aggregate profits are

$$\Pi(n) = n(ay - F) \tag{3}$$

Substituting (3) into (1) yields aggregate income as a function of the fraction of sectors industrializing:

$$y(n) = \frac{L - nF}{1 - na} \tag{4}$$

The numerator of (4) is the amount of labor used in the economy for actual production of output, after investment outlays. One over the denominator is the multiplier showing that an increase in effective labor raises income by more than one for one since expansion of low-cost sectors also raises profits. To see this more explicitly, note that

$$\frac{\mathrm{d}y(n)}{\mathrm{d}n} = \frac{\pi(n)}{1 - an} \tag{5}$$

where $\pi(n)$ is the profit of the last firm to invest. When the last firm earns this profit, it distributes it to shareholders, who in turn spend it on all goods and thus raise profits in all industrial firms in the economy. The effect of this firm's profit is therefore enhanced by the increases in profits of all industrial firms resulting from increased spending. Since there are a fraction $n$ of such firms, the multiplier is increasing in the number of firms that benefit from the spillover of the marginal firm. The more firms invest, the greater is the cumulative increase in profits and therefore income resulting from a positive net present value investment by the last firm.

For an alternative interpretation of (5), notice that since the price of labor is unity, the profit of the last firm, $\pi(n)$, is exactly equal to the net labor saved from its investment in cost reduction. The numerator of (5) is therefore the increase in labor available to the economy as a result of the investment by the last firm. In equilibrium, this freed-up labor moves into all sectors. However, its marginal product is higher in industrialized sectors than in nonindustrialized sectors. The more sectors industrialize (i.e., the higher is $n$), the greater is the increase in total output resulting from the inflow of freed-up labor into these sectors. In fact, the denominator of (5) is just the average of marginal labor costs across sectors, which is clearly a decreasing function of $n$. This interpretation connects (5) to (4), which explicitly states that income is a multiple of productive labor and that the multiplier is increasing in $n$.

Despite the fact that the firm ignores the profit spillover from its investment, it is easy to see that there is a unique Nash equilibrium in which either all firms industrialize or none of them do (i.e., there is no big push). In order for there to be a no-industrialization equilibrium, it must be the case that when aggregate income is equal to $L$, a single firm loses money from industrializing. But if no firm can break even from investing when income is $L$, then there cannot be an equilibrium in which any firms invest. For suppose that a single firm decides to invest. Since it loses money, it only reduces aggregate income, making the profit from industrialization in any other sectors even lower. Hence if it is unprofitable for a single firm to invest, it is even less profitable for more firms to do so, making the existence of the second equilibrium impossible. As is clear from (5), a firm's spillover is positive if and only if its own profits are positive. The multiplier changes only the magnitude of the effect of a firm's investment on income, and not the sign.

The remainder of the paper presents three modifications of this model in which a firm engaging in unprofitable investment can still benefit other sectors and make it more likely that they will find it profitable to invest. By doing so, we get away from the uniqueness result of this section and generate a big push.

## 4. A Model with a Factory Wage Premium

The first model of the big push we present comes closest in its spirit to Rosenstein-Rodan's (1943) paper. According to this theory, to bring farm laborers to work in a factory, a firm has to pay them a wage premium. But unless the firm can generate enough sales to people other than its own workers, it will not be able to afford to pay higher wages. If this firm is the only one to start production, its sales might be too low for it to break even. In contrast, if firms producing different products all invest and expand production together, they can all sell their output to each other's workers and so can afford to pay a wage premium and still break even. In this section, we construct a model along these lines.[6]

We assume that higher wages are paid in the factory to compensate workers for disutility of such work. Accordingly, we take utility to be $\exp[\int_0^1 \ln x(q)\mathrm{d}q]$ if a person is employed in cottage production and $\exp[\int_0^1 \ln x(q)\mathrm{d}q] - v$ if he or she is employed in a factory using increasing returns. Although factory workers earn higher wages, they have the same unit elastic demand curves for manufactures as cottage production workers, and so we can calculate demands based on the aggregate income, $y$.[7] Specifically, when the total profit and labor income is $y$, we can think of it as expenditure $y$ on each good. Workers engage in either constant returns to scale (CRS) cottage production of manufactures or in factory work in which increasing returns to scale (IRS) technologies are used.[8] Cottage production wage is set to one as numeraire, and total labor supply is fixed at $L$.

As before, the cottage technology for each good yields one unit of output for each unit of labor input. Cottage producers who use this technology are competitive. In contrast, the IRS technology requires a fixed cost of $F$ units of labor to set up a factory but then yields $\alpha > 1$ units of output for one unit of labor input. We assume that access to the IRS technology is restricted to a separate monopolist in each sector.

The monopolist will choose to operate his technology only if he expects to make a profit taking the demand curve as given. If he does operate, he could not raise his price above one without losing the business to the fringe. But he also would not want to cut the price since demand is unit elastic.

Since all prices are always kept at unity, it is easy to calculate the competitive factory wage, $w$. Each monopolist must pay a wage that makes a worker indifferent between factory and cottage production employment:

$$w = 1 + v > 1 \tag{6}$$

In this pure compensating differentials model, factory employees get the minimum wage necessary to get them out of cottage production and hence get no surplus from industrialization except as profit owners.

When aggregate income is $y$, the monopolist's profit is given by

$$\pi = y\left(1 - \frac{1+v}{\alpha}\right) - F(1+v) \tag{7}$$

where 1 is the price he gets and $(1 + v)/\alpha$ is his unit variable cost. The monopolist will incur $F(1 + v)$ only if he expects income to be high enough for this investment to make money.

As is clear from (7), for this model to be at all interesting, the productivity gain from using the IRS technology must exceed the compensating differential that must be paid to a worker, that is,

$$\alpha - 1 > v \tag{8}$$

If this condition does not hold, the factory will not be able to afford any labor even if it surrenders to it all the efficiency gain over the cottage technology. As a result, the factory could not possibly break even, whatever the level of income.

Under the conditions discussed below, this model can have two equilibria, one with and one without industrialization. In the first equilibrium, no firm incurs the fixed cost for fear of not being able to break even, and the population stays in cottage production. Income is equal to $L$, the wage bill of the cottage labor, since no profits are earned. For this to be an equilibrium, it must be the case that in no sector would a monopolist want to set up a factory if he has to pay the required factory wage. That is, for no industrialization to take place, we must have

$$L\left(1 - \frac{1+v}{\alpha}\right) - F(1+v) < 0 \tag{9}$$

In a second equilibrium, all sectors industrialize. By symmetry, the quantity of output produced in each sector is $\alpha(L - F)$, which at unit prices is also the value of output. Since the only input is labor, total factor payments are wages, which are equal to $L(1 + v)$. For this to be an equilibrium, profits must be positive:

$$\pi = \alpha(L - F) - L(1 + v) > 0 \tag{10}$$

When (10) holds, all firms expect a high level of income and sales resulting from simultaneous labor-saving industrialization of many sectors and are consequently happy to incur the fixed cost $F(1 + v)$ to set up a factory. This of course makes the expectation of industrialization self-fulfilling.

An examination of (9) and (10) suggests that there always exist some values of $F$ for which both equilibria exist, provided (8) holds. For these values of $F$, the economy is capable of a big push, whereby it moves from the unindustrialized equilibrium to one with industrialization when all its sectors coordinate investments. The reason for the multiplicity of equilibria is that a link between a firm's profit and its contribution to demand for products of other sectors is now broken. Because a firm that sets up a factory pays a wage premium, it increases the size of the market for producers of other manufactures, even if its investment loses money. Consequently, the firm's profit in this model is not an adequate measure of its contribution to the aggregate demand for manufactures since a second component of this contribution – the extra wages it pays – is not captured by the profits.

In this model, the Pareto superiority of the equilibrium with industrialization is apparent. Since prices do not change, workers are equally well off as wage earners in the second equilibrium, but they also get some profits. They have higher income at the same prices and hence must be better off. Firms making investment decisions in the no-industrialization equilibrium ignore the fact that, even when they lose money, the higher factory wages they pay generate profits in other industrializing sectors by increasing the demand for manufactures. As a result, these firms underinvest in the no-industrialization equilibrium, and an inefficiency results. As is commonly supposed in the discussion of industrialization, it indeed creates wealth and represents a better outcome.

The big push resulting from higher factory wages could also be obtained using a different but related model of industrialization. Instead of focusing on a compensating differential, we could assume that cottage production is located on the farm and factories are located in the cities, and that city dwellers' demand is more concentrated on manufactures. For example, living in a city might require consumption of processed food if fresh food is expensive to transport from the farm. Urbanization also leads to increased consumption of other manufactures, such as textiles, leather goods, and furniture (Reynolds, 1983). If these changes in demand are important, then urbanization in the process of industrialization leads to an increase in the demand for manufactures. In this way industrialization can be self-sustaining even if there is no compensating wage differential for factory work, but only a shift in the consumption bundle toward manufactures.

## 5. A Dynamic Model of Investment

This section presents a second example in which an investment that loses money nonetheless raises aggregate income. A firm that uses resources to invest at one point in time, but generates the labor savings from this investment at a later point, decreases aggregate demand today and raises it tomorrow. This shift in the composition of demand away from today's goods and toward tomorrow's goods can also give rise to multiple equilibria and inefficient underinvestment, unless the government coordinates investment or entrepreneurs are spontaneously "bullish."

One historical account (Sawyer, 1954; quoted in Cole, 1959) motivates this model in the context of nineteenth-century American economic growth. According to Sawyer, even when a cold economic calculation dictated otherwise, irrationally bullish and overoptimistic American entrepreneurs insisted on investing. But with enough people making this mistake, optimistic projections became self-fulfilling (cf. Keynes's (1936) account of entrepreneurial optimism):

> To the extent that it worked in an economic sense – that an over-anticipation of prospects in fact paid off in either a private or social balance sheet, we find ourselves on the perilous edge of an "economics of euphoria" – a dizzy world in which if enough people make parallel errors of over-estimation, and their resulting investment decisions fall in reasonable approximation to the course of growth, they may collectively generate the conditions of realizing their original vision. It suggests, historically, a sort of self-fulfilling prophecy, in which the generalized belief in growth operated to shift the marginal efficiency of capital schedule to the right, and in which the multiple centers of initiative, acting in terms of exaggerated prospects of growth, pulled capital and labor from home and from the available reservoirs abroad, and so acted as to create the conditions on which their initial decisions were predicated (Sawyer 1954, pt. C, p. 3).

Our model shows that Sawyer's ideas about self-fulfilling expectations of growth do not really rely on assuming entrepreneurial irrationality.

A two-period model suffices to illustrate the big push in a dynamic context. Consider a representative consumer with preferences defined over the same unit interval of goods in both the first and the second periods. If we denote by $x_1(q)$ and $x_2(q)$, with $q$ between zero and one, his consumption of good $q$ in periods 1 and 2, respectively, the consumer's utility is given by

$$U = \left[ \int_0^1 x_1^\gamma(q) dq \right]^{\frac{\theta}{\gamma}} + \beta \left[ \int_0^1 x_2^\gamma(q) dq \right]^{\frac{\theta}{\gamma}} \tag{11}$$

In this expression, $1/(1-\theta)$ is the intertemporal elasticity of substitution, and $1/(1-\gamma)$ is the elasticity of substitution between different goods within a period. For example, in the special case in which $\gamma = 0$ and $\theta = 1$, to which we return below, the consumer has unit elastic demand for each good $q$ and is indifferent about when to consume his income. The representative consumer is endowed with $L$ units of labor each period that he supplies inelastically, and he owns all the profits. Without loss of generality, each period's wage is set equal to one.

Each good $q$ in the first period must be produced using a CRS technology converting one unit of labor into one unit of output. The same technology is also available in the second period. The CRS technology is used by a competitive fringe of firms. In addition to this CRS technology, each sector $q$ has a potential monopolist who can invest $F$ units of labor in the *first* period and then produce $\alpha > 1$ units of output per unit of labor in the *second* period. Each monopolist in this model thus has an intertemporal investment decision since the benefits of the IRS technology obtain only with a lag. His decision whether or not to invest depends both on the equilibrium interest rate and on income in period 2.

To analyze the decision of a monopolist in a representative sector, denote his profits by $\pi$, equilibrium discount factor by $\beta^*$,[9] and periods 1 and 2 aggregate incomes by $y_1$ and $y_2$ respectively. As before, the price the monopolist can charge in the second period if he invests is bounded above by one, the price of the competitive fringe. We assume that

$$\alpha < \frac{1}{\gamma} \tag{12}$$

The demand curve in each sector is sufficiently inelastic that the monopolist does not want to cut the price below one. If we denote by $a = 1 - (1/\alpha)$ the marginal profit rate of the monopolist per dollar of sales, his profits can now be written as

$$\pi = \beta^* a y_2 - F \tag{13}$$

The monopolist will incur the fixed cost $F$ in the first period whenever the net present value of his profits given by (13) is positive.

For some parameter values, this model has two equilibria. In the first equilibrium, no sector incurs the fixed cost $F$ in period 1, and no industrialization takes place. Income each period is equal to wage income:

$$y_1 = y_2 = L \tag{14}$$

Furthermore, the equilibrium discount factor at which the consumers are willing to accept the constant expenditure $L$ on consumption in both periods is equal to $\beta$. For this to be an equilibrium, it must not pay a monopolist in a representative sector to incur $F$ in the first period if he expects income in the second period to be $L$ and if the discount factor is $\beta$. By (13), the monopolist will not invest if

$$\pi = \beta a L - F < 0 \tag{15}$$

When this condition holds, the demand that firms expect to obtain in the second period is too low for them to break even on their investments. Since they do not invest, the realized level of income is indeed low, and the no-industrialization equilibrium is sustained.

An important feature of this model is that, whereas what matters for a firm is the present value of its profits, what matters for its contribution to aggregate demand in the second period is its second-period cash flow. Thus even if an investing firm loses money, it still raises second-period income. Put differently, even an unprofitable investment transfers income from the first to the second period and thereby makes investment for other firms, which sell only in the second period, more attractive, *ceteris paribus*. Of course, this shift of income across periods resulting from investment is in part offset by an increase in the interest rate. Nonetheless, the income effect is in many cases more important than the interest rate effect, and, as a result, simultaneous investment by many firms can become profitable even when each loses money investing in isolation. This gives rise to a second equilibrium, in which the economy makes the "big push."

In this equilibrium with industrialization, each sector incurs the fixed cost $F$ in the first period, and as a result the first-period income is

$$y_1 = L - F \tag{16}$$

The second-period income is higher because of higher profits:

$$y_2 = L + \pi = L + a y_2 = \alpha L \tag{17}$$

One way to think about these equations for income is that, in the first period, there are no markups charged, and hence the multiplier is one, while in the second period the multiplier is $\alpha$ because each sector marks up the price over cost.

For the consumer to accept a higher level of consumption in period 2 than in period 1, the discount factor in this equilibrium must be

$$\beta^* = \beta \left( \frac{\alpha L}{L - F} \right)^{\theta - 1} \tag{18}$$

The interest rate rises in equilibrium to prevent the consumer from wanting to smooth his consumption. The higher $\theta$ is, the less averse the consumer is to intertemporal substitution, and hence the lower is the interest rate needed to equilibrate the loan market at zero. In the limiting case in which $\theta = 1$ and the consumer is perfectly happy to substitute consumption across time, the equilibrium discount rate is simply his rate of time preference $\beta$.

For the proposed allocation to be an equilibrium, it must pay the firm expecting income $y_2$ from (17) and faced with a discount rate from (18) to invest in the first period. This will be the case provided

$$(a\alpha L)\beta\left(\frac{\alpha L}{L-F}\right)^{\theta-1} - F > 0 \qquad\qquad (19)$$

When condition (19) holds, the interest rate does not rise too much when consumption is growing. As a result, there exists an equilibrium in which firms expect other firms to invest and income to rise, and all firms in fact invest in anticipation of profiting from the higher income. Our interpretation of the possibility of the big push is the coexistence of both equilibria for the same parameter values. In that case, firms invest if they expect other firms to do the same and income to grow, and they do not invest if they expect the economy to remain stationary.

The key to the coexistence of the two equilibria is the fact that a firm's profits are not an adequate measure of its contribution to demand for manufactures. An investing firm, even if it loses money, reduces period 1 income and raises period 2 income. Aside from the effect of this investment on the rate of interest, the main consequence of this action by the firm is to reduce the demand for manufactures in the first period – which is irrelevant for investment – and to raise the demand for manufactures of other firms in the second period – which is key to their investment decisions. As a result, the investment by a firm makes investment by other firms more attractive. All that is needed for this to be the case is that the second-period cash flow of the firm be positive. Then the whole cash flow contributes to the second-period demand for manufactures and raises the profitability of investment of all other firms in the economy (as long as the interest rate does not rise too much). The result of the investment, then, is to shift the composition of demand across periods in a way that makes the investment by other firms more attractive. This shift of income makes the big push possible, even if the net present value of a firm investing alone in the economy is negative. As before, the possibility of the big push turns on the divergence between the firm's profits and its contribution to the demand for manufactures of other investing firms.

In this model, the equilibrium with industrialization is Pareto-preferred to that without industrialization. This can be most easily seen from the fact that spot prices of manufacturing goods are the same in the two equilibria in both periods, but that the present value of income is higher in the second equilibrium even though the interest rate has risen. The reason for the Pareto ranking has to do with the difference in multipliers across the two periods. An investing firm uses up labor in the first period, when the contribution of labor to income is exactly equal to its wage. The same firm saves labor in the second period, which goes on to generate *both* wages and profits in other sectors. Hence the firm undervalues the labor it saves in the second period when making its investment decision. This is equivalent to saying that a dollar of a firm's positive cash flow in the second period generates more than a dollar in income since the dividends the firm pays become a source of demand and hence of profits in other sectors. In contrast, a dollar of negative cash flow in the first period reduces income by only a dollar. Both the labor market version of the story and the demand generation version explain why a dollar of the firm's profit in the second period raises income by $\$\alpha$, that is, has a multiplier associated with it. Because the firm ignores this multiplier in making its investment decision, it will in general underinvest in the no-industrialization equilibrium. The variation of multipliers across periods thus explains the Pareto ranking of the two equilibria.

We stress that the reasons for multiplicity of equilibria and for their Pareto ranking are not the same. To see this, suppose that the first-period technologies are also used by monopolists in the various sectors, who mark up the price over cost but get imitated by the competitive fringe in the second period. As before, monopolists can also further reduce costs and stay ahead of competition in the second period if they invest $F$ in the first period. If the markup in the first period is larger, the multiplier in the first period will be larger than the multiplier in the second period, even if monopolists invest to cut second-period costs below the competitive price. In this case, we might still have two equilibria. In the first, firms do not invest because they expect too few others to invest and raise second-period income. In the second equilibrium, firms invest and shift income from period 1 to period 2 and thus create high enough period 2 cash flows for other firms to justify their investments. In this case, however, the high investment equilibrium might be less efficient since firms are using up labor to build plants in the first period, when markups elsewhere in the economy are high, and saving labor in the second period, when the wage is closer to its contribution to income.[10] The point is that multiplicity is affected by gross cash flows in the two periods, whereas the relative efficiency of equilibria is determined by the difference in the multipliers.

At least at the initial stages of industrialization, it is plausible to think of the economy as moving from the use of competitive CRS backstop technologies to the use of less competitive IRS technologies. In this case, our model yields both a positive and a normative result concerning the big push. First, the big push indeed might take the form of simultaneous industrialization of many sectors, each generating future income that helps the profitability of other sectors. The mutual reinforcement of sectors is thus a key property of this big push. Second, the big push, or simultaneous industrialization, is good in this economy because it uses up labor when it is least productive (i.e., when it is stuck in backstop) and frees up labor when it is most productive (i.e., when industrialization has occurred).

The inefficiency of unindustrialized equilibrium raises the possibility of a government role either in encouraging agents to invest or, alternatively, in discouraging current consumption. In our model, persuasion and encouragement of investment alone might be an effective enough tool since these steps might coordinate agents' plans on a better equilibrium. Alternatively, the government can use investment subsidies as long as they are widely enough spread to bring about a critical mass of investment needed to sustain a big push.[11]

## 6. A Model of Investment in Infrastructure

For a large infrastructure project, such as a railroad, the size of the market can be particularly important since most of the costs are fixed. As a result, the building of a railroad often depends on the demand from potential users. These users, in turn, can access much larger markets if they can cheaply transport their goods using a railroad. It is not surprising in this context that infrastructure in general and railroads in particular have been commonly credited with being an important component of the big push (Rostow, 1960; Rosenstein-Rodan, 1961), although there is some debate on whether they have been absolutely pivotal (Fogel, 1964; Fishlow, 1965).

In our context, building a railroad is especially important because it interacts so closely with industrialization. In particular, since many sectors share in paying for the railroad and the railroad brings down effective production costs, an industrializing sector essentially has the effect of reducing the total production costs of the other sectors. These external effects of an investment are not captured by the firm making it, and hence we again have room for multiple equilibria. The railroad might not get built and industrialization might not take place unless there are enough potential industrial customers.

There are two separate reasons why a railroad might not get built even when it is socially efficient to build it. First, if a railroad is unable to price-discriminate between its users, it can extract only part of the social surplus that it generates. This reflects just the usual reason why a monopolist underinvests in a new technology. If the railroad could extract from each firm all the profits obtained through the use of its services, this inefficiency would not result. In addition, a railroad might not get built if, once it is built, there still remains extrinsic uncertainty about whether the economy industrializes. As in the model of the previous section, if it pays a sector to build a factory only when other sectors do the same even after the railroad is built, then there is always a chance of the bad equilibrium with no industrialization. If the railroad builder is sufficiently averse to this outcome, in which he gets no customers, the railroad will not be built.

We illustrate these results using a modified version of the intertemporal investment model from the previous section. First, we use the same utility function (11) as before, but since we do not care about the interest rate effects, we assume that $\theta = 1$ and $\gamma = 0$. The representative consumer is indifferent about when he consumes his income and spends equal shares of his income in each period on all goods. We also assume that the consumers' time discount factor $\beta$ is equal to one, so that the equilibrium interest rate is always zero.

It is natural to suppose that the CRS cottage technologies can be set up in all locations and hence do not require the use of a railroad. In contrast, IRS technologies are operated in only one location, and hence each unit of output produced with these technologies must be transported to get sold. We assume that industrialization cannot take place in the absence of the railroad. We also assume for simplicity that the transportation input is the same for all units manufactured using IRS.

In addition, we assume that there are now two types of IRS technologies. A fraction $n$ of sectors (1-firms) requires the fixed cost $F_1$ to be incurred in the first period to build a factory, whereas the fraction $1 - n$ (2-firms) requires the fixed cost $F_2 > F_1$. In the second period, all fixed-cost firms have labor productivity $\alpha$. We introduce the two types of sectors in order to address the case in which the railroad fails to extract all the surplus it generates. We also assume that it takes a fixed cost of $R$ units of labor in the first period to build the railroad and that the marginal cost of using it is zero. The latter assumption is used only for simplicity.

To address the question of surplus extraction by the railroad, we note that if the railroad does not observe the fixed cost of each firm, all firms look the same in the first period. As a result, the railroad cannot price-discriminate between them. A further issue is that to the extent that costs $F_1$ are sunk in the first period, a railroad that extracts all the period 2 cash flows from the investing firms will make all their investments money-losing.

Accordingly, we assume that the railroad can commit itself to a price it will charge in the second period before the potential industrial firms make their investments.

Throughout this section we also assume that there is no way that low-fixed-cost firms, even if they could profitably industrialize alone, would generate enough surplus to pay for the railroad; both types must industrialize to pay for it. This assumption amounts to

$$n\left(\frac{aL}{1 - an} - F_1\right) < R \tag{20}$$

which is essentially an upper bound on the profits 1-firms can generate. Note that (20) is also an efficiency condition for 1-firms industrializing alone since we are assuming that the railroad extracts all the surplus.

Under our assumptions, the price the railroad charges enables it to extract all the profits from high-but not low-fixed-cost firms. This seems to us to be the easiest way to model the realistic notion that the railroad owners do not capture all the social benefits of the investment.

A necessary and sufficient condition for there to exist an equilibrium in which a railroad is built and all sectors industrialize is

$$a\alpha L - F_2 > R \tag{21}$$

Condition (21) implies that the railroad can cover its costs when it charges each firm the amount equal to the profit of a 2-firm. Since the railroad cannot price-discriminate, each high-fixed-cost firm will then earn a zero profit, and each low, fixed-cost firm will earn a profit of $F_2 - F_1$. Condition (21) also implies that the high-fixed-cost firms can break even since period 2 income is $\alpha L$. It is easy to see, then, that (21) guarantees both that all firms are prepared to invest when the railroad is built and other firms invest, and that the railroad can be paid for by tariffs charged to investing firms.

In some circumstances, building of the railroad and industrialization of all sectors will not take place even if this outcome is efficient. Building the railroad is efficient whenever the surplus from industrialization is positive, which happens if

$$a\alpha L - nF_1 - (1 - n)F_2 > R \tag{22}$$

Since (22) is less stringent than (21), the railroad sometimes is not built even when it is efficient. This happens precisely because the railroad can charge each firm only the amount equal to the profits of 2-firms, which are smaller than the profits of 1-firms. At the same time, it would be efficient to build the railroad if it can break even extracting both the surplus of 1-firms and that of 2-firms. The imposibility of price discrimination gives rise to the outcome in which the railroad is not built and industrialization does not take place even when efficiency dictates otherwise.

This is a very simple reason for a failure of an efficient industrialization. When (22) holds but (21) fails, the market for railroad services is too small in the sense that some users do not end up paying as much as the services are worth to them, even if all firms would industrialize with a railroad. If the railroad could price-discriminate better, the efficient outcome would be achieved and there would be a large increase in income due to the large amount of producer and consumer surplus created by the railroad. As it is, there is a unique equilibrium in which the railroad is not built because it is privately unprofitable, even though it is socially very desirable.

The discussion thus far leaves open the question whether (21) suffices for the railroad to be built. In other words, will the railroad be built for sure if once it is built industrialization is a feasible equilibrium? The answer of course is no since industrialization need not be the only equilibrium that can occur once the railroad is built. What would keep the railroad from being built is the extrinsic uncertainty over whether or not the potential users of the railroad do in fact make their fixed-cost investments and thus become actual users. This uncertainty thus concerns the selection of equilibrium between sectors. If the railroad must be built without a prior knowledge of the actions of manufacturing sectors, its organizers might refuse to accept the uncertainty about the future demand, in which case the railroad is not built and industrialization does not occur.

For both equilibria to exist after the railroad is built, it suffices to look at parameter values for which (21) holds, and it also does not pay a 1-firm to invest when expected income is $L$, that is,

$$aL - F_1 < 0 \qquad (23)$$

For these parameter values, the railroad will make money on its first-period investment if the economy industrializes but will incur a large loss if no industrialization takes place and there are no consumers of its services. The investment $R$ might then not be made because the proprietors of the railroad are averse to the possibility that the bad equilibrium obtains. We then have a standoff in which the railroad is not built for fear that an insufficient number of sectors will industrialize, and this in turn ensures that firms do not make the large-scale investments needed to industrialize.

This discussion reveals two ways in which investment by a sector benefits other sectors in a way that is not captured by profits. First, just as in the previous section, an investing firm raises the demand in the second period and hence helps other firms make money. Second, by using railroad services, an investing firm helps pay for the fixed cost of the railroad. The railroad, in turn, reduces the production costs of other sectors. Indirectly, then, an investing firm contributes to the reduction of total costs of the other industrializing sectors. These effects give rise to the possibility that a firm actually benefits other firms even if it loses money, and so to big push type results. Furthermore, for reasons identical to those in the previous section, the equilibrium with industrialization is Pareto-preferred.

The failures of an efficient railroad to be built suggest some clear functions for the government in this model. Subsidizing the railroad might be helpful but not sufficient. What is also needed is a coordination of investments by enough private users of the railroad to get to the equilibrium with industrialization. Without industrialization by such users, the railroad can become a classic "white elephant" project that is not needed when it is built. This problem can of course be ameliorated if railroad users are sufficiently optimistic that they are eager to invest: this might be the description of America's nineteenth-century experience. The problem can also be solved if one large sector of the economy demands enough railroad services to cover the fixed cost:

Colombia's coffee boom in the 1880s is a case in point. In the absence of such favorable circumstances, however, government intervention in support of the railroad might be essential.

The railroad is one of a number of examples of infrastructure projects that require substantial demand by industry (or by other customers) to break even and that might need public subsidies if built ahead of demand. Other examples include power stations, roads, airports, and perhaps, most important, training facilities (Rosenstein-Rodan, 1961). One reason for underinvestment in such facilities is the inability of firms to prevent workers they train from moving to other firms and so appropriating the returns from training. A second important reason why a country with little industry will have too few training facilities concerns the ignorance of untrained workers about what they are good at. Some education is necessary to discover one's comparative advantage. A worker will invest in such education only if a broad range of different industries offer employment, so that he can take advantage of his skills. But a broad range of industries is less likely to develop in the first place if the labor force is uneducated.

In the context of market size models, infrastructure can be a particularly appealing area for state intervention. First, coordination issues are especially important since the infrastructure serves many sectors simultaneously. Second, the projects tend to be large and time-consuming, so that capital market constraints and substantial uncertainty can deter private participation. Third, projects are fairly standard, and hence "local knowledge" (von Hayek, 1945), which is perhaps the main advantage of private entrepreneurs over government, is not as essential as in other activities. It is not surprising then that most governments support infrastructure, and the most successful ones – such as Korea – coordinate that support with general industrial development.

# 7. Conclusion

The analysis of this paper has established some, though by no means all, conditions under which a backward economy can make a big push into industrialization by coordinating investments across sectors. The principal idea is that the big push is possible in economies in which industrialized firms capture in their profits only a fraction of the total contribution of their investment to the profits of other industrializing firms. In our examples, a firm adopting increasing returns must be shifting demand toward manufactured goods, redistributing demand toward the periods in which other firms sell, or paying part of the cost of the essential infrastructure, such as a railroad. In these cases, the firm can help to foster a mutually profitable big push even when it would lose money industrializing alone. All out models have the common feature that complementarities between industrializing sectors work through market size effects. In the first two models, industrialization of one sector raises the demand for other manufactures directly and so makes large-scale production in other sectors more attractive. In the railroad model, industrialization in one sector increases the size of the market for railroad services used by other sectors and so renders the provision of these services more viable.

The analysis may also have some implications for the role of government in the development process. First, a program that encourages industrialization in many sectors simultaneously can substantially boost income and welfare even when investment in any one sector appears unprofitable. This is especially true for a country whose access to foreign markets is limited by high transportation costs or trade restrictions. The net payoff from a program of simultaneous industrialization can also be high when all markets are open, but a shared infrastructure – such as a railroad or a stock of managers – is necessary to operate profitably in any given sector. In the latter case, simultaneous development of many export sectors may be necessary to sustain any one of them.

Our analysis also suggests that countries such as South Korea that have implemented a coordinated investment program can achieve industrialization of each sector at a lower explicit cost in terms of temporary tariffs and subsidies than a country that industrializes piecemeal. The reason is that potentially large implicit subsidies flow across sectors under a program of simultaneous industrialization. Any cost–benefit analysis of subsidies or of temporary protection should reflect both the lower direct costs and the higher net benefit of a program that is coordinated across sectors.

### Notes

1   The pecuniary externalities analyzed in this paper should be contrasted with technological externalities that can also give rise to interesting growth paths (Romer, 1986a; Lucas, 1988). Romer and Lucas also look at increasing returns, except in their models increasing returns are external to the firm. Earlier attempts outside the development literature to model pecuniary externalities in the growth context include important work of Young (1928) and Kaldor (1966) and recent work of Romer (1986b) and Shleifer (1986). Also related is some work in macro-economics, e.g., Hart (1982), Weitzman (1982), and Kiyotaki (1988).

2   Farrell and Saloner (1985) suggest that multiplicity of equilibria is not a problem if one redefines the game to be sequential. We believe that for the problem we address the multiple equilibrium model we present captures the essential aspects of reality.

3   Our own calculations are based on table 6.3 in Chenery et al. (1986).

4   The discussion that follows partly draws on Shleifer and Vishny (1988).

5   The assumption that each monopolist maximizes profits rather than the welfare of his share-holders is what allows pecuniary externalities to matter. Shleifer (1986) justifies this assumption in some detail.

6   Factory employment is usually associated with working in a city. Lewis (1967) and many others confirm the empirical validity of the assumption that higher real wages are paid in cities.

7   All the models we study assume unit elastic demand. Historically, however, price-elastic demand for manufactures has played an important role in growth of industry (Deane, 1979). Price-elastic demand leads to price cuts by a monopolist and the increase in consumer surplus, which is an additional reason for a big push.

8   For simplicity, there is no agricultural sector, although one could be added (see Murphy, Shleifer and Vishny, 1989).

9   If $r$ is the equilibrium interest rate, then $\beta^* = 1/(1 + r)$.

10   An example demonstrating this possibility is available from the authors.

11   Policies coordinating private investment across sectors appear in Rosenstein-Rodan's (1943) proposal for the East European Investment Trust. According to that proposal, foreign lenders and donors should insist that the money they lend to the economy be spent on investment and not on consumption. This is entirely consistent with this concern for the welfare of aid recipients as well as with a concern for getting their money back.

## References

Chenery, H. B., Robinson, S. and Syrquin, M. (1986): *Industrialization and Growth: A Comparative Study*. New York: Oxford University Press (for World Bank)

Chenery, H. B. and Syrquin, M. (1975): *Patterns of Development, 1950–1970*. London: Oxford University Press (for World Bank).

Cole, A. H. (1959): *Business Enterprise in Its Social Setting*. Cambridge, Mass.: Harvard University Press.

Deane, P. (1979): *The First Industrial Revolution*. 2nd edn. Cambridge: Cambridge University Press.

Farrell, J. and Saloner, G. (1985): "Standardization, Compatibility, and Innovation," *Rand Journal of Economics*, 16, Spring, 70–83.

Fishlow, A. (1965): *American Railroads and the Transformation of the Ante-Bellum Economy*. Cambridge, Mass.: Harvard University Press.

Fleming, J. M. (1955): "External Economies and the Doctrine of Balanced Growth," *Economic Journal*, 65, June, 241–56.

Fogel, R. W. (1964): *Railroads and American Economic Growth: Essays in Econometric History*. Baltimore: Johns Hopkins Press.

Hart, O. D. (1982): "A Model of Imperfect Competition with Keynesian Features," *Quarterly Journal of Economies*, 97, February, 109–38.

Kaldor, N. (1966): *Causes of the Slow Rate of Economic Growth of the United Kingdom: An Inaugural Lecture*. Cambridge: Cambridge University Press.

Keynes, J. M. (1936): *The General Theory of Employment, Interest and Money*. London: Macmillan.

Kiyotaki, N. (1988): "Multiple Expectations Equilibria under Monopolistic Competition," *Quarterly Journal of Economics* 103, November, 695–714.

Lewis, W. A. (1967): "Unemployment in Developing Countries," *World Today*, 23, January, 13–22.

Lucas, R. E., Jr. (1988): "On the Mechanics of Economic Development," *Journal of Monetary Economics*, 22, July, 3–42.

Murphy, K. M., Shleifer, A. and Vishny, R. W. (1989): "Income Distribution, Market Size, and Industrialization," *Quarterly Journal of Economics*, 104, August.

Nurkse, R. (1953): *Problems of Capital Formation in Underdeveloped Countries*. New York: Oxford University Press.

Reynolds, L. G. (1983): "The Spread of Economic Growth to the Third World: 1850–1980," *Journal of Economic Literature*, 21, September, 941–80.

Romer, P. M. (1986a): "Increasing Returns and Long-Run Growth," *Journal of Political Economy*, 94, October, 1002–37.

—— (1986b): "Increasing Returns, Specialization, and External Economies: Growth as Described by Allyn Young," manuscript, Rochester, N.Y.: University of Rochester.

Rosenstein-Rodan, P. N. (1943): "Problems of Industrialisation of Eastern and South-eastern Europe," *Economic Journal*, 53, June–September, 202–11.

—— (1961): "Notes on the Theory of the 'Big Push'," in H. S. Ellis and H. C. Wallich (eds) *Economic Development for Latin America*, New York: St. Martin's.

Rostow, W. W. (1960): *The Stages of Economic Growth: A Non-Communist Manifesto*. Cambridge: Cambridge University Press.

Sawyer, J. E. (1954): "Entrepreneurship in Periods of Rapid Growth: The United States in the 19th Century," paper presented at a conference on Entrepreneurship and Economic Growth, Cambridge, Mass., November 12–13.

Scitovsky, T. (1954): "Two Concepts of External Economies," *Journal of Political Economy*, 62, April, 143–51.

Shleifer, A. (1986): "Implementation Cycles," *Journal of Political Economy*, 94, December, 1163–90.
Shleifer, A. and Vishny, R. W. (1988): "The Efficiency of Investment in the Presence of Aggregate Demand Spillovers," *Journal of Political Economy*, 96, December, 1221–31.
von Hayek, F. A. (1945): "The Use of Knowledge in Society," *American Economic Review*, 35, September, 519–30.
Weitzman, M. L. (1982): "Increasing Returns and the Foundations of Unemployment Theory," *Economic Journal*, 92, December, 787–804.
Young, A. A. (1928): "Increasing Returns and Economic Progress," *Economic Journal*, 38, December, 527–42.

CHAPTER 2

# Increasing Returns and Long-run Growth

PAUL M. ROMER

This paper presents a fully specified model of long-run growth in which knowledge is assumed to be an input in production that has increasing marginal productivity. It is essentially a competitive equilibrium model with endogenous technological change. In contrast to models based on diminishing returns, growth rates can be increasing over time, the effects of small disturbances can be amplified by the actions of private agents, and large countries may always grow faster than small countries. Long-run evidence is offered in support of the empirical relevance of these possibilities.

## 1. Introduction

Because of its simplicity, the aggregate growth model analyzed by Ramsey (1928), Cass (1965), and Koopmans (1965) continues to form the basis for much of the intuition economists have about long-run growth. The rate of return on investment and the rate of growth of per capita output are expected to be decreasing functions of the level of the per capita capital stock. Over time, wage rates and capital–labor ratios across different countries are expected to converge. Consequently, initial conditions or current disturbances have no long-run effect on the level of output and consumption. For example, an exogenous reduction in the stock of capital in a given country will cause prices for capital assets to increase and will therefore induce an offsetting increase in investment. In the absence of technological change, per capita output should converge to a steady-state value with no per capita growth. All these presumptions follow directly from the assumption of diminishing returns to per capita capital in the production of per capita output.

The model proposed here offers an alternative view of long-run prospects for growth. In a fully specified competitive equilibrium, per capita output can grow without bound, possibly at a rate that is monotonically increasing over time. The rate of investment and the rate of return on capital may increase rather than decrease with increases in the capital stock. The level of per capita output in different countries need not converge; growth may be persistently slower in less developed countries and may even fail to take place at all. These results do not depend on any kind of exogenously specified technical change or differences between countries. Preferences and the technology are stationary and identical. Even the size of the population can be held constant. What is crucial for all of these results is a departure from the usual assumption of diminishing returns.

While exogenous technological change is ruled out, the model here can be viewed as an equilibrium model of endogenous technological change in which long-run growth is driven primarily by the accumulation of knowledge by forward-looking, profit-maximizing agents. This focus on knowledge as the basic form of capital suggests natural changes in the formulation of the standard aggregate growth model. In contrast to physical capital that can be produced one for one from forgone output, new knowledge is assumed to be the product of a research technology that exhibits diminishing returns. That is, given the stock of knowledge at a point in time, doubling the inputs into research will not double the amount of new knowledge produced. In addition, investment in knowledge suggests a natural externality. The creation of new knowledge by one firm is assumed to have a positive external effect on the production possibilities of other firms because knowledge cannot be perfectly patented or kept secret. Most important, production of consumption goods as a function of the stock of knowledge and other inputs exhibits increasing returns; more precisely, knowledge may have an increasing marginal product. In contrast to models in which capital exhibits diminishing marginal productivity, knowledge will grow without bound. Even if all other inputs are held constant, it will not be optimal to stop at some steady state where knowledge is constant and no new research is undertaken.

These three elements – externalities, increasing returns in the production of output, and decreasing returns in the production of new knowledge – combine to produce a well-specified competitive equilibrium model of growth. Despite the presence of increasing returns, a competitive equilibrium with externalities will exist. This equilibrium is not Pareto optimal, but it is the outcome of a well-behaved positive model and is capable of explaining historical growth in the absence of government intervention. The presence of the externalities is essential for the existence of an equilibrium. Diminishing returns in the production of knowledge are required to ensure that consumption and utility do not grow too fast. But the key feature in the reversal of the standard results about growth is the assumption of increasing rather than decreasing marginal productivity of the intangible capital good knowledge.

The paper is organized as follows. Section 2 traces briefly the history of the idea that increasing returns are important to the explanation of long-run growth and describes some of the conceptual difficulties that impeded progress toward a formal model that relied on increasing returns. Section 3 presents empirical evidence in support of the model proposed here. Section 4 presents a stripped-down, two-period version of the model that illustrates the tools that are used to analyze an equilibrium with externalities and increasing returns. Section 5 presents the analysis of the infinite-horizon, continuous-time version of the model, characterizing the social optimum and the competitive equilibrium, both with and without optimal taxes.

The primary motivation for the choice of continuous time and the restriction to a single state variable is the ease with which qualitative results can be derived using the geometry of the phase plane. In particular, once functional forms for production and preferences have been specified, useful qualitative information about the dynamics of the social optimum or the suboptimal competitive equilibrium can be extracted using simple algebra. Section 6 presents several examples that illustrate the extent to which conventional presumptions about growth rates, asset prices, and cross-country comparisons may be reversed in this kind of economy.


## 2. Historical Origins and Relation to Earlier Work

The idea that increasing returns are central to the explanation of long-run growth is at least as old as Adam Smith's story of the pin factory. With the introduction by Alfred Marshall of the distinction between internal and external economies, it appeared that this explanation could be given a consistent, competitive equilibrium interpretation. The most prominent such attempt was made by Allyn Young in his 1928 presidential address to the Economics and Statistics section of the British Association for the Advancement of Science (Young, 1969). Subsequent economists (e.g., Hicks, 1960; Kaldor, 1981) have credited Young with a fundamental insight about growth, but because of the verbal nature of his argument and the difficulty of formulating explicit dynamic models, no formal model embodying that insight was developed.

Because of the technical difficulties presented by dynamic models, Marshall's concept of increasing returns that are external to a firm but internal to an industry was most widely used in static models, especially in the field of international trade. In the 1920s the logical consistency and relevance of these models began to be seriously challenged, in particular by Frank Knight, who had been a student of Young's at Cornell.[1] Subsequent work demonstrated that it is possible to construct consistent, general equilibrium models with perfect competition, increasing returns, and externalities (see, e.g., Chipman, 1970). Yet Knight was at least partially correct in objecting that the concept of increasing returns that are external to the firm was vacuous, an "empty economic box" (Knight, 1925). Following Smith, Marshall, and Young, most authors justified the existence of increasing returns on the basis of increasing specialization and the division of labor. It is now clear that these changes in the organization of production cannot be rigorously treated as technological externalities. Formally, increased specialization opens new markets and introduces new goods. All producers in the industry may benefit from the introduction of these goods, but they are goods, not technological externalities.[2]

Despite the objections raised by Knight, static models of increasing returns with externalities have been widely used in international trade. Typically, firm output is simply assumed to be increasing, or unit cost decreasing, in aggregate industry output. See Helpman (1984) for a recent survey. Renewed interest in dynamic models of growth driven by increasing returns was sparked in the 1960s following the publication of Arrow's (1962) paper on learning by doing. In his model, the productivity of a given firm is assumed to be an increasing function of cumulative aggregate investment for the industry. Avoiding the issues of specialization and the division of labor, Arrow argued that increasing returns arise because new knowledge is discovered as investment and production take place. The increasing returns were external to individual firms because such knowledge became publicly known.

To formalize his model, Arrow had to face two problems that arise in any optimizing model of growth in the presence of increasing returns. The first, familiar from static models, concerns the existence of a competitive equilibrium; as is now clear, if the increasing returns are external to the firm, an equilibrium can exist. The second problem, unique to dynamic optimizing models, concerns the existence of a social optimum and the finiteness of objective functions. In a standard optimizing growth model that maximizes a discounted sum or integral over an infinite horizon, the presence of increasing returns raises the possibility that feasible consumption paths may grow so fast that the objective function is not finite. An optimum can fail to exist even in the sense of an overtaking criterion. In the model of Arrow and its elaborations by Levhari (1966a, 1966b) and Sheshinski (1967), this difficulty is avoided by assuming that output as a function of capital and labor exhibits increasing returns to scale but that the marginal product of capital is diminishing given a fixed supply of labor. As a result, the rate of growth of output is limited by the rate of growth of the labor force. Interpreted as an aggregate model of growth (rather than as a model of a specific industry), this model leads to the empirically questionable implication that the rate of growth of per capita output is a monotonically increasing function of the rate of growth of the population. Like conventional models with diminishing returns, it predicts that the rate of growth in per capita consumption must go to zero in an economy with zero population growth.

The model proposed here departs from both the Ramsey–Cass–Koopmans model and the Arrow model by assuming that knowledge is a capital good with an increasing marginal product. Production of the consumption good is assumed to be globally convex, not concave, as a function of stock of knowledge when all other inputs are held constant. A finite-valued social optimum is guaranteed to exist because of diminishing returns in the research technology, which imply the existence of a maximum, technologically feasible rate of growth for knowledge. This is turn implies the existence of a maximum feasible rate of growth for per capita output. Over time, the rate of growth of output may be monotonically increasing, but it cannot exceed this upper bound.

Uzawa (1965) describes an optimizing growth model in which both intangible human capital and physical capital can be produced. In some respects, the human capital resembles knowledge as described in this paper, but Uzawa's model does not possess any form of increasing returns to scale. Instead, it considers a borderline case of constant returns to scale with linear production of human capital. In this case, unbounded growth is possible. Asymptotically, output and both types of capital grow at the same constant rate. Other optimizing models took the rate of technological change as exogenously given (e.g., Shell, 1967b). Various descriptive models of growth with elements similar to those used here were also proposed during the 1960s (e.g., Phelps, 1966; von Weizsäcker, 1966; Shell, 1967a). Knowledge is accumulated by devoting resources to research. Production of consumption goods exhibits constant returns as a function of tangible inputs (e.g., physical capital and labor) and therefore exhibits increasing returns as a function of tangible and intangible inputs. Privately produced knowledge is in some cases assumed to be partially revealed to other agents in the economy. Because the descriptive models do not use explicit objective functions, questions of existence are generally avoided, and a full welfare analysis is not possible. Moreover, these models tend to be relatively restrictive, usually constructed so that the analysis could be carried out in terms of steady states and constant growth rate paths.

Continuous-time optimization problems with some form of increasing returns are studied in papers by Weitzman (1970), Dixit, Mirrlees, and Stern (1975), and Skiba (1978). Similar issues are considered for discrete-time models in Majumdar and Mitra (1982, 1983) and Dechert and Nishimura (1983). These papers differ from the model here primarily because they are not concerned with the existence of a competitive equilibrium. Moreover, in all these papers, the technical approach used to prove the existence of an optimum is different from that used here. They rely on either bounded instantaneous utility $U(c)$ or bounds on the degree of increasing returns in the problem; for example, the production function $f(k)$ is assumed to be such that $f(k)/k$ is bounded from above. The results here do not rely on either of these kinds of restrictions; in fact, one of the most interesting examples analyzed in section 6 violates both of these restrictions. Instead, the approach used here relies on the assumptions made concerning the research technology; the diminishing returns in research will limit the rate of growth of the state variable. A general proof that restrictions on the rate of growth of the state variable are sufficient to prove the existence of an optimum for a continuous-time maximization problem with nonconvexities is given in Romer (1986).

Because an equilibrium for the model proposed here is a competitive equilibrium with externalities, the analysis is formally similar to that used in dynamic models with more conventional kinds of externalities (e.g., Brock, 1977; Hochman and Hochman, 1980). It also has a close formal similarity to perfect-foresight Sidrauski models of money demand and inflation (Brock, 1975) and to symmetric Nash equilibria for dynamic games (e.g., Hansen, Epple, and Roberds, 1985). In each case, an equilibrium is calculated not by solving a social planning problem but rather by considering the maximization problem of an individual agent who takes as given the path of some endogenously determined aggregate variable. In the conventional analysis of externalities, the focus is generally on the social optimum and the set of taxes necessary to support it as a competitive equilibrium. While this question is addressed for this growth model, the discussion places more stress on the characterization of the competitive equilibrium without intervention since it is the most reasonable positive model of observed historical growth. One of the main contributions of this paper is to demonstrate how the analysis of this kind of suboptimal equilibrium can proceed using familiar tools like a phase plane even though the equations describing the equilibrium cannot be derived from any stationary maximization problem.

## 3. Motivation and Evidence

Because theories of long-run growth assume away any variation in output attributable to business cycles, it is difficult to judge the empirical success of these theories. Even if one could resolve the theoretical ambiguity about how to filter the cycles out of the data and to extract the component that growth theory seeks to explain, the longest available time series do not have enough observations to allow precise estimates of low-frequency components or long-run trends. When data aggregated into decades rather than years are used, the pattern of growth in the United States is quite variable and is apparently still influenced by cyclical movements in output (see figure 1). Cross-country comparisons of growth rates are complicated by the difficulty of controlling for political and social variables that appear to strongly influence the growth process. With these qualifications in mind, it is useful to ask whether there is anything in the data that should cause economists to choose a model with diminishing returns, falling rates of growth, and convergence across countries rather than an alternative without these features.

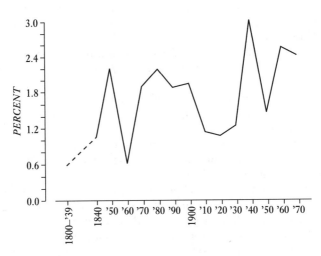

**Figure 1**   Average annual compound growth rate of per capita GDP in the United States for the inverval 1800–1839 and for 14 subsequent decades

*Source*:   Maddison (1979)

Consider first the long-run trend in the growth rate of productivity or per capita gross domestic product (GDP). One revealing way to consider the long-run evidence is to distinguish at any point in time between the country that is the "leader," that is, that has the highest level of productivity, and all other countries. Growth for a country that is not a leader will reflect at least in part the process of imitation and transmission of existing knowledge, whereas the growth rate of the leader gives some indication of growth at the frontier of knowledge. Using GDP per man-hour as his measure of productivity, Maddison (1982) identifies three countries that have been leaders since 1700: the Netherlands, the United Kingdom, and the United States. Table 1 reports his estimates of the rate of growth of productivity in each country during the interval when it was the leader. When the productivity growth rate is measured over intervals several decades long and compared over almost three centuries, the evidence clearly suggests that it has been increasing, not decreasing. The rate of growth of productivity increases monotonically from essentially zero growth in eighteenth-century Netherlands to 2.3 percent per year since 1890 in the United States.

Similar evidence is apparent from data for individual countries over shorter horizons. Table 2 reports growth rates in per capita GDP for the United States over five sub-periods from 1800 to 1978. (The raw data used here are from Maddison (1979).) These rates also suggest a positive rather than a negative trend, but measuring growth rates over 40-year intervals hides a substantial amount of year-to-year or even decade-to-decade variation in the rate of growth. Figure 1 presents the average growth rate over the interval 1800–1839 (for which no intervening data are available) and for the subsequent 14 decades. Identifying a long-run trend in rates measured over decades is more problematical in this case, but it is straightforward to apply a simple nonparametric test for trend.

**Table 1** Productivity growth rates for leading countries

| Lead country | Interval | Annual average compound growth rate of GDP per man-hour (%) |
|---|---|---|
| Netherlands | 1700–1785 | −0.07 |
| United Kingdom | 1785–1820 | 0.5 |
| United Kingdom | 1820–90 | 1.4 |
| United States | 1890–1979 | 2.3 |

*Source*:  Maddison (1982)

**Table 2**  Per capita growth in the United States

| Interval | Average annual compound growth rate of real per capita GDP (%) |
|---|---|
| 1800–1840 | 0.58 |
| 1840–80 | 1.44 |
| 1880–1920 | 1.78 |
| 1920–60 | 1.68 |
| 1960–78 | 2.47 |

*Source*:  Raw data are from Maddison (1979).

Table 3 reports the results of this kind of test for trend in the per capita rate of growth in GDP for several countries using raw data from Maddison (1979). The sample includes all countries for which continuous observations on per capita GDP are available starting no later than 1870. As for the data for the United States graphed in Figure 1, the growth rates used in the test for trend are measured over decades where possible. The statistic $\pi$ gives the sample estimate of the probability that, for any two randomly chosen decades, the later decade has a higher growth rate.

Despite the variability evident from Figure 1, the test for trend for the United States permits the rejection of the null hypothesis of a nonpositive trend at conventional significance levels. This is true even though growth over the four decades from 1800 to 1839 is treated as a single observation. However, rejection of the null hypothesis depends critically on the use of a sufficiently long data series. If we drop the observation on growth between 1800 and 1839, the estimate of $\pi$ drops from .68 to .63 and the *p*-value increases from .03 to .11.[3] If we further restrict attention to the 11 decades from 1870 to 1978, $\pi$ drops to .56 and the *p*-value increases to .29, so it is not surprising that studies that focus on the period since 1870 tend to emphasize the constancy of growth rates in the United States. Rejection does not appear to depend on the use of the rate of growth in per capita GDP rather than the rate of growth of productivity. Reliable measures of the work force prior to 1840 are not available, but using data from Kuznets (1971) for the period 1840– 1960 and from the 1984 Economic Report of the President for 1960–80, one can construct a similar test for trend in the rate of growth of productivity over successive decades. The results of this test, $\pi$ equal to .64 with a *p*-value of .10, correspond closely to those noted above for growth in per capita GDP over the similar interval, 1840–1978.

**Table 3**   A test for trend in per capita GDP growth rates

|  | Date of first observation | Number of observations | π | p-Value |
|---|---|---|---|---|
| United Kingdom | 1700 | 20 | 0.63 | 0.06 |
| France | 1700 | 18 | 0.69 | 0.01 |
| Denmark | 1818 | 16 | 0.70 | 0.02 |
| United States | 1800 | 15 | 0.68 | 0.03 |
| Germany | 1850 | 13 | 0.67 | 0.06 |
| Sweden | 1861 | 12 | 0.58 | 0.25 |
| Italy | 1861 | 12 | 0.76 | 0.01 |
| Australia | 1861 | 12 | 0.64 | 0.11 |
| Norway | 1865 | 12 | 0.81 | 0.002 |
| Japan | 1870 | 11 | 0.67 | 0.07 |
| Canada | 1870 | 11 | 0.64 | 0.12 |

$\pi$ is the sample estimate for each country of the probability that, for any two growth rates, the later one is larger. The $p$-value is the probability of observing a value of $\pi$ at least as large as the observed value under the null hypothesis that the true probability is .5. Except in the early years when data are sparse, per capita rates of growth of GDP were measured over successive decades. (Only two observations on growth rates are available for France prior to 1820; for the United Kingdom, only two prior to 1800; for the United States, only one from 1800 to 1840.) For the calculation of the $p$-value, see Kendall (1962). Data are from Maddison (1979).

Over the entire sample of 11 countries, the estimated value for $\pi$ ranges from .58 to .81, with a $p$-value that ranges from .25 to .002. Five out of 11 of the $p$-values are less than .05, permitting rejection at the 5 percent level in a one-sided test of the null hypothesis that there is a nonpositive trend in the growth rate; eight out of 11 permit rejection at the 10 percent level.

For less developed countries, no comparable long-run statistics on per capita income are available. Reynolds (1983) gives an overview of the pattern of development in such countries. Given the paucity of precise data for less developed countries, he focuses on the "turning point" at which a country first begins to exhibit a persistent upward trend in per capita income. The timing of this transition and the pace of subsequent growth are strongly influenced by the variations in the world economy. A general pattern of historically unprecedented growth for the world economy is evident starting in the last part of the 1800s and continuing to the present. This general pattern is interrupted by a significant slowdown during the years between the two world wars and by a remarkable surge from roughly 1950 to 1973. Worldwide growth since 1973 has been slow only by comparison with that surge and appears to have returned to the high rates that prevailed in the period from the late 1800s to 1914.

Although all less developed countries are affected by the worldwide economy, the effects are not uniform. For our purposes, the key observation is that those countries with more extensive prior development appear to benefit more from periods of rapid worldwide growth and suffer less during any slowdown. That is, growth rates appear to be increasing not only as a function of calendar time but also as a function of the level of development. The observation that more developed countries appear to grow relatively faster extends to a comparison of industrialized versus less developed countries as well. In the period from 1950 to 1980, when official estimates for GDP are generally available, Reynolds reports that the median rate of growth of per capita income for his sample of 41 less developed countries was 2.3 percent, "clearly below the median for the OECD countries for the same period" (1983, p. 975).

If it is true that growth rates are not negatively correlated with the level of per capita output or capital, then there should be no tendency for the dispersion in the (logarithm of the)[4] level of per capita income to decrease over time. There should be no tendency toward convergence. This contradicts a widespread impression that convergence in this sense has been evident, especially since the Second World War. Streissler (1979) offers evidence about the source of this impression and its robustness. For each year from 1950 to 1974, he measures the variance across countries of the logarithm of the level of per capita income. In a sample of ex post industrialized countries, those countries with a level of per capita income of at least $2,700 in 1974, clear evidence of a decrease in the dispersion over time is apparent. In a sample of *ex ante* industrialized countries, countries with a per capita income of at least $350 in 1950, no evidence of a decrease in the variance is apparent. The first sample differs from the second because it includes Japan and excludes Argentina, Chile, Ireland, Puerto Rico, and Venezuela. As one would expect, truncating the sample at the end biases the trend toward decreasing dispersion (and at the beginning toward increasing dispersion). When a sample of all possible countries is used, there is no evidence of a decrease in variance, but the interpretation of this result is complicated by the changing number of countries in the sample in each year due to data limitations.

Baumol (1985) reports similar results. When countries are grouped into industrialized, intermediate, centrally planned, and less developed economies, he argues that there is a tendency toward convergence in the level of productivity within groups, even though there is no tendency toward overall convergence. The tendency toward convergence is clear only in his group of industrialized economies, which corresponds closely to the sample of *ex post* industrialized countries considered by Streissler. In any case, he finds no obvious pattern in his entire sample of countries; if anything, there is a weak tendency toward divergence.[5]

The other kind of evidence that bears directly on the assumption of increasing returns in production comes from growth accounting exercises and the estimation of aggregate production functions. Economists believe that virtually all technical change is endogenous, the outcome of deliberate actions taken by economic agents. If so and if production exhibits constant returns to scale, one would expect to be able to account for the rate of growth of output in terms of the rates of growth of all inputs. The difficulty in implementing a direct test of this assertion lies in correctly measuring all the inputs to production, especially for intangible capital inputs such as knowledge. In a comprehensive attempt to account for the rates of growth in output in terms of rates of growth of all inputs, including human and nonhuman, tangible and intangible stocks of capital, Kendrick (1976) concluded that rates of growth of inputs are not sufficient to explain the rate of growth of output in the 40-year interval 1929–69. For various sectors and levels of aggregation, the rate of growth of output is 1.06–1.30 times the appropriate aggregate measure of the rate of growth for inputs. This kind of estimate is subject to substantial, unquantified uncertainty and cannot be taken as decisive support for the presence of increasing returns. But given the repeated failure of this kind of growth accounting exercise, there is no basis in the data for excluding the possibility that aggregate production functions are best described as exhibiting increasing returns.

## 4. A Simple Two-Period Model

Even in the presence of increasing returns and externalities, calculating a social optimum is conceptually straightforward since it is equivalent to solving a maximization problem. Standard mathematical results can be used to show that a maximum exists and to characterize the solution by means of a set of necessary conditions. Despite the presence of global increasing returns, the model here does have a social optimum. The next section illustrates how it can be supported as a competitive equilibrium using a natural set of taxes and subsidies. This optimum is of theoretical and normative interest, but it cannot be a serious candidate for describing the observed long-run behaviour of per capita output. To the extent that appropriate taxes and subsidies have been used at all, they are a quite recent phenomenon.

The model here also has an equilibrium in the absence of any governmental intervention. Much of the emphasis in what follows focuses on how to characterize the qualitative features of this suboptimal dynamic equilibrium. Although it is suboptimal, the competitive equilibrium does satisfy a constrained optimality criterion that can be used to simplify the analysis much as the study of the social optimization problem simplifies the analysis in standard growth models.

The use of a constrained or restricted optimization problem is not a new approach to the analysis of a suboptimal dynamic equilibrium. For example, it has been widely used in the perfect-foresight models of inflation. Nonetheless, it is useful to describe this method in some detail because previous applications do not highlight the generality of the approach and because the dynamic setting tends to obscure its basic simplicity. Hence, I start by calculating a competitive equilibrium for a greatly simplified version of the growth model.

Specifically, consider a discrete-time model of growth with two periods. Let each of $S$ identical consumers have a twice continuously differentiable, strictly concave utility function $U(c_1, c_2)$, defined over consumption of a single output good in periods 1 and 2. Let each consumer be given an initial endowment of the output good in period 1. Suppose that production of consumption goods in period 2 is a function of the state of knowledge, denoted by $k$, and a set of additional factors such as physical capital, labor, and so forth, denoted by a vector $\mathbf{x}$.[6] To restrict attention to a choice problem that is essentially one-dimensional, assume that only the stock of knowledge can be augmented; the factors represented by $\mathbf{x}$ are available in fixed supply. To capture the basic idea that there is a trade-off between consumption today and knowledge that can be used to produce more consumption tomorrow, assume that there is a research technology that produces knowledge from forgone consumption in period 1. Because the economy here has only two periods, we need not be concerned with the problem that arises in an infinite-horizon model when consumption grows too fast and discounted utility goes to infinity. Thus we do not need diminishing returns in research to limit the rate of growth of knowledge, and we can choose a simple linear technology with units such that one unit of forgone consumption produces one unit of knowledge. A more realistic diminishing returns research technology is described in the infinite-horizon model presented in the next section.

Since newly produced private knowledge can be only partially kept secret and cannot be patented, we can represent the technology of firm $i$ in terms of a twice continuously differentiable production function $F$ that depends on the firm-specific inputs $k_i$ and $x_i$ and on the aggregate level of knowledge in the economy. If $N$ is the number of firms, define this aggregate level of knowledge as $K = \sum_{i=1}^{N} k_i$.

The first major assumption on the production function $F(k_i, K, x_i)$ is that, for any fixed value of $K$, $F$ is concave as a function of $k_i$ and $x_i$. Without this assumption, a competitive equilibrium will not exist in general. Once concavity is granted, there is little loss of generality in assuming that $F$ is homogeneous of degree one as a function of $k_i$ and $x_i$ when $K$ is held constant; any concave function can be extended to be homogeneous of degree one by adding an additional factor to the vector $x$ if necessary (Rockafellar 1970, p. 67). McKenzie (1959) refers to this additional factor as an entrepreneurial factor. It can be interpreted as an accounting device that transforms any profits into factor payments.

By the homogeneity of $F$ in $k_i$ and $x_i$ and by the assumption that $F$ is increasing in the aggregate stock of knowledge, $K$, it follows that $F$ exhibits increasing returns to scale. For any $\psi > 1$,

$$F(\psi k_i, \psi K, \psi x_i) > F(\psi k_i, K, \psi x_i) = \psi F(k_i, K, x_i)$$

The second major assumption strengthens this considerably. It requires that $F$ exhibit global increasing marginal productivity of knowledge from a social point of view. That is, for any fixed $x$, assume that $F(k, Nk, x)$, production per firm available to a dictator who can set economywide values for $k$, is convex in $k$, not concave. This strengthening of the assumption of increasing returns is what distinguishes the production function used here from the one used in the models of Arrow, Levhari, and Sheshinski.

The equilibrium for the two-period model is a standard competitive equilibrium with externalities. Each firm maximizes profits taking $K$, the aggregate level of knowledge, as given. Consumers supply part of their endowment of output goods and all the other factors $x$ to firms in period 1. With the proceeds, they purchase output goods in period 2. Consumers and firms maximize taking prices as given. As usual, the assumption that agents treat prices and the aggregate level $K$ as given could be rationalized in a model with a continuum of agents. Here, it is treated as the usual approximation for a large but finite number of agents. Because of the externality, all firms could benefit from a collusive agreement to invest more in research. Although this agreement would be Pareto-improving in this model, it cannot be supported for the same reasons that collusive agreements fail in models without externalities. Each firm would have an incentive to shirk, not investing its share of output in research. Even if all existing firms could be compelled to comply, for example, by an economywide merger, new entrants would still be able to free-ride and undermine the equilibrium.

Because of the assumed homogeneity of $F$ with respect to factors that receive compensation, profits for firms will be zero and the scale and number of firms will be indeterminate. Consequently, we can simplify the notation by restricting attention to an equilibrium in which the number of firms, $N$, equals the number of consumers, $S$. Then per firm and per capita values coincide. Assuming that all firms operate at the same level of output, we can omit firm-specific subscripts.

Let $\ddot{\mathbf{x}}$ denote the per capita (and per firm) endowment of the factors that cannot be augmented; let $e$ denote the per capita endowment of the output good in period 1. To calculate an equilibrium, define a family of restricted maximization problems indexed by $K$:

$$P(K)\colon \max_{k\in[0,\bar{e}]} U(c_1,c_2)$$

subject to $c_1 \leq \bar{e} - k, c_2 \leq F(k,K,\mathbf{x}), \mathbf{x} \leq \ddot{\mathbf{x}}$.

Since $U$ is strictly concave and $F(k,K,\mathbf{x})$ is concave in $k$ and $\mathbf{x}$ for each value of $K$, $P(K)$ will have a unique solution $k$ for each value of $K$. (The solution for $\mathbf{x}$ is trivially $\ddot{\mathbf{x}}$.) In general, the implied values for $c_1, c_2$, and $k$ have no economic meaning. If $K$ differs from $Sk$, then $F(k,K,\ddot{\mathbf{x}})$ is not a feasible level of per capita consumption in period 2. Equilibrium requires that the aggregate level of knowledge that is achieved in the economy be consistent with the level that is assumed when firms make production decisions. If we define a function $\Gamma : \mathbb{R} \to \mathbb{R}$ that sends $K$ into $S$ times the value of $k$ that achieves the maximum for the problem $P(K)$, this suggests fixed points of $\Gamma$ as candidates for equilibria.

To see that any fixed point $K^*$ of $\Gamma$ can indeed be supported as a competitive equilibrium, observe that $P(K^*)$ is a concave maximization problem with solution $k^* = K^*/S, c_1^* = \bar{e} - k^*$, and $c_2^* = F(k^*,Sk^*,\ddot{\mathbf{x}})$. Since it is concave, standard necessary conditions for concave problems apply. Let $\mathcal{L}$ denote a Lagrangian for $P(K^*)$ with multipliers $p_1$, $p_2$, and $w$:

$$\mathcal{L} = U(c_1,c_2) + p_1(\bar{e} - k - c_1) + p_2[F(k,K,\mathbf{x}) - c_2] + w(\ddot{\mathbf{x}} - \mathbf{x})$$

When an interior solution is assumed, familiar arguments show that

$$p_j = D_j U\left(c_1^*, c_2^*\right) \qquad \text{for } j = 1,2$$

that

$$p_1 = p_2 D_1 F(k^*,Sk^*,\ddot{\mathbf{x}})$$

and that[7]

$$w = p_2 D_3 F(k^*,Sk^*,\ddot{\mathbf{x}})$$

As always, the shadow prices $w$ and $p_j$ can be interpreted as equilibrium prices. To see this, consider first the maximization problem of the firm:

$$\max_{k} p_2 F(k,Sk^*,\mathbf{x}) - p_1 k - w \cdot \mathbf{x}$$

Since the firm takes both prices and the aggregate level $Sk^*$ as given, a trivial application of the sufficient conditions for a concave maximization problem demonstrates that $k^*$ and $\ddot{x}$ are optimal choices for the firm. By the homogeneity of $F$ with respect to its first and third arguments, profits will be zero at these values. Consider next the problem of the consumer. Income to the consumer will be the value of the endowment,

$$I = p_1 \bar{e} + w \cdot \ddot{x} = p_2 F(k^*, Sk^*, \ddot{x}) + p_1(\bar{e} - k^*)$$

(The second equality follows from the homogeneity of $F$ in $k$ and x.) When the necessary conditions $p_j = D_j U(c_1^*, c_2^*)$ from the problem $P(K^*)$ are used, it follows immediately that $c_1^*$ and $c_2^*$ are solutions to the problem max $U(c_1, c_2)$ subject to the budget constraint

$$p_1 c_1 + p_2 c_2 \leq I$$

Note that the marginal rate of substitution for consumers will equal the private marginal rate of transformation perceived by firms,

$$\frac{D_1 U(c_1^*, c_2^*)}{D_2 U(c_1^*, c_2^*)} = D_1 F(k^*, Sk^*, \ddot{x})$$

Because of the externality, this differs from the true marginal rate of transformation for the economy,

$$D_1 F(k^*, Sk^*, \ddot{x}) + SD_2 F(k^*, Sk^*, \ddot{x})$$

Arguments along these lines can be used quite generally to show that a fixed point of a mapping like $\Gamma$ defined by a family of concave problems $P(K)$ can be supported as a competitive equilibrium with externalities. The necessary conditions from a version of the Kuhn–Tucker theorem generate shadow prices associated with any solution to $P(K)$. The sufficient conditions for the problems of the consumer and the firm can then be used to show that the quantities from the solution will be chosen in an equilibrium in which these prices are taken as given. Conversely, an argument similar to the usual proof of the Pareto optimality of competitive equilibrium can be used to show that any competitive equilibrium with externalities for this kind of economy will satisfy the restricted optimality condition implicit in the problem $P(K)$ (Romer, 1983). That is, if $K^*$ is an equilibrium value of aggregate knowledge, then $K^*/S$ will solve the problem $P(K^*)$. Thus equilibria are equivalent to fixed points of the function $\Gamma$.

This allows an important simplification because it is straightforward to characterize fixed points of $\Gamma$ in terms of the underlying functions $U$ and $F$. Substituting the constraints from $P(K)$ into the objective and using the fact that x will be chosen to be $\ddot{x}$, define a new function

$$V(k, K) = U(\bar{e} - k, F(k, K, \ddot{x}))$$

Because of the increasing marginal productivity of knowledge, $V$ is not a concave function; but for any fixed $K$, it is concave in $k$. Then the optimal choice of $k$ in any problem $P(K)$ is determined by the equation $D_1 V(kK) = 0$. Fixed points of $\Gamma$ are then given by substituting $Sk$ for $K$ and solving $D_1 V(k, Sk) = 0$. Given functional forms for $U$ and $F$, this equation can immediately be written in explicit form. The analysis can therefore exploit a three-way equivalence between competitive equilibria with externalities, fixed points of $\Gamma$, and solutions to an explicit equation $D_1 V(k, Sk) = 0$.

The key observation in this analysis is that equilibrium quantities can be characterized as the solution to a concave maximization problem. Then prices can be generated from shadow prices or multipliers for this problem. The complete statement of the problem must be sought simultaneously with its solution because the statement involves the equilibrium quantities. But since $P(K)$ is a family of concave problems, solving simultaneously for the statement of the problem and for its solution amounts to making a simple substitution in a first-order condition.

## 5. Infinite-Horizon Growth

### 5.1. Description of the model

The analysis of the infinite-horizon growth model in continuous time proceeds exactly as in the two-period example above. Individual firms are assumed to have technologies that depend on a path $K(t), t \geq 0$, for aggregate knowledge. For an arbitrary path $K$, we can consider an artificial planning problem $P_\infty(K)$ that maximizes the utility of a representative consumer subject to the technology implied by the path $K$. Assume that preferences over the single consumption good take the usual additively separable, discounted form, $\int_0^\infty U(c(t)) e^{-\delta t} dt$, with $\delta > 0$. The function $U$ is defined over the positive real numbers and can have $U(0)$ equal to a finite number or to $-\infty$, for example, when $U(c) = \ln(c)$. Following the notation from the last section, let $F(k(t), K(t), \mathbf{x}(t))$ denote the instantaneous rate of output for a firm as a function of firm-specific knowledge at time $t$, economywide aggregate knowledge at time $t$, and the level of all other inputs at $t$. As before, we will assume that all agents take prices as given and that firms take the aggregate path for knowledge as given.

Additional knowledge can be produced by forgoing current consumption, but the trade-off is no longer assumed to be one-for-one. By investing an amount $I$ of forgone consumption in research, a firm with a current stock of private knowledge $k$ induces a rate of growth $\dot{k} = G(I, k)$. The function $G$ is assumed to be concave and homogeneous of degree one; the accumulation equation can therefore be rewritten in terms of proportional rates of growth,

$$\frac{\dot{k}}{k} = g\left(\frac{I}{k}\right)$$

with $g(y) = G(y, 1)$. A crucial additional assumption is that $g$ is bounded from above by a constant $\alpha$. This imposes a strong form of diminishing returns in research. Given the private stock of knowledge, the marginal product of additional investment in research, $Dg$, falls so rapidly that $g$ is bounded. An inessential but natural assumption is that $g$ is bounded from below by the value $g(0) = 0$. Knowledge does not depreciate, so zero research implies zero change in $k$; moreover, existing knowledge cannot be converted back into consumption goods. As a normalization to fix the units of knowledge, we can specify that $Dg(0) = 1$; one unit of knowledge is the amount that would be produced by investing one unit of consumption goods at an arbitrarily slow rate.

Assume as before that factors other than knowledge are in fixed supply. This implies that physical capital, labor, and the size of the population are held constant. If labor were the only other factor in the model, exponential population growth could be allowed at the cost of additional notation; but as was emphasized in the discussion of previous models, a key distinguishing feature of this model is that population growth is not necessary for unbounded growth in per capita income. For simplicity it is left out. Allowing for accumulation of physical capital would be of more interest, but the presence of two state variables would preclude the simple geometric characterization of the dynamics that is possible in the case of one state variable. If knowledge and physical capital are assumed to be used in fixed proportions in production, the variable $k(t)$ can be interpreted as a composite capital good. (This is essentially the approach used by Arrow (1962) in the learning-by-doing model.) Given increasing marginal productivity of knowledge, increasing marginal productivity of a composite $k$ would still be possible if the increasing marginal productivity of knowledge were sufficient to outweigh the decreasing marginal productivity associated with the physical capital.

Within the restrictions imposed by tractability and simplicity, the assumptions on the technology attempt to capture important features of actual technologies. As noted in section 2, estimated aggregate production functions do appear to exhibit some form of increasing returns to scale. Assuming that the increasing returns arise because of increasing marginal productivity of knowledge accords with the plausible conjecture that, even with fixed population and fixed physical capital, knowledge will never reach a level where its marginal product is so low that it is no longer worth the trouble it takes to do research. If the marginal product of knowledge were truly diminishing, this would imply that Newton, Darwin, and their contemporaries mined the richest veins of ideas and that scientists now must sift through the tailings and extract ideas from low-grade ore. That knowledge has an important public good characteristic is generally recognized.[8] That the production of new knowledge exhibits some form of diminishing marginal productivity at any point in time should not be controversial. For example, even though it may be possible to develop the knowledge needed to produce usable energy from nuclear fusion by devoting less than 1 percent of annual gross national product (GNP) to the research effort over a period of 20 years, it is likely that this knowledge could not be produced by next year regardless of the size of the current research effort.

## 5.2. Existence and characterization of a social optimum

Before using necessary conditions to characterize the solutions to either the social optimization problem, denoted as $PS_\infty$, or any of the artificial optimization problems $P_\infty(K)$, I must verify that these problems have solutions. First I state the problems precisely. Let $k_0$ denote the initial stock of knowledge per firm for the economy. As in the last section, I will always work with the same number of firms and consumers. Because the choice of $\mathbf{x} = \ddot{\mathbf{x}}$ is trivial, I suppress this argument, writing $f(k, K) = F(k, K, \ddot{\mathbf{x}})$. Also, let

$$\mathscr{F}(k) = f(k, Sk) = F(k, Sk, \ddot{\mathbf{x}})$$

denote the globally convex (per capita) production function that would be faced by a social planner. In all problems that follow, the constraint $\dot{k}(t) \geq 0$ for all $t \geq 0$ and the initial condition $k(0) = k_0$ will be understood:

$$PS_\infty : \max \int_0^\infty U(c(t)) e^{-\delta t} dt$$

subject to

$$\frac{\dot{k}(t)}{k(t)} = g\left(\frac{\mathscr{F}(k(t)) - c(t)}{k(t)}\right)$$

$$P_\infty(K) : \max \int_0^\infty U(c(t)) e^{-\delta t} dt$$

subject to

$$\frac{\dot{k}(t)}{k(t)} = g\left(\frac{f(k(t), K(t)) - c(t)}{k(t)}\right)$$

Note that the only difference between these two problems lies in the specification of the production function. In the first case, it is convex and invariant over time. In the second, it is concave but depends on time through its dependence on the path $K(t)$. I can now state the theorem that guarantees the existence of solutions to each of these problems.

THEOREM 1    *Assume that each of U, f, and g is a continuous real-valued function defined on a subset of the real line. Assume that U and g are concave. Suppose that $\mathscr{F}(k) = f(k, Sk)$ satisfies a bound $\mathscr{F}(k) \leq \mu + k^\rho$ and that $g(z)$ satisfies the bounds $0 \leq g(\mathbf{x}) \leq \alpha$ for real numbers $\mu, \rho$, and $\alpha$. Then if $\alpha\rho$ is less than the discount factor $\delta$, $PS_\infty$ has a finite-valued solution, and $P_\infty(K)$ has a finite-valued solution for any path $K(t)$ such that $K(t) \leq K(0)e^{\alpha t}$.*

The proof, given in an appendix available on request amounts to a check that the conditions of theorem 1 in Romer (1986) are satisfied. Note that if $\alpha$ is less than $\delta$ the inequality $\alpha\rho < \delta$ allows for $\rho > 1$. Thus the socially feasible production function $\mathscr{F}$ can be globally convex in $k$, with a marginal social product and an average social product of knowledge that increase without bound.

The analysis of the social planning problem $PS_\infty$ in terms of a current-valued Hamiltonian and a phase plane follows along familiar lines (see, for example, Arrow, 1967; Cass and Shell, 1976a, 1976b). Define

$$H(k, \lambda) = \max_c U(c) + \lambda \left\{ kg\left(\frac{\mathscr{F}(k) - c}{k}\right) \right\}$$

For simplicity, assume that the functions $U, f,$ and $g$ are twice continuously differentiable. The first-order necessary conditions for a path $k(t)$ to be a maximum for $PS_\infty$ are that there exists a path $\lambda(t)$ such that the system of first-order differential equations

$$\dot{k} = D_2 H(k, \lambda) \qquad \text{and} \qquad \dot{\lambda} = \delta\lambda - D_1 H(k, \lambda)$$

are satisfied and that the paths satisfy two boundary conditions: the initial condition on $k$ and the transversality condition at infinity,[9]

$$\lim_{t \to \infty} \lambda(t)k(t)e^{-\delta t} = 0$$

Under the assumption that $\lim_{c \to 0} DU(c) = \infty$, maximizing over $c$ in the definition of $H(k, \lambda)$ implies that

$$Du(c) = \lambda Dg\left(\frac{\mathscr{F}(k) - c}{k}\right)$$

whenever the constraint $\dot{k} \geq 0$ is not binding; otherwise, $c = \mathscr{F}(k)$. This gives $c$ as a function of $k$ and $\lambda$. Substituting this expression in the equations for $\dot{k}$ and $\dot{\lambda}$ gives a system of first-order equations that depends only on $k$ and $\lambda$.

Because of the restriction that $\dot{k}$ be nonnegative, the plane can be divided into two regions defined by $\dot{k} = 0$ and $\dot{k} \geq 0$ ( Figure 2). In a convenient abuse of the terminology, I will refer to the locus of points dividing these two regions as the $\dot{k} = 0$ locus. Along this locus, both the conditions

$$c = \mathscr{F}(k) \quad \text{and} \quad DU(c) = \lambda Dg\left(\frac{\mathscr{F}(k) - c}{k}\right)$$

must hold. Thus the $\dot{k} = 0$ locus is defined by the equation $DU(\mathscr{F}(k)) = \lambda$. By the concavity of $U$, it must be a nonincreasing curve in the $k - \lambda$ plane.

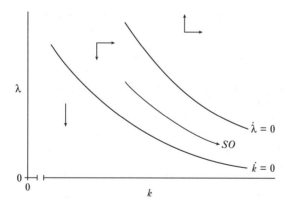

**Figure 2** Geometry of the phase plane for a typical optimum. Arrows indicate directions of trajectories in different sections of the plane. The rate of change of the stock knowledge, $\dot{k}$, is zero everywhere on or below the locus denoted by $\dot{k} = 0$; $SO$ denotes the socially optimal trajectory that stays everywhere between the lines $\dot{\lambda} = 0$ and $\dot{k} = 0$

As usual, the equation $\dot{\lambda} = 0$ defines a simple locus in the plane. When the derivative $D_1 H(k, \lambda)$ is evaluated along the $\dot{k} = 0$ locus, the equation for $\dot{\lambda}$ there can be written

$$\frac{\dot{\lambda}}{\lambda} = \delta - D\mathscr{F}(k)$$

If $D\mathscr{F}$ increases without bound, there exists a value of $\hat{k}$ such that $D\mathscr{F}(k) > \delta$ for all $k$ larger than $\hat{k}$, and for all such $k$, the $\dot{\lambda} = 0$ locus lies above the $\dot{k} = 0$ locus. It may be either upward or downward sloping. If $\mathscr{F}$ were concave and satisfied the usual Inada conditions, $\dot{\lambda} = 0$ would cross $\dot{k} = 0$ from above and the resulting steady state would be stable in the usual saddle-point sense. Here, $\dot{\lambda} = 0$ may cross $\dot{k} = 0$ either from above or from below. If $D\mathscr{F}(k)$ is everywhere greater than $\delta$, the $\dot{\lambda} = 0$ locus lies everywhere above the $\dot{k} = 0$ locus, and $\hat{k}$ can be taken to be zero. (This is the case illustrated in Figure 2.) Starting from any initial value greater than $\hat{k}$, the optimal trajectory $(\lambda(t), k(t)), t \geq 0$, must remain above the region where $\dot{k} = 0$. Any trajectory that crosses into this region can be shown to violate the transversality condition. Consequently, $k(t)$ grows without bound along the optimal trajectory.

This social optimum cannot be supported as a competitive equilibrium in the absence of government intervention. Any competitive firm that takes $K(t)$ as given and is faced with the social marginal products as competitive prices will choose not to remain at the optimal quantities even if it expects all other firms to do so. Each firm will face a private marginal product of knowledge (measured in terms of current output goods) equal to $D_1 f$; but the true shadow price of capital will be

$$D_1 f + S D_2 f > D_1 f$$

Given this difference, each firm would choose to acquire less than the socially optimal amount of knowledge.

## 5.3. Existence and characterization of the competitive equilibrium

Under a general set of conditions, this economy can be shown to have a suboptimal equilibrium in the absence of any intervention. It is completely analogous to the equilibrium for the two-period model. As in that model, it is straightforward to show that there is a three-way equivalence between competitive equilibria, fixed points of the mapping that sends a path $K(t)$ into $S$ times the solution to $P_\infty(K)$, and solutions to an equation of the form $D_1 V(k, Sk) = 0$.[10] In the infinite-horizon case, this equation consists of a system of differential equations, which can be represented in terms of a phase plane, and a set of boundary conditions.

To derive these equations, consider the necessary conditions for the concave problem $P_\infty(K)$. Define a Hamiltonian, denoted as $\tilde{H}$ to distinguish it from the Hamiltonian $H$ for the social planning problem $PS_\infty$:

$$\tilde{H}(k, \lambda, K) = \max_c U(c) + \lambda \left[ kg \left( \frac{f(k, K) - c}{k} \right) \right]$$

Then the necessary conditions for $k(t)$ to be a solution to $P_\infty(K)$ are that there exists a path $\lambda(t)$ such that

$$\dot{k}(t) = D_2\tilde{H}(k(t), \lambda(t), K(t))$$

and

$$\dot{\lambda}(t) = \delta\lambda(t) - D_1\tilde{H}(k(t), \lambda(t), K(t))$$

and such that the paths $k(t)$ and $\lambda(t)$ satisfy the boundary conditions

$$k(0) = k_0 \qquad \text{and} \qquad \lim_{\to\infty} \lambda(t)k(t)e^{-\delta t} = 0$$

Substituting $Sk(t)$ for $K(t)$ yields an autonomous system of differential equations,

$$\dot{k}(t) = D_2\tilde{H}(k(t), \lambda(t), Sk(t))$$

$$\dot{\lambda}(t) = \delta\lambda(t) - D_1\tilde{H}(k(t), \lambda(t), Sk(t))$$

that can be characterized using the phase plane. The two boundary conditions must still hold. Any paths for $k(t)$ and $\lambda(t)$ that satisfy these equations and the boundary conditions will correspond to a competitive equilibrium, and all competitive equilibria can be characterized this way.

Before considering phase diagrams, I must show that a competitive equilibrium exists for some class of models. Standard results concerning the existence of solutions of differential equations can be used to prove that the equations for $\dot\lambda$ and $\dot k$ determine a unique trajectory through any point $(k, \lambda)$ in the phase plane. The difficulty arises in showing that for any given value of $k_0$ there exists some value of $\lambda_0$ such that the transversality condition at infinity is satisfied along the trajectory through $(k_0, \lambda_0)$. As opposed to the case in which these equations are generated by a concave maximization problem known to have a solution, there is no assurance that such a $\lambda_0$ exists.

The basic idea in the proof that such a $\lambda_0$ exists, and hence that a competitive equilibrium exists, is illustrated in example 1 from the next section. To state the general result, I need additional conditions that characterize the asymptotic behavior of the functions $f$ and $g$. This is accomplished by means of an asymptotic exponent as defined by Brock and Gale (1969). Given a function $h(y)$, define the asymptotic exponent $e$ of $h$ as

$$e = \lim_{y\to\infty} \log_y |h(y)|$$

Roughly speaking, $h(y)$ behaves asymptotically like the power function $y^e$. Also, recall that $\alpha$ is the maximal rate of growth for $k$ implied by the research technology.

THEOREM 2    *In addition to the assumptions of Theorem 1, assume that $U$, $f$, and $g$ are twice continuously differentiable. Assume also that $\mathscr{F}(k) = f(k, Sk)$ has an asymptotic exponent $\rho$ such that $\rho > 1$ and $\alpha\rho < \delta$. Finally, assume that $Dg(\mathbf{x})$ has an asymptotic exponent strictly* *less than* $-1$. *Let* $\tilde{k}$ *be such that* $D_1 f(k, Sk) > \delta$ *for all* $k > \tilde{k}$. *Then if* $k_0 > \tilde{k}$, *there exists a competitive equilibrium with externalities in which* $c(t)$ *and* $k(t)$ *grow without bound.*

The proof is given in Romer (1983, theorem 3). The assumption on the asymptotic growth of $\mathscr{F}$ is self-explanatory. The assumption on the asymptotic exponent of $Dg$ is sufficient to ensure the boundedness of $g$. The condition on $D_1 f$ will be satisfied in most cases in which $\mathscr{F}(k) = f(k, Sk)$ is convex. Examples of functions satisfying these assumptions are given in the next section.

Once the conditions for the existence of a competitive equilibrium have been established, the analysis reduces once again to the study of the phase plane summarizing the information in the differential equations. In many respects, this analysis is similar to that for the social optimum for this economy. The phase plane can once again be divided into regions where $\dot{k} = 0$ and $\dot{k} > 0$. Since by definition $\mathscr{F}(k) = f(k, Sk)$, the equations for $c$ as a function of $k$ and $\lambda$ will be identical to those in the social optimum:

$$DU(c) = \lambda Dg\left(\frac{f(k, Sk) - c}{k}\right)$$

if $\dot{k} > 0$, $c = f(k, Sk)$ if $\dot{k} = 0$. As a result, the boundary locus for the region $\dot{k} = 0$ will also be identical with that from the social optimum. The only difference arises in the equation for $\dot{\lambda}$. Although the equality

$$H(k, \lambda) = \tilde{H}(k, \lambda, Sk)$$

does hold, the derivatives $D_1 H(k, \lambda)$ and $D_1 \tilde{H}(k, \lambda, Sk)$ differ. In the first case, a term involving the expression

$$D\mathscr{F}(k) = D_1 f(k, Sk) + SD_2 f(k, Sk)$$

will appear. In the second case, only the first part of this expression, $D_1 f(k, Sk)$, appears. Therefore, $D_1 H(k, \lambda)$ is always larger than $D_1 \tilde{H}(k, \lambda, Sk)$. Consequently, the $\dot{\lambda} = 0$ locus for the competitive equilibrium must lie below that for the social optimum.

As was true of the social optimum, the $\dot{\lambda} = 0$ locus can be either upward or downward sloping. If $D_1 f(k, Sk) > \delta$ for all $k$ greater than some value $\tilde{k}$, the $\dot{\lambda} = 0$ locus will lie above $\dot{k} = 0$ for values of $k$ to the right of $\tilde{k}$. Then the qualitative analysis is the same as that presented for the social optimum. Starting from an initial value $k_0 > \tilde{k}$, the only candidate paths for equilibria are ones that stay above the $\dot{k} = 0$ region; as before, paths that cross into this region will violate the transversality condition. A trajectory lying everywhere in the region where $\dot{k} > 0$ can fail to have $k(t)$ grow without bound only if the trajectory asymptotically approaches a critical point where $\dot{\lambda}$ and $\dot{k}$ are both zero, but no such point exists to the right of $\tilde{k}$. Hence, all the trajectories that are possible candidates for an equilibrium have paths for $k(t)$ that grow without bound. The existence result in theorem 2 shows that at least one such path satisfies the transversality condition at infinity.

## 5.4. *Welfare analysis of the competitive equilibrium*

The welfare analysis of the competitive equilibrium is quite simple. The intuition from simple static models with externalities or from the two-period model presented in section 3 carries over intact to the dynamic model here. In the calculation of the marginal productivity of knowledge, each firm recognizes the private return to knowledge, $D_1 f(k, Sk)$, but neglects the effect due to the change in the aggregate level, $SD_2 f(k, Sk)$; an increase in $k$ induces a positive external effect $D_2 f(k, Sk)$ on each of the $S$ firms in the economy. Consequently, the amount of consumption at any point in time is too high in the competitive equilibrium and the amount of research is too low. Any intervention that shifts the allocation of current goods away from consumption and toward research will be welfare-improving. As in any model with externalities, the government can achieve Pareto improvements not available to private agents because its powers of coercion can be used to overcome problems of shirking.

If the government has access to lump-sum taxation, any number of subsidy schemes will support the social optimum. Along the paths $k^*(t)$ and $\lambda^*(t)$ from the social optimum, taxes and subsidies must be chosen so that the first partial derivative of the Hamiltonian for the competitive equilibrium with taxes equals the first partial derivative of the Hamiltonian for the social planning problem; that is, the taxes and subsidies must be chosen so that the after-tax private marginal product of knowledge is equal to the social marginal product. This can be accomplished by subsidizing holdings of $k$, subsidizing accumulation $\dot{k}$, or subsidizing output and taxing factors of production other than $k$. The simplest scheme is for the government to pay a time-varying subsidy of $\sigma_1(t)$ units of consumption goods for each unit of knowledge held by the firm. If this subsidy is chosen to be equal to the term neglected by private agents,

$$\sigma_1(t) = SD_2 f(k^*(t), Sk^*(t))$$

private and social marginal products will be equal. A subsidy $\sigma_2(t)$ paid to a firm for each unit of goods invested in research would be easier to implement but is harder to characterize. In general, solving for $\sigma_2(t)$ requires the solution of a system of differential equations that depends on the path for $k^*(t)$. In the special case in which production takes the form $f(k, K) = k^\nu K^\gamma$, the optimal subsidy can be shown to be constant, $\sigma_2 = \gamma/(\nu + \gamma)$. (This calculation is also included in the appendix, available on request.)

While it is clear that the social marginal product of knowledge is greater than the private marginal product in the no-intervention competitive equilibrium, this does not necessarily imply that interest rates in the socially optimal competitive equilibrium with taxes will be higher than in the suboptimal equilibrium. In each case, the real interest rate on loans made in units of output goods can be written as

$$r(t) = -\left(\frac{\dot{p}}{p}\right)$$

where

$$p(t) = e^{-\delta t} DU(c(t))$$

is the present value price for consumption goods at date $t$. When utility takes the constant elasticity form

$$U(c) = \frac{c^{(1-\theta)} - 1}{(1 - \theta)}$$

this reduces to

$$r(t) = \delta + \theta\left(\frac{\dot{c}}{c}\right)$$

In the linear utility case in which $\theta = 0$, $r$ will equal $\delta$ regardless of the path for consumption and in particular will be the same in the two equilibria. This can occur even though the marginal productivity of knowledge differs because the price of knowledge in terms of consumption goods (equal to the marginal rate of transformation between knowledge and consumption goods) can vary. Holders of knowledge earn capital gains and losses as well as a direct return equal to the private marginal productivity of knowledge. In the case of linear utility, these capital gains and losses adjust so that interest rates stay the same.

This logical point notwithstanding, it is likely that interest rates will be higher in the social optimum. On average, $\dot{c}/c$ will be higher in the social optimum; higher initial rates of investment with lower initial consumption must ultimately lead to higher levels of consumption. If there is any curvature in the utility function $U$, so that $\theta$ is positive, interest rates in the optimum will be greater than in the no–intervention equilibrium. In contrast to the usual presumption, cost–benefit calculations in a suboptimal equilibrium should use a social rate of discount that is higher than the market rate of interest.


## 6. Examples

To illustrate the range of behavior possible in this kind of model, this section examines specific functional forms for the utility function $U$, the production function $f$, and the function $g$ describing the research technology. Because the goal is to reach qualitative conclusions with a minimum of algebra, the choice of functional form will be guided primarily by analytical convenience. For the production function, assume that $f$ takes the form noted above, $f(k, K) = k^{\nu}K^{\gamma}$. This is convenient because it implies that the ratio of the private and social marginal products,

$$\frac{D_1 f(k, Sk)}{D_1 f(k, Sk) + SD_2 f(k, Sk)} = \frac{\nu}{\nu + \gamma}$$

is constant. Nonincreasing private marginal productivity implies that $0 < \nu \leq 1$; increasing social marginal productivity implies that $1 < \gamma + \nu$. With these parameter values, this functional form is reasonable only for large values of $k$. For small values of $k$, the private and social marginal productivity of knowledge is implausibly small; at $k = 0$, they are both zero. This causes no problem provided we take a moderately large initial $k_0$ as given. An analysis starting from $k_0$ close to zero would have to use a more complicated (and more reasonable) functional form for $f$.

Recall that the rate of increase of the stock of knowledge is written in the homogeneous form

$$\dot{k} = G(I, k) = kg\left(\frac{I}{k}\right)$$

where $I$ is output minus consumption. The requirements on the concave function $g$ are the normalization $Dg(0) = 1$ and the bound $g(I/k) < \alpha$ for all $I/k$. An analytically simple form satisfying these requirements is

$$g(z) = \alpha z/(\alpha + z)$$

Recalling that $\delta$ is the discount rate, note that the bound required for the existence of a social optimum as given in theorem 1 requires the additional restriction that $\alpha(\nu + \gamma) < \delta$. Given the stated parameter restrictions, it is easy to verify that $f$ and $g$ satisfy all the requirements of theorems 1 and 2.

## 6.1. Example 1

With this specification of the technology for the economy, we can readily examine the qualitative behavior of the model for logarithmic utility $U(c) = \ln(c)$. The Hamiltonian can then be written as

$$\tilde{H}(k, \lambda, K, c) = \ln(c) + \lambda kg\left(\frac{f(k, K) - c}{k}\right)$$

Along (the boundary of the region in which) $\dot{k} = 0$, $Dg(0) = 1$ implies that $c = \lambda^{-1}$, so $\dot{k} = 0$ is determined by the equation

$$\lambda = [f(k, Sk)]^{-1} = S^{-\gamma}k^{-(\nu+\gamma)}$$

The exact form for the locus $\dot{\lambda} = 0$ is algebraically complicated, but it is straightforward to show that, for large $k$, $\dot{\lambda} = 0$ lies above the $\dot{k} = 0$ locus since $D_1 f(k, Sk)$ will be greater than $\delta$. Also, if we define the curve $L_1$ in the phase plane by the equation $\lambda = [1/(\delta - \alpha)]k^{-1}$, the $\dot{\lambda} = 0$ locus must cross $L_1$ from above as indicated in Figure 3. (Details are given in the appendix, available on request.) Thus $\dot{k} = 0$ behaves as $k$ to the power $-(\nu + \gamma) < -1$, and $\dot{\lambda} = 0$ is eventually trapped between $\dot{k} = 0$ and a line described by $k$ to the power $-1$. In figure 3, representative trajectories $t_1$ and $t_2$ together with the competitive equilibrium trajectory $CE$ are used to indicate the direction of trajectories in the various parts of the plane instead of the usual arrows.

Because the line $L_1$ is of the form $\lambda = [1/(\delta - \alpha)]k^{-1}$, any trajectory that eventually remains below $L_1$ will satisfy the transversality condition

$$\lim_{\to\infty} e^{-\delta t}k(t)\lambda(t) = 0$$

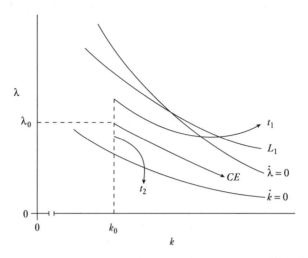

**Figure 3**   Geometry of the competitive equilibrium for example 1. The line $L_1$ is defined by the equation $\lambda = 1/(\delta - \alpha)k$; $t_1$ and $t_2$ denote representative trajectories in the phase plane;. $CE$ denotes the competitive equilibrium trajectory, which stays everywhere between the $\dot\lambda = 0$ and $\dot k = 0$ loci; $\lambda_0$ denotes the initial shadow price of knowledge corresponding to the initial stock of knowledge $k_0$

Given the geometry of the phase plane, it is clear that there must exist a trajectory that always remains between the loci $\dot\lambda = 0$ and $\dot k = 0$. Given the initial value $k_0$, index by the value of $\lambda$ all the trajectories that start at a point $(k_0, \lambda)$ between the two loci. The set of $\lambda$s corresponding to trajectories that cross $\dot\lambda = 0$ can have no smallest value, the set of $\lambda$s that correspond to trajectories that cross $\dot k = 0$ can have no largest value, and the two sets must be disjoint. Thus there exists a value $\lambda_0$ such that the trajectory through $(k_0, \lambda_0)$ crosses neither locus and must therefore correspond to an equilibrium.[11]

In fact, the path resembles a conventional equilibrium in which the trajectory remains between the $\dot\lambda = 0$ and $\dot k = 0$ loci as it converges to a saddle point, although here it is as if the saddle point has been moved infinitely far to the right. Since the optimal trajectory cannot stop, capital grows without bound. Since the trajectory is downward sloping and since consumption is increasing in $k$ and decreasing in $\lambda$, it is easy to see that consumption also grows without bound. Because of the difficulty of the algebra, it is not easy to describe the asymptotic rates of growth.

## 6.2. Example 2

Suppose now that utility is linear, $U(c) = c$. In the algebra and in the phase plane for this case, we can ignore the restriction $c \geq 0$ since it will not be binding in the region of interest. Maximizing out $c$ from the Hamiltonian

$$H(k, \lambda, K, c) = c + \lambda k g\left(\frac{(f - c)}{k}\right)$$

implies that

$$c = f - \alpha k(\lambda^{.5} - 1)$$

Then $f - c$ is positive (hence $\dot{k}$ is positive) if and only if $\lambda > 1$.

In this example, it is possible to put tighter bounds on the behavior of the $\dot{\lambda} = 0$ locus and, more important, on the behaviour of the equilibrium trajectory. As demonstrated in the appendix (available on request), $\dot{\lambda} = 0$ is upward sloping and behaves asymptotically like the power function $\lambda = Bk^{\nu+\gamma-1}$ for some constant $B$. For this economy, the equilibrium trajectory will lie above the $\dot{\lambda} = 0$ locus, so it is convenient to define an additional curve that will trap the equilibrium trajectory from above. For an appropriate choice of the constant $A$, the line $L_2$ defined by $\lambda = Ak^{\nu+\gamma-1}$ will lie above $\dot{\lambda} = 0$ and will have the property that trajectories must cross it from below (see figure 4). Since trajectories must cross $\dot{\lambda} = 0$ from above, the same geometric argument as used in the last example demonstrates that there exists a trajectory that remains between these two lines. Consequently it must also behave asymptotically like $k^{\nu+\gamma-1}$. Since $k(t)$ can grow no faster than $e^{\alpha t}$, the product $\lambda(t)k(t)$ will be bounded along such a trajectory by a function of the form $e^{\alpha(\nu+\gamma)t}$. Since $\delta > (\nu + \gamma)\alpha$, this trajectory satisfies the transversality condition and corresponds to an equilibrium.

Along the equilibrium trajectory, $\lambda$ behaves asymptotically like $k^{\nu+\gamma-1}$. Given the expression noted above for $c$ in terms of $\lambda$ and $k$, $c$ behaves asymptotically like $k^{\nu+\gamma} - \alpha k^{1+(.5)(\nu+\gamma-1)}$ and $I = f - c$ behaves like $k^{1+(.5)(\nu+\gamma-1)}$. Then $c$, $I$, $C/k$, and $I/k$ go to infinity with $k$. By the assumptions on the research technology, $I/k$ going to infinity implies that $\dot{k}/k$ approaches its upper bound $\alpha$. Consequently, the percentage rate of growth of output and of consumption will be increasing, both approaching the asymptotic upper bound $\alpha(\nu + \gamma)$.

Because the equilibrium trajectory is upward sloping, this economy will exhibit different stability properties from either the conventional model or the economy with logarithmic

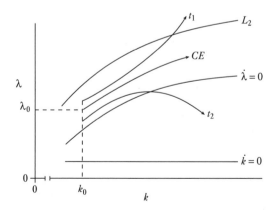

**Figure 4**  Geometry of the competitive equilibrium for example 2. The line $L_2$ is defined by an equation of the form $\lambda = Ak^{\nu+\lambda-1}$; $t_1$ and $t_2$ denote representative trajectories in the phase plane; $CE$ denotes the competitive equilibrium trajectory, which stays everywhere between $L_2$ and $\dot{\lambda} = 0$; $\lambda_0$ denotes the initial shadow price of knowledge

utility described above. Figure 5 illustrates a standard exercise in which a perfect-foresight equilibrium is perturbed. Suppose that at time 0 it is known that the stock of knowledge will undergo an exogenous increase of size $\Delta$ at time $T$ and that no other exogenous changes will occur. Usual arbitrage arguments imply that the path for any price like $\lambda(t)$ must be continuous at time $T$. The path followed by the equilibrium in the phase plane starts on a trajectory like $t_1$ such that at time $T$ it arrives at a point exactly $\Delta$ units to the left of the trajectory $CE$ from figure 4, which would have been the equilibrium in the absence of any exogenous change in $k$. As the economy evolves, it moves along $t_1$ then jumps $\Delta$ units to the right to the trajectory $CE$ at time $T$. Since $e^{-\delta t}\lambda(t)$ can be interpreted as a time 0 market price for knowledge, a foreseen future increase in the aggregate stock of knowledge causes a time 0 increase in the price for knowledge and a consequent increase in the rate of investment in knowledge. Because of the increasing returns, the private response to an aggregate increase in the stock of knowledge will be to reinforce its effects rather than to dampen them. Since the rate of growth of the stock of knowledge is increasing in the level, this kind of disturbance causes the stock of knowledge to be larger at all future dates. Moreover, the magnitude of the difference will grow over time. Thus small current or anticipated future disturbances can potentially have large, permanent, aggregate effects.

As a comparison with the first example shows, this result requires not only that increasing returns be present but also that marginal utility not decrease too rapidly with the level of per capita consumption. If we had restricted attention to the class of bounded, constant elasticity utility functions, $[c^{(1-\theta)} + 1]/(1 - \theta)$ with $\theta > 1$, this phenomenon would not be apparent. The specific example here uses linear utility for convenience,

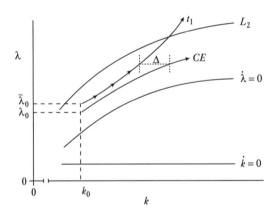

**Figure 5**   Geometry for the economy in example 2 when an exogenous increase of size $\Delta$ in the stock of knowledge is known to occur at a time $T > 0$. The equilibrium trajectory moves along $t_1$ until Time $T$, at which point it is $\Delta$ units to the left of the trajectory $CE$, at time T, the economy jumps horizontally to $CE$ with the change in the capital stock, but the path for $\lambda(t)$ is continuous. The equilibrium then proceeds along $CE$. $\tilde{\lambda}_0$ denotes the initial price of knowledge in the case in which the exogenous increase will take place; $\lambda_0$ denotes the lower value that obtains in an economy in which exogenous increase will take place

but similar results will hold for constant elasticity utility function $[c^{(1-\theta)} - 1]/(1 - \theta)$ for values of $\theta$ close enough to zero.

## 6.3. Example 3

The analysis of the previous example suggests a simple multicountry model with no tendency toward convergence in the level of per capita output. Suppose each country is modeled as a separate closed economy of the type in example 2. Thus no trade in goods takes place among the different countries, and knowledge in one country has external effects only within that country. Even if all countries started out with the same initial stock of knowledge, small disturbances could create permanent differences in the level of per capita output. Since the rate of growth of the stock of knowledge is increasing over time toward an asymptotic upper bound, a smaller country $s$ will always grow less rapidly than a larger country $l$. Asymptotically, the rates of growth $(\dot{k}/k)_s$ and $(\dot{k}/k)_l$ will both converge to $\alpha$, but the ratios $k_l/k_s$ and $c_l/c_s$ will be monotonically increasing over time, and the differences $k_l(t) - k_s(t)$ and $c_l(t) - c_s(t)$ will go to infinity.

It is possible to weaken the sharp separation assumed between countries in this discussion. In particular, neither the absence of trade in consumption goods and knowledge nor the sharp restriction on the extent of the externalities is essential for the divergence noted above. As in the Arrow (1962) learning-by-doing model, suppose that all knowledge is embodied either in physical capital or as human capital. Thus $k$ denotes a composite good composed of both knowledge and some kind of tangible capital. In this embodied form, knowledge can be freely transported between two different countries. Suppose further that the external effect of knowledge embodied in capital in place in one country extends across its border but does so with diminished intensity. For example, suppose that output of a representative firm in country 1 can be described as

$$f(k, K_1, K_2) = k^{\nu}(K_1^a + K_2^b)$$

where $k$ is the firm's stock of the composite good, $K_1$ and $K_2$ are the aggregates in the two countries, and the exponent $a$ on the domestic aggregate $K_1$ is strictly greater than the exponent $b$ on the foreign aggregate $K_2$. Production in country 2 is defined symmetrically. Then for a specific form of the research technology, Romer (1983) shows that the key restriction on the equilibrium paths $Sk_1$ and $Sk_2$ in the two countries comes from the equality of the marginal product of private knowledge imposed by the free mobility of the composite good $k$:

$$D_1 f(k_1, Sk_1, Sk_2) = D_1 f(k_2, Sk_2, Sk_1) \tag{1}$$

With the functional form given above, it is easy to verify that, in addition to the symmetric solution $k_1 = k_2$, there exists an asymmetric solution. In that solution, if $k_1$ is larger than $k_2$ and growing (e.g., country 1 is industrialized and country 2 is not), the path for $k_2$ that satisfies this equation either can grow at a rate slower than that for country 1 or may shrink, exporting the composite good to the more developed country.[12]

This kind of steady, ongoing "capital flight" or "brain drain" does not require any fundamental difference between the two countries. They have identical technologies. If we assume that there is perfect mobility in the composite $k$, it can even take place when both countries start from the same initial level of $k$. If all agents are convinced that country 2 is destined to be the slow-growing country in an asymmetric equilibrium, a discrete amount of the composite good will jump immediately to country 1. Thereafter, the two countries will evolve according to equation (1), with country 2 growing more slowly than country 1 or possibly even shrinking.

This kind of model should not be taken too literally. A more realistic model would need to take account of other factors of production with various degrees of less than perfect mobility. Nonetheless, it does suggest that the presence of increasing returns and of multiple equilibria can introduce a degree of instability that is not present in conventional models. This identifies a second sense in which small disturbances can have large effects. In addition to the multiplier-type effect for a closed economy as described in the last example, a small disturbance or a small change in a policy variable such as a tax rate could conceivably have a decisive effect on which of several possible equilibria is attained.

## 7. Conclusion

Recent discussions of growth have tended not to emphasize the role of increasing returns. At least in part, this reflects the absence of an empirically relevant model with increasing returns that exhibits the rigor and simplicity of the model developed by Ramsey, Cass, and Koopmans. Early attempts at such a model were seriously undermined by the loose treatment of specialization as a form of increasing returns with external effects. More recent attempts by Arrow, Levhari, and Sheshinski were limited by their dependence on exogenously specified population growth and by the implausible implication that the rate of growth of per capita income should be a monotonically increasing function of the rate of population growth. Incomplete models that took the rate of technological change as exogenously specified or that made it endogenous in a descriptive fashion could address neither welfare implications nor positive implications like the slowing of growth rates or the convergence of per capital output.

The model developed here goes part way toward filling this theoretical gap. For analytical convenience, it is limited to a case that is the polar opposite of the usual model with endogenous accumulation of physical capital and no accumulation of knowledge. But once the operation of the basic model is clear, it is straightforward to include other state variables. The implications for a model with both increasing marginal productivity of knowledge and decreasing marginal productivity of physical capital can easily be derived using the framework outlined here; however, the geometric analysis using the phase plane is impossible with more than one state variable, and numerical methods for solving dynamic equation systems must be used.[13] Since the model here can be interpreted as the special case of the two-state-variable model in which knowledge and capital are used in fixed proportions, this kind of extension can only increase the range of possible equilibrium outcomes.

### Notes

1   For an account of the development of Young's ideas and of his correspondence with Knight, see Blitch (1983).

2  For a treatment of increasing returns based on specialization, see Ethier (1982). Although the model there is essentially static, it demonstrates how specialization can be introduced in a differentiated products framework under imperfect competition.

3  The $p$-value gives the probability of observing a value of $\pi$ at least as large as the reported value under the null hypothesis that the true probability is .5.

4  Examining the dispersion in the logarithm of the level of per capita income, not dispersion in the level itself, is the correct way to test for convergence in the growth rates. If the rate of growth were constant across countries that start from different levels, the dispersion in the logarithm of the levels will stay constant, but dispersion in the levels will increase.

5  Baumol (1985) argues that the convergence he observes among the industrialized countries results from a transmission process for knowledge that takes place among the industrialized countries but does not extend to centrally planned or less developed countries. He would not agree that the apparent convergence is an artifact of an *ex post* choice of the industrialized countries. Since he does not treat this issue directly, it is difficult to resolve it from his data. He does admit that his groupings are "somewhat arbitrary."

6  For most of the subsequent discussion, $k$ will be treated as a stock of disembodied knowledge, i.e., knowledge in books. This is merely an expositional convenience and is not essential. For example, if one wants to assume that all knowledge is embodied in some kind of tangible capital such as conventional physical capital or human capital, $k$ can be reinterpreted throughout as a composite good made up of both knowledge and the tangible capital good.

7  Here, $D$ denotes a derivative, $D_i$ the partial derivative with respect to the $i$th argument.

8  See, e.g., Bernstein and Nadiri (1983) for estimates from the chemical industry suggesting that spillover effects can be quite large.

9  Proving the necessity of the transversality condition for a maximization problem that is not concave takes relatively sophisticated mathematical methods. Ekeland and Scheinkman (1983) prove the necessity of the transversality condition for nonconcave discrete-time problems. In continuous time, a proof that requires a local Lipschitz condition is given by Aubin and Clarke (1979).

10  An explicit proof of this result is given in Romer (1983). The method of proof is exactly as outlined in the two-period model. A generalized Kuhn–Tucker theorem is used to derive the necessary conditions that yield shadow prices for the maximization problems $P_\infty(K)$. Suppose $K^*$ is a fixed point. If the consumer and the firm are faced with the shadow prices associated with $P_\infty(K^*)$, the sufficient conditions for their maximization problems are shown to be satisfied at the quantities that solve $P_\infty(K^*)$.

11  This is the essence of the proof of theorem 2.

12  Details are available in an appendix available from the author.

13  For an example of this kind of numerical analysis in a model with a stock of knowledge and a stock of an exhaustible resource, see Romer and Sasaki (1985). As in the growth model, increasing returns associated with knowledge can reverse conventional presumptions; in particular, exhaustible resource prices can be monotonically decreasing for all time.

## References

Arrow, K. J. (1962): "The Economic Implications of Learning by Doing," *Review of Economic Studies*, 29, June, 155–73.

——(1967): "Applications of Control Theory to Economic Growth," in G. B. Dantzig and A. F. Veinott (eds), *Mathematics of the Decision Sciences*, vol. 1. Providence, R.I.: American Math. Soc.

Aubin, J. P. and Clarke, F. H. (1979): "Shadow Prices and Duality for a Class of Optimal Control Problems," *SIAM Journal of Control and Optimization*, 17, September, 567–86.

Baumol, W. J. (1985): "Productivity Growth, Convergence and Welfare: What the Long Run Data Show," research report no. 85–27, New York: New York University, C. V. Starr Center.

Bernstein, J. I. and Nadiri, M. I. (1983): "Research and Development, Spillovers and Adjustment Costs: An Application of Dynamic Duality at the Firm Level," working paper. New York: New York University.

Blitch, C. P. (1983): "Allyn Young on Increasing Returns," *Journal of Post Keynesian Economics*, 5, Spring 359–72.

Brock, W. A. (1975): "A Simple Perfect Foresight Monetary Model," *Journal of Monetary Economics*, 1, April, 133–50.

——(1977): "A Polluted Golden Age," in Vernon L. Smith (ed.), *Economics of Natural and Environmental Resources*, New York: Gordon and Breach.

Brock, W. A., and Gale, D. (1969): "Optimal Growth under Factor Augmenting Progress," *Journal of Economic Theory*, 1, October, 229–43.

Cass, D. (1965): "Optimum Growth in an Aggregative Model of Capital Accumulation," *Review of Economic Studies*, 32, July, 233–40.

Cass, D. and Shell, K. (1976a): "Introduction to Hamiltonian Dynamics in Economics," *Journal of Economic Theory*, 12, February, 1–10.

——(1976b): "The Structure and Stability of Competitive Dynamical Systems," *Journal of Economic Theory*, 12 February, 31–70.

Chipman, J. S. (1970): "External Economies of Scale and Competitive Equilibrium," *Quarterly Journal of Economics*, 84, August, 347–85.

Dechert, W. D. and Nishimura, K. (1983): "A Complete Characterization of Optimal Growth Paths in an Aggregated Model with a Non-concave Production Function," *Journal of Economic Theory*, 31, December, 332–54.

Dixit, A. K., Mirrlees, J. A. and Stern, N. (1975): "Optimum Saving with Economies of Scale," *Review of Economic Studies*, 42, July, 303–25.

Ekeland, I. and Scheinkman, J. A. (1983): "Transversality Conditions for Some Infinite Horizon Discrete Time Maximization Problems," technical report 411, Stanford, Ca.: Stanford University, IMSSS.

Ethier, W. J. (1982): "National and International Returns to Scale in the Model Theory of International Trade," *American Economic Review*, 72, June, 389–405.

Hansen, L. P., Epple, D. and Roberds, W. (1985): "Linear-Quadratic Duopoly Models of Resource Depletion," in T. J. Sargent (ed.), *Energy, Foresight and Strategy*, Washington: Resources for the Future.

Helpman, E. (1984): "Increasing Returns, Imperfect Markets, and Trade Theory," in W. Jones and P. B. Kenen (eds), *Handbook of International Economics*, vol. 2, New York: North-Holland.

Hicks, J. R. (1960): "Thoughts on the Theory of Capital: The Corfu Conference," *Oxford Economic Papers*, 12 June, 123–32.

Hochman, O. and Hochman, E. (1980): "Regeneration, Public Goods, and Economic Growth," *Econometrica*, 48, July, 1233–50.

Kaldor, N. (1981): "The Role of Increasing Returns, Technical Progress and Cumulative Causation in the Theory of International Trade and Economic Growth," *Économie Appliquée*, 34(4), 593–617.

Kendall, M. G. (1962): *Rank Correlation Methods*. New York: Hafner.

Kendrick, J. W. (1976): *The Formation and Stocks of Total Capital*. New York: Columbia University Press (for N.B.E.R.).

Knight, F. H. (1925): "On Decreasing Cost and Comparative Cost: A Rejoinder," *Quarterly Journal of Economics*, 39, February, 331–3.

Koopmans, T. C. (1965): "On the Concept of Optimal Economic Growth," in *The Econometric Approach to Development Planning*, Amsterdam: North-Holland (for Pontificia Acad. Sci.).

Kuznets, S. (1971): "Notes on the Pattern of U.S. Economic Growth," in R. W. Fogel, and S. L. Engerman (eds), *The Reinterpretation of American Economic History*, New York: Harper and Row.

Levhari, D. (1966a): "Extensions of Arrow's 'Learning by Doing,'" *Review of Economic Studies*, 33, April, 117–31.

——(1966b): "Further Implications of Learning by Doing," *Review of Economic Studies*, 33, January, 31–8.

McKenzie, L. W. (1959): "On the Existence of General Equilibrium for a Competitive Market," *Econometrica*, 27, January, 54–71.

Maddison, A. (1979): "Per Capita Output in the Long Run," *Kyklos*, 32 (1, 2), 412–29.

——(1982): *Phases of Capitalist Development*. New York: Oxford University Press.

Majumdar, M. and Mitra, T. (1982): "Intertemporal Allocation with a Nonconvex Technology: The Aggregative Framework," *Journal of Economic Theory*, 27, June, 101–36.

——(1983): "Dynamic Optimization with a Non-convex Technology: The Case of a Linear Objective Function," *Review of Economic Studies*, 50, January, 143–51.

Phelps, E. S. (1966): "Models of Technical Progress and the Golden Rule of Research," *Review of Economic Studies*, 33, April, 133–45.

Ramsey, F. P. (1928): "A Mathematical Theory of Saving," *Economic Journal*, 38, December, 543–59.

Reynolds, L. G. (1983): "The Spread of Economic Growth to the Third World: 1850–1980," *Journal of Economic Literature*, 21, September, 941–80.

Rockafellar, R. T. (1970): *Convex Analysis*. Princeton, N.J.: Princeton University Press.

Romer, P. M. (1983): "Dynamic Competitive Equilibria with Externalities, Increasing Returns and Unbounded Growth," Ph.D. dissertation, University of Chicago.

——(1986): "Cake Eating, Chattering and Jumps: Existence Results for Variational Problems," *Econometrica*, 54, July.

Romer, P. M. and Sasaki, H. (1985): "Monotonically Decreasing Natural Resource Prices under Perfect Foresight," working paper 19, Rochester, N.Y.: University of Rochester, Center for Economic Research.

Shell, K. (1967a): "A Model of Inventive Activity and Capital Accumulation," in Karl Shell (eds), *Essays on the Theory of Optimal Growth*, Cambridge, Mass.: MIT Press.

——(1967b): "Optimal Programs of Capital Accumulation for an Economy in which there is Exogenous Technological Change," in K. Shell (ed.), *Essays on the Theory of Optimal Growth*, Cambridge, Mass.: MIT Press.

Sheshinski, E. (1967): "Optimal Accumulation with Learning by Doing," in K. Shell (ed.), *Essays on the Theory of Optimal Growth*, Cambridge, Mass.: MIT Press.

Skiba, A. K. (1978): "Optimal Growth with a Convex–Concave Production Function," *Econometrica*, 46, May, 527–39.

Streissler, E. (1979): "Growth Models as Diffusion Processes: II. Empirical Illustrations," *Kyklos*, 32(3), 571–86.

Uzawa, H. (1965): "Optimum Technical Change in an Aggregative Model of Economic Growth," *International Economic Review*, 6, January, 18–31.

von Weizsäcker, C. C. (1966): "Tentative Notes on a Two Sector Model with Induced Technical Progress," *Review of Economic Studies*, 33, July, 245–51.

Weitzman, M. L. (1970): "Optimal Growth with Scale Economies in the Creation of Overhead Capital," *Review of Economic Studies*, 37, October, 555–70.

Young, A. A. (1969): "Increasing Returns and Economic Progress," in K. J. Arrow and T. Scitovsky (eds), *Readings in Welfare Economics*, Homewood, Ill.: Irwin (for American Economic Association).

CHAPTER 3

# History and Coordination Failure

ALÍCIA ADSERÀ AND DEBRAJ RAY

An extensive literature discusses the existence of a virtuous circle of expectations that might lead communities to Pareto-superior states among multiple potential equilibria. It is generally accepted that such multiplicity stems fundamentally from the presence of positive agglomeration externalities. We examine a two-sector model in this class and look for intertemporal perfect foresight equilibria. It turns out that under some plausible conditions, positive externalities must coexist with external *dis*economies elsewhere in the model, for there to exist equilibria that break free of historical initial conditions. Our main distinguishing assumption is that the positive agglomeration externalities appear with a time lag (that can be made vanishingly small). Then, in the absence of external diseconomies elsewhere, the long-run behavior of the economy resembles that predicted by myopic adjustment. This finding is independent of the degree of forward-looking behavior exhibited by the agents.

## 1. Introduction

An extensive literature discusses the existence of a virtuous circle of expectations that might lead communities to Pareto-superior states among multiple potential equilibria. It is generally accepted that such multiplicity stems fundamentally from the presence of positive agglomeration externalities. The purpose of this article is to examine the role of agglomeration externalities in a fully dynamic model in which agents exhibit perfect foresight. Under plausible conditions that we describe below, we show that the generation of equilibria that break free of initial historical conditions must critically depend on the presence of *congestion* externalities elsewhere in the model.

The role of externalities in the process of economic development has occupied a central place in theories of growth and development. Perhaps the first study along these lines is due to Paul Rosenstein-Rodan (1943). Authors such as Tibor Scitovsky (1954), Albert Hirschman (1958), and Gunnar Myrdal (1957) developed these notions further. More recently, Murphy, Shleifer, and Vishny (1989) have formalized some aspects of the Rosenstein-Rodan viewpoint, making precise the conditions that are needed for multiplicity of equilibria. The study of such multiplicity exhibits agglomeration externalities in its own right: a recent issue of the *Journal of Development Economics* concentrated entirely on this topic.

By and large, this literature ignores a central question raised by Rosenstein-Rodan and by Hirschman: how does an economy move from a bad to a good equilibrium? This question is imprecise: so-called transitions from one equilibrium to another must themselves be viewed as the equilibria of some encompassing intertemporal process. But this question is problematic for game theorists (and, *a fortiori*, for applied economists as well). In pure coordination games (such as those studied by Cooper and John (1988); see also Diamond (1982); Bryant (1983); Chatterjee and Cooper (1989), Chatterjee, Cooper, and Ravikumar, 1990), which essentially underly these models, where is the role of history? Why would an initial coordination failure transmit itself, or persist, over time? This is the fundamental issue raised (though not answered) by Rosenstein-Rodan and by Hirschman.

We study this issue by placing the static coordination game in the explicit context of an intertemporal process. Our two-sector migration model has already served as the canonical parable in part of this literature. In one of the sectors (the traditional sector), the return to each agent is exogenously given. In the other, modern sector, there are agglomeration externalities: the return to each agent depends positively on the number of agents located there. Viewed as a static model of locational choice, the model exhibits two equilibria – one in which everyone is located in the traditional sector and the other in which everyone is located in the modern sector. Viewed as a dynamic model of locational choice, agents take the intertemporal paths of returns in each sector as given and then make rational migration decisions to maximize the sum of discounted utility. Such decisions might include, in principle, the option to move back and forth several times. Each migratory step is costly. A perfect foresight equilibrium has the additional property that the joint migration decisions generate precisely the intertemporal path of returns that each agent takes as given.

A similar model has been used by Matsuyama (1991) and Krugman (1991a)[1] to discuss the role played by discounting in the generation of ahistorical equilibria. If agents discount the future heavily enough, then the intertemporal equilibrium resembles the path obtained through myopic tatonnement. Initial conditions (and thereafter the current discrepancy in the intersectoral rates of return) determine migratory flows. The sector with the initial advantage will come to dominate. On the other hand, for discount rates close to zero, other perfect foresight equilibria appear. These equilibria can break free of initial conditions, provided that agents harbor common expectations of optimism (or pessimism) about the eventual fate of the modern sector.

There is merit and insight to these arguments. They certainly allow for outcomes that we do sometimes see – a burgeoning, self-fulfilling move away from one type of activity (or location, or technology) to another. Our objective is to make explicit an aspect of these models, and possibly of the coordination framework in general, that remains hidden in the literature that we have seen. The observation is this:

> to generate equilibria that break free of historical conditions, negative agglomeration externalities must be present somewhere, in addition to the positive agglomeration externalities that are needed to create the problem in the first place.

Most important, this result is *independent* of the size of the degree of forward-looking behavior exhibited by the economic agents, as captured by their discount factors.

To make this point, we make an assumption that we believe to be eminently plausible. We assume that the positive agglomeration externalities must manifest themselves with a time lag.[2] We do not restrict the size of this lag in any way.[3]

In this model, for any positive discount rate, if relocation costs are constant and independent of the intersectoral allocation of agents, the final outcome of any perfect foresight equilibrium depends entirely on initial conditions. The equilibrium paths turn out to be (essentially) the same as if agents were short-sighted. The same result is true if the relocation cost depends *negatively* on the number of agents in the destination sector (which amounts to positive externalities as well). Thus, paradoxically enough, equilibria that break free of initial history can exist only if there are diseconomies elsewhere. In this model, such equilibria might exist if relocation costs depend *positively* on the number of agents in the destination sector (congestion). We do not construct such equilibria for our model, as this is not our main focus, but it is easy enough to do so along the lines discussed by Krugman and Matsuyama.

Once stated, the intuition behind such a result is easy enough to see. Suppose, for instance, that the rate of return in the traditional sector is initially higher, and then lower, along some equilibrium path. This implies that some migration must have occurred from the traditional to the modern sector. But because externalities are lagged, the initial migration must have occurred when current returns were unfavorable. Such migrants can benefit from postponing their migration decision, and they will certainly do so if the cost of relocation is not adversely affected in the process. But this means no one will migrate in this interim period, and so the positive externalities can never be generated in the first place. With diseconomies in relocation costs, this argument is no longer valid and such equilibria can be constructed (under some conditions).

In describing myopic tatonnement, Krugman (1991a, p. 657) writes: "The usefulness of this kind of heuristic approach to dynamics for thinking about models is so great that we would not propose abandoning it." In this article, we argue that the prediction of myopic tatonnement may have more than just heuristic appeal on its side. In economies of atomistic agents, the path of myopic adjustment may still be the most likely equilibrium outcome if no congestion cost is added to the model.

## 2. The Model

An economy has two regions, $A$ and $B$. A total capital (or labor) endowment of $\bar{K}$ is split at date 0 between the two regions. Denote by $K$ the capital in region $B$, so that $\bar{K} - K$ is the capital stock in region $A$. Capital invested in region $A$ yields a fixed rate of return, normalized to zero. Region $B$'s rate of return $r$ is taken to depend positively on its capital endowment:

$$r = f(K) \tag{1}$$

where $f$ is continuous, strictly increasing, and $f(0) < 0 < f(\bar{K})$.

Imagine that there is a continuum of agents, and each agent owns a single unit of capital. Capital is free to move between regions, but each relocation entails a nonnegative cost. Assume that the cost of moving from $B$ to $A$ is given by a nondecreasing function

$\hat{c}_A(K)$ and that the cost of moving from $A$ to $B$ is given by a nonincreasing function $\hat{c}_P(K)$, where $K$ is to be interpreted, in each case, as the population of capital in the destination region. Say that either of these cost functions exhibits *congestion* if it increases, at least over some interval, in $K$. Agents make decisions in the way described below.

First let us track the relevant prices. Let

$$\gamma \equiv \{r(t), c_A(t), c_B(t)\}_{t=0}^{\infty}$$

be some point expectation about the path (measurable in time) of returns and relocation costs in each region. Future returns are discounted in the standard way, using a discount rate $\rho$. Denote by $V(\gamma, i, t)$ the *optimal value* to an agent in region $i$, $i = A$, $B$, beginning at time $t$, when the commonly anticipated path of returns is $\gamma$. Then by standard dynamic programming arguments, an agent in region $i$ will switch sectors at time $t$ if

$$V(\gamma, i, t) < V(\gamma, j, t) - c_j(t)$$

will stay if the opposite inequality holds, and will be indifferent if equality holds.

A path $\gamma$ is an *equilibrium* if it is generated by the optimal decisions of (almost) all agents in response to $\gamma$.

To discuss the generation of $\gamma$, consider now some exogenously given measurable path $K(t)_{t=0}^{\infty}$.[4] We assume that there is *some* lag (however small) in the speed at which external effects induced by incoming/outgoing factors affect the going rates of return. From this point of view, we regard the return function $f(K)$ as representing a long-run level of the rate of return, once the economy has settled at a certain level of capital $K$. We assume that at date 0, $r(0)$ is precisely $f(K(0))$ (see (1)). Thereafter, we introduce an increasing function $g$, with $g(0) = 0$, such that

$$\dot{r}(t) = g(f(K(t)) - r(t)) \qquad (2)$$

Thus, the rate of return at any date chases the appropriate rate of return corresponding to the division of the capital endowment at that date. The specific functional form of $g(\cdot)$ determines the speed at which returns adjust. In any case, capital owners will always get paid $r(t)$, in accordance to their real marginal productivity at that point of time.

Several economic situations conform quite naturally to this specification. In models of search or matching, the productivity of some fixed amount of capital may depend on the ability of that capital to find partners (with more capital), say, because of minimum scale requirements in production. This ability, in turn, will depend on the total amount of capital in the economy (see, e.g., Diamond, 1982). Note that a discontinuous jump in the capital stock will lead to a smooth intertemporal increase in productivity as long as the process of matching partners takes place in continuous time. Likewise, if one replaces capital by population and rate of return by utility, the concentration of population in a particular geographical region may provoke large amounts of productive activity and a variety of goods and services, attracting still more people because of the greater utility to be had (Krugman, 1991b). Again, the degree of productive activity might react smoothly to a sudden influx of population (perhaps because the information regarding a larger market needs time to permeate to all the producers).

Appendix A provides a highly stylized example that makes explicit the process through which intertemporal smoothing can occur.

Thus a path of capital allocations $\{K(t)\}$ generates a path of returns $\{r(t)\}$ using (2), and a path $\{c_A(t), c_B(t)\}$ using the relationships $c_i(t) = \hat{c}_i(K(t))$ for all $t$. Note that we could introduce lags into the $c$ functions as well. We do not do this: it keeps the notation simple, and in any case our focus is primarily on lags in the flow rates of return.

Note that the literature on coordination (for example, Cooper and John, 1988) and on the role of history versus expectations (for example, Matsuyama, 1991; Krugman, 1991a) effectively assumes that $g$ is infinitely sensitive, so that $r(t)$ is always *exactly* equal to $f(K(t))$.[5]

## 3. History and Coordination Failure

If agents migrate only in response to current rate differentials, the resulting equilibrium is equivalent to myopic tatonnement. For instance, if $K(0)$ is such that $f(K(0)) < 0$, capital in $B$ will move to $A$ to cash in on the rate differential, and the process will ultimately lead to the specialization of the economy in sector $A$. The reverse will be true whenever $f(K(0)) > 0$. With positive relocation costs, there is an interval of initial conditions that will persist; no one finds it worthwhile to switch sectors. However, as Matsuyama (1991) and Krugman (1991a) observe, this strong history-dependence is driven by myopia. There might be forward-looking equilibria that lead, for instance, to ultimate specialization in either sector even though initial conditions do not favor this sector. It turns out, though, that such outcomes are impossible in the model of the previous section, irrespective of the degree of farsightedness.

To state this result, say that an intertemporal equilibrium is *exclusively history dependent* if the long-run outcome either equals the initial allocation, or entails migration *only* to the sector that is initially profitable. Note that myopic tatonnement has the same properties, though obviously the exact path may be different. The main similarity is that no room is left for farsighted expectations.

PROPOSITION 1    *Assume $f(K(0)) \neq 0$. Unless the cost of relocation exhibits congestion, every equilibrium must be exclusively history dependent, irrespective of the discount rate.*

This proposition summarizes the main point of the article: unless rates of return reflect *instantaneously* the external effects of incoming factors, the ability to generate "ahistorical equilibria" and to attain Pareto superior outcomes depends critically on how relocation costs are affected by intersectoral allocation. In particular, proposition 1 shows that if each agent faces a relocation cost that is *nonincreasing* in the number of destination agents, the long-run behavior of the economy is fully determined by initial conditions. Note that this argument includes the case in which movement is costless or in which the costs of migration are fixed, independent of intersectoral allocation. If rates of return adjust to going factor endowments with a lag, however small, agents will want to postpone their migration decisions to currently unprofitable areas, until returns rise sufficiently to justify the move. With a continuum of agents, this externality cannot be internalized, so that all equilibria with a historical steady states are knocked out. In particular, adverse initial conditions are perpetuated. Thus, the only equilibria that survive involve either perpetuation of the initial allocation or movement to initially profitable areas.[6]

Our observation is independent of the magnitude of discounting and of the degree of responsiveness of returns (as long as it is not instantaneous). Thus by a minor and reasonable weakening of one of the assumptions in the literature, we obtain a class of models where expectations are dwarfed by history, where initial conditions determine the final equilibrium. Of course, if rates of return adjust *instantaneously*, then expectations-driven equilibria are possible.

Our claim is not that ahistorical equilibria are impossible but that, in this class of models, in addition to the intersectoral agglomeration externalities, the migration technology is crucial to understand the sources of such equilibria. The only way in which such outcomes can occur is by introducing a cost to postponement – that is, by making future relocation costs increase in the stock of settlers in our case.

Thus it appears (though we have not provided a formal proof of this) that in this general approach, expectations can dominate history only through an interesting juxtaposition of *agglomeration* externalities in one sector (production) and *congestion* externalities in another (migration).[7] The reason that migrants might move to a currently unfavored sector, despite the lag in the realization of externalities, is that a later move will involve a higher cost. It is in this sense that the technology of adjustment costs is crucial to the existence of expectations-driven equilibrium.

## 4. Concluding Comments

Why some countries or regions develop and others do not crucially depends on when the benefits from the investment/migration decision will accrue and how costly the move is. It is unclear that congestion in relocation is always a good assumption. To the extent that this is the case, it may be difficult to invoke coordination games to explain some great migrations. For instance, being one of the first settlers in the Far West was possibly far more costly than arriving there later by train. In other cases, such as in the sudden growth of new cities in developing countries, congestion may well be a reasonable postulate.

In a similar way, the results of this article shed some light on the problem of technology adoption (see, e.g., Arthur, 1984; David, 1985; Chamley and Gale, 1994; Gale, 1995). A technology already in place may be dominated by an alternative technology if the latter is adopted by a significant group of firms. However, if these potential returns appear only over time and the cost of adoption decreases with the number of entrants, everyone waits for others to move first, negating the adoption of the technology even with forward-looking agents. If, on the other hand, the costs of adoption increase with the spread of the new technology, such equilibria are possibly sustainable.[8] Thus society may gain by being organized in such a way that being the first in the business matters.

The standardized role for intervention, which is weakened by the possibility of ahistorical equilibria, may need to be reexamined. As usual, we may think of the government as involved in the task of building up a critical mass in cases where history acts as a constraint. But the focus of this article reveals another role as well. The initial losses that migrating agents incur in moving to a poor region may be partially alleviated by subsidies (such as tax holidays) in the hope of more than recovering the cost in future fiscal revenues. The idea is to mimic or create the equivalent of congestion in the initial costs of relocation.

## APPENDIX A

Suppose that $n$ workers in a region have productivity $a_1, a_2, \ldots, a_n$. Let $a$ be the average productivity. If individual productivity is not observed by competitive employers and the production technology is linear with production coefficient normalized to one, then the equlibrium wage will be $\tilde{a}$, where this is the expectation of average productivity that employers calculate given common beliefs about the probability distribution of each individual's productivity.

Now suppose that the productivity of an individual is positively affected by meeting other individuals that he has not met before. Specifically, suppose that every encounter with a new individual adds $\delta$ to productivity.

Encounters take place in the following way. There is a Poisson process with given parameter: whenever a realization occurs, two (or more pairs of) individuals are taken randomly from the population and matched. A productivity upgrade occurs if and only if a match is new.

Take as given the following initial conditions. Each individual located in the region at date 0 has an initial productivity $b$. There is some initial number $n$ (0) of such individuals. Thereafter migration occurs as a function $n(t)$ that starts at time 0, jumps upward periodically, and finally flattens out when $n(t) = N$ (think of $N$ as total population).

The productivity of each individual is a random variable: for any such individual $i$ at date $t$

$$a_i(t) = b_i + \delta m_i(t)$$

where $b_i$ is the initial productivity of the migrant (which is $b$ for the original settlers at date 0), and $m_i(t)$ is the number of new meetings $i$ has had with other incumbents in the region up to date $t$. Clearly $a_i(t)$ is a random variable that begins at the initial productivity $b_i$, exhibits jumps at random dates along its sample paths, and converges almost surely to the value $b(t_0) + \delta(N - 1)$.

We assume that each new migrant (after date 0) is initially housed by an incumbent relative. These relatives are uniformly distributed among the incumbent settlers. The existing productivity of the relative is assumed to be instantly transmitted to the newcomer at the time of migration. Thereafter, the new migrant becomes an incumbent with something to teach as well as something to learn, exactly the same way as described in the previous paragraph.

Let $a(t)$ be the average productivity of all members of the region at date $t$; of course, $a(t)$ is still a random variable in its own right (with jumps on its sample paths). It is easy to check that $a(0) = b$ and (given the assumptions about new arrivals), $a(t)$ increases up to the limit $b + \delta(N - 1)$. But employers do not know the average productivity at date $t$ for sure because they do not know about the pattern of meetings that have occurred economy-wide, neither do they know the pattern of initial matchings between migrants and relatives, which they take to be random. Take the expectation of $a(t, n)$ at each date $t$

using the characteristics of the underlying Poisson process; call this $\tilde{a}(t)$. The (straightforward) proof of the following fact is omitted but is available on request:

> $\tilde{a}(t)$ is a deterministic, continuous function of $t$, which starts at $b$ and converges monotonically to $b + \delta(N-1)$.

REMARK 1    The assumption that new migrants costlessly acquire the productivity of the incumbents they go and live with, and thereafter proceed to teach and learn just as the incumbents do, is used only to ensure that a jump in $n$ does not instantly (and temporarily) lower expected average productivity at the date of the jump (as it would, for instance, if new migrants came in with a productivity of $b$). (This sort of temporary downward jump, it should be added, would only strengthen the results of the main model.)

REMARK 2    As written down, this example is unrealistic and is meant only to capture the process of intertemporal smoothing in the rates of return in the simplest possible way. In particular, to completely fit our model, it should be the case that if there is migration *out* of the region, then productivity in the region should fall over time. This sort of extension is easy enough to accomplish by putting in a depreciation factor for productivity that is constantly compensated for by new encounters with other incumbents. Then it will be the case that a lowering of $n$ will cause an economywide depletion of average productivity, as encounters become fewer, and the economy must move down to its new steady-state level of productivity.

## APPENDIX B: PROOF OF PROPOSITION 1

Consider the case in which $f(K(0)) < 0$. The case $f(K(0)) > 0$ can be settled by a parallel argument.

Fix any equilibrium $\gamma$. We claim that $K(t) \leq K(s)$ for all $t \geq s$, which establishes exclusive history-dependence.

Suppose this is false for some $t'$ and $s'$. Then, indeed, there is some $t$ and $s$ with $t > s$, $K(t) > K(s)$, and $r(\tau) < 0$ for all $s \leq \tau \leq t^*$ for some $t^* > t$ (this last observation uses the assumption that returns do not adjust instantaneously).

First note that

$$K(t^*) \geq K(\tau) \quad \text{for all } \tau \in [s, t^*] \tag{3}$$

For suppose this is not true; then $K(t^*) < K(\tau)$ for some $\tau \in [s, t^*)$. Because $K(t) > K(s)$ by assumption and $t \in [s, t^*)$, we may conclude that there exist $\{t_1, t_2, t_3\}$ in the interval $[s, t^*]$ such that $K(t_1) < K(t_2) > K(t_3)$, while $r(\tau) < 0$ for all $\tau \in [s, t^*]$. This means that (at least) two costly switches between sectors $A$ and $B$ are optimal while sector A earns a higher return throughout, a contradiction.

Now return to the main proof. So far, we know that there is a positive measure of agents between $s$ and $t$ such that for each of them, at the time $\tau$ of their move,

$$V(\gamma, B, \tau) - \hat{c}_B(K_\tau) \geq V(\gamma, A, \tau)$$

But for each such person, denoting the discount rate by $\rho$, we see that

$$
V(\gamma, A, \tau) \geq e^{-\rho(t^*-\tau)}[V(\gamma, B, t^*) - \hat{c}_B(K(t^*))]
$$

$$
> \int_\tau^{t^*} e^{-\rho(z-\tau)}r(z)\mathrm{d}z + e^{-\rho(t^*-\tau)}[V(\gamma, B, t^*) - \hat{c}_B(K(t^*))]
$$

$$
> \int_\tau^{t^*} e^{-\rho(z-\tau)}r(z)\mathrm{d}z + e^{-\rho(t^*-\tau)}V(\gamma, B, t^*) - \hat{c}_B(K(\tau))
$$

$$
= V(\gamma, B, \tau) - \hat{c}_B(K(\tau))
$$

The first inequality follows from the agent's option to stay in sector $A$ until $t^*$, and then switch. The second inequality follows from the fact that $t^* > \tau$ for all $s \leq \tau \leq t$ and $r(z) < 0$ for all $\tau \leq z \leq t^*$. The third inequality follows from discounting and (3), so that

$$
\hat{c}_B(K_\tau) > e^{-\rho(t^*-\tau)}\hat{c}_B(K_{t^*})
$$

and the last equality follows from the observation that two or more switches between $\tau$ and $t^*$ are clearly suboptimal.

Thus we have a contradiction to our presumption that

$$
V(\gamma, B, \tau) - \hat{c}_B(K_\tau) \geq V(\gamma, A, \tau)
$$

which completes the proof.

### Notes

1  See also Fukao and Benabou (1993) in this context, and in a related scenario, Chamley and Gale (1994) and Gale (1995).
2  Empirical work on such lags include the study by Henderson (1994), which reveals the specific lag structure with which changes in own-industry employment affect growth in some manufacturing sectors (at the metropolitan level). Literature on technology investment also stresses the fact that benefits from investment may take time to flow (Farrell and Saloner, 1985; Katz and Shapiro 1986, 1992).
3  To be more precise, our assumption of a continuum of agents (as in the Matsuyama and Krugman studies) allows us to handle arbitrarily small lags. If this is not clear now, it will be as soon as we state our main result.
4  Note that we do not *a priori* restrict it to be a continuous path, so that self-fulfilling jumps are, in principle, permitted.
5  This is to be contrasted with the more recent work of Gale (1995) and Chamley and Gale (1994), where lags also play a role.
6  This does not rule out multiplicity. It is possible, for instance, that if $f(K(0)) > 0$, both the initial allocation and a jump to the B region by everybody in A belong to a set of simultaneously sustainable equilibria. If initially $f(K(0)) < 0$, there is always a unique equilibrium: either the initial allocation or the complete abandonment of region B.
7  In the case where the adjustment cost depends on the *flow* of migration, it turns out that the existing literature that we are aware of (see, for example, Kemp and Wan, 1974; Mussa, 1978; Krugman, 1991a) *also* invoke congestion (rather than agglomeration) in migration costs.

8  Perhaps this explains why new software, such as Internet browsers, need to be given away, with prices rising later as the number of devotees to that software swell.

## References

Arthur, B. (1984): "Competing Technologies and Lock-in by Historical Small Events: The Dynamics of Allocation Under Increasing Returns," Stanford: CEPR Publication, Stanford University.
Bryant, J. (1983): "A Simple Rational Expectations Keynes-Type Model," *Quarterly Journal of Economics*, 97, 525–8.
Chamley, C. and Gale, D. (1994): "Information Revelation and Strategic Delay in a Model of Investment," *Econometrica*, 62, 1065–86.
Chatterjee, S. and Cooper, R. (1989): "Multiplicity of Equilibria and Fluctuations in Dynamic Perfectly Competitive Economies," *AEA Papers and Proceedings*, 79, 353–7.
Chatterjee, S., Cooper, R. and Ravikumar, B. (1990): "Participation Dynamics: Sunspots and Cycles," NBER Working Paper 3438.
Cooper, R. and John, A. (1988): "Coordinating Coordination Failures in a Keynesian Model," *Quarterly Journal of Economics*, 103, 441–64.
David, P. (1985): "Clio and the Economics of QWERTY," *American Economic Review, Papers and Proceedings*, 75, 332–7.
Diamond, P. (1982): "Aggregate Demand Management in Search Equilibrium," *Journal of Political Economy*, 90, 881–94.
Farrell, J. and Saloner, G. (1985): "Standardization, Compatibility and Innovation," *Rand Journal of Economics*, 16, 70–83.
Fukao, K. and Benabou, R. (1993): "History Versus Expectations: A Comment," *Quarterly Journal of Economics*, 108, 535–42.
Gale, D. (1995): "Dynamic Coordination Games," *Economic Theory*, 5, 1–18.
Henderson, J. V. (1994): "Externalities and Industrial Development," NBER Working Paper 4730.
Hirschman, A. (1958): *The Strategy of Economic Development*. New Haven: Yale University Press.
Katz, M. L. and Shapiro, C. (1986): "Technology Adoption in the Presence of Network Externalities," *Journal of Political Economy*, 94, 822–41.
—— (1992): "Product Introduction with Network Externalities," *Journal of Industrial Economics*, 40, 55–83.
Kemp, M. C. and Wan, H. Y. (1974): "Hysteresis of Long-Run Equilibrium from Realistic Adjustment Costs," in G. Horwich and P. A. Samuelson (eds), *Trade, Stability and Macroeconomics*, New York: Academic Press.
Krugman, P. (1991a): "History Versus Expectations," *Quarterly Journal of Economics*, 106, 651–67.
—— (1991b): "Increasing Returns and Economic Geography," *Journal of Political Economy*, 99, 483–99.
Matsuyama, K. (1991): "Increasing Returns, Industrialization, and Indeterminacy of Equilibrium," *Quarterly Journal of Economics*, 106, 616–50.
Murphy, K., Shleifer, A. and Vishny, R. (1989): "Industrialization and the Big Push," *Journal of Political Economy*, 97, 1003–26.
Mussa, M. (1978): "Dynamic Adjustment in the Heckscher–Ohlin–Samuelson Model," *Journal of Political Economy*, 68, 775–91.
Myrdal, G. (1957): *Economic Theory and Underdeveloped Regions*. London: Duckworth.
Rosenstein-Rodan, P. (1943): "Problems of Industrialization of Eastern and Southern Europe," *Economic Journal*, 55, 202–11.
Scitovsky, T. (1954): "Two Concepts of External Economies," *Journal of Political Economy*, 62, 143–51.

# B: Inequality and Underdevelopment

CHAPTER 4

# Income Distribution and Macroeconomics

ODED GALOR AND JOSEPH ZEIRA

This paper analyzes the role of wealth distribution in macroeconomics through investment in human capital. It is shown that in the presence of credit markets' imperfections and indivisibilities in investment in human capital, the initial distribution of wealth affects aggregate output and investment both in the short and in the long run, as there are multiple steady states. This paper therefore provides an additional explanation for the persistent differences in per-capita output across countries. Furthermore, the paper shows that cross-country differences in macroeconomic adjustment to aggregate shocks can be attributed, among other factors, to differences in wealth and income distribution across countries.

## 1. Introduction

This paper explores the theoretical linkage between income distribution and macroeconomics, through investment in human capital. Our main interest is how income and wealth distributions are related to long-run macroeconomic issues, like economic growth and sectorial adjustment. It is shown that distribution of wealth can significantly affect aggregate economic activity both in the short and in the long run. Countries which have different historically determined wealth distributions follow different growth paths and may even converge to different steady states. Hence the paper suggests an explanation for the differences in growth patterns between countries.

One of the major motivations to study the relationship between income distribution and aggregate economic activity is the empirical data, which persistently shows a strong correlation between income distribution and income per-capita. Kravis (1960) and Lydall (1968) have shown that income is more equally distributed within wealthier countries. Recent statistics provided by the World Bank (1988, 1989, 1990, 1991) suggest that this is still the case. Recently Persson and Tabellini (1990) have provided empirical evidence that equity is positively correlated not only with the level of income but with the rate of growth as well. Such observations call for an explanation.

In modern macroeconomic thought, the theoretical analysis of the relationships between income distribution and aggregate economic activity has gone through a number of phases.

Keynes (1936) stressed the effect of income distribution on aggregate demand. During the 1950s and 1960s attention shifted to the relationship between distribution and economic growth.[1] Most of this literature focused on the effect of income distribution on consumption and saving. During the 1970s and the 1980s macroeconomic theory lost interest in issues of distribution, partly due to the decline of interest in growth, and partly due to increased use of models of representative agents and overlapping generations. The recently renewed interest in growth and development, has led to new interest in distributional issues as well. This paper explores one possible relationship between distribution and growth, through investment in human capital in the presence of imperfect credit markets.[2]

The paper develops an equilibrium model of open economies with overlapping generations and inter-generational altruism. A single good can be produced by either a skill-intensive or an unskilled-intensive process. Individuals live for two periods. In the first they may either invest in human capital and acquire education or else work as unskilled. In the second period they work as skilled or unskilled – according to their education level – consume and leave bequests. Individuals are assumed to be identical with regard to their potential skills and preferences and differ only with respect to their inherited wealth.[3] It is further assumed in the paper that there are enforcement and supervision costs on individual borrowers and hence the borrowing interest rate is higher than the lending rate. Consequently, the inheritance of each individual determines whether she invests in human capital. Hence, the distribution of wealth determines the aggregate levels of investment, of skilled and unskilled labour and of output.[4] But the effect of wealth distribution is not only short run, as the different levels of investment in human capital in turn determine the distribution of income, which gradually changes the distribution of wealth through time.[5] It is shown in the paper that the economic dynamics of dynasties depend on initial wealth. There are rich dynasties, in which all generations invest in human capital, work as skilled and leave a large bequest. There are poor dynasties, in which people inherit less, work as unskilled, and leave less to their children. Hence the initial distribution of wealth determines how big these two groups of dynasties are, and therefore what is the long-run equilibrium in the economy. Wealth distribution, therefore, carries long-run as well as short-run implications.

There are two major assumptions in the paper. One is that credit markets are imperfect, as the interest rate for individual borrowers is higher than that for lenders. The second important assumption is that investment in human capital is indivisible, namely that there is a technological non-convexity. The result that wealth distribution affects economic activity in the short run is due to the assumption that credit markets are imperfect. This result is quite intuitive. If borrowing is difficult and costly, those who inherit a large initial wealth and do not need to borrow have better access to investment in human capital, as has already been noticed by Becker (1975) and Atkinson (1975). Hence the distribution of wealth affects the aggregate amounts of investment in human capital and of output. This result was first shown by Loury (1981).[6] In his important contribution Loury also shows, that under credit market imperfection the effect of wealth distribution disappears in the long run, as all initial wealth distributions in his model converge to a unique ergodic distribution. This paper shows that if we add a second assumption, that technology is non-convex, the inherited distribution of wealth affects the economy not only in the short run but in the long run as well. As a result of this assumption there are multiple long-run equilibria and dynamics are no longer ergodic.[7]

From the above description it is clear that this paper is related to the new wave of research on economic growth, pioneered by Romer (1986) and Lucas (1988). Like these, we attempt to examine why differences between economies persist. Contrary to most previous studies, we do not attribute these differences to technology or knowledge, but rather to differences in investment in human capital, due to credit market imperfection.[8] An additional similarity between our model and the new growth models is the existence of non-convexities in production. In our model it is the indivisibility of individual investment in human capital, a non-convexity at the individual level.[9]

The paper also deals, by use of an extension to the basic model, with the issues of the relationship between national income and income distribution and of the adjustment to aggregate shocks. We show that richer economies tend to have smaller wage differentials and a more equal distribution of income. This result is indeed consistent with the stylized facts described above. We also show that income and wealth distributions affect the adjustment of the economy to aggregate shocks, when this adjustment calls for investment in human capital and sectorial shifts.

The paper is organized as follows. Section 2 presents the basic model. Section 3 describes the short-run equilibrium where wealth distribution affects output and investment. Section 4 examines the long-run equilibrium where economic inequality can be persistent. Section 5 contains a discussion of the role of the various assumptions of the model. Section 6 extends the basic model to incorporate variable wages for unskilled workers. Section 7 studies the relationship between income distribution and national income. Section 8 examines the adjustment to exogenous shocks. Section 9 offers some concluding remarks.

## 2. The Basic Model

Consider a small open economy in a one-good world. The good can be used for either consumption or investment. The good can be produced by two technologies, one which uses skilled labour and capital and the other using unskilled labour only. Production in the skilled labour sector is described by:

$$Y_t^s = F(K_t, L_t^s) \tag{1}$$

where $Y_t^s$ is output in this sector at time $t$, $K_t$ is the amount of capital and $L_t^s$ is labour input. $F$ is a concave production function with constant returns to scale. It is assumed that investment in human capital and in physical capital is made one period in advance. For the sake of simplicity it is assumed that there are no adjustment costs to investment and no depreciation of capital. Production in the unskilled labour sector is described by:

$$Y_t^n = w_n \cdot L_t^n \tag{2}$$

where $Y_t^n$ and $L_t^n$ are output and unskilled labour input respectively, and $w_n > 0$ is marginal productivity in this sector.

Individuals in this economy live two periods each in overlapping generations. They can either work as unskilled in both periods of life or invest in human capital when young and be skilled workers in the second period of life. The amount of investment in human capital is $h > 0$. An individual supplies one unit of labour in each of the working periods. Note that the indivisibility of the amount of investment implies that there is a region of increasing returns to scale.

Each individual has one parent and one child, which creates the connection between generations within dynasties. This assumption also means that there is no population growth. In each generation there is a continuum of individuals of size $L$. People care about their children and leave them bequests. It is also assumed, for the sake of simplicity, that people consume in the second period of life only. Formally, we assume that an individual derives utility both from consumption in the second period of life and from any bequest to his/her offspring:[10]

$$u = \alpha \log c + (1 - \alpha) \log b \tag{3}$$

where $c$ is consumption in second period, $b$ is bequest, and $0 < \alpha < 1$. Notice that all individuals are born with the same potential abilities and with the same preferences. They differ only in the amounts they inherit from their parents.

Capital is assumed to be perfectly mobile so that both firms and individuals have free access to the international capital markets. The world rate of interest is equal to $r > 0$ and is assumed to be constant over time. Individuals can lend any amount at this rate. As for borrowing, we assume that a borrowing individual can evade debt payments by moving to other places etc., but this activity is costly. Lenders can avoid such defaults by keeping track of borrowers, but such precautionary measures are costly as well. Assume that if lenders spend an amount $z$ at keeping track of a borrower, this borrower can still evade the lenders but only at a cost of $\beta z$, where $\beta > 1$. As is later shown in the paper, these costs create a capital market imperfection, where individuals can borrow only at an interest rate higher than $r$.

Unlike individuals, firms are unable to evade debt payment, due to reasons such as immobility, reputation, etc.[11] Hence, firms can borrow at the lenders' interest rate $r$. Due to the absence of adjustment costs to investment, and to the fact that the number of skilled workers is known one period in advance, the amount of capital in the skilled labour sector is adjusted each period so that:

$$F_K\left(K_t, L_t^s\right) = r \tag{4}$$

Hence, there is a constant capital–labour ratio in this sector, which determines the wage of skilled labour $w_s$, which is constant as well. This wage $w_s$ depends on $r$ and on technology only.

We further assume that both labour markets and the good market are perfectly competitive and expectations are fully rational.

## 3. Wealth Distribution and Short-run Equilibrium

Let us first examine the capital market equilibrium for individual borrowers. It is clear that lenders to individuals must have positive costs of keeping track of each borrower, since otherwise everyone defaults. Hence, the individual must borrow at a rate higher than

$r$, to cover these tracking costs. An individual who borrows an amount $d$ pays an interest rate $i_d$ which covers lenders' interest rate and lenders' costs $z$, as competitive financial intermediation operates on zero profits:

$$d \cdot i_d = d \cdot r + z \tag{5}$$

Lenders choose $z$ to be high enough to make evasion disadvantageous:

$$d(1 + i_d) = \beta z \tag{6}$$

This is an incentive compatibility constraint. Equations (5) and (6) determine $i_d$:

$$i_d = i = \frac{1 + \beta r}{\beta - 1} > r \tag{7}$$

The borrowing interest rate $i$ is, therefore, independent of the amount borrowed $d$, as tracking costs rise with the amount borrowed $d$. This result is quite intuitive: as the amount borrowed increases, the incentive to default rises and hence tracking costs rise.

We now turn to describe individual optimal decisions. Consider an individual who inherits an amount $x$ in first period of life. If this individual decides to work as unskilled and not invest in human capital, his (her) lifetime utility is:

$$U_n(x) = \log[(x + w_n)(1 + r) + w_n] + \varepsilon \tag{8}$$

where:

$$\varepsilon = \alpha \log \alpha + (1 - \alpha)\log(1 - \alpha)$$

This unskilled worker is a lender who leaves a bequest of size:

$$b_n(x) = (1 - \alpha)[(1 + r)(x + w_n) + w_n] \tag{9}$$

An individual with inheritance $x \geq h$, who invests in human capital, is a lender with utility:

$$U_s(x) = \log[w_s + (x - h)(1 + r)] + \varepsilon \tag{10}$$

and a bequest of:

$$b_s(x) = (1 - \alpha)[w_s + (x - h)(1 + r)] \tag{11}$$

An individual who invests in human capital but has inheritance $x$ smaller than $h$ is a borrower, with lifetime utility:

$$U_s(x) = \log[w_s + (x - h)(1 + i)] + \varepsilon \tag{12}$$

and a bequest of:

$$b_s(x) = (1 - \alpha)[w_s + (x - h)(1 + i)] \tag{13}$$

It is clear that if $w_s - h(1 + r) < w_n(2 + r)$ all individuals prefer to work as unskilled. Since this is a case with limited interest we assume that:[12]

$$w_s - h(1 + r) \geqq w_n(2 + r) \tag{14}$$

Hence, as investment in human capital pays back more than unskilled labour, lenders prefer to invest in human capital, as is seen from equations (8) and (10). Borrowers invest in human capital as long as $U_s(x) \geqq U_n(x)$, that is as long as:

$$x \geqq f = \frac{1}{i - r}[w_n(2 + r) + h(1 + i) - w_s] \tag{15}$$

Individuals who inherit an amount smaller than $f$ would prefer not to invest in human capital but work as unskilled. Education is, therefore, limited to individuals with high enough initial wealth, due to a higher interest rate for borrowers.

The amount an individual inherits in first period of life, therefore, fully determines his (her) decisions whether to invest in human capital or work as unskilled, and how much to consume and bequeath. Let $D_t$ be the distribution of inheritances by individuals born in period $t$. This distribution satisfies:

$$\int_0^\infty dD_t(x_t) = L \tag{16}$$

The distribution $D_t$, therefore, fully determines economic performance in period $t$. It determines the amount of skilled labour:

$$L_t^s = \int_f^\infty dD_t(x_t) \tag{17}$$

and unskilled labour:

$$L_t^n = \int_0^f dD_t(x_t) \tag{18}$$

Hence the distribution of wealth determines aggregate output as well and it therefore has a strong effect on the macroeconomic equilibrium. This result is due to the credit market imperfection. But we can question the relevance of this result in the following way: the effect of wealth distribution is relevant only if this distribution differs substantially from one country to the other. This is not reasonable if the dynamic process is ergodic, namely if all initial distributions converge to the same distribution in the long-run, as in the works of Loury (1981) and Banerjee and Newman (1991). In the next section we show that the second assumption in the paper, of indivisibilities in investment in human capital, leads to non-ergodic dynamics and to multiple long-run wealth distributions. Hence it becomes more meaningful to examine the effect of wealth distribution in the short run as well.

## 4. The Dynamics of Wealth Distribution

The distribution of wealth not only determines equilibrium in period $t$, but also determines next period distribution of inheritances $D_{t+1}$:

$$x_{t+1} = \begin{cases} b_n(x_t) = (1-\alpha)[(x_t + w_n)(1+r) + w_n] & \text{if } x_t < f \\ b_s(x_t) = (1-\alpha)[w_s + (x_t - h)(1+i)] & \text{if } f \leq x_t < h \\ b_s(x_t) = (1-\alpha)[w_s + (x_t - h)(1+r)] & \text{if } h \leq x_t \end{cases} \tag{19}$$

In order to illustrate the dynamic evolution of wealth distribution through time we present in figure 1 the curves $b_n$ and $b_s$ which describe the dynamic relationships between inheritance and bequest for unskilled and skilled workers, respectively. Notice that $f$ is determined by the intersection of $b_n$ and $b_s$.

Individuals who inherit less than $f$ work as unskilled and so are their descendants in all future generations. Their inheritances converge to a long-run level $\bar{x}_n$:

$$\bar{x}_n = \frac{1-\alpha}{1-(1-\alpha)(1+r)} w_n(2+r) \tag{20}$$

Individuals who inherit more than $f$ invest in human capital but not all their descendants will remain in the skilled labour sector in future generations. The critical point is $g$ in figure 1:

$$g = \frac{(1-\alpha)[h(1+i) - w_s]}{(1+i)(1-\alpha) - 1} \tag{21}$$

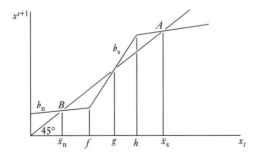

**Figure 1**

Individuals who inherit less than $g$ in period $t$ may invest in human capital, but after some generations their descendants become unskilled workers and their inheritances converge to $\bar{x}_n$. Individuals who inherit more than $g$ invest in human capital and so do their descendants, generation after generation. Their bequests converge to $\bar{x}_s$:

$$\bar{x}_s = \frac{1-\alpha}{1-(1-\alpha)(1+r)}[w_s - h(1+r)] \tag{22}$$

Thus, dynasties in this economy are concentrated in the long run in two groups: rich dynasties, where generation after generation invests in human capital, and poor ones, where generation after generation are unskilled workers.

Notice that the slopes of $b_n$ and $b_s$ in figure 1 are lower than one, at $\bar{x}_n$ and $\bar{x}_s$ respectively, and that means that we assume that $\alpha$ and $r$ satisfy:

$$(1-\alpha)(1+r) < 1 \tag{23}$$

This additional assumption guarantees that the process of bequest from generation to generation is stable and does not explode. Another additional assumption which is implicit in figure 1 is that enforcement costs are rather high so that the spread between the lending and borrowing interest rates is high too:

$$(1-\alpha)(1+i) = \frac{\beta}{\beta-1}(1+r)(1-\alpha) > 1 \tag{24}$$

so that the $b_s$ curve is drawn in its steep part with a slope higher than one. If (24) does not hold, all long-run distribution of labour are concentrated in either the unskilled labour sector or in the skilled sector. Since this is both unrealistic and uninteresting analytically, we restrict ourselves to the case described by (24).[13] It is also assumed in figure 1 that $g$ lies between $\bar{x}_s$ and $\bar{x}_n$, for similar reasons.

The dynamic evolution of the aggregate economy can be deduced from individual dynamics, as presented in figure 1. The economy converges to a long-run equilibrium in which the population is divided into two groups: skilled workers with wealth $\bar{x}_s$ and unskilled workers with wealth $\bar{x}_n$. The relative size of these two groups depends on the initial distribution of wealth, since the long-run number of unskilled workers $L_\infty^n$ is equal to $L_t^g$, the number of individuals who inherit less than $g$ in period $t$:

$$L_t^g = \int_0^g dD_t(x_t) \tag{25}$$

The long-run level of average wealth is:

$$\bar{x}_s - \frac{L_t^g}{L}(\bar{x}_s - \bar{x}_n) \tag{26}$$

which is decreasing with $L_t^g/L$.

Hence, the long-run levels of income and wealth are positively related to the initial number of individuals who inherit more than $g$. Thus, an economy which is initially poor, ends up poor in the long run as well. An economy which is initially rich and its wealth is distributed among many, ends up rich. But an economy with a large initial amount of wealth, which is held by few, ends up poor in the long run. If we would like to describe these results in more popular terms, we could say that a country has better growth prospects if it has a relatively larger middle class.

The long-run equilibrium in this model, therefore, depends on the initial distribution of wealth and is as a result historically dependent. There are multiple long-run equilibria and the specific one the economy converges to depends on the initial distribution of wealth.

Note that these results can be applied to a growth model with continuous technological innovations. Assume that productivity in the non-skilled sector $w_n$ grows at a rate $\alpha_n$, and in the skilled sector $w_s$ and $h$ grow at a higher rate $\alpha_s$. Then the rate of growth of output per capita is a weighted average of $\alpha_s$ and $\alpha_n$, where the weights depend on the initial distribution of wealth. Hence, wealth distribution can affect not only the long-run level of output, but the rate of growth as well.[14]

Let us now examine the issue of Pareto-efficiency in equilibrium in our model. It is obvious that wealth redistribution can raise output and income both in the short and in the long run, but it is not a Pareto-improvement. A Pareto-improvement in our economy is possible, if intertemporal exchange can be facilitated at a lower cost than the costs of monitoring borrowers. Let us consider for example the following policy. The government can subsidize education, which reduces individual costs of investment in human capital $h$, and finance these costs by a tax on skilled workers in the next period. Such a policy shifts the $b_s$ curve in figure 1 to the left, lowers both $f$ and $g$ and increases investment and output in the short and in the long run. This policy can be Pareto-improving if debt collection costs are higher than tax collection costs. This is a plausible assumption for two reasons. The first reason is that the government avoids the need to keep track of each individual borrower, by giving the subsidy to all students and by taxing all those who have a higher income, without even knowing how much each individual borrows. The second reason is that in most cases the tax system already operates for other purposes, and the above policy only raises the taxes already collected.

## 5. Discussion of the Basic Assumptions

Let us now examine more closely the role of various assumptions of the basic model. Examine first the role of the specific form of utility function assumed in equation (3). The logarithmic function greatly simplifies the analysis, but does not affect any of the major results. Even if utility is a general function of consumption and bequest, $u(c, b)$, it is clear that indirect utility depends on the amount the individual has in second period of life and so is his (her) bequest. Hence lifetime utility and bequest are monotonically related and hence the dynamic analysis is basically the same and so are the results.

In the basic model the altruistic intergenerational bequest motive is modeled as utility from the size of bequest. There is an alternative way to model this motive, by assuming that individuals' utility depends not on the size of bequest but on their offspring's utility, as in Barro (1974) and Loury (1981). Is it possible that if poor parents care about the utility of future generations they will save more to enable them in some stage to jump over the hurdle, invest in human capital and become high skilled? The answer is that even under such specification of utility the basic results of the paper hold as well. In an appendix to a former version of this paper (Galor and Zeira, 1990), we show that if the borrowing rate is higher than lenders' interest rate and investment in human capital is indivisible, then even under the Barro specification there are dynasties who remain unskilled workers forever, if their initial wealth is relatively small. We therefore conclude, that the major results of the paper are robust to changes in the specification of utility.

Another specific assumption in the paper is the type of credit market imperfection. We have analyzed the dynamics of the economy under alternative types of credit market imperfections, such as credit constraints due to asymmetric information etc., and the basic results still hold. Under any specification, as long as borrowing is not fully free and costless, those who inherit large amounts have easier access to investment in human capital than those with small bequests.

The results of our model are also robust to the introduction of individual uninsured risk. Even if wages of skilled and non-skilled workers vary randomly, as a result of different skills, the main results of the paper still hold. In order to see that, imagine that $w_s$ and $w_n$ are random but bounded. We can draw the $b_s$ and $b_n$ curves, as in figure 1, for the upper bounds of $w_s$ and $w_n$ and for the lower bounds. That determines a dynamic band instead of the dynamic curve in figure 1. If the variability of wages is not too high, the qualitative results are as follows: dynasties with high initial wealth will invest in human capital in every generation and remain rich. Dynasties with low initial wealth will never invest in human capital and remain poor. There is some intermediate domain, in which dynasties may fluctuate between the skilled and non-skilled sector. Hence initial wealth distribution affects the economy in the short and in the long run, even when skills are heterogenous.

As already mentioned in the paper, imperfection in credit markets is sufficient for wealth distribution to be effective in the short run, but in order to maintain this result in the long run we add an element of non-convexity to the model, namely indivisibility in investment in human capital. How necessary is this additional assumption? We believe that it is crucial for the major results of the paper. This can be verified by examining carefully the results of Loury (1981). In his model credit markets are imperfect, both due to infinite rate of interest for borrowers and due to lack of insurance, but the production function of human capital is smooth and convex. As a result the distribution of wealth converges to a unique long-run distribution. If we translate this result to our model, then all dynasties invest the same amount in human capital in the long run. This is very different from our results. Hence the results of our model require both assumptions, namely that credit markets are imperfect and that there are non-convexities in human capital.

## 6. Variable Wages

In this section we extend the basic model to include variable wages for unskilled workers. This extension has two goals. The first is to make the model more realistic, as it introduces greater mobility between sectors and relaxes the strong segmentation between dynasties in the basic model. The second intention is to enable us to analyze additional issues, such as the correlation between wealth and equality and the adjustment of the economy to aggregate shocks.

Let us, therefore, examine the basic model described in section 2 with one additional assumption, that production by unskilled labour involves a second factor of production, land. Let production by unskilled labour and land be described by:

$$Y_t^n = G(L_t^n, N) \tag{27}$$

where $N$ is land and $G$ is a standard constant return to scale production function. Let the aggregate amount of land be fixed at $\bar{N}$, so that wages of unskilled workers are:

$$w_t^n = G_L(L_t^n, \bar{N}) = P(L_t^n) \tag{28}$$

where $P$ is a function that describes the diminishing marginal productivity of unskilled labour. We assume that land is traded in a perfectly competitive market, which operates each period after production takes place. Due to lack of uncertainty in this deterministic economy, land is an asset which is equivalent to lending.[15]

We now turn to describe the supply of unskilled workers. Let us slightly change the basic model and assume, for simplification only, that the unskilled work only in the first period of life. The supply of unskilled workers is determined by the number of individuals who prefer not to invest in human capital:

$$S_t = \int_0^{f(w_t^n)} dD_t(x_t) \tag{29}$$

where $f(w_t^n)$ is the threshold level for investment in human capital, which has been defined in section 3 in equation (15), and which is equal in this case to:

$$f(w_t^n) = \frac{1}{i-r}\left[w_t^n(1+r) + h(1+i) - w_s\right] \tag{30}$$

Figure 2 presents demand $P$, supply $S_t$ and the equilibrium in the unskilled labour market. Notice that at

$$w_t^n = w_s 1 + r - h$$

individuals are indifferent between investing in human capital and working as unskilled, hence the supply curve becomes flat at this wage. The supply curve $S_t$ is upward sloping but can contain horizontal as well as vertical segments. If there is a group of positive measure who inherit the same amount in period $t$, then there is a horizontal segment in the supply curve. If the distribution $D_t$ is such that there are no inheritances between $f(w_0)$ and $f(w_1)$, then the supply curve is vertical between $w_0$ and $w_1$. The equilibrium in the market for unskilled labour, as described in figure 2, determines the wage of unskilled, the number of investors in human capital. It is clear from figure 2 that this equilibrium

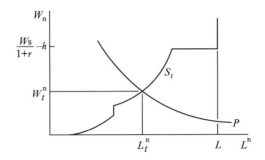

Figure 2

depends on the distribution of inheritances $D_t$. In the next section we show that the historically given distribution of wealth $D_t$ affects the equilibrium not only in the short run, but in the long run as well.

## 7. Wealth Distribution and National Income

In order to examine the dynamics of the economy let us first describe the dynamic evolution of wealth within dynasties:

$$x_{t+1} = \begin{cases} b_n(x_t) = (1-\alpha)\left[(x_t + w_t^n)(1+r)\right] & \text{if } x_t < f(w_t^n) \\ b_s(x_t) = (1-\alpha)\left[w_s + (x_t - h)(1+i)\right] & \text{if } f(w_t^n) \leq x_t < h \\ b_s(x_t) = (1-\alpha)\left[w_s + (x_t - h)(1+r)\right] & \text{if } h \leq x_t \end{cases} \quad (31)$$

These dynamics are similar to those in the basic model with one exception, that $w_t^n$ is no longer fixed, but is endogenous and depends on the distribution of wealth itself. This significantly complicates the dynamic analysis, but as we show later on, our diagrams enable us to describe these dynamics in a fairly simple way.

Figure 3 describes individual bequest dynamics as given in equation (31). As in figure 1, $b_s$ describes the bequests of investors in human capital while $b_n$ describes bequests of

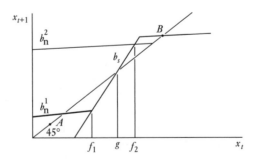

Figure 3

unskilled workers. Figure 3 differs from figure 1 in one respect: the $b_n$ line is no longer fixed but shifts with $w_t^n$, which is now endogenous.

Let us define an economy as "developed" if the equilibrium wage of unskilled workers in period $t$, $w_t^n$, is high and satisfies: $f(w_t^n) > g$, where $g$ is given by equation (21). Intuitively an economy is developed if the number of individuals who have high inheritances in $t$ is large.[16] Such a case is described by the $b_n^2$ curve in figure 3. It can be shown that an economy is developed if and only if $w_t^n > w_g$ where $w_g$ is defined by:

$$w_g = \frac{1}{1+r} \frac{\alpha + \alpha r - r}{\alpha + \alpha i - i} [w_s - h(1+i)] \tag{32}$$

Similarly an economy is defined as "less developed" if $w_t^n \leqq w_g$.

Let us now examine the dynamics of a less developed economy. Individual bequests in this economy in period $t$ are described by the curves $b_n^1$ and $b_s$ in figure 3. Notice that individuals who inherit more than $g$ leave a bequest which is larger than what they have inherited, while individuals who inherit less than $g$ leave a bequest which is smaller than what they have inherited.[17] Hence we infer from equation (29) that the supply curve of unskilled labour in period $t+1$, $S_{t+1}$, is rotated relative to $S_t$ around $w_g$, as described in figure 4. Hence, the wage of unskilled workers falls and $b_n$ shifts downward. This process continues and the economy converges to the long-run equilibrium at point $A$ in figure 4, where the wage is $w_\infty^n$, the number of unskilled workers is $L_\infty^n$ and $S_\infty$ is the supply curve. The long-run wealth of the unskilled is $\bar{x}_n$, given by point $A$ in figure 3. Notice that the long-run number of unskilled workers $L_\infty^n$ equals precisely the number of those who inherit less than $g$ in the initial period, $L_t^g$. Notice that this variable is time independent and remains constant for all $t$, so that the above results are time-consistent.

Consider now a developed economy where initial unskilled wage is higher than $w_g$, as described by $b_n^2$ in figure 3. In this case every individual (in the relevant domain) bequeaths more than she has inherited. Hence, the supply curve in next period shifts everywhere to the left. As a result wages rise: $w_{t+1}^n > w_t^n$, as is shown in figure 5. This process continues until equilibrium is reached at $B$, where the unskilled wage rate is equal

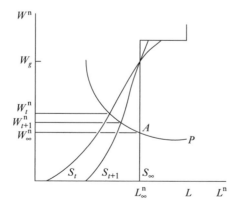

Figure 4

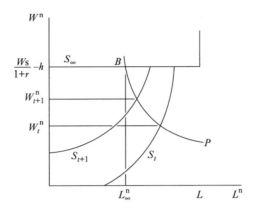

**Figure 5**

to $w_s/(1+r) - h$, and $b_n$ coincides with $b_s$. This is, therefore, an egalitarian long-run equilibrium, where net life-time incomes of skilled workers and of unskilled workers are equal.

The long-run economic dynamics in this model, therefore, crucially depend on the number of individuals who inherit less than $g$ in period $t, L_t^g$. It can be shown that a country is developed if and only if $P(L_t^g) > w_g$.

We can now summarize the results of this section in the following theorem:

THEOREM 1    *If an economy satisfies:* $0 < g < \bar{x}_s$, *its dynamics depend on the number of individuals who inherit less than $g$ in period $t, L_t^g$.*

    (a)   *A less developed economy, where $P(L_t^g) \leqq w_g$, converges to an unequal distribution of income, where:*

$$w_\infty^n < \frac{w_s}{1+r} - h$$

    (b)   *A rich economy, where $P(L_t^g) > w_g$, converges toward an equal distribution of lifetime income, where:*

$$w_\infty^n = \frac{w_s}{1+r} - h$$

Theorem 1 assumes that: $0 < g < \bar{x}_s$. If $g \leqq 0$ all countries are developed and converge to an equal distribution of income, while if $\bar{x}_s \leqq g$ all are poor and converge to an unequal distribution. Since we are interested in a situation where income distribution varies across countries we concentrate on the more interesting case and assume that: $0 < g < \bar{x}_s$. It can be shown that $g < \bar{x}_s$ iff $(1 - \alpha)w_s > h$ and $g > 0$ iff $h(1 + i) > w_s$.

In this section we, therefore, show that wealth and equality are highly correlated and affect one another. On the one hand, countries with greater income per capita have a more equal distribution of income and smaller wage differentials. On the other hand, countries with a more equal initial distribution of wealth grow more rapidly and have a higher income level in the long run. These results shed a new light on the empirical findings on income distribution across countries. It has long been noticed that income tends to be more equally distributed in developed countries than in less-developed countries, as described in the introduction. One of the early explanations for this correlation has been suggested by Kuznets (1955), who claimed that the distribution of income changes along the development path of a country.[18] Thus his theory implied that the changes in observed distributions are due to the fact that countries are at different stages on their growth path. A similar line is adopted in a theoretical study by Greenwood and Jovanovic (1990). Contrary to this approach, which assumes convergence of economies to a unique steady state, our theory presents a very different interpretation of the data. It is claimed that distributions of income differ among countries, since these countries are in different long-run equilibria. Our explanation, of course, does not rule out the existence of a Kuznets curve. It only adds an additional explanation for the correlation between income distribution and aggregate income.[19]

## 8. Exogenous Shocks and Income Distribution

In this section we continue to study the extended model, where wages are variable, in order to examine how the economy reacts to exogenous shocks. Let us first consider an adverse supply shock to productivity in the unskilled workers' sector, namely a reduction in $P$.

Let us assume for simplicity that the shock is unanticipated and that the economy is already in long-run equilibrium at the time of the shock.[20] Consider first the case of a developed economy where wealth is equally distributed. This case is described in figure 6 by the labour supply curve $S_1$. The shock reduces the demand for unskilled labour and shift the economy from $A_1$ to $B_1$. It has therefore no effect on the wage of unskilled workers but only on their number. The economy adjusts immediately through a structural

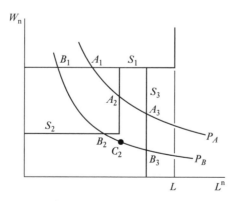

Figure 6

shift, from unskilled to skilled labour, by increased investment in human capital. Notice that income falls on impact, even if wages do not fall, due to an increase in investment in human capital, but this is a temporary fall in income. Net discounted income remains unchanged and there are no utility losses either.

Consider now an economy with unequal distribution of income – a less-developed country. This case is described by the supply curves $S_2$ and $S_3$ in figure 6. The long-run adjustment to the shock is through a decline in unskilled wages and no sectoral shifts, to points like $C_2$ or $B_3$. Convergence to the long-run equilibrium can be immediate, as in the case of $B_3$, when the economy is very poor, or through a temporary rise in skilled labour, as in $B_2$, but the final result is similar. Hence, economies with unequal income distribution suffer a permanent income and utility loss as a result of the shock, and their distribution of income becomes even more unequal.

Hence, we can conclude that economies with more equal distribution of income adjust better, with smaller income losses, to macroeconomic shocks than economies with highly unequal distribution of income. The intuitive reason for that is that the larger the wealth of an unskilled worker, the easier it is for his/her offspring to shift to the other sector if wages fall.

This analysis can shed some light on the long-run implications of the supply shocks in the seventies. Most studies of these events have concentrated on short-run adjustments to the shocks through wage reduction. Thus, Bruno and Sachs (1985) stress the role of real wage flexibility as an important factor in a country's adjustability to such shocks. In this section we look more into the long-run adjustment to a shock via investment in human capital and structural change in the economy. In the long run it is the initial distribution of income which determines how the economy adjusts to the shock, as described above. It may, therefore, be interesting to examine the patterns of structural adjustments to the supply shocks of the seventies in developed vs. less-developed countries.

Let us now consider another type of exogenous shocks, namely a technological innovation in the skilled labour sector which raises the wage level of skilled workers $w_s$. For the sake of simplicity we assume again that the economy is in a long-run equilibrium when the change occurs. The patterns of adjustment to the technological innovation are presented in figure 7. The technological change raises the bequests of skilled workers and shifts the $b_s$ curve from $b_s^1$ to $b_s^2$. Consider first a developed country with an equal distribution of income. In the long run such an economy moves from $A$ to $B$ in figure 7.

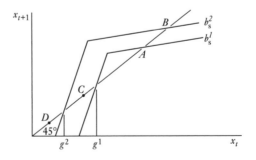

Figure 7

Hence unskilled workers' wages rise in order to remain equal to the higher net income of skilled workers, as $w_n = w_s/(1 + r) - h$. Investment in human capital in such an economy is increased since the number of unskilled workers is reduced. Both income and wealth increase.

Consider now a country with unequal distribution of income. Assume first that the country is not too poor, with unskilled workers concentrated before the change at a point $C$ in figure 7, where $g_2 < \bar{x}_n \leqq g_1$. In this case, the technological innovation pushes this economy across the threshold to converge to the equal distribution of income, at point $B$. In such an economy there is a rise in wages in both sectors and a vast investment in human capital. Imagine now that the economy is very poor and unskilled workers are concentrated at a point $D$, where $\bar{x}_n \leqq g_2$, before the innovation. In this case, the wage and number of unskilled workers remain the same and there is no change in investment in human capital. In fact, the only change in such a poor economy is a rise of income and wealth of skilled workers, while the income gap in society increases.

Thus, the way an economy adjusts to a technological improvement also depends on the initial distribution of income. In countries with fairly equal distribution the rise in skilled labour wage attracts more people to invest in human capital, since they have large enough initial wealth. In poor countries with a very unequal distribution of income there will be no increase in investment in human capital and the economic benefits from the innovation are limited.

## 9. Concluding Remarks

This paper analyzes the role of income distribution in macroeconomics through investment in human capital. The study demonstrates, that in the face of capital market imperfections the distribution of wealth significantly affects the aggregate economic activity. Furthermore, in the presence of indivisibilities in investment in human capital, these effects are carried to the long run as well. Hence, growth is affected by the initial distribution of wealth, or more specifically by the percentage of individuals who inherit a large enough wealth to enable them to invest in human capital. Thus, we can represent our results as describing the importance of having a large middle class for the purpose of economic growth.

In general, this study shows that the distributions of wealth and income are very important from a macroeconomic point of view. They affect output and investment in the short and in the long run and the pattern of adjustment to exogenous shocks. It is, therefore, our belief, that this relationship between income distribution and macroeconomics will attract more studies in the future.

### Notes

1   See Kaldor (1956), Kuznets (1955) and a later survey by Cline (1975).
2   Other recent papers which examine the relationship between growth and distribution are Greenwood and Jovanovic (1990), Murphy, Shleifer and Vishny (1989), Perotti (1990) and Persson and Tabellini (1990). These papers suggest other channels through which distribution effects growth.

3   According to Becker's (1975) terminology, individuals differ with respect to "opportunities" and not "abilities".

4   Notice that what matters is not only relative wealth, but the size distribution of absolute wealth. In this respect the model is very different from recent papers which emphasize the role of distribution through the political mechanism, as in Alesina and Drazen (1991), Perotti (1990) and Persson and Tabellini (1990).

5   Empirical evidence on the effect of investment in human capital on the distribution of income has been extensively documented in the literature. The central studies in this field are those of Becker (1975) and Mincer (1974).

6   Similar results are reached by Scheinkman and Weiss (1986) and by Banerjee and Newman (1991).

7   The result that there are multiple long-run wealth distributions is important in order to justify the existence of various distributions in the short run as well. Hence this result also gives more content to the former result, that wealth distribution has effect in the short run.

8   For empirical evidence, that points at the importance of investment in human capital in explaining differences in output among countries, see Mankiw, Romer and Weil (1992).

9   The existence of non-convexities in production plays an important role in some other recent models, which display multiple long-run equilibria, as in Azariadis and Drazen (1990) and Tsiddon (1992).

10  There are alternative ways to model the bequest motive, but it can be shown that they yield similar results. This issue is discussed in section 5.

11  This assumption is not critical to any of the results of the paper. Removing it can even strengthen our results. This assumption though reflects, in a somewhat extreme way, the fact that individuals are usually more credit constrained than firms.

12  If (14) does not hold, individuals all over the world prefer to work as unskilled. Hence, there is no capital and an excess supply of loans prevails. This drives the world rate of interest down until (14) is satisfied. Hence (14) is a reasonable assumption.

13  The assumption that interest rate for individual borrowers who invest in human capital is much higher than for lenders is also supported by the interesting survey by Tilak (1989) on education. According to studies he cites the estimated yearly social returns to investment in education in developing countries are very high: 26% for primary education, 17% for secondary education and 13% for higher education.

14  Persson and Tabellini (1990) present empirical evidence that supports this result, where they show that a more equal distribution of income tends to increase growth.

15  Hence, if the unit price of land in period $t$ is $Q_t$, we get:

$$Q_t(1 + r) = Q_{t+1} + G_N\left(L_{t+1}^n, \bar{N}\right)$$

in each period $t$, where $L_{t+1}^n$ is the expected number of unskilled workers in next period.

16  It is later shown that the definition of a developed economy is independent of the initial period $t$ (unless there are exogenous shocks or government intervention).

17  This is not true everywhere but in a large neighbourhood of $g$, but it is sufficient for the analysis which follows.

18  The Kuznets hypothesis had been empirically examined in numerous works. See for examples the surveys of Summers, Kravis and Heston (1984) and Lindert and Williamson (1985).

19  According to Cline (1975), the evidence on changes in income distribution in developing countries does not support the Kuznets hypothesis, but rather that of stable distributions.

20  We also assume that the shock is only in this country and not elsewhere in the world. An analysis of world-wide shocks would yield similar results, but would be more cumbersome to analyze, as it would affect world interest rates.

## References

Alesina, A. and Drazen, A. (1991): "Why are Stabilizations Delayed?," *American Economic Review*, 81, 1170–88.

Atkinson, A. B. (1975): *The Economics of Inequality*. Oxford: Clarendon Press.

Azariadis, C. and Drazen, A. (1990): "Threshold Externalities in Economic Development," *Quarterly Journal of Economics*, 105, 501–26.

Banerjee, A. V. and Newman, A. F. (1991): "Risk-Bearing and the Theory of Income Distribution," *Review of Economic Studies*, 58, 211–35.

Barro, R. J. (1974): "Are Government Bonds Net Wealth?," *Journal of Political Economy*, 82, 1095–117.

Becker, G. S. (1975): *Human Capital*. New York: NBER and Columbia University Press.

Bruno, M. and Sachs, J. (1985): *Economics of Worldwide Stagflation*. Cambridge: Harvard University Press.

Cline, W. R. (1975): "Distribution and Development," *Journal of Development Economics*, 1, 359–400.

Galor, O. and Zeira, J. (1990): "Income Distribution and Macroeconomics," mimeo. Department of Economics, Brown University.

Greenwood, J. and Jovanovic, B. (1990): "Financial Development, Growth and the Distribution of Income," *Journal of Political Economy*, 98, 1076–107.

Kaldor, N. (1956): "Alternative Theories of Distribution," *Review of Economic Studies*, 23, 83–100.

Keynes, J. M. (1936): *The General Theory of Employment, Interest and Money*. London: Macmillan.

Kravis, I. B. (1960): "International Differences in the Distribution of Income," *Review of Economics and Statistics*, 42, 408–16.

Kuznets, S. (1955): "Economic Growth and Income Equality," *American Economic Review*, 45, 1–28.

Lindert, P. H. and Williamson, J. G. (1985): "Growth, Equality, and History," *Explorations in Economic History*, 22, 341–77.

Loury, G. C. (1981): "Intergenerational Transfers and the Distribution of Earnings," *Econometrica*, 49, 843–67.

Lucas, R. E., Jr. (1988): "On the Mechanics of Economic Development," *Journal of Monetary Economics*, 3–42.

Lydall, H. (1968): *The Structure of Earnings*. Oxford: Clarendon Press.

Mankiw, G. N., Romer, D. and Weil, D. N. (1992). "A Contribution to the Empirics of Economic Growth," *Quarterly Journal of Economics*, 107, 407–37.

Mincer, J. (1974): *Schooling, Experience, and Earnings*. New York: NBER and Columbia University Press.

Murphy, K. M., Shleifer, A. and Vishny, R. (1989): "Income Distribution, Market Size, and Industrialization," *Quarterly Journal of Economics*, 104, 537–64.

Perotti, R. (1990): "Political Equilibrium, Income Distribution and Growth," mimeo, MIT.

Persson, T. and Tabellini, G. (1990): "Politico-Economic Equilibrium Growth: Theory and Evidence," mimeo.

Romer, P. M. (1986): "Increasing Returns and Long-Run Growth," *Journal of Political Economy*, 94, 1002–37.

Scheinkman, J. and Weiss, L. (1986): "Borrowing Constraints and Aggregate Economic Activity," *Econometrica*, 54, 23–45.

Summers, R., Kravis, I. B. and Heston, A. (1984): "Changes in the World Income Distribution," *Journal of Policy Modeling*, 6, 237–69.

Tilak, J. B. G. (1989): "Education and its Relation to Economic Growth, Poverty and Income Distribution," World Bank Discussion Paper.
Tsiddon, D. (1992): "A Moral Hazard Trap to Growth," *International Economic Review*, 33, 299–321.
The World Bank (1988): *World Development Report, 1988*. New York: Oxford University Press.
The World Bank (1989): *World Development Report, 1989*. New York: Oxford University Press.
The World Bank (1990): *World Development Report, 1990*. New York: Oxford University Press.
The World Bank (1991): *World Development Report, 1991*. New York: Oxford University Press.

CHAPTER 5

# Occupational Choice and the Process of Development

ABHIJIT V. BANERJEE AND ANDREW F. NEWMAN

This paper models economic development as a process of institutional transformation by focusing on the interplay between agents' occupational decisions and the distribution of wealth. Because of capital market imperfections, poor agents choose working for a wage over self-employment, and wealthy agents' become entrepreneurs who monitor workers. Only with sufficient inequality, however, will there be employment contracts; otherwise, there is either subsistence or self-employment. Thus, in static equilibrium, the occupational structure depends on distribution. Since the latter is itself endogenous, we demonstrate the robustness of this result by extending the model dynamically and studying examples in which initial wealth distributions have long-run effects. In one case the economy develops either widespread cottage industry (self-employment) or factory production (employment contracts), depending on the initial distribution; in the other example, it develops into prosperity or stagnation.

## 1. Introduction

Why does one country remain populated by small proprietors, artisans, and peasants while another becomes a nation of entrepreneurs employing industrial workers in large factories? Why should two seemingly identical countries follow radically different development paths, one leading to prosperity, the other to stagnation? Questions like these are of central concern to both development economists and economic historians, who have been interested in the study of the evolution of institutional forms, particularly those under which production and exchange are organized. Yet most of these institutional questions have resisted formal treatment except in a static context (see Stiglitz (1988) for a review), whereas the dynamic issues that are peculiarly developmental have for the most part been restricted to the narrower questions of output growth or technical change. This paper takes a first step in the direction of providing a dynamic account of institutional change by focusing on the evolution of occupational patterns, the contractual forms through which people exchange labor services.[1]

There are several ways in which the dynamics of occupational choice influence the process of development. Most obvious among them is the effect on the distribution of income and wealth. Insofar as distribution can affect saving, investment, risk bearing, fertility, and the composition of demand and production, there is a clear link with the economy's rate of growth and hence with development in its narrowest sense.

Just as important is the connection that arises when one considers development to mean institutional transformation as well as economic growth (Stiglitz, 1988; Townsend, 1988; Khan, 1989). One of the most significant elements of the institutional structure of any economy is the dominant form of organization of production: it has "external" consequences considerably beyond the efficiency of current production. Some of these effects may be politico-economic, but there are also some that are purely economic. It has been argued, for example, that the introduction of the factory system in the early years of the Industrial Revolution left the technology unaffected and generated little efficiency gain initially. But it seems very likely that in the long run this new form of production organization helped to make possible the major innovations of the Industrial Revolution; see, for example, Cohen (1981), Millward (1981) and North (1981).

Conversely, the process of development also affects the structure of occupations. It alters the demand for and supply of different types of labor and, hence, the returns to and allocations of occupations. It transforms the nature of risks and the possibilities for innovations. And, of course, it changes the distribution of wealth. Since one's wealth typically affects one's incentives to enter different occupations, the effect on the wealth distribution generates a parallel effect on the occupational structure.

Our aim here is to build a model that focuses directly on this interplay between the pattern of occupational choice and the process of development. The basic structure of interaction is very simple. Because of capital market imperfections, people can borrow only limited amounts. As a result, occupations that require high levels of investment are beyond the reach of poor people, who choose instead to work for other, wealthier, employers; thus wage contracts are viewed primarily as substitutes for financial contracts. The wage rate and the pattern of occupational choice are then determined by the condition that the labor market must clear.[2] Depending on labor market conditions and on their wealth, other agents become self-employed in low-scale production or remain idle.

The pattern of occupational choice is therefore determined by the initial distribution of wealth, but the structure of occupational choice in turn determines how much people save and what risks they bear. These factors then give rise to the new distribution of wealth. We shall be concerned with the long-run behavior of this dynamic process.

Despite its simplicity, our model's structure is somewhat nonstandard. As a rule, the dynamics are nonlinear and the state space – the set of all wealth distributions – is very large, so that reasonably complicated behavior may be expected. While a complete mathematical analysis of the model is beyond the scope of this paper, we confine our attention to two special cases that admit considerable dimensional reduction. These examples afford complete study: they are simple enough to allow diagrammatic exposition in which we trace out entire paths of development, including institutional evolution, and with them we generate robust and natural instances of hysteresis or long-run dependence on initial conditions.

In one of our examples (section 4.4), the ultimate fate of the economy – prosperity or stagnation – depends in a crucial way on the initial distribution of wealth. If the economy initially has a high ratio of very poor people to very rich people, then the process of development runs out of steam and ends up in a situation of low employment and low wages (this may happen even when the initial per capita income is quite high, as long as the distribution is sufficiently skewed). By contrast, if the economy initially has few very poor people (the per capita income can still be quite low), it will "take off" and converge to a high-wage, high-employment steady state.

That an economy's long-term prosperity may depend on initial conditions is a familiar idea in the development literature, and some recent papers capture different aspects of this phenomenon in a formal model (e.g., Romer, 1986; Lucas, 1988; Murphy, Shleifer, and Vishny, 1989a, 1989b; Matsuyama, 1991; Galor and Zeira, in 1993). Our paper differs from these in several respects. First, most of the papers study technological increasing returns, originating either in the production technology itself or in various kinds of productivity spillovers. We consider instead a kind of "pecuniary" increasing returns stemming from an imperfect capital market (Galor and Zeira also follow this tack). Second, distribution tends not to play a causal role in this literature. A notable exception is Murphy et al. (1989a), but there the mechanism is the structure of demand for produced commodities rather than the occupational choice mediated by the capital market: moreover, their model is static and therefore does not endogenize the distribution.

Third, and most important, none of these papers emphasizes the endogeneity of economic institutions as part of the process of development. This distinction is highlighted by the example we examine in section 4.3, in which there appears a different kind of dependence on initial conditions. We show that the economy might converge to a steady state in which there is (almost) only self-employment in small-scale production; alternatively, it may end up in a situation in which an active labor market and both large- and small-scale production prevail. Which of the two types of production organization eventually predominates once again depends on the initial distribution of wealth. Specifically, an economy that starts with a large number of relatively poor people is more likely to develop wage employment and large-scale production than an economy with few very poor people. This result provides a formalization of the classical view that despite the fact that capitalism is the more dynamic economic system, its initial emergence does depend on the existence of a population of dispossessed whose best choice is to work for a wage.

In Section 2 we set up the basic model. Section 3 examines single-period equilibrium. The main results on the dynamics of occupational choice and the process of development are in section 4. We conclude in section 5 with a brief discussion of some qualitative properties of this class of models.

## 2. The Model

### 2.1. Environment

There is a large population (a continuum) of agents with identical preferences; the population at time $t$ is described by a distribution function $G_t(w)$, which gives the measure of the population with wealth less than $w$.

At the beginning of life, agents receive their initial wealth in the form of a bequest from their parents. They also have an endowment of one unit of labor; the effort they actually exert, however, is not observable except under costly monitoring by another agent.

When agents become economically active, they may apply for a loan. Enforcement of loan contracts is imperfect, and agents immediately have an opportunity to renege; lenders will limit borrowing and require collateral in order to ensure that agents do not. The agents choose an occupation, which determines how they invest their labor and capital. They then learn investment outcomes and settle outside claims. Finally, they bequeath to their children, consume what remains, and pass from the scene.

Although the model is naturally recursive, we prefer to study dynamics in continuous time and to impose an overlapping demographic structure. These modifications permit us to avoid unrealistic jumps and overshooting, which can arise as artifacts of discrete time and simultaneous demographics. We therefore shall assume that all the economic activity other than inheritance – borrowing, investment, work, and bequests – takes place at the instant the agents reach maturity. The age of maturity in turn is distributed exponentially with parameter $\lambda$ across the population and independently from wealth.[3] The total population is stationary and is normalized to unity; that is, a cohort of size $\lambda$ is active at each instant.

These assumptions, though artificial, greatly simplify the analysis. For instance, they imply that in an interval of time $dt$, a measure $\lambda G_t(w)dt$ of agents with wealth below $w$ are active: the measure of active agents in a wealth interval is always proportional to the measure of the entire (immature) population in that interval. Thus differential changes in the wealth distribution at each instant will depend only on the current distribution. Moreover, the differential dynamics will be related to the recursive dynamics in a transparent manner so that it will be easy to switch attention from the (recursive) dynamics of a lineage to the (continuous) dynamics of the economy.

Agents are risk-neutral: preferences over commodities are represented by $c^\gamma b^{1-\gamma} - z$, where $c$ is an agent's consumption of the sole physical good in the economy, $b$ is the amount of this good left as a bequest to his offspring (the "warm glow" (Andreoni, 1989) is much more tractable than other bequest motives), and $z$ is the amount of labor he supplies. Denote the income realization by $y$; utility then takes the form $\delta y - z$, where $\delta \equiv \gamma^\gamma (1 - \gamma)^{1-\gamma}$.

## 2.2. Production technology and occupations

The economy's single good may be used for consumption or as capital. There are three ways to invest. First, there is a divisible, safe asset that requires no labor and yields a fixed gross return $\hat{r} < 1/(1 - \gamma)$.[4] One may think of it as financial claims mediated by foreign banks that borrow and lend at the fixed international interest rate $\hat{r} - 1$.[5] Agents may invest in this asset regardless of how they use their labor. Anyone who invests only in the safe asset is said to be idle or to be subsisting.

Second, there is a risky, indivisible investment project such as a farm or machine that requires no special skill to operate. To succeed, it must have an initial investment of $I$ units of capital and one unit of labor; with any lower level of either input, it will not generate any returns. If the project succeeds, it generates a random return $rI$, where $r$ is $r_0$ or $r_1$ with probabilities $1 - q$ and $q$, respectively $(0 < r_0 < r_1)$, and has mean $\bar{r}$. Such a project may be operated efficiently by a self-employed agent insofar as it produces enough output to cover its labor cost:

$$I(\bar{r} - \hat{r}) - \frac{1}{\delta} \geq \max\{0, I(r_0 - \hat{r})\}$$

Finally, there is a monitoring technology that permits aggregated production. By putting in an effort of one, one entrepreneur can perfectly monitor the actions of $\mu > 1$ individuals; less effort yields no information. This activity is indivisible, and it is impossible to monitor another monitor.

Using this technology, an entrepreneur can hire $\mu$ workers, each at a competitive wage $v$. Workers undertake projects that require $I'$ units of capital and one unit of labor and generate random returns $r'I'$; $r'$ takes on the values $r_0'$ and $r_1'$ (also with $0 < r_0' < r_1'$) with probabilities $1 - q'$ and $q'$. It is natural to imagine that the projects individual workers are running are similar to the projects being run by the self-employed. To facilitate this interpretation, we assume that $I' = I$ and that $r'$ and $r$ have the same mean (note that $q' \neq q$, however). The returns on each of the projects belonging to a single entrepreneur are perfectly correlated. Entrepreneurial production is feasible in the sense that at the lowest possible wage rate (which is $1/\delta$, since at a lower wage the worker is better off idle) it is more profitable than self-employment:

$$\mu\left[I(\bar{r} - \hat{r}) - \frac{1}{\delta}\right] - \frac{1}{\delta} \geq \max\left\{I(\bar{r} - \hat{r}) - \frac{1}{\delta}, \mu\left[I(r_0' - \hat{r}) - \frac{1}{\delta}\right]\right\}$$

The main difference between the two types of production lies not so much in the technology but rather in the contracts under which output is distributed. In one, the worker runs a project for himself: he is the claimant on output and therefore needs no monitoring. In the other, the worker runs it for someone else, which entails the monitoring function of the entrepreneur.

To summarize, there are four occupational options:

(1)  subsistence
(2)  working
(3)  self-employment, and
(4)  entrepreneurship.

There may be a question of how we rule out other possibilities. Entrepreneurs cannot control more than $\mu$ projects because one cannot monitor a monitor. Being a part-time entrepreneur (sharing with someone else) is ruled out by the indivisible monitoring technology and in any case would not be attractive because of risk neutrality. Raising capital through partnership is precluded by the same contract enforcement problems that exist between the bank and borrowers: one partner could as easily default on another partner as default on the bank (thus without loss of generality we need consider only debt and can ignore equity). The same arguments rule out combining self-employment with any other activity.

## 2.3. Markets

In the market for labor, demand comes from entrepreneurial production and supply from individuals' occupational choices. This market is competitive, with the wage moving to equate supply and demand. The goods market is competitive as well, but it is otherwise pretty trivial.

It remains to discuss the market for loans. We assume that lenders can enter freely; what distinguishes this market is the possibility that a borrower might renege on a debt. The story we have in mind is similar to that proposed by Kehoe and Levine in 1993). To abstract from bankruptcy issues, assume that project returns are always high enough to ensure that borrowers can afford repayment. Suppose that an agent puts up all his wealth $w$ (the maximum he can provide) as collateral and borrows an amount $L$. He may now attempt to avoid his obligations by fleeing from his village, albeit at the cost of lost collateral $w\hat{r}$; flight makes any income accruing to the borrower inaccessible to lenders. Fleeing does not diminish investment opportunities, however, and having $L$ in hand permits the agent to achieve $V(L)$ in expected gross income net of effort (under our assumptions, his ensuing decisions and therefore $V(L)$ are independent of his choice whether to renege). At the end of the production period, he will have succeeded in escaping the lender's attempts to find him with a large probability $1 - \pi$, in which case he avoids paying $L\hat{r}$. Should he be caught, though, he will have had ample time to dispose of his income, and therefore he can be subjected to only a nonmonetary punishment $F$ (such as flogging or imprisonment), which enters additively into his utility. Reneging therefore yields a payoff of $V(L) - \pi F$, and repaying yields $V(L) + w\hat{r} - L\hat{r}$; the borrower will renege whenever $w\hat{r} + \pi F < L\hat{r}$. Knowing this, lenders will make only loans that satisfy

$$L \leq w + \pi \frac{F}{\hat{r}}$$

All loans made in equilibrium will satisfy this constraint, and the borrower will never renege.[6]

The only reason to borrow in this model is to finance self-employment or entrepreneurship. The target levels of capital are therefore $I$ and $\mu I$ (we assume that wages are paid at the end of the period so there is no need to finance them). Someone with a wealth level $w < I$ who wants to become self-employed therefore uses $w$ as collateral and needs to borrow $I$.[7] He will be able to borrow this amount if and only if $I \leq w + (\pi F/\hat{r})$. Thus the minimum wealth level $w^*$ necessary to qualify for a loan large enough to finance self-employment is equal to $I - (\pi F/\hat{r})$ (the escape probability $1 - \pi$ is large enough that $w^* > 0$). The smallest wealth needed to borrow enough to be an entrepreneur, denoted $w^{**}$, is derived by a parallel argument and is equal to $\mu I - (\pi F/\hat{r})$. Since $\mu$ exceeds unity, $w^{**}$ is greater than $w^*$; moreover, neither of these values depends on the wage.

The model of the capital market we have chosen here yields a rather extreme version of increasing returns to wealth. In effect, it is not terribly different from the models of Sappington (1983) and Bernanke and Gertler (1989, 1990) or the numerous discussions of credit markets in the development literature; see Bell (1988) for a survey. Using such models would not alter the dependence of borrowing costs on wealth or of occupational structure on distribution. But as we shall see, the present model is simple enough in some cases to allow reduction to a dynamical system on the two-dimensional simplex, a procedure that would be impossible with a more elaborate specification.

## 3. Static Equilibrium

Recall that the distribution of wealth at time $t$ is denoted by $G_t(w)$ and that because the age to maturity is exponentially distributed and independent of wealth, $\lambda G_t(w)$ represents the distribution of wealth for the cohort active at $t$. The (expected) returns to self-employment and subsistence are given exogenously by the model's parameters; the wage $v$ determines the returns to the other two occupations. The returns and the borrowing constraints determine the occupational choice made at each level of wealth. Integrating these choices with respect to $\lambda G_t(w)$ gives us the demand for and the supply of labor. To find the instantaneous equilibrium, we need only find the wage that clears the labor market (we can assume that the goods market clears; as for the capital market, the interest rate has already been fixed at $\hat{r}$).

All agents who do not choose subsistence will have the incentive to expend full effort. Therefore, the payoffs to each occupation (for someone who can choose any of them) are

subsistence, $\delta w \hat{r}$
worker, $\delta(w\hat{r} + v) - 1$
self-employed, $\delta[w\hat{r} + I(\bar{r} - \hat{r})] - 1$
entrepreneur, $\delta[w\hat{r} + \mu I(\bar{r} - \hat{r}) - \mu v] - 1$

Since only entrepreneurs demand labor, these expressions imply that demand will be positive only if the wage does not exceed

$$\bar{v} \equiv \frac{\mu - 1}{\mu} I(\bar{r} - \hat{r})$$

Moreover, since only agents with $w \geq w^{**}$ will be entrepreneurs, the labor demand correspondence is

0                              if $v > \bar{v}$
$[0, \mu\lambda[1 - G_t(w^{**})]]$    if $v = \bar{v}$
$\mu\lambda[1 - G_t(w^{**})]$      if $v < \bar{v}$

Similar reasoning tells us that the supply of labor is (denote the minimum wage $1/\delta$ by $\underline{v}$)

0                                if $v < \underline{v}$
$[0, \lambda G_t(w^*)]$              if $v = \underline{v}$
$\lambda G_t(w^*)$                  if $\underline{v} < v < I(\bar{r} - \hat{r})$
$[\lambda G_t(w^*), \lambda]$          if $v = I(\bar{r} - \hat{r})$
$\lambda$                            if $v > I(\bar{r} - \hat{r})$

The equilibrium wage will be $\underline{v}$ if

$$G_t(w^*) > \mu[1 - G_t(w^{**})]$$

and $\bar{v}$ if

$$G_t(w^*) < \mu[1 - G_t(w^{**})]$$

The singular case in which $G_t(w^*) = \mu[1 - G_t(w^{**})]$ gives rise to an indeterminate wage in $[\underline{v}, \bar{v}]$. The facts that the wage generically assumes one of only two values, that it depends on no more information about the distribution $G_t(\cdot)$ than its value at $w^*$ and $w^{**}$, and that $w^*$ and $w^{**}$ do not depend on any endogenous variables of the model are the keys to the dimensional reduction that so simplifies our analysis below.

To summarize, the pattern of occupational choice that is generated in equilibrium is as follows:

(1)  Anyone with initial wealth less than $w^*$ will be a worker unless wages are exactly $\underline{v}$, in which case the labor market clears by having some of the potential workers remain idle.

(2)  Agents with initial wealth between $w^*$ and $w^{**}$ will become self-employed; although they could choose working, they would do so only if $v \geq I(\bar{r} - \hat{r})$, which cannot occur in equilibrium.

(3)  Anybody who starts with wealth at or above $w^{**}$ will be an entrepreneur as long as $v < \bar{v}$. If $v = \bar{v}$, all the potential entrepreneurs are equally happy with self-employment, so

$$1 - \frac{G_t(w^*)}{\mu} - G_t(w^{**})$$

of them opt for the latter, and the labor market clears.

Thus despite the fact that everybody has the same abilities and the same preferences, different people choose different occupations. What is more, the occupational choices made by individuals depend on the distribution of wealth. For example, if everyone is above $w^*$, everyone will be self-employed. Employment contracts emerge only if some people are below $w^*$ and others are above $w^{**}$. With everyone below $w^*$, subsistence becomes the only option. Thus, as in Newman (1991), the institutional structure of the economy, represented by the pattern of occupations, depends on the distribution of wealth.[8] The question, of course, is whether this dependence of institutional structure on distribution that obtains in the short run also obtains in the long run, when the distribution itself is endogenous.

## 4. Dynamics

We have described how the equilibrium wage and occupational choices at time $t$ are determined, given an initial wealth distribution. Knowledge of the realization of project returns then gives us each person's income and bequests, from which we can calculate the rate of change of this distribution.

### 4.1. Individual dynamics

A person active at $t$ leaves $1 - \gamma$ of his realized income as a bequest $b_t$. The intergenerational evolution of wealth is then represented as follows:

(1)   subsistence: $b_t = (1 - \gamma)w_t\hat{r}$
(2)   working: $b_t = (1 - \gamma)(w_t\hat{r} + v)$
(3)   self-employment: $b_t = (1 - \gamma)[w_t\hat{r} + I(r - \hat{r})]$, which is random; and
(4)   entrepreneurship: $b_t = (1 - \gamma)\{w_t\hat{r} + \mu[I(r' - \hat{r}) - v]\}$, also random.

The transition diagram in figure 1 represents the dynamics of lineage wealth for the case $v = \bar{v}$. Everybody with wealth between zero and $w^*$ will choose working, and their offspring's wealth as a function of their own wealth is given by the line segment $AB$. Agents between $w^*$ and $w^{**}$ will be self-employed, and their wealth dynamics are given by the two parallel lines $CD$ and $C'D'$, each indicating one realization of the random variable $r$. Since the wage is $\bar{v}$, everyone above $w^{**}$ will either be an entrepreneur or be self-employed; the two parallel lines $DE$ and $D'E'$ represent the dynamics for a self-employed person and $FG$ and $F'G'$ represent those for an entrepreneur.

A similar diagram can be constructed for the case in which $v = \underline{v}$. The specific positions of the different lines in these diagrams depend, of course, on the parameters of the model.

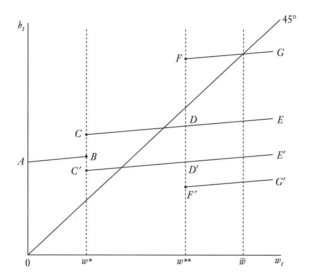

**Figure 1**   Individual recursion diagram for $v = \bar{v}$

## 4.2.  The dynamics of distribution and occupational choice

From the point of view of an individual lineage, wealth follows a Markov process. If this process were stationary, we could go ahead and use the standard techniques (see, e.g., Stokey and Lucas, 1989) to establish existence and global stability of an ergodic measure on the wealth space and, since we are assuming a continuum of agents, reinterpret this to be the limiting wealth distribution for the economy. Under the stationarity assumption, one can study Markov processes by considering (deterministic) maps from the space of distributions to itself; such maps are well known to be linear.

In our model, however, the stationarity assumption is not justified. At the time a lineage is active, its transition rule depends on the prevailing wage. The wage in turn depends on the current distribution of wealth across all active agents in the economy (which, as we have said, is the same as that for the entire population); as the distribution changes over time, so does the wage, thereby destroying the stationarity of the process.

In short, the state space for our model is not simply the wealth interval, but the set of distributions on that interval: this is the smallest set that provides us with all the information we need to fully describe the economy and predict its path through time. We have already shown that given the current distribution of wealth, we can determine the equilibrium level of wages and the pattern of occupational choices. Then, using the transition equations, the current distribution of wealth $G_t(\cdot)$, and the fact that we have a large number of agents receiving independent project returns, we can in principle derive the (deterministic) change in the distribution of wealth at time $t$. We therefore have a well-defined, deterministic, dynamical system on the space of wealth distributions.

Ordinarily, the dynamical system so derived may be quite complex, and unlike a system induced by the familiar stationary Markov process, which is defined on the same space, it is nonlinear. The nonlinearity already tells us that uniqueness, global stability, and other nice, easy-to-verify properties of linear systems are unlikely to obtain. But we want to say more about our economy than to simply state abstractly that it might display hysteresis, nonuniqueness, cycles, or other nonlinear behavior.[9]

Fortunately, if we restrict attention to certain sets of parameter values, we can achieve a rather precise characterization of the economy's behavior using methods that are elementary. In the rest of this section we shall look at two examples that obtain when the individual transition diagrams like figure 1 have certain configurations; these cases are illustrative of interesting historical patterns of development and occupational structure.

### 4.3. The cottage versus the factory

Consider the case in which the transition diagrams for $v = \underline{v}$ and $v = \bar{v}$ are given by figure 2. The configuration represented in these diagrams will obtain when $\bar{v}$ is relatively high, $1 - \gamma$ is relatively low, and the riskiness of production (given by $r_1 - r_0$ and $r_1' - r_0'$) is quite large.

Look now at figure 2(a). Define $\bar{w}$ to be the fixed point of the intergenerational wealth transition map

$$b(w_t) = (1 - \gamma)\{w_t \hat{r} + \mu[I(r_1' - \hat{r}) - \underline{v}]\}$$

and observe that this is the highest possible wealth level that can be sustained in the long run (any lineage with wealth greater than this value is sure to fall below it eventually). Without loss of generality then, we restrict all our attention to wealth distributions on the interval $[0, \bar{w}]$.

Observe now that in figure 2(a), a lineage currently with wealth in $[0, w^*)$ remains in that range in the next period. Any lineage initially in $[w^*, w^{**})$ either goes to $[w^{**}, \bar{w}]$ (if the project return is high) or remains in $[w^*, w^{**})$ (if the project return is low). Finally, the offspring of an agent who is in $[w^{**}, \bar{w}]$ either remains there (if lucky) or goes to $[w^*, w^{**})$ (if unlucky). The important point is that these transitions depend only on what interval

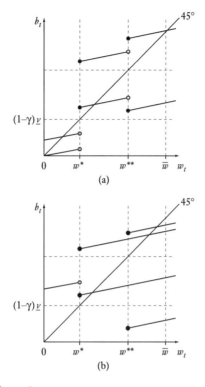

**Figure 2** (a) $v = \underline{v}$; (b) $v = \bar{v}$

one is in and not on the precise wealth level within that interval. Similarly, inspection of figure 2(b) shows that when the prevailing wage is $\bar{v}$, the transitions between the same three intervals also depend only on those intervals and not on the wealth levels within them.

As we showed in section 3, the equilibrium wage and the occupational structure depend only on the ratio of the number of people in $[0, w^*)$ and the number of people in $[w^{**}, \bar{w}]$, and not on any other properties of the distribution. Identify the three intervals $[0, w^*)$, $[w^*, w^{**})$, and $[w^{**}, \bar{w}]$ with three "classes" $L$, $M$, and $U$ (for lower, middle, and upper); wealth distributions (fractions of the population in the three classes) are then given by probability vectors $\mathbf{p} = (p_L, p_M, p_U)$, that is, points in $\Delta^2$, the two-dimensional unit simplex. The state space for our economy is then just this simplex: for our purposes, it contains all the information we need.[10]

Now suppose that at some instant $t$, $\lambda p_L > \mu \lambda p_U$ so that there is excess supply in the labor market and $v = \underline{v}$. In an interval of time $dt$ a measure $\lambda p_U dt$ of the current upper class is active. The people in this class are replaced by their children, of whom a fraction $q'$ will have parents who are lucky with their investment and therefore remain in the upper class. Among the children in the currently active middle class, $q$ have lucky parents and ascend into the upper class. The change in the upper-class population in this interval is therefore

$$dp_U = \lambda(qp_M dt + q'p_U dt - p_U dt)$$

The evolution of the entire wealth distribution can be represented by a dynamical system on $\Delta^2$, which may be written

$$\frac{d\mathbf{p}}{dt} = \mathbf{A}(\mathbf{p}(t))\mathbf{p}(t) \tag{1}$$

where $\mathbf{A}(\mathbf{p}(t))$ is a $3 \times 3$ matrix that depends on the current distribution $\mathbf{p}(t)$ in the sense that it takes two different forms depending on whether $p_L$ is greater or less than $\mu p_U$. If $\lambda p_L > \mu \lambda p_U$ so that $v = \underline{v}$, then we have (for brevity, we set $\lambda = 1$ for the remainder of the paper)

$$\mathbf{A}(\mathbf{p}) = \begin{bmatrix} 0 & 0 & 0 \\ 0 & -q & 1-q' \\ 0 & q & q'-1 \end{bmatrix} \qquad p_L \text{ for } > \mu p_U \tag{2}$$

For the case $v = \bar{v}$, the situation is slightly more complicated since the individual transition probabilities for members of the class $U$ depend on their occupation:

$$\mathbf{A}(\mathbf{p}) = \begin{bmatrix} -1 & 0 & (1-q')\dfrac{p_L}{\mu p_U} \\ 1 & -q & (1-q)\left[1-\left(\dfrac{p_L}{\mu p_U}\right)\right] \\ 0 & q & q+(q'-q)\left(\dfrac{p_L}{\mu p_U}\right)-1 \end{bmatrix} \qquad \text{for } p_L < \mu p_U \tag{3}$$

The third column of this matrix is derived by noting that $p_L/\mu p_U$ of the agents with wealth greater than $w^{**}$ become entrepreneurs; of these, $q'$ get the high return and remain above $w^{**}$, and $1 - q'$ fall below $w^*$; the remaining agents in $U$ become self-employed and enter $L$ and $U$ in the proportions $1 - q$ and $q$.

Now it will be convenient to study the dynamics of our economy by using a phase diagram; to do so we restrict our attention to the two variables $p_L$ and $p_U$, since knowledge of them gives us $p_M$. This procedure gives us a piecewise-linear system of differential equations:

$$\dot{p}_L = \begin{cases} 0 & p_L > \mu p_U \\ \left(\dfrac{1-q'}{\mu} - 1\right)p_L & p_L < \mu p_U \end{cases} \tag{4}$$

and

$$\dot{p}_U = \begin{cases} q - qp_L + (q' - q - 1)p_U & p_L > \mu p_U \\ q - \left(q + \dfrac{q}{\mu} - \dfrac{q'}{\mu}\right)p_L - p_U & p_L < \mu p_U \end{cases} \tag{5}$$

The phase diagram for this set of differential equations is given in figure 3(a). The upper triangle represents distributions for which $v = \bar{v}$, and the lower triangle represents those

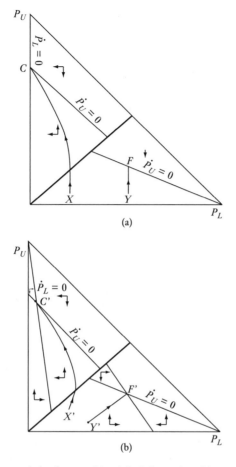

**Figure 3** The cottage and the factory: (a) original dynamics; (b) perturbed dynamics

for which $v = \underline{v}$. The heavy line is the "boundary" $p_L = \mu p_U$ between the two linear systems.[11]

In the upper triangle the point $C$ represents a stationary distribution that is locally stable. In the lower triangle there is a continuum of stationary distributions since the $\dot{p}_L = 0$ locus includes the whole lower triangle. This is a consequence of the fact that there is no way in or out of state $L$. Hysteresis of a degenerate sort is therefore built into this model.

Since our interest lies in hysteresis generated by the workings of the labor market, we feel that it is best to eliminate the degeneracy. This is legitimate since all we need to do to get rid of it is to perturb the dynamics slightly by allowing individuals very small probabilities of moving from state $L$ to the other two states and from the other two states to $L$.[12] The phase diagram for one such perturbation is given in figure 3(b). As expected, the $\dot{p}_U = 0$ loci in both triangles have moved only very slightly, as has the $\dot{p}_L = 0$ locus in the upper triangle. The most significant change is that now we have a $\dot{p}_L = 0$ locus in the lower triangle that intersects the $\dot{p}_U = 0$ locus in that triangle at the point $F'$.

Both $F'$ and $C'$ represent stationary distributions, and both are locally stable. But they represent very different social situations. Point $F'$ is an economy in which there are three distinct classes with very little social mobility between the top two and the bottom one (all mobility in and out of $L$ is due to the small random perturbations we used to eliminate the degeneracy). The principal reason behind the limited mobility is that the ratio of workers to entrepreneurs is high; the consequent low wage rate makes it virtually impossible, given the propensity to bequest, for workers to accumulate enough wealth to enter state $M$. At the same time, the wage rate is low enough and the project returns (in particular the low ones) are high enough to ensure the self-employed and entrepreneurs against going to $L$.

By contrast, $C'$ is a situation in which there is really only one occupation in the economy: the overwhelming majority of the population (in the unperturbed version of the model, *everyone*) is self-employed. While there are a substantial number of people in class $U$ who therefore are wealthy enough to be entrepreneurs, most of them are self-employed because they cannot find any workers. Since the low outcome for the self-employed is still high enough to keep the next generation in state $M$, the supply of people in state $L$ remains small and the original configuration is able to reproduce itself.

The economy always converges to one of these stationary states. Which of the two will result depends on the initial conditions. With the aid of the phase diagram we see what types of economies converge to $C'$ rather than to $F'$. Roughly speaking, economies with a small fraction of poor relative to middle- and upper-class people tend to converge to $C'$.

By looking at some trajectories, we can be more precise and better understand the dynamics. The points $X'$ and $Y'$ are two points close to each other in the lower triangle that both have a small upper class but have slightly different mixes of the classes. Consider the trajectory starting at $X'$, which has the relatively smaller lower class. Since the middle class is large and the upper class small, those moving up from $M$ to $U$ outnumber those who are moving the other way. The upper class grows. Because the size of the lower class changes very slowly, the ratio of the upper class to the lower class increases over time until $\mu p_U$ becomes greater than $p_L$. At this point the wage increases to $\bar{v}$ and the dynamics change. The workers start rising into the middle class, reducing the fraction of potential entrepreneurs who can find workers. The rest of the upper class now adopts self-employment and the transitions into the lower class decline (the self-employed remain in the middle class even when they are unlucky). The fraction of the lower class in the population thus continues to decline, and the economy converges to a distribution like $C'$.

The trajectory that starts at $Y'$ also moves in the same direction at first, but since the initial fraction of the middle class was smaller, the rate of increase in the upper class will be smaller. For this reason, and also because the initial fraction of the lower class was larger, $p_L$ remains larger than $\mu p_U$, wages do not rise, and employing people remains profitable. Instead of converging to $C'$, the economy ends up at $F'$, which is a situation with both self-employment and entrepreneurial production.

If we identify self-employment with self-sufficient peasants and cottage industries and entrepreneurial production with large-scale capitalist agriculture and factory production, the dynamic patterns we describe above have historical parallels. The most famous of these might be the instance of England and France, which in terms of the level of development and technology were roughly comparable at the middle of the eighteenth century (O'Brien and Keyder, 1978; Crafts, 1985; Crouzet, 1990) and yet went through radically different paths of development. England went on to develop and benefit hugely from the factory system and large-scale production, whereas France remained a nation of small farms and cottage industries for the next hundred years. In terms of our model, one possible explanation would be that England started at a point like $Y'$ and France started at a point like $X'$.[13]

## 4.4. Prosperity and stagnation

A somewhat different set of development paths can be generated with an alternative configuration of parameter values. Consider the case in which the transition map is as in figure 4 (corresponding once again to the cases $v = \underline{v}$ and $v = \bar{v}$). As before, the aggregate dynamic behavior can be reduced to a two-dimensional dynamical system in the simplex. Using the same definitions for the states as above, we follow a similar procedure to derive the dynamics of the wealth distribution. This process is described by the following system of piecewise-linear differential equations:

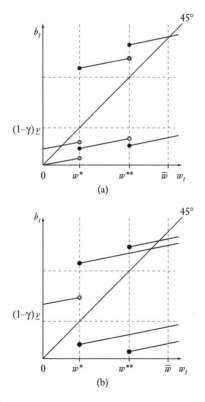

Figure 4   (a) $v = \underline{v}$; (b) $v = \bar{v}$

$$\dot{p}_L = \begin{cases} 1 - q - (1-q)p_L + (q - q')p_U & p_L > \mu p_U \\ 1 - q - \left(2 - q + \dfrac{q'}{\mu} - \dfrac{q}{\mu}\right)p_L & p_L < \mu p_U \end{cases} \tag{6}$$

and

$$\dot{p}_U = \begin{cases} q - qp_L + (q' - q - 1)P_U & p_L > \mu p_U \\ q - \left(q + \dfrac{q}{\mu} - \dfrac{q'}{\mu}\right)p_L - p_U & p_L < \mu p_U \end{cases} \tag{7}$$

The corresponding phase diagram appears in figure 5. There are two stationary distributions, labeled $S$ and $P$, and both are locally stable, with large basins of attraction.[14] Again, these stationary distributions are very different from each other. The distribution $S$ is a state of economic collapse or stagnation: $p_L = 1$, so all agents have low wealth, which entails that they all remain in the subsistence sector. By contrast, $P$ is a prosperous economy with both self-employment and an active labor market in which workers receive high wages; since the transition probabilities between the states are relatively high, there is also considerable social mobility. This contrasts with the case of factory production discussed above (point $F'$ in figure 3($b$)) in which there is little mobility between $L$ and the other two states.

As before, the long-run behavior of this economy depends on the initial conditions: economies in which the initial ratio of workers to entrepreneurs is low are more likely to be above the boundary line, where they will be subject to the high-wage dynamics, and are therefore more likely to converge to $P$. Where the initial ratio of poor to wealthy is high, the economy will be subject instead to the low-wage dynamics.

Of course, by examining figure 5, we can see that even if an economy initially has a high ratio of poor to wealthy, it is not necessarily doomed to stagnate, particularly if the middle

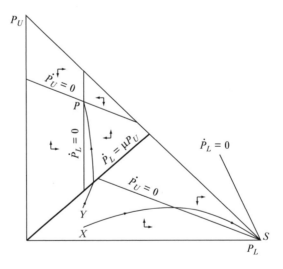

**Figure 5**   Prosperity and stagnation

class is sufficiently large (distributions with a large middle class are located near the origin). Consider the path starting at the point $Y$. Here most agents in the economy are self-employed, and the few workers that there are receive low wages because there are so few entrepreneurs demanding their labor (recall that some agents in state $L$ must be idle). Over time, some of the self-employed become entrepreneurs and the rest fall into the lower wealth class. Along this particular path, the number of agents in $U$ grows sufficiently fast that all agents in $L$ are eventually hired as workers, and the economy is brought to the boundary. Now there is excess demand for labor and the high-wage dynamics take over, with the number of wealthy agents growing rapidly (the number of workers declines slightly along this part of the development path, from which we infer that the ranks of the self-employed must be growing). Thus even though this economy begins with a high ratio of poor to wealthy, it eventually achieves prosperity.

Notice, however, that if we start at the nearby point $X$ instead of $Y$, the upper class grows slightly faster than the lower class, with both growing at the expense of the middle class of self-employed. The wage remains low, however, and eventually the lower class begins to dominate until the economy collapses to the stationary point $S$.

We can also check whether an economy might adhere to standard accounts of development such as the Kuznets hypothesis. The present example shows that the path to prosperity need not follow this pattern. Along the path emanating from $Y$, equality, measured by the relative size of the middle class, declines all the way to the prosperous steady state $P$. We can, however, easily generate versions of figure 5 in which some paths to prosperity are indeed of the Kuznets type. An example is shown in figure 6, which is obtained when the probability $q'$ of high returns for entrepreneurs is fairly large. Beginning at $Y$, the middle class declines until point $Z$, after which it grows as the economy

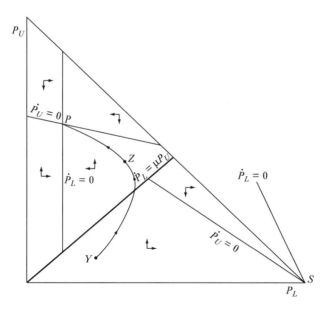

**Figure 6**   A development path that follows a Kuznets curve

converges to $P$. Thus, as Kuznets suggested, while mean wealth rises along the entire development path, inequality first increases and then decreases.

## 5. Conclusion

In dynamic studies of income and wealth distribution, economists have tended to rely on what we have referred to as linear models, in which individual transitions are independent of aggregate variables; see Banerjee and Newman (1991) and the references therein. Our model of a developing economy, by contrast, is nonlinear because it violates this property of individual dynamics; see also Aghion and Bolton (1991). While it seems unlikely that other nonlinear models will admit the kind of dimensional reduction we have exploited, our examples do illustrate some of the fundamental differences between the two types of model.

For one thing, they may have distinct policy implications. Under the guidance of the linear model, which usually displays global stability, one is led to conclude that continual redistributive taxation, with the distortion it often entails, is required for achieving equity. The nonlinear model, by contrast, raises the possibility that one-time redistributions may have permanent effects, thereby alleviating the need for distortionary policy.

The nonlinear model also provides a way to capture the empirically appealing notion that the same individual characteristics (e.g., wealth levels) can be observed under different stationary distributions. For all practical purposes, the very richest people in India are as wealthy as the very richest in the United States, and the very poorest Americans are no wealthier than their Indian counterparts. Yet standard Markov process models (including deterministic representative agent models) that give rise to multiple steady states or hysteresis preclude this possibility: any state observed under one stationary distribution cannot be observed under another, so that if India and the United States correspond to different equilibria of the same standard model, then no Indian can enjoy the same wealth as any American.

Our examples (particularly $C'$ and $F'$ in figure 3(b)) underscore a related point. Individual lineages can travel all over the wealth space under two very different stationary distributions.[15] Moreover, random perturbations to the individual-level dynamics will not significantly affect these distributions and cannot destroy the dependence of aggregate behavior on initial conditions. Contrary to the lessons of linear models, there need be no contradiction between individual mobility and aggregate hysteresis.

### Notes

1   We use the term "occupation" to mean a contractual arrangement rather than a productive activity. A bricklayer and an accountant are in the same occupation if each is an independent contractor or if each works for a wage.

2   This static model of occupational choice is a simplified version of the one in Newman (1991), which also discusses the advantages of the capital market imperfections approach over preference-based approaches such as that of Kihlstrom and Laffont (1979). See also the related work of Eswaran and Kotwal (1989).

3   That is, an agent born at $s$ is "immature" with probability $e^{\lambda(s-t)}$ at time $t > s$ ($1/\lambda$ is the average age of maturity of the population). These demographics resemble those in Blanchard (1985), although he does not assume instantaneous economic activity.

4   The restriction on the safe return ensures that the long-run dynamics are reasonable in the sense that people's wealth levels do not grow without bound.

5   Of course, $\hat{r}$ might instead represent the return to some physical subsistence activity that requires wealth but no effort; arbitrage considerations then dictate that this also be the return on loans.

6   An alternative interpretation is that $\pi F$ is equal to a moving cost incurred by the borrower when he flees, with no chance for the lender to catch him.

7   By using all his wealth as collateral, the borrower maximizes the size of the loan he can obtain.

8   So does static efficiency. In this model, a first-best Pareto optimum is achieved only when everyone is self-employed. Even though the employment contract is optimal from the point of view of the parties involved, an equilibrium with employment contracts cannot be first-best efficient (some resources are being spent on monitoring instead of direct production).

9   As this article was going to press, we became aware of the work of Conlisk (1976) on interactive Markov chains, to which our model is closely related. His results do not apply to our case, however.

10   Thus if $G(\cdot)$ is the current wealth distribution, then

$$p_L = G(w^*)$$
$$p_M = G(w^{**}) - G(w^*)$$

and

$$p_U = 1 - G(w^{**})$$

Of course, some information is lost by our dimensional reduction: if $H(\cdot)$ is another distribution with

$$H(w^*) = G(w^*) \qquad \text{and} \qquad H(w^{**}) = G(w^{**})$$

then it will be indistinguishable from $G(\cdot)$, even if the two distributions have different means. The limits to which they converge will generally differ as well but will be equal at $w^*$ and $w^{**}$.

11   We have assumed that on the boundary the high-wage dynamics apply. The behavior at the boundary is, of course, affected by which wage prevails there. Making alternative assumptions will not significantly change our results.

12   Think of these small probabilities as corresponding to winning the lottery and having a thunderbolt hit your house and factory.

13   A full study of the relevant data would be the subject of another paper, but there seems to be abundant evidence both for the poor performance of credit markets, at least in England (Deane, 1965; Shapiro, 1967; Ashton, 1968), and for a more equal land distribution in France (especially after the Revolution) than in England (where the enclosure movement had generated a large population of landless poor). See Clapham (1936), Grantham (1975), and Soltow (1980).

14   Figure 5 is not the only possible phase diagram that can correspond to the configurations in figure 4. If $q, q'$, and $\mu$ satisfy

$$\mu q(1 - q) < 1 + q' + q(q - q')$$

the stationary point of the high-wage dynamics will actually lie *below* the $p_L = \mu p_U$ boundary. Then there is a unique steady state since in converging to the high-wage stationary point, the economy crosses the boundary and the low-wage dynamics take over: the economy inevitably stagnates.

15   The idea that a stationary economy is one in which aggregate characteristics are fixed, but in which individuals may occupy different states over time, is already common in economics (examples are Loury (1981), Banerjee and Newman (1991), and Hopenhayn (1992)); it is one

motivation for seeking ergodic distributions. What is new here is the presence of multiple ergodic distributions with common support.

## References

Aghion, P. and Bolton, P. (1991): "A Trickle-down Theory of Growth and Development with Debt Overhang," manuscript, Paris: DELTA.

Andreoni, J. (1989): "Giving with Impure Altruism: Applications to Charity and Ricardian Equivalence," *Journal of Political Economy*, 97, December, 1447–58.

Ashton, T. S. (1968): *The Industrial Revolution, 1760–1830.* London: Oxford University Press.

Banerjee, A. V. and Newman, A. F. (1991): "Risk-Bearing and the Theory of Income Distribution," *Review of Economic Studies*, 58, April 211–35.

Bell, C. (1988): "Credit Markets, Contracts and Interlinked Transactions," in H. Chenery and T. N. Srinivasan (eds), *Handbook of Development Economics*, New York: North-Holland.

Bernanke, B. and Gertler, M. (1989): "Agency Costs, Net Worth, and Business Fluctuations," *American Economic Review*, 79, March, 14–31.

—— (1990): "Financial Fragility and Economic Performance," *Quarterly Journal of Economics*, 105, February, 87–114.

Blanchard, O. J. (1985): "Debt, Deficits, and Finite Horizons," *Journal of Political Economy*, 93, April, 223–47.

Clapham, J. H. (1936): *Economic Development of France and Germany, 1815–1914*, 4th edn. Cambridge: Cambridge University Press.

Cohen, J. S. (1981): "Managers and Machinery: An Analysis of the Rise of Factory Production," *Australian Economic Papers*, 20, June 24–41.

Conlisk, J. (1976): "Interactive Markov Chains," *Journal of Mathematical Sociology*, 4, July, 157–85.

Crafts, N. F. R. (1985): "Industrial Revolution in England and France: Some Thoughts on the Question, 'Why Was England First?'," in J. Mokyr (ed.), *The Economics of the Industrial Revolution*, Totowa, N.J.: Rowman & Allanheld.

Crouzet, F. (1990): *Britain Ascendant: Comparative Studies in Franco-British Economic History.* Cambridge: Cambridge University Press.

Deane, P. (1965): *The First Industrial Revolution.* Cambridge: Cambridge University Press.

Eswaran, M. and Kotwal, A. (1989): "Why Are Capitalists the Bosses?," *Economic Journal*, 99, March, 162–76.

Galor, O. and Zeira, J. (1993): "Income Distribution and Macroeconomics," *Review of Economic Studies*, 60(1), 35–52.

Grantham, G. W. (1975): "Scale and Organization in French Farming, 1840–1880," in W. N. Parker and E. L. Jones (eds), *European Peasants and Their Markets: Essays in Agrarian Economic History*, Princeton, N.J.: Princeton University Press.

Hopenhayn, H. A. (1992): "Entry, Exit, and Firm Dynamics in Long Run Equilibrium," *Econometrica*, 60, September, 1127–50.

Kehoe, T. J. and Levine, D. K. (1993): "Debt-Constrained Asset Markets," *Review of Economic Studies*, 60(4), October, 865–88.

Khan, M. A. (1989): "In Praise of Development Economics," manuscript, Baltimore: Johns Hopkins University.

Kihlstrom, R. E. and Laffont, J. J. (1979): "A General Equilibrium Entrepreneurial Theory of Firm Formation Based on Risk Aversion," *Journal of Political Economy*, 87, August, 719–48.

Loury, G. C. (1981) "Intergenerational Transfers and the Distribution of Earnings," *Econometrica*, 49, July, 843–67.

Lucas, R. Jr. (1988): "On the Mechanics of Economic Development," *Journal of Monetary Economy*, 22, July, 3–42.

Matsuyama, K. (1991): "Increasing Returns, Industrialization, and Indeterminacy of Equilibrium," *Quarterly Journal of Economics*, 106, May, 617–50.

Millward, R. (1981): "The Emergence of Wage Labor in Early Modern England," *Explorations Economic History*, 18, January, 21–39.

Murphy, K. M., Shleifer, A. and Vishny, R. W. (1989a): "Income Distribution, Market Size, and Industrialization," *Quarterly Journal of Economics*, 104, August, 537–64.

—— (1989b): "Industrialization and the Big Push," *Journal of Political Economy*, 97, October, 1003–26.

Newman, A. F. (1991): "The Capital Market, Inequality, and the Employment Relation," manuscript, Evanston, Ill.: Northwestern University.

North, D. C. (1981): *Structure and Change in Economic History*. New York: Norton.

O'Brien, P. K. and Keyder, C. (1978): *Economic Growth in Britain and France, 1780–1914: Two Paths to the Twentieth Century*. London: Allen & Unwin.

Romer, P. M. (1986): "Increasing Returns and Long-Run Growth," *Journal of Political Economy*, 94, October, 1002–37.

Sappington, D. (1983): "Limited Liability Contracts between Principal and Agent," *Journal of Economic Theory*, 29, February, 1–21.

Shapiro, S. (1967): *Capital and the Cotton Industry in the Industrial Revolution*. Ithaca, N.Y.: Cornell University Press.

Soltow, L. (1980): "Long-Run Changes in British Income Inequality," in A. B. Atkinson (ed.) *Wealth, Income, and Inequality*, 2nd edn. Oxford: Oxford University Press.

Stiglitz, J. E. (1988): "Economic Organization, Information, and Development," in H. Chenery and T. N. Srinivasan (eds) *Handbook of Development Economics*, New York: North-Holland.

Stokey, N. L. and Lucas, R. E., Jr. (1989): *Recursive Methods in Economic Dynamics*. Cambridge, Mass.: Harvard University Press.

Townsend, R. M. (1988): "Models as Economies," *Economic Journal*, 98, supplement, 1–24.

CHAPTER 6

# Economic Underdevelopment: The Case of a Missing Market for Human Capital

LARS LJUNGQVIST

This paper demonstrates that the coexistence of developed and underdeveloped countries can be a stationary equilibrium in a world economy with free trade in consumption goods and physical capital. An underdeveloped country is characterized by a high ratio of unskilled workers in the labor force, a small stock of physical capital, a low gross national product, a high rate of return on human capital and a corresponding large wage differential between skilled and unskilled workers. The critical assumptions are that future labor earnings cannot serve as collateral on a loan and indivisibilities in education.

## 1. Introduction

Dualism is a term often used in the characterization of underdeveloped countries. It refers to asymmetries in these societies which cannot be found in the developed world. A commonly asserted dualism is the coexistence of a modern industrial sector and a backward agricultural sector. Another economic asymmetry has to do with earnings differentials between various types of labor. Such an example is provided by Psacharopoulos (1973), who, in the 1960s, compared the relative average earnings of individuals by educational level for a group of developed and less developed countries. In the latter countries he found that workers with a university education on the average earned 6.4 times as much as the typical worker who had completed primary school, while the corresponding figure for the developed countries was 2.4.[1] A related empirical observation is the significantly higher private and social rates of return on education in the less developed countries compared to the developed ones as documented in a comprehensive survey article by Psacharopoulos (1985). It seems therefore puzzling that substantially higher relative wage differences in the underdeveloped world do not trigger a reallocation of labor which would reduce those differentials. Or stated as a more general question, is the existence of a dual economy consistent with individual rationality?

In the classic Lewis (1954) model of a dual economy, the level of wages in the urban industrial sector is assumed to be constant and determined as a fixed premium over a constant subsistence level of wages in the traditional agricultural sector. The earnings differential is such that a rural worker is indifferent between keeping his current employment or starting to work in the industrial sector. The model's inadequacy to deal with "excessive" relative wage differences is addressed by Harris and Todaro (1970), who assume a politically determined minimum urban wage at levels substantially higher than agricultural earnings. The resulting urban unemployment acts as an equilibrating force by reducing the expected earnings in the urban industry. Calvo (1978) shows how the urban wage can be determined endogenously after introducing a trade union into the Harris–Todaro model. However, it remains to be explored whether substantial relative wage differences can exist under pure competition. In doing so, we will combine Lewis' idea of economic dualism with Schultz's emphasis on the importance of human capital for understanding the situation in low-income countries. When these two economists shared the Nobel Prize in 1979, Schultz (1980) stressed also that poverty does not impair rationality and "poor people are no less concerned about improving their lot and that of their children than rich people are."

In the human capital literature, whose early contributors included Becker (1962) and Mincer (1958), educational decisions are based on maximizing behavior. A common assumption has also been that a perfect market for educational loans exists. This seems questionable, since the embodiment of human capital in people ought to affect its value as security for a loan. As Friedman (1962) pointed out, the productivity of human capital depends on the cooperativeness of the original borrower, and the prohibition of slavery makes it impossible to seize the capital from a borrower who does not honor his debt. It follows that credit constraints may be an important source of educational differences, which is also the conclusion in empirical work by Behrman et al. (1989) using U.S. data. Our paper adopts therefore the assumption of Loury (1981), which is that future labor earnings cannot serve as collateral on a loan.

The world economy in our model is assumed to be inhabited by agents who are identical with respect to preferences and innate abilities. An agent maximizes utility over an infinite horizon and can be thought of as representing a dynastic family. All countries have access to the same technologies concerning the production of a single good and education. The good can be used for consumption or investment. It is produced with physical capital, skilled workers and unskilled workers as inputs in a constant-returns-to-scale production function. Any unskilled agent can become skilled when being educated by an already skilled worker. The international economy exhibits free trade in consumption goods and physical capital, while labor is assumed to be completely immobile between countries.

Within this framework we ask the question, can developed and underdeveloped countries coexist indefinitely in a competitive world equilibrium? That is, can we find an allocation and price system supporting such a dynamic general equilibrium? It should be noted that the model itself makes it feasible for a country to reach the development level of any other country. The countries are assumed to be identical with respect to technology and the innate abilities of their labor forces. Moreover, all countries have access to the international capital market to finance their stocks of physical capital or as an outlet for net national savings. It is therefore not a foregone conclusion how there can exist underdeveloped countries in a stationary world equilibrium. Finally, the focus on stationary outcomes is meant to further our understanding of economic development by first exploring under what circumstances economic underdevelopment can persist over time.

Given indivisibilities in education, this paper establishes a continuum of steady states depending on the distribution of human and nonhuman wealth. An underdeveloped country is characterized by a high ratio of unskilled workers in the labor force, a small stock of physical capital, a low gross national product, a high rate of return on human capital and a corresponding large wage differential between skilled and unskilled workers. The perpetuation of such a situation can be explained as follows. In a country with a high ratio of unskilled labor, the wage of an uneducated worker is very low relative to the wage of a skilled worker. This means that the cost of education is high in comparison to the labor earnings of an unskilled agent. It turns out that an unskilled worker with no or few assets chooses not to obtain an education. The loss of utility from foregone consumption while saving for educational expenditures outweighs the welfare from higher future earnings.[2]

The precise structure of the model is set out in the following section. Equilibrium prices and quantities in a country are characterized in section 3. Section 4 studies individuals' optimization behavior. Section 5 proves the existence of multiple steady states for a country, while a stationary world equilibrium is described in section 6. Section 7 discusses economic growth in the context of our model, and section 8 contains the conclusions.

## 2. The Model

Consider a world economy inhabited by a continuum of infinitely lived agents. All agents are identical with respect to preferences and innate abilities. An agent's preferences at time $t_0$ over consumption streams take the usual additively separable, discounted form,

$$\int_{t_0}^{\infty} e^{-\rho t} U(c_t) \mathrm{d}t \quad \rho > 0 \tag{1}$$

The instantaneous utility function $U(c)$ is strictly increasing, concave and differentiable over the positive real numbers. The utility function is also assumed to satisfy the Inada condition

$$\lim_{c \to 0} U'(c) = \infty \tag{2}$$

Each agent is endowed with a constant flow of time that can be devoted to work. As can be seen from the agent's preferences, there is no disutility associated with working.

The world economy produces a single good which can be used for either consumption or investment. A country's output at time $t$ depends on its capital stock $K_t$ and the employment levels in two different job categories. Let $L_{st}$ denote the employment level for the skill-intensive type of work, which can only be performed by skilled workers. On the other hand, the employment in the labor-intensive job category, $L_{ut}$, can be made up of both unskilled and skilled workers. The good is then produced according to the aggregate production function

$$F(L_{st}, L_{ut}, K_t) = G(L_{st}, L_{ut})^\alpha K_t^{1-\alpha} \qquad 0 < \alpha < 1 \tag{3}$$

The production function exhibits constant returns to scale with positive marginal products, i.e., the function $G(L_{st}, L_{ut})$ is linearly homogeneous with positive first derivatives. It is also assumed that the marginal rate of substitution between different labor is diminishing everywhere:

$$\frac{F_1(L_s, L_u, K)}{F_2(L_s, L_u, K)} = \frac{G_1(L_s, L_u)}{G_2(L_s, L_u)} \qquad \text{is strictly decreasing} \qquad \text{in} \frac{L_s}{L_u} \tag{4}$$

(An integer $i$ as a subscript on a function denotes the partial derivative with respect to the $i$th argument.) Moreover the marginal product of unskilled labor approaches zero when the fraction of skilled labor to unskilled labor goes to zero, while the marginal product of skilled labor remains strictly positive in that limit (for any positive stock of physical capital). The corresponding restrictions on the function $G$ are

$$\lim_{L_s/L_u \to 0} G_1(L_s, L_u) > 0 \tag{5a}$$

$$\lim_{L_s/L_u \to 0} G_2(L_s, L_u) = 0 \tag{5b}$$

For simplicity, physical capital is assumed to not depreciate over time unless it is being consumed. Concerning the skilled labor force, there is an education technology which is also common across countries. A number $\gamma$ of skilled workers can instantaneously transform an unskilled worker into a skilled worker. This education allows the worker to remain skilled for $\tau$ units of time.

The consumption good and physical capital are internationally traded without any transportation costs. However, labor is completely immobile between countries. Another critical assumption on feasible trades is that an agent's future labor earnings cannot serve as collateral on a loan. Physical capital can still be used as collateral security, but that is equivalent to selling and repurchasing capital in this world without uncertainty.[3]

We will focus on stationary equilibria for the described world economy. It turns out that a steady state, or, for that matter, a Pareto-optimal stationary allocation, will only exist if the education technology is sufficiently productive. In particular, the parameters must satisfy

$$1 - \rho\gamma > e^{-\rho\tau} \tag{6}$$

which implies that $\tau > \gamma$.[4] If condition (6) is not satisfied, any constant stock of human capital would be unprofitable in an equilibrium. The rate of return would fall short of the subjective discount factor $\rho$ as will be shown in (17) below. Even feasibility is violated if $\tau < \gamma$ as will be seen in (11) below. Such economies where human capital must necessarily vanish over time are left out from our analysis, i.e., condition (6) is assumed to hold throughout the paper.

## 3. Equilibrium Prices and Quantities in a Country

Let $w_{st}$ and $w_{ut}$ denote the real wages at time $t$ for the country's workers employed in the skill-intensive and labor-intensive jobs, respectively. In a competitive equilibrium, these two production factors are paid their marginal products:

$$w_{st} = F_1(L_{st}, L_{ut}, K_t) = \alpha G_1(L_{st}, L_{ut}) G(L_{st}, L_{ut})^{\alpha-1} K_t^{1-\alpha} \tag{7a}$$

$$w_{ut} = F_2(L_{st}, L_{ut}, K_t) = \alpha G_2(L_{st}, L_{ut}) G(L_{st}, L_{ut})^{\alpha-1} K_t^{1-\alpha} \tag{7b}$$

Since skilled workers can perform both types of work, it must also be true that $w_{st}$ is at least as high as $w_{ut}$. A similar argument implies that the wage of educators is equal to $w_{st}$.

In a stationary world equilibrium, the internationally determined real interest rate will be equal to the rate of time preference $\rho$. Given this interest rate and the employment levels in the two job categories, we can find an expression for the equilibrium stock of capital,

$$\rho = F_3(L_{st}, L_{ut}, K_t)$$

i.e.,

$$K_t = [\rho^{-1}(1-\alpha)]^{1/\alpha} G(L_{st}, L_{ut}) \tag{8}$$

Since the production technologies for goods and education exhibit constant returns to scale, another implication of perfect competition is that "pure" profits are zero and, therefore, the ownership of these industries is immaterial.

Normalize the country's total labor endowment to unity and let $L_{et}$ denote the number of skilled workers employed as educators. Since agents supply all labor inelastically, market clearing in the country's labor market is obtained when

$$L_{st} + L_{ut} + L_{et} = 1 \tag{9}$$

If we let $H_t$ denote the number of skilled workers at time $t$, feasibility requires also that

$$L_{st} + L_{et} \leqq H_t \tag{10}$$

Due to international trade, there are no "domestic" market clearing conditions for goods and physical capital. However, any flows of resources between countries must be consistent with individual agents satisfying their budget constraints as shown in section 4.

Since we will only analyze stationary equilibria, it is convenient to drop the time subscript from all variables. A country's steady state will then turn out to be fully characterized by its ratio of skilled workers $H$. This quantity is obviously related to the number of educators $L_e$. After noting that rational agents will not incur the cost of education as long as their skills are intact, it follows that

$$H = \int_0^\tau \gamma^{-1} L_e dt = \frac{\tau L_e}{\gamma}$$

i.e.,

$$L_e(H) = \frac{\gamma H}{\tau} \in (0, H) \tag{11}$$

$L_e(H)$ is strictly less than $H$ by assumption (6), which ensures that any stationary ratio of skilled workers is feasible. Due to the resource cost associated with education, it must also be true in a steady state that no skilled workers are employed in the labor-intensive job category. After substituting (11) into (10) at equality, it can be seen that

$$L_s(H) = \frac{\tau - \gamma}{\tau} H \in (0, H) \tag{12a}$$

and by also using (9),

$$L_u(H) = 1 - H \tag{12b}$$

It is then straightforward to express the capital stock in terms of $H$ by substituting (12) into (8),

$$K(H) = [\rho^{-1}(1 - \alpha)]^{1/\alpha} G\left(\frac{\tau - \gamma}{\tau} H, 1 - H\right) \tag{13}$$

Similarly, the steady-state output level can be written as a function of $H$ by substituting (12) and (13) into (3):

$$F(L_s(H), L_u(H), K(H)) = [\rho^{-1}(1 - \alpha)]^{(1-\alpha)/\alpha} G\left(\frac{\tau - \gamma}{\tau} H, 1 - H\right) \tag{14}$$

The steady-state wages can also be expressed in terms of $H$ by substituting (12) and (13) into (7):

$$w_s(H) = \alpha[\rho^{-1}(1 - \alpha)]^{(1-\alpha)/\alpha} G_1\left(\frac{\tau - \gamma}{\tau} H, 1 - H\right) \tag{15a}$$

$$w_u(H) = \alpha[\rho^{-1}(1 - \alpha)]^{(1-\alpha)/\alpha} G_2\left(\frac{\tau - \gamma}{\tau} H, 1 - H\right) \tag{15b}$$

Finally, let $r(H)$ denote the rate of return on human capital in a steady state, which can be computed from

$$\gamma w_{\rm s}(H) = \int_0^\tau e^{-r(H)t}[w_{\rm s}(H) - w_{\rm u}(H)]dt \tag{16}$$

The left-hand side of this expression is the cost of education, while the right-hand side represents the present value of the increase in future labor income due to education.

## 4. Individuals' Optimization Behavior

This section examines what stationary prices are consistent with individuals' optimization behavior. In a steady state, it must be true that both skilled and unskilled workers *choose* to retain their respective educational status. We also know that an individual would prefer a constant consumption stream, since the rate of time preference is equal to the real interest rate.

Let us first examine for what stationary wages a skilled worker is willing to continue to bear the cost of education. The answer is simply; whenever the rate of return on human capital is at least as high as the rate of return on the alternative of investing in physical capital, i.e., $r(H) \geq \rho$. After using (16), this weak inequality can be rearranged to a restriction on the relative wage:

$$\frac{w_{\rm s}}{w_{\rm u}} \geq \frac{1 - e^{-\rho t}}{1 - e^{-\rho t} - \rho\gamma} \equiv \left(\frac{w_{\rm s}}{w_{\rm u}}\right)^* > 1 \tag{17}$$

Condition (17) ensures that the wage differential between skilled and unskilled labor is high enough to compensate skilled workers for their investment in human capital. Given that (17) is satisfied, it is straightforward to derive the optimal consumption and savings of a skilled worker. The mentioned desire to smooth consumption over time leads the individual to choose a constant flow of savings $q$ out of labor income, which together with compound interest is exactly sufficient to finance the educational expenditure $\gamma w_{\rm s}$ every $\tau$ units of time, i.e.,

$$\int_0^\tau e^{\rho t} q dt = \gamma w_{\rm s}$$

The necessary flow of savings is therefore equal to

$$q = \frac{\rho\gamma w_{\rm s}}{e^{\rho t} - 1} \tag{18}$$

In addition, let $\bar{a}$ denote the individual's assets in excess of those used for financing education. It follows that the optimal consumption flow of such a skilled worker can be written as

$$c_s(\bar{a}) = w_s - q + \rho\bar{a} \qquad (19)$$

We now turn to the optimization behavior of an unskilled worker. Let $a_0$ denote his assets. Given that the agent remains uneducated forever, the optimal consumption flow is

$$c_u(a_0) = w_u + \rho a_0 \qquad (20)$$

with a corresponding life-time utility of

$$\int_0^\infty e^{-\rho t} U(c_u(a_0)) dt = \rho^{-1} U(c_u(a_0)) \qquad (21)$$

Any unskilled worker is able to become skilled by acquiring education. However, if his assets are less than the educational expenses of $\gamma w_s$, the agent must first accumulate sufficient funds. During this accumulation phase it will once again be optimal for the individual to choose a constant consumption stream, let say $\hat{c} < w_u + \rho a_0$.[5] This consumption level will then determine the length of the accumulation period, denoted $T(\hat{c})$. The pair $\hat{c}$ and $T(\hat{c})$ represents a trade-off between the reduction in consumption while assets are being accumulated and the rapidity at which the higher income of a skilled worker is realized. In particular, a shorter accumulation period enables an individual to acquire an education faster but reduces also his consumption level as an unskilled worker. The formal relationship is

$$\int_0^{T(\hat{c})} e^{\rho t}(w_u - \hat{c}) dt + e^{\rho T(\hat{c})} a_0 = \gamma w_s$$

i.e.,

$$T(\hat{c}) = \rho^{-1} \ln\left(\frac{w_u - \hat{c} + \rho\gamma w_s}{w_u - \hat{c} + \rho a_0}\right) \qquad (22)$$

When the unskilled worker has obtained an education, the optimal consumption level is $c_s(0)$ as defined in (19). The equality between the discount rate and the real interest rate makes it unattractive to acquire any assets in excess of those used for financing education. The optimal $\hat{c}$ is therefore found by solving the following optimization problem:

$$\max_{\hat{c}} \int_0^{T(\hat{c})} e^{-\rho t} U(\hat{c}) dt + \int_{T(\hat{c})}^\infty e^{-\rho t} U(c_s(0)) dt \qquad (23)$$

subject to

$$\hat{c} < w_u + \rho a_0$$

$c_s(0)$ and $T(\hat{c})$ as defined in (19) and (22) given $a_0$.

The limiting value of the objective function when $\hat{c}$ approaches $w_u + \rho a_0$ is clearly the life-time utility of an agent who remains uneducated forever, given by (21). If this latter utility level cannot be improved upon by obtaining a future education, an unskilled worker with insufficient assets, $a_0 < \gamma w_s$, *chooses* to remain uneducated forever. After substituting (22) into (23), the condition for this can be seen to be

$$U(c_u(a_0)) \geqq \rho \frac{\gamma w_s - a_0}{w_u - \hat{c} + \rho \gamma w_s} U(\hat{c}) + \frac{w_u - \hat{c} + \rho a_0}{w_u - \hat{c} + \rho \gamma w_s} U(c_s(0)) \tag{24}$$

for all $\hat{c} < w_u + \rho a_0$.

## 5. Steady States and Welfare in a Country

As demonstrated in section 3, a country's steady state is fully characterized by its ratio of skilled workers $H$. We will now prove that there exist equilibrium wages as defined in (15), which are consistent with individuals' optimization behavior. Proposition 1 establishes what is the highest possible $H$ in a steady state, while a continuum of steady states is proven to exist in proposition 2. Proposition 3 compares prices and quantities across such stationary equilibria. Proposition 4 concludes that a Pareto-optimal stationary allocation is only obtained for the steady state with the highest ratio of skilled workers.

PROPOSITION 1    *The highest ratio of skilled workers consistent with a steady state in a country is $H^*$ implied by*

$$\frac{G_1((\tau - \gamma)/\tau^{-1}H^*, 1 - H^*)}{G_2((\tau - \gamma)/\tau^{-1}H^*, 1 - H^*)} = \left(\frac{w_s}{w_u}\right)^* \tag{25}$$

*where $(w_s/w_u)^*$ is defined in (17). If (25) is not satisfied for any ratio of skilled workers in the unit interval, $H^*$ is equal to one.*

PROOF    After substituting (15) into (17), the resulting expression (25) determines the highest $H$ for which skilled workers would choose to remain educated. At this composition of the labor force, the equilibrium wages are such that the return on education net of "depreciation" is equal to the real interest rate $\rho$. People are therefore indifferent between acquiring an education or investing in physical capital. This means also that unskilled workers have no incentive to change their educational status. An unskilled worker's life-time utility is even reduced if education would have to be preceded by a period of asset accumulation.

The existence of a unique $H^* \in (0, 1]$ is guaranteed by assumptions (4) and (5). The latter assumption implies that the limit of the left-hand side of (25) is infinity when $H$

approaches zero, and the expression is decreasing in $H$ by the former assumption. However, the model does not preclude the possibility that the rate of return on education does not fall below $\rho$ even if all workers are educated. $H^*$ would then be equal to one.

In addition to the highest possible steady state $H^*$ in proposition 1, the following proposition guarantees the existence of a continuum of steady states.

PROPOSITION 2    *There exists $H \in (0, 1]$ such that any ratio of skilled workers $H \in (0, \bar{H}]$ can be a steady state in a country whenever the unskilled workers have no assets.*[6]

PROOF    See appendix.

The continuum of steady states may seem surprising in light of assumption (4) that the relative wage of unskilled labor is lower the smaller $H$ is. One might therefore think that unskilled workers would like to educate themselves and start earning the higher wage. But at very low ratios of skilled workers in the economy, the educational cost is also high compared to the labor income of an unskilled worker. It turns out that the loss of utility from foregone consumption while saving for educational expenditures outweighs the welfare gain from higher future earnings. Moreover, the proof of proposition 2 is 'continuous' with respect to the unskilled workers' asset holdings. It can therefore be shown that a ratio of skilled workers strictly less than $\bar{H}$ is consistent with a steady state as long as the unskilled workers have sufficiently few assets.

PROPOSITION 3    *The steady-state output level and stock of physical capital are increasing in the ratio of skilled workers in the labor force, while the wage of skilled labor in terms of unskilled labor and the rate of return on education are decreasing.*

PROOF    See appendix.

PROPOSITION 4    *Given lump-sum transfers being available, a Pareto-optimal stationary allocation is only obtained when the ratio of skilled workers is equal to $H^*$ as defined in proposition 1.*

PROOF    Since all agents have the same discount factor $\rho$, a Pareto-optimal stationary allocation must implement all investment opportunities with a rate of return greater than or equal to $\rho$. The international market for physical capital can be said to accomplish this objective for nonhuman capital. But according to the proofs of propositions 1 and 3, there are investment opportunities in human capital earnings a rate of return greater (less) than $\rho$ whenever $H$ is less (greater) than $H^*$. It is straightforward to construct a Pareto-superior allocation for any stationary ratio of skilled workers other than $H^*$ by gradually adjusting that ratio towards $H^*$.

# 6. World Equilibrium

The existence proofs of a country's steady states were partial equilibrium arguments, since they only imposed market clearing in the domestic labor market. A world equilibrium requires also that the international good market and physical capital market clear. We will now examine under what circumstances, supply is equal to demand in the world capital market. It then follows that market clearing for international trade in goods is ensured by Walras' Law.

Consider any number of countries and suppose that each country has a stationary ratio of skilled workers consistent with a steady state as discussed in section 5. The steady-state capital stock in a country is then given by expression (8), which depends on the composition of the country's labor force. A condition for a stationary world equilibrium is that the implied world capital stock is willingly held by the agents. First of all, assets are demanded by skilled workers who are saving for future educational expenditures. These agents have been shown to optimally accumulate assets until it is time for them to obtain a new education. Despite this sawtooth time pattern of each skilled agent's asset holdings, it is straightforward to verify that a country's total assets used for financing education stay constant over time in a steady state. After summing up all such assets across countries, this demand for assets cannot be allowed to exceed the supply, i.e., the world capital stock. It follows that a stationary world equilibrium with interest rate $\rho$ will only exist if the implied stock of physical capital is at least as large as agent's savings for future educational expenditures.

Any physical capital not used for financing education can be owned by anyone in the world, as long as the ownership is consistent with all agents choosing to retain their educational status. In particular, it has been shown that unskilled workers in an under-developed country must be relatively poor, since they would otherwise like to obtain an education. On the other hand, unskilled workers in a country with the highest possible ratio of skilled workers can own any amount of assets. At this composition of the labor force, the rates of return on human and nonhuman capital are equalized. As a result, agents are indifferent between obtaining an education or investing in physical capital.

In a steady state, countries' aggregate asset holdings and individuals' consumption levels stay constant over time. Any net flows of goods between countries will only arise from factor payments for foreign-owned physical capital. The international capital market equalizes the rates of return on physical capital across countries. Agents are therefore indifferent to the location of their savings, and the allocation of the world's physical capital depends solely on countries' stocks of human capital. It follows that economic under-development is caused by underinvestment in human capital. A reflection of this is the higher rates of return on education in less developed countries, which also correspond to larger relative wage differences between skilled and unskilled labor in these countries.

## 7. Economic Growth

We have studied the implications of a missing credit market for human capital in a stationary environment. It is clearly desirable to extend the analysis to an economy exhibiting economic growth. The following proposition is suggestive with respect to the effects of neutral technological change.

PROPOSITION 5 *Suppose the production function in (3) is multiplied by a 'technology level' A, and assume that the marginal utility of consumption remains strictly positive in the limit when consumption approaches infinity. It is then possible to eliminate any steady state other than $H^*$ by choosing A sufficiently large.*

PROOF    See appendix.

The proof uses the fact that neutral technological change raises the marginal products of all inputs by the same factor. This implies that the rate of return on education is unchanged for any given ratio of skilled workers in the labor force. However, the higher wage of unskilled workers makes economic underdevelopment less likely. At a sufficiently high income level, everyone would like to save for an education as long as the rate of return on human capital exceeds the interest rate in the market for physical capital.

Even though economic growth may eventually loosen the impact of a missing market for human capital, it leaves open the question how the process of growth itself is affected by such a market imperfection. The answer will depend on which "growth mechanism" is chosen. The exogenous technological change in Solow's (1956) original neoclassical model has been superseded by the endogenous growth literature. Uzawa (1965) assumes that both intangible human capital and physical capital can be accumulated without limits making unbounded growth possible, while Arrow (1962) examines the effects of learning by doing. A more recent exploration of these concepts can be found in Romer (1986) and Lucas (1988). Another example of an endogenous growth model is the attempt by Becker and Barro (1988) to analyze fertility and capital accumulation decisions simultaneously within a general equilibrium framework. In future work, we intend to reexamine the implications of these models when markets for human capital are incomplete.

## 8. Conclusions

This paper has examined the effects of indivisibilities in education and a missing market for human capital, in a world economy with free trade in consumption goods and physical capital. Although technology and individuals' preferences are identical across countries, it is shown that both developed and underdeveloped countries can coexist in a stationary equilibrium. In fact, there is a continuum of steady states for the world economy corresponding to different distributions of human and nonhuman wealth. The perpetuation of economic underdevelopment is due to the inability to use future labor earnings as collateral on a loan and the nonconvexity in education. As a result, unskilled workers with little assets living in underdeveloped countries choose to remain uneducated despite the higher rates of return on education in these countries. The reason being that the loss of utility from foregone consumption while saving for educational expenditures, outweighs the welfare from higher future earnings.

Another model of an international economy with both skilled and unskilled labor is presented by Findlay and Kierzkowski (1983). Given a perfect student loan market, they show that skilled and unskilled workers attain the same utility level. This case corresponds to our unique Pareto-optimal production structure in proposition 4, where an individual's welfare depends on the sum of his human and nonhuman assets but not on his educational status *per se*. The reason that the composition of the labor force can differ across countries in the model of Findlay and Kierzkowski, is the assumption of exogenously given levels of a specific educational input. Under our assumption that skilled labor is used to transform unskilled workers into skilled workers, it is shown with identical preferences that all countries are clones of each other. The market imperfection for human capital is therefore crucial for explaining economic underdevelopment in this framework when educational inputs are reproducible.

The constraint that future labor earnings cannot serve as collateral on a loan is also analyzed by Loury (1981), who writes down a model with human capital as the only intertemporal good. In the face of stochastic shocks to individuals' abilities, the economy is seen to converge to a unique income distribution. An important reason for multiple distributions being ruled out is the assumption that the recurrent education decision is a continuous choice variable. We have instead shown that indivisibilities in education can explain the persistence of economic underdevelopment, even when all agents can earn the market interest rate on any amount of savings chosen. We believe that the assumption of a lumpy education technology parallels more closely to actual circumstances. The common practice, for whatever reason, is to provide education in "packages" like high school and college degrees.

Our multiplicity of steady states resembles the idea of an underdevelopment trap by Azariadis and Drazen (1990). They assume that the technological rate at which individuals can accumulate human capital depends positively on the existing economy-wide stock of human resources. It is shown that a country can converge to a steady state with or without investments in human capital depending on whether or not the initial stock of human capital exceeds a critical threshold value. The positive externality of human capital, as in the earlier development paper by Lucas (1988), implies that rates of return on education are lower in less developed countries than in developed ones. Our model has the opposite implication, which is also supported by empirical work as mentioned in the introduction. To appreciate the differences in mechanism between the two types of models, we consider why an uneducated worker in an underdeveloped country would like to migrate to a developed country. In a model with technological externalities, the agent would enhance his own productivity by working in close proximity to highly educated individuals. In our model, his ability would not change, but he would earn a higher wage in the developed country because of the relative scarcity of unskilled labor compared to the stock of human and nonhuman capital.

Another implication of our analysis is a positive correlation between economic under-development and income inequality within a country. The relationship is even exact when income derived from nonhuman assets is excluded. The income inequality can be said to reflect the severity of the credit constraint on human capital investments. This result is at variance with Kuznets' (1955) idea that inequality tends to increase in the early stages of economic development and to decrease in the later stages, the so-called "Kuznets curve." However, Fields and Jakubson (1990) argue that the existing empirical support of the Kuznets curve is entirely an artifact of the econometric method used. The inference is reversed as soon as country-specific effects are introduced in the estimation. Their conclusion that inequality tends to decrease with economic development is shown to be robust to alternative samples and functional form specifications.

The income distribution matters also in the model of industrialization by Murphy et al. (1989). They interpret industrialization as the introduction of increasing returns technologies. The assumption that international trade is costly attaches then importance to the size and composition of domestic demand. Industrialization is seen to take place if incomes are distributed broadly enough to materialize as demand for mass-produced domestic manufactures. A higher concentration of incomes to the very rich is not conducive to industrialization, since it means a shift of aggregate demand away from high volumes to more variety of goods. As a consequence, fewer industries may find it profitable to incur the fixed costs of introducing increasing returns technologies. These demand considerations are clearly absent in our model with unhampered international trade in goods, and the focus in instead on a relationship between the income distribution and the supply of human capital. At any rate, both models can be said to highlight economic interdependencies which are not present in a representative agent framework.

The fact that the steady state with the highest ratio of skilled workers is the only Pareto-optimal allocation implies that benevolent governments can do away with economic underdevelopment in our model. However, this may only be true if lump-sum transfers are available. Suppose, instead, that the economic reform must take the form of a student loan program. This would not only benefit the additional agents being educated but also the wage of workers remaining unskilled would increase due to the change in the labor force. On the other hand, the originally skilled workers would face a lower wage in terms of unskilled labor, and if there is an absolute decline in their income they would oppose the reform. Such an argument brings us back to the two economists referred to in the motivation of our paper. Both Lewis (1954, p. 409) and Schultz (1964, p. 196) spoke about underinvestment in human capital because of some agents' vested interests in maintaining the status quo. Romer (1990) resorts to similar reasoning when explaining import restrictions on producer durables, which slow down a country's economic growth but benefit domestic capital owners.

Lucas (1990) mentions that capital market imperfections can be a reason for countries remaining underdeveloped. Capital flows between countries are too small when there is no effective mechanism for enforcing international borrowing agreements. Our paper has shown that a similar constraint on households' financing of human capital can explain the same macroeconomic situation of underdevelopment. The analysis suggests that the observed migration pressure between countries due to restrictions on immigration has its counterpart in a lack of "occupational migration" within underdeveloped economies because of imperfections in the process of human capital accumulation. The model is therefore consistent with Adelman's (1977) observation that newly industrialized countries, such as South Korea and Taiwan, implemented educational policies prior to their growth takeoffs in the early 1960s.

APPENDIX

## Proof of proposition 2

As shown in the proof of proposition 1, skilled workers choose to remain educated for any $H \in (0, H^*]$. We will now have to prove the existence of $H^u$ such that an unskilled worker without assets would not like to acquire an education for any $H \in (0, H^u]$. The proposition is then obviously true for $\bar{H} = \min\{H^*, H^u\}$.

According to (24), an unskilled worker without assets would not like to change his educational status if

$$U(c_u(0)) \gtreqless \frac{\rho \gamma w_s}{w_u - \hat{c} + \rho \gamma w_s} U(\hat{c}) + \frac{w_u - \hat{c}}{w_u - \hat{c} + \rho \gamma w_s} U(c_s(0)) \qquad \text{for all } \hat{c} < w_u$$

A sufficient condition is therefore that

$$U(c_u(0)) \gtreqqless U(\hat{c}) + \frac{w_u - \hat{c}}{\rho\gamma w_s} U(c_s(0)) \qquad \text{for all } \hat{c} < w_u$$

After imposing (18)–(20), this weak inequality can be written as

$$\frac{U(w_u) - U(\hat{c})}{w_u - \hat{c}} \gtreqqless \frac{U(\phi w_s)}{\rho\gamma w_s} \qquad \text{for all } \hat{c} < w_u \tag{A.1}$$

where

$$\phi = 1 - \frac{\rho\gamma}{e^{\rho t} - 1} > 0$$

Assumption (6) ensures that the constant $\phi$ is positive. By using (2), (5) and (15), the limits of the two sides can be found for $H$ approaching zero:

$$\lim_{w_u \to 0} \left. \frac{U(w_u) - U(\hat{c})}{w_u - \hat{c}} \right|_{\hat{c} < w_u} = \lim_{c \to 0} U'(c) = \infty \tag{A.2a}$$

$$\lim_{w_s \to \underline{w}_s} \frac{U(\phi w_s)}{\rho\gamma w_s} \tag{A.2b}$$

where

$$\underline{w}_s = \alpha \left[\rho^{-1}(1 - \alpha)\right]^{(1-\alpha)/\alpha} \lim_{L_s/L_u \to 0} G_1(L_s, L_u) > 0$$

The limit in (A.2b) is always finite. This is obvious when $\underline{w}_s$ is finite or the utility function is bounded from above. If $\underline{w}_s$ is infinite and the utility function is unbounded, L'Hôpital's rule can be applied to obtain the limit $(\rho\gamma)^{-1}\phi U'(\infty)$ which is still finite. We can then conclude that condition (A.1) is satisfied for some interval $(0, H^u]$, i.e., an unskilled worker without assets chooses to remain uneducated if the ratio of skilled workers in the labor force is less than or equal to $H^u$.

## Proof of proposition 3

Given the equilibrium expressions for the allocation of labor in (12) and the wages in (15), assumption (4) implies that the wage of skilled labor in terms of unskilled labor is decreasing in the ratio of skilled workers in the labor force. After dividing both sides of (16) by $w_s(H)$, it then also follows that the rate of return on education is decreasing in $H$. To establish that the steady-state output level and stock of physical capital are increasing in $H$, it must be shown according to (13) and (14) that the function $G$ is increasing in $H$ for the relevant domain, i.e., for all values of $H$ which can constitute steady states. When totally differentiating $G$ with respect to $H$, it can be seen that $G$ is an increasing function as long as

$$\frac{G_1\left(\frac{\tau-\gamma}{\tau}H,1-H\right)}{G_2\left(\frac{\tau-\gamma}{\tau}H,1-H\right)} > \frac{\tau}{\tau-\gamma} \tag{A.3}$$

In a steady state, the left-hand side is equal to relative wage of skilled labor in terms of unskilled labor. The proof can therefore be completed by demonstrating that the lower bound on the steady-state wage in (17) is greater than the right-hand side of (A.3), i.e.,

$$\left(\frac{w_s}{w_u}\right)^* \equiv \frac{1-e^{-\rho\tau}}{1-e^{-\rho\tau}-\rho\gamma} > \frac{\tau}{\tau-\gamma} \Leftrightarrow e^{-\rho\tau} > 1-\rho\tau$$

The inequality holds trivially for $\rho\tau \geqq 1$. If $\rho\tau \in (0,1)$, take the natural logarithm of both sides and calculate the Taylor series expansion of the right-hand side around $\rho\tau = 0$. The result is the obviously true statement that

$$0 > -\sum_{i=2}^{\infty} i^{-1}(\rho\tau)^i$$

## Proof of proposition 5

Let $H$ be a steady state for some given technology level $A$, i.e. conditions (17) and (24) are satisfied for the corresponding equilibrium wages $w_s$ and $w_u$. It can then be shown that condition (24) will eventually be violated when $A$ goes to infinity unless $H$ is equal to $H^*$. In particular, we will show that even unskilled workers without assets would like to start saving for an education at a sufficiently high $A$. First, choose an arbitrary savings plan implied by some consumption level $\hat{c} < w_u$. Second, multiply the resulting consumption allocation by the same factor as the contemplated increase in $A$, let say $\lambda$. This is clearly feasible since all wages are raised by $\lambda$ in the case of neutral technological change. Our new version of (24) becomes

$$U(\lambda c_u(0)) \geqq \frac{\rho\gamma\lambda w_s}{\lambda w_u - \lambda\hat{c} + \rho\gamma\lambda w_s} U(\lambda\hat{c}) + \frac{\lambda w_u - \lambda\hat{c}}{\lambda w_u - \lambda\hat{c} + \rho\gamma\lambda w_s} U(\lambda c_s(0))$$

After imposing (18)–(20), this can be rearranged to read

$$\frac{U(\lambda w_u) - U(\lambda\hat{c})}{U(\lambda\phi w_s) - U(\lambda w_u)} \geqq \frac{w_u - \hat{c}}{\rho\gamma w_s} \tag{A.4}$$

where $\phi$ is defined in (A.1). The limit of the left-hand side when $A$, and therefore $\lambda$, goes to infinity is

$$\lim_{\lambda\to\infty} \frac{U(\lambda w_u) - U(\lambda\hat{c})}{U(\lambda\phi w_s) - U(\lambda w_u)} = \lim_{\lambda\to\infty} \frac{w_u U'(\lambda w_u) - \hat{c}U'(\lambda\hat{c})}{\phi w_s U'(\lambda\phi w_s) - w_u U'(\lambda w_u)}$$

$$= \frac{w_u - \hat{c}}{\phi w_s - w_u} \tag{A.5}$$

Besides applying L'Hôpital's rule, we have used the assumption in proposition 5 that the marginal utility of consumption remains positive when consumption approaches infinity.

The marginal utilities in the numerator and denominator of (A.5) must therefore converge to the same number and cancel out. Finally, substitute this limit back into (A.4),

$$\frac{w_\mathrm{u} - \hat{c}}{\phi w_\mathrm{s} - w_\mathrm{u}} \gtreqless \frac{w_\mathrm{u} - \hat{c}}{\rho \gamma w_\mathrm{s}} \Leftrightarrow \frac{w_\mathrm{s}}{w_\mathrm{u}} \lesseqgtr \frac{1 - e^{-\rho \tau}}{1 - e^{-\rho \tau} - \rho \gamma} \equiv \left( \frac{w_\mathrm{s}}{w_\mathrm{u}} \right)^* \tag{A.6}$$

A limiting stationary equilibria with skilled and unskilled labor must satisfy both conditions (17) and (A.6), i.e. the only permissible relative wage is $(w_\mathrm{s}/w_\mathrm{u})^*$ and $H^*$ is the unique steady state according to proposition 1. [If $H^*$ is equal to one, there are no unskilled workers and condition (A.6) becomes irrelevant.]

## Notes

1  United States, Canada, Great Britain, Netherlands, France and Norway constitute the group of developed countries, while the less developed countries include Malaysia, Philippines, Ghana, South Korea, Kenya, Uganda, Nigeria and India. See table 8.4 in Psacharopoulos (1973).
2  An economist from Ghana questioned the relevance of this model for his country where education is publicly subsidized. However, he later acknowledged that the low participation of the rural population in higher schooling was due to various costs related to education. These costs included tutoring necessary for passing entrance exams, lost labor income while studying, and higher living expenses in urban areas where institutes of higher learning are located.
3  Ljungqvist (1989) derives results similar to this paper in an overlapping generations framework. Following the approach of Becker (1974) and Barro (1974), the two-period lived agents in that model maximize an infinite-horizon objective function due to concern about their offspring. The critical assumption on feasible trades is that parents can only pass on nonnegative inheritance to their children.
4  The parameters $\rho$ and $\gamma$ are both strictly positive, so assumption (6) implies that $\rho \gamma \in (0, 1)$. After taking the natural logarithm of (6) and calculating the Taylor series expansion of the left-hand side around $\rho \gamma = 0$, we arrive at

$$- \sum_{i=1}^{\infty} \frac{1}{i} (\rho \gamma)^i > -\rho \tau \Rightarrow \gamma + \sum_{i=2}^{\infty} \frac{1}{i} \rho^{i-1} \gamma^i < \tau \Rightarrow \gamma < \tau$$

5  Any uneven consumption flow while saving for educational expenditures can be improved upon by cutting off the peaks and filling in the troughs at the interest rate $\rho$. It is clearly feasible for the individual to delay consumption by investing in physical capital. The ongoing accumulation of educational funds implies also that consumption smoothing is possible in the opposite direction through a reduction of early savings.
6  Please note that the highest possible steady state $H^*$ in proposition 1 may or may not be included in the set (0, A) since $H^* \geqq A$.

## References

Adelman, I. (1977): Redistribution before growth – A strategy for developing countries, Inaugural lecture Leyden University, Leyden, The Netherlands.
Arrow, K. J. (1962): "The Economic Implications of Learning by Doing," *Review of Economic Studies*, 29, 155–73.
Azariadis, C. and Drazen, A. (1990): "Threshold Externalities in Economic Development," *Quarterly Journal of Economics*, 105 (2), 501–26.

Barro, R. J. (1974): "Are Government Bonds Net Wealth?," *Journal of Political Economy*, 82(6), 1095–117.

Becker, G. S. (1962): "Investment in Human Capital: A Theoretical Analysis," *Journal of Political Economy*, 70 (5), 9–49.

——(1974): "A Theory of Social Interactions," *Journal of Political Economy*, 82 (6), 1063–93.

Becker, G. S. and Barro, R. J. (1988): "A Reformulation of the Economic Theory of Fertility," *Quarterly Journal of Economics*, 103 (1), 1–25.

Behrman, J. R., Pollak R. A. and Taubman, P. (1989): "Family Resources, Family size, and Access to Financing for College Education," *Journal of Political Economy*, 97 (2), 398–419.

Calvo, G. A. (1978): "Urban Unemployment and Wage Determination in LDCs: Trade Unions in the Harris–Todaro Model," *International Economic Review*, 19 (1), 65–81.

Fields, G. S. and Jakubson, G. H. (1990): "The Inequality–Development Relationship in Developing Countries," manuscript Cornell University, Ithaca, NY.

Findlay, R. and Kierzkowski, H. (1983): "International Trade and Human Capital: A Simple General Equilibrium Model," *Journal of Political Economy*, 91 (6), 957–78.

Friedman, M. (1962): Capitalism and Freedom. Chicago: University of Chicago Press.

Harris, J. R. and Todaro, M. P. (1970): "Migration, Unemployment and Development: A Two Sector Analysis," *American Economic Review*, 60 (1), 126–42.

Kuznets, S. (1955): "Economic Growth and Income Inequality," *American Economic Review*, 45 (1), 1–28.

Lewis, W. A. (1954): "Economic Development with Unlimited Supplies of Labour," Manchester School of Economic and Social Studies, 22 (2), 139–91, in A.N. Agarwala and S.P. Singh (1958) (eds), *The Economics of Underdevelopment*, London: Oxford University Press

Ljungqvist, L. (1989): Insufficient Human Capital Accumulation resulting in a Dual Economy caught in a Poverty Trap, SSRI workshop series no. 8902, Madison, WI. University of Wisconsin-Madison.

Loury, G. C. (1981): "Intergenerational Transfers and the Distribution of Earnings," *Econometrica*, 49 (4), 843–67.

Lucas, R. E., Jr. (1988): "On the Mechanics of Economic Development," *Journal of Monetary Economics*, 22 (1), 3–42.

——(1990): "Why Doesn't Capital Flow from Rich to Poor Countries?," *American Economic Review Papers and Proceedings*, 80 (2), 92–6.

Mincer, J. (1958): "Investment in Human Capital and Personal Income Distribution," *Journal of Political Economy*, 66 (4), 281–302.

Murphy, K. M., Shleifer, A. and Vishny, R. W. (1989): "Income Distribution, Market Size, and Industrialization," *Quarterly Journal of Economics*, 104 (3), 537–64.

Psacharopoulos, G. (1973): *Returns to Education: An International Comparison*. San Francisco, CA: Elsevier-Jossey Bass.

——(1985): "Returns to Education: A Further International Update and Implications," *Journal of Human Resources*, 20 (4), 583–604.

Romer, P. M. (1986): "Increasing Returns and Long-Run Growth," *Journal of Political Economy*, 94 (5), 1002–37.

——(1990): Trade, Politics, and Growth in a Small, Less Developed Economy, paper presented at a CEPR/IIES Conference in Stockholm, June.

Schultz, T. W. (1964): *Transforming Traditional Agriculture*. New Haven, CT: Yale University Press.

——(1980): "Nobel Lecture: The Economics of Being Poor," *Journal of Political Economy*, 88 (4), 639–51.

Solow, R. M. (1956): "A Contribution to the Theory of Economic Growth," *Quarterly Journal of Economics*, 70 (1), 65–94.

Uzawa, H. (1965): "Optimum Technical Change in an Aggregative Model of Economic Growth," *International Economic Review*, 6 (1), 18–31.

# C: Slow Convergence

CHAPTER 7

# Was Prometheus Unbound by Chance? Risk, Diversification, and Growth

Daron Acemoglu and Fabrizio Zilibotti

This paper offers a theory of development that links the degree of market incompleteness to capital accumulation and growth. At early stages of development, the presence of indivisible projects limits the degree of risk spreading (diversification) that the economy can achieve. The desire to avoid highly risky investments slows down capital accumulation, and the inability to diversify idiosyncratic risk introduces a large amount of uncertainty in the growth process. The typical development pattern will consist of a lengthy period of "primitive accumulation" with highly variable output, followed by takeoff and financial deepening and, finally, steady growth. "Lucky" countries will spend relatively less time in the primitive accumulation stage and develop faster. Although all agents are price takers and there are no technological spillovers, the decentralized equilibrium is inefficient because individuals do not take into account their impact on others' diversification opportunities. We also show that our results generalize to economies with international capital flows.

## 1. Introduction

The advance occurred very slowly over a long period and was broken by sharp recessions. The right road was reached and thereafter never abandoned, only during the eighteenth century, and then only by a few privileged countries. Thus, before 1750 or even 1800 the march of progress could still be affected by unexpected events, even disasters (Braudel 1973, p. xi).

This view of slow and uncertain progress between the tenth and early nineteenth centuries is shared by many economic historians. North and Thomas (1973, p. 71) describe the fourteenth and fifteenth centuries as times of "contractions, crisis and depression," and DeVries (1976) refers to this period as "an Age of Crisis." The same phenomenon is observed today: Lucas (1988, p. 4) writes that whereas "within the advanced countries, growth rates tend to be very stable over long periods of time," for poorer countries, "there are many examples of sudden, large changes in growth rates, both up and down." Why are the early stages of development slow and subject to so much randomness? Models of economic development based on threshold effects (e.g., Azariadis and Drazen, 1990) may be modified to predict a slow development process, but even then, these models have no implications regarding randomness of growth. In contrast, this paper argues that these patterns are predicted by the neoclassical growth model augmented with the natural assumptions of micro-level indivisibilities and micro-level uncertainty.

We begin with a number of observations that will be elaborated and empirically supported in the next section. First, most economies have access to a large number of imperfectly correlated projects; thus a significant part of the risks they face can be diversified. Second, a large proportion of these projects are subject to significant indivisibilities, especially in the form of minimum size requirements or start-up costs. Third, agents dislike risk. Fourth, there exist less productive but relatively safe investment opportunities. And finally, societies at the early stages of development have less capital to invest than developed countries. These features lead to a number of important implications.

(i)   At the early stages of development, owing to the scarcity of capital, only a limited number of imperfectly correlated projects can be undertaken, and agents will seek insurance by investing in safe but less productive assets. As a result, poor countries will endogenously have lower productivity, and this will contribute to their slow development.

(ii)  Since the diversification opportunities are limited, existing activities will bear more of the diversifiable risks. This will make the earlier stages of development highly random and slow down economic progress further since many runs toward takeoff will be stopped by crises.

(iii) Chance will play a very important role; economies that are lucky enough to receive good draws at the early stages will have more capital and thus will achieve better risk diversification and higher productivity. Therefore, although Prometheus will not be unbound accidentally, chance will always play a key role in his unchaining.

In our model, agents decide how much to save and how much of their money to invest in a safe asset with lower return. The rest of the funds are used to invest in imperfectly correlated risky projects. However, not all risky projects are available to agents at all points in time because of the minimum size requirements that affect some of these sectors. The more "sectors" (projects) that are open, the higher the proportion of their savings that agents are willing to put in risky investments. In turn, when the capital stock of the economy is larger, there will be more savings, and more sectors can be opened. Therefore, development goes hand in hand with the expansion of markets and with better diversification opportunities. Nevertheless, this process is full of perils because with limited investments in imperfectly correlated projects, the economy is subject to considerable randomness and spends a long time fluctuating in the stage of low accumulated capital. Only economies that receive "lucky draws" will grow, whereas those that are unfortunate enough to receive a series of "bad news" will stagnate. As lucky economies grow, the takeoff stage will be reached eventually, and full diversification of idiosyncratic risks will be achieved.

Theoretically, our model corresponds to an economy with endogenous commodity space because the set of traded financial assets (or open sectors) is determined in equilibrium. We use the competitive equilibrium concept suggested by Hart (1979) and Makowski (1980) for this type of economy. This equilibrium is Walrasian conditional on the set of sectors that are open, and the number of open sectors is determined through a free-entry condition. Although all agents are price takers and there are no unexploited gains in any activity, the competitive equilibrium is inefficient and too few projects are undertaken. The underlying problem is that the opening of an additional sector creates a positive *pecuniary externality* on other open projects since consumers now bear less risk when they buy these securities. Not only do we show that the competitive equilibrium is inefficient, but we establish the stronger result that under plausible assumptions on commitment, there exists no decentralized market structure that can avoid this inefficiency.

It may be conjectured that since our mechanism is related to capital shortages, its validity will be limited in the presence of international capital flows. In section 5, we show that decreasing return to capital would make foreign funds flow toward poor economies. But counteracting this, better insurance opportunities in richer countries could make domestic capital flow out. In a two-country generalization of our model, these forces lead to an interesting pattern that matches the historical facts of Western European development: At the early stages, funds flow into one of the countries; thus capital flows create divergence. But as the world economy becomes richer, the direction of capital flows is reversed, and there is rapid convergence (Neal, 1990).

Our model is related to the growing literature on credit and growth (among others, Greenwood and Jovanovic, 1990; Bencivenga and Smith, 1991; Saint-Paul, 1992; Greenwood and Smith, 1993; Zilibotti, 1994). Like these papers, our work shows that capital accumulation is associated with an increase in the volume of intermediation and financial activities as a proportion of the gross domestic product; see the empirical findings of Goldsmith (1969), Atje and Jovanovic (1993), and King and Levine (1993). However, while most existing theories derive their dynamics from the presence of fixed costs of financial intermediation, in our model there are no explicit costs of financial relations. Instead, all costs arise endogenously because of the diversification efforts of agents. We show that better diversification opportunities enable a gradual allocation of funds to their most productive uses while reducing the variability of growth. The intuition that risk diversification will lead to more productive specialization was first expressed by Gurley and Shaw (1955) and is modeled in Saint-Paul (1992). Greenwood and Jovanovic (1990) also show that the variability of growth may decrease with development. Our paper differs from these contributions because the degree of diversification and the extent of market incompleteness in the aggregate economy are endogenized and because there are no exogenous costs of financial intermediation. Further, the inefficiency of equilibrium with price-taking agents and the links between credit markets and international capital flows are also novel.

Another important literature that relates to our work is the one pioneered by Townsend (1978, 1983), Boyd and Prescott (1986), and Allen and Gale (1988, 1991), which studies financing decisions in general equilibrium. As in Allen and Gale, we endogenize the market structure, but without explicit costs of issuing securities. Furthermore, we focus mainly on the interaction between the incompleteness of markets, the opportunities for diversification, and the process of development. We follow the work of Townsend and others in allowing coalitions to internalize financial externalities. However, in contrast to these papers, we show that the efficient allocation is extremely hard to sustain as a decentralized equilibrium. The reason for these different conclusions will be explained in section 5.

The paper is organized as follows. Section 3 lays out the basic model and characterizes the equilibrium. Section 4 shows that the decentralized equilibrium is not Pareto-efficient and characterizes the Pareto-optimal allocation. Section 5 demonstrates that the inefficiency result is robust to the formation of financial coalitions. Section 6 analyzes international capital flows, and Section 7 presents a conclusion.

## 2. Motivation and Historical Evidence

Many economic historians (e.g., Braudel, 1973, 1982; North and Thomas, 1973; DeVries, 1976) emphasize the high variability of performance at the early stages of development. McCloskey (1976) calculates that the coefficient of variation of output net of seed in medieval England was 0.347 and that "famines" were occurring on average every 13 years. Part of this variability is certainly due to the fact that agricultural productivity was largely dependent on weather. But this heavy reliance on agriculture is itself a symptom of an undiversified economy. Additionally, there is considerable evidence that nonagricultural activities were also subject to large uncertainties. Braudel describes the development of industry before 1750 as "subject to halts and breakdowns" (1982, p. 312). He points out the presence of failed takeoffs: "three occasions in the West when there was an expansion of banking and credit so abnormal as to be visible to the naked eye [Florence 1300s, Genoa late 1500s, and Amsterdam 1700s] . . . three substantial successes, which ended every time in failure or at any rate in some kind of withdrawal" (p. 392). The pattern of these failures is also informative. While these cities grew gradually by expanding the scope of industrial and commercial activities, the collapse took the form of an abrupt end ignited by a few bankruptcies, suggesting the presence of large undiversified risks.

Poor countries today also exhibit considerably higher variability of output than more developed economies. Figure 1 plots the logarithm of the standard deviation of each

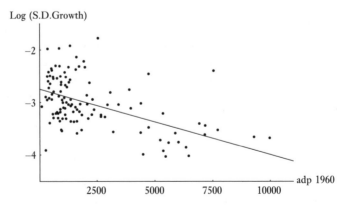

**Figure 1**   Variability of growth

country's GDP per capita growth rate over the period 1960–85 versus the GDP per capita in 1960 for 117 countries from the data set in Summers and Heston (1991). The solid curve traces the regression line, calculated excluding Saudi Arabia, a rich country with highly volatile growth due to oil prices. This line has a negative and highly significant coefficient ($t$-statistic, $-6.68$) and an $R^2$ of .29. When we drop five outliers (Iran, Iraq, Gabon, Somalia, and Uganda) for which political unrest and wars appear to have been the main source of their exceptionally high variability, the fit of the regression increases to $R^2 = .34$. A 1 percent increases in the initial GDP is associated, on average, with a 0.25 percent decrease in the standard deviation of growth, a very large quantitative effect.

Similar results are obtained by pooling cross-sectional and time-series information. We consider pairs of observations $\{GDP_{t,i}, |\epsilon_{t+1,i}|\}$, where $|\epsilon_{t+1,i}|$ is the absolute value of the one-period-ahead deviation from the average growth rate in country $i$. We then divide our $117 \times 25$ pairs of observations into four groups according to increasing GDP per capita ranges ($\bar{X}_1 = [0, 700]$, $\bar{X}_2 = [700, 1,500]$, $\bar{X}_3 = [1,500, 4,500]$, and $\bar{X}_4 = [4,500, \infty]$) and assign each deviation to one group so that $\{|\epsilon_{i^*, t^*+1}|\} \in \{GROUP_k\}$ if and only if $GDP_{i^*, t^*} \in \bar{X}_k$ (GDP per capita in 1980 U.S. dollars). Finally, we compute the sample mean for the (pooled) absolute value of deviations in each group. The results are reported in table 1, with the standard error of the mean in parentheses. Column 1 shows that the average size of deviation from the mean growth rate decreases with the income range; hence a low-income country or period is associated with higher variability. In column 2 (with fixed effects), we report the sample means for the corresponding income ranges after controlling for fixed country and time effects by subtracting from each observation the respective country and time means (averaged, respectively, across $t$ and $i$). Since we are computing deviations from averages, some observations will now be negative. The negative correlation between GDP levels and growth variability remains very significant. Therefore, not only is this negative correlation driven by cross-country variations, but the time-series variations are also consistent with our prediction.[1]

Recent empirical work by others also provides support. Ramey and Ramey (1995) find a negative correlation between variability of growth rates and average growth both in a subsample of the countries we study and within OECD countries. Quah (1993) analyzes the cross-country dynamics of growth by estimating a Markov chain transition matrix after

Table 1   Variability of growth rates (Panel)

| GDP per capita | Average deviation | | Observations (3) |
| --- | --- | --- | --- |
| | No fixed effects (1) | With fixed effects (2) | |
| $0 < GDP_{i,t} < 700$ | .048 | .0072 | 448 |
| | (.0025) | (.0048) | |
| $700 < GDP_{i,t} < 1,500$ | .047 | .0067 | 766 |
| | (.0018) | (.0034) | |
| $1,500 < GDP_{i,t} < 4,500$ | .041 | $-.0011$ | 964 |
| | (.0014) | (.0026) | |
| $4,500 < GDP_{i,t}$ | .031 | $-.0098$ | 743 |
| | (.0013) | (.0026) | |

Standard errors are in parentheses.

classifying countries in four groups according to their GDP per capita relative to the world average (p. 431). Table 2 reports a summary of his results for a 23-year transition matrix, 1962–85 (where $z$ stands for GDP per capita relative to world average, and the different columns report the estimated probability that a country belonging to a certain group falls to a relatively poorer group, remains in the same group, or moves up to a richer group). When we consider higher-income ranges, the probability of falling to a poorer group decreases (a finding also confirmed by Benhabib and Gali (1995)). These results give further support to the claim that the process of development is perilous at the early stages.

A possible explanation for decreasing variability is technological. At the early stages of development, countries may have access to only risky and low-productivity technologies. However, this does not seem to be the whole story. The adoption of new technologies is as often subject to economic as to scientific constraints. North and Thomas (1973) and Rosenberg and Birdzell (1986) argue that many technologies that were used later were actually known in medieval Europe, but failed to be adopted because of a lack of monetary incentives. Hobsbawm (1968) goes further and asserts that there was nothing new in the technology of the British Industrial Revolution, and the new productive methods could have been developed 150 years before.

In accord with this view, there exist many instances in which capital scarcities and limited savings appear to have been a major obstacle to expansion and growth. Bagehot (1873, p. 4) more than a century ago wrote that "in poor countries, there is no spare money for new and great undertakings" (see also Gerschenkron, 1962, p. 14). In line with this view, Wrigley (1988) argues that the main reason for heavy reliance on agriculture and an important constraint on industrialization were the shortages of energy caused by scarcities of capital. The size of the required activity was certainly a relevant factor in the minds of entrepreneurs. Scherer (1984, p. 13) quotes Matthew Boulton, James Watt's partner, writing to Watt that the production of the engine was not profitable for just a few countries, but would be so if the whole world were the market.

Our mechanism also relies on agents' changing their behavior in order to reduce the risks they bear. The importance of risk aversion is confirmed by the institutions developed in many societies to deal with the problems of insurance and risk pooling (Persson, 1988; Townsend, 1994) and by the extensive use of storage technology and scattering of fields chosen for their relative safety. Braudel (1982) notes the presence of unproductive hoarding in undiversified economies and writes that "every society accumulates capital which is then at its disposal, either to be saved and hoarded unproductively, or to replenish the channels of the active economy.... If the flow was not strong enough to open all the

**Table 2**   Transition matrix

| Relative GDP per capita | Prob (↓) | Prob (∼) | Prob (↓) |
|---|---|---|---|
| $z < \frac{1}{4}$ | ... | .76 | .24 |
| $\frac{1}{4} < z < \frac{1}{2}$ | .52 | .31 | .17 |
| $\frac{1}{2} < z < 1$ | .29 | .46 | .26 |
| $1 < z < 2$ | .24 | .53 | .24 |
| $2 < z$ | .05 | .95 | ... |

*Source*: Quah (1993)

sluice-gates, capital was almost inevitably immobilized, its true nature as it were unrealized" (p. 386). The pattern of change in the British portfolios between the eighteenth and nineteenth centuries also documents that as per capita income increased, the use of relatively safe assets decreased and the array of available assets expanded considerably (Kennedy, 1987, table 5.1).

Finally, this paper stresses that lack of diversification at early stages of development leads to an important role of "chance," especially regarding the success of large and risky projects. In this context, the impact of railways on economic development is interesting. In the United States, the success of railways is hailed as opening the way for the financing of large projects (e.g., Chandler, 1977), whereas in Spain, where railways attracted 15 times as much capital as total manufacturing, the heavy losses on railway investments are argued to have led to serious capital scarcities for decades (Tortella, 1972, pp. 118–21). Regarding this episode and a similar one in Italy, Cameron (1972, p. 14) writes that "in both cases the result was a fiasco which set back the progress of industrialization and economic development by at least a generation."

## 3. The Model and the Decentralized Equilibrium

We consider an overlapping generations model with competitive markets and nonaltruistic agents (households) who live for two periods. There is a continuum of agents with mass $a > 1$ in each living generation, and agents of the same generation are all identical. The production side of the economy consists of a single final-good sector and a continuum one of intermediate sectors (projects). The final-good sector transforms capital and labor into final output. Intermediate sectors transform savings of time $t$ into capital to be used at time $t + 1$ without using labor. In their youth, our agents work in a final-sector firm and receive the wage rate of this sector. At the end of this period they make their consumption, saving, and portfolio decisions. Their savings can be invested in risky securities or in a safe asset that has a nonstochastic gross rate of return equal to $r$. After the investment decisions, the uncertainty unravels, and the security returns and the amount of capital

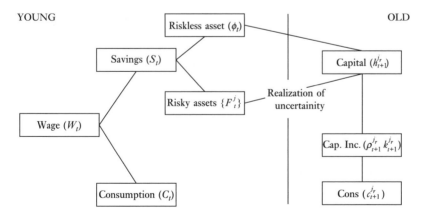

**Figure 2**    Timing of events ($j_r$ stands for the realized state of nature)

brought forward to the next period are determined. Capital that agents own in their retirement period is sold to final-sector firms and fully depreciates after use. Old agents consume this capital income. Figure 2 summarizes the sequence of events in our model.

## 3.1. Uncertainty

There is a continuum of equally likely states represented by the unit interval. Intermediate sector $j \in [0, 1]$ pays a positive return only in state $j$ and nothing in any other state. Therefore, investing in a sector is equivalent to buying a basic Arrow security that pays in only one state of nature. More formally, an investment of $F^j$ in sector $j$ pays the amount $RF^j$ if state $j$ occurs *and* $F^j \geq M_j$, and nothing otherwise. In our model, $R > r$, so these projects are more productive than the safe investment. The requirement $F^j \geq M_j$ implies that all intermediate sectors have linear technologies, but some require a certain minimum size, $M_j$, before being productive. The distribution of minimum size requirements is given by

$$M_j = \max\left\{0, \frac{D}{1 - \gamma}(j - \gamma)\right\}$$

Sectors $j \leq \gamma$ have no minimum size requirement, and for the rest of the sectors, the minimum size requirement increases linearly (see figure 3 on page 171 for a diagrammatic representation). The results are not dependent on this linear specification, and the ranking of projects from lower to higher size occurs without loss of generality and imposes no timing constraint.

This formalization contains the two features that will drive our results:

(i)   risky investments have a higher expected return than the safe asset (i.e., $R > r$), and
(ii)  different projects are imperfectly correlated so that there is safety in variety.

A convenient implication of this formulation is that if a portfolio consists of an equiproportional investment $F$ in all projects $j \in \bar{\mathcal{J}} \subseteq [0, 1]$ and the measure of the set $\bar{\mathcal{J}}$ is $p$, then the portfolio pays the return $RF$ with probability $p$ and nothing with probability $1 - p$. Note that if the aggregate production set were convex (i.e., $D = 0$), the allocation problem of the economy would be trivial: all agents would invest an equal amount in all intermediate goods sectors and diversify all the risks. However, in the presence of nonconvexities, as captured by our minimum size requirements, there is a trade-off between insurance and high productivity.

## 3.2. Preferences, technology, and factor prices

The preferences of consumers over final goods are defined as

$$E_t U(c_t, c_{t+1}) = \log(c_t) + \beta \int_0^1 \log\left(c_{t+1}^j\right) \mathrm{d}j \tag{1}$$

where $j$ represents the states of nature, which are assumed, as noted above, to be equally likely. Each agent discounts the future at the rate $\beta$ and has a rate of relative risk aversion equal to one. Although the realization of the state of nature does not influence the productivity of the final-good sector, it affects consumption since it determines how much capital each agent takes into the final-good production stage and the equilibrium price of capital.

Output of the final-good sector is given by

$$Y_t = A K_t^\alpha L_t^{1-\alpha} \tag{2}$$

We normalize the labor endowment of each young worker to $1/a$. Since the mass of agents is $a$ and labor supply is inelastic, we have $L_t = 1$. The aggregate stock of capital depends on the realization of the state of nature. If the state of nature is $j$, then

$$K_{t+1}^j = \int_{\Omega_t} \left( r\phi_{h,t} + RF_{h,t}^j \right) dh$$

where $F_{h,t}^j$ is the amount of savings invested by agent $h \in \Omega_t$ in sector $j$, $\phi_{h,t}$ is the amount invested in the safe asset, and $\Omega_t$ is the set of young agents at time $t$. Since both labor and capital trade in competitive markets, equilibrium factor prices in state $j$ are given as

$$W_{t+1}^j = (1-\alpha)A\left(K_{t+1}^j\right)^\alpha \equiv (1-\alpha)A\left[\int_{\Omega_t} \left( r\phi_{h,t} + RF_{h,t}^j \right) dh\right]^\alpha \tag{3}$$

and

$$\rho_{t+1}^j = \alpha A\left(K_{t+1}^j\right)^{\alpha-1} \equiv \alpha A\left[\int_{\Omega_t} \left( r\phi_{h,t} + RF_{h,t}^j \right) dh\right]^{\alpha-1} \tag{4}$$

The wage earning of a young agent conditional on the realization of state $j$ will then be $w_t^j = W_t^j/a$.

## 3.3. Intermediate goods and portfolio decisions

We assume that intermediate sector firms are run by agents who compete to get funds by issuing financial securities and sell them to other agents in the stock market. Each agent can run at most one project, although more than one agent can compete to run the same project (see section 5 for generalizations).

Decisions are made in two stages.[2] In the first stage, each agent $h \in \Omega_t$ takes the announcements of all other agents as given and announces his plan to run at most one project in the intermediate sector and sell an unlimited quantity of the associated basic Arrow security. Securities are labeled by the indices of the project to which they are attached. Therefore, one unit of security $j$ entitles its holder to $R$ units of $t+1$ capital in state of nature $j$. We denote the unit price of security $j$ (in terms of savings of time $t$) by $P_{j,h,t}$, and subscript $h$ implies that this security is issued by agent $h$. Put differently, agent

$h$ is managing investments in project $j$ on behalf of other agents, and for every unit of savings he collects from others, he invests $1/P_{j,h,t}$ and keeps the remaining $(P_{j,h,t} - 1)/P_{j,h,t}$ as his commission. A first-stage strategy for agent $h$ at time $t$ is an announcement

$$Z_{h,t} = \left( j, P_{j,h,t} \right) \in [0,1] \times \mathbb{R}^+$$

specifying the project $h$ intends to run and the price at which he sells the corresponding security. If an agent $h'$ decides to run no project, then $Z_{h',t} = \emptyset$. The function $Z_t: \Omega_t \to [0,1] \times \mathbb{R}^+$ summarizes the announcements of all agents at time $t$. We also denote the subset of all projects that at least one agent proposes to run at time $t$ by $\mathcal{J}_t(Z_t) \subseteq [0,1]$; thus

$$\mathcal{J}_t(Z_t) = \left\{ j \in [0,1] | \exists h \text{ s.t.} Z_{h,t} = \left( j, P_{j,h,t} \right) \right\}$$

Finally, we define $P_t(Z_t): \mathcal{J}_t(Z_t) \to \mathbb{R}^+$ as the function that summarizes the minimum price for each security $j \in \mathcal{J}_t(Z_t)$ induced by the set of announcements $Z_t$. Formally,

$$P_t(Z_t) = \left\{ P^j(Z_t) \right\}_{j \in \mathcal{J}} \qquad \text{and} \qquad P^j(Z_t) = \min_{\{h \text{ s.t.} Z_{h,t} = (j,\, P_{j,h,t})\}(P_{j,h,t})}$$

From now on, the index $h$ will be dropped whenever this will cause no confusion.

In the second stage, all agents behave competitively, take as given the set of securities offered and the price of each security announced in the first period, and announce their savings $S_t$, their demand for the safe asset $\phi_t$, and their demand for each security $j$, $F_t^j$.[3] Therefore, optimal consumption, savings, and portfolio decisions can be characterized by

$$\max_{s_t, \phi_t, \{F_t^j\}_{0 \le j \le 1}} \log(c_t) + \beta \int_0^1 \log\left( c_{t+1}^j \right) \mathrm{d}j \tag{5}$$

subject to

$$\phi_t + \int_0^1 P_t^j(Z_t) F_t^j \mathrm{d}j = S_t \tag{6}$$

$$c_{t+1}^j = \rho_{t+1}^j \left( r\phi_t + R F_t^j \right) \tag{7}$$

$$F_t^j = 0 \qquad \forall j \notin \mathcal{J}_t(Z_t) \tag{8}$$

and

$$c_t + s_t \le \omega_t + \upsilon_t \tag{9}$$

where $P_t^j(Z_t)$ is the minimum price at which security $j$ is offered, $\rho_{t+1}^j$ is the price of capital in state $j$ (see eqn (4)), and $v_t$ is the commission the agent obtains for running a project. For all $h \in \Omega$ such that $Z_{h,t} = \emptyset$, $v_{h,t} = 0$, and for an agent who runs project $j$,

$$v_{h,t} = \frac{P_{j,h,t} - 1}{P_{j,h,t}} \hat{F}^{j,h,t}$$

where $\hat{F}^{j,h,t}$ is the total amount of funds that he raises. In this stage, each agent takes $\omega_t$, $P_t^j$, $\rho_{t+1}^j$, and the set of risky assets $\mathcal{J}_t(Z_t)$ as given.[4]

We now define a static equilibrium given wage earnings of young agents, $\omega_t$ (or given $K_t$). A full dynamic equilibrium is a sequence of static equilibria linked to each other through (3).

DEFINITION 1   *An equilibrium at time $t$ is a set of first-stage announcements $Z_t^*$; second-stage saving and portfolio decisions $s_t^*$, $F_t^*$, and $\phi_t^*$; and factor returns $\{W_{t+1}^j\}_{j \in [0,1]}$ and $\{\rho_{t+1}^j\}_{j \in [0,1]}$ such that*

(a)   *given any $Z_t$, $\omega_t$, and $\{\rho_{t+1}^j\}$, each agent $h$ chooses $s_h^*(P_t(Z_t), \mathcal{J}_t(Z_t))$, $\phi_h^*(P_t(Z_t), \mathcal{J}_t(Z_t))$, and $F_h^{j*}(P_t(Z_t), \mathcal{J}_t(Z_t))$ in the second stage to solve (5) subject to (6)–(9);*

(b)   *in the first stage, given the set of first-stage announcements and the decision rules $s^*(P_t(Z_t), \mathcal{J}_t(Z_t))$, $\phi^*(P_t(Z_t), \mathcal{J}_t(Z_t))$, and $F_j^*(P_t(Z_t), \mathcal{J}_t(Z_t))$ of all other agents in the second stage, every agent $h$ makes the optimal announcement $Z_{h,t}^*$; and*

(c)   $\{W_{t+1}^j\}$ *and* $\{\rho_{t+1}^j\}$ *are given by (3) and (4).*

This is essentially a competitive equilibrium. All agents take prices as given and maximize their utility. The only difference from a standard competitive equilibrium is that before the trading stage, the set of traded securities (open sectors) has to be determined, and this is accomplished by imposing a free-entry condition. We can therefore characterize the equilibrium by solving the maximization problem in (5) and then use the asset demands of agents and free entry to find out which sectors will be open.

We start the characterization of equilibrium with two useful observations. First, because preferences are logarithmic, the following saving rule is obtained irrespective of the risk-return trade-off:

$$s_t^* \equiv s^*(\omega_t) = \frac{\beta}{1+\beta} \omega_t \tag{10}$$

Given this result, an agent's optimization problem can be broken into two parts: the amount of savings is determined, and then an optimal portfolio is chosen. Second, free entry into the intermediate good sector implies that $v_{h,t} = 0$ for all $t$, $h$. To see why, suppose $v_{h,t} > 0$; then since there are more agents than projects, there exists $h'' \in \Omega_t$ with $Z_{h'',t} = \emptyset$ who can offer to run the same project as $h'$ but sell the corresponding security at a lower price. Thus $v_{h',t} > 0$ cannot be an equilibrium, and we must have $P_t(Z^*) = 1$. Therefore, in the program (5)–(9), we can substitute $P^j = 1$ for all $j \in \mathcal{J}_t$ and $v_t = 0$. Next we have the following important result.

LEMMA 1   *Let $Z_t^*$ be the set of equilibrium announcements at time t. Then*

(i)   $F_t^{j*} = F_t^{j'*}$ *for all* $j, j' \in \mathcal{J}_t(Z_t^*)$, *and*
(ii)  $\mathcal{J}_t(Z_t^*) = [0, n_t(Z_t^*)]$ *for some* $n_t(Z_t^*) \in [0, 1]$.

Like all other results in sections 3–5, this lemma is proved in appendix A.

The first part establishes that since each individual is facing the same price for all the traded *symmetric* Arrow securities, he would want to purchase an equal amount of each. We refer to this portfolio consisting of an equal amount of all traded securities as a *balanced portfolio.* The second part states that when only a subset of projects can be opened in equilibrium, "small projects" are opened before "large projects." As a result, if a sector $j^*$ is open, all sectors $j \leq j^*$ must also be open.

Given lemma 1 and (8), the problem of maximizing

$$\int_0^1 \log\left[\rho_{t+1}^j\left(RF_t^j + r\phi_t\right)\right] dj$$

with respect to $\phi_t$ and $\{F_t^j\}$ can be written as

$$\max_{\phi_t, F_t} n_t \log\left[\rho_{t+1}^{qG}(RF_t + r\phi_t)\right] + (1 - n_t) \log\left[\rho_{t+1}^{qB}(r\phi_t)\right] \tag{11}$$

subject to

$$\phi_t + n_t F_t = s_t^* \tag{12}$$

where $n_t$ and $\rho_{t+1}^j$ are taken as parametric by the agent, and $s_t^*$ is given by (10). The term $\rho_{t+1}^{(q\text{B})} = \alpha(r\phi_t)^{\alpha-1}$ is the marginal product of capital in the "bad" state, when the realized state is $j > n_t$ and no risky investment pays off; $\rho_{t+1}^{(q\text{G})} = \alpha(RF_t + r\phi_t)^{\alpha-1}$ applies in the "good state," that is, when the realized state is $j \leq n_t$. Simple maximization gives

$$\phi_t^* = \frac{(1 - n_t)R}{R - rn_t} s_t^* \tag{13}$$

and

$$F_t^{j,*} = \begin{cases} F_t^* \equiv \dfrac{R - r}{R - rn_t} s_t^* & \forall j \leq n_t \\ 0 & \forall j > n_t \end{cases} \tag{14}$$

Figure 3 expresses the aggregate demand for each risky asset, $aF^*(n_t)$, as a function of the proportion of securities that are offered, which is obtained by aggregating (14) over all agents. Demand for *each asset* grows as the measure of open sectors increases because when more securities are available, the risk diversification opportunities improve and consumers become willing to reduce their investments in the safe asset and increase

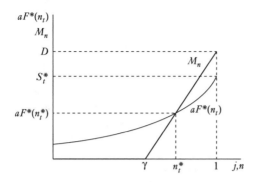

**Figure 3**  Static equilibrium

their investments in risky projects. Equations (10), (13), and (14) completely characterize the second-stage decision rules of savers.

Let us also introduce an additional assumption, which will be discussed below.

ASSUMPTION 1   $R \geq (2 - \gamma)r$.

The following proposition characterizes the static equilibrium conditional on $K_t$.

PROPOSITION 1  *Suppose that assumption 1 holds and let*

$$n_t^*(K_t) =$$

$$\begin{cases} \dfrac{(R + r\gamma) - \left\{(R + r\gamma)^2 - 4r\left[(R - r)(1 - \gamma)\frac{\Gamma}{D}K_t^\alpha + \gamma R\right]\right\}^{1/2}}{2r} & \text{if } K_t \leq \left(\frac{D}{\Gamma}\right)^{1/\alpha} \\[4mm] 1 & \text{if } K_t > \left(\frac{D}{\Gamma}\right)^{1/\alpha} \end{cases}$$

*where $\Gamma \equiv A(1 - \alpha)[\beta/(1 + \beta)]$. Then there exists a unique equilibrium such that, in the first stage, for all $h \in \Omega_t$, either $Z_{h,t}^* = \emptyset$ or $Z_{h,t}^* = (j, 1)$, where $j \in [0, n_t^*]$; and, for all $j \in [0, n_t^*]$, there exists $h \in \Omega_t$ such that $Z_{h,t}^* = (j, 1)$. In the second stage,*

$$s_t^* = \frac{\beta}{1 + \beta}\frac{(1 - \alpha)AK_t}{a}$$

*and $\phi_t^*$ and $F_t^{j*}$ are given by (13) and (14). Factor returns are given by (3) and (4).*

This equilibrium is expressed as the intersection of the aggregate demand of each risky asset, $aF^*(n_t)$, with the thick curve that traces minimum size requirements in figure 3. When $K_t > (D/\Gamma)^{1/\alpha}$, aggregate savings $S_t^* \geq D$, there are sufficient funds to open all the projects, and $n_t^* = 1$. In contrast, when aggregate savings $S_t^* (= as_t^*) < D$, $n_t^*(K_t) < 1$. In this case, only projects in $[0, n_t^*(K_t)]$ are open. The intuition for why $n_t^*(K_t)$ is the equilibrium is given by the figure. If an agent proposed to open one more sector, each agent would invest more in risky projects but not sufficiently to cover the minimum size requirement of the next project because minimum size requirements grow faster than asset demands. But for all $n < n_t^*$, an agent can offer to open one more project, raise enough funds, and make some positive profit $v$; thus the equilibrium must be at $n_t^*$.

Assumption 1 is important in ensuring uniqueness.[5] In figure 3, when $S_t^* < D$, there is only one intersection; thus the equilibrium is unique irrespective of this assumption. However, if $R < (2 - \gamma)r$ and $S_t^* \geq D$, $aF^*(n_t)$ would cross $M_n$ twice, and there would be multiple equilibria: although the amount of savings is sufficient to open all sectors so $n_t^* = 1$ is an equilibrium, there will also exist another equilibrium: each agent, expecting others to invest part of their savings in the safe asset, reduces his investment in the risky projects; therefore, there are not sufficient funds to open all risky projects. Assumption 1 rules out this possibility. In section 5, we shall show that when financial coalitions are allowed, this coordination failure equilibrium can be ruled out and assumption 1 is unnecessary. Until then, it simplifies out exposition.

## 3.4. The dynamic equilibrium path

Proposition 1 characterizes the equilibrium allocation and prices for given $K_t$. To obtain the full stochastic equilibrium process, the equilibrium law of motion of $K_t$ needs to be determined. From (3), (10), (13), and (14), this stochastic process is obtained as

$$
K_{t+1} = \begin{cases} \dfrac{r(1 - n_t^*)}{R - rn_t^*} R\Gamma K_t^\alpha & \text{prob. } 1 - n_t^* \\[2em] R\Gamma K_t^\alpha & \text{prob. } n_t^* \end{cases} \tag{16}
$$

where $n_t^* = n^*(K_t)$ is given by (15). The capital stock follows a Markov process in which the level of capital next period depends on whether the economy is lucky in the current period (which happens when the risky investments pay off, with probability $n_t^*$). Moreover, the probability of this event changes over time. As the economy develops, it can afford to open more sectors, and the probability of transferring a large capital stock to the next period, $n_t^*$, increases. Also from (16), the expected productivity of an economy depends on its level of development and diversification. To see this, define expected "total factor productivity" (conditional on the proportion of sector open) by

$$
\sigma^e(n^*(K_t)) = (1 - n^*)\frac{r(1 - n^*)}{R - rn^*} R + n^* R \tag{17}
$$

Simple differentiation establishes that as $n_t^*$ increases, this measure also increases.

To formalize the dynamics of development, we define the following concepts:

(i)  QSSB: The "quasi steady state" of an economy that *always has unlucky draws*. An economy would converge to this quasi steady state if it follows the optimal investments characterized above but the sectors invested never pay off because of bad luck.

(ii)  QSSG: The "quasi steady state" of an economy that *always receives good news*.

The capital stocks of these two quasi steady states are (figure 4)

$$K^{QSSB} = \left\{ \frac{r[1 - n^*(K^{QSSB})]}{R - rn^*(K^{QSSB})} R\Gamma \right\}^{1/(1-\alpha)}$$

$$K^{QSSG} = (R\Gamma)^{1/(1-\alpha)} \tag{18}$$

If uncertainty could be completely removed, that is, $n(K^{QSSG}) = 1$, then there would never be bad news, and the good quasi steady state would be a real steady state; a point, if reached, from which the economy would never depart. From equations (15) and (18), the condition for this steady state to exist is that the saving level corresponding to $K^{QSSG}$ be sufficient to ensure a balanced portfolio of investments, of at least $D$, in all the intermediate sectors. Thus if

$$D < \Gamma^{1/(1-\alpha)} R^{\alpha/(1-\alpha)} \tag{19}$$

a steady state will exist, which we denote by $K^{SS}$.

Next, note that at very low levels of capital (region I in figure 4), the Inada conditions of the production function guarantee positive growth even conditional on bad news (both curves lie above the 45-degree line). Then there is a range (region II) in which growth occurs conditional on only good draws (the bad-draws curve is below the 45-degree line). Regions I and II are separated by $K^{QSSB}$. Although this level of capital is not a steady state, it is a point around which the economy will spend some time. When they are below this level, all economies will grow toward it. When they are above this level, their output will fall when they receive bad shocks, and the probability of bad news is very high when the economy has a level of capital stock just above $K^{QSSB}$. Yet, as good news is received, the capital stock will grow and the probability of a further

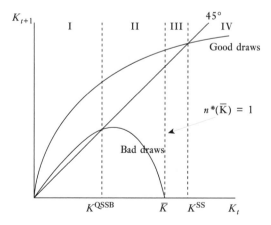

**Figure 4**   Capital accumulation

lucky draw will increase.[6] Note that even when it grows, the economy is still exposed to large undiversified risks and will typically experience some setbacks. Finally, provided that (19) is satisfied, the economy will eventually enter region III, where all idiosyncratic risks will be removed (since all sectors are open and an equal amount is invested in all sectors), and there will be deterministic convergence to $K^{SS}$. We have the following proposition.

PROPOSITION 2   *Suppose that (19) is satisfied. Then*

$$\operatorname*{p\,lim}_{t\to\infty} K_t = K^{SS}$$

As figure 4 suggests, when (19) is satisfied, the equilibrium stochastic process has a unique ergodic set, which in this case is just a point, $K^{SS}$ (a previous version of the paper, available on request, has preferences that lead to nonergodic dynamics and underdevelopment traps). Therefore, takeoff will occur almost surely, though it will take longer and may be painfully slow for countries that are unfortunate.

## 3.5. *Variability of growth rates*

To determine what happens to the variability of performance over the development process, the natural variable to look at is the conditional variance of the total factor productivity defined above. Let $\sigma(n^*(K_t))$ be a random variable that takes the values

$$r\left(\frac{1 - n_t^*}{R - rn_t^*}\right)R \qquad \text{and} \qquad R$$

with respective probabilities $1 - n^*$ and $n^*$. The mean of this random variable is given by (17). Then, taking logs, we can rewrite (16) as

$$\Delta \log(K_{t+1}) = \log \Gamma + (\alpha - 1) \log(K_t) + \log[\sigma(n^*(K_t))] \tag{20}$$

It is clear from this equation that capital (and output) growth volatility, after removal of the deterministic "convergence effects" induced by the neoclassical technology, will be entirely determined by the stochastic component $\sigma$. Define the variance of $\sigma$ given $K_t$ as $V_n$. We want to determine how this volatility measure evolves as a function of $n^*$ (and $K$). Two forces have to be considered:

(i)   as the economy develops, more savings are invested in risky assets; and
(ii)  as more sectors are opened, idiosyncratic risks are better diversified.

PROPOSITION 3

$$V_n \equiv \operatorname{var}[\sigma(n^*, \cdot) \mid n^*] = n^*(1 - n^*)\left[R\left(\frac{R - r}{R - rn^*}\right)\right]^2$$

(a) If $\gamma \geq R/(2R-r)$, then $\partial V_n/\partial K_t \leq 0$, for all $K_t$.
(b) If $\gamma < R/(2R-r)$, then there exists $K'$ such that $n^*(K') = R/(2R-r) < 1$ and

$$\frac{\partial V_n}{\partial K_t} \begin{cases} \leq 0 & \forall K_t \geq K' \\ > 0 & \forall K_t < K' \end{cases}$$

Therefore, our model predicts that the variance of the growth rate is uniformly decreasing with the size of the accumulated capital (case a) if either $\gamma$ is large enough or the productivity of risky projects is sufficiently higher than that of the safe asset. Otherwise, variability exhibits an inverse U-shaped relation with respect to the capital stock (case b) and is decreasing for $K_t$ large enough. In either case, the prediction of our model is that at the later stages of development variability is decreasing in the level of income.

## 3.6. Are the effects quantitatively significant?

Our theoretical analysis so far has established that the interaction between micro indivisibilities and risk aversion leads to a slow and random path of development. An economy fluctuates in a state of low productivity before achieving full diversification and higher productivity. How important and long-lasting are these effects? Although a more detailed analysis of this issue is left for future research, some simple calibrations would give a sense of the empirical relevance of our theory. With this purpose, we now use some reasonable parameter values to compute how many periods it takes for a set of simulated economies to start from $K^{\mathrm{QSSB}}$, the quasi steady state conditional on bad draws, and reach "full diversification."

We shall study three cases, characterized by different degrees of diminishing returns to capital (the only accumulable factor in our economy), $\alpha$. In the three series of experiments, we shall set $\alpha$ equal to 0.35, 0.5, and 0.65, respectively. The population size will be the same in all economies, and in all cases we shall have $R = 2, \gamma = 0.25$, and $\Gamma = 2$. The parameter $r$ will be chosen so as to have

$$\frac{Y^{\mathrm{SS}}}{L} = 15\left(\frac{Y^{\mathrm{QSSB}}}{L}\right)$$

This means that the steady-state income per capita is 15 times larger than the income of an economy that always receives bad draws. The 15-fold difference corresponds, approximately, to the gap between the U.S. per capita income and that of an average low-income country (e.g., Senegal) in 1985. To keep this gap constant across the three series of experiments, we choose $r$ equal to 0.019, 0.184, and 0.6, respectively. Furthermore, we adjust the size of the parameter $D$ so as to ensure that in all cases $n(K^{\mathrm{SS}}) = 1$ – that is, $D < \Gamma^{1/(1-\alpha)} R^{\alpha/(1-\alpha)}$ – and that the distance between $K^{\mathrm{SS}}$ and the minimum capital level corresponding to full diversification is "small."[7]

For each of the three parameter configurations, we run 100 simulations and calculate a number of statistics on the speed of convergence to full diversification (to $K$ such that $n(K) = 1$). Each simulation is associated with a different independent sequence of random realizations drawn from the uniform distribution over [0, 1]. The summary results are reported in table 3.

In column 1, we report the average number of periods the set of simulated economies take to go from the initial condition (bad quasi steady state) to full diversification. Column 2 reports the standard deviation of this number of periods across the 100 experiments. Column 3 reports the number of periods that the tenth-fastest and the tenth-slowest economies take to reach full diversification. Finally, column 4 reports how long an economy that always receives favorable draws would require to complete the transition. Given the structure of the model, this is identical to the time an economy subject to no indivisibilities would take to converge to full diversification.

The results show that in all cases the effects of indivisibilities are rather long-lasting, though less so when there are strong diminishing returns to capital. We can assess the importance of nonconvexities on the dynamics of growth by comparing the convergence speed of the deterministic neoclassical model (col. 4) with the average convergence speed in our model (col. 1) under the same parameters. The convergence speed decreases by a factor of three when $\alpha = 0.35$, by a factor of five when $\alpha = 0.5$, and by a factor of 10 when $\alpha = 0.65$. It is also interesting to observe that the differences between the transition length of lucky versus unlucky countries (col. 3) are very large. For instance, in all cases the tenth-most unlucky country would take more than three times as long to "industrialize" as the tenth-luckiest economy. Overall, under reasonable parameters, the effects described by this model appear very persistent and quantitatively significant.

**Table 3**   Simulations: Speed of convergence

| Case | Mean (T) (1) | Standard deviation (T) (2) | [$Q_t$ (10 %), $Q_t$ (90%)] (3) | min [T] (4) |
|------|------|------|------|------|
| $\alpha = .35$ | 19.47 | 11.56 | [7, 30] | 6 |
| $\alpha = .50$ | 44.91 | 23.67 | [21, 72] | 9 |
| $\alpha = .65$ | 116.24 | 63.04 | [65, 195] | 11 |

## 4. Optimal Portfolio Choice and Inefficiency

In this section we shall explain why the equilibrium of section 3 is not Pareto-optimal and characterize the optimal portfolio decision. To focus on our main interest, we shall deal only with the issue of static efficiency. We shall therefore consider the portfolio allocation that a social planner maximizing the welfare of the current generation of savers would choose, taking the amount of savings as given.[8] In contrast, in the decentralized equilibrium, $\mathcal{J}_t$ (thus $n_t$) will also be a choice variable, $F_t^j$ no longer has to equal $F_t^j$, and the marginal product of capital in different states is no longer taken as parametric. It is straightforward to see that the subset of projects in which the planner will invest will have the form $\mathcal{J}^{FB} = [0, n^{FB}]$. Therefore, subject to feasibility, she will solve

$$\max_{n_t, \phi_t, [F_t^j]_{0 \le j \le n_t}} \int_0^{n_t} \log\left(RF_t^j + r\phi_t\right)dj + (1 - n_t)\log(r\phi_t) \tag{21}$$

This maximization problem leads to the following result.

**Proposition 4**    *Let $n^*(K_t)$ be given by (15) and let $S_t^* = as_t^*$ denote total savings. Then, for all $S_t^* < D$,*

$$n^{FB}(K_t) > n^*(K_t)$$

$$\phi^{FB}(K_t) < \phi^*(K_t)$$

*and each agent receives the following portfolio of assets:*

$$\exists \, j_t^* < n^{FB}(S_t^*) \text{ s.t. } F_t^{j,\,FB} = \begin{cases} \dfrac{M_j^*}{a} > \dfrac{M_j}{a} & \text{if } j_t < j_t^* \\[2mm] \dfrac{M_j}{a} & \text{if } n^{FB}(K_t) \geq j_t \geq j_t^* \\[2mm] 0 & \text{if } j_t > n^{FB}(K_t) \end{cases} \tag{22}$$

*And for all $S_t^* \geq D, n^{FB}(K_t) = n^*(K_t)$ and $F_t^{j,\,FB} = S_t^*/a$, for all $j$.*

Figure 5 gives the diagrammatic form of the first-best portfolio (represented by the shaded area). The qualitative properties of the first-best portfolio are similar to that in the decentralized equilibrium. The dynamics of the economy are still characterized by three stages: primitive accumulation, takeoff, and steady growth. But progress is faster on average because a larger share of savings is invested in high-productivity risky projects. The transition equation looks considerably more complicated than (16) because the total return is different in each state.

The reason for the failure of the decentralized economy to reach the first-best allocation is a *pecuniary externality* due to missing markets. As an additional sector opens, all existing projects become more attractive relative to the safe asset because the amount of undiversified risks they carry is reduced, and as a result, risk-averse agents are more willing to buy

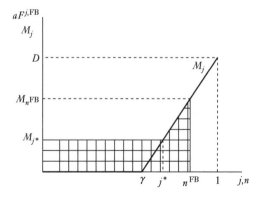

**Figure 5**    Pareto–optimal portfolio

the existing securities. Since each agent ignores his impact on others' diversification opportunities, the externality is not internalized. It is important to reiterate at this point that in this model markets are not assumed to be missing; instead, the range of open markets is endogenously determined in equilibrium.

The pecuniary externality is not internalized in our economy because project level indivisibilities make the aggregate production set nonconvex (this is also the reason why lotteries would not be useful in this setting). As a result, a full Arrow–Debreu equilibrium does not exist. A full Arrow–Debreu equilibrium is defined as a price mapping $P^A : [0, 1] \rightarrow \mathbb{R}^+$ that assigns a price to each commodity (project) in each time period such that, for all $j \in [0, 1]$ such that $P_t^{A_j} > 0$, the excess demand for security $j$ at time $t$, $\mathrm{ed}_t^j(P_t^A)$, is equal to zero, and for all $j \in [0, 1]$ such that $P_t^{A_j} = 0$, $\mathrm{ed}_t^j(P_t^A) \leq 0$. Note that this concept of equilibrium assigns a price level to all commodities irrespective of whether they are being traded.

The nonexistence of a full Arrow–Debreu equilibrium can be explained in terms of supply and demand. For a sector with a positive minimum size requirement, the supply is discontinuous, because if $x$ is less than the minimum size requirement, $x$ units of this security cannot be supplied at any price. This is the reason why a decentralized equilibrium exists only conditional on the set of open sectors. This result is related to the general equilibrium literature with endogenous commodity spaces (Hart, 1979; Makowski, 1980), which, for the same reason, uses weaker versions of the Arrow–Debreu equilibrium similar to our equilibrium concept. The equilibrium concept we use captures all the salient features of a competitive situation. In particular, in our equilibrium, all agents are price takers, there is unfettered competition at all stages, and all the gains from trade that can be exploited via a decentralized trading procedure are exploited. The main distinction is that the requirement that markets that are closed must have $\mathrm{ed}_t^j(P_t) \leq 0$ at $P_t^j = 0$ is replaced by the condition that the number of open markets is determined by a forward-looking and fully rational free-entry condition.[9]

To conclude, also note that government policy can restore efficiency by subsidizing large projects. It is interesting that this policy appears similar to the industrial policies sometimes adopted at the earlier stages of development, for instance the policy of the German government that, despite the absence of any obvious technological spillovers, subsidized large undertakings at the expense of light industries (Gerschenkron, 1962, p. 15; Cameron, 1972).

## 5. Inefficiency with Alternative Structures

### 5.1. General motivation

Would the market failure in portfolio choices be overcome if some financial institution could coordinate agents' investment decisions? Imagine that rather than all agents acting in isolation and ignoring their impact on each others' decisions – which is the source of inefficiency in section 3 – funds are invested through a financial intermediary. This intermediary can collect all the savings and offer to each saver a *complex* security (different from a basic Arrow security) that pays

$$RF_t^{j,\mathrm{FB}} + r\phi_t^{\mathrm{FB}}$$

in each state $j$, where $F_t^{j,\text{FB}}$ and $\phi_t^{\text{FB}}$ are as described in proposition 4. Holding this security would make each consumer better off compared to the equilibrium of proposition 1. Although from this discussion it could appear that the inefficiency we identified may not be robust to the formation of more complex financial institutions, we shall show that this is not the case. Unless some rather strong assumptions are made about the set of contracts that a financial intermediary can offer, the unique equilibrium allocation with unfettered competition among intermediaries will be identical to the one we characterized in proposition 1.

The role of financial intermediaries and coalitions in overcoming various types of trade frictions and informational imperfections has been studied by a number of authors, e.g., Townsend (1978, 1983), Boyd and Prescott (1986), Greenwood and Jovanovic (1990), Greenwood and Smith (1993). The approach followed in this subsection closely resembles that of Townsend (1983), who also constructs a multistage game in order to model how coalitions of agents will form to internalize some of the externalities of imperfect information and to reduce the costs of trade. However, in contrast to these papers, in our economy financial coalitions will not be able to restore efficiency.

## 5.2. Coalitions as investment funds

In order to model endogenous formation of coalitions, we now assume that savings can be intermediated by agents who decide to act as middlemen and run an *investment fund*. Put differently, some agents initiate the formation of a coalition of agents that buys securities on behalf of its members. In return, participants in the financial coalition can be charged an intermediation fee, $\bar{v}$. Projects are still run by agents. We now introduce the following three assumptions for our coalition formation game.

ASSUMPTION 2   *An agent cannot be part of two coalitions at the same time.*

ASSUMPTION 3   *Coalitions at all points maximize a weighted utility of their members. In particular, a coalition cannot commit to a path of action that will be against the interests of its members in the continuation game.*

ASSUMPTION 4   *Coalitions cannot exclude other agents (or coalitions) from investing in a particular project.*

Assumption 2 is introduced to simplify the objective function of coalitions; see Townsend (1983) for more discussion of the case in which agents belong to multiple coalitions. As discussed below, our results hold when this assumption is relaxed. The most important assumption for our purposes is assumption 3. We view this as a very natural restriction along the lines of subgame perfection, and its importance will be discussed further below. Assumption 4 is also mainly expositional. We shall see that as long as assumption 3 holds, *coalitions would never want to exclude others*, and thus this assumption is imposed only to simplify the exposition.

Formally, the game played among the savers at time $t$ now has three stages. To simplify the notation, we shall suppress time subscripts. In the first stage, each agent $h \in \Omega$ can announce that he is willing to act as an intermediary for a specified set of agents $\Theta_h$ (where

$\Theta_h \in Y$, the set of all subsets of $\Omega$, and we define $\mu$ as the Lebesque measure over $Y$). In general, only a subset of agents belonging to $\Theta_h$ will accept the offer of the intermediary. Let $\Theta_h^a \subseteq \Theta_h$ denote this subset of agents. Note that because of assumption 2, in equilibrium, $Y$ will be partitioned into disjoint coalitions. The intermediary $h$ will invest the savings he collects in the shares of both risky and safe projects so as to maximize the total utility of the agents belonging to $\Theta_h^a$. A first-stage strategy for agent $h$ is an announcement

$$Z_h^{(1)} = (\bar{V}_h, \Theta_h) \in \mathbb{R}^+ \times Y$$

If agent $h$ announces that he will not act as an intermediary, then $Z_h^{(1)} = \varnothing$. Among the possible nonnull announcements, there is autarky; that is, $Z_h^{(1)} = (0, \{h\})$, which means that $h$ will intermediate only (at most) his own savings. Finally, we denote the set of first-stage announcements of all agents by

$$Z^{(1)} : \Omega \to \mathbb{R}^+ \times Y$$

In the second stage, each agent $h \in \Omega$ can announce his plan to run at most one project and sell the corresponding basic Arrow security; that is, $h$ announces a pair $(j, P_{j,h})$, as in the game discussed in section 3. But now, securities are sold to financial intermediaries rather than directly to agents. Formally, the second-stage announcement for agent $h$ is

$$Z_h^{(2)} = (j, P_{j,h}) \in [0, 1] \times \mathbb{R}^+$$

and

$$Z^{(2)} : \Omega \to [0, 1] \times \mathbb{R}^+$$

is the set of all second-period announcements. We shall also denote the set of minimum security prices announced in the second stage of the game by $P = \{P_{j \in \mathcal{J}}^j\}$ (see section 3).

In the third stage, each agent takes the set of prior announcements, $Z^{(1)}$ and $Z^{(2)}$, as given and chooses which coalition to join. Or, equivalently, $Z_h^{(3)}$ is $h$'s choice of an intermediary from

$$M_h\left[Z^{(1)}\right] \equiv \{i \in \Omega | Z_i^{(1)} = (\bar{V}_i, \Theta_i) h \in \Theta_i\}$$

the set of coalitions that announced his name. Note that although the set $M_h[Z^{(1)}]$ could be empty, this will never be the case in equilibrium, since any agent can costlessly make the *autarky* announcement in the first stage. Finally, after all agents announce which coalition-intermediary they will belong to, *each intermediary makes the optimal investment decision.* We still use the notation $\phi_h$ and $F_h^j$ to denote the investment of an agent (through a coalition) in the safe and risky assets. More precisely, if a coalition $\Theta$ invests $F_\Theta^j$ in project $j$, then $F_h^j$ will be the share of agent $h$ in this coalition times $F_\Theta^j$.

DEFINITION 2    *A perfect equilibrium is a set of announcements*

$$Z^* = \left( Z^{(1)*}, Z^{(2)*}, Z^{(3)*} \right)$$

*at each stage of the game; a price function $P^*(Z^*)$ for all basic Arrow securities; a saving decision $s_h^*(Z^*)$; induced holdings of the safe asset $\phi_h^*(Z^*)$ and securities $F_h^{j*}(Z^*)$ for all agents; and factor payments $W^*$ and $\rho^*$ such that, given the announcements of the previous stage(s) and the announcements of all other agents in the current stage, every agent chooses $Z_h^{(i)}$ that maximizes his utility as given by (5) and factor returns are determined by (3) and (4).*

Note that the definition of equilibrium used so far was also subgame perfect. Here we emphasize perfection in order to reiterate the importance of assumption 3 in our analysis.

## 5.3. Equilibrium with coalitions

The first observation is that free entry will drive profits (commissions) to zero in both the first and second stages. This is established by the following lemma (proof omitted).

LEMMA 2    *In equilibrium,*

(i)   $P^{j,*}(Z^*) = 1$, *for all $j$, and*
(ii)  $\bar{\nu}_h = 0$, *for all $h \in \Omega$.*

With this remark, it is now possible to establish the following proposition.

PROPOSITION 5    *The set of (perfect) equilibria is nonempty, and all allocations in this set have the following characteristics:*

(1)  *For all $h \in \Omega$, $M_h \neq \emptyset$ (all agents are included in some coalition).*
(2)  *Let $n_t^*$ be defined as in (15). Then, for all $h \in \Omega$, either $Z_h^{(2)*} = \emptyset$ or $Z_h^{(2)*} = (j, 1)$, where $j \in [0, n_t^*]$. And for all $j \in [0, n_t^*]$, there exists $h \in \Omega$ such that $Z_h^{(2)}* = (j, 1)$.*
(3)  *In the third stage, all coalitions $\Theta_h^a \neq \emptyset$ will choose a portfolio that induces $\phi_t^*$ and $F_i^{j*} = F_i^*$ as given by equations (13) and (14).*

The most important feature of this set of equilibria is that they all give rise to the same allocation as the competitive equilibrium of section 3. Note in particular that *the first-best allocation is not an equilibrium* of the game with intermediaries, whereas one of the equilibria has $\Theta_h = \{h\}$ for all $h$; that is, *all agents choose autarky*, which is identical to the situation without intermediaries (i.e., proposition 1). First, consider an allocation in which there is only one active intermediary, a "grand coalition" of all savers (i.e., $Z_{h^g}^{(1)} = (0, \Omega)$ for one agent $h^g$, and $Z_h^{(1)} = \emptyset$ for all $h \neq h^g$), which will invest in the optimal portfolio in the third stage of the game. If all agents agree to take part in this grand coalition, then the resulting allocation would be Pareto-optimal. However, an agent $h' \neq h^g$ can do better by announcing $Z_{h'}^{(1)} = (0, \{h'\})$ and holding a balanced portfolio of all the available assets since in the second stage he cannot be excluded from investing his savings in the traded securities, $\mathcal{J}^{FB}$. Because only one agent has deviated, what the grand coalition can achieve has not changed. Therefore, maximizing the utility of its remaining members, $\Omega/h'$, the grand coalition will choose to open $\mathcal{J}^{FB}$, and its members will have utility $U^{FB}$. On the other hand, $h'$ could hold a balanced portfolio of all $j \in \mathcal{J}^{FB}$ and would get utility $U_{h'} > U^{FB}$. Therefore, all agents would prefer to deviate, and the first-best portfolio cannot be sustained as an equilibrium. The intuition for why the grand coalition is not successful is that it is trying to induce its members to hold a portfolio that *cross-subsidizes* large projects by investing more in them than in small projects. But, from lemma 1, when each agent takes the set of traded securities as given, he prefers to hold a balanced portfolio; thus any agent $h'$ can *free-ride* by not becoming part of this coalition and investing his funds individually in the form of a *balanced portfolio*. This intuition also reveals why coalitions could deal with market failures much more effectively in the previous analyses. In the studies referenced above (e.g., Townsend, 1983; Boyd and Prescott, 1986), there was no issue of free-riding or cross-subsidization; therefore, all agents wanted to belong to some coalition to avoid informational problems or economize on transaction costs. In contrast, here they can free-ride by not taking part in the coalition that invests in large projects.

Next, consider the allocation in which every agent intermediates his own funds and invests them in a balanced portfolio as in proposition 1. A coalition, $\Theta_{h'}$, of a positive measure of agents could improve on this allocation by carrying out some degree of cross-subsidization, that is, by holding an unbalanced portfolio. However, if we start from complete autarky and $h'$ announces $Z_{h'}^{(1)} = (\nu_{h'}, \Theta_{h'})$, not to join $\Theta_{h'}$ is a dominant strategy for all $h'' \in \Theta_{h'}$. Intuitively, given *any third-stage choice* of all other agents belonging to $\Theta_{h'}$, $h''$ would find it optimal to let other members do the cross-subsidization and just free-ride on their actions by choosing a balanced portfolio. Note that autarky (each agent intermediating his own funds) is not the unique equilibrium. Other equilibria also exist, but they all lead to exactly the same allocation as in proposition 1.

It is worth noting that if assumption 2 were relaxed, the results would not change. Irrespective of whether they have to belong to only one coalition or not, given assumptions 3 and 4, agents would always free-ride by not joining any coalition that holds an unbalanced portfolio. Thus first-best would never be sustained and autarky would remain an equilibrium.

There is, however, one difference between the equilibrium of proposition 1 and the one here. In proposition 1, without assumption 1, multiple equilibria were possible for $S_t^* \geq D$. In one equilibrium, all risky projects would be open and all the idiosyncratic risks would be diversified ($n_t = 1$ and $\phi_t = 0$); in another, $n_t$ would be less than one (and $\phi_t > 0$). It is straightforward to see that in this case, the equilibrium with all sectors open is Pareto-superior. Now if, instead of the decentralized equilibrium concept of definition 1, we used the coalitional approach of this section, the equilibrium with $\phi_t > 0$ would disappear because the coordination failure that led to this equilibrium would be prevented by the entry of an intermediary proposing the grand coalition and offering a riskless portfolio with return $R$. Since in this case the grand coalition also holds a balanced portfolio, there is no scope for free-riding and all agents would agree to take part. Therefore, although the formation of coalitions does not enable cross-subsidization to be sustained in equilibrium, it can avoid other sources of inefficiency such as coordination failures.

## 5.4. Robustness under alternative assumptions

This discussion also suggests that there are some alternative assumptions under which the first-best portfolio could be implemented as a decentralized equilibrium.

First, it is easy to see that if a coalition can commit to a *nonsubgame perfect path of action*, then the first-best can be implemented by a grand coalition of all savers. For instance, imagine that the grand coalition can commit to the following course of action: If all agents join (i.e., $\Theta_{GC} = \Omega$), then we invest in $\mathcal{J}^{FB}$. If even only one agent does not join (i.e., $\Theta_{GC} \neq \Omega$), then $\phi_t = s_t$; that is, all savings are invested in the safe asset. In this case, agent $h'$, who contemplates free-riding, will realize that by opting out of the grand coalition, he would not get a balanced portfolio of $[0, n_t^{FB}]$ but one that has a low rate of return that is naturally dominated by taking part in the grand coalition. Therefore, this type of commitment can implement the first-best. However, this is a commitment to take a course of action that would hurt all the members of the coalition. If, after $h'$'s deviation, the members had the option to revise their plans, they would *always* prefer to do so and invest in an unbalanced portfolio of $n^{FB}$ assets. Consequently, we view such a commitment as extremely strong and noncredible.

Second, consider relaxing assumption 4. In particular, suppose that coalitions can buy up projects and *exclude* all other intermediaries from investing in the projects they control. Then the grand coalition can form and make potential members a *take-it-or-leave-it* offer of the following form: Either you invest all your savings in this coalition or you will be excluded. This arrangement would sustain the first-best portfolio as an equilibrium. However, such exclusion would again run into credibility problems. To see why, consider a deviation from the grand coalition such that agent $h'$ offers to form a coalition for a set of agents $\Theta_{h'}$ with $0 < \mu(\Theta_{h'}) < \frac{1}{2}$. After this deviation, the new coalition $\Theta_{h'}$ offers to invest part of its funds in the high-minimum size projects controlled by $\Omega \backslash \Theta_{h'}$. At this stage, as in the previous case discussed above, it is in the interest of all the members of $\Omega \backslash \Theta_{h'}$ to accept these investments, because otherwise they will have to run many fewer projects and bear a lot more risk. If these investments by $\Theta_{h'}$ are accepted, then the members of $\Theta_{h'}$ are better off than they would have been in the grand coalition. Therefore, again, unless $\Omega$ can commit to a path of behavior that does not maximize its members' utility in the continuation game, there is a profitable deviation that breaks the first-best allocation. This argument shows that, as long as assumption 3 holds, assumption 4 is not important in deriving the results of this section.

As well as raising credibility/commitment issues we have just discussed, both cases sketched above have the unrealistic implication that only one large intermediary would be active in equilibrium. With more realistic intermediation technologies (e.g., increasing average operational costs for the intermediaries), not even these strong commitments would be sufficient to implement the first-best allocation. Therefore, this section establishes that the cross-subsidization of large projects that is required for an efficient allocation is extremely hard to achieve even when coalitions and intermediaries are allowed to form freely.

## 6. International Capital Flows

In this section, we extend our model to a two-country world. Since capital shortages play a crucial role, it is important to understand whether a world of many countries behaves as a single economy or whether there would be more subtle interactions between these countries. The results will depend on the extent of capital mobility and trade. There are many different ways of modeling the interactions of two countries in this setting, and we choose the following:

(1) The final good is tradable. This has two implications. First, there is full capital (savings) mobility in the sense that agents can invest their savings in the assets offered in any country.[10] Second, final output produced in country $i$ can be consumed in country $i'$.

(2) Intermediate goods cannot be traded or transported from one country to another. Thus if intermediate good $j$ is produced in country $i$, it has to be used in the final-good sector of country $i$.

Also, both countries face identical technologies and uncertainty as described in section 3; in particular, if the (world) state of nature is $j$, then only sectors $j_1$ and $j_2$ are productive, where $j_i$ is sector $j$ in country $i$. As an example, imagine the case in which it is not known whether railways are a good investment; if they are, then they will have high returns in both countries. These assumptions imply that there are two forces to be taken into account when comparing the profitability of investments in two different countries: *risk diversification* and *differential prices for intermediate goods*. To see how these two forces work, consider two closed economies such that country 1 has a larger stock of savings than country 2. According to proposition 1, country 1 has both more open sectors – that is, there will be some sector $j'$ that is open in country 1 but not in country 2 – and a larger amount of intermediate goods in (at least) all realizations in which one of the open projects is successful. Given the production function (2), the marginal product of investment in country 2 will be higher. Now, introduce capital mobility. Ideally, agents would have liked to invest all their savings in one country and then transfer half of the produced intermediate goods to the other, thus maximizing both diversification and productivity. But this is not possible because intermediate goods are not traded. In terms of the example suggested above, if all railway investments are in country 1 and they are successful, the final-good production of country 2 will not benefit from this success. Therefore, there will be a trade-off between a force that tends to collect funds in one country (the diversification motive) and another that pushes toward more spread-out investments (the decreasing marginal product of capital). In the remainder of this section, we shall set up the maximization problem of an agent $h$ (which will be the same problem irrespective of where the individual lives); then we shall prove that in this context a modified "balanced portfolio" condition will hold (lemma 3). The equilibrium solution will be characterized in proposition 6. The key results of this section are that, first, the general features of equilibrium derived in the previous section will continue to hold with international capital flows, and, second, at the early stages of development, international capital flows will serve to increase the GDP of one of the countries relative to the world average (*divergence*) but will later contribute to faster *convergence*.

The definition of equilibrium is the same as in section 3, and all agents can announce to run any of the intermediate sector firms of this world economy. Also to simplify notation, we drop time subscripts throughout this section. The total mass of agents in the world is $2a$, and agents are equally distributed between the two countries. Each agent is free to invest his funds in any combination of the two safe assets and $2 \times [0, 1]$ risky assets. It is straightforward to see that free entry implies $P^*_{j_i} = 1$, for all $j_i \in \mathcal{J}_i$, $i = 1, 2$; thus all traded securities will be sold at the unit price (we drop time subscripts). Also, in each country, small sectors will open before larger ones, so $\mathcal{J}_i = [0, n_i]$. Then, without loss of any generality, we suppose that a larger (or equal) number of projects are open in country 1 ($n_1 \geq n_2$). Since all agents can buy any security issued in either country, the portfolio choice that maximizes the utility of an agent $h \in \Omega_1 \cup \Omega_2$ can be written as

$$
\max_{\phi_{1h}, \phi_{2h}, \{F^j_{1h}\}, \{F^j_{2h}\}} \int_0^{n_2} \log\left[\rho^j_1(r\phi_{1h} + RF^j_{1h}) + \rho^j_2(r\phi_{2h} + RF^j_{2h})\right] dj
$$

$$
+ \int_{n_2}^{n_1} \log\left[\rho^j_1(r\phi_{1h} + RF^j_{1h}) + \rho^j_2(r\phi_{2h})\right] dj \qquad (23)
$$

$$
+ \int_{n_1}^1 \log\left[\rho^j_1(r\phi_{1h}) + \rho^j_2(r\phi_{2h})\right] dj
$$

subject to the constraint

$$
\int_0^{n_1} F^j_{1h} dj + \int_0^{n_2} F^j_{2h} + \phi_{1h} + \phi_{2h} = s^*_h \qquad (24)
$$

where

$$
s^*_h = \frac{\beta}{1+\beta} w_h = \begin{cases} \dfrac{\beta}{1+\beta} \dfrac{(1-\alpha)A[K^{(1)}]^\alpha}{a} & \text{if } h \text{ lives in country 1} \\[3ex] \dfrac{\beta}{1+\beta} \dfrac{(1-\alpha)A[K^{(2)}]^\alpha}{a} & \text{if } h \text{ lives in country 2} \end{cases} \qquad (25)
$$

is the optimal saving of individual $h$ that depends on the wage rate in the country he lives in, and $K^{(i)}$ is the stock of capital inherited by country $i$.

Let us briefly explain the terms that make up (23). Recall that $n_1 \geq n_2$. Then if the realized state of nature is $j \in q_1 \equiv [0, n_2]$, a risky investment in both countries will have a positive payoff. If $j \in q_2 \equiv [n_2, n_1]$, then only risky investments in country 1 will have a positive payoff. Finally, if $j \in q_3 \equiv [n_1, 1]$, no risky projects will be successful. Note also that when making their decisions, all agents take the price of intermediate goods (capital) $\rho$ as given. However, it is important to note that in contrast to section 3, these prices are not necessarily equalized between countries (i.e., $\rho^j_1 \neq \rho^j_2$) because intermediate goods are nontradable. The next lemma parallels lemma 1 of section 3. (The proof of this lemma and the proofs of all the other results in this section are contained in Appendix B, which is available from the authors on request.)

LEMMA 3

(i)   *For all $h$ and for all $j, j' < n_2$, we have*

$$F^j_{1h} = F^{j'}_{1h} \equiv F_{1h} \qquad and \qquad F^j_{2h} = F^{j'}_{2h} \equiv F_{2h}$$

(ii)   *For all h and for all $j, j' \in [n_2, n_1]$, we have*

$$F^j_{1h} = F^{j'}_{1h} \equiv G_h$$

This lemma is a weaker version of lemma 1. If two projects $j$ and $j'$ are open in both countries, then in each country, they should receive the same amount of investment because they have the same probability of success, the same return when they are successful (i.e., $\rho^j_i = \rho^{j'}_i$, and the same equilibrium price. If two projects are open only in country 1, then, with a similar reasoning, they should again receive the same level of investment. Given lemma 3, we can reduce program (23) to

$$\max_{F_{1h}, F_{2h}, G_h, \phi_{1h}, \phi_{2h}} n_2 \log\left[\rho^{(q1)}_1(r\phi_{1h} + RF_{1h}) + \rho^{(q1)}_2(r\phi_{2h} + RF_{2h})\right]$$

$$+(n_1 - n_2) \log\left[\rho^{(q2)}_1(r\phi_{1h} + RG_h) + \rho^{(q2)}_2(r\phi_{2h})\right] \qquad (26)$$

$$+(1 - n_1) \log\left[\rho^{(q3)}_1(r\phi_{1h}) + \rho^{(q3)}_2(r\phi_{2h})\right]$$

subject to

$$n_2(F_{1h} + F_{2h}) + (n_1 - n_2)G_h + \phi_{1h} + \phi_{2h} = s^*_h \qquad (27)$$

where $\rho^{(q_t)}_i$ denotes the price of intermediate goods in country $i$ and in the subject of states $q_t$. For instance,

$$\rho^{(q3)}_1 = \alpha A(r\phi^w_1)^{\alpha-1}$$

and

$$\rho^{(q1)}_2 = \alpha A(r\phi^w_2 + RF^w_2)^{\alpha-1}$$

where $\phi^w_1$ denotes total world investment in the safe asset issued in country 1, $F^w_2$ denotes total world investment in each open sector in country 2, and so forth. By analogy, we define $c^{(q1)}_h$ as the of agent $h$ in states $q_t$. We also let

$$S^w_t = (1 - \alpha)A\left\{[K^{(1)}_t]^\alpha + [K^{(2)}_t]^\alpha\right\}$$

denote the stock of world savings. We can now fully characterize the equilibrium of this two-country world.

PROPOSITION 6. *The unique equilibrium allocation is as follows:*

(i)   *If $n^*_2 < 1$, then*

$$RF_{1h}^* + r\phi_{1h}^* = RF_{2h}^* + r\phi_{2h}^*(\Rightarrow \rho_1^{(q1)} = \rho_2^{(q1)} \equiv \rho^{(q1)})$$

$$\phi_{1h}^* < \phi_{2h}^*(\Rightarrow \rho_1^{(q3)}) \geq \rho_2^{(q3)}$$

*and*

$$G_h^* > F_{1h}^* > F_{2h}^*(\Rightarrow \rho_2^{(q2)} > \rho^{(q1)} > \rho_1^{(q2)}$$

(ii)   *If $n_2^* < 1$, then*

$$c_h^{(q1)} > c_h^{(q2)} > c_h^{(q3)} \qquad \textit{for all } h \in \Omega_1 \cup \Omega_2$$

(iii)   *There exists $\bar{S}^{\mathrm{w}} \in (D, 2D)$ such that*:

*if $S^{\mathrm{w}} < \bar{S}^{\mathrm{w}}$ then $n_2^* < n_1^* < 1$ and $\phi_{1h}^* > 0$*

*if $S^{\mathrm{w}} > \bar{S}^{\mathrm{w}}$, then $n_2^* < n_1^* = 1$ and $\phi_{1h}^* = 0$*

*if $S^{\mathrm{w}} > 2D$, then $n_2^* = n_1^* = 1$.*

The first part of proposition 6 is obtained from the first-order conditions of the program (26)–(27). The general form of the resulting aggregate equilibrium investments is plotted in figure 6 (where $G^{*w} = \int_{\Omega_1 \cup \Omega_2} G_h^* dh$, etc.). The first equality of part (i) ensures that the marginal return of investment is the same in both countries for the subset of states $[0, n_2^*]$. If this were not the case, an agent could increase his return in those states by just reshuffling $F_{1h}$ and $F_{2h}$. To see why $\phi_{1h}^* < \phi_{2h}^*$, note that the insurance role of the safe asset is less important in country 1 than in country 2. Finally, in states $j \in [n_2^*, n_1^*]$, the higher minimum size requirement forces $G_h^* > F_{1h}^*$.

Part (ii) of proposition 6 reveals the most salient features of this equilibrium. In the closed-economy model of section 3, savers always chose a balanced portfolio that gave them the same consumption level in all states of nature (except those states for which they could not buy the associated security). Here, instead, they accept a lower consumption

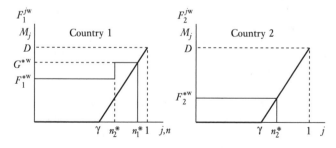

**Figure 6**   A two-country world

when $j \in [n_2^*, n_1^*]$ than when $j \in [0, n_2^*]$, although a market exists for securities that pay off when $j \in [n_2^*, n_1^*]$. The reason is that they are facing a risk-return trade-off that was absent in the closed economy. Although all existing securities are sold at the same price and have the same expected return in terms of intermediate goods, the expected return in terms of consumption is not the same for all securities. In particular, the first part of the lemma establishes that $\rho_2^{(q_2)} > \rho^{(q_1)} > \rho_1^{(q_2)}$; that is, the price of intermediate goods is not equalized between countries when $j \in [n_2^*, n_1^*]$. But a market for securities with a positive payoff in these states exists only in country 1, where the price of intermediate goods is low. Thus $1.00 invested by a risky asset $j \in [0, n_2^*]$ (issued in either country) gives an expected return of $R\rho^{(q_1)}$, whereas $1.00 invested in an asset $j \in [n_2^*, n_1^*]$ (issued in country 1) yields the lower expected return $R\rho_1^{(q_2)}$. This observation makes it clear that the nature of the equilibrium crucially depends on the assumption that intermediate goods are not traded; otherwise the price of intermediate goods in different countries would be equalized in all states.

Part (iii) of proposition 6 states that there is a range of world saving levels *smaller than* 2D such that one country, but not both, opens all projects. In this case, there is no demand for the safe asset of country 1. However, since $G^{*w} > F_1^{*w}$, in the range in which $S^w > \bar{S}^w$, country 1 is still subject to output variability. Nevertheless, it can be formally proved that, for at least all $S^w > \bar{S}^w$, the variance of GDP growth conditional on the world saving level is higher in country 2 than in country 1 (see Appendix B available from the authors). So, the prediction that growth is more volatile in poorer countries carries over to this two-country extension. Finally, as the stock of savings reaches 2D, all projects will open, all risks will be diversified, and the allocation of resources will be exactly the same in the two countries.

The dynamic implications of international capital flows are interesting and can be seen by considering the following example. Suppose that the world consists of two closed economies with equal capital stock, and the total stock of savings is larger than $\bar{S}^w$ but less than 2D, so that without capital flows both countries have $n^* < 1$. Then consider the introduction of international capital mobility. First, funds will flow from country 2 to country 1, and country 1 will open all the sectors. Now, if a state $j \in [0, n_2^*]$ occurs, the realized income and next generation's wages will be the same in the two countries. However, if $j \in [n_2^*, 1]$, GDP in country 1 will be higher than in country 2.[11] Therefore, international capital flows lead to *divergence* between the two countries. Nevertheless, after some time, as the world economy becomes sufficiently rich, the direction of net capital flows will be reversed, and this time the relative GDP of country 2 will increase. In particular, as $S^w \rightarrow 2D$, the two countries will converge to the same level of GDP. Therefore, the typical pattern we predict is *divergence* first with capital flowing to the richer country, and then a reversal of capital flows and *convergence* (at a faster rate than if the two economies were closed). This is similar to the pattern that Neal (1990) documents over the eighteenth and nineteenth centuries in Western Europe as the direction of capital flows between Amsterdam and London reversed.

Overall, this section shows that, conditional on no trade in intermediate goods, the two-country world does not behave like a large closed economy, and the introduction of international capital flows both enriches our framework and yields additional implications that appear consistent with historical developments. We believe that this case has empirical relevance since many intermediate goods appear to be nontraded (e.g., railways).

However, if we allowed trade in intermediate goods as well as full mobility of savings, the world economy would behave like a large closed economy.


## 7. Conclusion

We argued in this paper that a model of development linking capital accumulation to the extent of market incompleteness yields a number of new insights. In a growth model with micro-level nonconvexities and uncertainty, we showed that the process of development goes hand in hand with better diversification opportunities and more productive use of funds. We demonstrated how primitive accumulation is followed by takeoff and financial deepening, how failed takeoffs can occur, how variability of growth decreases with development, and how productivity endogenously increases as the diversification opportunities improve. We also established that although all agents are price takers and there are no technological externalities, the process of financial development will be inefficient because of a pecuniary externality that we identify. This is not only a new source of inefficiency, but also one that, in contrast to many others that previous literature studied, cannot be internalized even when costless formation of complex intermediaries is allowed.


Appendix A

To simplify the notation in the proofs, we shall drop the time subscripts when this will cause no confusion.


### *Proof of lemma 1*

(i)  We have $P_j = 1$ for all $j \in \mathcal{J}(Z^*)$. Now let $\Lambda$ be the Lagrangean of (5) subject to (6) – (9). Then it is straightforward that $\partial \Lambda / \partial F^j = \partial \Lambda / \partial F^{j'}$, for all $j, j' \in \mathcal{J}(Z^*)$; thus for all $j, j' \in \mathcal{J}(Z^*)$, $F^j = F^{j'} = F$.

(ii)  First, observe that

    (a)  $s = [\beta/(1+\beta)]w$ (from (10))

    (b)  $P_j = 1$ for all $j \in \mathcal{J}(Z^*)$; and

    (c)  for all $j, j' \in \mathcal{J}(Z^*)$, $F^j = F^{j'} = F$ (from part (i)).

Let $I^j \in [0,1]$ be an index denoting whether sector $j$ is open or not. Then any competitive equilibrium given the prices (as in part (b)) and the demand functions of individuals (as in parts (a) and (c)) must be a solution to the following second-best planning problem:

$$\max_{\phi, F, \{I^j\}_{0 \le j \le 1}} \int_0^1 \log\left[\rho^j(r\phi + RFI^j)\right] dj \tag{A1}$$

    subject to

$$\frac{\beta}{1+\beta} w \geq F \int_0^1 I^j + \phi$$

$$F \geq M_{j_{max}} \qquad \text{where } j_{max} = \max\{j : I^j = 1\} \qquad (A2)$$

where $\rho^j$s are taken as given. In other words, given prices and demand functions, the equilibrium must maximize the welfare of the representative consumer.

Let

$$\Psi_\phi \equiv \left[\frac{\beta}{1+\beta}\right] w - \phi$$

Conditional on $\phi$, the problem is equivalent to choosing $F$ and $\{I^j\}_{0 \leq j \leq 1}$ to maximize (A1) subject to the constraints $F \int_0^1 I^j = \Psi_\phi$ and $F \geq M_{j_{max}}$.

Next note that irrespective of $\{I^j\}$, given $\psi_\phi$ all feasible portfolios have exactly the same return, but the variability is a decreasing function of $\int_0^1 I^j$. Since agents are risk-averse, the optimum must therefore maximize $\int_0^1 I^j$ subject to feasibility. This is achieved by setting $F = M_{j_{max}}(\phi)$ and $I^j = 1$ for all $j \leq j_{max}(\phi)$, and $j_{max}(\phi)$ is such that

$$\frac{j_{max}(\phi) = \min(\psi_\phi)}{M_{j_{max}}(\phi), 1}$$

This argument applies for any $\phi$; thus, *a fortiori*, it applies for the $\phi$ that is the solution to the program, that is, $\phi = \phi^*$. Let $n^* = j_{max}(\phi^*)$. Then $\mathcal{J}(Z^*) = [0, n^*]$. This completes the proof of the lemma. Q.E.D.

## *Proof of proposition 1*

The terms $\phi^*$ and $F^*$ are the unique solutions to (11) – (12), and $s^*$ is given from (10) and (3). To prove that $n^*(K)$ as defined by (15) is the unique equilibrium, we shall use the aggregate demand function $aF^*(n)$ as drawn in figure 3. We shall first show that, when $S^* \leq D, aF^*(n) = M_n$ for a unique value of $n \in [0, 1]$, and when $S^* > D, aF^*(n) > M_n$ for all $n \in [0, 1]$.

Observe that the solutions to $aF^*(n) = M_n$ can be given as the roots of a quadratic:

$$n_{(1), (2)} = \frac{(R + r\gamma) \pm \sqrt{(R + r\gamma)^2 - 4r\left[\frac{(R - r)(1 - \gamma)}{D} S_t^* + \gamma R\right]}}{2r} \qquad (A3)$$

where we denote the smaller root by $n_{(1)}$. When $S^* < D$, inspection of (A3) shows that $0 < n_{(1)} < 1 < n_{(2)}$, and both roots are real. In contrast, when $S^* > D$ and assumption 1 is satisfied, it is straightforward to see that neither $n_{(1)}$ nor $n_{(2)}$ belongs to the real interval [0, 1]. Since

$$aF^*(0) = \left(\frac{R-r}{R}\right)S^* > M_0 = 0$$

and both $aF^*(n)$ and $M_n$ are continuous in $n$ in the range $[0, 1]$, $aF^*(n) > M_n$ for all $n \in [0, 1]$.

To show that, when $S^* \leq D, n^* = n_{(1)}$ (as in eq. (15)) is the unique equilibrium, recall that, from lemma 1, $\mathcal{J}(Z^*) = [0, \bar{n}]$. Next suppose that $\bar{n} < n_t^*$ as given by (15). Then there exists $h$ with $Z_h = \varnothing$ who can deviate to $Z_k = (\bar{n} + \epsilon, 1 + \epsilon)$; and for $\epsilon$ sufficiently small, $|F^* - F^{n+\epsilon}| < \delta_\epsilon$, which implies that $Z_h$ is feasible and $v_h > 0$, a contradiction. The same argument can be used to establish that when $S^* > D, n < 1$ cannot be an equilibrium; thus $n^* = 1$ is the unique equilibrium. Next, going back to the case in which $S^* < D$, suppose that $\mathcal{J}(Z^*) = [0, \tilde{n}]$ such that $\tilde{n} > n^*$. Note that

$$\frac{\partial aF^*(n)}{\partial n} = \frac{r(R-r)}{(R-rn)^2} > 0$$

$$\frac{\partial^2 aF^*(n)}{\partial n^2} = -\frac{2r(R-r)}{(R-rn)^3} < 0 \qquad\qquad (A4)$$

When assumption 1 holds

$$\frac{\partial aF^*(1)}{\partial n} = \frac{r}{R-r} < \frac{D}{1-\gamma}$$

thus

$$\frac{\partial aF^*(n)}{\partial n} < \frac{D}{1-\gamma} \qquad \text{for all } n \in [0, 1]$$

Thus at the point of intersection $n^*$ (figure 3), $aF^*(n)$ is less steep than $M_n$. Then $aF^*(\tilde{n}) < M_n$; hence this allocation is not feasible. Therefore, $\mathcal{J}(Z^*) = [0, n^*]$ is the unique equilibrium. It is then straightforward, from free entry at stage 1, that, for all $j \in [0, n^*]$, there exists $h$ such that $Z_h = (j, 1)$. Q.E.D.

### Proof of proposition 2

Let $\bar{K} = (D/\Gamma)^{1/\alpha}$. Then (15) implies that, for all $K_t \geq \bar{K}, n^*(K_t) = 1$. Next, (19) implies that

$$\bar{K} < K^{SS} = (R\Gamma)^{1/(1-\alpha)}$$

thus if $K_t \geq \bar{K}$, then $K_{t+1} = R\Gamma K_t^\alpha$ and $K_t$ converges deterministically to $K^{SS}$. Equations (15) and (16) imply that the set $[0, \bar{K}]$ has no absorbing subset (except for the point zero) since, for all $K_t > 0, K_{t+1} = R\Gamma K_t^\alpha > K_t$ with probability $n^*(K_t) > 0$ (the economy grows conditional on good news). Therefore, we need only to show that from any point in $(0, \bar{K})$ there is a positive probability that $\bar{K}$ will be reached. We already observed that, conditional on good news, $K_{t+1} = R\Gamma K_t^\alpha$ and $K_t \to K^{SS} > \bar{K}$. Hence, for all $K_0 > 0$, there exists a sequence of $N(K_0)$ good draws such that $K_{N(K_0)} > K$, and this sequence occurs with positive probability. Therefore, $\text{plim}_{t\to\infty} K_t = K^{SS}$. Q.E.D.

## Proof of proposition 3

The variance of $\sigma(n^*(K))$ is

$$V_n = (1 - n^*)\left[\frac{r(1 - n^*)R}{R - rn^*} - \sigma^e(n^*(K))\right]^2 + n^*[R - \sigma^e(n^*(K))]^2$$

where $\sigma^e(n^*(K))$ is defined by (17) in the text.

Simple algebra establishes that

$$V_n = n^*(1 - n^*)\left(\frac{R(R - r)}{R - rn^*}\right)^2$$

and

$$\text{sign}\left(\frac{\partial V_n}{\partial n^*}\right) = \text{sign}\ (R - 2n^*R + rn^*)$$

Thus if $n^* > R/(2R - r)$, then $\partial V_n/\partial n^* < 0$. We also know from (15) that $n^* > \gamma$. Therefore, if $\gamma > R/(2R - r)$, then $V_n$ is decreasing in $n^*$ everywhere. Otherwise, it will be nonmonotonic (inverse U-shaped with $n^* = R/[2R - r]$ maximizing $V_n$). Since (15) implies $\partial n^*/\partial K \geq 0$ for all $K$, the rest of the proof follows. Q.E.D.

## Proof of proposition 4

We shall first prove that no allocation with a balanced portfolio can be optimal and then show that the optimal allocation will look as in figure 5.

The expected utility from second-period consumption for the representative agent, when individual savings are equal to $s^*$ and $\mathcal{J} = [0, n]$, can be written as

$$U(n, \{F^j\}, s^*) = \int_0^n \log\left[RF^j + r\left(s^* - \int_0^n F^j dj\right)\right] dj$$

$$+ (1 - n) \log\left[r\left(s^* - \int_0^n F^j dj\right)\right]$$

(A5)

Taking partial derivatives of $U(\cdot)$ with respect to $n$ and $\{F^j\}$ and evaluating them at the decentralized equilibrium, $n = n^*$ and $F^j = F^*$, we obtain

$$\frac{\partial U(n^*, \{F^*\}, s^*)}{\partial F^j} = 0 \qquad \forall j \in \left(0, n_t^*\right)$$

(A6)

and

$$\frac{\partial U(n^*, \{F^*\}, s^*)}{\partial n} = \log[RF^* + r(s^* - n^*F^*)]$$

$$- \log[r(s^* - n^*F^*)] + \frac{F^* + r(s^* - n^*F^*) + RF^*(1 - n^*)}{[RF^* + r(s^* - n^*F^*)](s^* - n^*F^*)} \quad \text{(A7)}$$

$$> 0$$

Now let us reduce $F^j$ for $j \leq \gamma$ below $F^*$ and increase $n$ (such that $\gamma dF \simeq F^* dn$). From (A4) and (A5), this will increase $U(\cdot)$. Therefore, the decentralized equilibrium is not Pareto-optimal. By evaluating $\partial U / \partial n$ and $\partial U / \partial F$ at any $\bar{n} \leq S^*/F^*(\bar{n})$ and applying the same argument, we can establish that no feasible allocation with a balanced portfolio of risky assets can be a Pareto optimum when $n < 1$. Moreover, this argument also establishes that the planner would open more sectors than the decentralized equilibrium; thus $n^{FB}(K) > n^*(K)$ whenever $n^*(K) < 1$.

To characterize the first-best, let us construct the Lagrangian

$$\Lambda\left(n, \{F^j\}, \phi, \lambda, \{\mu^j\}\right) = \int_0^n \log\left(RF^j + r\phi\right) dj + (1 - n)\log(r\phi)$$

$$+ \lambda\left(s - \int_0^n F^j dj - \phi\right) + \mu^j\left(aF^j - M_j\right) \quad \text{(A8)}$$

The first-order condition with respect to $F_t^j$ is

$$\frac{R}{RF_t^j + r\phi_t} - \lambda_t + a\mu_t^j = 0 \qquad \forall j \in (0, n_t) \quad \text{(A9)}$$

Now, if two sectors $j', j'' \in [0, n]$ do not have a binding minimum size requirement, then optimality requires that $\mu^{j'} = \mu^{j''} = 0$ and (by eqn (A9)) $F^{j', FB} = F^{j'', FB}$. For the rest of the sectors, $\mu^j > 0$ and $F^{j, FB} = Mj/a$. Next, we prove the following three claims:

(i)  $j > j'$ and $\mu^{j'} > 0 \Rightarrow \mu^j > 0$
(ii)  $j < j'$ and $\mu^{j'} = 0 \Rightarrow \mu^j = 0$
(iii)  $\mu^{j'} > \mu^j = 0 \Rightarrow F^{j', FB} > F^{j, FB}$

Suppose that claim (i) were not true, so that $\mu^{j'} > 0$ and $\mu^j = 0$. It must then be the case that

$$aF^j > M_j > aF^{j'} = M_{j'}$$

But then it would be feasible for the planner to give each agent more insurance and the same expected return by simply reducing $F^j$ and increasing $F^{j'}$ by the same amount, and this portfolio could not be optimal. So claim (i) must be true. A similar argument can be applied to prove claims (ii) and (iii). These three facts imply that we can define

$$n^{\text{FB}} = \max\{j \in [0, 1] \text{ s.t. } F^{j, \text{FB}} > 0\}$$

where from the first part of this proof we know that $n^* < n^{\text{FB}} \le 1$. Then there exists $j^* \in [0, n^{\text{FB}}]$ such that, for all $j < j^*$, $F^{j, \text{FB}} = M_{j^*}/a$ (the minimum size requirement is not binding), whereas for all $j \in [j^*, n^{\text{FB}}]$, $F^{j, \text{FB}} = M_j/a$ (the minimum size requirement is binding).

For expression (22) in proposition 4 (and the allocation described by figure 5) to follow, we have to show only that $0 < j^* < n^{\text{FB}}$ (with strict inequalities). Assume that $j^* = n^{\text{FB}}$. Then agents would be holding a balanced portfolio, which was shown above never to be a Pareto optimum. Thus $j^* < n^{\text{FB}}$. Assume $j^* = 0$. This would be equivalent to not opening sectors with no minimum size requirement, and it is straightforward to see that the planner could reduce the risk borne by the agents by increasing the measure of the set $\mathcal{J}^{\text{FB}}$. So $j^* > 0$. Finally, from $n^{\text{FB}} > n^*$ and the first-order conditions, it easily follows that $\phi^{\text{FB}} < \phi^*$. Q.E.D.

## *Proof of proposition 5*

We shall first establish that all equilibrium allocations must satisfy parts 1–3; then we shall show that the set of equilibrium allocations is nonempty.

Part 1 is straightforward, since an agent $h$ who has $M_h = \emptyset$ can always choose $Z_h^{(1)} = (0, \{h\})$ (autarky). Next, consider part 3. Define $U_h(\Theta_h^a, n)$ as the utility of agent $h$ when he joins coalition $\Theta_h^a$ and $\mathcal{J}(Z^{(2)}) = [0, n]$. Suppose that there is an equilibrium in which there exists $\Theta_h^a$ with $\mu(\Theta_h^a) > 0$ holding an unbalanced portfolio. Consider an agent $h' \in \Theta_h^a$. By lemma 1, given $n$, $h'$ maximizes his utility by holding a balanced portfolio $[0, n]$. Since by assumption 4 there is no exclusion from the open sectors, $h'$ can choose autarky and hold a balanced portfolio of all the open sectors. By assumption 3, after $h'$ leaves, $\Theta_h^a$ would still invest in the same portfolio (or if the set of agents who did not join had positive measure $\epsilon$, the coalition would invest in a portfolio that would be only a small distance away from the previous choice, and exactly the same argument would apply with $\epsilon$ small enough). Therefore, by leaving, agent $h'$ would receive $U_{h'}(h', n) > U_{h'}(\Theta_h^a, n)$. Then, in the first stage, $Z_{h'}^{(1)} = (0, \{h'\})$ and $Z_{h'}^{(3)} = \{h'\}$ is a beneficial deviation for all $h'$. Therefore, there can be no equilibrium in which the set of announcements induces an agent to hold an unbalanced portfolio. Next, lemma 2 implies that second-stage announcements will induce $P(Z^*) = 1$ and that there can be no positive commissions. This result combined with a balanced portfolio for all agents immediately implies that $\mathcal{J}(Z^*) = [0, n^*]$, where $n^*$ is given by (15) and $\phi^*$ and $F^*$ are given by (13) and (14). Therefore, all equilibria have to be as described in proposition 5.

Next, to prove that the set of equilibrium allocations in nonempty, it is sufficient to show that the "autarky" allocation in which $Z_h^{(1)} = (0, \{h\})$, for all $h \in \Omega$, together with parts 1–3 is in the equilibrium set. Suppose that $Z_h^{(1)} = (0, \{h\})$, for all $h \in \Omega$, and that in the second stage, for all $j \le n^*(K)$, there exists $h' : Z_{h'} = (0, j)$ and all agents choose a balanced portfolio over $[0, n^*(K)]$ as given by (13) and (14) in the third stage. It is clear that, given the announcements of the first stage, we are in the same situation as in proposition 1; thus $Z_h^{(2)}$ and $Z_h^{(3)}$ as described are optimal for all $h$. Therefore, we need only to show that there is no profitable first-stage deviation. Suppose that $h'$ deviates to $Z_{h'}^{(1)} = (\epsilon, \Theta_{h'})$, where $\epsilon > 0$ but can be arbitrarily small. Consider first $\mu(\Theta_{h'}) = 0$; then the optimal policy for this coalition in the third stage is to hold a balanced portfolio. Thus for all $\epsilon > 0$, the best response of all $h$ is *not* to join this coalition since they would hold exactly the same portfolio in autarky and would save the intermediation cost $\epsilon$. Now consider $\mu(\Theta_{h'}) > 0$. Then either this coalition will still hold a balanced portfolio, in which case the same argument applies, or it will hold an unbalanced portfolio over some set $\mathcal{J}' = [0, n']$ with $n' > n^*(K)$. But then by the argument we used above, each $h$ will prefer not to join this coalition and hold a balanced portfolio over $[0, n']$ in autarky. Therefore, autarky (with the allocation characterized in proposition 1) is in the equilibrium set. Q.E.D.

## Notes

1   The findings presented here are robust. We obtained very similar results when the variability of growth for each country was measured by the standard deviation of the estimated innovations from a second-order autoregressive process for the growth rate.

2   Some care needs to be taken since we have a continuum of choice variables and a continuum of agents. First, we have to restrict all agents to measurable strategies. Second, rigorous statements have to consider a deviation not only by a single agent but by a set of agents with positive but small measure, and optimality conditions have to read "almost everywhere." These technical details do not affect our analysis, and all results would go through with countable sets of agents and projects. The continuum representation is adopted to reduce notation, and we think of it as an approximation to an economy with a large but finite number of agents and projects.

3   If some agent $h$ ends up with insufficient funds to cover the minimum size requirement for the project he announced to run ("bankruptcy"), no trade occurs, $h$ suffers a punishment, and the game goes back to the first stage. Otherwise securities are traded. Note that bankruptcy will never be observed in equilibrium, and this specification is chosen only for the characterization of the out-of-equilibrium behavior. In particular, this specification ensures that agents do not have to worry about whether other agents believe that a certain announcement is feasible; thus they act taking the security prices and returns as given.

4   The wage earning of the agent depends on the realization of the state of nature in the previous period, i.e., eqn (3). To simplify notation, we suppress this dependence.

5   It is possible that, along the equilibrium path, an agent makes an announcement of the form $Z_h = (j, P_j)$ for some $j \in \mathcal{J}_t(Z^*)$, where $P_j > 1$; as long as another agent $h'$ has $Z_h' = (j, 1)$, no consumer will buy security $j$ from $h$. Therefore, this announcement is equivalent to $Z_h = \emptyset$. To economize on notation, we ignore these announcements in the statement of proposition 1.

6   But bad news now becomes more damaging since more funds are invested in risky projects. This feature of the model can be avoided by altering the specification for the structure of returns of the risky assets. An example would be to assume that in every period a fixed measure $z > 0$ of all possible projects have positive return. We shall show in proposition 3 that the variability of economic performance decreases as $n \rightarrow 1$. The reason is that although bad news becomes more damaging, its likelihood falls even faster.

7   This is achieved by setting $D$ equal to 4.1, 7.9, and 25 in the three cases. The choice of $D$ is of no major importance and serves only to have indivisibilities of similar relative size in the different experiments. The initial, full diversification, and steady-state capital levels are, respectively:

$$\alpha = 0.35 \rightarrow K_0 = 0.0037; K(n = 1) = 7.78; K^{SS} = 8.44$$

$$\alpha = 0.5 \rightarrow K_0 = 0.071; K(n = 1) = 15.6; K^{SS} = 16$$

$$\alpha = 0.65 \rightarrow K_0 = 0.814; K(n = 1) = 48.7; K^{SS} = 52.5.$$

8   With some abuse of terminology, we shall refer to this allocation as *first-best*. Although Pareto-optimal allocations of this economy will have a portfolio decision as characterized in this section, saving decisions would in general differ. This is due in part to the overlapping generations specification. But even if we were to restrict attention to a planner maximizing only the welfare of the current generation, the saving rate would be different. First, the planner would realize that by saving more she could open more projects. Second, she would also recognize that by saving less she would increase the rate of return on capital, $\rho_{t+1}$, and, therefore, the old-age consumption of the current generation.

9   The closest equilibrium concept is that of full Walrasian equilibrium proposed by Makowski (1980). Makowski defines a full Walrasian equilibrium as a feasible competitive allocation sustained by the set of traded commodities such that "no firm sees that it can increase its profits by altering its trade decisions assuming that the set of marketed commodities other than its own will remain the same" (p. 228). Allen and Gale (1991) also obtain a similar inefficiency. In their model the possibility of short sales implies that financial innovators will not receive the full benefits of the new assets they introduce. However, in Allen and Gale's economy, even when transaction costs are infinitesimal and there are no entry barriers, not all agents are price takers. In contrast, in our model, inefficiency arises with price-taking behavior and without short sales.

10   To simplify the terminology, throughout the paper we referred to the total amount of inter-mediate goods plus the output of the safe technology as "capital." However, in the current context, this terminology could be misleading. We therefore depart from this terminology slightly and use *capital mobility* to refer to the case in which savings can be freely invested in the assets of the other country and use the term *no trade in intermediate goods* to stand for a situation in which the output of the sector that transforms savings into capital goods (through both risky and safe technologies) in country $i$ can be used only by final-good firms located in country $i$.

11   Note that there is an important difference between GDP and gross national product in this model. Since both countries are assumed to have the same level of savings, even if country 1 has a higher GDP. GNP (and consumption) will be equal because agents are choosing identical portfolios. However, this is true only for the first generation, because, later, wages will differ in the two countries. Also, the implications about the randomness of growth depend on whether we use GDP or GNP. In particular, the variability of GNP will be the same for both countries. though it will also decrease over time. With more realistic preferences (e.g., bequests or longer horizons), it is easy to generate more GNP variability in poor countries.

## References

Allen, F. and Gale, D. (1988): "Optimal Security Design," *Review of Financial Studies*, 1 (3), 230–63.

——(1991): "Arbitrage, Short Sales, and Financial Innovation," *Econometrica*, 59, July, 1041–68.

Atje, R. and Jovanovic, B. (1993): "Stock Markets and Development," *European Economic Review*, 37, April, 632–40.

Azariadis, C. and Drazen, A. (1990): "Threshold Externalities in Economic Development," *Quarterly Journal of Economics*, 105, May, 501–26.

Bagehot, W. (1873): *Lombard Street: A Description of the Money Market*. New York: Scribner Reprint. Homewood, Ill.: Irwin, 1962.

Bencivenga, V. R. and Smith, B. D. (1991): "Financial Intermediation and Endogenous Growth," *Review of Economic Studies*, 58, April, 195–209.

Benhabib, J. and Gali, J. (1995): "On Growth and Indeterminacy: Some Theory and Evidence," manuscript, New York: New York University.

Boyd, J. H. and Prescott, E. C. (1986): "Financial Intermediary-Coalitions," *Journal of Economic Theory*, 38, April, 211–32.

Braudel, F. (1973): *Capitalism and Material Life, 1400–1800*. New York: Harper and Row.

——(1982): *Civilization and Capitalism, 15th–18th Century*, vol. 2. *The Wheels of Commerce*. New York: Harper and Row.

Cameron, R. E. (1972): "Introduction," in R. E. Cameron (eds), *Banking and Economic Development: Some Lessons of History*, New York: Oxford University Press.

Chandler, A. D. Jr. (1977): *The Visible Hand: The Managerial Revolution in American Business*. Cambridge, Mass.: Belknap Press.

DeVries, J. (1976): *The Economy of Europe in an Age of Crisis, 1600–1750*. Cambridge: Cambridge University Press.

Gerschenkron, A. (1962): *Economic Backwardness in Historical Perspective: A Book of Essays*. Cambridge: Cambridge University Press.

Goldsmith, R. W. (1969): *Financial Structure and Development*. New Haven, Conn.: Yale University Press.

Greenwood, J. and Jovanovic, B. (1990): "Financial Development, Growth, and the Distribution of Income," *Journal of Political Economy*, 98 (5), October, 1076–107.

Greenwood, J. and Smith, B. D. (1993): "Financial Markets in Development and the Development of Financial Markets," manuscript, Rochester, N.Y.: University of Rochester; Ithaca, N.Y.: Cornell University.

Gurley, J. G. and Shaw, E. S. (1955): "Financial Aspects of Economic Development," *American Economic Review*, 45, September, 515–38.

Hart, O. D. (1979): "On Shareholder Unanimity in Large Stock Market Economies," *Econometrica*, 47, September, 1057–83.

Hobsbawm, E. J. (1968): *Industry and Empire: An Economic History of Britain since 1750*. New York: Penguin.

Kennedy, W. P. (1987): *Industrial Structure, Capital Markets, and Origins of British Economic Decline*. Cambridge: Cambridge University Press.

King, R. G. and Levine, R. (1993): "Finance and Growth: Schumpeter Might Be Right," *Quarterly Journal of Economics*, 108, August, 717–37.

Lucas, R. E., Jr. (1988): "On the Mechanics of Economic Development," *Journal Monetary Economics*, 22, July, 3–42.

McCloskey, D. N. (1976): "English Open Fields as Behavior towards Risk," in Paul Uselding (ed.) *Research in Economic History*, vol. 1, Greenwich, Conn.: JAI.

Makowski, L. (1980): "Perfect Competition, the Profit Criterion, and the Organization of Economic Activity," *Journal of Economic Theory*, 22, April, 222–42.

Neal, L. (1990): *The Rise of Financial Capitalism: International Capital Markets in the Age of Reason*. Cambridge: Cambridge University Press.

North, D. C. and Thomas, R. P. (1973): *The Rise of the Western World: A New Economic History*. Cambridge: Cambridge University Press.

Persson, K. G. (1988): *Pre-industrial Economic Growth, Social Organization and Technological Progress in Europe*. Oxford: Blackwell.

Quah, D. (1993): "Empirical Cross-section Dynamics in Economic Growth," *European Economic Review*, 37, April, 426–34.

Ramey, G. and Ramey, V. A. (1995): "Cross-Country Evidence on the Link between Volatility and Growth," *American Economic Review*, 85, December 1138–51.

Rosenberg, N. and Birdzell, L. E., Jr. (1986): *How the West Grew Rich: The Economic Transformation of the Industrial World*. New York: Basic Books.

Saint-Paul, G. (1992): "Technological Choice, Financial Markets and Economic Development," *European Economic Review*, 36, May, 763–81.

Scherer, F. M. (1984): *Innovation and Growth: Schumpeterian Perspectives*. Cambridge, Mass.: MIT Press.

Summers, A. and Heston, R. (1991): "The Penn World Table (Mark 5): An Expanded Set of International Comparisons, 1950–1988," *Quarterly Journal of Economics*, 106, May, 327–68.

Tortella, G. (1972): "Spain, 1829–1874," in R. E. Cameron (ed.), *Banking and Economic Development: Some Lessons of History*, New York: Oxford University Press.

Townsend, R. M. (1978): "Intermediation with Costly Bilateral Exchange," *Review of Economic Studies*, 45, October, 417–25.

——(1983): "Theories of Intermediated Structures," *Carnegie-Rochester Conference Series Public Policy*, 18, Spring, 221–72.

——(1994): "Risk and Insurance in Village India," *Econometrica*, 62, May, 539–91.

Wrigley, E. A. (1988): *Continuity, Chance and Change: The Character of the Industrial Revolution in England*. Cambridge: Cambridge University Press.

Zilibotti, F. (1994): "Endogenous Growth and Intermediation in an 'Archipelago' Economy," *Economic Journal*, 104, March, 462–73.

# PART II:

# Market Incompleteness and Informal Institutions: Microeconomic Analysis

# A: Agrarian Organization

CHAPTER 8

# Access to Capital and Agrarian Production Organisation

MUKESH ESWARAN AND ASHOK KOTWAL

There are two problems, both universal, that entrepreneurs in any economy must contend with. Firstly, an agent generally has access only to a limited amount of working capital. Secondly, workers hired by an agent are subject to moral hazard, and this necessitates their supervision. This paper models, for an agrarian economy, the constraints imposed on entrepreneurs' activities by these two problems and endogenously determines the various organisational forms of production, as well as the allocation of resources that will obtain. With a simple model we endeavour to explain a diverse set of empirical observations pertaining to the less developed countries in terms of the general processes that determine the distribution of income among the various agents and the hierarchical relationships that develop among them.

Agricultural production typically involves a period of several months between the time the inputs are purchased and the time the output is marketed. Access to working capital and hence to the credit market thus plays an important role in a farmer's production decisions; the distribution of access to credit, in turn, tends to be an important determinant of income distribution. In poor agrarian economies, credit is invariably rationed according to the ability to offer collateral.[1] The amount of working capital a farmer can mobilise, therefore, depends on the amount of land he owns, which is often a good proxy for his overall wealth and, thus, his ability to offer collateral. Further, since hired hands have a propensity to shirk, they need to be supervised, and, therefore, the labour time that can be hired on the market is only an imperfect substitute for one's own time. The time endowment of a farmer thus becomes a crucial constraint on his decisions and, consequently, how he allocates it becomes an important determinant of the organisation of production.

The theoretical framework constructed in this paper focuses on the effects of the constraints discussed above on the behaviour of utility-maximising agents. In the partial equilibrium form of our model, we show that agents, through their optimal time alloca-tion, determine the organisation of production they adopt. In this we follow in the footsteps of Roemer (1982) who was the first to formally analyse class structure (i.e. classification of agents according to their activities) in terms of non-uniform distributions of the means of production. Access to credit, as modelled here, is functionally equivalent to ownership of the means of production. We show that the introduction of moral hazard on the part of hired labour increases the explanatory power of Roemer's scheme.

The framework is used to understand the formation of agrarian class structure. It is also used to provide an explanation of the inverse relationship between farm size and the labour input per acre. In its general equilibrium form, the framework allows us to carry out comparative static exercises that help us to analyse in a formal way the consequences of institutional policy actions. We have examined the effects of land and credit reform on social welfare, income distribution, the number of people in poverty, the proletarianisation of marginal cultivators and the welfare of the landless class.

## 1. The Partial Equilibrium

In this section, we assume that the factor prices are exogenously given and then consider the optimisation problem facing an agent who is constrained by the credit available to him and by his time endowment. The optimal time allocation made by each agent determines the mode of cultivation he will adopt.

We assume that the production process entails the use of two inputs land ($h$) and labour ($n$), both of which are essential. The production function, $f(h, n)$, is assumed to be linearly homogeneous, increasing, strictly quasi-concave and twice-continuously differentiable in its arguments. We can write the output, $q$, of a farm as

$$q = \epsilon f(h, n) \tag{1}$$

where $\epsilon$ is a positive random variable with expected value unity, embodying the effect of such stochastic factors as the weather. Land and labour can be hired in competitive markets at (exogenously given) prices $v$ and $w$, respectively. The price, $P$, of output is also exogenously given – determined, say, in the world market.

We assume that production entails the incurrence of fixed set-up costs, $K$. While we are abstracting from all inputs other than land and labour, we introduce $K$ as a proxy to represent the fixed component of the costs associated with other inputs. An example might be the fixed costs associated with the sinking of tube-wells for irrigation. $K$ is a set-up cost associated with each farm. While the production function itself is linearly homogenous, these costs, required to initiate production, will render unprofitable the cultivation of extremely small plot sizes. We shall see later on that these costs are also partly responsible for the existence of a class of pure agricultural workers in the economy. The amount of working capital, $\bar{B}$, to which a farmer has access, is typically determined by the assets he possesses – mainly the amount of land, $\bar{h}$, he owns.[2] Note that since land can be leased in or leased out, $h$ can be greater than or less than $\bar{h}$. Thus the scale of operation of a farmer is bounded by the working capital constraint.

$$vh + w(n - l) \leqslant \bar{B} - K + v\bar{h} + wt \tag{2}$$

where $n$ is the total amount of labour applied, $l$ the amount of labour he himself supplies, $h$ is the amount of land he cultivates, and $t$ the amount of time he sells on the labour market. The use of owned land and own labour in cultivation are valued at the going prices. In writing down (2) we have implicitly assumed that all capital outlays are incurred at the beginning of the production period.[3] The interest rate per crop season (which does not play a substantive role in our model), is assumed to be exogenously fixed at some level $r \geqslant 0$.

It is well recognised that the potential for moral hazard on the part of hired workers makes their supervision imperative. Implicit in (1) is the assumption that $n$ is the number of efficiency units of labour applied. The presence of the stochastic variable $\epsilon$ in (1) renders it impossible to infer from the knowledge of any two of $q$, $h$ and $n$, the value of the third. Thus even a supervisor will have the incentive to shirk and will need to be monitored – unless he is a residual claimant (Alchian and Demsetz, 1972). It follows that the entrepreneur must himself undertake the task of supervision – the only substantive implication of uncertainty in our model, since we shall be abstracting from risk preferences.

We assume that each agent is endowed with one unit of time. Let $R$ denote the amount of leisure ('rest') he consumes (to be endogenised below). The agent can then allocate the remaining amount of time $(1 - R)$ across three activities:

(a)   selling his services (for an amount of time $t$) in the labour market,
(b)   working on his own farm (for an amount of time $l$),
(c)   supervising hired labour on his farm (for an amount of time $S$, say).

We assume that the amount of time required of the entrepreneur to supervise $L$ hired workers is an increasing and strictly convex function of $L$:

$$S = s(L) \qquad s' > 0, S'' > 0 \tag{3}$$

with $s(0) = 0$ and, to ensure that the supervision of hired labour is not prohibitively costly for all $L$, $s'(0) < 1$. Strict convexity of the supervision function is rationalised on the traditional grounds that it renders finite the size of the enterprise despite linear homogeneity of the production function. We discuss later the consequences of relaxing the assumption of strict convexity of $s(L)$.

The time endowment constraint facing an entrepreneur may now be written.

$$1 - R - t - s(L) \geqslant 0 \tag{4}$$

The left-hand side of (4) is the amount of time, $l$, the entrepreneur works on own farm as a labourer.

To complete the specification of the model we posit that all agents have identical preferences defined over the present value earnings, $Y$, of the period and leisure. For tractability, the utility function is posited to have the additive structure:

$$U(Y, R) = Y + u(R) \tag{5}$$

with $u' > 0, u'' < 0$. Further, we shall take it that the marginal utility of leisure is infinite at $R = 0$. Note that the linearity of the utility function in income implies that the agent is risk-neutral.

We now turn to the optimisation problem facing an agent. For the moment we shall examine the agent's choices assuming that he opts to cultivate. We shall subsequently analyse his choice between being a cultivator and an agricultural worker. First, note that according to (3) the supervision time required of the entrepreneur depends only on the aggregate amount of labour he hires. Thus the time spent on supervision cannot be lowered by operating two separate plots of land rather than one. The existence of positive set-up costs associated with each operation then renders it suboptimal for an agent to operate two or more separate farming establishments.[4] We first consider the problem confronting an agent who has sufficient capital to cultivate. (Later, we will address the question as to whether he will, in fact, *opt* to do so.) An entrepreneur seeking to maximise his expected utility by cultivation will thus solve

$$\max_{R,h,t,L} P\beta f(h, l + L) + wt - \nu(h - \bar{h}) - wL - K + u(R) \tag{6}$$

$$\text{s.t.} B + wt \geqslant \nu h + wL \tag{7}$$

$$l \equiv 1 - R - t - s(L) \geqslant 0 \qquad L \geqslant 0, t \geqslant 0 \tag{8}$$

where $\beta \equiv 1/(1 + r)$ is the discount factor per crop period, and

$$B \equiv \bar{B} - K + \nu\bar{h}$$

Given our assumptions on $u(\cdot)$ and $f(\cdot, \cdot)$, the problem stated in (6) has the classic Kuhn–Tucker form and admits of only one solution. Thus for given $v$, $w$ and $B$ there exists a unique solution to the optimisation problem in (6). This solution can be parameterised by the working capital, $B$, available to the entrepreneur and the various exogenous prices. We shall denote the solution by the quartet $[R^*(B, v, w), h^*(B, v, w), t^*(B, v, w), L^*(B, v, w)]$, and the associated expected utility by $U^*(B, v, w, K)$, which is non-decreasing in $B$. Note that since the constant term $\nu\bar{h}$ appears additively in the maximand (6), we can always write

$$U^*(B, v, w, K) = U^+(B, v, w, K) + \nu\bar{h}$$

where $U^+$ is non-decreasing in $B$ – a property we note here for future reference.

The following proposition demonstrates that there are four potential modes of cultivation that can arise:[5]

PROPOSITION 1   *The solution to (6) admits of four distinct modes of cultivation, separated by three critical values, $B_1$, $B_2$, $B_3$ (with $0 < B_1 < B_2 < B_3$) of $B$, such that the entrepreneur is a*

    (I)   *labourer–cultivator* $(t > 0, l > 0, L = 0)$ *for* $0 \leqslant B < B_1$
    (II)  *self-cultivator* $(t = 0, l > 0, L = 0)$ *for* $B_1 \leqslant B < B_2$
    (III) *small capitalist* $(t = 0, l > 0, L > 0)$ *for* $B_2 \leqslant B < B_3$
    (IV) *large capitalist* $(t = 0, l = 0, L > 0)$ *for* $B \geqslant B_3$.

The intuition for proposition 1 becomes clear if we reason through, as we do below, how different activities become optimal at different levels of capital.

An agent with severely restricted access to capital can lease in only a small amount of land; the marginal revenue product of his labour on this piece of land would be correspondingly small. He thus finds it optimal to sell his services on the labour market for part of the time, thereby augmenting his working capital. He then earns a return on this capital by expanding his operation. Such agents are the labourer–cultivators, who are wage-earners cum entrepreneurs. The amount of leisure they consume is determined by the condition that the utility derived from the marginal unit of leisure equals the income from cultivation that is foregone as a result. Since the latter is constant for a linearly homogeneous production function, it follows that all labourer–cultivators consume the same amount of leisure.

The greater the working capital a labourer–cultivator has access to, the greater the amount of land he can rent and, therefore, the larger is the marginal product of his own labour. Since all labourer–cultivators consume the same amount of leisure, it follows that those with larger budgets will sell less of their labour services and devote more time to cultivation. The agent with a budget $B = B_1$ altogether ceases to transact in the labour market: he devotes all of his non-leisure time to cultivation. If hired and own labour had the same price, an agent with a budget marginally greater than $B_1$ would hire outside help. This, however, is not so. While the wage rate earned by the agent in the labour market would be $w$, the cost to him of hiring the first worker on his own farm is $w + s'(0)u'(R)$, which is strictly greater than $w$ since $s'(0) > 0$. Thus this agent will not hire outside help; he will expend his entire budget on hiring land and opt to be a self-cultivator. Agents with greater access to working capital will (self-) cultivate larger farms by consuming less leisure.

Since each agent has a limited amount of time endowment, the price of own-labour (i.e. the marginal utility of leisure foregone) becomes increasingly higher at higher levels of working capital. The ratio of the effective price of hired to own labour, i.e. $[(w + s'(0)u'(R))]/u'(R)$, declines. An agent with some sufficiently high budget $B_2(> B_1)$ will thus find it optimal to hire and supervise outside help, apart from applying some of his own labour on the farm. This agent marks the transition from the class of self-cultivators to the class of small capitalists. We thus see that the capitalist mode of cultivation emerges as a natural response to the need of entrepreneurs to circumvent their time-endowment constraints. Agents with budgets greater then $B_2$ will hire greater amounts of labour and spend more time in supervision. At some level of working capital $B_3(> B_2)$ it pays the agent to specialise in supervision, all labour is hired labour and the agent maximises the returns to his access to working capital by only supervising hired hands. Agents with $B \geqslant B_3$ comprise the class of large capitalists.

In proposition 1 we have merely derived all the modes of cultivation that are potentially observable. We have presumed that the agent in question in fact opts to cultivate. Whether or not he will do so will depend on whether or not his maximised utility $U^*(B, v, w, K)$, in cultivation exceeds his maximised utility in the next best alternative: being a pure agricultural worker. As an agricultural worker, the maximised utility, $U_0^*(v, w, \bar{h})$, of an agent who owns (and leases out) an amount of land $\bar{h}$ is given by

$$U_0^*(v, w, \bar{h}) = \max_R w(1 - R) + u(R) + v\bar{h} \tag{9}$$

The agent will opt to cultivate if and only if

$$U^*(B, v, w, K) > U_0^*(v, w, \bar{h}) \tag{10}$$

If set-up costs, $K$, were zero, all agents (including those with $B = 0$) will opt to cultivate if the technology is at all viable at prices $(P, v, w)$. However, if set-up costs are positive and sufficiently large, agents with meagre working capital would find it more attractive to join the labour force on a full-time basis than to cultivate on a scale so small as to be unprofitable. Those agents for whom (10) is violated will form the class of pure agricultural workers. There thus emerges a fivefold class structure in our model of an agrarian economy.[6] In reality, cultivation may not be feasible for the poorest agents because they have to assure themselves of a minimum subsistence before they can expend resources to engage in cultivation. Thus a pure labourer class could obtain even in the absence of scale economies. However, for expediency in modelling we shall continue with our assumption of positive set-up costs in cultivation.

For the rest of this section we shall assume that all the modes of cultivation we have discussed are mainfest. In other words, if $B_{max}$ denotes the largest amount of capital that a single entrepreneur can profitably utilise in agriculture, then $B_{max} > B_3$. The quantity $B_{max}$ is determined as the smallest value of $B$ for which the capital constraint ceases to bind in (6), and will depend on $P$, $v$ and $w$ in general.

We now turn our attention to the land-to-labour ratio of farms as a function of the entrepreneurs' access to working capital. The following proposition records our results comparing the land-to-labour ratio and the average productivity per acre across farms spanning the four modes of cultivation.

PROPOSITION 2    *As a function of* $B$,

(a)   *the land-to-labour ratio is constant over the labourer-cultivator class and strictly increasing over all other classes,*
(b)   *the (expected) output per acre of farms is constant over the labour cultivator class and strictly decreasing over all other classes.*

Intuition for the above proposition can be readily had. By equating the marginal utility per dollar spent on the two factors, the agents are, in effect, setting the ratio of the marginal products of land and labour equal to the ratio of their perceived prices. The perceived price of land is the same for all agents, and equals its market price. We have seen that all labourer-cultivators consume the same amount of leisure, so that the perceived price of (own) labour is constant for all $B \leqslant B_1$. Since the price ratio of the factors (land and own labour) is constant for $B \leqslant B_1$, production from a linearly homogeneous technology will use the factors in a fixed ratio. We have also seen that, beyond $B_1$, increases in $B$ induce the entrepreneurs to consume less leisure, resulting in a rising perceived price of own labour. Since the price of land is constant, we shall observe a bias towards land in the use of factors under self-cultivation: the land-to-labour ratio will increase with $B$. In the capitalistic mode of production, this effect is further reinforced by the fact that the cost of supervising hired labour increases at an increasing rate with the amount of labour hired. Part (b) of the above proposition follows directly from part (a) and the linear homogeneity of the production function. To the extent that our thinking is conditioned by the implicit assumption that markets are perfect, these results would appear counter-intuitive. If agents were not constrained in their borrowing, for example, it would be Pareto-efficient for those agents currently operating inefficiently large farms to lease out some of their land to agents with smaller (and hence more efficient) farms. In equilibrium, we would then expect all agents to operate farms of identical sizes.

We now briefly discuss how the results of these propositions would be affected by relaxing our assumptions regarding the nature of the supervision function $s(L)$ and the set-up costs $K$. Our results are driven by the assumption of increasing marginal disutility of effort. Even if the supervision function $s(L)$ were not strictly convex in $L$ but the cost of supervision in terms of the entrepreneur's utility were so, these results would still obtain. Thus if, as might be argued for share tenancy, the supervision function is linear, the results of propositions 1 and 2 would be quite unaffected except for one minor qualification: the land-to-labour ratio is constant for the small capitalist class. On the other hand, if the supervision function is strictly concave, the labour costs in terms of the entrepreneur's utility may not be convex. The results of proposition 2 may then not obtain.

It is conceivable that the set-up costs (e.g. irrigation) increase with the size of the plot cultivated. This would be equivalent to altering the effective price of land with the plot-size. If the set-up costs increase less than proportionately with the plot-size then the effective price of land is declining with the plot-size, and the results of proposition 2 are further strengthened. If the set-up costs rise proportionately with the plot-size then again our results are intact, since the effective price of land is constant. Finally, if the set-up costs rise more than proportionately with the plot-size, the results are ambiguous because the effective prices of both land and labour are rising with the scale of operation.

Among the hypotheses alternative to the one proposed in this paper for the inverse relationship between size and labour usage per acre, the most celebrated one is the dual labour-cost hypothesis of Sen (1975). According to Sen, small farms make extensive use of family labour whereas larger farms engage a greater proportion of hired labour. Family workers perceive a lower cost to working on their own farms due to psychological and other factors, and this results in greater use of labour per acre compared to larger farms. Ahmed (1981), Cline (1970) and Ghose (1979) provide evidence that a negative relationship between size and labour per acre can exist even within samples comprised of only family operated farms and also within samples comprised of farms that operate with only hired labour. In other words, the inverse relationship exists independently in the self-cultivation and the capitalist modes of production – consistent with our result in proposition 2. Our results are also consistent with the implications of Sen's hypothesis that family farmers (i.e. self-cultivators) perceive a lower cost of labour than do capitalist farmers.

The empirical evidence on the inverse relationship between farm size and land productivity is, however, less clear. In Brazil, Cline (1970) and Kutcher and Scandizzo (1982) have found a clear evidence for the inverse relationship. In India, the evidence is mixed. The less capital intensive agriculture depicted in Farm Management Surveys of 1955-6, which Bharadwaj (1974) analysed, shows a more prominent inverse size-productivity relationship than does the much more capital intensive agriculture of present day Punjab (Rao, 1977; Bhalla and Chadha, 1981; Rudra, 1982). In a recent paper Carter (1984) has confirmed the existence of the inverse relationship between farm size and productivity in data gathered in Haryana (India) during the years 1969–72. Rao (1977) observes that the inverse relationship is weakening, and perhaps becoming direct, over time in the prosperous regions of India that have adopted the new High Yielding Variety technology. In

Mexico (World Bank, 1978) the size-productivity relationship for foodgrains such as rice and wheat certainly seems to have changed from being inverse to being direct over the past thirty years. It is our contention that the greater use of physical capital over time is responsible for this change in Mexico and Punjab (India). Labour-displacing capital not only mitigates the scale diseconomies introduced by the heavy supervision requirement of large farms, but it also introduces scale economies due to indivisibilities. Since only large farms can utilise such capital, it is not surprising that the more recent data reveal a positive size-productivity relationship.

## 2. The General Equilibrium

In this section we set up a general equilibrium version of the model we considered in the previous section. Agents are allowed to choose the activities they undertake, their choices being dictated by the going prices and their access to working capital. The present value of the output price, $P\beta$, is normalised to unity. The factor prices are determined as those which clear the labour and land-rental markets, given the decisions of the agents in the economy. The general equilibrium framework, in which factor prices and class structure are endogenously thrown up, enables us to evaluate the income-distribution and welfare effects of policy actions such as land reform and credit reform. Since analytic results are difficult to obtain in general equilibrium, we are forced to resort to specific functional forms.

We assume that the production function in (1) takes the Cobb-Douglas form.

$$f(h,n) = Ah^{\frac{1}{2}} n^{\frac{1}{2}} \qquad A > 0 \tag{11}$$

and that the sub-utility function $u(R)$ has the constant-elasticity form

$$u(R) = DR^{\frac{1}{2}} \qquad D > 0 \tag{12}$$

As discussed in previous sections, an agent's access to capital in an agrarian economy is largely determined by the amount of land he owns. We posit that an agent whose owned-land holding is $h$ has available to him a maximum amount of credit, $\bar{B}(h)$, given by

$$\bar{B}(\bar{h}) = \theta\bar{h} + \phi \qquad \theta \geqslant 0, \phi \geqslant 0 \tag{13}$$

If $\phi$ is positive, even landless agents have access to some credit.

We assume that the total amount of land in the economy is exogenously given to be $H$, and that it is distributed across $N_0 + N_1$ agents, $N_1$ of whom own strictly positive amounts of land; the remaining $N_0$ agents are landless. The distribution of ownership across the landed agents is not necessarily egalitarian. We can index a landed agent by the proportion, $p$, of the landed agents who own smaller holdings than he does. We posit that the proportion, $F(p)$, of that is held by all landed agents $p' < p$ is given by Pareto distribution:

$$F(p) = 1 - (1-p)^{\delta} \qquad 0 < \delta \leqslant 1 \tag{14}$$

The larger the value of the parameter $\delta$, the more egalitarian is the distribution of ownership across the $N_1$ landed agents. The amount of land, $\bar{h}(p)$, agent $p$ owns is obtained from the density function associated with (14):

$$\bar{h}(p) = H\delta(1 - p)^{\delta-1} \tag{15}$$

Together, (13) and (15) determine the amount of credit available to every agent in the economy.

Finally, we assume that the supervision function, $s(L)$, is a quadratic in the amount of hired labour:

$$s(L) = bL + cL^2 \qquad 0 < b < 1, c \geqslant 0 \tag{16}$$

We are now ready to address the choice facing a typical agent: Given his owned land holding (and, therefore, the credit he has access to), the set-up costs, $K$, and parametric prices $v$ and $w$, should he lease out his land and join the labour force, or should he cultivate? In case he opts for the latter, there is no presumption that his operational holding will equal his owned holding. Consider agent $p$ of the landed class. If he cultivates, he will solve the optimisation problem (6), with $f(h, n)$ given by (11), $u(R)$ by (12), $s(L)$ by (16) and

$$B[\bar{h}(p)] = \phi - K + (\theta + v)\bar{h}(p)$$

The solution to (6) will thus be parameterised by $B[\bar{h}(p)]$, $v$ and $w$. This solution, described at length in the previous section, will generate the agent's demand for land, $h^*\{B[\bar{h}(p)], v, w\}$ and (net) demand for labour,

$$L^*\{B[\bar{h}(p)], v, w\} \equiv L^*\{B(\bar{h}(p), v, w\} - t^*\{B[\bar{h}(p)], v, w\}$$

He will choose to cultivate or become a pure agricultural worker, respectively, depending on whether

$$U^*\{B[\bar{h}(p)], v, w, K\} \gtrless U_0^*[v, w, \bar{h}(p)] \tag{17}$$

Recalling that

$$U_0^*(B, v, w, K) = U^+(B, v, w, K) + v\bar{h}$$

and that

$$U_0^*(v, w, \bar{h}) = U_0^*(v, w, 0) + v\bar{h}$$

(17) may be rewritten as

$$U + \{B[\bar{h}(p)], v, w, K\} \gtrless U_0^*(v, w, o) \tag{18}$$

Since the left-hand side is non-decreasing in $B$ and hence in $p$, it follows that if when agent $p$ opts to cultivate then all agents $p'$, with $p' > p$, will do likewise. The marginal cultivator, $p_m(v, w, K)$, is determined as the agent for whom (17) holds with equality: he is indifferent between being a cultivator and a pure agricultural worker. If $p_m(v, w, K) > 0$, then landed agents with $p < p_m(v, w, K)$ and all of the landless agents will be pure agricultural workers.

It is possible, however, that $p_m(v, w, K) = 0$, i.e. all landed agents opt to cultivate. Further, it is also possible that the landless agents might prefer to cultivate by leasing in land. This would be the case if

$$U + (\phi - K, v, w, K) > U_0^*(v, w, 0) \tag{19}$$

Note that since all of the landless agents are identical in every respect, their choices will also be identical.

We are now ready to write down the conditions that characterise the general equilibrium of this agrarian economy. Given the optimising choices of individual agents elaborated on above, these conditions are essentially the market clearing conditions for land and labour:

$$N_0 h^*(\phi - K, v, w) + N_1 \int_0^1 h^*\{B[\bar{h}(p)], v, w\} \mathrm{d}p - H = 0 \tag{20a}$$

$$N_0 \tilde{L}^*(\phi - K, v, w) + N_1 \int_0^1 \tilde{L}^*\{B[\bar{h}(p)]v, w\} \mathrm{d}p = 0 \tag{20b}$$

with

$$p_m(v, w, K) \geqslant 0 \qquad U^+\{B[\bar{h}(p_m)], v, w, K\} - U_0^*(v, w, 0) \geqslant 0 \tag{20c}$$

$$p_m(v, w, K) = 1 \qquad \text{if } U^+[B_{max}, v, w, K] - U_0^*(v, w, 0) < 0 \tag{20d}$$

where $B_{max}$, as defined in the previous section, is the largest amount of capital that can be profitably utilised in agriculture. In writing down (20c) we have followed the convention that if one of the inequalities is strict the other must hold with equality. Condition (20d) says that cultivation is the less attractive option for all agents in the economy, i.e. cultivation is not viable at these prices.

The simultaneous solution to conditions (20a)–(20d) determines the general equilibrium. Exogenous to the model are the parameters $A$ (of the production function), $K$ (the set-up cost), $b$ and $c$ (of the supervision function), $D$ (of the utility function), $\theta$ and $\phi$ (of the borrowing constraint), $\delta$ (of the land-ownership distribution function), $N_0$ (the number of landless agents), $N_1$ (the number of landed agents), and $H$ (the total supply of land). Endogenous to the model are the land-rental and wage rates ($v$ and $w$), each agent's net demand for land and labour, the utilities of the agents, the proportion of the landed agents who become pure agricultural workers ($p_m$) and, more generally, the class structure of the economy. These in turn determine the income distribution and welfare of the society. As our measure of welfare, we adopt the Benthamite welfare function:

$$W = N_0 \tilde{U}(\phi - K, v, w, K) + N_1 \int_0^1 \tilde{U}\{B[\bar{h}(p), v, w, K\} \mathrm{d}p \tag{21}$$

where

$$\tilde{U}\{B[\bar{h}(p)]v, w, K\} \equiv \max(U^*\{B[\bar{h}(p)]v, w, K, U_0^*[v, w, \bar{h}(p)]\}) \tag{22}$$

This completes the specification of the general equilibrium model. For parametric prices, the demand and supply choices of each agent we can determine analytically. To solve the market clearing equations $(20a)$–$(20d)$, however, we have had to resort to numerical methods. We now present the general equilibrium comparative statics of the model.[7]

Figures 1 and 2 show the percentage of total land operated in equilibrium under different modes of production as a function of the parameter, $\delta$, which characterises the distribution of land ownership. The parameter values are noted at the bottom of the figures. Figure 1 corresponds to a case when there are no landless people, while figure 2 corresponds to a case when there are landless agents. We can see from the two figures that if the ownership distribution is extremely unequal $(\delta \approx 0)$, the dominant mode of production is large capitalist farming whether or not there exists a class of landless people. The 'latifundia' agriculture of north-east Brazil would correspond to this case. At the other extreme, in the agrarian areas of present-day Taiwan and Japan, which are characterised by relatively uniform distributions of land ownership $(\delta \approx 1)$ and an absence of landless rural workers, the dominant mode of production is self-cultivation as shown in figure 1. In the limit when the distribution is perfectly uniform $(\delta = 1)$, the credit available will be identical for all cultivators. This symmetry will yield, for moderate values of the set-up cost, an equilibrium involving only self-cultivators, owning and operating identical amounts of land. This is consistent with Rosenzweig's (1978) empirical finding in Indian agriculture that participation in the labour market declines with decreases in landholding inequality. If there exists a class of landless workers, however, the egalitarian landed class will be able to hire these workers to supplement their own labour and the landed agents will thus all be capitalists – a situation depicted in figure 2 for values of $\delta$ approaching unity.[8] Note that when the dominant mode of cultivation is large capitalism – as is the case here when distribution of land ownership is highly skewed $(\delta \approx 0)$ – there

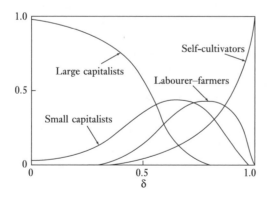

**Figure 1** Proportion of land operated under various modes of cultivation as a function of $\delta$. Parameter values: $A = 5$, $b = 0.1$, $c = ?$, $D = 0.1$, $K = 0.5$, $\theta = 1$, $\phi = 0$, $H = 0.5$, $N_0 = 0$, $N_1 = 1$

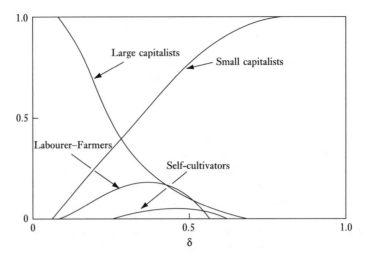

**Figure 2** Proportion of land operated under various modes of cultivation as a function of $\delta$. Parameter values: $A = 5$, $b = 0.3$, $c = 0.01$, $D = 0.1$, $K = 0.5$, $\theta = 1$, $\phi = 0$, $H = 1$, $N_0 = 0.5$, $N_1 = 1$

must exist, correspondingly, a sizeable class of agricultural labourers. This is consistent with Bardhan's (1982) findings in West Bengal, India. He observed that the proportion of wage labourers in the rural labour force is 'positively and very significantly associated with the index of inequality of distribution of cultivated land in the region'.

We now turn our attention to the question of land reform, which we define, in a narrow sense, to be an increase in the land distribution parameter $\delta$. Figure 3 allows us to evaluate the impact of land reform on social welfare (using the Benthamite welfare measure defined above), the relative income distribution (as measured by the Gini index $G_i$) and absolute poverty, $z$ (measured as the proportion of total population below an arbitrarily selected poverty line income, $Y_p$). In the figure we also present the Gini coefficient for the land-ownership distribution, $G_h[= (1 - \delta)/(1 + \delta)]$. We see from the figure that an increase in the distributional parameter $\delta$ (i.e. greater equity) not only unambiguously reduces the Gini coefficient on income and reduces the proportion of the rural population below the poverty line, but it also simultaneously causes an increase in social welfare.[9] The increase in social welfare is a direct consequence of the inverse relationship between farm size and land productivity discussed in the previous section; a move towards a more egalitarian land-ownership distribution increases the aggregate output.[10] This result is significant in the light of the present debate on land reform. The record of successful land reforms carried out in Japan (Dore, 1959) and Taiwan (King, 1977, ch. 9) and Cline's predictions (Cline, 1970) on the impact of land redistribution on Brazilian agricultural output are quite consistent with our general equilibrium results.

An interesting outcome of land reform in the presence of a landless class is depicted in figure 4. The utility of a landless worker increases continuously as the distribution of ownership is made more uniform among the *landed* agents. This follows from the increase in the demand for labour and, thus in wages that results from the land reform, since

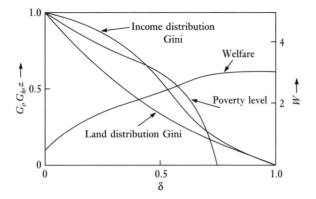

**Figure 3**  Impact of land reform on the poverty level, income distribution and social welfare. Parameter values are the same as in figure 1. The poverty line is set as $Y_p = 1.3$

smaller farms demand greater amounts of labour per acre. This is supported by the empirical results of Rosenzweig (1978); he found, in Indian agriculture, that rural wages decrease with inequality in land-ownership. For extremely unequal distributions (low values of $\delta$) we see from figure 4 that any increase in $\delta$ brings about substantial increases in the welfare of landless workers. The relationship becomes concave as the distribution gets more uniform. Clearly, the benefits of land reform for the landless are quite marked when the ownership distribution among the landed is highly skewed.

Figure 5 illustrates the results of a credit reform in which the total volume of the credit is held constant, while $\theta$ (the parameter which determines the extent to which the access to credit is dependent on land ownership) is varied. When $\theta = 0$, the access to credit is completely independent of land ownership; when $\theta$ is large, the access to credit is, of course, extremely sensitive to land ownership. In order to ensure that the aggregate credit, $B_T$, available to the agrarian economy is constant, we vary $\phi$ according to the rule $\phi = B_T - \theta H$;

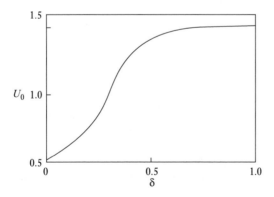

**Figure 4**  Impact of land reform amongst only the landed agents on the utility level of a landless agent. Parameter values are the same as those in figure 2

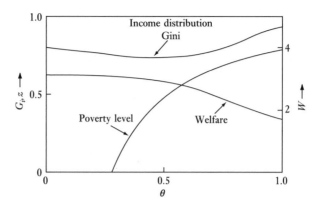

**Figure 5**  Impact of credit reform on poverty, income distribution and social welfare. Total credit is fixed at $B_T = 0.5$. Other parameter values: $A = 5$, $b = 0.3$, $c = 0.1$, $D = 0.1$, $K = 0.2$, $\delta = 0.1$, $N_0 = 0$, $N_1 = 1$, $Y_p = 1.0$

thus when $\theta$ changes, credit is merely redistributed, remaining constant in aggregate. The results show that social welfare monotonically decreases and the proportion of rural population under the poverty line monotonically increases with an increase in $\theta$. (Since the change in welfare following credit reform is mainly due to the change in aggregate output, we may interpret the welfare function in figure 5 as an approximation of GNP.) This provides the theoretical rationale for the argument that the creation of institutions capable of accepting as collateral future crops rather than owned land-holdings would prove to be an effective tool for removing poverty as well as for improving efficiency.

## 3. Conclusions

The cornerstones of the model presented in this paper are the two constraints facing each agent in his optimisation problem:

(1)   the amount of working capital (or credit) available to him and
(2)   his limited time endowment.

The constraint on the availability of working capital arises from the characteristics of capital markets in which credit is rationed according to the ability to offer collateral. The fact that the total time available to an agent is fixed matters because the (unsupervised) time purchased from another agent on the market is an imperfect substitute for one's own time. The allocative process is thus influenced by imperfections in two key markets – imperfections in the sense that agents cannot purchase desired amounts of working capital or effective labour at given prices.

   In an economy in which agents are bound by the above two constraints, we have demonstrated that in equilibrium there is a misallocation of resources: land-to-labour ratios differ across farm sizes and there is scope for welfare- and output-improving transfers of resources across agents. It is important to note that this misallocation arises because of imperfections in two markets. If agents could borrow unlimited amounts of capital at a given interest rate, all farms would be of the same size, using land and labour in the same proportion – thus yielding a Pareto-efficient outcome. If, on the other hand, there were no moral hazard on the part of hired labour (i.e. hired and own labour were perfect substitutes), then in the absence of set-up costs, differently credit-constrained agents would operate farms on different scales but with the same land-to-labour ratios[11] – again achieving a Pareto efficient outcome. With a constant returns to scale technology, a Pareto inefficient allocation of resources requires imperfection in at least two markets – for example, labour and land markets, or credit and land markets, etc.

The modern theory of organisation revolves around the issue of moral hazard of hired labour. The hierarchical relationship between an employer and his employee within a capitalist firm has been rationalised as a way of mitigating moral hazard in team production (Alchian and Demsetz, 1972). In our model, however, workers are not hired because of any technological superiority of team production. An agent who has access to large amounts of credit cannot earn positive returns on it by re-lending the money unless he has a more effective way of curbing moral hazard on the part of the potential borrower than does the credit agency. Therefore, when an agent engaged in self-cultivation is given access to a larger amount of credit, he must use the additional credit for cultivation on a larger scale. Given the increasing marginal cost of his own time, he seeks to stretch his time constraint by hiring labour, which must be supervised. The agents who are selling their services on the labour market are those whose lack of access to credit prevents them from becoming cultivators. Hierarchical relationship can thus come about due to a non-uniform distribution of access to credit rather than any technological superiority of team production. Our argument remains valid even when set-up costs are zero. Agriculture is one sector for which the explanation of hierarchical employment relationships on the basis of a presumed technological advantage of team production is not compelling. Since the various production activities are necessarily spread out over time, it is possible for individual agents to operate as efficiently as would a team (Dorner, 1972, p. 103).

Our model implies that richer employers typically consume smaller amounts of leisure. This implication, however, is not generally borne out. The reason for this is not hard to see. Those agents with access to large amounts of credit have incentives to come up with organisations and technologies that facilitate production on a large scale. The creation of pyramidal hierarchies and the use of labour-displacing mechanisation are two examples of how such agents can use more hired factors to economise on their supervision time.

We conclude by observing some serious limitations of the model presented in this paper. If the supervision requirement increases at a decreasing – rather than increasing – rate with the size of the hired labour force, our results on the welfare effects of land and credit reform may not obtain. The same qualification must be made if the set-up costs have a variable component that increases less than proportionately with the plot-size cultivated. The irrigation technology employed is particularly relevant to this point. Finally, note that tenancy in our model is explicitly fixed rental tenancy. An attempt to introduce share tenancy into our framework would pose two problems. First, it would require a precise understanding of the way in which share tenancy alters the supervision technology. Secondly, it might violate our assumption that the credit ceiling of a cultivator is determined by the amount of land he owns; a share tenant may obtain his credit from the landlord. It is, however, conceivable that share tenancy arises to circumvent imperfections in capital markets. In particular, it may be an arrangement whereby the tenant acquires access to the use of land prior to the payment of its rental. Since the crop would stand on the landlord's own land, tenancy would be tantamount to accepting future crops as collateral. If this is so, it is yet another indication that imperfections of capital markets can have significant consequences for agrarian institutions.

## Notes

1   Good recent sources on this are Von Pischke et al. (1983) and Rudra (1982, ch. 4). Binswanger and Siller (1983) offer an insightful analysis of how differential ownership of collateral (mainly land) determines differential access to credit and gives rise to credit-rationing in an agrarian setting.

2   In most agrarian economies the total wealth of an agent is strongly correlated with land-ownership. The use of other assets besides land for collateral would not change our results qualitatively. Note that we take the distribution of land-ownership as exogenously given. Binswanger and Rosenzweig (1982) offer a compelling explanation for the relative infrequency of land sales in the less-developed countries.

3   Seasonal consumption loans by landlords – a frequent practice in subsistence agriculture – could be construed as advance wage payments. Tenants, however, are not necessarily required to pay the rent in advance. But requiring this to be so in our two-factor model provides a way of simulating the working capital necessitated by the existence, in reality, of numerous intermediate inputs.

4   If we allow the supervision requirement on each plot to depend only on the number of hired workers on that plot, it is conceivable that an agent might contemplate operating two separate farms, However, this feature would render our model intractable. In view of this, we can interpret $K$ as the set-up cost per farm and also as the set-up cost per agent.

5   The proof of this and the following proposition is given in Eswaran and Kotwal (1984).

6   In a *tour de force* in Marxian economics, Roemer (1982) was the first to derive analytically a fivefold class structure in an economy in which agents have differential access to the means of production. There is one essential difference between Roemer's analysis of class structure and ours. If only a single crop is produced, the class in Roemer's framework which is the analogue of what we call self-cultivators in our formulation is a set of measure zero. This arises from his implicit assumption that own and (unsupervised) hired labour are perfect substitutes. We have seen above that if agents are arranged in the order of increasing budgets, the agent with a budget $B_1$ will be the first one to self-cultivate. Further, if $s'(0) = 0$ he would also be the only on to self-cultivate since all agents with budgets exceeding $B_1$ will find it optimal to hire outside help. If the distribution of the access to capital across the agents of the economy is continuous, it follows that self-cultivators would form a set of zero measure. In our formulation, this anomaly does not arise. As long as hired labour requires supervision, there exists an interval $[B_1, B_2]$ of strictly positive length such that all agents with budgets in this range would choose to self-cultivate. Bardhan (1982) presents an enlightening empirical analysis of agrarian class structure in West Bengal, India, based on Roemer's theoretical framework.

7   In the exercises that follow, our intention is to obtain some comparative static results numerically, since analytic methods are infeasible. The parameter values are chosen with the purpose of illustrating various possible general equilibrium outcomes. Note, however, that we cannot interpret specific parameter values as being 'large' or 'small'.

8   Note that although small capitalist production dominates for $\delta = 1$ in figure 2, if there were a larger number of landless agents the dominant mode of production could conceivably be large capitalism.

9   Notice that in figure 3, $G_i$ exceeds $G_\lambda$. In the absence of set-up costs, the opposite would be true since the profits per acre would be declining in the farm size (Rao, 1977, p. 148). For significant set-up costs, however, this would not remain so.

10   Note that land reform, by equalising access to credit across agents, increases the number of cultivators. This would increase the aggregate set-up cost incurred by the economy. If the set-up cost $K$ is inordinately large, it is conceivable that social welfare could in fact decline following a land reform. This, however, is unlikely. Moreover, if the class of pure labourers arises due to minimal consumption requirements (as pointed out in the text) rather than due to set-up costs in cultivation, social welfare will unambiguously increase following land reform.

11   With positive set-up costs and an otherwise linearly homogeneous production function, it would be socially optimal to have only a single farm if supervision were redundant.

## References

Ahmed, I. (1981): "Farm Size and Labour Use: Some Alternative Explanations," *Oxford Bulletin of Economics and Statistics*, 43, 73–88.

Alchian, A. and Demsetz, H. (1972): "Production, Information Costs, and Economic Organisation," *American Economic Review*, 62, 777–95.

Bardhan, P. (1982): "Agrarian Class Formation in India," *Journal of Peasant Studies*, 10, 73–94.

Bhalla, G. and Chadha, G. (1981): "Structural Changes in Income Distribution: A Study of the Impace of Green Revolution in the Punjab," *Report on the ICSSR Project*, New Delhi: Jawaharlal Nehru University.

Bharadwaj, K. (1974): *Production Conditions in Indian Agriculture*. London and New York: Cambridge University Press.

Binswanger, H. and Rosenzweig, M. (1982): "Behavioural and Material Determinants of Production Relations in Agriculture," discussion paper, Research Unit, Agriculture and Development Department, Operational Policy Staff, World Bank, Report No: ARU5.

Binswanger, H. and Siller, D. A. (1983): "Risk Aversion and Credit Constraints in Farmers' Decision-making: A Reinterpretation," *Journal of Development Studies*, 20, 5–21.

Carter, M. R. (1984): "Identification of the Inverse Relationship between Farm Size and Productivity: An Empirical Analysis of Peasant Agricultural Production," *Oxford Economic Papers*, 36, 131–45.

Cline, W. (1970): *Economic Consequences of a Land Reform in Brazil*. Amsterdam: North-Holland.

Dore, R. (1959): *Land Reform in Japan*. London: Oxford University Press.

Dorner, P. (1972): *Land Reform and Economic Development*. Baltimore: Penguin.

Eswaran, M. and Kotwal, A. (1984): "Access to Capital as a Determinant of the Organization of Production and Resource Allocation in an Agrarian Economy," University of British Columbia discussion paper, 84–06, July.

Ghose, A. (1979): "Farm Size and Land Productivity in Indian Agriculture: A Reappraisal," *The Journal of Development Studies*, 16, 27–49.

King, R. (1977): *Land Reform – A World Survey*. London: G. Bell.

Kutcher, G. and Scandizzo, P. (1982): *The Agricultural Economy of Northwest Brazil*. Baltimore: Johns Hopkins University Press.

Rao, C. (1977): *Technological Change and Distribution of Gains in Indian Agriculture*. Delhi: Macmillan Company of India.

Roemer, J. (1982): *A General Theory of Exploitation and Class*. Cambridge: Harvard University Press.

Rosenzweig, M. (1978): "Rural Wages, Labor Supply, and Land Reform: A Theoretical and Empirical Analysis," *American Economic Review*, 68, 847–61.

Rudra, A. (1982): *Indian Agricultural Economics*. New Delhi: Allied Publishers.

Sen, A. (1975). *Employment, Technology and Development*. London: Oxford University Press.

Von Pischke, J., Adams, D. and Donald, G. (eds) (1983): *Rural Financial Markets in Developing Countries*. Baltimore: Johns Hopkins University Press.

World Bank (1978): *Land Reform in Latin America: Bolivia, Chile, Mexico, Peru and Venezuela*. Staff Working Paper 275 Washington: World Bank.

# B: Labor

# Inequality as a Determinant of Malnutrition and Unemployment: Theory

PARTHA DASGUPTA AND DEBRAJ RAY

> But it was only in the last generation that a careful study was begun to be made of the effects that high wages have in increasing the efficiency not only of those who receive them, but also of their children and grandchildren . . . the application of the comparative method of study to the industrial problems of different countries of the old and new worlds is forcing constantly more and more attention to the fact that highly paid labour is generally efficient and therefore not dear labour; a fact which, though it is more full of hope for the future of the human race than any other that is known to us, will be found to exercise a very complicating influence on the theory of distribution.
>
> *Alfred Marshall (1920, p. 510)*

## 1. The Issues

Even by conservative estimates well over three hundred million people in the world are thought to be seriously undernourished today.[1] International data on the incidence of malnutrition are in large parts only sketchy. Moreover, those that are available are not readily interpretable, for the science of nutrition is relatively new.[2] In particular, it is known that the food-adequacy standard for a person depends not only on the sorts of activities in which he is engaged, but also on his location and on his personal characteristics, of which the last includes his prior history. This makes the subject particularly difficult.[3]

The general effects of malnutrition vary widely. In children they are especially severe. It can cause muscle wastage and growth retardation (thus future capability), increased illness and vulnerability to infection. There is evidence that it can affect brain growth and development. Chronic malnutrition in adults diminishes their muscular strength, immunity to disease and the capacity to do work. Persons suffering thus are readily fatigued. There are also marked psychological changes, manifested by mental apathy, depression, introversion lower intellectual capacity and lack of motivation; see, for example, Read (1977). Life expectancy among the malnourished is low, but not nil. Such people do not face immediate death. Malnutrition is this side of starvation. For this reason the world can indefinitely carry a stock of undernourished people, living and breeding in impaired circumstances.

Not surprisingly, an overwhelming majority of the world's undernourished live in the low-income developing countries (FAO, 1974, p. 66). Not a negligible number of economists have gone on to emphasise that it is the absolute-poor who go hungry.[4] But then who *are* the absolute poor? The available evidence suggests that they are among the landless, or near-landless people; see Da Costa (1971), Reutlinger and Selowsky (1976), and Fields (1980, p. 161), for example. Presumably this is because they have no non-wage income, or if they do it is precious little. But then why do they not get employed and earn a wage? One answer is that, they do, but that because the economy is resource-poor, the low level of prevailing wages does not provide the necessary escape from absolute poverty and malnutrition (Leibenstein, 1957); see also Fei and Chiang (1966) and Prasad (1970). But this must be an incomplete answer, for some *do* escape; while others, who are similar in all other respects, do not. To put it another way, the labour market often does not clear in such economies, and the non-clearance manifests itself in the form of involuntary unemployment. Thus, some obtain employment at wages that enable them to purchase an adequate diet while others languish in activities that keep them undernourished. But this begs the question, for why does the labour market not clear? In particular, why do frustrated job-seekers not undercut the employed?

In this essay and its sequel (Dasgupta and Ray, 1987; chapter 9, part 2, this volume) we will attempt to provide a rigorous theory that links involuntary unemployment to the incidence of malnutrition, relates them in turn to the production and distribution of income and thus ultimately to the distribution of assets. The basic descriptive features of the model used to illustrate the theory will be presented in this essay. In the sequel we will for the most part study policy implications. The model used to illustrate the theory is a fully 'general equilibrium' one. Involuntary unemployment will be shown to exist in the construct, not assumed; that is, wage rigidities will be explained, not hypothesised.[5]

We want to emphasise that the concept of undernourishment plays a central, *operational*, role in the model that we will develop here; and it is as well to make clear what we mean by this. Poverty, inequality, malnutrition and involuntary unemployment (or, more generally, surplus labour) have all been much discussed in the development literature. For example, the idea of 'basic needs', as it occurs in Streeten (1981), or the more general notion of 'capabilities', as developed in Sen (1983), patently subsume the concept of food-adequacy standard in their net. Now, malnutrition is not the same as hunger. There is not only discomfort in being malnourished, there is impairment in the capacity to engage in physical and mental activities, through illness or plain weakness. (If this is denied one must accept that malnutrition as a distinct concept is vacuous.) Any theory that incorporates 'basic needs' or 'capabilities' must then as a minimum acknowledge that at low nutrition levels there is some link between food intake and work capacity. For this reason it is a puzzle to us that the recent theoretical literature on absolute poverty has made little use of this link to its advantage when discussing the efficacy of food transfers (that is, their effect on growth of output). Reading this valuable literature is rather like seeing the grin but not the Cheshire Cat. Thus it is a commonplace to argue that food transfers to the very poor may lower growth rates in national product because of their detrimental influence on savings and investment, incentives and so forth. But this is only one side of the picture. The other side is what concepts such as 'basic needs' and 'capabilities' try among other things to capture, that a transfer from the well-fed to the undernourished will enhance output via increased work capacity of the impoverished. One does not know in advance which is the greater effect, but to ignore the latter is certain to yield biased estimates. We are fully aware that these are difficult estimates to make, if only because data are sparse. But to date we do not even possess a theoretical scheme to tell us how we might go about thinking on the matter. For it is not obvious what is the pattern of resource allocation in a decentralised environment if and when the link between nutrition and work capacity assumes potency. The point is that the incidence of both malnutrition and involuntary unemployment need to be endogenous in a model which is used for the purposes of policy debates. One wants the model to identify which category of people will suffer from undernourishment. In particular, one wants it to identify those people who will be denied access to work that pays enough to enable them to produce enough for an employer to wish to hire them in the first place.

So as to keep the formal model as simple as possible we will consider a timeless world in which work capacity is related to food intake in the manner postulated by Leibenstein (1957) in his pioneering work. In section 2 we will present the ingredients of our construction. The central theorems concerning the existence and general characteristics of involuntary unemployment equilibrium will be presented in section 3. In section 4 we postulate that the food and work capacity relation is a simple step-function and we then present a two-class economy in which equilibrium is unique and can be computed explicitly. Readers wishing to avoid the general arguments in section 3 can go direct from section 3.2. (where market equilibrium is defined) to section 4.

The link between nutrition and work capacity is a most complex one and on reading some of the literature one detects that passions among analysts can run deep. A simple timeless model in this area will be found otiose even by some who find timeless models of normal production theory readily palatable. In section 5 we therefore discuss several objections that can be raised about the reasonableness of our basic model and we argue that the general features that are highlighted in section 3 are robust against generalisation. Section 5 contains a summary of our main conclusions. Proofs of theorems are relegated to the Appendix.

The model that we will develop in this essay postulates frictionless markets for all capital assets and a flawless competitive spirit among employers and workers. We wish to emphasise this point, because at the level of *theoretical* discourse it will not do to explain poverty, malnutrition and unemployment by an appeal to monopsonistic landlords, or predatory capitalists, or a tradition-bound working class and leave it at that. That is far too easy, but more to the point, one is left vulnerable to the argument that this merely shows that governments should concentrate their attention on freeing markets from restrictive practices. It does not provide an immediate argument as to why governments, if they are able to, should intervene to ensure directly that people are not malnourished. Our formal model is a classical one. There are no missing markets. In particular, involuntary unemployment arising in it is not due to demand deficiency. To seal this point we will show in the sequel that equilibria in our model are Pareto-efficient. This means in particular that there are no policy options open to the government other than consumption or asset transfers. In the sequel, therefore, we will also study the impact of such policies.

## 2. The Model

We begin by distinguishing labour-*time* from labour-*power* and observe that it is the latter which is an input in production. We consider a timeless construct and eschew uncertainty (see section 5 for extensions). Consider a person who works in the economy under analysis for a fixed number of 'hours' – the duration of the analysis. Denote the labour power he supplies over the period by $\lambda$ and suppose that it is functionally related to his consumption, $I$, in the manner of the bold-faced curve in figure 1(a). (We should emphasise that we are thinking of labour power as an aggregate concept, capturing not only power in the thermodynamic sense, but also motivation, mental concentration, cognitive faculty, morbidity and so forth.)

The key features of the functional relationship are that it is increasing in the region of interest, and that at low consumption levels it increases at an *increasing* rate followed eventually by diminishing returns to further consumption.

An alternative specification of the functional relationship, used, for example, by Bliss and Stern (1978*b*), is drawn in figure 1(b). Here, $\lambda$ is nil until a threshold level of consumption, $I^*$, the resting metabolic rate (RMR). $\lambda(I)$ is an increasing function beyond $I^*$, but it increases at a diminishing rate.

Two factors, *land* and *labour-power*, are involved in the production of *rice*.[6] Land is homogeneous, workers are not. Denoting by $T$ the quantity of land and by $E$ the *aggregate*

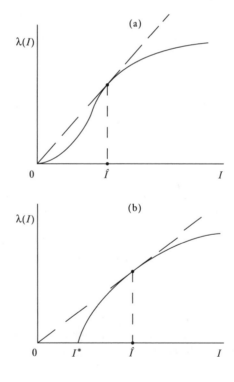

Figure 1

labour-power employed in production (i.e. the sum of individual labour powers employed) let $F(E, T)$ be the output of rice, where the aggregate production function $F(E, T)$ is assumed to be concave, twice differentiable, constant-returns-to-scale, increasing in $E$ and $T$, and displaying diminishing marginal products.[7] Total land in the economy is fixed, and is $\hat{T}$. Aggregate labour power in the economy is, of course, endogenous.

Total population, assumed without loss of generality to be equal to the potential work force, is $N$. We take it that $N$ is large. We can therefore approximate and suppose that people can be numbered along the unit interval $[0, 1]$. Each person has a label, $n$, where $n$ is a real number between 0 and 1. In this interval the population *density* is constant and equal to $N$. We may therefore normalise and set $N = 1$ so as not to have to refer to the population size again. A person with label $n$ is called an $n$-person. The proportion of land he owns is $t(n)$, so that $\hat{T}t(n)$ is the *total amount* of land he owns; $t(n)$ is thus a density function. Without loss of generality we label people in such a way that $t(n)$ is nondecreasing in $n$. So $t(n)$ is the land distribution in the economy and is assumed to be continuous. In figure 2 a typical distribution is drawn. All persons labelled 0 to $\underline{n}$ are landless. From $\underline{n}$ the $t(n)$ function is increasing. Thus all persons numbered in excess of $\underline{n}$ own land, and the higher the $n$-value of a person the greater the amount of land owned by him.

We will suppose that a person either does not work in the production sector or works for one unit of time.[8] There are competitive markets for both land and labour power. Let $r$ denote the rental rate on land. Then $n$-person's non-wage income is $r\hat{T}t(n)$. Each person has a reservation wage which must as a minimum be offered if he is to accept a job in the competitive labour market. For high $n$-persons this reservation wage will be high because they receive a high rental income. (Their utility of leisure is high.) For low $n$-persons, most especially the landless, the reservation wage is low, though possibly not nil. We are concerned with malnutrition, not starvation. In other words, we are supposing that these are normal times that are being modelled. The landless do not starve if they fail to find jobs in the competitive labour market. They beg, or at best do odd jobs *outside* the economy under review, which keep them undernourished. But they do not die. Thus the reservation wage of even the landless exceeds their RMR. All we assume is that at this reservation wage a person is malnourished.

Denote by $\bar{w}(R)$ the reservation wage function, where the argument $R$ denotes non-wage income. We are supposing here that the $\bar{w}(\cdot)$ *function* is exogenously given (continuous and non-decreasing), though of course, non-wage income is endogenous to the model. For

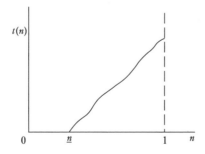

Figure 2

a given rental rate on land, $r > 0$, $\bar{w}[rt(n)\hat{T}]$ is constant for all $n$ in the range $0$ to $\underline{n}$ (since all these people are identical). Thereafter, $\bar{w}[rt(n)\hat{T}]$ increases in $n$ (figure 3).[9] Given the options that an individual faces he chooses the one which maximises his income.

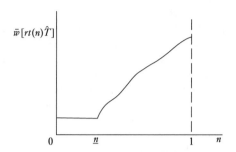

**Figure 3**

For our purpose a precise definition of malnutrition is not required, even for the model economy under study. But for concreteness we are going to choose $\hat{I}$ – the consumption level in figure 1 at which marginal labour power equals average labour power – as the cut-off consumption level below which a person will be said to be undernourished. $\hat{I}$ is then the food-adequacy standard. Nothing of analytical consequence depends on this choice, but since the choice of $\hat{I}$ does have a rationale (see the example in section 4) we may as well adopt it. All we need, for our purpose, is the assumption that the reservation wage of a *landless* person is one at which a person is undernourished, and thus less than $\hat{I}$.

We are then left with the concept of involuntary unemployment, which has yet to be defined. It is sharper than the notion of surplus labour, much discussed in the development literature. We have postulated the existence of a continuum of people with good reason. Involuntary unemployment in the sense that we want to think about here has to do with differential treatment meted out to similar people. Formally we have:

DEFINITION 1   *A person is involuntarily unemployed if he cannot find employment in a market which does employ a person very similar to him and if the latter person, by virtue of his employment in this market, is distinctly better off than him.*

Notice that definition 1 subsumes the case where the persons in question are identical, in which case dissimilar treatment may arise due to rationing in the labour market (see section 3.5). But it has been noted that no two persons are ever identical. The natural generalisation of the idea is therefore definition 1.

## 3. Market Outcome

### 3.1. Efficiency wage

From the example studied by Mirrlees (1975), Rodgers (1975) and Stiglitz (1976) we may infer that a Walrasian (or Arrow–Debreu) equilibrium does not exist in our model economy under a wide class of cases (see section 3.5). The point is that the labour market may not clear. So we assume in what follows that the market has the ability to *ration* labour power if supply of labour power exceeds its demand. A precise mechanism will be suggested below.

In order to keep the exposition simple we will for the rest of the paper specialise somewhat and suppose that $\lambda(I)$ is of the form given in figure 1(b) and is, barring $I^*$, continuously differentiable at all points.[10] We begin by defining $w^*(n, r)$ as:

$$w^*(n, r) \equiv \arg \min_{w \geq \bar{w}[rt(n)\hat{T}]} \left\{ \frac{w}{\lambda[\bar{w} + r\hat{T}t(n)]} \right\} \tag{1}$$

In words, $w^*(n, r)$ is that wage rate (i.e. wage per unit of labour-*time*) which, at the land-rental rate $r$, minimises the wage per unit of labour *power* of $n$-person, conditional on his being willing to work at this wage rate.[11] $w^*(n, r)$ is the *efficiency wage* of $n$-person. It is a function of $n$. We have introduced labour heterogeneity in the model not by assuming that the $\lambda$ function differs from person to person, but by allowing different people to possess different landholdings. This explains why a person's efficiency wage depends in general on the rental rate on land. (A person's efficiency wage depends on his non-labour income.) Since by hypothesis $\hat{I}$ exceeds the reservation wage of the landless, $w^*(n, r) = \hat{I}$ for the landless. For one who owns a tiny amount of land,

$$\bar{w}[rt(n)\hat{T}] < w^*(n, r) < \hat{I}$$

For one with considerable amount of land,

$$w^*(n, r) = \bar{w}[rt(n)\hat{T}]$$

Finally, for one who owns a great deal of land we would expect,

$$w^*(n, r) = \bar{w}[rt(n)\hat{T}] > \hat{I}^{12}$$

Next, define $\mu^*(n, r)$ as:

$$\mu^*(n, r) \equiv \frac{w^*(n, r)}{\lambda\left[w^*(n, r) + r\hat{T}t(n)\right]} \tag{2}$$

Given $r$, $\mu^*(n, r)$ is therefore the minimum wage per unit of labour power for $n$-person, subject to the constraint that he is willing to work. In figure 4(a) a typical shape of $\mu^*(n, r)$ has been drawn. $\mu^*(n, r)$ is 'high' for the landless because they have no non-wage income. In fact, for such people

$$\mu^*(n, r) = \frac{\hat{I}}{\lambda(\hat{I})}$$

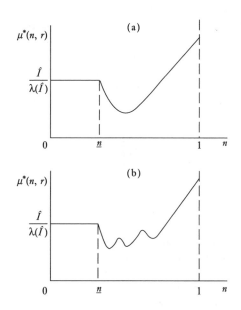

**Figure 4**

It is relatively 'low' for 'smallish' landowners because they *do* have some nonwage income and because their reservation wage is not too high. $\mu^*(n, r)$ is 'high' for the big land-owners because their reservation wages are very 'high'.

While a 'typical' shape of $\mu^*(n, r)$, as in figure 4(a), is used to illustrate the arguments in the main body of the paper, it must be pointed out that our assumptions do *not*, in general, generate this 'U-shaped' curve. Figure 4(b) illustrates other possible configurations of the $\mu^*(n, r)$ function, which are perfectly consistent with the assumptions we have made.[13] What *is* common to all $\mu^*(n, r)$ functions that are obtained from (2) are these features: for a given $r$,

(a)   $\mu^*(n, r)$ is constant for all landless $n$-persons and falls immediately thereafter.
(b)   $\mu^*(n, r)$ continues to decrease in $n$ as long as the reservation wage constraint is not binding in equation (1). (Therefore, whenever $\mu^*(n, r)$ increases with $n$ the reservation wage constraint in (1) *is* binding.)
(c)   Once the reservation wage binds for some $n$-person it continues to do so for all $n$-persons with more land.[14]
(d)   $\mu^*(n, r)$ 'finally' rises as the effect of the increasing reservation wage ultimately outweighs the (diminishing) increments to labour power associated with greater land-ownership.

Having said this, though, we will continue to use the simpler figure 4(a) for the purpose of exposition. The interested reader is referred to the Appendix and Dasgupta and Ray (1984) for the more rigorous arguments.

Bliss and Stern (1978a, b) interpreted $\lambda(I)$ as the (maximum) *number* of *tasks* a person can perform by consuming $I$. In this interpretation we may regard $\mu^*(n, r)$ in equation (2) as the *efficiency-piece-rate* of $n$-person. In what follows we will so regard it.

## 3.2. Market equilibrium

By hypothesis markets are competitive, and there are two factors of production, land and labour power (or tasks). There are thus two competitive factor prices to reckon with. The rental rate on land is $r$. Let $\mu$ denote the price of a unit of labour power, that is, the *piece rate*. (By normalisation, the price of output is unity.) Let $D(n)$ be the market *demand* for the *labour time* of $n$-person, and let $S(n)$ be his labour (time) *supply*. (By assumption $S(n)$ is either zero or unity.) Let $w(n)$ be the wage rate for $n$-person and let $G$ denote the set of $n$-persons who find employment. Production enterprises are profit maximising and each person aims to maximise his income given the opportunities he faces.[15] We now have

DEFINITION 2   *A rental rate $\tilde{r}$, a piece rate $\tilde{\mu}$, a subset $\tilde{G}$ of [0, 1] and a real-valued function $\tilde{w}(n)$ on $\tilde{G}$ sustain a competitive equilibrium if (and only if):*

- (i)   *for all $n$-persons for whom $\tilde{\mu} > \mu^*(n, \tilde{r})$, we have $S(n) = D(n) = 1$;*
- (ii)   *for all $n$-persons for whom $\tilde{\mu} < \mu^*(n, \tilde{r})$, we have $S(n) = D(n) = 0$;*
- (iii)   *for all $n$-persons for whom $\tilde{\mu} = \mu^*(n, \tilde{r})$, we have $S(n) \geqslant D(n)$, where $D(n)$ is either $0$ or $1$ and where $S(n) = I$ if $\tilde{w}(n) > \bar{w}(n, \tilde{r})$ and where $S(n)$ is either $0$ or $1$ if $\tilde{w}(n) = \bar{w}(n, \tilde{r})$; (here we have written $\bar{w}(n, \tilde{r})$ for $\bar{w}[\tilde{r}\hat{T}t(n)]$);*
- (iv)   $\tilde{G} = \{n/D(n) = 1\}$ *and $\tilde{w}(n)$ is the larger of the (possibly) two solutions of $w/\lambda[w + \tilde{r}\hat{T}t(n)] = \tilde{\mu}$, for all $n$ with $D(n) = 1$;[16]*
- (v)   $\tilde{\mu} = \partial F(\tilde{E}, \hat{T})/\partial E$, *where $\tilde{E}$ is the aggregate labour power supplied by all who are employed; that is*

$$\tilde{E} = \int_{\tilde{G}} \lambda[\tilde{w}(n) + \tilde{r}\hat{T}t(n)]dv(n)$$

- (vi)   $\tilde{r} = \partial F(\tilde{E}, \hat{T})/\partial T.$

Now for a verbal account. Since 'production enterprises' are competitive, $\tilde{r}$ must in equilibrium equal the marginal product of land and $\tilde{\mu}$ the marginal product of aggregate labour-power. These are conditions (vi) and (v). Moreover, we should conclude at once from (v) that the market demand for the labour time of an $n$-person whose efficiency-piece-rate exceeds $\tilde{\mu}$ must be nil. Equally, such a person cannot, or, given his reservation wage, will not, supply the labour quality the market bears at the going piece rate $\tilde{\mu}$. (To see this suppose he were employed at wage $w \geqslant \bar{w}[\tilde{r}\hat{T}t(n)]$. For this to be feasible it must be that

$$w + \tilde{r}\hat{T}t(n) \leqslant \tilde{\mu}\lambda[w + \tilde{r}\hat{T}t(n)] + \tilde{r}\hat{T}t(n)$$

and so $w \leqslant \tilde{\mu}\lambda[w + \tilde{r}\hat{T}t(n)]$. This contradicts the fact about this person that $\mu^*(n, \tilde{r}) > \tilde{\mu}$.) This is stated as condition (ii). But what of an $n$-person whose efficiency-piece-rate is less than $\tilde{\mu}$? Plainly every enterprise wants his service. Speaking metaphorically, his *wage rate* is bid up by competition to the point where the piece rate he receives equals $\tilde{\mu}$. Demand for his time is positive. Since the wage he is paid exceeds his reservation wage $(\tilde{\mu} > \mu^*(n, \tilde{r}))$, and so

$$\tilde{w}(n) > w^*(n, \tilde{r}) \geqslant \bar{w}(n, \tilde{r})$$

he most willingly supplies his unit of labour time which, in equilibrium, is what is demanded. This is stated as conditions (i) and (iv). Finally, what of an $n$-person whose efficiency-piece-rate equals $\tilde{\mu}$? Enterprises are indifferent between employing such a worker and not employing him. He is, of course, willing to supply his unit of labour time: with eagerness if the wage he receives in equilibrium exceeds his reservation wage, and as a matter of indifference if it equals it. This is stated in conditions (iii) and (iv). Since the production function is constant-returns-to-scale, production enterprises earn no profits after factor payments have been made. Finally, it is clear that aggregate demand and supply of rice are equal. This follows from Walras' Law which has been incorporated directly into the definition of an equilibrium. We may now state

THEOREM 1 *Under the conditions postulated, a competitive equilibrium exists.*

PROOF   See appendix.

A competitive equilibrium in our economy is not necessarily Walrasian. It is not Walrasian when, for a positive fraction of the population, condition (iii) in definition 2 holds; see section 3.5.[17] Otherwise it is. If in equilibrium, condition (iii) holds for a positive fraction of the population the labour market does not clear and we take it that the market sustains 'equilibrium' by rationing; that is, of this group a fraction is employed while the rest are kept out. For concreteness we may think of a lottery system which accomplishes the rationing.

What do individuals need to know in equilibrium? The information structure in our economy is no different from that required in the Arrow–Debreu theory. All observe the market signals $\tilde{r}$ and $\tilde{\mu}$. The production sector knows the production function $F(\cdot)$, knows the quantity of land it rents and can observe the number of tasks performed by all who are employed by it. (For simplicity of exposition we are postulating a single entrepreneur for the moment.) Each individual knows how much land he possesses and knows his own potential; that is, the $\lambda(I)$ function. Finally, as in the Arrow–Debreu theory, all contracts must, by assumption, be honoured. This means in particular that an $n$-person who finds employment asks for and receives $\tilde{w}(n)$ as a wage and promises to supply $\lambda[\tilde{w}(n) + \tilde{r}\hat{T}t(n)]$ units of labour power (or tasks).

## 3.3. *Simple characteristics of market equilibrium*

In what follows we will characterise equilibria diagrammatically. To do this we merely superimpose the horizontal curve $\mu = \tilde{\mu}$ on to figure 4(a). There are *three* different types of equilibria, or *regimes*, depending on the size of $\hat{T}$, the parameter we vary in the next three subsections. Specifically, we have

THEOREM 2    *A competitive equilibrium is in one of three possible regimes, depending on the total size of land, $\hat{T}$, and the distribution of land. Given the latter:*

(1)    *If $\hat{T}$ is sufficiently small, $\tilde{\mu} < \hat{I}/\lambda(\hat{I})$, and the economy is characterised by malnourishment among all the landless and some of the near-landless (figure 5(a)).*

(2)    *There are ranges of moderate values of $\hat{T}$ in which $\tilde{\mu} = \hat{I}/\lambda(\hat{I})$, and the economy is characterised by malnourishment and involuntary unemployment among a fraction of the landless (figure 5(b)).*

(3)    *If $\hat{T}$ is sufficiently large, $\tilde{\mu} > \hat{I}/\lambda(\hat{I})$, and the economy is characterised by full employment and an absence of malnourishment (figure 5(c)).*

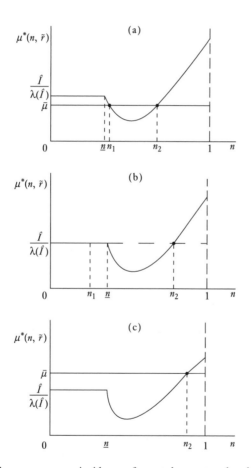

**Figure 5**    (a) Land-poor economy: incidence of unemployment and malnutrition; (b) moderate land endowment: incidence of involuntary unemployment and malnutrition; (c) rich economy: full employment and no malnutrition

PROOF   See appendix.

We will discuss these equilibrium regimes successively in sections 3.4–3.6. But first we note that among those in employment persons owning more land are doubly blessed: they not only enjoy greater rental income, their wages are higher.

THEOREM 3   *Let* $n_1, n_2 \in \tilde{G}$ *with* $t(n_1) < t(n_2)$. *Then* $\tilde{w}(n_1) < \tilde{w}(n_2)$.

PROOF   See appendix.

A strong implication of this result is that competition, in some sense, *widens* the initial disparities in asset ownership by offering larger (employed) landowners a higher *wage* income. Contrast this with the results of Bliss and Stern (1978*a*). There, a monopsonist landlord narrows initial asset disparities in his quest to equalise marginal labour power across all labour types. Competition, by placing productive asset-holders at a premium in the job market, has exactly the opposite effect.

## 3.4. *Regime 1: Malnourishment among the landless and near-landless*

Figure 5(a) depicts a typical equilibrium under regime 1. ($\hat{T}$ is small and so from the first part of theorem 2, $\tilde{\mu} < \hat{I}/\lambda(\hat{I})$.) From condition (i) of definition 2, one notes that all $n$-persons between $n_1$ and $n_2$ are employed in the production of rice. Typically, the borderline $n_1$-person will be one for whom the market wage $\tilde{w}(n_1)$ will exceed his reservation wage $\bar{w}[\tilde{r}t(n_1)\hat{T}]$. We will assume this in the exposition. From condition (ii) of definition 2, we observe that all $n$-persons below $n_1$ and above $n_2$ are out of the market: the former because their labour power is too expensive, the latter because their reservation wages are too high – they are too rich.

It should also be noted that in this regime, all the landless are malnourished. Indeed, it can be verified that (if, as we are assuming in this essay, malnourishment incomes are defined to be those below $\hat{I}$) *all* persons between $\underline{n}$ and $n_1$ are also malnourished, their rental income is too meagre. Finally, note that some of the *employed* are also malnourished, which is verifiable by noting that employed persons slightly to the right of $n_1$ consume less than $\hat{I}$.

To be sure, there are no job queues in the labour market; nevertheless, there is involuntary unemployment in the sense of definition 1. To see this note first that $\tilde{w}(n_1) > \bar{w}[\tilde{r}t(n_1)\hat{T}]$. This implies that $\tilde{w}(n) > \bar{w}[\tilde{r}t(n)\hat{T}]$ for all $n$ in a neighbourhood to the *right* of $n_1$. Such people are employed. They are therefore *distinctly* better off than $n$-persons in a neighbourhood to the *left* of $n_1$, who suffer their reservation wage. This means that the equilibrium income schedule is discontinuous at $n_1$. Such a discontinuity is at odds with the Arrow–Debreu theory with convex structures.

Finally, observe that $n$-persons above $n_2$ are *voluntarily* unemployed. Call them the pure rentiers, or the landed gentry. They *are* capable of supplying labour at the piece-rate $\tilde{\mu}$ called for by the market, but *choose* not to: their reservation wages are too high. They are to be contrasted with unemployed people below $n_1$, who are *incapable* of supplying labour at $\tilde{\mu}$.

### 3.5. Regime 2: Malnourishment and involuntary unemployment among the landless

The relevant curves are as drawn in figure 5(b). Here $\tilde{\mu} = \hat{I}/\lambda(\hat{I})$. It is not a fluke case: it pertains to certain intermediate ranges of $\hat{T}$. (We are keeping land distribution fixed here.) The economy equilibrates by rationing landless people in the labour market. (We may suppose that it does so by means of a lottery.) In figure 5(b) all $n$-persons between $\underline{n}$ and $n_2$ are employed ((i) of definition 2). All $n$-persons above $n_2$ are out of the labour market because their reservation wages are too high ((ii) of definition 2). A fraction of the landless, $n_1/\underline{n}$, is involuntarily unemployed, the remaining fraction, $I - n_1/\underline{n}$, is employed. The size of this fraction depends on $\hat{T}$. Those among the landless that are employed are paid $\hat{I}$. Those who are unemployed suffer their reservation wage. They are malnourished. The labour market does not clear.

Finally, we observe that, by our definition of malnourishment incomes as being those below $\hat{I}$, the group of unemployed and malnourished people *coincide* under this regime. This is to be contrasted with regime 1.

### 3.6. Regime 3: The full employment equilibrium

Figure 5(c) presents the third and final regime, pertinent for large values of $\hat{T}$. Here, $\tilde{\mu} > \hat{I}/\lambda(\hat{I})$. From part (i) of definition 2 we conclude that all persons from zero to $n_2$ are employed. From (ii) we note that those above $n_2$ are not employed. But, as before, they are not involuntarily unemployed: they are the landed gentry. Thus this regime is characterised by full employment, and no one is undernourished. This corresponds to a standard Arrow–Debreu equilibrium.

### 3.7. Growth as a means of reducing the incidence of malnourishment and unemployment

It is difficult to resist extending the conclusions of the timeless structure and introducing time. So we will not try. One can imagine an economy with a small $\hat{T}$ and a given distribution of land, $t(n)$. An equilibrium is characterised by figure 5(a). If the propertied class, which is well-to-do at the equilibrium, accumulates in land improvement – that is, in capital that improves the productivity of land – $\hat{T}$ will increase. Assuming that land distribution, $t(n)$, remains approximately the same, it would follow that with $\hat{T}$ increasing more and more, the economy will after some time enter the regime depicted by figure 5(b), and eventually the final regime of figure 5(c).[18] It is only in the final regime that no one is undernourished. We take it that this is what 'trickle-down' theory amounts to.

Of course, if we introduce time we must also introduce a capital market and allow peasants to borrow. As accumulation (increase in $\hat{T}$) takes place one expects the equilibrium piece-rate to increase in regime 1. Thus borrowing will, *ceteris paribus*, accelerate the transition from regime 1 to regime 2, since a peasant who borrows and is employed, consumes in excess of his current income and thus increases his productivity. On the other hand, if the economy is a closed one this borrowing must be from high $n$-persons and loans are an alternative to land improvement. This will lower the progress of the economy.

In regime 2, accumulation raises employment rather than the piece-rate. As the end of regime 2 approaches, all landless peasants may wish to borrow. A capital market will modify the 'trickle', but it will not eliminate any of the three regimes.

## 4. An Example

We assume

$$
\lambda(I) = \begin{cases} \bar{\lambda} > 0 & \text{if } I \geqslant \hat{I} > 0 \\ 0 & \text{if } I < \hat{I} \end{cases} \tag{3}
$$

$$
t(n) = \begin{cases} \dfrac{1}{1 - \underline{n}} & \text{for } n \geqslant \underline{n} \geqslant 0 \\ 0 & \text{for } 0 \leqslant n < \underline{n} \end{cases} \tag{4}
$$

$$
\bar{w}(R) = 0 \qquad \text{for all } R \geqslant 0 \tag{5}
$$

$$
F(E, T) = E^a T^{1-a} \qquad 0 < a < 1 \tag{6}
$$

In words, (3) says that the food–productivity relationship is a step-function, (4) says that it is a two-class economy, (5) says that the reservation wage is nil for all persons, and (6) postulates a Cobb–Douglas production function. (3) and (4) violate the conditions assumed in section 3.1. (For example, both $\lambda(I)$ and $t(n)$ have so far been assumed to be continuous.) Clearly, though, we can approximate them by functions satisfying those conditions as closely as we like. The example is thus a valid one to use for illustrating the theory. It also indicates that assumptions of continuity, etc. are essentially simplifying devices for the model.

Using (3)–(5) in equation (1) we find the efficiency-wage of $n$-person to be

$$
w^*(n, r) = \begin{cases} \hat{I} & \text{for } 0 \leqslant n < \underline{n} \\ \max\left[0, \hat{I} - \dfrac{r\hat{T}}{1-n}\right]/\bar{\lambda} & \text{for } 1 \geqslant n \geqslant \underline{n} \end{cases} \tag{7}
$$

Likewise, using (3)–(5) in equation (2) yields the efficiency-piece-rate as

$$
\mu^*(n, r) = \begin{cases} \hat{I}/\bar{\lambda} & \text{for } 0 \leqslant n < \underline{n} \\ \max\left[0, \hat{I} - \dfrac{r\hat{T}}{1-n}\right]/\bar{\lambda} & \text{for } 1 \geqslant n \geqslant \underline{n} \end{cases} \tag{8}
$$

We will first vary $\hat{T}$ so as to illustrate theorem 2 and the claims made in sections 3.4–3.6. It is in fact simplest to write down the equilibrium conditions for regime 2 (section 3.5 and figure 5(b)), because $\tilde{\mu}$ is anchored to $\hat{I}/\lambda(\hat{I})$. So, on using (3)–(8) in theorem 2 we note that the equilibrium conditions in regime 2 are:

$$
\tilde{E} = \bar{\lambda}(1 - n_1) \tag{9}
$$

where $0 < n_1 < \underline{n} < 1$

$$\tilde{r} = \bar{\lambda}^a (1 - n_1)^a (1 - a) \hat{T}^{-a} \tag{10}$$

$$\tilde{\mu} = a \bar{\lambda}^{(a-1)} (1 - n_1)^{(a-1)} \hat{T}^{(1-a)} \tag{11}$$

and

$$\tilde{\mu} = \frac{\hat{I}}{\bar{\lambda}} \tag{12}$$

Note that $\tilde{G} = [n | D(n) = 1] = [n_1, 1]$.

Equations (9)–(12) are four in number, and there are four unknowns, $\tilde{E}$, $\tilde{r}$, $\tilde{\mu}$ and $n_1$, to solve for. Using (11) and (12) we note that

$$n_1 = 1 - \left[\frac{a \bar{\lambda}^a \hat{T}^{(1-a)}}{\hat{I}}\right]^{1/(1-a)} \tag{13}$$

Now, in regime 2 one must have $0 < n_1 < \underline{n} < 1$. Using this in equation (13) we conclude that *given* $\underline{n}$, for the economy to be in regime 2, $\hat{T}$ must satisfy the inequalities:

$$(1 - \underline{n}) \left(\frac{\hat{I}}{a \bar{\lambda}^a}\right)^{1/(1-a)} < \hat{T} < \left(\frac{\hat{I}}{a \bar{\lambda}^a}\right)^{1/(1-a)} \tag{14}$$

that is, if $\hat{T}$ is neither too large nor too small (section 3.5).

From (14) we conclude that the economy is in regime 3 if $\hat{T} \geqslant (\hat{I}/a\bar{\lambda}^a)^{1/(1-a)}$, no matter what the distribution of land holdings is, a result which we will generalise in the sequel. Since $n_1 = 0$ in regime 3 (figure 5(c)) competitive equilibrium can be explicitly computed to be

$$\tilde{E} = \bar{\lambda}$$

$$\tilde{r} = \bar{\lambda}^a (1 - a) \hat{T}^{-a}$$

and $\tag{15}$

$$\tilde{\mu} = a \bar{\lambda}^{(a-1)} \hat{T}^{(1-a)} > \frac{\hat{I}}{\bar{\lambda}}$$

From (14) we also conclude that the economy is in regime 1 (section 3.4 and figure 5(a)), if

$$\hat{T} \leqslant (1 - \underline{n}) \left(\frac{\hat{I}}{a \bar{\lambda}^a}\right)^{1/(1-a)}$$

The regime 1 equilibrium exhibits employment of all from $\underline{n}$ to 1 as long as $\hat{T}$ is not too small. To calculate this bound, assume first that the equilibrium set $\tilde{G} = [\underline{n}, 1]$; then

$$
\begin{aligned}
\tilde{E} &= \bar{\lambda}(1 - \underline{n}) \\
\tilde{r} &= \bar{\lambda}^a (1 - \underline{n})^a (1 - a) \hat{T}^{-a}
\end{aligned}
\tag{16}
$$

and

$$
\tilde{\mu} = a[\bar{\lambda}(1 - \underline{n})]^{a-1} \hat{T}^{-a} < \frac{\hat{I}}{\bar{\lambda}}
$$

And this is an equilibrium as long as $\tilde{\mu} \geqslant \mu^*(n, \tilde{r})$ for all $n \in [\underline{n}, 1]$, or if

$$
a[\bar{\lambda}(1 - \underline{n})]^{a-1} \hat{T}^{1-a} \geqslant \frac{\hat{I} - \dfrac{\tilde{r}\hat{T}}{1 - \underline{n}}}{\bar{\lambda}}
\tag{17}
$$

Substituting for $\tilde{r}$ and rearranging, one obtains

$$
\hat{T} \geqslant a^{1/(1-a)} (1 - \underline{n}) \left( \frac{\hat{I}}{a\bar{\lambda}^a} \right)^{1/(1-a)}
\tag{18}
$$

Note that, since $a < 1$, the right-hand side of (18) is smaller than the left-hand side of (14), which is the borderline for regime 1.

If $\hat{T}$ does not satisfy (18), then we are in regime 1 where only a subset of $[\underline{n}, 1]$ is employed. No generality is lost by choosing this subset to be $[n_1, 1]$, where $n_1 > \underline{n}$.

For such equilibria, $\tilde{\mu} = \mu^*(n, \tilde{r})$; in other words, defining

$$
\begin{aligned}
\tilde{E} &= \bar{\lambda}(1 - n_1) \\
\tilde{r} &= \bar{\lambda}^a (1 - n_1)^a (1 - a) \hat{T}^{-a}
\end{aligned}
\tag{19}
$$

and

$$
\tilde{\mu} = a\left[\bar{\lambda}(1 - n_1)\right]^{a-1} \hat{T}^{1-a} < \frac{\hat{I}}{\bar{\lambda}}
$$

as the equilibrium magnitudes, we solve for $n_1$ by using (8) and (19) to obtain

$$
a\left[\bar{\lambda}(1 - n_1)\right]^{a-1} \hat{T}^{1-a} = \frac{\hat{I} - \dfrac{\tilde{r}\hat{T}}{1 - \underline{n}}}{\bar{\lambda}}
\tag{20}
$$

Rearranging, $n_1$ is the solution to

$$a\bar{\lambda}^a(1 - n_1)^{a-1}\hat{T}^{1-a} + \frac{(1 - a)\bar{\lambda}^a(1 - n_1)^a\hat{T}^{1-a}}{1 - \underline{n}} = \hat{I} \tag{21}$$

This describes the regimes.

## 5. Commentary

How robust are our general conclusions against relaxation of the underlying assumptions in the model? Five obvious extensions suggest themselves and we discuss them briefly.[19]

HETEROGENEITY  People differ. So the food-productivity relation $\lambda(\cdot)$ should depend on the characteristics of the person in question, including his history. (Climate matters too, but we are keeping that fixed for all people.) Let $m$ (for simplicity, a real number) denote an additional index characterising an individual and let the function $\lambda$ depend on the parameter $m$. A person is then denoted by a pair of numbers $(m, n)$ and in the obvious notation, $\lambda = \lambda(I_n, m)$ where $I_n = w + r\hat{T}t(n)$. We may now define the population to be a uniform bivariate distribution on $(m, n)$ pairs and reconstruct our analysis. Nothing of substance will change.

HOUSEHOLD DECISIONS  Notice that this device can also be used to distinguish people by their family size and thus their family commitments. A person with a family does not consume the entire income he collects. He shares with his family. *Ceteris paribus* the larger is his family the less he consumes of the income he collects. If it is reasonable to simplify and suppose that members in a household share total income in some fixed manner, the foregoing index scheme will suffice. If not, we will need to formulate the manner in which a typical household decides to share its income and then label people as well by their household size. The number of dependants (and this will of course be endogenous in the model because the person in question may have a spouse or a sibling who also is in search of a job outside) and the sharing rule will (endogenously) tell us how much of a person's income will be consumed by him. The rest of the argument is monumentally tedious, but routine.

It is often thought that the concept of involuntary unemployment is of necessity restricted to a wage economy and that a recognition that people do household chores and cultivate family plots, will spell ruin for the concept and that we will need to rethink the entire issue. Not so. The concept has to do with *work options* open to a person and to those who are *similar* to him. It is a special case of a concern with consumption options open to a person and to those who are similar to him. The concept has to do with *localised* inequality in available options, or horizontal inequity in work options. Definition 1 can easily be generalised for non-market environments.

It is a profound tragedy that a family in absolute poverty not only has to make do with so little, it cannot even afford to share its poverty equally. In his highly original analytical work Mirrlees (1975) pointed out that a poor family is forced to divide its consumption unequally among its members when the relation between food intake and work capacity assumes the forms we have considered in this essay. These considerations and the related issue of gender-bias in nutrition-status within the household bear on household decisions. Including them in an analysis will not affect our general conclusions regarding *interfamily* transactions, the subject of this essay.

MORAL HAZARD   How can an employer tell how much of his income the worker will himself consume? Should he not expect leakage? Furthermore, what guarantee is there that the worker will not shamefully waste his calories by playing and dancing in his spare time? Neither matters for our theory if, as we have assumed, contracts are always honoured. An employer does not care *what* a worker does with his calories so long as the piece-rate that he is paid does not exceed the market rate. (Of course, the employer must be able to observe the number of tasks the worker actually completes. Otherwise, piece rates cannot be implemented.) Recall that we are here discussing *competitive* markets. A *monopsonistic* landlord *will* care and will take steps to see that wages are not frittered away in frivolous activities.[20] But that is a different matter.

NOISY λ   People cannot possibly know their own $\lambda(\cdot)$ function. So then how can a person commit himself to performing the tasks he undertakes to accomplish? He cannot of course. He, like his employer, will be taking risks when agreeing on a contract. Their attitudes to risk, the availability of risk markets and so forth, will influence the final outcome. These are familiar terrains, similar to the uncertainty one faces in production theory. Protestations notwithstanding, food-productivity relations are no more an abstraction than are production functions, input–output tables and 'books of blue-prints'. The fact that we may *think* we know less about them does not make them any the less real. (We have explored these issues further in Dasgupta and Ray, 1987.)

TIME AND HISTORY   Sukhatme (1978), among others, has argued that a person's metabolic efficiency in the *use* of energy adjusts over time to alterations in his energy intake. Put another way, there are multiple metabolic equilibria for a person; in particular, even hungry people operate sometimes with 'metabolic slack'. It is easy to misuse this observation. It does *not* say (and it would be totally absurd if it said otherwise) that this adjustment can occur indefinitely with vanishing food intake. The food–productivity relation used in this paper captures in the simplest manner possible the fact that humans are biological entities. Of *course* a person's history matters; that is, $\lambda$ at any date for a person depends on his entire nutrition and work history. This complicates things, but does not alter our general conclusions; so long, that is, as the $\lambda$ function has regions of increasing-returns.

A person's past nutritional status is like a capital asset and when this affects present and future productivity there is a problem of intertemporal externality. Unless long-term labour contracts can be signed – and the existence of casual labour suggests that they often are not – employers will not be able to appropriate all the future benefits from employing persons. As one would expect, such missing markets will tend to depress wages (Mazumdar, 1959). But nothing of substance will be affected in our analysis.

A person's history can be telling and very pernicious for him. For example, it has been suggested to us by a referee that if our model economy of section 3 languishes in a stationary state (no accumulation) in regime 2 then our concept of involuntary unemployment is useless because *on average* all the landless will be employed the same *number* of periods. (This would be so if in each period a lottery is used to ration the labour market.) So then over the long haul there is equality among the landless. This is certainly so. But now introduce a tiny bit of history. Suppose a person's nutrition status in one period affects his $\lambda$ function in the next period. Suppose the landless are all identical to begin with. In the first period a fraction will be employed. Which particular people we cannot tell in advance because a lottery is in use. But in the next period the previously employed have a slight advantage (because of their better nutrition history). From then on, most of these same people will find employment, and all of those who languished in the first period, through bad luck, will continue to languish; no longer through bad luck but through *cumulative causation*. The evils of malnutrition and involuntary unemployment cannot be exorcised by mathematical sophistry.

## 6. Conclusions

People without assets are doubly cursed. Not only do they not enjoy non-labour income, they are at a disadvantage in the labour market relative to those who do possess assets. If the efficiency-piece-rate of a wealthy man is too high for anyone to wish to hire him it is because his reservation wage is too high. He is not unemployed. Not so for the assetless. Such a man's efficiency-piece-rate is high not because he does not *want* to work but because his entire food intake must be wage-based. Thus he either cannot offer the labour quality the market demands and so must languish in a state of malnourishment (section 3.4, regime 1), or can, but is, if unlucky, prevented from joining the labour force because of rationing (section 3.5, regime 2). In the latter case he is involuntarily unemployed and malnourished. The central purpose of this essay has been to illustrate these points and to explore their ramifications.

We have argued in this essay that the market may force identical persons to be treated differently – in particular to award some a job and adequate nutrition and to keep others out in a state of malnourishment – and in the sequel we will show that this can happen even if the economy is rich enough in assets to feed all adequately. The reason is that because a large fraction of the population is landless the market cannot 'afford' to employ all. Inequality as such is not the worst of evils. But malnourishment in the midst of potential plenty (as in theorem 4 of the sequel) is not far from being one. While it is true that if accumulation – e.g., via an improvement in land – proceeds, unemployment, and thus malnutrition, will be eradicated in the model economy in time (theorem 2). However, it may be a long while coming. For the immediate future the 'quantity' of land cannot be altered much. But the extreme inequality in food consumption which the market inflicts *can* be countered. For economies not generously endowed with physical assets the competitive market mechanism must be judged an unmitigated disaster. The policy implications in the model economy are clear enough and will be explored in the sequel.

At the mathematical level it is easy to see why, despite pure competition, there is involuntary unemployment when the number of landless people is large. It is because of the inherent increasing-returns-to-scale in the food–productivity relation of a person at low consumption levels (Figure 1).[21] It is because of this that the theory outlined here is so different from the Arrow–Debreu theory of perfect competition with convex structures. We have argued that given the land distribution function $t(n)$, it is only when the total quantity of land is large (when $\hat{T}$ is large) that pure competition in the economy in question merges with the standard Arrow–Debreu theory (theorem 2, regime 3). In the sequel (theorem 4) we will show that if there is sufficient land to feed all but it is not a land-rich country then competitive equilibrium in our model economy merges with the standard Arrow–Debreu equilibrium only if land distribution is sufficiently equal. In the sequel we will also show (see theorem 5 in the sequel) that if the aggregate quantity of land is very large land distribution does not matter as regards employment and malnutrition: an equilibrium is a conventional Arrow–Debreu one. We take this to mean that the Arrow–Debreu theory pertains only to an economy which is asset-rich. This is not to say that an Arrow–Debreu equilibrium has much to commend it from the point of view of the distribution of welfare. There is, however, nothing new in this point and it is not the one we want to make here. The point we *are* making here is that the Arrow–Debreu theory does not have a *vocabulary* either for malnutrition or for involuntary unemployment.[22] The central purpose of this essay has been to provide here a simple theory that can accommodate these notions, and in particular to expose their link with the inequality in asset ownership.

## APPENDIX

In what follows we present proofs of the theorems stated in the text. On occasion we will, for brevity, only sketch an argument. For details, see Dasgupta and Ray (1984), Appendix.

We assume that the food–productivity curve, $\lambda(I)$, has the properties displayed in figure 1(b); that is, $\lambda(I) = 0$ for $0 \leqslant I \leqslant I^*$, with $I^* > 0$, $\lambda(I)$ is increasing and strictly concave on $[I^*, \infty)$, and barring $I^*$, $\lambda$ is continuously differentiable at all points. Finally, assume that $\lambda(I)$ is bounded above.

We turn to the production function $F(E, T)$. We take it that in addition to the assumption made in the text, $F(E, T)$ satisfies the Inada conditions, that is:

$$F_E(E, \hat{T}) \to 0 \text{ as } E \to \infty$$

$$F_E(E, \hat{T}) \to \infty \text{ as } E \to 0$$

$$F_T(E, \hat{T}) \to 0 \text{ as } \hat{T} \to \infty$$

$$F_T(E, \hat{T}) \to \infty \text{ as } \hat{T} \to 0$$

## *Proof of theorem I*

For each $r > 0$ define $E(r)$ by the condition

$$r = F_T[E(r), \hat{T}] \tag{22}$$

Note that $E(r)$ is unique for each $r$ and that $E(r) \to 0$ as $r \to 0$ and $E(r) \to \infty$ as $r \to \infty$. Likewise, for each $r > 0$ define $\mu(r)$ by the condition

$$\mu(r) \equiv F_E[E(r), \hat{T}] \tag{23}$$

Note that $\mu(r)$ is unique for each $r$ and that $\mu(r) \to \infty$ as $r \to 0$ and $\mu(r) \to 0$ as $r \to \infty$.

Let $B(r) \equiv [n|\mu^*(n, r) < \mu(r)]$ and $G(r) \equiv [n|\mu^*(n, r) \leqslant \mu(r)]$. Notice that $G(r)$ is *not*, in general, the closure of $B(r)$. Now define

$$H(r) \equiv \{G \subseteq [0, 1] | \ G \text{ is closed and } B(r) \subseteq G \subseteq G(r)\} \tag{24}$$

If $G(r)$ is non-empty, then for each $n \in G(r)$ it is possible to define $w(n, r)$ uniquely by the pair of conditions

$$\frac{w(n, r)}{\lambda[w(n, r) + r\hat{T}t(n)]} = \mu(r) \tag{25}$$

and

$$w(n, r) \geqslant w^*(n, r)$$

Note that $w(n, r)$ is continuous in $n$ and $r$. Finally, define the correspondence $M(r)$ as follows:

$$M(r) = \begin{cases} \{E \in R^1 | E = \int_G \lambda[w(n, r) + r\hat{T}t(n)]d\nu(n), G \in H(r)\} & \text{if } G(r) \text{ is not empty} \\ \{0\} & \text{if } G(r) \text{ is empty} \end{cases} \tag{26}$$

It is possible to show that for all $r > 0$, $M(r)$ is an *interval* (possibly a degenerate interval, a singleton); see Dasgupta and Ray (1984, appendix, lemma 1). It is also possible to show that if $\{r^l\}$ is a positive sequence, with $r^l \to r > 0$ as $l \to \infty$, and if $E^l \in M(r^l)$, with $E^l \to E$ as $l \to \infty$, then $E \in M(r)$; see Dasgupta and Ray (1984, appendix, lemma 2).

Now, for $r > 0$ but sufficiently small, we have for all $n \in [0, 1]$,

$$\mu^*(n, r) \leqslant \mu^*(n, 0) = \frac{\hat{I}}{\lambda(\hat{I})} < \mu(r)$$

Using this we note that for $r$ small enough, min $M(r)$ is bounded away from zero, so that near zero, min $M(r) > E(r)$, for recall that $E(r) \to 0$ as $r \to 0$. Since $\lambda(\cdot)$ is bounded, so is max $M(r)$ for all $r$.

Furthermore, since $E(r) \to \infty$ as $r \to \infty$ we have for large $r$, max $M(r) < E(r)$. It is easy to verify that there exists a $\tilde{r} > 0$ and $\tilde{E} \in M(\tilde{r})$ such that $\tilde{E} = E(\tilde{r}) > 0$. Thus $G(\tilde{r})$ is non-empty. Now pick $\tilde{G} \in H(\tilde{r})$ such that

$$\tilde{E} = \int_{\tilde{G}} \lambda[w(n, \tilde{r}) + \tilde{r}\hat{T}t(n)]d\nu(n) \tag{27}$$

and define $\tilde{w}(n) \equiv w(n, \tilde{r})$ for all $n \in \tilde{G}$. Finally define $\tilde{\mu} = \tilde{\mu}(\tilde{r})$ from (23). The quartet $\{\tilde{r}, \tilde{\mu}, \tilde{w}(n), \tilde{G}\}$ sustain a competitive equilibrium, as can easily be checked from definition 2.

## Proof of theorem 2

Parts (1) and (3) follow directly from the Inada conditions on the production function, $F(\cdot, \cdot)$ and the fact that $\tilde{E}$ in (27) is bounded above (since $\lambda(\cdot)$ is bounded above). What remains to be proved is that regime 2 occurs over at least one non-degenerate interval of values for $\hat{T}$. This can be confirmed by noting that the proof of theorem 1 can be easily extended to demonstrate that the equilibrium correspondence is upper hemicontinuous in $\hat{T}$.

## Proof of theorem 3

Write $I(n) = w(n) + r\hat{T}t(n)$ for $n \in G$. Clearly $\lambda[I(n)] > 0$. Since $\lambda(I)$ is strictly concave when $\lambda(I) > 0$, we have

$$\tilde{w}(n_2) - \tilde{w}(n_1) = \tilde{\mu}\{\lambda[\tilde{I}(n_2)] - \lambda[\tilde{I}(n_1)]\}$$
$$> \tilde{\mu}[\tilde{I}(n_2) - \tilde{I}(n_1)]\lambda'[\tilde{I}(n_2)]$$

which on rearrangement, yields

$$[\tilde{w}(n_2) - \tilde{w}(n_1)]\{1 - \tilde{\mu}\lambda'[\tilde{I}(n_2)]\} = \hat{T}\tilde{\mu}\lambda'[\tilde{I}(n_2)][t(n_2) - t(n_1)]\tilde{r} > 0 \tag{28}$$

Now, the first-order condition for the maximisation problem (1) in the text is,

$$\frac{\lambda(w^* + \bar{R})}{w^*} \geqslant \lambda'(w^* + \bar{R}) \qquad \text{for all } \bar{R} \geqslant 0$$

This and the fact that $\tilde{w}(n_2) \geqslant w^*(n_2, \tilde{r})$ imply

$$\lambda[\tilde{I}(n_2)] \geqslant \tilde{w}(n_2)\lambda'[\tilde{I}(n_2)] \tag{29}$$

It is simple to check from characteristics (b) and (c) of $\mu^*(n, r)$ in the text that if $n_1, n_2 \in \tilde{G}$ and $t(n_2) > t(n_1)$ then *either* $w^*(n_2, \tilde{r}) = \tilde{w}(n_2, \tilde{r})$ *or* $\tilde{w}(n_2) > w^*(n_2, \tilde{r})$. In either case (29) is a *strict* inequality. Using this and condition (iv) of definition 2 it follows that $I > \tilde{\mu}\lambda'[\tilde{I}(n_2)]$ in (28).

### Notes

1   See Lipton (1983). By undernourishment we mean here, following Lipton, calorie deficiency only, recognising of course that a food-adequacy-standard must meet other requirements as well, such as protein, vitamins and minerals, and that a person's *state of health* depends also on education (see Behrman and Wolfe, 1984) and on the medical and sanitation facilities available to him and made use of by him. These, among other reasons, are why Lipton's estimates are conservative.

2   See FAO (1957, 1963, 1973, 1974) for systematic, downward revisions of the energy needs of the 'reference man'. Their 1973 assessment – a daily need of 2,600 kilocalories for maintenance and 400 kilocalories for moderate activity for an average male aged between 20 and 39, weighing 65 kilograms and living in a mean ambient temperature of 10 °C – is now acknowledged to be too high and is, in any case, not the basis on which global estimates of the extent of under-nutrition ought to be based. As a consequence the 1973 assessment has been the cause of much heated, and often misdirected, debate. For an assessment of the implication of the clinical literature, see Dasgupta and Ray (1986).

3   A sustained national case-study on these matters is the continuing series of reports by C. Gopalan and his associates, for India. A brief summary of his group's findings is in Gopalan (1983). A great deal of the controversy generated by the publication of national estimates (such as those in India) of numbers of people below the poverty line has centred on the point that there are inter-regional and interpersonal variations in basic nutrition needs. It should also be noted that there is evidence that a person's metabolic efficiency in the *use* of energy adjusts, *up to a point*, to alterations in his energy intake. But even when such corrections are allowed for, worldwide incidence of undernourishment assumes an awesome figure well in excess of three hundred million people.

4   One may of course ask in what sense a person can be said to be rich and yet be hungry – unless it is by anorexic or other compulsion.

5   There is now, following Harris and Todaro (1970), a large development literature that has studied the implications of wage rigidities on migration decisions. But for the most part such wage rigidities are not explained in this literature.

6   Since we will be thinking of a wage-based economy it would be more appropriate to think of the output as a cash crop which can be traded internationally at a fixed price for rice. It should be added that the one-good structure bars us from addressing a number of important related issues concerning the composition of consumption among different income groups, in particular the silent food wars that are being fought among them. On this, see Yotopolous (1985).

7   We also suppose that $F(E, T)$ satisfies the Inada conditions (see Appendix). These are technical conditions designed to streamline proofs. They are innocuous.

8   'Smoother' labour–leisure choices can easily be built in, but it would violate the spirit of the exercise so much that we do not introduce it.

9   It would add complications to the notation enormously were we to 'endogenise' the reservation wage by, say, modelling a 'begging market' and it would add nothing by way of insights. So we take the reservation wage schedule as exogenously given. Furthermore, the assumption that the reservation wage is an increasing function of $n$ is not at all important for the model. We postulate it for realism and to allow for the establishment of a leisure-class.

10  The theory that we are developing here can certainly accommodate figure 1(a), but it requires additional, fairly complicated exposition. So we avoid it. The reader can extend the arguments that follow to this case. Indeed, we will indicate some of these extensions as we go along. In the text we shall continue to describe properties of various functions by the help of diagrams. In the Appendix these properties will be formally stated.

11  Given that the $\lambda$ function is of the form depicted in figure 1(b), the right-hand side of equation (1) has a unique value. If the $\lambda$ function is of the $s$-shaped form of figure 1(a) the right-hand side of (1) is not necessarily unique. When not, we would choose the largest solution (which in fact exists) and define $w^*(n, r)$ as the largest solution.

12  The reader can easily check this by translating the curve in figure 1(b) to the *left* by the amount $r\hat{T}t(n)$ and then using equation (1).

13  We have not been able to find reasonable assumptions that will generate the U-shape, so we do not impose any such structure in the mathematical arguments of the Appendix. This necessitates the use of some fairly complicated technical arguments.

14   This is not, in general, true for the more complicated consumption-ability curve of figure 1(a), but that does not affect the main arguments.

15   Or more precisely, he compares his maximal income if he is working in the economy in question to the sum of his reservation wage and maximal non-wage income if he is not working in this economy.

16   All relevant functions such as $D(n)$ are taken to be measurable. Lebesgue measure is denoted by $\nu(\cdot)$. Observe that the two stated conditions regarding $w(n)$ define it uniquely for each employed $n$-person.

17   Equilibrium, as we have defined it, is equivalent to a *quasi-equilibrium* in Debreu (1962) and is for our model, also equivalent to the concept of *compensated equilibrium* in Arrow and Hahn (1971). A formal identification would involve an infinity of commodities, each different value of $\lambda$ (or labour 'quality') being identified as one such commodity.

18   We have not been able to prove that under general conditions the economy moves monotonically from regime 1 to 2 and then to 3 with increasing $\hat{T}$. The example in section 4 does, however, display this feature.

19   We will not discuss relaxation of the competitive hypothesis for reasons that we mentioned in section 1. Bliss and Stern (1978a) have discussed some of the consequences of there being a monopsonistic landlord.

20   An extreme case is slavery On the constraints imposed on the activities of slaves see Miller and Genovese (1974). Rodgers (1975) and Stiglitz (1976) analysed an economy in which the landowners' reservation wage is in effect infinity. Thus the only possible workers are the landless. But in this case it makes no difference whether there is a single employer (i.e. labour monopsony) or many: *the outcome is the same*! Because of this happy analytical coincidence Rodgers and Stiglitz did not need to develop the apparatus required to discuss non-monopsonistic markets, a need which cannot be avoided if one wishes to explore the implications of land reform (see the sequel); for, *after* a reform the labour market cannot be monopsonistic.

21   This is conjunction with the fact that the initial endowment points of the landless lie on the boundary of their consumption-possibility sets.

22   The Arrow–Debreu theory does not ever claim to do so. It is of course the great power of the Arrow–Debreu analysis to have found (sufficient) conditions under which involuntary unemployment will *not* occur.


## References

Arrow, K. and Hahn, F. (1971): *General Competitive Analysis*. San Francisco: Holden Day.

Behrman, J. R. and Wolfe, B. L. (1984): "More Evidence on Nutrition Demand: Income Seems Overrated and Women's Schooling Underemphasized," *Journal of Development Economics*, 14, 105–28.

Bliss, C. J. and Stern, N. H. (1978a): "Productivity, Wages and Nutrition, 1: The Theory," *Journal of Development Economics*, 5, 331–62.

——and——(1978b): "Productivity, Wages and Nutrition, 2: Some Observations," *Journal of Development Economics*, 5, 363–97.

Da Costa, E. P. W. (1971): "A Portrait of Indian Poverty," in A. J. Fonsaca (ed.), *Challenge of Poverty in India*, Delhi: Vikas Publications.

Dasgupta, P. and Ray, D. (1984): "Inequality, Malnutrition and Unemployment: A Critique of the Competitive Market Mechanism," IMSSS technical report 454, Stanford University, and CEPR discussion paper 50, 6 Duke of York Street, London.

——and——(1986): "Adjusting to Undernutrition: The Clinical Evidence and Its Implications," mimeo, Helsinki: World Institute for Development Economics Research.

——and——(1987): "Inequality as a Determinant of Malnutrition and Unemployment: Policy," *Economic Journal*, 97 March, 385.

Debreu, G. (1962): "New Concepts and Techniques for Equilibrium Analysis," *International Economic Review*, 3, 257–73.

FAO (1957): *Calorie Requirements*. Nutritional Studies, 15, Rome.

——(1963): *Third World Food Survey*. Freedom from Hunger Campaign Basic Study, 11, Rome.

——(1973): *Energy and Protein Requirements*. Nutrition Meetings Report, series 52, Rome.

——(1974): *Assessment of the World Food Situation, Present and Future*. World Food Conference (Item 8 of the Provisional Agenda), United Nations.

Fei, J. C. H. and Chiang, A. C. (1966): "Maximum-Speed Development Through Austerity," in I. Adelman and E. Thorbecke (eds), *The Theory and Design of Economic Development*, Baltimore: Johns Hopkins University Press.

Fields, G. S. (1980): *Poverty, Inequality, and Development*. Cambridge: Cambridge University Press.

Gopalan, C. (1983): "Development and Deprivation," *Economic and Political Weekly*, 18, December, 2163–8.

Harris, J. R. and Todaro, M. (1970): "Migration, Unemployment and Development: A Two-Sector Analysis," *American Economic Review*, 60, 126–42.

Leibenstein, H. (1957): *Economic Backwardness and Economic Growth*. New York: Wiley.

Lipton, M. (1983): "Poverty, Undernutrition and Hunger," World Bank Staff working paper, 597, Washington, D.C.

Marshall, A. (1920): *The Principles of Economics*. London: Macmillan.

Mazumdar, D. (1959): "The Marginal Productivity Theory of Wages and Disguised Unemployment," *Review of Economic Studies*, 26, 190–7.

Miller, E. and Genovese, E. D. (1974): *Plantation, Town and Country: Essays on the Local History of American Slave Society*. Urbana, Illinois: University of Illinois Press.

Mirrlees, J. A. (1975): "A Pure Theory of Underdeveloped Economies," in L. Reynolds (ed.), *Agriculture in Development Theory*, New Haven, Connecticut: Yale University Press.

Prasad, P. H. (1970): *Growth with Full Employment*. Bombay: Allied Publishers.

Read, M. S. (1977): "Malnutrition and Human Performance," in L. S. Greene (ed.), *Malnutrition, Behaviour and Social Organization*, New York: Academic Press.

Reutlinger, S. and Selowsky, M. (1976): *Malnutrition and Poverty*. World Bank Staff occasional paper, 23, Baltimore: Johns Hopkins University Press.

Rodgers, G. (1975): "Nutritionally Based Wage Determination in the Low Income Labour Market," *Oxford Economic Papers*, 27, 61–81.

Sen, A. K. (1983): "Development: Which Way Now?" *Economic Journal*, 93, 745–62.

Stiglitz, J. E. (1976): "The Efficiency Wage Hypothesis, Surplus Labour and the Distribution of Income in LDCs," *Oxford Economic Papers*, 28, 185–207.

Streeten, P. (1981): *First Things First: Meeting Basic Needs in Developing Countries*. New York: Oxford University Press.

Sukhatme, P. (1978): "Assessment of Adequacy of Diets at Different Economic Levels," *Economic and Political Weekly*, special number, August.

Yotopolous, P. A. (1985): "Middle-income Classes and Food Crises: The 'New' Food–Feed Competition," *Economic Development and Cultural Change*, 33, 463–83.

# Inequality as a Determinant of Malnutrition and Unemployment: Policy

PARTHA DASGUPTA AND DEBRAJ RAY

In the predecessor to this article (Dasgupta and Ray, 1986; chapter 9, part 1, this volume), we developed a theory which provides a link between persistent involuntary unemployment and the incidence of undernourishment, relates them in turn to the production and distribution of income and thus ultimately to the distribution of assets. The theory is founded on the much-discussed observation that at low levels of nutrition-intake there is a positive relation between a person's nutrition status and his ability to function; or to put it at once more generally and more specifically, a person's consumption-intake affects his productivity.

The central idea which we pursued in part 1 is that unless an economy in the aggregate is richly endowed with physical assets it is the assetless who are vulnerable in the *labour market*. Potential employers – or speaking metaphorically, the 'market' – find attractive those who enjoy non-wage income, for in effect they are cheaper workers. Put another way, those who enjoy non-wage income can undercut those who do not, and if the distribution of assets is highly unequal even competitive markets are incapable of absorbing the entire labour force: the assetless are too expensive to employ in their entirety, as there are too many of them (part 1, theorem 2.)

A simple example may help. Suppose each person requires precisely 2000 calories per day to be able to function: anything less and a person's productivity is nil, anything more and his productivity is unaffected. Consider two people, one of whom has no non-wage income while the other enjoys 1500 calories per day of such income. The first person needs a full 2000 calories of wages per day in order to be employable, the latter only 500 calories per day. It is for this reason the assetless is disadvantaged in the labour market. To be sure, if employers compete for the service of people with assets their wages will be bid up and the consequent analysis will be a great deal more complicated than the corresponding analysis of a monopsonistic labour market. In part 1 we provided this analysis and we showed the precise way in which asset advantages translate themselves into employment advantages. But this suggests strongly that certain patterns of egalitarian asset redistributions may result in greater employment and indeed greater aggregate output. The purpose of this article is to confirm such possibilities, and to explore in some detail public policy measures which ought to be considered in the face of massive market-failure of the kind identified in part 1. In the following section we will reintroduce the notation and redefine certain terms. Section 2 will contain the heart of our analysis of public policy options. Section 3 presents our main conclusions. As in part 1, proofs are relegated to the Appendix.

## 1. Notation and The Model

We distinguish labour-*time* from labour-*power* and observe that it is the latter which is an input in production. Consider a person who works in the economy under analysis for a fixed number of 'hours' – the duration of the analysis. Denote the labour power he supplies over the period by $\lambda$ and suppose that it is functionally related to his consumption, $I$, in the manner of the bold-faced curve in figure 1(b) of chapter 9, part 1.

Two factors, *land* and *labour-power*, are involved in the production of *rice*. Land is homogeneous, workers are not. Denoting by $T$ the quantity of land and by $E$ the *aggregate* labour-power employed in production (i.e. the sum of individual labour powers employed) let $F(E, T)$ be the output of rice, where the aggregate production function $F(E, T)$ is assumed to be concave, twice differentiable, constant-returns-to-scale, increasing in $E$ and $T$, and displaying diminishing marginal products. Total land in the economy is fixed, and is $\hat{T}$. Aggregate labour power in the economy is, of course, endogenous.

We represent a large population, normalised at unity, by the unit interval [0, 1], so that each person has a label $n$, where $n$ is a number between 0 and 1. A person with label $n$ is called an $n$-person, and we assume that the quantity of land he owns is $\hat{T}t(n)$. We assume that there are a great many landless persons. Thus we suppose that there is some number $\underline{n} > 0$ such that all persons labelled between 0 and $\underline{n}$ are landless, and that $t(n)$, the proportion of aggregate land $n$-person owns, is an increasing function of $n$ beyond $\underline{n}$. (See figure 2 in chapter 9, part 1.)

A person either does not work in the production sector or works for one unit of time. There are competitive markets for both land and labour power. Let $r$ denote the rental rate on land. Then $n$-person's non-wage income is $r\hat{T}t(n)$. Each person has a reservation wage which must as a minimum be offered if he is to accept a job in the competitive labour market. $\bar{w}(R)$ denotes the reservation wage, where $R$ denotes non-wage income. In our model $R = r\hat{T}t(n)$. We take it that $\bar{w}$ is constant for all $n$ in the range 0 to $\underline{n}$ and that thereafter it is an increasing function of $n$ (see figure 3 in chapter 9, part 1). In figure 1 (b) of chapter 9, part 1, $\hat{I}$ is the *efficiency-wage* of a landless person. We take it that the reservation wage of a landless person is less than $\hat{I}$. This is a crucial assumption, and we made much use of it earlier.

To present our results in a sharp form we will suppose that the curvature of the $\lambda$ function in figure 1 (b) of chapter 9, part 1 is great at $\hat{I}$. We will therefore be justified in referring to $\hat{I}$ as the food-adequacy standard. A person consuming less than $\hat{I}$ is thus malnourished.

Finally define

$$w^*(n, r) \equiv \arg_{w \geq \bar{w}[r\hat{T}t(n)]} \min\{\frac{w}{\lambda[w + r\hat{T}t(n)]}\} \tag{1}$$

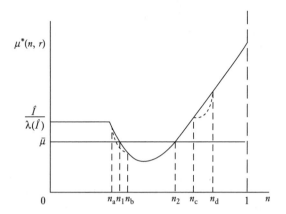

**Figure 1**   Partial land reform: $n$-persons between $n_a$ and $n_b$ gain land, and rentiers between $n_c$ and $n_d$ lose land

and

$$\mu^*(n,r) \equiv \frac{w^*(n,r)}{\lambda[w^*(n,r) + r\hat{T}t(n)]} \tag{2}$$

Equation (1) defines the *efficiency-wage rate* of an $n$-person, and equation (2) defines his *efficiency-piece rate*. (See figure 1 for a typical functional form of $\mu^*(n,r)$ for a given value of $r$.) The reader can obtain a detailed account of these functions in part 1 of chapter 9.

In part 1 we defined a competitive equilibrium allocation in the economy under review and proved its existence (definition 2 and theorem 1 in chapter 9, part 1). Stated verbally, a competitive equilibrium is an allocation sustained by a land rental rate $\tilde{r}$, a piece rate $\tilde{\mu}$, a set of employed persons, $\tilde{G}$, and a wage rate $\tilde{w}(n)$ on offer to an $n$-person belonging to the set $\tilde{G}$, such that:

(i)   $\tilde{r}$ equals the marginal product of land and $\tilde{\mu}$ equals the marginal product of aggregate labour power employed;

(ii)  a person whose efficiency piece rate falls short of $\tilde{\mu}$ finds employment;

(iii) a person whose efficiency piece rate exceeds $\tilde{\mu}$ supplies no labour and is not on demand either; and

(iv)  employers are indifferent between employing and not employing a person whose efficiency piece rate equals $\tilde{\mu}$.

We noted that equilibrium is compatible with the presence of widespread involuntary unemployment and the incidence of undernourishment. In particular, we showed that given the land distribution $t(n)$, if the aggregate quantity of land in the economy is neither too small nor too large, equilibrium entails rationing in the labour market: a fraction of the landless find employment at its efficiency wage $\hat{I}$, while the remaining fraction are disfranchised and suffer their reservation wage, which is nutritionally inadequate (regime 2 in section 2.5 of chapter 9, part 1). We also noted that if the aggregate quantity of land is small all the landless and the marginal landholders are malnourished and unemployed (regime 1 in section 2.4 of chapter 9, part 1). Finally, it was noted that if the aggregate quantity of land is large there is no involuntary unemployment in equilibrium and the landless receive a wage in excess of their efficiency wage (regime 3 in section 2.6 of chapter 9, part 1).

Figure 1 illustrates an equilibrium outcome in regime 1. (The efficiency piece rate, $\mu^*(n,\tilde{r})$ as a function of $n$, is given by the unbroken U-shaped curve.) The equilibrium piece rate, $\tilde{\mu}$, is less than the efficiency piece rate of the landless, $\hat{I}/\lambda(\hat{I})$. Persons labelled between 0 and $n_1$ are unemployed, as are people labelled between $n_2$ and 1, but the latter group choose not to work: their reservation wages are too high.

In what follows we will, as in part 1, denote equilibrium values of economic variables by tildes. Thus $\tilde{r}$, $\tilde{\mu}$ and so on denote equilibrium values of the rental rate, the piece rate, and so forth.

In part 1, we studied the implications of aggregate asset accumulation in the economy in question. The distribution of assets was held fixed (theorem 3 in chapter 9, part 1). In this essay we study, for the most part, the implication of asset redistribution.

## 2. Public Policy

Growth, seen as a means of removing poverty and unemployment, has long dominated the development literature. We want now to argue that in certain circumstances it is the *inequality* in the distribution of assets which is the *cause* of poverty and malnutrition and thus in turn involuntary unemployment. To analyse this we will, in this section, hold the aggregate quantity of land fixed and alter the land distribution.[1] But first we must check that redistributive policies are the only ones that are available. This is confirmed by

THEOREM 1   *Under the conditions postulated, a competitive equilibrium is Pareto-efficient.*

PROOF  See appendix.

### 2.1. Partial land reforms

A variety of different redistribution schemes can be studied. For ease of exposition, we will first look at a simple, though important case: that of land transfers from the landed gentry (i.e. those who do not enter the labour market because their reservation wage is too high) to those who are involuntarily unemployed. Such redistributions need not (and, in general, will not) lead to full equalisation of asset holdings. To distinguish them from *full land redistributions* (to perfect equality) which we shall discuss below, call them *partial land reforms*.

In figure 1, a partial land reform, where land is transferred to some of the unemployed as well as those 'on the margin' of being unemployed, is depicted.[2] The diagram displays the changes evaluated at the original equilibrium $(\tilde{\mu},\tilde{r})$. People between $n_a$ and $n_b$ gain land; for them, the $\mu^*(\cdot,\tilde{r})$ function shifts downward; that is, their efficiency-piece-rate is lowered. The losers, between $n_c$ and $n_a$, also experience a downward shift in $\mu^*(\cdot,\tilde{r})$, but for entirely different reasons – their reservation wages have been lowered.

Of course, a new equilibrium will now be established, one with a different wage schedule and rental rate. Can the two be compared? A partial answer is given in

THEOREM 2. *Suppose that for each parametric specification, the competitive equilibrium is unique.*[3] *Then a partial land reform of the kind just described necessarily leads to at least as much output in the economy (strictly more, if $\mu^*(n, \tilde{r})$ is of the form in figure 1).*

PROOF   See appendix.

The result implies that there is no necessary conflict between equality-seeking moves and aggregate output in a resource-poor economy. Such redistributions have three effects. First, the unemployed become more attractive to employers as their non-wage income rises. Second, those among the poor who are employed are more productive to the extent that they, too, receive land. Finally, by taking land away from the landed gentry, their reservation wages are lowered, and if this effect is strong enough, this could induce them to forsake their state of voluntary unemployment and enter the labour market. For all these reasons, the number of employed efficiency units in the economy rises, pushing it to a higher-output equilibrium.

Note, however, that theorem 2 is silent on how the *set* of employed persons changes. Do previously unemployed persons necessarily find unemployment? Does the *number* of involuntarily unemployed fall?

Unfortunately, the answer to this question can go either way. There is a natural tendency for employment to rise, because of the features mentioned above. However – and this is characteristic of all *partial* (as opposed to *full*) land reforms – there is a 'displacement effect' at work, whereby newly productive workers are capable of displacing previously employed, less productive workers in the labour market. (An example is given in Dasgupta and Ray (1984), using an economy in regime 2.)

## 2.2.  *Full land reform*

This displacement effect cannot exist in the case of *full* land reforms, our final object of analysis. So as to highlight the detrimental effects of unequal land distributions we assume in what follows that the economy is productive enough to feed everyone adequately. To make this precise assume that land is socially managed and that there is complete equality in the treatment of all. If $I$ denotes the consumption level of each person under such a scheme, $\lambda(I)$ is the labour-power of the representative person, and aggregate output is $F[\lambda(I), \hat{T}]$. For such an allocation to be viable, there must be a solution (in $I$) to the equation

$$I = F[\lambda(I), \hat{T}] \tag{3}$$

It is easy to see that if there is a solution to (3), in general there are two.[4] Concentrate on the *larger* of the two solutions and call it $I(\hat{T})$, and let $\hat{T}_1$ be the smallest value of $\hat{T}$ such that

$I(\hat{T}) = \hat{I}$. Thus at $\hat{T}_1$ we have a formalisation of the idea that the economy is productive enough (just about) to feed all adequately (i.e. at the level of the food adequacy standard $\hat{I}$).

To set the stage, we first state:

THEOREM 3   *Let $[\hat{T}, I(\hat{T})]$ be an equal division solution. Then, if reservation wages are low enough,*[5] this is achievable as a competitive equilibrium under full equality of land distribution.

PROOF   See appendix.

To complete our analysis of full land redistributions, we will show that for each size of land in some range above $\hat{T}_1$, there are unequal distributions of that land that sustain involuntary unemployment and malnourishment (i.e. equilibrium is in either regime 1 or 2; see chapter 9, part 1, even though full redistributions are associated with full employment and no malnourishment.

THEOREM 4   *There exists an interval $(\hat{T}_1, \hat{T}_2)$ such that if $\hat{T}$ is in this interval, full redistributions yield competitive equilibria with full employment and no malnourishment. Moreover for each such $\hat{T}$, there are unequal land distributions which give rise to involuntary unemployment and malnourishment.*

PROOF   See appendix.

In other words, we have identified a class of cases, namely, a range of moderate land endowments, where *inequality* of asset ownership can be pinpointed as the *basic* cause of involuntary unemployment and malnourishment. In such circumstances judicious land reforms, or food transfers, can *increase* output and *reduce* both unemployment and the incidence of undernourishment. Indeed, if land were equally distributed the market mechanism would sustain this economy in regime 3 (section 2.6 in chapter 9, part 1) in which undernourishment and unemployment are things of the past.

Finally, note that it is perfectly possible that unequal distribution of 'adequate' aggregate land (in the sense of theorem 4) leads the economy to, say, regime 2 unemployment. In this case, as we have observed, partial land reforms may well have perverse effects on employment. At the same time, full land redistributions lead to full employment (theorem 4). This observation suggests that in some cases partial reform movements may not serve the desired purpose as well as a more aggressive, total, redistributive policy.

Our last result deals with 'rich' economies, for the sake of completeness. Theorem 5, below, states that for all land endowments greater than or equal to $\hat{T}_2$ (see the statement of theorem 4), inequality in asset holdings cannot lead to malnourishment and involuntary unemployment through the mechanism highlighted in this paper.[6]

THEOREM 5   *For all $\hat{T} \geqslant \hat{T}_2$, there is no land distribution which involves involuntary unemployment or malnutrition.*

PROOF   See appendix.

## 3. Conclusion

In this article and its predecessor we have analysed the implications of the effect of nutrition on a person's capacity to function on employment, production and distribution. Our approach has been very much 'pure theory', but this is because a proper theoretical foundation for these links was not available to us. It has been customary in welfare economics to view the distribution of consumption as a primary social good, and to locate public policies that promote both it and other social goods. Our purpose has been to provide a complementary analysis: the *instrumental* value of redistribution policies. We have so chosen our model economy that asset redistributions (or equivalently, food transfers) are the only public policies worth considering (see theorem 1 above). Theorem 2 goes some way towards showing how certain Lorentz-improving asset redistributions result in lower aggregate unemployment and greater aggregate output. The analysis, however culminates in theorem 4, where this idea is really nailed down: an economy which is moderately endowed and capable of employing everyone and feeding everyone adequately will fail to do so if the distribution of assets is highly unequal. It follows that asset-redistribution policies, or food transfer programmes, can be highly potent as regards aggregate output and employment in moderately endowed economies.

The theory of unemployment we have offered here is, we believe, a descendant of classical theories. And in theorem 5 we provide the link between our theory and that of the now-standard competitive one by showing that the chain connecting asset distribution and aggregate employment is snapped if the economy is richly endowed in assets. But some of the most influential doctrines today concerning material prospects for less developed countries would seem to be based on the efficacy of the market mechanism. We would not argue that there is anything wrong in planners trying 'to get prices right'. But as theorem 4 makes plain, this may be far from the most potent option available, for even if one were to get them right (as in theorem 4) the market mechanism could be an unmitigated disaster.

APPENDIX

Competitive equilibrium has been defined formally in chapter 9, part 1 (see definition 2). $\tilde{G}$ is the set of persons who, in equilibrium, are employed and $\tilde{w}(n)$ is the wage rate of an $n$-person who is employed. Finally, $\nu(n)$ is the Lebesgue measure on $[0, 1]$.

### *Proof of theorem 1*

Let $\{\tilde{r}, \tilde{\mu}, \tilde{G}, \tilde{w}(n)\}$ be an equilibrium. It sustains a 'utility' schedule $\tilde{Y}(n)$ given by

$$\tilde{Y}(n) = \begin{cases} \tilde{w}(n) + \tilde{r}\hat{T}t(n) & \text{for } n \in \tilde{G} \\ \tilde{w}[\tilde{r}\hat{T}t(n)] + \tilde{r}\hat{T}t(n) & \text{for } n \notin \tilde{G} \end{cases} \tag{4}$$

Let $\tilde{I}(n)$ be the income accruing to $n$-person from the economy under review. Then $\tilde{I}(n) = \tilde{Y}(n)$ for $n \in \tilde{G}$ and $\tilde{I}(n) = \tilde{r}\hat{T}t(n)$ for $n \notin \tilde{G}$.

Suppose $[\tilde{r}, \tilde{\mu}, \tilde{G}, \tilde{w}(n)]$ is *not* Pareto-efficient. Then there is a set $AC$ $[0, 1]$, with $\nu(A) = 1$, and a feasible 'utility' schedule $Y(n)$ for $n \in [0, 1]$ such that $Y(n) \geqslant \tilde{Y}(n)$ on $n \in A$, and a set $B$, with $\nu(B) > 0$, such that $Y(n) > \tilde{Y}(n)$ for $n \in B$. We want to show that this cannot be; that any such $Y(n)$ is infeasible.

Let $G$ be the set of persons who are employed in the economy at this Pareto-superior allocation. Let $\tilde{G}^c \equiv A - \tilde{G}$ and $G^c \equiv A - G$, and write $C \equiv \tilde{G} \cap G^c$, $D \equiv \tilde{G}^c \cap G$, $K \equiv \tilde{G}^c \cap G^c$ and $\mathcal{J} \equiv \tilde{G} \cap G$. We then have

$$Y(n) = \begin{cases} \tilde{w}[I(n)] + I(n) & \text{for } n \in G^c \\ I(n) & \text{for } n \in G \end{cases} \tag{5}$$

where $I(n)$ is the income given to $n$-person from the economy at this Pareto-superior allocation. Let $E \equiv \int_G \lambda[I(n)] dv(n)$. We wish to show that

$$\int_A I(n) dv(n) > F(E, \hat{T}) \tag{6}$$

Now, note that $C \cup D \cup K \cup \mathcal{J} = A$. Moreover,

$$I(n) \geqslant \tilde{r}\hat{T}t(n) \qquad \text{for } n \in K \tag{7}$$

(This follows from the fact that $\tilde{w}'(R) \geqslant 0$ for all $R \geqslant 0$.)

It is possible to show that $E > \tilde{E}$ (see Dasgupta and Ray, 1984, appendix). Consider first $n \in \mathcal{J}$. The additional consumption that he enjoys in the Pareto-superior allocation is $I(n) - \tilde{I}(n)$. We show that this is no less than his contribution to the addition in output $F(E, \hat{T}) - F(\tilde{E}, \hat{T})$.

We begin by noting that this latter contribution does not exceed $F_E(\tilde{E}, T)$ $\lambda'[\tilde{I}(n)][I(n) - \tilde{I}(n)]$.[7] From (1) and $\lambda[\tilde{I}(n)] > 0$, we know that

$$\lambda[\tilde{I}(n)] \geqslant \tilde{w}(n)\lambda'[\tilde{I}(n)] \tag{8}$$

Using (8) and conditions (iv) and (v) of definition 2 in chapter 9, part 1 we conclude that $n$'s contribution to the addition in aggregate output cannot exceed $I(n) - \tilde{I}(n)$. In particular, if the latter is positive the increase in his consumption *exceeds* his contribution to additional output.

Next consider $n \in D$. It follows from (1) above and condition (ii) of definition 2 in part 1 of chapter 9 that

$$F_E(\tilde{E}, \hat{T}) \leqslant \frac{w}{\lambda[w + \tilde{R}(n)]} \qquad \text{for } w \geqslant \tilde{w}[\tilde{R}(n)] \tag{9}$$

where $\tilde{R}(n) = \tilde{r}\hat{T}t(n)$. But by hypothesis $I(n) - \tilde{I}(n) \geqslant \tilde{w}[\tilde{R}(n)]$, (see (4) and (5)). And so (9) applies for $w = I(n) - \tilde{I}(n)$. It follows that the contribution of this $n$-person to the addition in output is less than or equal to the left-hand side of

$$F_E(\tilde{E}, \hat{T})\lambda[I(n)] = F_E(\tilde{E}, \hat{T})\lambda[I(n) + \tilde{R}(n) - \tilde{I}(n)] \leqslant I(n) - \tilde{I}(n) \tag{10}$$

(since $\tilde{R}(n) = \tilde{I}(n)$ for $n \in \tilde{G}^c$). Moreover, if $\nu(D) > 0$, it follows from the *strict* concavity of $F$ in $E$, and from (10) that the contribution to the increase in total output by all $n \in D$ is *less* than the increase in the total consumption of all $n \in D$.

Next note that if $n \in K$, he works in neither allocation, and so he adds nothing to the increase in production. Suppose then that $C = \mathbf{\Phi}$. We are then done, because by hypothesis $\nu(B) > 0$. So we must have $\nu(B \cap D) > 0$, or $\nu(B \cap J) > 0$, or $\nu(B \cap K) > 0$. Under any of these circumstances the total increase in output must fall short of the total increase in consumption. It follows that the allocation $Y(n)$ is infeasible.

If, on the other hand, $C \neq \mathbf{\Phi}$, the argument is a little bit more complicated. For details see Dasgupta and Ray (1984, appendix).

## *Proof of theorem 2*

As in the proof of theorem 1, in chapter 9, part 1 correspondence $M'(r)$ as in equation (26) there, corresponding to the new land distribution $t'(n)$ after a partial land reform. In what follows we use primes on all relevant variables (functions) corresponding to the new equilibrium. We also borrow other notation from that theorem.

Note first min $M'(r) >$ min $M(r)$. To see this observe that in moving from $t(n)$ to $t'(n)$ none of the people who were previously employed *loses* land. Moreover, the gain in land-holding among some who were involuntarily unemployed pushes their $\mu^*(n, \tilde{r})$ down to $\mu^*(n, \tilde{r})$, below $\tilde{\mu}$. This means that $\nu[B'(r) - B(r)] > 0$. Hence min $M'(r) >$ min $M(r)$. A similar argument establishes that $\nu[G'(r) - G(r)] > 0$ and so max $M'(r) >$ max $M(r)$.

If $\tilde{E} \in M'(\tilde{r})$, then the original labour power-output configuration continues to be the unique equilibrium. Otherwise

$$E(r) = \tilde{E} < \min M'(\tilde{r}) \tag{11}$$

By virtue of the properties established in the proof of theorem 1 in part 1 of chapter 9 of the correspondence $M(r)$, we conclude that there is $\tilde{r}' > \tilde{r}$ and $\tilde{E}' \in M'(\tilde{r}')$ such that $\tilde{E}' = E(\tilde{r}')$. But since $E(r)$ is an increasing function $\tilde{E}' > \tilde{E}$. From $\tilde{E}'$ construct the new (unique) equilibrium as in the proof of theorem 1 in part 1 of chapter 9. This equilibrium thus sustains greater output.

Finally, observe that if the original equilibrium was in regime 1, $\tilde{G} = \bar{B}(\tilde{r})$ and so $\tilde{G} \subseteq B'(\tilde{r})$, where $\bar{B}(\tilde{r})$ is the closure of $B(\tilde{r})$. But this proves that (11) must hold and therefore that the new equilibrium sustains higher aggregate output.

## *Proof of theorem 3*

Let $[\hat{T}, I(\hat{T})]$ be an equal division solution. Define

$$\hat{\mu} = F_E\{\lambda[I(\hat{T}), \hat{T}\}$$

and

$$\hat{r} = F_T\{\lambda[I(\hat{T})], \hat{T}\}$$

Choose the reservation-wage function low enough so that, in particular

$$\bar{w}(\hat{r}\hat{T}) < \lambda[I(\hat{T})]\hat{\mu}$$

and let $\tilde{G} = [0,1]$, with $\hat{w}(n) \equiv \hat{w} \equiv \lambda[I(\hat{T})]\hat{\mu}$ for all $n \in [1,0]$. (Recall that by the equal distribution postulate, $t(n) = 1$.) It remains to check that this allocation satisfies the conditions of definition 2 in part 1 of chapter 9. (See Dasgupta and Ray, 1984, appendix.)

### Proof of theorem 4

Define $\hat{T}_0$ as the minimum value of $\hat{T}$ for which equation (3) has a positive solution. It is easy to check that

$$F_E\{\lambda[I(\hat{T}_0)], \hat{T}_0\}\lambda'[I(\hat{T}_0)] = 1 \tag{12}$$

By equations (3) and (12) and Euler's Theorem we have

$$
\begin{aligned}
I(\hat{T}_0) = F\{\lambda[I(\hat{T}_0)], \hat{T}_0\} &= F_T\hat{T}_0 + F_E\lambda[I(\hat{T}_0)] \\
&> F_E\lambda[I(\hat{T}_0)] = \lambda[I(\hat{T}_0)]/\lambda'[I(\hat{T}_0)]
\end{aligned}
\tag{13}
$$

From (13) we conclude that $I(\hat{T}_0) < \hat{I}$ and since $I(\hat{T})$ is an increasing and unbounded function of $\hat{T}$, we have $\hat{T}_1$, well defined and $\hat{T}_1 > \hat{T}_0$. Given this last we have, from (12), that for all $\hat{T} \geqslant \hat{T}_1$,

$$F_E\{\lambda[I(\hat{T})], \hat{T}\}\lambda'[I(\hat{T})] < 1 \tag{14}$$

Moreover, $I(\hat{T}) > \hat{I}$ for $\hat{T} > \hat{T}_1$. Now define

$$\mu(\hat{T}) \equiv F_E\{\lambda[I(\hat{T})], \hat{T}\} \tag{15}$$

We may now use (14) to show that $\mu(\hat{T})$ is an increasing and unbounded function of $\hat{T} \geqslant \hat{T}_1$. But $\mu(\hat{T}_1) < \hat{I}/\lambda(\hat{I})$. Therefore there exists $\hat{T}_2 > \hat{T}_1$ such that $\mu(\hat{T}_2) = \hat{I}/\lambda(\hat{I})$.

Finally, we will show that for $\hat{T} \in [\hat{T}_1, \hat{T}_2)$ equal distribution of $\hat{T}$ generates equilibria involving full employment and an absence of malnutrition while there exist *unequal* distributions of $\hat{T}$ which generate equilibria in regime 1 or 2 (see chapter 9, part 1). The first part of the claim follows trivially from theorem 3 and the fact that $I(\hat{T}) > \hat{I}$ for $\hat{T} > \hat{T}_1$. We establish the second part now.

Let $\hat{T} \in [\hat{T}_1, \hat{T}_2]$. Consider the equilibrium resulting from an equal distribution of this. It is in regime 3. Let $\hat{r}, \hat{\mu}$ and $\hat{w}$ be the rental rate on land, the piece rate and the wage rate, respectively. Then clearly

$$\frac{\hat{w}}{\lambda(\hat{w} + \hat{r}\hat{T})} = \hat{\mu} > \min\left[\frac{w}{\lambda(w + \hat{r}\hat{T})}\right] \qquad w \geqslant \bar{w}(\hat{r}\hat{T}) \tag{16}$$

We conclude that $M(r)$ in equation (26) of chapter 9, part 1 is a singleton at $\hat{r}$. It also follows that in a small neighbourhood of $\hat{r}$, say $[r_a, r_b]$, $M(r)$ remains a singleton. Since $\hat{\mu} = \hat{\mu}(\hat{r}) < \hat{I}/\lambda(\hat{I})$, we can also ensure that $\mu(r_a) < \hat{I}/\lambda(\hat{I})$.

Now let $\delta$ be a small positive number and define a 'slightly' unequal land distribution $t(n, \delta)$ as:

$$t(n, \delta) = \begin{cases} 0 & \text{for } n \in [0, \delta] \\ 2(n - \delta)/(2 - 3\delta)\delta & \text{for } n \in [\delta, 2\delta] \\ 2/(2 - 3\delta) & \text{for } n \in [2\delta, 1] \end{cases} \tag{17}$$

Now choose a small positive number $\delta_0$ such that $t(n, \delta)$ in (17) is well-defined for all $\delta \in [0, \delta_0)$. In theorem 3 and the first part of the theorem being proved reservation wages were chosen to be sufficiently small so that they were not a binding constraint. Choose $\delta_0$ small enough so that they remain non-binding for all $r \in [r_a, r_b]$. Now define a corresponding $M(r, \delta)$ on $[r_a, r_b] \times [0, \delta_0]$ analogous to equation (26) in chapter 9, part 1, for the land distribution $t(n, \delta)$. Then notice that $M(r, 0) = M(r)$. It is easy to verify that if $r_a, r_b$ and $\delta_0$ are chosen suitably $M(r, \delta)$ is a singleton (i.e. a function). It is also continuous in $\delta$ at $\delta = 0$. We conclude that for $\delta$ close to zero but positive, there is $\hat{r}(\delta) \in [r_a, r_b]$ so that

$$M[\hat{r}(\delta), \delta] = M[\hat{r}(\delta)] \tag{18}$$

It is a simple matter to check that this is an equilibrium. But because $\hat{r}(\delta) \geqslant r_a$ and $\mu(r_a) < \hat{I}/\lambda(\hat{I})$, it must be true that the new equilibrium piece rate, $\mu[\hat{r}(\delta)]$, is less than $\hat{I}/\lambda(\hat{I})$.

## *Proof of theorem 5*

Suppose not. Then for some $\hat{T} \geqslant \hat{T}_2$ there exists a land distribution $t(n)$ such that $\tilde{\mu} < \hat{I}/\lambda(\hat{I})$. By definition of $\hat{T}_2$ and the fact that $\mu(\hat{T})$ is an increasing function of $\hat{T}$ for $\hat{T} > \hat{T}_1$ (see proof of theorem 4 and equation (15)) we have $\mu(\hat{T}) \geqslant \hat{I}/\lambda(\hat{I})$ for $\hat{T} \geqslant \hat{T}_2$, so that combining all this with the strict concavity of $F$ in $E$, we note

$$\int_{[0, 1]} \lambda[\tilde{I}(n)] d\nu(n) > \lambda[I(\hat{T})] \tag{19}$$

Now consider the maximisation problem

$$\max_{I(n)} \int_{[0, 1]} \lambda[I(n)] d\nu(n) \tag{20}$$

subject to the feasibility constraint

$$\int_{[0, 1]} I(n) d\nu(n) = F\left\{ \int_{[0, 1]} \lambda[I(n)] d\nu(n), \hat{T} \right\} \tag{21}$$

One can then show (Dasgupta and Ray, 1984, appendix) that the solution, $I(n)$ say, is unique and equals $I(\hat{T})$ for $n$ almost everywhere in [0, 1]. But this contradicts (19).

## Notes

1  It should be emphasised that although we will talk of land redistribution, *consumption* redistribution – via lump-sum food transfers – is all that the model requires.
2  Figure 2 looks at a land reform in regime 1; clearly, the case of regime 2 can be similarly analysed. See sections 2.4 and 2.5 in chapter 9, part 1.
3  The assumption of a unique competitive equilibrium can be dropped, but then one would have to look at the stable equilibria. We avoid these to rule out unnecessary technical complications.
4  This excludes the 'tangency case' where there is exactly one solution. One can show that the smallest $\hat{T}$ for which a solution to (3) exists involves an $I(\hat{T}) < \hat{I}$. So $\hat{T}_1$, to be described below is uniquely defined.
5  It helps to think of the reservation wage function as being identically zero in the relevant range, for this final section, as its presence adds nothing to the development of our basic point.
6  This statement should *not* be taken to mean that there is no connection between inequality and unemployment in resource-rich economies, only that the causal chain running through *our* analysis is not of the first importance for rich economies.
7  This follows from the strict concavity of $F(E, \hat{T})$ as a function of $E$.

## References

Dasgupta, P. and Ray, D. (1984): "Inequality, Malnutrition and Unemployment: A Critique of the Competitive Market Mechanisms," IMSS technical report 454, Stanford University and CEPR discussion paper 50, Duke of York Street, London.
——and——(1986): "Inequality as a Determinant of Malnutrition and Unemployment: Theory," *Economic Journal*, 96, December.

CHAPTER 10

# A Theory of Two-tier Labor Markets in Agrarian Economies

MUKESH ESWARAN AND ASHOK KOTWAL

Economic analysis of agricultural tenancy has yielded rich insights into the institutional mechanisms that evolve as rational responses to the state of market development and production technology. In many respects, the study of tenancy has been a forerunner of the modern literature that is attempting to create a theory of organization based on the analysis of incentive mechanisms underlying the contractual structure. It may be quite fruitful, therefore, to study premodern institutions, especially if they have recurred in diverse environments or at different time periods, and have proved to be historically tenacious. The more anomalous they seem, at first glance, the more rewarding may their analysis prove to us.

One such institution that has not been subjected to economic analysis until recently (Alan Richards, 1979; Pranab Bardhan 1983) is the institution of permanent workers. Permanent workers (alternatively referred to as tied laborers, estate laborers, farm servants, or attached workers) have existed in agrarian economies as diverse as those of thirteenth-century England, Tokugawa Japan, East Elbian Germany (1750–1860), the Egyptian Delta (1850–1940), pre-1930 Central Chile, and present day India. This institution has exhibited certain common features across different time periods and regions. First, in sharp contrast to the so-called "casual workers" hired on a daily basis, permanent workers are engaged on long-term contracts that span entire crop periods, years, and, sometimes, lifetimes. Second, the employment relationship between the landlords and these laborers is highly personalized and involves patronage benefits such as homesteads, consumption credit, holiday gifts, and emergency aid in return for total loyalty. A permanent worker is expected to remain loyal to the landlord and further the landlord's interests even in periods of strife between the landlord and casual workers (Sheila Bhalla, 1976; Bardhan and Ashok Rudra, 1981; Richards, 1979). Third, the incidence of this seemingly backward institution appears to increase in response to what may be construed as modernizing stimuli. The opening up of new markets for Chilean agrarian products in the nineteenth century and the consequent increase in labor demand resulted in an increase in the number and proportion of permanent labor contracts (Richards, 1979). Those regions in North India (Haryana) with wider diffusion of new technology and consequently higher labor demand also exhibit greater proportion of permanent labor contracts (Bhalla). A theory of the institution of permanent labor should, therefore, simultaneously explain:

(a)   why the landlord places such a premium on loyalty,
(b)   the choice of the instruments he uses to elicit such loyalty, and
(c)   the increase in the incidences of permanent labor contracts in response to an increase in labor demand.

Bardhan (1983) has recently proposed an explanation for the institution of permanent labor, based on the following idea. Risk-averse workers faced with an uncertain spot wage can engage in long-term contracts with risk-neutral landlords for a prenegotiated wage, albeit at a rate lower than the expected spot rate. Workers, who are assumed to have heterogeneous opportunity incomes, self-select into the permanent and casual labor markets. The main comparative static result of this model explains the well-acknowledged empirical finding that the proportion of permanent workers is higher in tighter labor markets.[1] In an earlier paper (1979a), Bardhan proposed an alternative explanation for the existence of permanent contracts that was based on differential recruitment costs. Although he noted the importance of the patron–client aspects of the institution of permanent labor, the focus of his two models was to explain the longer duration of the contract. Patron–client aspects, such as loyalty, which are distinctive and inalienable features of the institution of permanent labor, are yet to be formally analyzed.

In this paper we follow the lead of Richards (1979), who has analyzed the institution of permanent labor in the widely different agrarian economies of East Elbian Germany, Egypt, and Chile. His investigation led him to the hypothesis that this institution emerged as a subtle means of supervising labor. A cursory examination of the differences in the tasks assigned to the two kinds of hired labor reveals that important tasks that require judgement, discretion, and care (and are difficult to monitor) are seldom, if ever, assigned to casual workers.[2] Permanent workers, on the other hand, are often entrusted with such responsibilities, almost as if they were family members. Our theory of the institution of permanent labor is based on the hypothesis that it is an attempt by the landlords to transform hired labor into workers whose behavior would approximate that of family labor, thus reducing the burden of on-the-job supervision. Do any of the stylized facts available on the terms of permanent contracts suggest a mechanism that could elicit such behavior from hired workers?

A significant and yet puzzling observation reported by Prafulla Sanghavi (1969) and Bardhan (1979a) is that permanent workers in Indian agriculture typically enjoy a significantly higher annual income (despite a lower daily wage) than casual workers.[3] In addition, permanent workers get consumption loans, homesteads, and other patronage benefits while casual workers face a great deal of uncertainty on the labor markets (Bardhan, 1983; Bhalla, 1976). It seems inconceivable that workers close to subsistence and without either employment opportunities or savings could be indifferent between a permanent contract that assures employment and consumption even in slack seasons and a precarious dependence on casual markets. To a worker at subsistence, neither the greater burden of responsibility and more work, nor the distaste for the serf-like existence under the close control of the landlord are reasons compelling enough to render the two types of contracts equivalent in utility.[4] On the other hand, it is equally puzzling that landlords would find it necessary to pay higher-than-opportunity incomes to their permanent workers. It might be natural to presume that the permanent workers are more able and, therefore, earn higher incomes than casual workers. The income differential between the two classes would be explained as ability-rent only if there is no excess supply of able people. In that case, the composition of the labor force would be insentive to intensification of agriculture, contradicting the observations of Richards (1979).

An explanation of why employers are sometimes found to pay higher-than-opportunity incomes to their employees has recently been proposed by B. Curtis Eaton and William White (1983). The idea, put simply, is that an income differential maintained over the opportunity income of the worker serves as a monitoring device; any shirking by the worker would invite the threat of getting fired and losing the stream of income differentials.[5] By replacing the income differential with a utility differential and assuming that the opportunity utility of a permanent worker is the expected utility of a casual worker (i.e., assuming an environment with no other employment opportunity), we can adapt the Eaton–White framework to answer the questions we posed earlier. The landlords transform some of the hired laborers into loyal laborers by keeping them at a higher utility level than what they could otherwise attain. The excess demand for permanent jobs thus created is sustained in equilibrium, since it enables the landlords to entrust responsible tasks to an artificially created cadre of loyal workers who would have been prohibitively expensive to supervise otherwise. The wage that minimizes the total labor costs (including wage and supervision costs) is higher than the wage that would minimize the wage costs alone. This framework explains the observation made by Bhalla (1976) and Richards (1979) that the permanent workers constitute a class within the class of agricultural workers – the upper tier in an artificially created "two-tiered" labor force. They receive superior benefits and tend to align themselves with their employers under most circumstances. It is important to note, however, that such contracts are viable only if they are long term and if reputation plays an important role so that the fired worker cannot secure another contract soon afterwards.

The above framework is an accurate representation of the institution of permanent labor as described by historians. For example, Arnold Bauer (1975, p. 56) observes that in nineteenth-century rural Chile:

> Numerically few, the *inquilinos* [permanent workers] were the cream of the rural labour.... This selectivity was made possible by the limited need for estate labour and the lack of alternatives open to the numerous rural families. The good fortune of being accepted on the hacienda was repaid by the inquilinos with service and loyalty.

Our assumption that permanent workers are kept at a higher utility level than casual workers is borne out by the accounts of Richards (1979) on the institution as it prevailed from 1850 to 1940 in Egypt, from 1750 to 1860 in East Elbian Germany, and in pre-1930 Central Chile. Richards also observes: "An Instmann [permanent worker] dismissed for insubordination would quickly find himself among the insecure ranks of Eigenkatner and Einlieger [casual workers]" (1979, p. 512).

A legitimate question that may be raised at this point is: why doesn't the landlord offer a tenancy contract to the worker? We have explained elsewhere our view that the choice among fixed rental, sharecropping, and fixed wage contracts are influenced by the distribution of certain unmarketed resources across landlords and workers (Eswaran and Kotwal, 1985). It is demonstrated there that this, together with the technology and the type of crops, determines the contractual structure that would prevail; even with a linearly homogeneous technology, tenancy contracts will not necessarily obtain. A permanent contract is essentially a wage contract in which the landlord undertakes management and employs a subtle supervision technique that avoids resorting to continuous monitoring, and we model it as such.[6] Such a supervision technique is viable only with long-term contracts since the landlord depends on imperfect indicators of the workers' efforts which are gathered almost costlessly as by-products of other management activities. Any meaningful judgment as to whether a worker has been supplying an acceptable level of effort can only be formed after reviewing the accumulated information on the worker's performance over the entire crop season. The landlord is then able to form a judgment on whether or not to fire the worker. For tractability, we shall assume that after the crop has been harvested and counted, the landlord has sufficient information accumulated to know with certainty if the worker has supplied an acceptable level of effort.

To sum up, we postulate that the institution of permanent labor exists in order to facilitate the assignment of important labor tasks to hired labor without having to devote inordinately large amounts of resources to supervision. It enables the landlord to utilize valuable information about the worker's performance that can be costlessly gathered while the landlord is engaged in performing other managerial activities. The permanent worker's income is maintained at a level that renders him a utility sufficiently greater than his opportunity utility that he would choose to supply the acceptable level of effort. Any change in the casual worker's wages, that are determined in a competitive market, results in a corresponding change in the permanent worker's wages.

In section 1, we present a general equilibrium model that incorporates the seasonal nature of agricultural production. The labor market consists of homogeneous workers allocated between permanent and casual workers according to the different tasks assigned. We work out the implications of the model assuming for the workers' utility function a specific form which gives rise to a labor supply function that is consistent with empirical observations. In section 2, we then carry out comparative static exercises and examine the link between the incidence of permanent labor and the different characteristics of the production technology. In the final section, we elaborate on the general applicability of the essential principle modeled in this paper to discourage morally hazardous behavior.

# 1. The Model

We assume that a single crop is produced each year; the crop takes two periods to produce, each period lasting for one-half year. The two periods posited for the production of a crop enable us to capture the variation in the demand for labor and capital over the year. For concreteness, the first period can be viewed as requiring such activities as soil preparation, tilling, sowing, etc., and the second as the period of harvesting, threshing, etc. Typically, the demand for labor and capital is considerably higher in the second period.

We envisage the production process as entailing the use of three inputs: land ($h$), capital ($K$), and labor. It is imperative for our purposes to disaggregate the labor input, and this we do according to the nature of the tasks performed. It is sufficient to consider two broad categories of tasks. Type 1 tasks are those that involve considerable care and judgment (such as water resource management, the application of fertilizers, maintenance of the draft animals and machines, etc.). Such tasks do not lend themselves to easy on-the-job supervision. Type 2 tasks are those that are routine and menial (such as weeding, harvesting, threshing, etc.). Since they involve little discretion, productivity on such tasks can be directly gauged from the extent of the workers' physical activity. In other words, type 2 tasks are by their very nature easy to monitor. All workers are assumed to have identical abilities. However, even though all workers are drawn from a homogeneous labor force, the tasks to which they are assigned are not necessarily the same.

We draw a distinction between the length of a worker's employment over a period ($l$) and the "intensity" of effort ($e$) with which he applies himself. Efficient performance of a task (either type 1 or type 2) requires an effort level $\bar{e} > 0$. Since effort is deemed a bad, a worker on a fixed wage will set $e = 0$ unless he is monitored. We shall take an efficiency unit of labor to be one worker hired for a whole period ($l = 1$) at an effort level $\bar{e}$. As will be explained below, type 1 tasks are performed by workers with long-term contracts, while workers hired on the spot market (casual workers) are entrusted with only type 2 tasks. Empirically, we observe that casual workers are hired mainly in the peak season (i.e., the second period). This is because the tasks to be performed in period 1 are mainly of type 1 variety – soil preparation, plowing (which entails the use of draft animals or tractors), application of fertilizers, etc. For simplicity we assume that no casual workers are hired in period 1. We let $L_p$ denote the number of efficiency units of permanent labor employed per period on a typical farm. A permanent worker's contract is over the infinite horizon unless he is found to shirk. We denote by $L_c$ the number of efficiency units of casual labor employed on the farm in period 2. A casual worker's contract lasts for the whole or part of this period.

We posit that the output, $q_1$, of period 1 can be written

$$q_1 = a \min\{g_1(K_1, L_p), bh\} \tag{1}$$

where $K_1$ is the amount of capital used in period 1, $h$ is the amount of land used, and $a, b > 0$, and $g_1(K_1, L_p)$ is a twice continuously differentiable, linearly homogeneous function that is increasing and strictly quasi concave in its arguments. The production function in (1) implies that there is no substitutability between land and the other two factors of production, and that the potential output of the farm is determined entirely by the amount of land. $g_1(K_1, L_p)$ can be interpreted as an aggregate of the capital and labor inputs in period 1. We assume that labor is an essential input in period 1, that is, that $g_1(K_1, 0) = 0$ for all $K_1$. The parameter $b$ is introduced to capture land-augmenting technical change, while $a$ is introduced to simulate Hicks-neutral technical change.

In period 2, the tasks performed by labor are mostly type 2 variety. We shall assume that in period 2, casual and permanent labor are perfect substitutes and both will be employed to do type 2 tasks. Now the output of the second period will depend nontrivially on the activities of the first period. More precisely, $q_1$ is an intermediate input and we write the second period's output (the final product), $q_2$, as

$$q_2 = \min\{g_2(K_2, L_p + L_c), q_1\} \tag{2}$$

where $K_2$ is the amount of capital used in period 2, and $g_2$ is a twice continuously differentiable, linearly homogeneous function, increasing and strictly quasi concave in its arguments. The motivation for (2) lies in the interpretation of $q_1$ as the quantity of unharvested crop and $q_2$ as the quantity of the final product, that is, the harvested and threshed crop; $q_1$ is thus a natural upper bound on $q_2$.

The price of the output is assumed to be exogenously fixed – set in the world market, say – and is normalized to unity. All farmers are assumed to be price takers in the labor and capital markets. For convenience, we assume that all farms are identical. Then in view of the linear homogeneity of (1) and (2), we can aggregate all farmers into a single price-taking farmer. The quantity $h$ now represents the total arable land in the economy and is assumed fixed; $L_p$, $L_c$, $K_1$, $K_2$, $q_1$, and $q_2$ can similarly be interpreted as aggregates. The wage rate of a permanent worker is $w_p$ per period, while that of a casual worker is $w_c$. The rental rate on capital equipment per period, assumed exogenous, is $r_i$, $i = 1, 2$. Since the types of capital used in the two periods are not necessarily the same, we can have $r_1 \neq r_2$.

## 1.1. Demand side

We now turn to the optimal choices of $L_p$, $L_c$, and $K_i$, $q_i$, $i = 1, 2$. Consider the production of a typical crop. First note that the optimal choice of factor inputs in period 2 depends on $L_p$ and the decisions of the first period. The landlord's decision making must thus be foresighted and must be made with full awareness of how the choice of $L_p$ and his period 1 decisions will impinge on period 2's choices. In what follows we shall adopt the convention that all expenses (wages and rentals) are incurred at the end of the period.

Given the nature of the production functions and the assumption of a constant and exogenously determined price for the final product, it follows that if production is at all viable, as we assume it is, it is profitable to cultivate all of the arable land. The profit-maximizing output levels in the two periods are

$$q_1 = q_2 = abh \tag{3}$$

Without loss of generality we shall set $h = 1$. The factor inputs will thus be determined so as to minimize the total present value cost of producing the outputs in (3). Since the landlord's choices of capital and casual labor are dependent on the amount of permanent labor hired, we first determine his demands of $K_1$, $K_2$, and $L_c$ conditional on his choice of $L_p$.

Define the cost functions

$$C_2(q_2, r_2, w_c) \equiv \min_{K_2, L_a} \{r_2 K_2 + w_c L_a \mid g_2(K_2, L_a) \geq q_2\} \tag{4}$$

where $L_a \equiv L_p + L_c$ is the aggregate amount of labor used in period 2, and

$$C_1\left(L_p, \frac{q_1}{a, r_1}\right) \equiv \min_{K_1} \left\{r_1 K_1 \mid g_1(K_1, L_p) \geq \frac{q_1}{a}\right\} \tag{5}$$

At the profit-maximizing output levels given by (3), Shephard's Lemma yields the following factor demands:

$$K_1^d\left(L_p, b, r_1\right) = \frac{\partial C_1}{\partial r_1}\left(L_p, b, r_1\right) \tag{6a}$$

$$K_2^d(ab, r_2, w_c) = \frac{\partial C_2}{\partial r_2}(ab, r_2, w_c) \tag{6b}$$

$$L_a^d(ab, r_2, w_c) = \frac{\partial C_2}{\partial w_c}(ab, r_2, w_c) \tag{6c}$$

The casual labor demand is thus given by

$$L_c^d\left(ab, L_p, r_2, w_c\right) = \max\left\{L_a^d(ab, r_2, w_c) - L_p, 0\right\} \tag{6d}$$

The optimal choice of $L_p$ is now determined as the solution to

$$\min_{L_p} r_1 K_1^d\left(L_p, b, r_1\right) + \beta r_2 K_2^d(ab, r_2, w_c) + (1 + \beta) w_p L_p$$
$$+ \beta w_c\left[L_a^d(ab, r_2, w_c) - L_p\right] \tag{7}$$

assuming that the amount of casual labor hired is strictly positive. In (7) $\beta(0 < \beta < 1)$ denotes the per period discount factor. The first-order condition associated with (7) is

$$-r_1\left(\frac{\partial K_1^d\left(L_p, b, r_1\right)}{\partial L_p}\right) = (1 + \beta) w_p - \beta w_c \equiv z \tag{8}$$

The demand for permanent labor, $L_p^d(b, r_1, z)$, is implicitly determined as the solution to (8). Twice continuous differentiability and the strict quasi concavity of $g_1(K_1, L_1)$ implies that the left-hand side of (8) is declining in $L_p$. Thus $L_p^d$ is decreasing in $z$ (see figure 1).

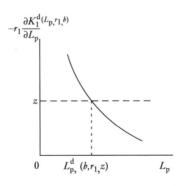

**Figure 1**   Determination of the demand for permanent labor

Together, $L_p^d(b, r, z)$ and the expressions (6a) – (6d) constitute the demand side of our model. We now turn to the supply side.

## 1.2. Supply side

Consistent with Bardhan's (1979b) empirical evidence that the agricultural labor supply exhibits low elasticity in the peak period, though it may be fairly elastic in the slack period, we posit the utility function of an agricultural worker to be of the form

$$U(y, e, l) = (y - el)^\gamma \qquad 0 < \gamma < 1 \tag{9}$$

where $y$ is the income received for the period and $l$ is the fraction of the period for which he is employed ($l = 1$ if he is hired for the entire period). For an arbitrarily given $e$ and wage rate $w$, the supply response $l^*(w, e)$, of a worker is obtained as the solution to

$$\max_l U(wl, e, l) \qquad \text{such that } l \le 1 \tag{10}$$

The maximization in (10) yields the labor supply response:

$$l^*(w, e) \begin{cases} = 0 & \text{for } w < e \\ \in (0, 1) & \text{for } w = e \\ = 1 & \text{for } w > e \end{cases} \tag{11}$$

and an indirect utility function

$$V(w, e) = \{(w - e)l^*(w, e)\}^\gamma \tag{12}$$

Since $V$ is a decreasing function of $e$, there is an obvious moral hazard problem under a fixed wage contract, which makes the monitoring of effort imperative. Since type 2 tasks are easy to monitor, we shall assume that workers performing these tasks can be costlessly supervised. There is thus little reason to hire these workers on long-term contracts, and the conventional means of hiring them, namely, on the spot markets, serves adequately.

With workers performing type 1 tasks the situation is, however, quite different. We have defined type 1 tasks as those that involve some discretion and judgment, and are difficult to monitor. Our discussion in the introduction leads to the following view on the nature of contracts given to workers performing type 1 tasks.

In order to provide a self-enforcing (incentive) contract, the landlord offers type 1 workers a permanent contract (over the infinite horizon),[7] in which the worker receives a wage $w_p$ per period in exchange for the worker's services for the fraction $l^*(w_p, \bar{e})$ of each period at an effort level $\bar{e}$. The worker's effort in period 1 is assumed to be accurately imputable at the end of the year. If the worker is found to have shirked, he is fired at the end of the crop.[8] He is, however, paid his wage, $w_p$ for each of the two periods. Once a type 1 worker is fired, he cannot be rehired except as a casual worker.[9] If $w_p$ is high enough that a worker's increase in utility from shirking in one period is more than offset by the discounted loss in his utility in having to join the casual labor force, he would never shirk.

It is important to spell out the terms required for the viability of such a contract to permanent workers. First, since a permanent worker's effort can be gauged only at the end of the second period, he can be fired only at the end of period 2. If the landlord concludes that the worker has shirked and decides to fire him, he must still be contractually committed to pay him the prenegotiated wage $w_p$ in each of the two periods. Without such a contractual commitment, the landlord cannot be trusted to pay even honest workers and no worker would accept the contract. It may be argued that the fear of notoriety and the consequent difficulty in finding labor would keep the landlord honest. We feel, however, that in a labor surplus economy, reputation can hardly be as effective a check on the behavior of the owner of the scarce factor (land) as it is on the behavior of laborers competing for permanent jobs. Reputation is an effective weapon against moral hazard only for the suppliers of those factors that are in excess supply. The method of eliciting the desired level of effort from an employee by keeping him over his opportunity utility serves precisely to create such an excess supply so that reputation matters.

Another valid question is why a casual worker who failed to secure a permanent contract does not entice the landlord into offering him such a contract by posting a bond, the present value of which is marginally less than the difference in the present values of the lifetime income streams of the permanent and casual workers. Once again, such an arrangement is not viable due to the possibility of moral hazard on the part of the landlord; he always has the incentive to claim at the end of the period that the worker has shirked and thus expropriate the bond. Besides, as Eaton and White (1982) have pointed out, a worker faced with asset constraints may be unable to raise the amount necessary to post such a bond.

We can determine $w_p$ in terms of $w_c$ as follows. Assuming, for simplicity, that workers discount their utility at the same rate $\beta$ as the landlord discounts profits, the present value utility of a permanent worker who is honest (i.e., who never shirks) is given by[10]

$$\mathcal{J}_p^h(w_p, \beta) = \frac{V(w_p, \bar{e})}{1 - \beta} \tag{13}$$

Now the opportunity utility of a permanent worker is the utility he would receive as a casual worker. Assume that the casual labor demand is spread uniformly across all the casual workers. Then the discounted lifetime utility of a casual worker is given by

$$\mathcal{J}_c(w_c, \beta) = \left(\frac{\beta}{1 - \beta^2}\right) V(w_c, \bar{e}) \tag{14}$$

We now turn to the possibility of shirking on the part of a permanent worker. Since any shirking is guaranteed to result in termination at the end of the second period of the same crop, a permanent worker who chooses to shirk will find it optimal to set $e = 0$ in the first period. Since in period 2 he performs only menial tasks, which can be costlessly monitored, shirking is not possible. His discounted utility over this crop (relative to the beginning of the crop) is

$$V(w_p, 0) + \beta V(w_p, \bar{e})$$

Further, assuming demand and supply conditions to be identical across all years, a permanent worker who contemplates shirking will do so in the very first year. Thus the discounted lifetime utility of a permanent worker who shirks is

$$J_p^s(w_p, w_c, \beta) = V(w_p, 0) + \beta V(w_p, \bar{e}) + \beta^2 J_c(w_c, \beta) \tag{15}$$

To ensure that a permanent worker never shirks, we simply require

$$J_p^h(w_p, \beta) \geq J_p^s(w_p, w_c, \beta) \tag{16}$$

For given $w_c$ and $\beta$, inequality (16) puts a lower bound on the permanent worker's wage, $w_p$, which will elicit the required level of effort. At any $w_p$ that satisfies (16) a worker obtains a strictly higher utility in a permanent contract than in a series of spot contracts:[11]

$$J_p^h(w_p, \beta) > J_c(w_c, \beta) \tag{17}$$

It follows that the number of permanent workers hired will be demand determined in general. Since a laborer strictly prefers being a permanent worker to being a casual worker, there will generally be an excess supply of workers seeking permanent contracts. This, however, will not result in a downward pressure on the permanent workers' wage, since any wage which is lower than the smallest $w_p$, say $\bar{w}_p(w_c, \beta)$, that satisfies (16) for given $w_c$ and $\beta$ is not credible: it leaves an incentive for the permanent worker to shirk. A casual worker who seeks to obtain a permanent contract by offering to work for a wage marginally less than $\bar{w}_p$ will find that the landlord will not entertain the offer.

In the next section, we shall find that the behavior of $\bar{w}_p(w_c, \beta)$ as a function of $w_c$ is of crucial importance in determining the response of the agricultural economy to various exogenous changes. This behavior is recorded in the following proposition.

PROPOSITION 1 *For $w_c \geq \bar{e}$, an increase in $w_c$ warrants a change in $w_p$, that is,*

(a) *positive, and*
(b) *if $\bar{w}_p(w_c, \beta) < w_c$, then*

$$\frac{d\bar{w}_p}{dw_c} < \frac{\beta}{1 + \beta} \tag{18}$$

PROOF See the appendix.

Part (a) of proposition 1 is eminently reasonable, since an increase in $w_c$ amounts to an increase in the permanent worker's opportunity income (and utility). According to part (b), when the permanent worker's per period wage rate $\bar{w}_p(w_c, \beta)$ is less than that of a casual worker's, $w_c$, the increase ($\Delta w_p$) that is required to compensate a permanent worker for an exogenous increase ($\Delta w_c$) in a casual worker's wage rate satisfies the inequality

$$(1 + \beta)\Delta w_p - \beta \Delta w_c < 0 \tag{19}$$

This implies that the increase in present value cost of engaging a permanent worker is less than that of a casual worker.

We now turn to the determination of the equilibrium. The equilibrium levels of capital in the two periods are demand determined. Since permanent workers are held above their opportunity utilities, their number, $L_p^*$, is also demand determined:

$$L_p^*(b, r_1, z) = L_p^d(b, r_1, z) \tag{20a}$$

The demand for casual workers, we have seen, is given by

$$L_c^d(L_p, ab, w_c, r_2) = L_a^d(ab, r_2, w_c) - L_p^*(b, r_1, z) \tag{20b}$$

assuming the demand to be strictly positive. Next, we have the condition (16), which translates into

$$\frac{V(w_p, \bar{e})}{1 - \beta} \geq V(w_p, 0) + \beta V(w_p, \bar{e}) + \frac{\beta}{\left(1 - \beta^2\right)} V(w_c, \bar{e}) \tag{20c}$$

For any $w_c$, (20c) determines the minimum $w_p$ that will prevent a permanent worker from shirking.

Note that an equilibrium must have $w_c \geq \bar{e}$ and $w_p \geq \bar{e}$, in view of (11). Note also that $w_p = \bar{e}$ is never a solution to (20c) when $w_c \geq \bar{e}$. Thus we must have $w_p > \bar{e}$, and consequently, $l^*(w_p, \bar{e}) = 1$ for a permanent worker. In other words, each permanent worker provides one efficiency unit of labor per period. Let $N$ be the (exogenously given) total number of workers in the agrarian economy. The aggregate supply of casual labor in the second period, $L_c$, is then given by

$$L_c^s \begin{cases} = 0, & \text{for } w_c < \bar{e} \\ \in \left(0, N - L_p^*\right) & \text{for } w_c = \bar{e} \\ = N - L_p^* & \text{for } w_c > \bar{e} \end{cases} \tag{20d}$$

This completes the specification of our model. Exogenous to the model are the production and utility functions, the discount factor, the rental rates on capital, and the total labor force. Endogenous to the model are the wage rate of the permanent and casual workers, the number of permanent workers, the number of efficiency units of casual workers hired in the second period, and the amounts of capital hired in each of the two periods. These are obtained as the solution to the general equilibrium system defined by (20a)–(20d). The employment of capital is demand determined, that is, by (6a) and (6b).

Since a permanent worker's contract extends over the infinite horizon, the hiring of a permanent laborer represents a sunk cost for the landlord. The choice of the labor mix between permanent and casual workers can thus be viewed as a choice between sunk and variable costs.

For an arbitrarily chosen value of $L_p$, the casual labor supply is given by the kinked curve $L_c^s$ in figure 2. The demand for casual labor, contingent on the choice of $L_p$, is

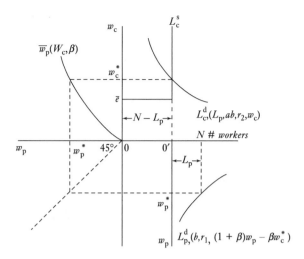

**Figure 2**   An equilibrium with unemployment in period 1 and full employment in period 2

obtained from (20b) and is also shown in the first quadrant of figure 2. The casual labor market clears at the wage rage $w_c^*$. (In what follows stars denote equilibrium values.) The second quadrant displays the solution for $w_p$ in terms of $w_c$ as obtained from (20c). Associated with a casual labor wage rate $w_c^*$ is a permanent labor wage rate $w_p^*$. The fourth quadrant displays the demand for permanent labor as a function of $w_p$ when the casual labor wage rate is $w_c^*$. For convenience this demand for permanent labor is measured from $0'$ (along the horizontal axis). If we have indeed located an equilibrium, the demand for permanent labor at $w_p^*$ will be exactly equal to the $L_p$ with which we began our construction. Thus the situation illustrated in figure 2 represents an equilibrium of the system of equations (20a) through (20d).

Given our assumption that the number of casual workers hired is strictly positive, two distinct situations can emerge as equilibria, although both of these are not equally relevant:

$$0 < L_p^* < N$$
*Case* 1: $0 < L_c^* < N$
$$L_p^* + L_c^* < N$$

This situation is illustrated in figure 3. The demand for casual labor in the peak season is not enough to warrant full employment: there is some unemployment at the equilibrium casual wage rate $w_c^* = \bar{e}$.

$$0 < L_p^* < N$$
*Case* 2: $0 < L_c^* < N$
$$L_p^* + L_c^* = N$$

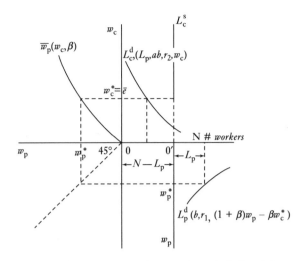

**Figure 3**   An equilibrium involving unemployment in periods 1 and 2

This is the situation we considered in figure 2. Here the supply of labor is a binding constraint in the second period and $w^* > \bar{e}$.

Of these two cases, the empirically relevant one is Case 2 – in which only part of the labor force is hired on a permanent basis, while in the peak season there is no unemployment. In what follows, therefore, we shall focus exclusively on this case.

## 2. Results

We now turn to the comparative static results of our model. These results depend crucially on whether the casual wage rate exceeds or falls short of the wage rate of the permanent workers. These are, of course, endogenously determined and our model allows for both possibilities. However, since our purpose here is to confront our predictions with what empirical evidence there is, we pursue the empirically relevant case. From Richards (1979), Sanghavi (1969), Ashok Rudra (1982), and Rakesh Basant (1984), we gather this case to be one where

$$w_c^* > w_p^* \tag{21}$$

In what follows we shall assume (21) to be true.[12] (The signs of the comparative static results below are reversed when (21) is violated.) Defining

$$z^* = (1 + \beta)w_p^* - \beta w_c^*$$

we see from (18) that

$$\frac{dz^*}{dw_c^*} = (1 + \beta)\left[\frac{dw_p^*}{dw_c^*} - \frac{\beta}{1 + \beta}\right] < 0 \tag{22}$$

That is, the difference in the present value cost of hiring a permanent worker over that of hiring a casual worker declines with $w_c^*$. This fact is used in establishing the comparative static properties of our model, which are recorded in the following proposition.

PROPOSITION 2: *In an equilibrium corresponding to Case 2,*

(a)  *an increase in $N$ decreases the proportion of permanent contracts,*
(b)  *an increase in $a$ (or $b$ or both) increases the number of permanent contracts,*
(c)  *an increase in $a$, with $ab$ held constant, decreases the number of permanent contracts,*
(d)  *an increase in $r_1$ or $r_2$ increase the number of permanent contracts.*

PROOF  See the appendix.

Parts (a) and (b) of proposition 2 provide explanations, alternative to Bardhan's (1983), for certain empirical observations on permanent labor. According to (a), the proportion of permanent workers is higher the tighter the labor market. A reduction in the supply of agricultural labor, $N$, increases the peak season casual wage rate, $w_c^*$. This results in an increase in the wage rate of the permanent workers, $w_p^*$. However, the increases satisfy inequality (19) – implying that the marginal permanent worker is becoming cheaper to hire relative to a casual worker in period 2 – inducing a substitution of permanent for casual workers. Part (a) above explains the dramatic increase in the percentage of permanent contracts in East Prussian agriculture in the first half of the nineteenth century. During this period there was an increase in the cultivated area by almost 90 percent between 1815 and 1849, and a simultaneous agrarian reform resulted in peasants losing land to large landlords. The loss of land forced the peasants into the labor market. Richards (1979), however, estimates that the total net loss of land by the peasants to the landlords may have been as low as 3 percent, implying an overall decrease in the labor-to-land ratio, resulting in a higher proportion of permanent workers.

Part (b) of proposition 2 implies that a yield-increasing improvement in the technology, either through a Hicks-neutral technical change (i.e., higher $a$) or through a land-augmenting technical change (i.e., higher $b$) would increase the proportion of permanent contracts. The intuition for this is the same as that for part (a), and hinges on the relative changes in the magnitudes of $w_c^*$ and $w_p^*$ triggered by the exogenous change. Bardhan (1983) provides empirical evidence based on the second Agricultural Labor Enquiry Data that the percentage of permanent labor in India is positively correlated with the index of land productivity.

The demand for permanent and casual labor is, of course, a derived demand. For simplicity we have assumed that the price of the output is exogenously given. It is clear, however, that any factor that affects the demand for output will have repercussions on the labor composition in equilibrium. In particular, an increase in the output price will induce an increase in the output for production functions more general than the ones we have adopted. The effects of an increase in the price of the output can, however, be simulated in our model by an increase in $a$. Part (b) of proposition 2 then explains the impact of the opening up of export markets on the labor composition in nineteenth-century Chile. In the 1860s, Chile began to export grain to European markets and this lasted until 1890. Bauer (1971) estimated that the percentage of casual workers in the rural labor force of central Chile fell from 72 percent in 1865 to 39 percent in 1895 – an observation that is consistent with the result in part (b) of the above proposition.

While part (b) is of empirical interest since it is easily verifiable, an exercise that is of theoretical interest is contained in part (c). Here the final output is held final and the burden of activity is shifted across the two periods. We see that an increase in $a$, implying a decrease in $b$, makes cultivation less intensive in the first period while increasing the activity in the peak season. Since in the second period casual and permanent labor are substitutable, we observe a shift from permanent to casual labor. Thus Jan Breman (1974) observes that a change in crops from rice (which has a relatively even distribution of tasks over the two periods) to mangoes (which has a very heavy labor demand in period 2) resulted in the replacement of permanent contracts by casual labor contracts in Gujarat, India. Kalpana Bardhan (1977) has also made similar empirical observations.[13]

Part (d) of proposition 2 indicates that a decrease in the rental cost of the type of capital used in the first period would displace permanent workers and consequently increase the use of casual labor in the second period. It could be argued that in India, in view of the notoriously imperfect capital markets, farms with tractors are those for which the owners face lower capital costs. If tractors were employed on such farms only during period 1 (for operations such as ploughing and sowing), the result would be a displacement of permanent workers and an increase in the use of casual workers. While the existing empirical literature (Rudra (1982); Bina Agarwal, 1981) bears out our prediction regarding permanent workers, there is conflicting evidence on the effect on the employment of casual workers. We conjecture that this conflict arises because tractors are used on some farms for period 1 operations only, while on others they are also used in period 2.

An interesting feature of the result in part (d) of proposition 2 is the implied complementarity between the capital used in the two periods. Since there are no sunk costs involved in the use of capital (they are presumed to be rented separately in each period), one might expect the choice of the amount of capital used in period 1 to be independent of $r_2$. This, however, is not so. A decline in $r_2$ increases the demand for $K_2$ and reduces the demand for casual labor. Given full employment in the second period, this lowers the casual wage rate, which in turn lowers the wage rate of permanent workers. In view of (18), however, permanent workers are becoming relatively more expensive than casual workers and this induces a substitution away from permanent labor. The reduction in the amount of permanent labor hired warrants an increase in $K_1$ since, in the first period, these two inputs are substitutable. A policy implication of this result is that any governmental effort to alleviate labor-supply bottlenecks in the peak period by lowering $r_2$ (through subsidies, for example) would have an adverse effect on the employment of labor in the slack period.

## 3. Conclusions

In this paper we have presented the view that the institution of permanent workers exists to elicit loyalty and trustworthiness from hired workers, so that they can be entrusted with important tasks that are inherently difficult to monitor. This is accomplished by holding them at a higher-than-opportunity utility, and thus creating in the process two tiers within a homogeneous labor force. Evidence of disloyal behavior (i.e., shirking) results in the termination of the permanent contract and the possibility of the consequent discrete fall in the utility keeps the worker loyal.[14]

A well-known result in the agency literature states that a threshold contract with a discontinuous reward system can be devised to elicit the optimal amount of effort from a worker. The incentive mechanism implicit in permanent contracts within a two-tiered labor force is, however, not a special case of this. A contract which stipulates the agent's reward in terms of his effort when the verdict on the latter is pronounced *ex post* by the principal will not be accepted by the agent. The possibility of morally hazardous behavior on the part of both the principal and the agent has to be explicitly recognized. In the institution we have discussed, the relationship between the principal and the agent involves repeated transactions and this facilitates the design of a contract which gets around the above difficulty. The landlord is contractually committed to pay the permanent worker the full stipulated income for the year even if he is fired at the end of the year. In other words, the compensation goes with the position; as long as a worker is in the higher tier he receives a compensation appropriate to this position. The contract is thus incentive compatible for both parties despite the inherent problem that there is no objective criterion by which to gauge the worker's effort level.

Long-standing relationships that involve repeated transactions between two parties and put a premium on loyalty and trust are referred to as patron–client relationships. These relationships are often sustained and strengthened by means of implicit contracts. The patron (the principal) maintains the client (the agent) at a higher-than-opportunity utility through patronage to win the client's loyalty and trust. The instruments used to effect this patronage will vary according to the needs of the client and the ability of the patron to supply these needs. Ideally, the instruments will bestow a large benefit on the client at a relatively low cost to the patron. Provision of land plots in labor-scarce economies, consumption credit in an environment of imperfect capital markets or protection in the dubious legal environment of Sicily are examples of instruments of patronage. As discussed in this paper, the seasonal nature of agriculture renders it relatively easy for landlords to maintain a utility-differential between permanent and casual workers.

Even in industrialized economies we observe contracts that resemble those of permanent workers. In particular, in sectors subject to seasonal demand (such as construction, services catering to tourism, recreational vehicle services, etc.) firms retain year-round a core of permanent workers selected from the same pool as the seasonal workers. We further conjecture that the most familiar type of employment contract, namely, the salaried contract of a white-collar worker (in a position that is inherently difficult to monitor), embodies a supervision mechanism similar to the one discussed in this paper.

The institution of permanent workers is a graphic manifestation of the consequences of the supervision principle proposed by Eaton and White (1983). This principle, however, is quite general in scope. For example, it explains a fact that forms the premise of numerous models in the migration literature: the substantial wage differential that exists between newly recruited factory workers and those in the informal urban sector from which they are recruited.

Indeed, this incentive mechanism does not even require that the transaction between the principal and agent be voluntary. The mechanism could work equally well in a slave economy. What is essential is that the agent be convinced in a credible fashion that there is a state of existence that is discretely worse than his current one. Even the miserable existence of a slave can be made worse by selling him and separating him from his family. More subtle means employed to create a favored status among slaves in the antebellum

South are discussed by Robert Fogel and Stanley Engerman (1974). Thus even when crude supervision devices such as physical punishment are permitted by society, subtle incentive mechanisms that reduce the cost of supervision have always played an important role. The study of historical institutions and their incentive structures could, therefore, be quite useful in the construction of a theory of economic organizations.

## APPENDIX

### *Proof of proposition 1*

(a) Substituting (13), (14), and (15) in (16), which holds with equality at $\bar{w}_p$, we have

$$\frac{V(\bar{w}_p, \bar{e})}{1 - \beta} = V(\bar{w}_p, 0) + \beta V(\bar{w}_p, \bar{e}) + \left(\frac{\beta^3}{1 - \beta^2}\right) V(w_c, \bar{e}) \tag{A1}$$

Differentiating the above expression totally with respect to $w_c$ and rearranging, we obtain

$$\frac{d\bar{w}_p}{dw_c} = \frac{\left(\dfrac{\beta^3}{1 + \beta}\right) \dfrac{\partial V}{\partial w_c}(w_c, \bar{e})}{\left(1 - \beta + \beta^2\right) \dfrac{\partial V}{\partial w_p}(\bar{w}_p, \bar{e}) - (1 - \beta) \dfrac{\partial V}{\partial w_p}(\bar{w}_p, 0)} \tag{A2}$$

The numerator of the right-hand side is clearly positive. Note that for (A1) to hold we must have $\bar{w}_p > \bar{e}$. Using (11), it follows from (12) that

$$\frac{\partial V}{\partial w_p}(\bar{w}_p, \bar{e}) > \frac{\partial V}{\partial w_p}(\bar{w}_p, 0) \tag{A3}$$

so that from (A2)

$$\frac{d\bar{w}_p}{dw_c} > 0 \tag{A4}$$

(b) From (A3), we see that the denominator of the right-hand side of (A2) exceeds

$$\left(1 - \beta + \beta^2\right) \frac{\partial V}{\partial w_p}(\bar{w}_p, \bar{e}) - (1 - \beta) \frac{\partial V}{\partial w_p}(\bar{w}_p, \bar{e}) = \beta^2 \frac{\partial V}{\partial w_p}(\bar{w}_p, \bar{e})$$

Thus from (A2) we have

$$\frac{d\bar{w}_p}{dw_c} < \frac{\beta}{1 + \beta} \left[ \frac{\dfrac{\partial V}{\partial w_c}(w_c, \bar{e})}{\dfrac{\partial V}{\partial w_p}(\bar{w}_p, \bar{e})} \right]$$

If $\bar{w}_p(w_c, \beta) < w_c$, it follows by differentiating (12) that the term in the square bracket is less than unity, so that $d\bar{w}_p/dw_c < \beta/(1+\beta)$.

## *Proof of proposition 2*

First, note that $K_1^d(L_p, b, r_1)$, which is obtained as the solution to the trivial optimization in (5) with $q_1 = ab$, has the following comparative static properties:

$$\frac{\partial K_1^d}{\partial L_p}(L_p, b, r_1) < 0$$

$$\frac{\partial K_1^d}{\partial b}(L_p, b, r_1) > 0 \tag{A5}$$

$$\frac{\partial K_1^d}{\partial r_1}(L_p, b, r_1) = 0$$

The comparative static properties of $L_p^d(b, r_1, z)$, obtained by differentiating (8), using (A5) and the strict quasi concavity of $g_1(K_1, L_p)$, are easily seen to be given by

$$\frac{\partial L_p^d}{\partial b}(b, r_1, z) > 0$$

$$\frac{\partial L_p^d}{\partial r_1}(b, r_1, z) > 0 \tag{A6}$$

$$\frac{\partial L_p^d}{\partial z}(b, r_1, z) < 0$$

If we let $\alpha$ denote an exogenous shift parameter whose comparative static effects we wish to determine, we may write

$$\frac{dL_p^*}{d\alpha} = \frac{\partial L_p^d}{\partial \alpha}(b, r_1, z^*) + \frac{\partial L_p^d}{\partial z^*}(b, r_1, z^*)\frac{dz^*}{dw_c^*}\frac{dw_c^*}{d\alpha} \tag{A7}$$

recalling that the number of permanent workers is demand determined. From (20b) and (20d), we have

$$L_a^d(ab, r_2, w_c^*) = N \tag{A8}$$

Totally differentiating this with respect to $\alpha$ and rearranging, we have

$$\frac{dw_c^*}{d\alpha} = \frac{\dfrac{dN}{d\alpha} - \dfrac{\partial L_a^d}{\partial \alpha}}{\dfrac{\partial L_a^d}{\partial w_c}} \tag{A9}$$

The comparative static properties of $L_a^d(ab, r_2, w_c)$, which is obtained as the solution to the optimization problem (4), are easily verified to be

$$\frac{\partial L_a^d}{\partial r_2}(ab, r_2, w_c) > 0$$

$$\frac{\partial L_a^d}{\partial w_c}(ab, r_2, w_c) < 0 \tag{A10}$$

$$\frac{\partial L_a^d}{\partial (ab)}(ab, r_2, w_c) > 0$$

(a) Since

$$\partial L_a^d / \partial N = 0 \text{ and } \partial L_a^d / \partial w_c < 0$$

(A9) yields $dw_c^*/dN < 0$. Further, since $\partial L_a^d/\partial N = 0$, we have from (A7) and (22) that $dL_p^*/dN < 0$.

$$\therefore \frac{d}{dN}\left(\frac{L_p^*}{N}\right) = -\frac{1}{N^2}L_p^* + \frac{1}{N}\frac{dL_p^*}{dN} < 0$$

(b) Since by (A10) $\partial L_a^d/\partial a > 0$, we have $dw_c^*/da > 0$ from (A9), so that from (A7) we have $dL_p^*/da > 0$. As above, $dw_c^*/db > 0$ since $\partial L_a^d/\partial b > 0$. Also, since $\partial L_p^d/\partial b > 0$, it follows from (A7) that $dL_p^*/db > 0$.

(c) When $a$ changes but $ab$ is held constant, we see from (A8) that $dw_c^*/da = 0$. Thus from (A7),

$$\text{sign}\left\{\frac{dL_p^*}{da}\bigg|_{ab=\text{constant}}\right\} = \text{sign}\left\{\frac{\partial L_p^d}{\partial a}\left(\frac{1}{a}, r_1, z\right)\right\} < 0$$

(d) Since $\partial L_a^d/\partial r_1 = 0$, we have from (A9) that $dw_c^*/dr_1 = 0$.

$$\frac{dL_p^*}{dr_1} = \frac{\partial L_p^d}{\partial r_1} > 0$$

Further, since $\partial L_a^d/\partial r_2 > 0$, it follows from (A9) that $dw_c^*/dr_2 > 0$. Since $\partial L_p^d/\partial r_2 = 0$, we have from (A7) that $dL_p^*/dr_2 > 0$.

## Notes

1  In addition to Bardhan's own work on East India (1979a, b), this finding has been found to be empirically valid in Chile (pre-1930), East Elbian Germany (1750–1860), and Egypt (1850–1940), as documented in Richards (1979).

2  See Shigemochi Hirashima (1978, p. 109) for a description of the differential tasks assigned to the two kinds of workers in Pakistan. Also see Thomas Smith (1959) on the tasks performed by permanent workers in Tokugawa Japan and M. M. Postan (1954) for a description of the duties of estate workers in thirteenth-century England.

3  In Sanghavi (1969) (Table 4.7, p. 100), the data on all states in North India, except for Uttar Pradesh, showed a higher annual income for male attached workers by a range of 15–100 percent. Bardhan (1979a) found that the average level of consumption for the family members of permanent workers in Bengal was Rs. 32/month/capita where as it was Rs. 24/month/capita for the family members of casual workers.

4  For persuasive accounts suggesting that permanent workers are better off than casual workers, see Richards on Egypt (1982, p. 63); Arnold Bauer on Chile (1971, p. 1072).

5  A similar idea also appears in Steven Stoft (1980) and, more recently, in Carl Shapiro and Joseph Stiglitz (1984).

6  Introducing the possibility of tenancy in this model would greatly complicate the formulation, and is a task to be accomplished in future research.

7  While the assumption of infinite time horizon is analytically convenient, it is also empirically appropriate when a permanent worker's status can be inherited.

8  It might be argued that the landlord would be indifferent between retaining the disloyal worker and replacing him with another who has exactly the same propensity to shirk. A permanent worker who realizes this cannot be deterred from shirking. Since the credibility of the system is at stake, however, the landlord would strictly prefer to replace the disloyal worker, establishing his reputation as a firm enforcer of contracts.

9  This is assumed for simplicity. For our purposes it is enough if he can secure another such contract only with a probability that is strictly less than unity. This would lead to a discretely lower present value expected earning if he is fired.

10  This assumes that there is no saving, so that consumption and income are identical.

11  This can be seen by rewriting inequality (16) as

$$\left(1 - \beta + \beta^2\right) V\left(w_p, \bar{e}\right)$$

$$\geq (1 - \beta) V\left(w_p, 0\right) + \frac{\beta^3}{1 + \beta} V\left(w_c, \bar{e}\right)$$

$$> (1 - \beta) V\left(w_p, \bar{e}\right) + \frac{\beta^3}{1 + \beta} V\left(w_c, \bar{e}\right)$$

by (12), so that

$$(1 + \beta) V\left(w_p, \bar{e}\right) > \beta V\left(w_c, \bar{e}\right)$$

12  Full employment in the peak period is a necessary condition for this to hold. It is also necessary that the permanent workers not discount the future too heavily.

13  Part (c) of proposition 2 is also consistent with empirical evidence that increases in the cropping intensity, which would result in a more even labor demand profile, are correlated with higher incidence of permanent contracts. See K. Bardhan (1977) on India, and Richards (1979) on East Prussia.

14  Note that the assumption of a homogeneous labor force is not essential to our theory. With heterogeneous alternative employment opportunities across workers, casual workers with high opportunity incomes may not prefer permanent contracts. Even so, our theory remains valid as long as there is an excess supply of some casual workers desiring permanent jobs. Bardhan and Rudra (1981) found, in a survey conducted in West Bengal (India), that the bulk of the casual workers preferred casual contracts and the bulk of the permanent workers preferred permanent contracts. However, a statistical test performed on their data leads us to

reject the hypothesis that there is no excess supply of workers desiring permanent contracts in favor of the hypothesis of a strictly positive excess supply.

## References

Agarwal, B. (1981): "Agricultural Mechanisation and Labour Use: A Disaggregated Approach," *International Labour Review*, 120, January–February, 115–27.

Bardhan, K. (1977): "Rural Employment, Wages and Labour Markets in India, A Survey of Research – III," *Economic and Political Weekly*, 12, July 9, 1101–18.

Bardhan, P. K. (1979a): "Wages and Unemployment in a Poor Agrarian Economy: A Theoretical and Empirical Analysis," *Journal of Political Economy*, 87, June, 479–500.

—— (1979b): "Labor Supply Functions in a Poor Agrarian Economy," *American Economic Review*, 69, March, 73–83.

—— (1983): "Labor-Tying in a Poor Agrarian Economy: A Theoretical and Empirical Analysis," *Quarterly Journal of Economics*, 98, August, 501–14.

—— and Rudra, A. (1981): "Terms and Conditions of Labor Contracts in Agriculture: Results of a Survey in West Bengal 1979," *Oxford Bulletin of Economics and Statistics*, 43, February, 89–111.

Basant, R. (1984): "Attached and Casual Labour Wage Rates," *Economic and Political Weekly*, 19, March, 390–6.

Bauer, A. J. (1971): "Chilean Rural Labor in the Nineteenth Century," *American History Review*, 76, October, 1059–83.

—— (1975): *Chilean Rural Society from the Spanish Conquest to 1930*. Cambridge: Cambridge University Press.

Bhalla, S. (1976): "New Relations of Production in Haryana Agriculture," *Economic and Political Weekly*, 11, March 27, A23–30.

Breman, J. (1974): *Patronage and Exploitation*. Berkeley: University of California Press.

Eaton, B. C. and White, W. D. (1982): "Agent Compensation and the Limits of Bonding," *Economic Inquiry*, 20 July, 330–43.

—— and —— (1983): "The Economy of High Wages: An Agency Problem," *Economica*, 50, May, 175–82.

Eswaran, M. and Kotwal, A. (1985): "A Theory of Contractual Structure in Agriculture," *American Economic Review*, 75(3), June, 352–67.

Fogel, R. W. and Engerman, S. L. (1974): *Time on the Cross*. Boston: Little, Brown.

Hirashima, S. (1978): *The Structure of Disparity in Developing Agriculture*. Tokyo: Institute of Developing Economies.

Postan, M. M. (1954): *The Famulus: The Estate Labourer in the Twelfth and Thirteenth Centuries*, Economic History Review, Supplement 2.

Richards, A. (1979): "The Political Economy of Gutswirtschaft: A Comparative Analysis of East Elbian Germany, Egypt, and Chile," *Comparative Studies in Society and History*, 21, October, 483–518.

—— (1982): *Egypt's Agricultural Development, 1800–1980*. Boulder: Westview Press.

Rudra, A. (1982): *Indian Agricultural Economics: Myths and Realities*. New Delhi: Allied Publishers.

Sanghavi, P. (1969): *Surplus Manpower in Agriculture and Economic Development*. New Delhi and New York: Asia Publishing.

Shapiro, C. and Stiglitz, J. E. (1984): "Equilibrium Unemployment as a Worker Discipline Device," *American Economic Review*, 74, June, 433–44.

Smith, T. C. (1959): *The Agrarian Origins of Modern Japan*. Palo Alto: Stanford University Press.

Stoft, S. (1980): "An Explanation of Involuntary. Unemployment, Sticky Wages and Labor Market Structures," unpublished doctoral dissertation, University of California-Berkeley.

# C: Credit and Land

# CHAPTER 11

# Credit Rationing in Developing Countries: An Overview of the Theory

PARIKSHIT GHOSH, DILIP MOOKHERJEE, AND DEBRAJ RAY

## 1. Introduction

Credit is essential in poor rural economies in a variety of ways. It is required to finance working capital and investment in fixed capital, particularly among farmers too poor to accumulate much saving. It is an important instrument for smoothing consumption, in a context where incomes typically experience large seasonal fluctuations. Moreover, unusual events such as illnesses or weddings often create a pressing need to borrow. Apart from the intrinsic benefit of being able to weather such shocks, availability of credit reduces reluctance to adopt technologies that raise both mean levels and riskiness of incomes.[1] The credit market thus affects output, investment, technology choices and inequality.

A significant fraction of credit transactions in underdeveloped countries still takes place in the informal sector, in spite of serious government efforts to channel credit directly via its own banks, or by regulating commercial banks.[2] This is largely because poorer farmers lack sufficient assets to put up as collateral – a usual prerequisite for borrowing from banks.[3] Numerous case studies and empirical analyses in a variety of countries have revealed that informal credit markets often display patterns and features not commonly found in institutional lending:

(i)   Loans are often advanced on the basis of oral agreements rather than written contracts, with little or no collateral, making default a seemingly attractive option.
(ii)  The credit market is usually highly segmented, marked by long-term exclusive relationships and repeat lending.
(iii) Interest rates are much higher on average than bank interest rates, and also show significant dispersion, presenting *apparent* arbitrage opportunities.
(iv)  There is frequent interlinkage with other markets, such as land, labor or crop.
(v)   Significant credit rationing, whereby borrowers are unable to borrow all they want, or some loan applicants are unable to borrow at all.

There are a number of different theoretical approaches that attempt to explain some or all of these features. Though differing in specific mechanisms proposed, they share a common general theme: that the world of informal credit is one of missing markets, asymmetric information, and incentive problems. There are a number of broad strands in the literature, focusing respectively on adverse selection (hidden information), moral hazard (hidden action), and contract enforcement problems. This article provides a sample of the latter two approaches, and argues that they are fundamentally similar in terms of their underlying logic and policy implications. These models have appeared in the work of many previous authors; our purpose is to provide a simple exposition, and identify the common underlying elements. The two theories focus respectively on involuntary and voluntary default risks, and associated borrower incentives. In the first model, defaults arise involuntarily, owing to adverse income or wealth shocks that make borrowers unable to repay their loans. The second model in contrast stresses problems with contract enforcement: borrowers may not repay their loans even if they have the means to do so. Both models explain how borrowing constraints endogenously arise in order to mitigate these incentive problems, even in the absence of exogenous restrictions on interest rate flexibility. The models also provide explanations for the features of informal credit markets listed above. Since their microfoundations are explicit – assumptions concerning underlying preferences, technology and information structure – they allow welfare and policy implications to be derived.

The adverse selection theory of credit markets originates with the paper by Stiglitz and Weiss (1981). The theory rests on two main assumptions: that lenders cannot distinguish between borrowers of different degrees of risk, and that loan contracts are subject to limited liability (i.e., if project returns are less than debt obligations, the borrower bears no responsibility to pay out of pocket). The analysis is restricted to *involuntary* default, i.e, it assumes that borrowers repay loans when they have the means to do so.

In a world with simple debt contracts between risk-neutral borrowers and lenders, the presence of limited liability of borrowers imparts a preference for risk among borrowers, and a corresponding aversion to risk among lenders. This is because limited liability on the part of borrowers implies that lenders bear all the downside risk. On the other hand, all returns above the loan repayment obligation accrues to borrowers. Raising interest rates then affects the profitability of low-risk borrowers disproportionately, causing them to drop out of the applicant pool. This leads to an adverse compositional effect – higher interest rates increase the average riskiness of the applicant pool. At very high interest rates, the only applicants are borrowers who could potentially generate very high returns (but presumably with small probability). Since lenders' preferences over project risk run counter to those of borrowers, they may hold interest rates at levels below market-clearing and ration borrowers in order to achieve a better composition and lower risk in their portfolio. Excess demand in the credit market may persist even in the face of competition and flexible interest rates.

Stiglitz and Weiss' theory was designed to apply quite generally, rather than in the specific context of informal credit in developing countries. In the latter context, the theory has often been criticized for its underlying assumption that lenders are not aware of borrower characteristics.[4] The close knit character of many traditional rural societies implies that lenders possess a great deal of information about relevant borrower characteristics, such as farming ability, size and quality of landholdings, cropping patterns and risk attitudes.[5]

However, if the distribution of returns from the investment is affected by the borrower's *actions*, observability and monitoring will be a problem even for lenders who live in close proximity. Limited liability could then increase default risk by reducing the borrower's effort in avoiding low yield states, rather than adversely affecting the composition of the loan applicant pool. This is precisely the moral hazard model, which we describe in section 2 of the paper.[6] The model illustrates the trade-off between extraction of rents and the provision of incentives to induce a good harvest. Higher interest rates cause the problem of *debt overhang* – a highly indebted farmer has very little stake in ensuring a good harvest (i.e., remaining solvent), since the large loan repayments this outcome occasions imply that he captures only a small portion of the returns from the harvest. Keeping this in mind, lenders will be reluctant to raise interest rates beyond some level. As in the adverse selection theory, the interest rate may not rise enough to guarantee that all loan applicants secure credit, in times when loanable funds are limited. In general, the volume of credit and level of effort is less than first-best. We also show how collateral affects effort and borrower returns. Borrowers who have greater wealth to put up as collateral obtain cheaper credit, have incentives to work harder, and earn more income as a result. Existing asset inequalities within the borrowing class are projected and possibly magnified into the future by the operation of the credit market, a phenomenon that may cause the persistence of poverty.[7]

In section 3, we consider problems arising from contract enforcement, and the attendant possibility of *voluntary* default. Loan contracts in the informal sector are rarely explicitly recorded and enforced by formal legal institutions. Repayments may be induced partially via informal enforcement mechanisms based on social sanctions, coercion or threats of violence. In large part, however, compliance is ensured by the threat of reduction or elimination of access to credit in the future. The natural model to study the enforcement problem is one of repeated interactions in the credit market, which is described in section 3. We first analyze a model of a single (monopolist) lender and a borrower, and show that in a (constrained) efficient stationary equilibrium, credit rationing arises unless the borrower has sufficient bargaining power. We then show that the same framework can be adapted to understand more realistic markets with multiple lenders. In such scenarios, *social norms* which prescribe that defaulters be boycotted by the entire market, can give rise to equilibria that sustain positive levels of borrowing and lending. However, credit rationing remains a pervasive phenomenon. At this point, we draw the reader's attention to two different forms of quantity constraints: *micro* credit rationing, which places credit limits on borrowers (below first-best levels), and *macro* credit rationing, which randomly denies access to *any* credit to a fraction of borrowers. The second form involves asymmetric treatment of otherwise identical agents. We show that both forms of rationing might coexist, and play complementary but distinct roles. It also becomes clear that the second form of rationing gains in importance when information flow within the lending community is poor (so that defaulters have a fair chance of escaping detection).

One lesson that emerges from both the debt overhang and enforcement stories is that the distribution of bargaining power across lenders and borrowers has strong implications for the degree of credit rationing, effort levels and efficiency. The effect is similar in both cases – greater bargaining power to the lender reduces available credit and efficiency.[8] The reason is that rent extraction motives can run counter to surplus maximization objectives beyond a certain point. The rent extractable from a marginal dollar loan or a marginal unit of effort induced may be less than the cost of funds, although the social returns might exceed it, leading to underinvestment. The implication is that social policies which empower the borrower and increase his bargaining strength are likely to increase efficiency.

## 2. Moral Hazard and Credit Rationing

Consider an indivisible project which requires funds of amount $L$ to be viable. Output is binary, taking values of either $Q$ (good harvest) or 0 (crop failure). The probability of a good harvest is $p(e)$, where $e$ is the effort level of the agent who oversees the project. We assume that $p'(e) > 0$ and $p''(e) < 0$, the latter representing usual diminishing returns. Effort cost is given by $e$, and all agents are risk neutral.

First, consider the problem of a self-financed farmer. If investment takes place at all, the effort level is chosen so as to

$$\max_{e} p(e) \cdot Q - e - L \tag{1}$$

The optimum choice $e^*$ is described by the first-order condition:

$$p'(e^*) = \frac{1}{Q} \tag{2}$$

This is the efficient, or first-best level of effort, which forms the benchmark against which all subsequent results will be compared.

Now consider a debt-financed farmer. Let $R = (1 + i)L$ denote total debt, where $i$ is the interest rate. To introduce moral hazard, we assume that $e$ is not verifiable by third parties, hence not contractible. Furthermore, there is limited liability: the borrower faces no obligations in the event of a crop failure (outcomes are verifiable, although effort is not). However, we allow for some collateral. Let $w$ denote the value of the borrower's transferable wealth that can be put up as collateral. To make the problem interesting, assume $w < L$. The effort choice of a borrower facing a total debt $R$ is given from:

$$\max_{e} p(e) \cdot (Q - R) + (1 - p(e)) \cdot (-w) - e \tag{3}$$

Denote the optimal choice by $\hat{e}(R, w)$, defined by the following first-order condition:

$$p'(e) = \frac{1}{Q + w - R} \tag{4}$$

Observe that $\hat{e}(R, w)$ is decreasing in $R$ and increasing in $w$.[9] A higher debt burden reduces the borrower's payoff in the good state, but not in the bad state, dampening incentive to apply effort. A bigger collateral, on the other hand, imposes a stiffer penalty in the event of crop failure, thus stimulating the incentive to avoid such an outcome.

The lender's profit is given by

$$\pi = p(e)R + [1 - p(e)]w - L \tag{5}$$

To find the Pareto frontier of possible payoffs, we hold the lender's expected profit at any given level $\pi$, and maximize the borrower's utility, subject to incentive compatible choice of effort level. Implicit in our formulation is the assumption that the opportunity cost of funds is zero, which is entirely innocuous and can be generalized without any problem. In determining equilibrium choices, we will treat $\pi$ as given, and will later see the comparative static effects of increasing it. The special case where $\pi = 0$ represents a perfectly competitive loan market with free entry. Since lenders can always choose not to lend, it makes sense to restrict attention only to cases where $\pi \geq 0$. This last condition, together with (5) (and the fact that $w < L$) immediately implies that $R > w$. Using this to compare (2) and (4), and remembering the concavity of the $p(\cdot)$ function, we conclude that $\hat{e} < e^*$.

PROPOSITION 1    *As long as the borrower does not have enough wealth to guarantee the full value of the loan, the effort choice will be less than first-best.*

This is the *debt overhang* problem: an indebted borrower will always work less hard on his project than one who is self-financed.

The variables determined in equilibrium are $R$ and $e$. Equations (5) (the isoprofit curve) and (4) (the incentive curve) jointly determine the outcome. It is easy to check that the locus described by each is negatively sloped. If the borrower works harder, the risk of default is reduced, and $R$ must be lower to hold down the lender's profit at the same level. On the other hand, a reduced debt burden increases the incentive to work hard.

Notice also that as we move downward along the incentive curve, the borrower's payoff is increasing. Lower debt ($R$) increases borrower payoff for any given choice of effort, and hence also after adjusting for optimal choice. If there are multiple intersections, only the lowest among these (the one associated with the lowest $R$) is compatible with Pareto efficiency. Further, the incentive curve should be steeper than the isoprofit line at the optimum point (otherwise, a small decrease in $R$ will increase both lender profit and borrower utility). Figure 1 depicts a typical situation, point $E$ representing the equilibrium.

We can now examine the comparative static effect of higher lender profit ($\pi$) or higher wealth ($w$). Figure 2 shows the effect of increasing $\pi$. The isoprofit curve shifts up; in the

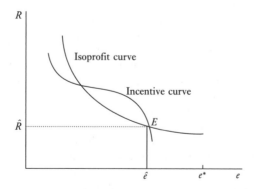

**Figure 1**    Equilibrium debt and effort in the credit market

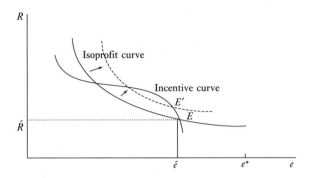

**Figure 2**   Effect of an increase in the lender's profit

new resultant Pareto efficient equilibrium, the debt burden $(R)$ increases, and so does the interest rate (since the loan size is fixed), while the effort level falls.

PROPOSITION 2    *(Pareto efficient) equilibria in which lenders obtain higher profits involve higher debt and interest rates, but lower levels of effort. Hence, these equilibria produce lower social surplus.*

It is instructive to ask why higher rent extraction is associated with lower overall efficiency. Lenders earn more profit by increasing the interest rate, which in itself is a pure transfer. However, a greater debt burden reduces the borrower's incentive to spend effort, increasing the chance of crop failure and creating a deadweight loss. Consider two extreme cases. The case of $\pi = 0$ represents perfect competition, and this situation generates the highest level of effort among all. Notice, however, that since the debt burden still exceeds $w$, effort will nevertheless be less than first-best. This tells us that the source of the inefficiency is not so much monopolistic distortion created by the lender's market power (although that certainly exacerbates the problem), but the agency problem itself, and the distortion in incentives created by limited liability. While the borrower shares in capital gains, he bears no part of the capital losses (beyond the collateral posted). Working with other people's money is not the same as working with one's own.

The other extreme case is that of monopoly. In this case, the value of $\pi$ is maximized from among all feasible and incentive compatible alternatives. In other words, the monopolistic lender will choose the point on the incentive curve that attains the highest isoprofit curve. The condition is the standard one of tangency between the two curves. This provides a ceiling on the interest rate, or debt level $(\bar{R})$, and the lender will not find it profitable to raise it above this level. In more competitive conditions, this ceiling will still apply. If, in a competitive credit market, there is excess demand for funds at $\bar{R}$, the interest rate will not rise to clear the market. We have an exact counterpart of Stiglitz–Weiss type of rationing (rationing of borrowers, or macro-rationing in our terminology) in the presence of moral hazard rather than adverse selection.[10]

The observation that borrower-friendly equilibria are more efficient has broad implications for social policy. Any change which reduces interest rates, or improves the bargaining power of the borrower will enhance effort and productivity. The latter involves institutional changes, such as a reallocation of property rights over relevant productive assets from lenders to borrowers, or an improvement in the latter's outside options (an issue elaborated by Mookherjee in chapter 13, this volume). Note, however, that such policy interventions cannot result in improvements in Pareto efficiency – since equilibrium contracts are by definition constrained Pareto-efficient – but result in higher levels of social surplus. In other words, they must make some agents in the economy worse off. Despite the fact that the gainers (borrowers) could potentially compensate the losers, such compensations cannot actually be paid, owing to the wealth constraints of the borrowers. Accordingly such policies will tend to be resisted by the losers, and may not actually be adopted.

Can the model also generate micro-rationing – a situation in which even those who succeed in obtaining credit still get too little? In other words, can there be underinvestment in debt-financed projects, in addition to under-supply of effort? We cannot address the issue in this simple model, since the project has been assumed to be indivisible. However, it is easy to see that the answer will be in the affirmative if the model is extended in a natural way to allow for variable size of investment. Suppose output (when harvest is good) is $Q(L)$, an increasing concave function of the amount of loan or investment, but zero in the event of crop failure. The complementarity between effort and investment will then generate suboptimal choices on both fronts.[11]

In particular the phenomenon of nonlinear interest rates – where the interest rate depends on loan size – may arise even when the credit market is competitive. An expansion in loan size increases the debt burden, reducing the borrower's stake in success, causing default risk to increase. This may outweigh the effect of a larger scale of borrowing, making the lender worse off. In order to remain commercially viable, the larger loan must be accompanied by a different interest rate and/or level of collateral that reduces lender risk. Increases in the interest rate can make matters worse, by raising debt burdens even further. While some loan increases may thus be feasible if accompanied by higher interest rates, the lender may be unwilling to lend beyond some level of loan size at *any* interest rate.[12] Both micro and macro forms of credit rationing can therefore arise, with credit ceilings depending on the collateral that the borrower can post.

Turn now to the role of collateral in the credit market. Figure 3 captures the effect of an increase in $w$ on equilibrium interest rates and effort choice. The incentive curve shifts to the right (there is more effort forthcoming at any $R$, since failure is more costly to the borrower), while the isoprofit curve shifts down (for any effort level $e$, since the return in the bad state is higher due to more collateral, the return in the good state, i.e, the interest charged, must be lower to keep profits the same).

PROPOSITION 3    *An increase in the size of collateral, $w$, leads to a fall in the equilibrium interest rate and debt, and an increase in the effort level. For a fixed $\pi$, the borrower's expected income increases; hence, the utility possibility frontier shifts outwards.*

The intuition is fairly simple. *Ceteris paribus*, a bigger collateral increases the incentive to put in effort, since failure is now more costly to the borrower. If lender's profits are to be preserved at the same level, the interest rate must fall, because there is lower default risk. This causes less debt overhang, further reinforcing the effect on incentives. Higher effort levels increase the total surplus, but since lender's expected profits are held

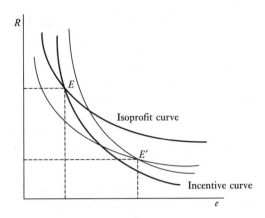

**Figure 3**   Effect of higher borrower wealth (collateral)

constant, borrowers must get more in net terms.

These results illustrate how interest rate dispersion might arise, even in competitive credit markets. In the presence of default risk and moral hazard, the interest rate will be closely tied to borrower characteristics such as wealth or ability to post collateral. Wealthier borrowers pose less risk for two reasons: these loans have better guarantees in case of default, plus lower default risk arising from better incentives. Hence, wealthier borrowers have access to cheaper credit. Arbitrage opportunities are illusory – the isoprofit line restricts lenders to the same profit level for different types of borrowers. The second point of interest is that the functioning of the credit market may exacerbate already existing inequalities. Those with lower wealth are doubly cursed: they not only face lower consumption potential from asset liquidation, but also lower income earning potential, owing to costlier (or restricted) access to credit. The reason is that the poor cannot credibly commit to refrain from morally hazardous behavior as effectively as the rich. This process of magnification of past inequalities through the operation of specific markets has been identified in different contexts by Dasgupta and Ray (chapter 9, this volume) and Galor and Zeira (chapter 4, this volume), among others.

Long-term exclusive relationships and social networks can be useful in mitigating these inefficiencies to some extent. When the lender and borrower enter a long-lived relationship, it expands the opportunity for the lender to relax limits on the borrower's current liability by extracting repayment in future successful periods (by the institution of debt), or by the threat of terminating the supply of credit (an issue further discussed in Dutta, Ray and Sengupta (1989)). A similar reason underlies the role of lending within social networks, where punishments can be imposed for loan defaults in other spheres of social interaction, and third-party community-based sanctions can be brought to bear on defaulters owing to the rapid flow of information within the community.

## 3. Repeated Borrowing and Enforcement

Results similar to those in the previous section can also arise from costly contract enforcement, where the principal problem faced by lenders is in preventing wilful default *ex post* by borrowers who do in fact possess the means to repay their loans. Most credit contracts in the developing world are not enforced by courts, but instead by social norms of reciprocal and third-party sanctions. Contracts have to be self-enforcing, where repayment of loans rely on the self-interest of borrowers, given the future consequences of a default. In this respect the problem is akin to that of sovereign debt where lender countries and international courts do not have the means of enforcing loan repayments by borrowing countries. Defaults are sought to be deterred solely by the threat of cutting the borrower off from future access to credit. Empirical and historical accounts of trade and credit in countries lacking a developed system of legal institutions amply document the role of such reputational mechanisms: see, for example, Clay (1997), Greif (1989, 1993, 1994), Greif, Milgrom and Weingast (1994) and McMillan and Woodruff (1999). Theoretical models of Eaton and Gersovitz (1981) and Ghosh and Ray (1996, 1999) have shown how such enforcement problems can also give rise to most of the phenomena described above: adverse incentive effects of raises in interest rates, credit rationing, long term relationships and the role of social networks.

To understand these issues, we turn our attention to the problem of *voluntary* default. In the absence of usual enforcement mechanisms (courts, collateral, etc.), compliance must be achieved through the use of dynamic incentives, i.e, from the threat of losing access to credit in the future. We use a simple infinite horizon repeated lending-borrowing game to illustrate such a mechanism, and derive its implications for rationing and efficiency in the credit market. Since bankruptcy and involuntary default are not the focus in this section, we remove any source of production uncertainty.

Each period, the borrower has access to a production technology which produces output $F(L)$, where $L$ is the value of inputs purchased and applied. The production function satisfies standard conditions: $F'(\cdot) > 0$ and $F''(\cdot) < 0$. Suppose production takes the length of one period, and let $r$ be the bank rate of interest (opportunity cost of funds). To set the benchmark, consider the case of a self-financed farmer. The optimum investment $L^*$ is given from the solution to

$$\max_{L} F(L) - (1+r)L \tag{6}$$

which yields the first-order condition

$$F'(L^*) = 1 + r \tag{7}$$

Next we turn to debt-financed farmers. We assume that such farmers do not accumulate any savings and have to rely on the credit market to finance investment needs every period. We can allow the possibility of saving by adding a probability of crop failure.[13] This will significantly complicate the analysis by introducing inter-temporal choices, without necessarily adding much insight, so we drop it here.[14] Borrowers live for an infinite number of periods, and discount the future by a discount factor $\delta$.

## 3.1. Partial equilibrium: Single lender

We first solve a partial equilibrium exercise. Suppose there is a single borrower and a single lender. We focus on a stationary subgame perfect equilibrium, where the lender offers a loan contract $\{L, R = (1 + i)L\}$ every period, and follows the trigger strategy of never offering a loan in case of default. The defaulting borrower still has an outside option that yields a payoff $v$ every period. For now, we treat $v$ as exogenous. Later, we show how $v$ can be "rationalized" as the value arising in a general equilibrium model with many borrowers and lenders.

Of course, as with all repeated games, there are many equilibria. We characterize the Pareto frontier of all stationary equilibria, in which the same loan contract is offered at all dates.[15] All such equilibria must satisfy the incentive constraint for the borrower:

$$(1 - \delta)F(L) + \delta v \leq F(L) - R \tag{8}$$

i.e., the borrower should not benefit from defaulting on the loan: the left-hand side represents the average per period long-run payoff from defaulting, and the right-hand side the corresponding payoff from not defaulting. In order to generate the Pareto frontier, we must maximize the borrower's per period net income, while satisfying the incentive constraint and holding the lender's profit at some fixed level $z$. Mathematically,

$$\max_{L, R} F(L) - R \tag{9}$$

subject to the constraints

$$R \leq \delta[F(L) - v] \tag{10}$$

$$z = R - (1 + r)L \tag{11}$$

(10) is simply the incentive constraint in (8), after rearrangement. The nature of the solution is illustrated in figure 4. The boundary of the incentive constraint is the positively sloped, concave curve with slope $\delta F'(L)$, while the lender's profit constraint (11) is represented by a straight line with slope $1 + r$. The points of intersection $A$ and $B$ are

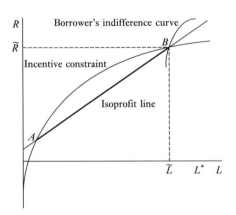

**Figure 4** Optimal solution to the enforcement problem

where both constraints bind. Clearly, the line segment $AB$ represents the feasible set. The borrower's indifference curves are rising, concave curves with slope $F'(L)$, lower indifference curves representing higher payoff. If these indifference curves attain tangency at some point on $AB$, it is the solution to the problem, and has the property: $L = L^*$, and $R = (1+r)L^* + z$. If not, the solution must be at the corner $B$. Let $\hat{L}(v, z)$ be the value of $L$ at $B$, and let $\tilde{L}(v, z)$ denote the solution to the problem above (the corresponding value of $R$ is given from (11)). The preceding discussion leads to the conclusion:

$$\tilde{L}(v, z) = \min\{L^*, \hat{L}(v, z)\} \tag{12}$$

If the second argument applies above (i.e, the solution is at the corner $B$), credit rationing will arise. We will show in a moment that this is possible. However, we first analyze the effect of a parametric shift in $z$ (lender's equilibrium profit) or $v$ (option value of default). If $z$ increases (figure 5), the isoprofit line shifts up and the point $B$ moves to the left, i.e, $\hat{L}(z, v)$ is decreasing in $z$. If this is indeed the solution, then the equilibrium volume of credit is reduced and rationing becomes more acute. If the solution is interior $(L^*)$ to begin with, a small increase in $z$ will raise the interest rate, but will leave the loan size unaffected. Notice that the interest rate rises in the first case too, as indicated by the fact that the ray connecting point $B$ to the origin becomes steeper.

Figure 6 illustrates the effect of increasing the borrower's outside option $v$. The curve representing the boundary of the incentive constraint undergoes a parallel downward shift, moving the corner point $B$ to the left. The effect on loan sizes and interest rates is nearly similar to the case of increasing $z$. If $\hat{L} = L^*$ to begin with, nothing changes (since $v$ affects only the incentive constraint, which is not binding). If $\tilde{L} = \hat{L}$, on the other hand, increasing $v$ has the implication that the equilibrium loan size falls and the interest rate rises.

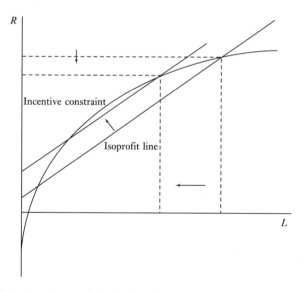

**Figure 5**   Effect of an increase in lender's profit

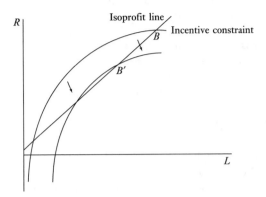

**Figure 6**   Effect of an increase in borrower's outside option

Can credit rationing arise in equilibrium? To see that the answer is in the affirmative, notice that if the value of $z$ (given $v$) or $v$ (given $z$) is too high, the problem does not have a solution, since the isoprofit line will lie everywhere above the boundary of the incentive region. The borderline case is one where the two are tangent, i.e, when the points $A$ and $B$ converge to each other and the feasible set of the constrained maximization problem described above becomes a singleton. The solution must then be this single feasible point. Tangency of (11) and (10) (the latter holding with equality) implies that $\delta F'(\tilde{L}) = 1 + r$ implying $\tilde{L} < L^*$ since $\delta < 1$ and $F$ is concave. There is credit rationing if $z$ (or $v$) is sufficiently high. Since the solution is continuous in $z$ (or $v$), and given the comparative static properties of the corner solution, it follows that there will be credit rationing if either $z$ or $v$ (given the other) is above a critical value.

We summarize these observations in the following proposition:

PROPOSITION 4   *There is credit rationing if $z$, the lender's profit (given $v$), or $v$, the borrower's outside option (given $z$), is above some threshold value. If rationing is present, a further increase in the lender's profit, or the borrower's outside option, leads to further rationing (i.e. a reduction in the volume of credit) as well as a rise in the interest rate.*

Notice that while changes in $z$ move us along the Pareto frontier, shifts in $v$ translate into a shift of the frontier itself. Equilibria which give more profit to the lender involve lower overall efficiency, because credit rationing is more severe in such equilibria. Increased bargaining power of lenders thus reduce productivity, echoing a similar result in the previous model involving involuntary default. The reason is also similar: marginal rents accruing to the lender fall below the social returns from increased lending, the difference accounted for by the incentive rents that accrue to the borrower.

## 3.2. General equilibrium: Multiple lenders

An obvious shortcoming of the model so far is that the outside option $v$ has been assumed exogenous. In a competitive setting with multiple lenders – which fits descriptions of informal credit in many developing countries[16] – a defaulting borrower can switch to a different lender. If there is a good deal of information flow within the lending community, the defaulting borrower could face social or market sanctions (as opposed to merely individual sanction from the past lender), thus restoring the discipline.[17] However, the strength and reliability of such information networks could vary from one context to another, and is a factor that needs to be taken into account. Accordingly the strength of such networks can be treated as a parameter of the model.

Suppose that following a default, the existing credit relationship is terminated. The borrower can then approach a new lender, who checks on the borrower's past and uncovers the default with probability $p$ (i.i.d. across periods).[18] In that case, the lender refuses the loan, and the borrower approaches yet another lender, whereupon the same story repeats itself. If, on the other hand, the lender fails to uncover the default, the borrower enters into a new credit relationship with the lender. Given the assumption of a symmetric (and stationary) equilibrium, the borrower receives the same contract $(L, R)$ as with previous lenders with payoff denoted $w$. Then $v$, the expected value of the outside option, is given by

$$v = p\delta v + (1-p)w = \frac{1-p}{1-\delta p}w \tag{13}$$

Then we can write $v = (1-\rho)w$, where

$$\rho \equiv \frac{p(1-\delta)}{1-\delta p} \tag{14}$$

can be viewed as the *scarring factor*. Notice that if $p$ gets very close to one, so that a default is always recognized, then the scarring factor converges to one as well. On the other hand, for any $p$ strictly between zero and one, the scarring factor goes to zero as $\delta$ goes to unity, or if $p$ itself goes to zero.

For the endogenous determination of $v$, we utilize our analysis of the partial equilibrium model in the previous section, to construct a function $\phi(v;z)$ whose fixed point denotes the equilibrium in this more general setting. Consider a given $z$ and any arbitrary value of $v$ for which the problem has a solution. The borrower's per period payoff (on the equilibrium path) in partial equilibrium is given by[19]

$$w(v, z) = (1-\delta)F(\tilde{L}(v, z)) + \delta v$$

If he defaults, his expected per period payoff thereafter is $(1-\rho)w(v, z)$. The original $v$ is "rationalized" if this latter value coincides with $v$ (i.e, the defaulting borrower's continuation payoff is precisely what he can expect to get from the market itself after termination by his current lender). Of course, our focus is on a stationary symmetric equilibrium in which all lenders offer the same package $(L, R)$ to borrowers in good standing. Hence, we define the following function:

$$\phi(v; z) = (1-\rho)w(v, z) \tag{15}$$

and note that, given $z$, any fixed point of $\phi$ (with respect to $v$) denotes an equilibrium.

Proposition 4 tells us that an exogenous increase in either $v$ or $z$ leads to a smaller loan size and higher interest rates, which adversely affects borrower payoffs. Hence the function $\phi(v, z)$ is decreasing in both its arguments. Further, if $v$ is higher than some threshold $\bar{v}(z)$, the problem has no solution, and the value of $\phi(v, z)$ can be taken to be 0 in that case. Take $z$ as given. Figure 7 shows the nature of the function $\phi$: it is downward sloping, with a downward jump at $\bar{v}$. There is an unique fixed point – $v^*$ in the diagram – if there is an intersection with 45 degree line before the point of discontinuity. Otherwise, no symmetric equilibrium exists.

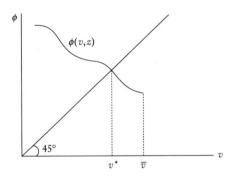

**Figure 7**    The function $\phi(v, z)$

We next show that if the scarring factor is sufficiently high (either the probability of detection $p$ is high enough, or borrowers are sufficiently patient), an equilibrium usually exists. However, note first that the lower bound on the equilibrium value of $v$ is zero, so there will be a maximal value of $z$ (say $\bar{z}$) that is consistent with a solution existing to the problem defined in (9) through (11). Suppose $z$ is held fixed at a value below this threshold. Then, it is easy to see from (15) that, as $\rho$ is increased, $\phi$ undergoes a downward shift, the point of discontinuity remaining the same (since the function $w(v, z)$ is independent of $\rho$). The discontinuity disappears as $\rho \to 1$; hence we conclude that there is a threshold value $\rho^*$ (dependent on $z$) such that an equilibrium exists if and only if $\rho \geq \rho^*$. The next proposition summarizes these findings.

PROPOSITION 5    *Suppose $z \leq \bar{z}$. There is a unique equilibrium in the credit market provided $\rho$ is greater than some threshold value $\rho^*$, i.e. provided either that borrowers are sufficiently patient, or the probability of detection is high enough.*

These results are fairly intuitive. A higher discount factor implies that the cost of (probabilistic) lack of access to credit in the future is more costly. A rise in the detection probability has a similar effect. The last point brings out the disciplining role of dissemination of information regarding borrower credit histories. Improved credit information networks lower outside options of borrowers: by proposition 4 this reduces both interest rates and credit constraints, consistent with the empirical results of McMillan and Woodruff (1999).

Finally, we wish to check whether equilibria that provide higher profits to the lender create more credit rationing and reduce efficiency. This was the feature that emerged in the partial equilibrium analysis, and we now demonstrate that it extends to this more general formulation. First, observe that a rise in $z$ shifts the $\phi$-function downwards, implying that the equilibrium value of $v$ must fall (see figure 8). Next, remembering that in equilibrium $\phi(v, z) = v$ and using (15), we can write:

$$v = (1 - \rho)[(1 - \delta)F(\tilde{L}) + \delta v]$$

which, on rearrangement, yields:

$$v = \frac{(1 - \rho)(1 - \delta)F(\tilde{L})}{1 - \delta(1 - \rho)} \tag{16}$$

where $\tilde{L}$ denotes the equilibrium loan. This establishes that in equilibrium, $v$ and $\tilde{L}$ are positively related. Since $v$ falls due to a parametric increase in lenders' profit $z$, so does $\tilde{L}$.

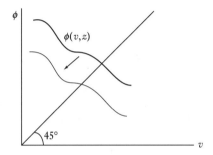

**Figure 8** Effect of an increase in lender's profit

We saw from proposition 5 that existence of equilibrium requires that the detection probability is sufficiently high. What if it is not? The immediate possibility is credit rationing at some macroeconomic level. To see how this fits, suppose that a past defaulter may be excluded from future loan dealings for two distinct reasons:

TARGETED EXCLUSION Incidence of past defaults are discovered by a new lender (with probability $p$), and he is refused a loan. This is already incorporated in the model above.

ANONYMOUS EXCLUSION Whether or not a potential borrower has actually defaulted in the past, he may face difficulty in getting a loan. This is macro rationing of credit, analogous to the equilibrium unemployment rate in Shapiro and Stiglitz (1984). Let us denote the probability of such exclusion (in any period) by $q$. Notice that to build a coherent model in which $q > 0$, we really have to answer the question of why the market may not clear. After all, if some borrowers are shut out of the market, an individual lender may be tempted to make profit by offering them credit at interest rates equal to or higher than the market interest rate.[20] One coherent model is given by the case in which lenders make zero expected profits, so that they are always indifferent between lending and not lending. In equilibrium, lenders can then mix between giving and not giving credit to a new borrower. Lending to a new borrower on market terms does not add to profits; attempting to earn positive profits by lending to rationed borrowers on stiffer terms leads to violation of the incentive constraint.[21]

The main point is that anonymous exclusion may be an equilibrium-restoring device. To see this, let us calculate $\rho$, the effective scarring factor, when there is both targeted and anonymous exclusion. The corresponding equation is

$$\rho \equiv \frac{\pi(1 - \delta)}{1 - \delta\pi} \tag{17}$$

where $\pi$, now, is the overall probability of being excluded at any date. It is easy to see that

$$\pi = 1 - (1 - p)(1 - q) \tag{18}$$

Now notice that irrespective of the value of $p$, $q$ can always adjust to guarantee that an equilibrium exists. (To be sure, the determination of $q$ becomes an interesting question, but this is beyond the scope of the present exercise.)

## 4. Concluding Comments

Despite their differences in detail, the two theories of credit rationing described above are similar in a number of broad respects. Both are driven by the positive effect of higher repayment burdens on default risk. Accordingly limiting default risks necessitate restrictions on repayment burdens. This is achieved by limiting loan sizes below what borrowers desire – the phenomenon of micro credit rationing, and preventing interest rates from rising to excessively high levels – which can precipitate macro credit rationing when loanable funds are scarce.

Access to credit is especially restricted for the poor, owing to their inability to provide collateral. Collateral both reduces default risk (for incentive reasons) and lender exposure in the event of default. Existing poverty and wealth inequalities may therefore tend to be perpetuated, an issue typically investigated in dynamic extensions of the models described here.

As for policy implications, macroeconomic stabilization policies often ignore the consequences of raising interest rates on default risks in times of financial crises: accordingly they may be ineffective or even counterproductive in attracting investors and restoring financial stability. In terms of structural reforms aimed at alleviating poverty in the long term, the models illustrate the possible perils of large infusions of subsidized credit by the public sector. If informal markets are competitive to start with, such credit programs will typically run into losses (even if government banks were as well informed about borrower characteristics and able to enforce loan repayments as are informal lenders, both questionable assumptions). For if existing loan contracts are constrained Pareto efficient, there is no scope for Pareto improvements from supplementary credit provision or subsidies.[22] Indeed, the provision of cheap credit from the formal sector can increase the outside options of borrowers in their informal credit relationships, thus disrupting the informal market seriously.[23] The government or other nonprofit institutions can, however, play a potentially useful role by altering the root cause of the market distortions: the institutional environment within which lenders and borrowers interact on the informal market. This involves measures to increase the bargaining power of borrowers, reduce asset inequality, and improve credit information networks.

## Notes

1   Rosenzweig and Binswanger (1993) for instance show the effect of weather uncertainty on divergence between cropping choices of poor and rich farmers in Indian ICRISAT villages, which presumably owes to differential risk attitudes induced partly by differences in credit access.

2   For further details, see Hoff and Stiglitz (1993).

3   Banks, in turn, have to rely on such guarantees because the impersonal nature of institutional lending reduces the ability to select or monitor borrowers effectively.

4   Other criticisms of the theory are discussed further in the Introduction to this volume.

5   See, however, our discussion later, as well as Aleem (1993), for arguments that the information available on borrowers is likely to decline over the course of development, due to increase in mobility and expansion of the market's domain.

6   Versions of this model appear in Aghion and Bolton (1997), Jaffee and Russell (1976), Mookherjee (chapter 13, this volume) and Piketty (1997).

7   The implications of the theory for the dynamics of poverty and inequality are explored in Aghion and Bolton (1997), Mookherjee and Ray (1999) and Piketty (1997).

8   It must be stressed that "efficiency" in this context refers to maximization of social surplus, not constrained Pareto efficiency. The latter feature is built into our analysis by construction, since we only look at the boundary of the set of possible equilibrium payoff vectors. The result reported here is that as we move along this boundary towards higher lender payoffs and lower borrower payoffs, the sum of payoffs (total social surplus) decreases along the way. Lender profits can be increased only by creating a more than offsetting loss for the borrower.

9   If the size of collateral is positive, or if the borrower has some outside option, there will be a participation constraint in addition to the incentive compatibility condition described here. However, the participation constraint only places a ceiling on the interest rate, and will be nonbinding if the values of collateral and outside option are low. Hence, we drop it from our analysis.

10  Stiglitz and Weiss (1981) discuss how their story can be recast as a moral hazard problem. However, the incentive problem suggested there is somewhat different. With limited liability, borrowers will prefer a mean preserving increase in spread in the distribution of returns. They will tend to pass up projects with secure returns, and will instead select projects with high possible returns but also high risk. An increase in the interest rate will reinforce this tendency.

11  It is easy to see that in any constrained efficient contract the loan size will be selected to maximize $p(e)Q(L) - L$.

12  For an explicit example, see Aghion and Bolton (1997).

13  This will disallow the strategy of defaulting on the first loan and rolling it over infinitely to finance investment forever after. A crop failure will cut short the process.

14  For an intemporal model of consumption-smoothing and credit, with default risk, see Eaton and Gersovitz (1981).

15  The assumption of stationarity is, surprisingly, not innocuous. Non-stationary equilibria can Pareto dominate equilibria which are efficient in the class of stationary equilibria. See Ray (2000) for an analysis of this issue. We confine ourselves to stationarity for simplicity and tractability.

16  See, for example, the case studies of Aleem (1993), Kranton and Swamy (1998), McMillan and Woodruff (1999) and Siamwalla et al. (1993).

17  For a rich description of such sanctions in practice, see Udry (1994) in the context of credit markets in northern Nigeria, and Greif (1993) for an analysis of medieval overseas trade and merchant networks.

18  Aleem (1993), McMillan and Woodruff (1999) and Siamwalla et al. (1993) document the importance of screening new borrowers among informal lenders in Pakistan, Vietnam and Thailand respectively.

19  This is obtained by treating (10) as binding.

20  Note, by the way, that the same issues come up when we attempt to explain why defaulting borrowers may be shut out from the market, without taking recourse to any reputational factors.

21  For a more careful analysis of how such rationed equilibria can be constructed, see Ghosh and Ray (1999).

22  However if lenders have market power then the provision of government credit or measures to encourage entry of new lenders can potentially increase the bargaining power of borrowers, with attendant improvement in borrower incentives and social efficiency.

23  For a more detailed exploration of these issues, see Hoff and Lyon (1995), Kahn and Mookherjee (1995, 1998), Kranton (1996), Kranton and Swamy (1998) and McMillan and Woodruff (1999).

## References

Aghion, P. and Bolton, P. (1997): "A Theory of Trickle-down Growth and Development," *Review of Economic Studies*, 64, 151–72.

Aleem, I. (1993): "Imperfect Information, Screening, and the Costs of Informal Lending: A Study of a Rural Credit Market in Pakistan," in K. Hoff, A. Braverman and J. Stiglitz (eds), *The Economics of Rural Organization: Theory, Practice and Policy*, London: Oxford University Press (for the World Bank).

Clay, K. (1997): "Trade Without Law: Private Order Institutions in Mexican California," *Journal of Law, Economics and Organization*, 13, 202–31.

Dutta, B., Ray, D. and Sengupta, K. (1989): "Contracts with Eviction in Infinitely Repeated Principal Agent Relationships," in P. Bardhan (ed.) *The Economic Theory of Agrarian Institutions*, Oxford: Clarendon Press.

Eaton, J. and Gersovitz, M. (1981): "Debt with Potential Repudiation: Theoretical and Empirical Analysis," *Review of Economic Studies*, 48, 289–309.

Ghosh, P. and Ray, D. (1996): "Cooperation in Community Interaction without Information Flows," *Review of Economic Studies*, 63, 491–519.

——(1999): "Information and Repeated Interaction: Application to Informal Credit Markets," mimeograph, Department of Economics, Texas A&M University.

Greif, A. (1989): "Reputation and Coalitions in Medieval Trade: Evidence on the Maghribi Traders," *Journal of Economic History*, 49, 857–82.

——(1993): "Contract Enforceability and Economic Institutions in Early Trade: The Maghribi Traders' Coalition," *American Economic Review*, 83, 525–48.

——(1994): "On the Political Foundations of the Late Medieval Commercial Revolution: Genoa during the Twelfth and Thirteenth Centuries," *Journal of Economic History*, 54, 271–87.

Greif, A., Milgrom, P. and Weingast, B. (1994): "Coordination, Commitment and Enforcement: The Case of the Merchant Guild," *Journal of Political Economy*, 102, 745–76.

Hoff, K. and Lyon, A. (1995): "Non-Leaky Buckets: Optimal Redistributive Taxation and Agency Costs," *Journal of Public Economics*, 58, 365–90.

Hoff, K. and Stiglitz, J. (1993): "Imperfect Information in Rural Credit Markets: Puzzles and Policy Perspectives," in K. Hoff, A. Braverman, and J. Stiglitz (eds), *The Economics of Rural Organization: Theory, Practice and Policy*, London: Oxford University Press (for the World Bank).

Jaffee, D. and Russell, T. (1976): "Imperfect Information, Uncertainty and Credit Rationing," *Quarterly Journal of Economics*, 90, 651–66.

Kahn, C. and Mookherjee, D. (1995): "Market Failure and Moral Hazard with Side Trading," *Journal of Public Economics*, 58, 159–84.

—— (1998): "Competition and Incentives with Nonexclusive Contracts," *Rand Journal of Economics*, 29 (3), 443–65.

Kranton, R. (1996): "The Formation of Cooperative Relationships," *Journal of Law, Economics and Organization*, 12, 214–33.

—— and Swamy, A. (1998): "The Hazards of Piecemeal Reform: British Civil Courts and the Credit Market in Colonial India," *Journal of Development Economics*, 58, 1–24.

McMillan, J. and Woodruff, C. (1999): "Interfirm Relationships and Informal Credit in Vietnam," *Quarterly Journal of Economics*, 114, 1285–320.

Mookherjee, D. and Ray, D. (1999): "Contractual Structure and Wealth Accumulation," mimeo, Boston University.

Piketty, T. (1997): "The Dynamics of the Wealth Distribution and the Interest Rate with Credit Rationing," *Review of Economic Studies*, 64, 173–89.

Ray, D. (2000): "The Time Structure of Unenforceable Agreements," mimeo, New York University.

Rosenzweig, M. and Binswanger, H. (1993): "Wealth, Weather Risk and the Composition and Profitability of Agricultural Investments," *Economic Journal*, 103, 56–78.

Shapiro, C. and Stiglitz, J. (1984): "Equilibrium Unemployment as a Worker Discipline Device", *American Economic Review*, 74, 433–44.

Siamwalla, A., Pinthong, C., Poapongsakorn, N., Satsanguan, P., Nettayarak, P., Mingmaneenakin, W. and Tubpun, Y. (1993): "The Thai Rural Credit System and Elements of a Theory: Public Subsidies, Private Information, and Segmented Markets," in K. Hoff, A. Braverman and J. Stiglitz (eds), *The Economics of Rural Organization: Theory, Practice and Policy*, London: Oxford University Press (for the World Bank).

Stiglitz, J. and Weiss, A. (1981): "Credit Rationing in Markets with Imperfect Information," *American Economic Review*, 71, 393–410.

Udry, C. (1994): "Risk and Insurance in a Rural Credit Market: An Empirical Investigation in Northern Nigeria," *Review of Economic Studies*, 61, 495–526.

CHAPTER 12

# Sharecropping and the Interlinking of Agrarian Markets

AVISHAY BRAVERMAN AND JOSEPH E. STIGLITZ

One of the often noted features of less-developed agrarian economies is the existence of interlinkages among the land, labor, credit, and product markets.[1] The landlord is often the supplier of credit; he frequently purchases and markets the output of the tenant farmers; and he often sells raw materials (fertilizers) and even consumption goods to his tenant farmers.

How do we explain this phenomenon? What are the welfare consequences of attempts to restrict these practices, which often seem to constitute restraints on free trade? These are the questions to which this paper is addressed.

In the past, theoretical discussions of interlinked contracts viewed them as a form of exploitation of less-powerful agents by more-powerful agents (for example, see Amit Bhaduri, 1973, 1977). The argument, however, was never very convincing: if a landlord could exploit his tenants to the point of reducing them to their subsistence level (as these arguments often suggested), why could the landlord not do so simply by reducing the share on the share contract? What more could he get through these other devices?

In this paper we present a general set of arguments applicable to both competitive and noncompetitive environments, to situations where all the terms of the contract are determined in an optimal way, as well as to situations where many of the terms are specified institutionally.[2]

Our analysis is based on two features commonly found in less-developed agrarian economies:

(a)   Individuals are not paid on the basis of their input (effort) since this, in general, is not observable; and they conventionally do not rent land for a fixed sum since that imposes too much risk on them.[3] Hence the contractual arrangements involve at least some form of sharecropping;[4] as a result, workers do not obtain the full marginal product of their efforts.

(b)   The landlord cannot completely specify the actions to be taken by the worker; the worker has considerable discretion both with respect to the level of effort and its allocation, and the choice of technique of production. Some of these decisions may, of course, be easily monitored by the landlord, but there are other actions, perhaps equally important, for which the cost of monitoring would be very high.

These two facts – that the worker has considerable discretion over his own actions, and that, because of the nature of the contractual arrangements between the worker and the landlord, the worker's actions have an important effect on the landlord's expected profits – have, in turn, some further important implications. In particular, it means that the landlord has an incentive to attempt to *induce* workers to behave in the way he would like them to behave. The behavior of the worker is affected, in important ways, by the amount he borrows and the terms at which he obtains credit, and by the goods he can purchase and the prices he pays.

Much of the formal analysis of this paper focuses on showing how the landlord, by altering, say, the terms at which he makes loans available to his tenants, not only can induce the tenant to borrow more but, more importantly, can induce the tenant to work harder or to undertake projects which are more to the liking of the landlord. For instance, if the landlord makes credit less expensive, the tenant (under quite reasonable conditions) will be induced to borrow more; under somewhat more restrictive conditions the tenant will be induced to increase his borrowing to such an extent that the amount which he must repay (including interest) increases. If there are severe penalties associated with default (for example, the tenant is put into bonded labor), the tenant will then need to work harder to avoid this contingency.[5]

Similarly the landlord may observe that his tenants are employing techniques of production which are too safe; the landlord's income might be increased if his tenants would be willing to employ techniques with higher means but higher variances. Again, he may note that his tenants are acting in a particularly risk-averse manner because they are concerned about the consequences of defaulting on outstanding loans. Thus, the landlord may require that his tenants only borrow from him. He will charge them an interest rate which is above the market rate and this will induce them to restrict their borrowing. As a result, he may be able to offer a tenancy contract which is much more attractive in some other dimensions.

The arguments for interlinkage with product markets are similar. The tenants may purchase less of inputs, such as fertilizer, than the landlord desires; some of the increased return to the input is appropriated by the landlords. As we show elsewhere (1981a), conventional cost-sharing rules, where the landlord pays a share of the cost equal to the share he receives of output, alleviate but do not fully correct for this distortion. When an increase in fertilizer induces tenants to increase their effort, there is an incentive for the landlord to encourage the utilization of fertilizer by contributing a higher share of the cost.

Similarly, consumption of certain commodities serves to increase effort while the consumption of other commodities (alcohol) may reduce it. It may be worthwhile for the landlord to subsidize the consumption of the former class of commodities, and to attempt to restrict the consumption of the latter class (either by charging high prices for these commodities at the landlord's store or by providing wages in kind).

Thus we establish that:

(i)  Interlinking markets can increase the expected utility of both landlords and workers; it unambiguously shifts the utility possibilities schedule outward;

(ii)   Accordingly, both competitive and monopoly markets will, in general, be char-
       acterized by interlinkages;

(iii)  Although interlinkage shifts the utility possibility frontier outwards, the competi-
       tive equilibrium with interlinkage *may* (but need not) entail tenants being worse off.

(iv)   While even with a monopoly landlord, interlinkage *may* (but need not) entail
       tenants being better off.

In providing a general analysis of interlinkage of markets, we are able at the same time
to obtain answers to several questions concerning the design of contractual arrangements
between landlords and tenants. In particular, we show that:

(v)    A monopolist gains nothing from controlling the markets for inputs and outputs,
       if he is unrestricted in adopting cost and crop sharing rules; if he is restricted,
       controlling the markets for inputs and outputs can be a valuable additional
       instrument for the monopolist;

(vi)   A monopolist only gains from controlling the consumption goods market to the
       extent that he uses it to change relative prices of different consumption goods.

It should be emphasized that our analysis applies equally well to situations where the
terms of the tenancy contract (the share, plot size, etc) are endogenous as well as
institutionally determined.[6] The employment of sharecropping arrangements need not,
however, be viewed (as interpreters of Marshall did)[7] as an inefficient contractual arrangement, even where it gives rise to the variety of problems which are the subject of this
paper. When information is costly and there are significant risks, sharecropping provides a
method by which some of the risks are borne by the landlord, and which, at the same time,
maintains incentives for the tenant.[8]

This paper is divided into the following: section 1 examines interlinked credit and
tenancy contracts; section 2 examines interlinked marketing and tenancy contracts; section
3 points out the possible interlinking between labor contracts and consumption goods
markets; and section 4 presents the different equilibrium frameworks discussed in this
paper, that is, monopoly, monopsony, competition, and equilibria with surplus labor.

# 1. Interlinked Credit and Tenancy Contracts

In this section we establish that whenever there is not a pure rental system so that the
landlord's income depends, in part, on the actions of the tenant, and the actions of the tenant
cannot be perfectly monitored,[9] the returns to the landowner are affected by the borrowing
decisions of the tenant.[10] In the following discussion we will be concerned both with the
tenant's allocation of effort and his choice of technique of production, for example, when and
how often he weeds, when he plants and harvests, the type of seed he plants, the amount and
kind of fertilizer he uses, when and how he applies it, etc. Some of these decisions may be
easily monitored by the landlord, but there are other actions, perhaps equally important, for
which the cost of monitoring would be very high. The fact that the tenant has some discretion
over his effort and choices, and that his behavior can thus affect the returns to the landlord, is
referred to as the moral hazard problem.

## 1.1. A general model

We begin our discussion by presenting a general model. The following subsections focus on a number of special, but important, specializations of this model.

We assume that there is a pure sharecropping agreement.[11] The tenant receives a share $\alpha$ of the gross output, the landlord receives $1 - \alpha$. Output, $Y$, is a function of:

(a)  the effort of the tenant, which we denote by $e$;[12]
(b)  environmental factors (the weather) denoted by $\theta$; and
(c)  the choice of technique, denoted by $\Omega$.

We let an increase in $\Omega$ represent an increase in risk (see discussion below). Thus

$$Y = Y(e, \theta, \Omega) \tag{1}$$

It will greatly simplify the analysis, however, if we write

$$Y = gf(e) \tag{1'}$$

where $g$ is a positive random variable with a density function $(Eg \equiv \bar{g})$: $h = h(g, \Omega)$.

The tenant's utility[13] can be expressed as a function of his income $y = \alpha Y$, his effort $e$, his technique of production, $\Omega$, of the other variables which are under his control, $z$, and of a set of variables which are under the control of the landlord which we denote by $q$:

$$u = u(y, e, \Omega, z, q) \tag{2}$$

In the subsequent analysis, we shall investigate several special cases of this general specification. For instance, if $z$ is the individual's consumption of some commodity purchased from the landlord, $q$ is the price charged by the landlord, and $c$ is the individual's consumption of other commodities, we can write

$$U = U(c, e, \Omega, z) = U(y - zq, e, \Omega, z) \tag{2'}$$

Similarly, consider an individual with initial wealth $W_0$ who wishes to borrow to finance current consumption. Assume the landlord charges an interest rate $r$ and the tenant borrows an amount $B$; denote the $i$th period consumption by $c_i$. We can then write

$$U = U(c_0, c_1, e, \Omega) = U(W_0 + B, \ y - (1 + r)B, e, \Omega) \tag{3}$$

(which is of the form (2)).[14]

The tenant chooses $e$, $z$, and $\Omega$ to maximize his expected utility, taking into account the production relationship (1),

$$\max_{\{e, z, \Omega\}} Eu(y, e, \Omega, z, q) \equiv V(\alpha, q) \tag{4}$$

where $\alpha$, the tenant's crop share, can be determined in a variety of ways; it may, for instance, be directly controlled by the landlord. From the first-order conditions for this maximization problem, we can solve for the level of effort, the choice of technique, and the level of $z$ as a function of the control variables at the disposal of the landlord, that is: $e = e(\alpha, q)$, $z = z(\alpha, q)$, $\Omega = \Omega(\alpha, q)$.

For simplicity, we shall assume that the landlord is risk neutral. His expected income, $\bar{P}$, has two parts: the direct receipts from the sharecroppers, $(1 - \alpha)f(e)Eg$, and the return from the interlinked activities (which may be negative), $\pi(q, z)$. Hence

$$\bar{P} = (1 - \alpha)f(e)\bar{g} + \pi(q, z) \tag{5}$$

Thus, for instance, in the first example where the landlord sold, say, alcohol to his tenants at a price of $q$,

$$\pi(q, z) = (q - q_0)z(q) \tag{6}$$

where $q_0$ is the price at which the landlord can purchase (or produce) the given commodity. In the second example, where the tenant borrows at the rate of interest $r$, the return to the interlinked activity is simply the difference between the rate of interest charged and what the landlord could obtain from his funds lent elsewhere, times the amount borrowed.[15]

The problem of the landlord is now simple: he chooses $q$ and $\alpha$ (if $\alpha$ is a control variable; $q$ may in fact represent a vector of control variables) to maximize his expected income, subject to the constraint of being able to obtain workers; that is:

$$\max_{\{q, \alpha\}} \bar{P}; \text{ such that } V(\alpha, q) \geqslant \bar{U} \tag{7}$$

The first-order conditions for this problem (for $q$) can be written as

$$\frac{d\bar{P}}{dq} = (1 - \alpha) \times \left[ \bar{g}f'(e)\frac{de}{dq} + f(e)\frac{d\bar{g}}{d\Omega}\frac{d\Omega}{dq} \right] + \pi_q + \pi_z\frac{dz}{dq} - \lambda\frac{\partial V}{\partial q} \tag{8}$$

where $\lambda$ is the Lagrange multiplier associated with the constraint in (7). What is critical about (8) is that the landlord realizes that changing $q$ has not only a direct effect (an effect on his return as a lender or as a shopkeeper), but an indirect effect on his income, through its effect on the level of effort or the choice of technique of the tenant. It is this which provides the fundamental motivation for interlinkage in our analysis.

The subsequent sections attempt to analyze in greater detail this argument, to ascertain, in particular, the conditions under which the landlord is likely to subsidize, say, borrowing, or those under which he will attempt to restrict it.

Although there is a kind of formal similarity between those cases where the landlord wishes to induce borrowing and thus subsidizes the rate of interest, and those cases where he wishes to restrict borrowing activity, there are important asymmetries in the costs of implementation. The latter requires a kind of monitoring of the tenant which the former does not.

The analysis proceeds in a number of steps. First, we analyze how the behavior of the tenant is affected by the presence of outstanding loan commitments. We analyze separately the effect on the level of effort (Parts 1.2 and 1.3) and on the choice of technique (Part 1.4). We then use these results to determine the optimal policy of the landlord (Parts 1.5 and 1.6). Part 1.7 considers the particular problems raised by default clauses (bonded labor). Part 1.8 argues that there is a symmetric argument, when there is a positive probability of default, for why lenders would wish to effect borrowers behavior in the land-tenancy market, thus strengthening the argument for interlinkage.

Although most of our discussion is couched in partial equilibrium terms, Part 1.9 shows how it may be extended to a general equilibrium framework.

## 1.2. The impact of the tenant's borrowing on his effort supply

In this section, we ask: How does the fact that the individual must repay an amount, $(1+r)B$, to a lender affect his supply of effort?

To analyze this question we specialize the general model presented earlier by assuming separability between consumption and effort at one date, and those at any other date. This enables us to address the question of the effect of outstanding loans, without asking how the outstanding debt was determined. We focus here only on effort, taking the choice of technique of production as given.

Defining $\hat{B} = (1+r)B$ as the fixed amount the tenant must pay to the landlord and letting $c$ denote the tenant's consumption, then

$$c = \alpha Y - \hat{B} \tag{9}$$

and the individual now chooses effort to maximize

$$\max EU(c, e) = \max_{\{e\}} EU(\alpha g f(e) - \hat{B}, \ e) \tag{10}$$

where $U$ is a concave function of $c$ and $e$. We obtain the first-order condition[16]

$$\alpha f'(e)EU_c g + EU_e = 0 \tag{11}$$

By total differentiation of (11) and using the concavity of $U$, it is evident that $de/d\hat{B} \gtrless 0$ as

$$\frac{d\left[\int (U_c \alpha g f' + U_e)h \, dg\right]}{d\hat{B}} = -E(U_{cc}\alpha g f' + U_{ec}) \gtrless 0 \tag{12}$$

Since $U_{cc} < 0$, condition (12) implies the following proposition:

Proposition 1   *Increased borrowing will increase the effort of tenants, and hence, the return to landlords provided that $U_{ec} \leqslant 0$.*

The condition $U_{ec} \leqslant 0$ is a very reasonable one. It states that increased consumption increases or leaves unchanged the marginal disutility associated with effort.[17]

## 1.3. Effort and default

Now consider the impact of two opposite institutional arrangements regarding the consequences of default: bonded labor and bankruptcy. A *bonded labor* clause in the loan agreement is an arrangement which states that if the tenant fails to repay his loan, he must provide certain labor services to the moneylender. We assume this to be an undesirable outcome for the tenant; hence, this implies that he will try to avoid situations or decisions which would increase the probability that his output will fall below a certain level such that he would no longer be able to repay his debt and would have to offer bonded labor services. Clearly, therefore, the impact of adding a bonded labor clause to the loan agreement is to *increase* the tenant's effort.

One formal way to model the bonded labor clause for a risk- averse tenant (figure 1(a)) is by assuming that the tenant's marginal utility of consumption, (or, alternatively, of income, for a given level of debt), $U_c$, is very high, that is, approaching infinity for very low values of $c$; see figure 1(b). In the extreme, we can depict the tenant as choosing the minimum level of effort required to avoid bondage. Thus, $e$ is chosen so that

$$\alpha f(e)g_{\min} = \hat{B} \tag{13}$$

when $g_{\min}$ = minimum value of $g$. Thus

$$\frac{de}{d\hat{B}} = \frac{1}{\alpha f' g_{\min}} > 0 \tag{14}$$

A *bankruptcy clause* is an arrangement whereby the borrower is allowed to default on his loan whenever his income is sufficiently low, and when he defaults he is guaranteed a level of consumption, $\hat{c}$, in excess of the starvation level.

The effect of adding a bankruptcy clause to the loan agreement is to *decrease* the tenant's effort since he does not have to bear fully the consequences of "bad" events. Formally, if the tenant utility function is not "too strictly" concave, the bankruptcy clause causes the utility function to become convex for certain regions; see figure 1(c). This change from a concave utility function to a convex function, implies that the bankruptcy clause changes the tenant's attitude towards risk from risk averter to risk lover.[18]

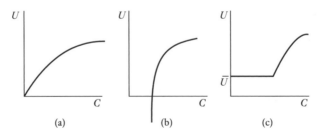

**Figure 1**   Utility as function of income (for given level of debt) under alternative default clauses

When bankruptcy is a possibility we can write

$$c = \max\{\alpha g f(e) - \hat{B}, \hat{c}\} \tag{15}$$

Let

$$\hat{g} = \frac{\hat{c} + \hat{B}}{\alpha f(e)} \tag{16}$$

be the critical value of $g$ below which bankruptcy occurs. Then the tenant's objective function (10) becomes

$$\max_{\{e\}}\left\{ \int_0^{\hat{g}} U(\hat{c}, e)h \, dg - \int_{\hat{g}}^{\infty} U(\alpha g f(e) - \hat{B}, e)h \, dg \right\} \tag{10'}$$

which leads to the first-order condition

$$\int_{\hat{g}}^{\infty} [U_c \alpha g f' + U_e]h \, dg + \int_0^{\hat{g}} U_e h \, dg = 0 \tag{11'}$$

and hence to

$$\frac{de}{d\hat{B}} \gtreqqless 0 \qquad \text{as} \qquad - U_c \alpha \hat{g} f' \frac{1}{\alpha f(e)} - \int_{\hat{g}}^{\infty} [U_{cc} \alpha g f' + U_{ce}]h \, dg \gtreqqless 0 \tag{12'}$$

An increase in borrowing makes bankruptcy more likely. This effect reduces the marginal return to effort and is expressed by the first term of (12') which is always negative. The sum total effect of increased borrowing on tenants' effort can still be positive only if the second set of terms dominates the first term. The following proposition and remark summarize this subsection.

PROPOSITION 2    *If the tenant's loan agreement includes a bonded labor clause, increased borrowing will increase the effort of tenants and, hence, the return to the landlords.*

REMARK    If the tenant's loan agreement includes a bankruptcy clause instead of a bonded labor clause, increased tenant borrowing may not increase his effort supply.
   Since landlords' expected returns are clearly dependent on the tenants' level of effort, it is clear that, in general, tenants' borrowing has an effect on landlords' expected returns; this effect is beneficial under the bonded labor system, but if bankruptcy is possible then increased borrowing may have a deleterious effect on landlords' returns.

## 1.4. The impact of the tenant's borrowing on his choice of technique of production

Now, let us assume that the only set of decisions available to the tenant is the choice of technique, $\Omega$. Effort is fixed (for example, to obtain any output requires a given level of effort; increased effort beyond that point bears little fruit). Since our main concern here is with risk taking, let us first consider a set of projects, all of which have the same mean, that is,

$$\int_0^\infty gh \, dg = \text{constant} \tag{17}$$

or

$$\int_0^\infty gh_\Omega \, dg = 0 \tag{18}$$

Therefore, riskier projects represent mean-preserving spreads $(MPS)$[19] of less-risky projects, that is, letting $H$ represent the distribution function, riskier projects are described by

$$\int_0^x H_\Omega \, dg \geqslant 0 \qquad \text{for all } x > 0 \tag{19}$$

$$\int_0^\infty H_\Omega dg = 0 \tag{20}$$

In figure 2 we graphically express an $MPS$ of the $H$ distribution, that is, the shifting of weight from the center to the tails. It is expressed both in terms of densities and cumulative distributions.

Making the same kind of separability assumption employed in Part 1.2, the first-order condition for the tenant's choice of technique is given by

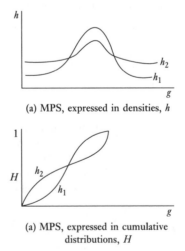

(a) MPS, expressed in densities, $h$

(a) MPS, expressed in cumulative
distributions, $H$

**Figure 2**  Mean-preserving spread in distribution of $g$: (a) MPS, expressed in densities, $h$; (b) MPS, expressed in cumulative distributions, $H$

$$\int Uh_\Omega \, dg + \int U_\Omega \, hdg = 0 \tag{21}$$

and assuming $U_{c\Omega} = 0,$[20] it immediately follows that

$$\frac{d\Omega}{d\hat{B}} \gtrless 0 \quad \text{as} \quad -\int_0^\infty U_c \, h_\Omega dg \gtrless 0 \tag{22}$$

Integrating twice by parts, and using (18) and (20), we obtain

$$\frac{d\Omega}{d\hat{B}} \gtrless 0 \quad \text{as} \quad -\int_0^\infty U_{ccc}\left[\int_0^x H_\Omega \, dg\right] dx \gtrless 0 \tag{23}$$

Using (19), it is thus apparent that

$$\frac{d\Omega}{d\hat{B}} \gtrless 0 \quad \text{as} \quad U_{ccc} \gtrless 0 \tag{24}$$

From (24) it is clear that an increase in borrowing will leave risk taking unaffected if and only if the utility function is quadratic, so $U_{ccc} = 0$. Otherwise, risk taking may either increase or decrease.

It is worth noting several special cases:

(a) Assume a *bonded labor* clause in the loan agreement, so that $U_c$ for very low values of $c$ is very high, that is, approaching infinity. Then from (22) it is apparent that an increase in borrowing reduces risk taking: individuals are concerned with only the lower tail of the distribution where $U_c$ is very high and $h_\Omega$, the shift in the density, is positive (figure 2(a)). Hence an increase in borrowing induces tenants to be more conservative.

In the limiting case described earlier, $\Omega^*$ is the largest value of $\Omega$ such that

$$\alpha g_{\min}(\Omega^*) = \hat{B} \tag{25}$$

where $g(\Omega^*)$ is the minimum value of $g$ for the technique $\Omega^*$. Thus,

$$\frac{d\Omega^*}{d\hat{B}} = \frac{1}{\alpha g'_{\min}} < 0 \tag{26}$$

since $g'_{\min}(\Omega)$ is negative; increasing $\Omega$ means an increasing spread of risk which implies that the smallest value of $g$ for given $\Omega$ declines.

(b) Assume that the individual has *decreasing absolute risk aversion*. Absolute risk aversion is defined by

$$A \equiv -\frac{U_{cc}}{U_c} \quad \text{so} \quad A' = -\frac{U_{ccc}}{U_c} + \frac{U_{cc}^2}{U_c^2}$$

Thus, decreasing absolute risk aversion implies $U_{ccc} > 0$. Therefore, from (24), risk taking is reduced by an increase in borrowing.

(c)  Assume a *bankruptcy* clause in the loan agreement. If the individual's utility function is linear in consumption (in the absence of bankruptcy, he would be risk neutral) he now becomes a risk lover; this holds more generally, provided he is not "too" risk averse (figure 3). Then the increase in borrowing may induce more risk taking.

According to our analysis, in which we focus on choices of techniques that leave the mean output unchanged but increase the spread of distribution, these changes in the choice of technique leave the risk-neutral landlord unaffected. However, in many cases techniques which are riskier also have higher means. This is true, for instance, of some of the HYV seeds of the "green revolution," which are more vulnerable to rain falls, under which circumstances their output is actually lower than that of more traditional seeds (see note 9 for another example).[21] If mean output is not increased too much, it will still be true that if tenants have decreasing absolute risk aversion (or if there is bonded labor), an increase in tenant's borrowing will result in a reduction in risk taking. This reduction in risk taking, however, will now have an effect on landlords; their expected income will be lowered.

Formally, we postulate that

$$Y = g\lambda(\Omega)f(e) \tag{27}$$

with $\lambda' > 0$ (recall that we have adopted the convention that an increase in $\Omega$ represents an increase in risk). Now the first-order condition for the tenant's modified objective function will be (instead of (21))

$$\int [Uh_\Omega + U_\Omega + U_c g\lambda'(\Omega)f(e)]dg = 0 \tag{28}$$

and then,

$$\frac{d\Omega}{d\hat{B}} \gtrless 0 \qquad \text{as} \qquad -\int [U_c h_\Omega + U_{cc} g\lambda' f]dg \gtrless 0 \tag{29}$$

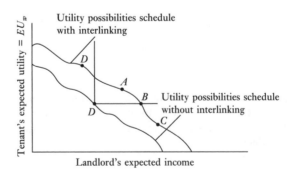

**Figure 3**  Welfare comparison of equilibrium with interlinking to equilibrium without interlinking

Thus our earlier results are unaffected, provided $\lambda'$ is sufficiently small (the bounds on $\lambda'$ are determined by the magnitude of $U_{ccc}$). We can summarize this subsection with the following proposition and remark.

PROPOSITION 3  *With a bonded labor clause in the loan agreement or with decreasing absolute risk aversion, an increase in the tenant's borrowing will reduce his risk taking. He will therefore not select some techniques which allow for higher mean output as well as higher risk. This reduces the returns of the risk-neutral landlord.*

REMARK  With a bankruptcy clause in the loan agreement the tenant may increase his risk taking with increased borrowing and, thus, may select riskier and higher mean output techniques than he would have chosen under a bonded labor clause. This choice increases a risk-neutral landlord's returns.

The above arguments establish clearly that the return to the landlord will depend critically on whether his tenant has borrowed, and if so, how much. Formally, the landlord could effect the same behavior by charging a rent paid at the end of the production period and equal to $\hat{B}$, in addition to the share. What is important is that the individual's behavior is affected by the total magnitude of the sum of rents and loan repayments, and that it is of value to the landlord to know their magnitude. In other words, although the form which the tenants' commitments take (whether rents or loans) may make little difference, it is important for the landlords to control the total and it is this which provides the motivation for interlinking. (Indeed, rent paid at the end of the production period can be viewed as a rent paid at the beginning of the period plus a loan from the beginning of the period to its end; in a sense, then, rent and loan commitments are equivalent.)

## 1.5. The equilibrium terms of loans from landlords to tenants

Let us first consider the case where an increase in borrowing reduces the expected return to the landlord – a negative externality. While he would like to restrict the amount of borrowing, he would not want to eliminate it altogether. The restriction on the amount of borrowing obviously reduces the expected utility of the tenant; thus, in a competitive environment, the tenant will require an alteration in some other provision of the contract to compensate for any such restriction. He might, for instance, be able to induce his tenants to accept a borrowing restriction by lending to the individual a given amount at a "favorable" interest rate, but beyond that point, charging a prohibitively high interest rate. Even if the landlord cannot directly monitor loans from the other creditors such a scheme may be very effective. To borrow supplementally from other lenders may then be very expensive: since the loan from his landlord has seniority over any supplemental loan, any potential lender would have to charge a very high interest rate.

If the amount which an individual borrows from other lenders is observable, then the competitive equilibrium contract will make the share (or other provisions of the contract) a function of the size of loans the worker has undertaken. In this case there would be no difference between the equilibrium which would emerge if the two markets were linked together, or if they were separated. If there are costs of monitoring and collection, however, there is a natural advantage for the landlord to undertake the loan.

In the case where there is a *positive externality*, there will be an incentive for the landlord to subsidize loans and to encourage the tenant to become indebted to him, so that he will work harder to repay the loan. (Bardhan and Rudra, 1978, report that in West Bengal landlords quite often offer tenants loans at interest rates below the market rate, sometimes even offering interest-free consumption loans.)

We now analyze formally the landlord's optimal contract. We write the tenant's utility function as $U^*(c_0, c_1, e)$ where $c_0 \equiv$ consumption in the 0th period $= W_0 + B$, $W_0$ denotes the individual's initial wealth[22] and $B$ denotes the amount borrowed, $c_1 = \alpha f(e)g - B(1 + r)$ where $c_1$ is consumption in the first period, and $r$ denotes the interest charged to the tenant.[23] In general, $r$ will be a function of $B$; the landlord specifies the "loan function" $r(B)$ and the tenant chooses the loan size, $B$. However, since in our analysis we assume that all tenants are identical, they will all choose the same value of $\{r, B\}$.[24] There are a large variety of loan functions which will induce the same choices of $\{r, B\}$ (and indeed, any $\{r, B\}$ which makes the tenant better off than he would be with $B = 0$, can be generated by some loan function). Hence, we analyze the behavior of the landlord assuming he controls $r$ and $B$ (or equivalently $B(1 + r)$ and $B$) directly.[25] If $\rho$ is the cost of capital to landlords, we can describe the optimal loan as the solution to the landlord's problem.[26]

$$\max_{\{B, B(1+r)\}} \bar{P} \equiv (1 - \alpha)f(e) + (1 + r - (1 + \rho))B \tag{30}$$

where, without loss of generality, we have assumed $Eg = 1$, subject to

$$EU^*(W_0 + B, \alpha f(e)g - (1 + r)B, e) \geqslant \bar{U}$$

As before, we assume that $U^*$ is separable in $c_0$ and $c_1$, that is, $U^* = u(c_0) + U(c_1, e)$. Then we obtain the following by using the envelope theorem and recalling $\hat{B} \equiv B(1 + r)$:

$$-\frac{\dfrac{dU^*}{d\hat{B}}}{\dfrac{dU^*}{dB}} = \frac{EU_c(c_1, e)}{u'(c_0)} = \frac{(1 - \alpha)f'(e)de/d\hat{B} + 1}{1 + \rho} = -\frac{\dfrac{d\bar{P}}{d\hat{B}}}{\dfrac{d\bar{P}}{dB}} \tag{31}$$

In contrast, in a competitive loan market, if the tenant and landlord had equal access to the capital market (an admittedly dubious assumption),

$$\frac{u'(c_\theta)}{EU_c(c_1, e)} = 1 + \rho \tag{32}$$

Comparing (31) and (32) we obtain the following proposition:

PROPOSITION 4    *The optimal contract offered by the landlord will entail farmers borrowing more (borrowing less) than they would in an unlinked market with equal access to capital, if $de/d\hat{B} > (<)0$, that is, if increased borrowing induces more (less) effort.*

In order for the landlord to control simultaneously both the amount borrowed ($B$) and the amount owed ($\hat{B}$), he must use a nonlinear loan function.[27] In note 27 we discuss the case where the landlord is restricted to charging a simple interest rate. (Clearly, intermediate cases, for example, where the landlord can restrict the maximum borrowing, can be treated within the same framework.)

In all of the above cases, notice that the tenant could have elected to keep some of his initial wealth in savings, or could have elected to borrow less to ensure adequate consumption in period one; yet the landlord manages to induce him to borrow the amount $B$ even though the tenant is fully aware of the consequences.[28]

## 1.6. Default clauses

The discussion in section 1.5 did not cover default clauses. As previously discussed, a bonded labor clause increases the tenant's effort but reduces his risk taking. Thus, the two effects go in opposite directions in their impact on the return to the risk-neutral landlord. The bankruptcy clause produces the opposite result: it reduces effort and increases risk taking. Hence the landlord's preference for one clause over another depends on the extent of the significance of the moral hazard problem regarding effort supply compared with the tenant's choice of technique. For example, if effort can be relatively easily monitored and enforced, and the moral hazard problem mainly involves the tenant's choice of technique, then a risk-neutral landlord will tend to prefer a bankruptcy clause to a bonded labor clause. On the other hand, if the moral hazard problem is more significant in the tenant's effort supply than in his choice of technique, then a bonded labor clause will be preferred by the landlord.

## 1.7. Production loans

For simplicity, the analysis to this point has assumed that loans are only used for consumption purposes. There is no interaction between the amount lent in the previous period and output in the current period. The modifications required to take this into account are straightforward;[29] we let output be a function not only of effort but of the amount borrowed:[30]

$$Y = gf(e, B) \tag{33}$$

Then, the first-order condition for the (appropriately modified version of the) maximization problem (30) can be written as

$$\frac{EU_c}{EU_c \alpha g f_B} = \frac{(1-\alpha)f_e \partial e/\partial \hat{B} + 1}{(1-\alpha)[f_e \partial e/\partial B + f_B] + (1+\rho)} \tag{34}$$

Thus the landlord takes into account that

(a)  he appropriates a fraction of the return from the increased input $((1-\alpha)f_B)$;
(b)  the increased inputs alter the level of effort; and

(c)   an increase in the amount lent increases the expected utility of the tenant (and
      thus enables him to alter some other term of the contract more to his liking while
      still being able to recruit tenants).

The effect of increased inputs on effort is ambiguous;[31] if effort and other inputs are
complements ($f_{eB} > 0$), as we might expect, the increased inputs increase the marginal
return to effort. But the increased output has an additional income effect which normally
decreases the level of effort.

In the absence of subsidization, the tenant would have set

$$EU_c(1 + \rho) = EU_c \alpha g f_B \tag{35}$$

Thus, whether the landlord prefers to subsidize or to restrict borrowing depends on
whether

$$\frac{f_e \partial e}{\partial B} + f_B \gtrless \frac{EU_c \alpha g f_B}{EU_c} \cdot f_e \frac{\partial e}{\partial \hat{B}} \tag{36}$$

Clearly either is possible, depending on the degree of complementarity ($f_{eB}$) and the
specifics of the utility function.

## 1.8. Externalities from the landlord to the lender in the absence of linkages

Our previous discussion emphasized the externality associated with the lending activity on
the income of the landlord. There is also a reverse externality in situations where there is a
positive probability of default, so long as the return to the lender is affected by default.
(Normally, we would assume that default reduces the expected income of the lender, but it
is possible that, with bonded labor, it increases his expected income.) The analysis is
similar to that presented earlier. What is relevant now, however, is not the mean output of
the farm, but the probability that the income of the tenant, after paying the landlord's
share, is sufficiently low so that the tenant goes into default. This is clearly affected by the
terms of the contract (the share, the plot size, the supply of complementary inputs), but
the landlord, in choosing the optimal contract, ignores the impact on the lender. Since the
landlord who lends funds to his own tenants can internalize this externality, he can obtain
a higher return from lending to his own tenants than he can obtain lending elsewhere.
This, then, provides a further motivation for interlinking the two markets.

## 1.9. General vs. partial equilibrium

The preceding analysis shows that, for any fixed level of expected utility of workers, the
landlord can increase his expected income by simultaneously controlling the credit market.
This argument establishes that the utility possibilities schedule, in an economy in where
the two markets are linked together, will be above that of an economy where (for example,
as a result of legal restrictions) the two are kept separate, and it establishes that in a
competitive equilibrium such linkages will, in fact, exist. However, it does not necessarily

imply that landlords are the only beneficiaries, or indeed, in general equilibrium, that landlords will be better off at all. The new equilibrium with linkages may lie to the northeast of the one without linkages (point *A*, figure 3), making both workers and landlords better off, but it need not.

In figure 3 we depict four possible situations: in *A*, the landlords and workers are both better off; they share in the gains from interlinking markets; in *B*, tenants have a subsistence utility level to which they are always driven; thus all the gains from interlinking accrue to landlords; in *C*, tenants are worse off as a result of interlinking markets; all the gains accrue to landlords – and then some; while *D* is the converse situation, where landlords are worse off as a result of interlinking; all the gains accrue to tenants.

Under competitive conditions, we can ascertain the conditions for *C* or *D* to occur. The effect of interlinkage on the welfare of tenants is, in principle, easy to ascertain. We can derive a pseudo demand curve for labor. There is now not a simple price of labor (the wage); but we can, instead, summarize the contract in terms of the expected utility that it generates to the tenant. At higher levels of expected utility, there will be a lower demand for labor, as depicted in figure 4 where the supply of *tenants* is assumed perfectly inelastic.[32] The competitive equilibrium is just the intersection of the demand and supply schedules (point O in figure 4). Interlinkage may shift the demand schedule upwards, in which case the tenants will be better off (point *D* in figure 4). If it shifts up the demand schedule enough, landlords will compete for tenants so fiercely that landlords will be worse off. However, it is possible for the demand curve to shift down, in which case tenants are worse off (point *C* in figure 4). If at a particular level of expected utility of tenants, the optimal "interlinked" contract entails a plot size for each tenant which is smaller (larger) than in the noninterlinked contract, then, at that level of expected utility of tenants, there is an excess supply (demand) for tenants; hence, in the competitive equilibrium with interlinkage the expected utility of tenants must be lower (higher) than in the equilibrium without interlinkage. The calculations of the relationship between the optimal plot size and interlinkage are complicated, and are presented in the Appendix. There we show that interlinkage can, under not implausible conditions, increase plot size (at a given level of utility of tenants) and make tenants worse off.

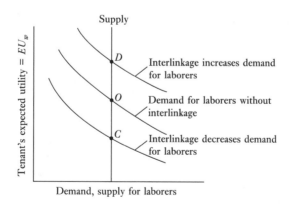

**Figure 4**   Competitive equilibria in the tenancy market with and without interlinkage

Consider, for instance, an economy with a Cobb–Douglas production function. It is known (Stiglitz, 1974) that in the optimal contract, the share of the tenant $\alpha$ equals the implicit share of labor $S_w$ (where $S_w$ is the exponent on labor in the Cobb–Douglas function). This share is optimal for all levels of borrowing. Changes in the credit terms, thus, must be offset by changes in plot size. If interlinkage attempts to restrict credit (as it would if the conditions of propositions 1 and 4 are satisfied) then tenants will be worse off; to compensate them (leave them at the same level of expected utility as they would have without interlinkage) plot size must be increased; this reduces the demand for tenants, and hence the general equilibrium effect corresponds to the partial equilibrium effect.

Conversely, if interlinkage attempts to encourage borrowing (see propositions 1 and 4) then tenants will be better off as a result of interlinkage; to leave them at the same level of expected utility, plot size must be reduced, and this increases the demand for labor, and, again, the general equilibrium effect conforms to the partial equilibrium effect. In more general cases, the partial and general equilibrium effects need not be qualitatively the same.[33]

In Section 4 below we analyze the effects of interlinkage in noncompetitive environments.

## 2. Interlinking Marketing and Tenancy Contracts

In the discussion above, we assumed that output and raw material prices are exogenously given to both landlords and tenants. Landlords and tenants therefore face identical prices; quite often, however, one observes that the landlord undertakes the marketing activity for his tenant and is involved in the provision of raw material inputs.[34] Is there an explanation for this interlinkage between marketing and tenancy contracts which is analogous to that presented earlier, for the interlinkage between credit markets and tenancy.[35] In this section, we focus on inputs, while in the next we consider interlinkages with consumption goods markets. Here we show

(i)   if there is a single input, and if the contract can specify the cost and output sharing formula without restriction, then interlinkage provides no advantages; but
(ii)  if there are restrictions on the cost-sharing formula (and, in particular, if the same cost-sharing formula must be employed for a variety of inputs), then there will be interlinkages.

It is widely believed that by marketing the output, the landlord may explicitly (by buying the product from the tenant at a lower price than at the market price) or implicitly (by charging high marketing costs), extract further surplus from the tenant. However, in a utility equivalent contract equilibrium framework where the landlord both possesses sufficient controls and gains from pushing the tenant down to his reservation utility, there is no possibility to extract further surplus from the tenant. Hence, in such a world the following question arises: Does the control of output and raw material prices provide an *additional* instrument for the landlord to motivate the tenant (and extract surplus) besides those already discussed?

Consider the tenant's problem in the absence of uncertainty. Assume that both the tenant and landlord face the same price for the raw material fertilizer, $P_x$ (for example, the fertilizer purchased from the village cooperative). For notational convenience, we shall define the fertilizer units such that $P_x = 1$. However, the landlord buys the output from the tenant at the price $P_T$ which is different from the market price at which the landlord sells the output, $P_L$. Thus, the tenant's income is

$$Y_T = \alpha P_T f(e, x) - \beta x \tag{37}$$

where $\alpha$ and $\beta$ denote the tenant's output share and cost share, respectively, and he maximizes

$$\max_{(e, x)} U(Y_T(e, x), e) \tag{38}$$

From the first-order conditions we obtain

$$f_x = \frac{\beta}{\alpha P_T} \tag{39}$$

$$f_e = -\frac{U_2(Y_T, e)}{U_1(Y_T, e) \cdot \alpha P_T} \tag{40}$$

Hence, the tenant's decisions are fully determined by the set of controls $\beta, \alpha P_T$. Let us therefore define $\hat{\alpha} \equiv \alpha P_T$, and write the tenant's effort and input supply functions $e = e(\hat{\alpha}, \beta)$, $x = x(\hat{\alpha}, \beta)$.

Now let us move to the landlord's problem and determine whether $P_T$ plays a separate role for him, in addition to its role in determining $\hat{\alpha}$. The landlord who faces the output price, $P_L$, at the market place maximizes his income subject to the utility equivalence constraint, that is,

$$\max_{\{\alpha, \beta, P_T\}} (1 - \alpha) P_L f[e(\hat{\alpha}, \beta), x(\hat{\alpha}, \beta)] - (1 - \beta) x(\hat{\alpha}, \beta) \tag{41}$$

subject to

$$U[Y_T(\hat{\alpha}, \beta, P_T), e(\hat{\alpha}, \beta)] = \bar{V}$$

Equation (41) can be rewritten as

$$\max_{\{\alpha, \beta, P_T\}} P_L f - x - Y_T \tag{42}$$

The last term is the tenant's income. By inverting the constraint in (41) we obtain

$$Y_T = \phi[\bar{V}, e(\hat{\alpha}, \beta)] \tag{43}$$

Substituting (43) into (42) we obtain

$$\max_{\{\hat{\alpha}, \beta\}} P_L f(\hat{\alpha}, \beta) - x(\hat{\alpha}, \beta) - \phi(\bar{V}, \hat{\alpha}, \beta) = \Pi(\hat{\alpha}, \beta) \qquad (44)$$

from which it is clear that the landlord cares only about $\hat{\alpha}$ rather than about $\alpha$ and $P_T$ separately. Hence

PROPOSITION 5    *In a utility equivalence world where shares are not restricted, the landlord can pay the tenant the market price for his output, that is, $P_T = P_L$. However, if shares are restricted either by social norms or laws, the landlord can extract the tenant's surplus by paying him a price lower than the market place, that is, $P_T < P_L$, without any loss in efficiency.*

A similar analysis suggests why it may be in the interests of a monopsonist marketing agent to attempt to interlink the credit markets with his marketing activity. Assume that he pays a single price for the output which he purchases from farmers. He sets this price so the marginal cost of purchasing an additional unit equals the marginal revenue he obtains from selling the good. But since the price he pays is, in general, less than the marginal cost, the tenants have (from his point of view) insufficient incentives to produce. If he can induce them to produce more at the given price, this will increase his profits. Thus it may, for instance, be worthwhile for him to subsidize credit.

A similar argument establishes that if there are many inputs, and if $P_i$ is the price at which the landlord sells the $i$th input to the tenant (we normalize the units so the purchase price of all inputs by the landlord is unity), and $\beta_i$ is the share of the $i$th input's cost borne by the tenant, then the tenant's behavior is fully determined by the set of controls $\{\beta_i P_i, \alpha P_T\}$. Similarly, the profits of the landlords are a function of the same variables. Thus, any equilibrium can be supported by the landlord setting $P_i = 1$ for every $i$, (the price the landlord must pay for the inputs). But again, if there are restrictions on $\beta_i$ (in particular, if the same cost-sharing formula must apply to all inputs), since the optimal value of $\{\beta_i P_i\}$ will differ from one input to another, so, too, must the optimal price. However, note that it is only through changes in the relative prices of inputs that the landlord achieves the advantages of interlinkages.

## 3. Interlinking of Labor and Consumption Good Markets

The argument of the previous section suggested that providing the landlord with additional instruments for exploiting workers through control of the product market would not, in fact, enable him to do so any better than he could have done by simply altering the "contract" which he imposed on his workers.[36] This is not true for the landlord's control of the consumption good market. We represent the typical worker by his indirect utility function $V = V(C, p)$. By the usual arguments, $V$ and $e$ are both homogeneous of degree zero in $C$ and $p$: so long as the monopolist does not change *relative prices*, the fact that he may also own the store at which his workers buy their goods has no effect on his ability to exploit his workers.

The landlord will, however, wish to change the relative prices of goods, to encourage the consumption of goods which are complementary to effort, and discourage the consumption of goods which are complementary to leisure.[37] Thus, giving the landlord this extra degree of control will increase his return. In addition, this argument provides a rationale for landlords providing workers with meals and some in-kind payments, rather than full money wages.[38]

## 4. Monopoly, Monopsony, Competition, and Equilibrium with Surplus Labor

For most of the analysis in this paper, we have not had to distinguish between a monopoly landlord and a competitive landlord. In either situation, the contract should be designed so as to maximize the expected profits of the landlord, given whatever level of expected utility the workers attain. The only distinction is the determination of the level of expected utility of workers. In the monopoly solution, it is at the subsistence level of workers; in the competitive equilibrium, it is at whatever level equates demand and supply of tenants.

There is, however, another quite different regime, in which, in equilibrium there is unemployment (surplus labor). In our earlier discussion, we characterized the equilibrium by having the landlord maximize his expected profits subject to the constraint of being able to obtain workers, that is, offering tenants a contract which generated a level of expected utility at least as great as the worker could obtain elsewhere. In a variety of situations, this constraint turns out not to be binding. For instance, in the efficiency wage model analyzed by Harvey Leibenstein (1957), James Mirrlees (1976) and Stiglitz (1976), there is a wage which minimizes labor costs per efficiency unit. Even though labor could be obtained at a lower wage, a landlord would not do so, since that would increase his labor costs. At a lower wage, workers are not only less efficient, but are sufficiently less efficient that wage costs per unit of effective labor are actually larger than they would have been at the "efficiency wage." Similarly, a landlord might be able to reduce the share or the size of plot he provides workers, but it would not pay him to do so, since his expected profits might be reduced as a result of such a move. In this case, even in a competitive market there may exist equilibrium in which the supply of labor exceeds the demand – that is, there is nonvoluntary unemployment. (For such an unemployment equilibrium to occur it is required that output per hectare increase with plot size. Braverman and Srinivasan (1981) have shown that with production functions with constant returns to scale in land and labor this can never occur.)

In such situations, interlinking has some interesting implications. Interlinking may increase the expected profits of landlords (in either competitive or noncompetitive situations) if, for instance, the landlord can induce a higher level of effort by providing loans at a subsidized rate. Although the welfare implications for landlords in this situation are clear, the implications for workers are ambiguous:

(i)   The number of workers employed may increase or decrease, depending on the effect of interlinkage on the optimal plot size; and

(ii)  Those workers who do succeed in getting land may be better or worse off.

Consider a case where the worker divides his consumption between alcohol, which decreases effort, and food, which increases it. Assume that by changing the relative price of alcohol to food, the landlord is able to induce a significant change in the relative proportion of income spent on the two goods (the elasticity of substitution between the two goods is very high). Then, not only may this increase the level of effort, but it may also increase the *marginal* return to increasing plot size, share, etc.; if, for instance, the efficiency wage increases significantly, as depicted in figure 5, the individual who succeeds in getting land may be *better off*. (Clearly, although the level of effort might increase, the marginal return to increasing wages might decrease; the monopolist may thus reduce the wage of his worker and the interlinking of the consumption market and the labor market would then *lower* the welfare of the worker.) Similarly, if the optimal plot size increases, the level of unemployment will increase; likewise if optimal plot size decreases so will unemployment.

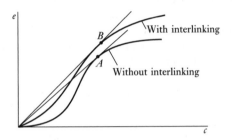

**Figure 5**  Example when interlinking goods and land/labor markets results in higher levels of consumption for workers

We have argued in this section that there is no fundamental difference in the structure of the analysis of interlinkage of markets between a competitive market and a market with a single landowner, but that there is a significant difference between those situations where the expected utility constraint of workers is binding and those where it is not. It is important to recognize, however, that whether the expected utility constraint is or is not binding, is itself affected by the market structure, that is, by whether there is a single landlord, or by the instruments for exploitation which are at the disposal of the landlord. In our earlier discussion, we suggested, for instance, that the landlord might like to employ a nonlinear lending schedule, where the rate of interest was a function of the amount borrowed. If, however, there is a secondary loan market so individuals can re-lend to each other, the landlord may be forced to lend at a single rate. Then, if he lowers the rate to induce workers to borrow more and is either restricted from decreasing the share or plot size, or finds it undesirable to do so, workers will enjoy an expected utility level exceeding their subsistence constraint. If the landlord could impose a lump sum tax on his workers, he could again drive them back to their subsistence constraint.

## 5.  Conclusion

This paper has provided an economic rationale for interlinking contracts in situations where there are important moral hazard problems. The analysis has focused on the case where the terms of the tenancy contract are determined optimally, but the argument for interlinkage is even stronger in those situations where convention or law restricts certain contractual arrangements (for example, usury laws which forbid or restrict interest rates).[39]

We also note that our analysis did not address the implications of heterogenous population of landlords and tenants for interlinking. The interlinkages of credit and tenancy contracts, for example, may serve landlords as a screening device to identify more able potential tenants (see Franklin Allen, 1980, and Braverman and Guasch, 1981). Furthermore, our analysis has focused on interlinkages within a set of markets at a given time; similar arguments can be put forward for interlinkages across markets over time. This may lead to the signing of long-term contracts between tenants and landlords-cum-lenders. In this case, although, there may be *ex ante* competition (before the contract has been signed), there is only limited *ex post* competition.[40] The implications of this are important, but unfortunately cannot be pursued here.

Although we have argued that the presence of interlinkages need not be taken as evidence that agrarian markets in less-developed countries are noncompetitive, it seems clear that such linkages have both distributive as well as allocative effects. Attempts to reduce the landlord's "power" by restricting his marketing or credit activities may, in certain circumstances, lower agrarian output and make tenants worse off. In other circumstances,[41] total agrarian output might increase, tenants could be better off, and only the landlords suffer. Further empirical work is clearly needed to distinguish which of the various possibilities is relevant in any particular situation. Yet, one of the conclusions of our study is that in many situations competitive and noncompetitive markets may look quite similar (say, with respect to the kinds of interlinkages employed). Thus, distinguishing among the various possibilities may require greater subtlety than is frequently employed in empirical and policy work in this area. We hope our study has shown that simplistic models (whether competitive or noncompetitive) which involve anonymous market places, homogeneous goods and perfect monitoring of inputs are likely to be very misleading.

APPENDIX: DETERMINATION OF THE EQUILIBRIUM PLOT SIZE, WITH VARIABLES SHARES IN UTILITY EQUIVALENT CONTRACT EQUILIBRIUM

Let $f(el)$ = output per hectare, so $f/l$ = output per worker. Let $\alpha$ and $l$ be variable. Let $Eg = 1$. The landlord must choose $\{\alpha, l\}$ to yield

$$EU\left(\frac{\alpha f(el)}{l}g - \hat{B}, e\right) = \bar{U} \tag{A1}$$

We thus obtain

$$\frac{d\alpha}{dl}\bigg|_{\bar{U}} = \frac{\alpha(f - f'el)}{lf} = \frac{\alpha(1 - S_w)}{l} \tag{A2}$$

where $1 - S_w = (f - f'el)/f$ is the implicit share of landlord. Moreover, recalling the first-order condition for effort

$$EU_c\alpha f'g + EU_e = 0 \tag{A3}$$

we observe that along the iso-utility contract, assuming for simplicity an additive utility function,

$$\frac{l}{e}\frac{de}{dl}\Big|_{\bar{u}} = -\frac{\alpha f'[1 - \gamma - S_w]EU_c g}{elEU_c\alpha f''(el)g + EU_{ee}e} = \frac{1 - S_w - \gamma}{\gamma + \nu} \tag{A4}$$

where $\gamma = -f''el/f'$ and $\nu = EU_{ee}e/EU_e$, which is the elasticity of effort supply.

Expected profits (per hectare) of the landlord are $(1 - \alpha)f(el)$. Hence, the optimal contract is such that

$$f\left[(1 - \alpha)S_w\left(1 + \frac{d\ln e}{d\ln l}\Big|_{\bar{U}}\right) - \alpha(1 - S_w)\right] = 0 \tag{A5}$$

that is,

$$\frac{\alpha}{1 - \alpha} = \frac{S_w}{1 - S_w}\left(1 + \frac{d\ln e}{d\ln l}\Big|_{\bar{U}}\right) \tag{A6}$$

For example, if $d\ln e/d\ln l\,|_{\bar{u}} = 0$, $\alpha = S_w$, and from (A4), if there is a Cobb–Douglas production function, that is, $\gamma = 1 - S_w$, then $d\ln e/d\ln l\,|_{\bar{u}} = 0$. Hence, for a Cobb–Douglas production function, the optimal share remains unchanged, as we change $(1 + r)B$. Thus, to obtain the same level of expected utility, as we increase the interest rate charged on a fixed level of borrowing, we increase plot size. Therefore, interlinkage reduces the demand for labor; and it leads tenants to be worse off.

More generally, we observe that the elasticity of substitution, $\sigma = (1 - S_w)/\gamma$. Substituting back into (A4), we obtain

$$\frac{d\ln e}{d\ln l}\Big|_{\bar{U}} = \frac{(1 - S_w)(1 - 1/\sigma)}{(1 - S_w)/\sigma + \nu} = \frac{(1 - S_w)(\sigma - 1)}{(1 - S_w) + \nu\sigma} \gtrless 1 \quad \text{as} \quad \sigma \gtrless \frac{2(1 - S_w)}{1 - S_w - \nu} \tag{A7}$$

Hence

$$\frac{\alpha}{1 - \alpha} = \frac{S_w}{1 - S_w} + \frac{S_w(\sigma - 1)}{1 - S_w + \nu\sigma} \tag{A8}$$

Although (A8) always characterizes the equilibrium, it is important to note that $\gamma, \alpha, S_w, \sigma$, and $\nu$ are all endogenous variables (except in some special cases). We can still use (A8), however, to obtain certain results concerning the effects of interlinking. First, let us assume that $B$ is unchanged, but the rate of interest charged is increased. (The borrowing was for an emergency which occurred the preceding period.) Assume $l$ were unchanged to keep $U$ at the same level, then $\alpha$ must be increased. Thus, $e$ will be increased, both because of the increased $\alpha$ and the increased value of $(1 + r)B$. If the elasticity of substitution exceeds unity, this increases $S_w$. Both the left-hand and the right-hand sides of (A8) have thus increased. If the right-hand side has increased more, it means that at the contract which generates equal expected utility with unchanged plot size, $\alpha$ is too small; thus $\alpha$ must be increased, and plot size decreased. Therefore the demand for tenants will increase and their expected utility will also increase. This will occur if the elasticity of substitution is very large. But if the elasticity of substitution is just slightly greater than unity, the left-hand side will exceed the right, and hence $\alpha$ will need to be reduced and plot size correspondingly increased (if individuals are to be at the same level of expected utility). These changes will increase effort, but less than proportionately to the increase in plot size; hence, $el$ will be reduced, which will reduce the right-hand side of (A8); $\alpha$ will continue to be reduced until the left- and right-hand sides of (A8) are equal. In this case, therefore, interlinkage has resulted in a decrease in the demand for labor and tenants' expected utility is decreased. (Other cases are left as exercises to the reader.)

## Notes

1   For a survey of such phenomena, see Pranab Bardhan (1980) and Hans Binswanger et al., (1983). For the nineteenth-century United States, see Joseph Reid (1979).

2   Other recent studies which have addressed this question include those of Clive Bell and Pinhas Zusman (1980), Pradeep Mitra (1983), Reid (1976), and Braverman and Srinivasan (1981). In particular, Mitra's study raises the central issue discussed, of the relationship between interlinking and moral hazard. For a more general discussion of equilibrium with moral hazard, including implications of moral hazard for the decentralization of the economy, see Richard Arnott and Stiglitz (1980).

3   Moreover, if there is some probability of their not being able to pay the fixed rent, which can be affected by the actions of the tenant, rental arrangements may not be desirable from the point of view of the landlord (Stiglitz and Andrew Weiss, 1981), and even with a rental agreement tenants do not obtain the full marginal benefit (or cost) of their actions.

4   See Alfred Marshall (1920), Steven Cheung (1969), Bardhan and T. N. Srinivasan (1971), Reid (1973), Stiglitz (1974), Bell and Zusman (1976), David Newbery (1977), and Newbery and Stiglitz (1979) for earlier discussions of sharecropping.

5   It is important to note that in our analysis, the worker is not myopic; at the time he undertakes the loan, he knows that he will want ("need") to work harder next period, and takes this into account in determining his demand for loans. If workers are myopic, the case for interlinkages may be even stronger than that presented here.

6   This applies to the situations which were previously discussed in the literature where interlinkage provides a mechanism by which legal restrictions (such as limits on usurious interest rates) and conventions (such as "fair" division of output between landlords and tenants) may be evaded (for example, Braverman and Srinivasan, 1981). Such situations can be viewed as special cases of the analysis provided here.

7   Marshall recognized the importance of share contracts in a world dominated by market imperfections and the absence of certain markets (see Christopher Bliss and Nickolas Stern, 1981, ch. 3; and Jerald Jaynes, (1983).

8   The optimal linear contractual arrangements are discussed in Stiglitz (1974) and Newbery (1977); the only variable which the worker alters is effort; in this paper, we also consider the problem of the choice of technique.

9    Although our results only require that the actions of the tenant not be perfectly monitored (and
     that the contractual arrangements, which could accordingly specify compensation based on the
     observed actions be perfectly enforced), in our model we will assume that these actions (effort
     or the choice of technique) cannot be monitored at all. Clearly, some actions (such as what crop
     is planted) are easily monitored, and thus there would, presumably, be little difficulty in
     enforcing deviations from the contract. Other actions, however, are more difficult to specify
     (either implicitly or explicitly) in a contract, to monitor and to enforce; for example, the
     "optimal" time to harvest will, in general be a complicated function of the weather conditions
     during the growing season as well as the expectations concerning weather during the harvest
     season. By harvesting earlier, the mean harvest may be smaller but there is likely to be less risk
     (of the crop being destroyed before it is harvested).

10   The argument is, in fact, even stronger; these moral hazard problems arise even with rental
     tenancy arrangements, if renters have insufficient capital to pay the rent in advance, and if there is
     sufficient variability in output that it may not be feasible for the renter to repay the promised rent.

11   The model, however, is far from being the most general one for which our conclusions are valid.
     Thus, although we limit ourselves to discussing pure sharecropping contracts, the results apply
     for virtually any contractual arrangement other than fixed rental contracts when there is no
     possibility of bankruptcy.

12   It should also be clear that $e$ could represent a vector of inputs, including fertilizer, machinery, etc.

13   As the following discussion will make clear, this is a *derived* utility function, analogous to the
     indirect utility function.

14   In these two examples "$q$" is the price at which the landlord makes goods or credit available to his
     tenant. The landlord need not, however, restrict himself to linear price systems; he may impose a
     variety of restrictions on his tenants, employ a nonlinear price system, etc. See note 21.

15   The returns from interlinked activities may be random; $\pi$ then denotes the mean value, also $\pi$
     may be a function of $e$ and $\Omega$. This would necessitate only minor modifications to the analysis.

16   We ignore corner solutions throughout this paper.

17   In the absence of uncertainty, normality in income of consumption and leisure suffice for the
     proposition. An alternative condition is that in addition to the normality condition, the variance
     of income be small enough.

18   This issue will be discussed in Part 1.4 to follow.

19   Consult Rothschild and Stiglitz (1970) and Diamond and Stiglitz (1974) for discussions of
     mean-preserving spreads.

20   Throughout the remainder of the paper we assume $U_{e\Omega} = 0$; if we write $U = U(c, e)$
     $-V(\Omega)$, $V(\Omega)$ can be thought of as the "cost" of technology $\Omega$. Furthermore, if all available
     technologies have the same mean, then for an interior solution (i.e., $\Omega > \Omega_{min}$, where $\Omega_{min}$ is
     the least risky technology), we require that $V'(\Omega)$ be sufficiently large.

21   Presumably, the choice of seed as a decision variable which could be specified by the
     contract between landlord and tenant. But as we noted in note 9, there are many other
     decisions concerning techniques which could not be so easily specified, or if specified, mon-
     itored and enforced. A fuller analysis would, of course, not simply dichotomize the actions
     into "observables" and "nonobservables." There are costs of observation, as well as costs
     entailed in decision making, contract specifications, monitoring and enforcement; these costs
     will for the landlord, depend, for instance, partly on whether he is an absentee landlord. Thus,
     what is specified in the contract should be treated as an endogenous variable.

22   For simplicity, we take $W_0$ here as simply a parameter. It represents, for instance, the amount
     the tenant has been able to save. Clearly, in a more general model, $W_0$ would be affected by the
     terms of the contract.

23   We ignored here the direct effect of borrowing on production. See Part 1.7.

24    See Braverman and Guasch (1981) for a discussion of a self-selection separating equilibrium, where heterogeneous tenants choose different pairs of $\{r, B\}$ from a loan function $r(B)$, offered by the landlords.

25    If the population is heterogeneous, then the precise specification of the loan function becomes more important. Even then, provided that there are only a finite number of types of borrowers, the same sets of choices can be induced by a large variety of loan functions. Only in the limiting case of a continuum of types, does the optimal loan function become determinate.

26    In the calculation, we take the share and the plot size as exogenously given; alternatively, we could view them as having been optimally chosen. For purposes of the ensuing analysis it makes no difference. See the Appendix.

27    The contract described in the preceding analysis entailed the landlord specifying $B$, the amount borrowed, and $\hat{B} = (1 + r)B$, the amount paid back. The landlord does not, however, allow the tenant to borrow as much as he would like at the interest rate $r = (\hat{B}/B) - 1$. Effectively the landlord is employing a nonlinear interest rate schedule to maintain the individual on the same expected utility curve. In Section 5, we consider what happens if the landlord is not allowed to use such schedules, and cannot decrease $\alpha$ or plot size to compensate for lowering in the interest rate. (Thus, the expected utility constraint will not be binding.) Note that if the landlord cannot restrict the level of credit or "force" credit, but can announce an $r$ different from $\rho$, and can alter $\alpha$, then instead of (31) we obtain

$$\frac{EU_c g}{EU_c} = \left[ 1 - \frac{1 - \alpha}{\alpha} \frac{f'e}{f} \frac{\partial \ln e}{\partial \ln \alpha} - \frac{(r - \rho)}{f} \frac{\partial B}{\partial \alpha} \right] \div \left[ 1 + \frac{(1 - \alpha)f'e}{\alpha} \frac{\partial \ln e}{\partial \ln \hat{B}} \frac{\partial \ln \hat{B}}{\partial \ln r} \frac{f}{rB} + \frac{dB}{dr} \frac{(r - \rho)}{B} \right]$$

Whether the landlord will set $r \lessgtr \rho$ depends on tenants' risk aversion, as well as the elasticity of effort with respect to share ($\alpha$) and with respect to indebtedness ($\hat{B}$), and the elasticity of indebtedness with respect to the interest rate.

28    It is possible, of course, that

$$\frac{EU_c(\alpha fg, e)}{u'(W_0)} > \frac{(1 - \alpha)f'(e) \left. \frac{de}{d\hat{B}} \right|_{B=\hat{B}=0} + 1}{1 + \rho}$$

In that case the landlord would like to induce the tenant to lend to him, but if this is not feasible, then $B = \hat{B} = 0$. Notice that it is still possible that

$$\left. \frac{EU_c(c_1, e)}{u'(c_0)} \right|_{B=\hat{B}=0} < \frac{1}{1 + \rho}$$

in which case the tenant may attempt to borrow elsewhere. The landlord will attempt to restrict this borrowing, if he can. If he cannot, he may still lend to the tenant. In either case, there is a kind of interlinking, although in the first case, no transactions occur in the interlinked market.

29    Similar modifications need to be made in the analysis of the consumption loan model when the utility function is not separable, so that changes in $c_0$ affect effort, $e$.

30    This formulation assumes that the marginal increment in input from a marginal increase in borrowing is unity. More generally, if output is a function of effort and an input, $z$, $f(e, z)$ and $z$ is a function of $B$, $z(B)$, then $f(e, B) \equiv \hat{f}(e, z(B))$. Equation (34) is unaffected, although the interpretation of $f_B$ needs to be modified.

31    Differentiating the first-order condition for effort with respect to $B$ (keeping $\hat{B}$ fixed) yields

$$\frac{\partial e}{\partial B} = -\{\alpha f_{Bc} EU_c g + \alpha^2 f_B f_e [E(U_{cc} g + U_{cc}) g]\} + \{\alpha f_{ee} EU_c g + \alpha f_e E[(U_{cc} \alpha f_e + U_{cc}) g] + EU_{cc}\}$$

32    The case with elastic supply of laborers may be handled analogously. There is one critical difference: if the supply schedule of tenants is upward sloping (as one might expect), and interlinkage increases plot size at a fixed level of expected utility, then in equilibrium, when land area is fixed, plot size will increase. The number of tenants will accordingly decrease. Conversely, if interlinkage decreases plot size the equilibrium number of tenants will increase. One can, thus, infer the welfare impact from observing the equilibrium effect on plot size.

33    This is a general property which arises in variety of situations where risk is involved. See, for instance, Newbery and Stiglitz (1982).

34    For simplicity we will focus in this section on interlinking of marketing of output and tenancy contracts while similar reasoning applies to discussion regarding marketing raw materials by the landlord to the tenant.

35    There are several other reasons why the landlord might market the tenant's output. If the landlord requires the tenant to market his output solely through himself (the landlord), then he creates a simple way to monitor the output and guarantee that he obtains the agreed share. Another reason is that marketing activity exhibits increasing returns to scale; hence, it is efficient for a specialized agency to market output of many production units together. The landlord may provide such an agency.

36    This is Newbery's (1975) point in response to Bhaduri's (1973) assertion that interlinked credit and tenancy contracts are an obstacle to technological innovation. See Srinivasan (1979) and our (1981b) paper on this issue.

37    We omit the details of the calculations describing the optimal pricing policy of the monopolist. That analysis is exactly parallel to the standard analysis of the optimal set of commodity taxes. There, the problem for the government is to maximize the welfare of consumers, subject to a given budget constraint; here, we are concerned with the dual problem, the maximization of the revenue (of the monopolist) subject to the subsistence level of utility of workers, where the constraint may not be binding.

38    There is an alternative argument for interlinking the consumption good market that is based on consumers' misperception of their "real" income associated with the whole interlinked contract, i.e., they may perceive certain subsidies which they receive immediately (for example, credit, food), more intensely than the disadvantageous terms, the impact of which will be felt only later.

39    In such situations, it is obvious that interlinkage provides one way of effectively circumventing these restrictions. Thus, interlinkages would occur even in the absence of the moral hazard problems, which we have focused on here: see Braverman and Srinivasan (1981).

40    See Stiglitz and Weiss (1980) on the question of *ex ante* vs. *ex post* competitivity in credit markets.

41    When there is a single landlord, and the expected utility constraint is not binding.

## References

Allen, F. (1980): "Control of Capital, Sharecropping, Ability and Information," mimeo, Nuffield College, Oxford.

Arnott, R. and Stiglitz, J. E. (1980): "Equilibrium in Competitive Insurance Markets – The Welfare Economics of Moral Hazard," paper presented to NSF-Bell Laboratories Conference on Information and Decentralization, May.

Bardhan, P. K. (1980): "Interlocking Factor Markets and Agrarian Development: A Review of Issues," *Oxford Economic Papers*, 32, March, 82–98.

——and Rudra, A. (1978): "Interlinkage of Land, Labour and Credit Relations: An Analysis of Village Survey Data in East India," *Economic and Political Weekly*, 13, February, 367–84.

—— and Srinivasan, T. N. (1971): "Crop Sharing Tenancy in Agriculture: A Theoretical and Empirical Analysis," *American Economic Review*, 61, March, 48–64.

Bell, C. and Zusman, P. (1976): "A Bargaining Theoretic Approach to Cropsharing Contracts," *American Economic Review*, 66, September, 578–88.

—— (1980): "On the Interrelationship of Credit and Tenancy Contracts," World Bank, Development Research Center, mimeo, March.

Bhaduri, A. (1973): "Agricultural Backwardness Under Semi-Feudalism," *Economic Journal*, 83, March, 120–37.

—— (1977): "On the Formation of Usurious Interest Rates in Backward Agriculture," *Cambridge Journal of Economics*, 1, December, 341–52.

Binswanger, H. P., Doherty, V. S., Balaramaiah, T., Bhende, M. J., Kshirsagar, K. G., Rao, V. B. and Raju, P. S. S. (1983): "Common Features and Contrasts in Labor Relations in the Semi-Arid Tropics of India," in H. Binswanger and M. Rosenweig (eds), *Rural Labor Markets in Asia: Contractural Arrangements, Employment and Wages*, New Haven: Yale University Press.

Bliss, C. J. and Stern, N. H. (1981): *Palanpur–Studies in the Economy of a North Indian Village*. New Delhi: Oxford University Press.

Braverman, A. and Guasch, J. L. (1981): "Capital Requirements and Interlinked Credit and Tenancy Contracts," discussion paper, World Bank, Development Economics Department, Public Finance Division, September.

—— and Srinivasan, T. N. (1981): "Credit and Sharecropping in Agrarian Societies," *Journal of Development Economics*, 9, December, 289–312.

—— and Stiglitz, J. E. (1981a): "Moral Hazard, Incentive Flexibility and Risk: Cost Sharing Arrangements Under Sharecropping," discussion paper, World Bank, Development Economics Department, Public Finance Division.

—— and —— (1981b): "Landlords, Tenants and Technical Innovations," discussion paper, World Bank, Development Economics Department, Public Finance Division.

Cheung, S. N. (1969): *The Theory of Share Tenancy*: Chicago: University of Chicago Press.

Diamond, P. and Stiglitz, J. E. (1974): "Increases in Risk and in Risk Aversion," *Journal of Economics Theory*, 8, July, 337–60.

Jaynes, J. (1983): "Economic Theory and Land Tenure," in H. Binswanger and M. Rosenzweig (eds), *Rural Labor Markets in Asia: Contractural Arrangements, Employment and Wages*, New Haven: Yale University Press.

Leibenstein, H. (1957): *Economic Backwardness and Economic Growth*. New York: Wiley.

Marshall, A. (1920): *Principles of Economics*. London: Macmillan.

Mirrlees, J. (1976): "A Pure Theory of Underdeveloped Economies," in L. Reynolds (ed) *Agriculture in Development Theory*, New Haven: Yale University Press.

Mitra, P. (1983): "A Theory of Interlinked Rural Transactions," *Journal of Public Economics*, 20, 167–91.

Newbery, D. M. G. (1975): "Tenurial Obstacles to Innovation," *Journal of Development Studies*, 11, July, 263–77.

—— (1977): "Risk Sharing, Sharecropping and Uncertain Labor Markets," *Review of Economic Studies*, 44, October, 585–94.

—— and Stiglitz, J. E. (1979): "Sharecropping, Risk Sharing and the Importance of Imperfect Information," in J. A. Roumasset, J-M. Boussard and I. Singh (eds), *Risk, Uncertainty and Agricultural Development*, SEARCA, A.D.C. Publication.

—— and —— (1982): "Risk Aversion, Supply Response and the Optimality of Random Prices – A Diagrammatical Analysis," *Quarterly Journal of Economics*, 97, February, 1–26.

Reid, J. (1973): "Sharecropping as an Understandable Market Response: The Post Bellum South," *Journal of Economic History*, 33, March, 106–30.

—— (1976): "Sharecropping and Agricultural Uncertainty," *Economic Development and Cultural Change*, 24, April, 549–76.

——(1979): "Tenancy in American History," in J. A. Roumasset, J-M. Boussard and I. Singh (eds), *Risk Uncertainty and Agricultural Development*, SEARCA, A.D.C. Publication.

Rothschild, M. and Stiglitz, J. E. (1970): "Increasing Risk I: A Definition," *Journal of Economic Theory*, 2, September, 225–43.

Srinivasan, T. N. (1979): "Agricultural Backwardness under Semi-Feudalism," *Economic Journal*, 89, June, 416–19.

Stiglitz, J. E. (1974): "Incentives and Risk Sharing in Sharecropping," *Review of Economic Studies*, 61, April, 219–56.

——(1976): "The Efficiency Wage Hypothesis, Surplus Labor and the Distribution of Income in LDCs," *Oxford Economic Papers*, 28, July, 185–207.

——and Weiss, A. (1981): "Credit Rationing in Markets with Imperfect Information," *American Economic Review*, 71, June 393–410.

——and——(1980): "Credit Rationing in Markets with Imperfect Information, Part II," unpublished mimeo.

# CHAPTER 13

# Informational Rents and Property Rights in Land

DILIP MOOKHERJEE

## 1. Introduction

The institution of sharecropping tenancy and its inefficiency has long fascinated development economists, especially following the famous footnotes on the subject in Marshall (1920).[1] The tendency for a landlord to appropriate a fraction of the crop tilled by a tenant, and to interlink the tenancy contract with monopoly provision of credit, appears to many people to be 'semi-feudal' in character, inducing low levels of agricultural productivity. This orthodoxy has been challenged in the last two or three decades on a number of conceptual grounds, following the critique of the Marshallian argument by Cheung (1969). Sharecropping is viewed as providing a reasonable compromise between the need for a wealthy landlord to share risks with a poor tenant, and to provide incentives to the latter to apply effort (Stiglitz, 1974; Newbery, 1977; Bell, 1989; Singh, 1989). Interlinking of tenancy and credit contracts is viewed as an efficient response to the problem of moral hazard on the part of the tenant, to avoid externalities between landlords and creditors (Braverman and Stiglitz, 1982; Bell, 1989).

Nevertheless, the more recent empirical evidence for India in, for example, the works of Bell (1977), Sen (1981) and Shaban (1987), suggests that sharecropping tenancy is characterized by significantly lower productivity compared to owner-cultivated farms based largely on family labour.[2] Moreover, this appears to be linked to greater application of labour input by owner-cultivators rather than variations in soil quality or irrigation. Similar results pertain to the comparison of small owner-cultivated farms relying primarily on family labour, with large ones relying primarily on hired labour. These outcomes are related to significant imperfections in labour markets, such as the divergence of marginal products from wage rates, particularly for small owner-cultivated farms (Bardhan, 1973; Sen, 1981). Compounding these are further imperfections in land markets which prevent the sale of land by landlords to their tenants or hired workers that might be intended to appropriate the productivity benefits of small-scale owner cultivation. These imperfections have motivated arguments for public intervention in land redistribution. These arguments, however, have not been based on a precise articulation of the nature of the market failure that creates a potential role for government.

In this chapter, we pose a set of questions that need to be answered for a better understanding of these issues. First of all, why are tenant farms characterized by lower application of labour effort than are owner-cultivated farms, when both are based on family labour? The typical argument for lower effort under tenancy is the Marshallian effect: tenants appropriate a fraction of the marginal product, whereas owner–cultivators are presumed to receive the entire marginal product. This argument overlooks the fundamental symmetry between the two ownership modes with respect to feasible contractual structures. For instance, what prevents the landlord from designing a tenurial contract that mimics the incentive system for an owner–cultivator? Indeed, a fixed rent contract would also provide tenants with their entire marginal product. Such contracts are believed to be not so widespread owing to the need for landlords to share risks with their tenants, and the limited wealth of the latter which causes tenants to default on fixed rent obligations in times of distress.

However, owner–cultivators are subject to similar risks and wealth constraints as well, which they will seek to alleviate by entering into formal and informal credit and insurance relationships. Townsend (1994), for instance, presents evidence for the substantial degree of consumption smoothing in three Indian villages achieved by such arrangements. These will also be subject to moral hazard, arising from the need to induce appropriate incentives for the cultivator to apply effort and thereby reduce the likelihood of default. Why should the incentive problem for owner–cultivators be any less severe than for tenant farmers? The usual Marshallian argument simply presumes that owner–cultivators obtain a greater share of their marginal product than do comparable tenant farmers, without explaining the underlying reasons.

Similar issues arise in attempting to explain why family labour is cheaper than hired labour. The conventional explanation runs in terms of the incentive problems with respect to hired labour, necessitating costly supervision. It is implicitly presumed that family labour is not subject to any incentive problems, overlooking the moral hazard inherent in the credit and insurance arrangements that owner–cultivators are involved in.

The answer to either of these questions could be sought in terms of owner–cultivators having less access to credit than do tenants or hired workers. If anything, the collateral value of the land owned should permit owner–cultivators *greater* access to credit, so it would be surprising if this hypothesis did turn out to be valid.[3] And even if it were empirically supported, the reasons for this specific form of credit market imperfection would have to be clearly understood.

Second, the fact that tenant farms are characterized by lower levels of labour effort does not imply anything about the relative *welfare* properties of *self-ownership* and *tenancy*. For instance, tenants may be better protected against weather uncertainties than are owner–cultivators, in which case the benefits of such risk-sharing should be weighed against the cost of reduced incentives. An argument for government intervention to promote a transfer of ownership of land to cultivators should be based on an explicit articulation of the nature of market failure inherent in tenancy or hired labour.

Third, what prevents landlords from selling their land to tenants or hired workers, if small owner-cultivated farms are significantly more productive? The empirical evidence suggests that land markets are thin, and that the institution of tenancy or wage labour tends to persist. A number of possible reasons may be advanced for the thinness of land markets: taxes, collateral value of land, risk diversification motives and legal difficulties: these are reviewed further in section 6. Nevertheless, the persistence of tenancy remains a bit of a puzzle, if one believes it to be a genuinely inefficient institution. This question forms part of a wider question concerning the evolution of economic institutions: what are the impediments to institutional changes that would appear to promote both efficiency and equity?

One explanation for the higher productivity of owner-cultivated farms could be based on the hypothesis that tenancy contracts are incomplete, and that cultivators must invest in farm specific assets – such as soil improvement or irrigation – to improve productivity, as in the theory developed by Grossman and Hart (1986), Hart and Moore (1990), Klein, Crawford and Alchian (1978) or Williamson (1975, 1985). In this theory, ownership can be identified with the possession of *ex post* bargaining power: for instance, when contracts are renegotiated. Anticipating that the landlord would opportunistically revise contractual terms at later dates to expropriate the rents from past investments, tenant farmers would have lower incentives to make such investments. In such contexts, a transfer of ownership to the cultivator would enhance farm productivity, as well as total surplus. Nevertheless, in such a setting it would be mutually advantageous for the landlord and the tenant to enter into a land sale. In other words, it would fail to address the third question outlined above.

Consequently, the objective of this chapter is to develop an alternative theory of ownership based on a complete contracting framework. We argue that ownership rights affect the allocation of *ex ante* bargaining power, at the stage where tenancy or credit contracts are initially negotiated. Any given ownership pattern thus generates an *ex ante* Pareto-efficient outcome, implying that different ownership patterns cannot be Pareto ranked. Hence there cannot be any scope for a mutually advantageous land sale from landlord to tenant.

This gives rise to the question: why may the allocation of bargaining power have an impact on effort incentives and farm productivity? Our answer is based on the presence of informational rents which need to be paid to the farmer in order to induce effort incentives. These rents arise from wealth constraints which limit the downside risk to which the farmer can be exposed. The wealth constraints cannot be circumvented by borrowing, since loan contracts are also subject to higher default risk owing to the limited ability for farmers to put up collateral. The informational rents that must accompany the provision of high effort incentives represent a payment from the landlord or moneylender to the farmer. These are pure transfers, with no accompanying deadweight losses. Under self-ownership the farmer earns higher bargaining power, thereby serving to better internalize the pecuniary externality arising from the informational rents.

The main results of the model are the following.

1. Increased *ex ante* bargaining power of the farmer *vis-à-vis* landlords or creditors results in a higher level of effort incentives.
2. Bargaining power is affected by ownership, in conjunction with the structure of tenancy and credit markets, alternative employment opportunities for farmers, and their wealth levels. The effects of ownership on efficiency therefore depend on market structure for tenancy and credit, on farmer wealth and on non-farm employment opportunities.
3. Provided population pressure on land is sufficiently great, landlords will have enough monopoly power on tenancy and labour markets to imply that self-ownership will induce greater bargaining power and therefore higher effort incentives.
4. In such contexts, owner-cultivation will be associated with a higher level of (utilitarian) welfare than tenancy or hired labour farms.

5. Despite this, there will never be any scope for mutually profitable land sales from landlords to tenants, as the latter will be unable to borrow enough to finance the purchase.

The implications for land redistribution policies are the following. Coercive land transfers from landlords to cultivators will result in productivity and welfare improvements, though not a Pareto improvement. As indicated above, the magnitude of such improvements will be higher the greater the population pressure on the land, and the lower the off-farm opportunities of the landless. The effects of such land reforms will then be similar to those of free trade, pollution control or increased competition in markets where losers cannot be compensated suitably for a variety of informational and implementational problems, despite the fact that the gains of those who benefit outweigh these losses. In the present context it is not feasible to require that farmers receiving land be made to compensate the landlords, owing to the limited wealth and borrowing capacity of the former. If the landlords are to be compensated suitably then some third party, such as urban taxpayers, must bear the cost of these compensations. In either case the reform is bound to have distributive consequences, and its success will predictably depend on the relative political strengths of different parties affected by it.

The structure of this chapter is as follows. Section 2 introduces the one-period model with risk-neutral farmers subject to a limited liability constraint. Section 3 then considers the case of a bilateral monopoly between a farmer and a landlord-cum-moneylender. The basic results of this chapter – that is, the productivity difference between the two ownership modes and the non-existence of mutually profitable land sales – are presented in this context. Section 4 discusses how the model can be extended to a market setting with numerous farmers and landlords, and the determinants of bargaining power. Section 5 describes extensions to risk-aversion and multi-period relationships. Finally, Section 6 discusses related empirical and theoretical literature, and concludes by discussing possible directions for future research.

## 2. The Model

We begin by focusing on a single plot of land, and the relationship between two agents: a cultivator or farmer (denoted by F), and a noncultivator (landlord or moneylender, denoted by L). For semantic convenience, we shall refer to the latter party as the lender. The plot can be owned either by the farmer or by the lender (in the latter case L becomes a landlord-cum-lender). When the farmer owns the land, the relationship between the two parties involves the supply of credit by the lender to the farmer; whereas if the lender owns the land, their relationship involves a combination of tenancy (or wage labour) and credit. In our model the tenancy relation is indistinguishable from a wage–labour relation, so the case where the farmer does not own the land can equally be viewed as one involving the management of cultivation by L and hiring in the labour supplied by the farmer.[4]

The nature of the production technology is as follows. There is a single period, which is divided into two points of time: $t = 0$ (beginning) and $1$ (end).[5] Only the farmer can till the land. A fraction $x$ of the overall plot can be farmed, where $x$ lies between 0 and 1. The basic technology is linear: at $t = 0$ a material input worth $Ix$ is needed to farm proportion

$x$ of the plot. At $t = 1$ the output of the farm is realized. Between $t = 0$ and 1, nature intervenes, so the crop output is uncertain. There are two possible values of the output: a normal value $nx$, or a disaster value $dx$, where $d < n$. The probability of a normal crop depends on the level of effort $e \geq 0$ selected by the farmer at $t = 0$, and is denoted by $p(e)$, where $p(\cdot)$ is a strictly increasing, continuously differentiable and concave function satisfying $1 > p(e) > 0$ for all $e$.[6] The value of the crop per unit area cropped, net of the material input requirement, in the normal state is denoted $s = n - 1$, and in the disaster state is $f \equiv d - 1$. Indeed, we shall frequently refer to the state by this value itself.

Agents consume at the end of the period, and no one discounts between beginning and end of the period. In order to survive, the farmer's consumption must be at least above a minimum subsistence level, denoted $\underline{s}$. In order to simplify the analysis, and stay as close as possible to the transferable utility context, we assume that both agents are risk-neutral.[7] So the utility of the lender can be equated with the expected income from lending money or leasing out land. The farmer's utility depends on his consumption $c$ and effort $e$, and is given by $c - D(e)$, where $D$ denotes the disutility of effort. We assume that $D(\cdot)$ is strictly increasing, continuously differentiable and strictly convex. Moreover, $D(0) = D'(0) = 0$.

Next we describe the nature of endowments. The farmer has an exogenous amount of wealth $w$ in the form of liquid assets, which can be used to purchase inputs at the beginning of the period. The remainder can either be used to repay loans or be consumed at the end of the period. The non-farm wealth of the lender, on the other hand, will be assumed to be large enough that she is not subject to any limited liability constraint.

The information structure is as follows. The non-farm wealth $w$ of the farmer, as well as the crop output of the farm, are assumed to be costlessly verifiable by the landlord or lender. On the other hand, the farmer's effort cannot be monitored. All other variables are contractable, such as the respective contributions of the two parties at $t = 0$, the scale of production $x$, and the returns to both parties at $t = 1$. Hence, there is no incompleteness in the contracts that can be feasibly enforced, in the sense of Grossman and Hart (1986).

A *contract* specifies the following: $x$, the scale of cultivation, $I_L$ and $I_F$ the respective contributions of the lender and the farmer to cover the inputs required at $t = 0$, and $F_i$ and $L_i$ their respective receipts from the crop output $ix$ at $t = 1$, where $i$ can equal either $s$ or $f$. Naturally, in order to be feasible, the contract must satisfy

$$I_L + I_F = Ix$$
$$F_i + L_i = (i + I)x$$

In addition, the farmer should be able to survive:

$$c_i \equiv F_i + w - I_F \geq \underline{s} \quad \text{for } i = s, f$$

where $c_i$ denotes his consumption at $t = 1$ when the crop return is $i$.

Such a contract will induce an effort level from the farmer, which maximizes his expected return

$$p(e)c_s + [1 - p(e)]c_f - D(e)$$

The farmer's optimal effort choice can therefore be described as follows: if $c_s \leq c_f$ then zero effort is selected; otherwise it is given by the solution to

$$p'(e)[c_s - c_f] = D'(e)$$

which is strictly positive. Conversely, given any desired level of effort $e$, the spread between consumption in the two states necessary to sustain this in an incentive compatible fashion, is given by

$$c_s - c_f = \alpha(e) \tag{1}$$

where $\alpha(e)$ denotes $D'(e)/p'(e)$, a continuous function which is strictly increasing and satisfies $\alpha(0) = 0$.

This incentive constraint will apply identically in either ownership mode, though the specific interpretations may differ. When the farmer owns the land, and acquires credit from the lender, his downside risk will be limited by virtue of the limited liability constraint $c_f \geq \underline{s}$. In other words, if the nominal repayment obligation is $L_s$, and the farmer cannot feasibly pay this amount in the disaster state, the latter will be interpreted as a default on the loan. The possibility of defaulting on the loan limits the liability of the borrower in the adverse state, therefore limiting his *ex ante* incentive to apply effort. Of course, the extent of loan default will depend on the residual wealth $w - I_F$ of the farmer, which can be interpreted as the loan collateral. Wealthier borrowers are therefore less likely to default, and so likely to apply more effort, which is why they will have greater access to credit. In the tenancy setting, on the other hand, the contract will typically take the interpretation of a cropsharing formula which for the traditional Marshallian reason affects the tenant's incentive to apply labour.

So far we have not discussed the nature of participation constraints. This is because these constraints depend partly on the nature of the market for credit or tenancy, and partly on the pattern of ownership. Nevertheless, there are some lower bounds to the outside opportunities of either party which are independent of ownership or market structure. For instance, the lender cannot obtain a negative return from a contract. Moreover, the farmer can decide to withdraw altogether from the activity of farming, whence he obtains an exogenous net utility of $\bar{U}$ from his next best alternative occupation.[8]

Given the incentive constraint (1), we can redefine a contract as follows: a triple $(x, c_f, e)$ describing respectively the scale of cultivation, consumption of the farmer in the disaster state, and the level of effort induced. The corresponding consumption level of the farmer in the good state is then given by

$$c_s = c_f + \alpha(e)$$

And given the eventual consumption of the farmer in either state, we can derive the net return $R_i$ to the lender in state $i$ as follows:

$$R_i \equiv L_i - I_L = (i + I)x - F_i - I_L = ix - c_i + w$$

since

$$c_i \equiv F_i + w - I_F$$

Letting

$$R(e) \equiv p(e)s + [1 - p(e)f]$$

denote the expected return (net of the material input) when the entire plot is farmed, the expected profit of the lender is thus given by

$$xR(e) + w - [p(e)c_s + \{1 - p(e)\}c_f] \equiv xR(e) + w - c_f - p(e)\alpha(e)$$

It is as if the lender appropriates the entire crop return and wealth of the farmer to start with, and then undertakes the responsibility of providing for the farmer's consumption. Moreover, the particular way in which input costs are shared is immaterial, by virtue of our assumption that there is no consumption need at $t = 0$.

Using the notation $c = (x, c_f, e)$ to denote a contract, the expected return to the lender is given by

$$U_L(c) = xR(e) + w - c_f - p(e)\alpha(e)$$

and to the farmer is

$$U_F(c) = c_f + p(e)\alpha(e) - D(e)$$

For the two parties to enter into such a contract, it must be the case that each obtains at least the (lower bound on their) utility from not participating. Therefore, the set of *feasible contracts* C is defined as comprising contracts $c = (x, c_f, e)$ satisfying the conditions

$$c_f \geq \underline{s}, \qquad U_L(c) \geq 0 \qquad U_F(c) \geq \bar{U} + w \tag{2}$$

However, since the actual benefit from non-participation may exceed the lower bounds $(0, \bar{U} + w)$ incorporated in the above definition of feasibility, not all feasible contracts will be individually rational: either party may have outside points (such as a contract with a different party in a market setting), and disagreement pay-offs need not coincide with 0 and $\bar{U} + w$, depending on the pattern of ownership. The precise level of non-participation utilities will be addressed in subsequent sections.

Finally, we introduce some assumptions that will be retained throughout the rest of the chapter. First, the expected return $R(e)$ from the land net of material input costs is strictly positive at all effort levels. Efficient contracts must then necessarily involve cultivation at the maximal scale $x = 1$, or no cultivation at all. This is true both in a first-best setting (where the effort of the farmer is contractable) as well as in a second-best setting. The first-best must therefore necessarily involve the effort level $e^*$ which maximizes the sum of utilities $R(e) - D(e)$ of the farmer and the lender. For the model to remain interesting, we assume that it is always jointly profitable to farm the land in a first-best setting:

$$R(e^*) - D(e^*) \geq \bar{U} \tag{3}$$

## 3. Bilateral Monopoly

We now consider the simple case where there is exactly one lender and one farmer. In other words, if the two parties fail to agree, then neither can enter into any trade at all, as there are no alternative trading partners. Nevertheless disagreement pay-offs may depend on the pattern of ownership and wealth levels, as explained below.

When the land is owned by the lender, the absence of a contract implies that the farmer cannot till the land, and must necessarily earn his outside opportunity of $\bar{U} + w$. In such a case, the set of feasible contracts coincides with the set of individually rational contracts. But when the farmer owns the land, the absence of contracts merely denies him credit: he can still farm the land if he so wishes. Hence while the lender earns zero in this situation, the farmer may conceivably obtain an expected return in excess of his alternative opportunity by farming the land on the basis of his own resources. In such a case the set of individually rational contracts will be a subset of feasible contracts.

Let $\mathcal{U}$ denote the set of expected utility combinations $(U_F(c), U_L(c))$ corresponding to feasible contracts $c \in C$. Owing to moral hazard, this set could conceivably be non-convex. It may therefore be desirable to allow randomized contracts. In our setting, however, the only randomizations which may be worthwhile will involve *ex ante* randomizations over the effort level. Let the set of such randomized contracts be denoted $C^*$, and the corresponding expected utility combinations be denoted $\mathcal{U}^*$, the convex hull of $\mathcal{U}$ as shown in figure 1.

Under either ownership mode, the chosen contract will be decided on the basis of bargaining between the farmer and the lender. We will assume that the expected pay-off

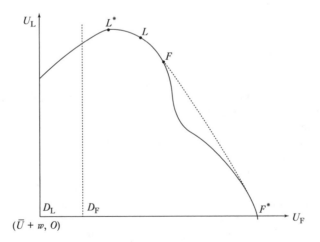

**Figure 1**   [Figure 1.1] Feasible pay-off sets

functions of either are common knowledge. Hence the chosen contract must be Pareto efficient within the class of feasible contracts. So we can restrict attention to the set of efficient points of $\mathcal{U}^*$. Both ownership modes are characterized by the same set of Pareto-efficient contracts. However, since ownership will typically affect the allocation of bargaining power, the precise contract chosen will depend on the nature of ownership.

By virtue of our assumption that $R(e)$ is strictly positive for all effort levels, all efficient contracts must necessarily involve $x = 1$, that is, the entire plot of land ought to be tilled. Therefore, the outcome of either ownership mode will always be the maximal scale of cultivation. The scale of cultivation may, however, be nonmaximal in the event of the two agents failing to agree on a contract (for example, when the farmer owns the land and does not have access to credit).

We now discuss the precise outcomes of disagreement under either ownership mode. When farmers do not own the land, the absence of a contract corresponds to the case where there is no farming nor supply of credit:

$$x = I_L = I_F = F_i = L_i \qquad \text{for } i = s, f$$

In this case the disagreement pay-offs are 0 and $\bar{U} + w$ respectively for lenders and farmers, so the set of feasible contracts coincides with the set of individually rational contracts. However, when farmers own the land, then the absence of a contract means that there is no credit available:

$$I_L = 0 = L_i \qquad i = s, f$$

But farmers can farm the land on the basis of their own resources, that is, at any scale satisfying $Ix \leq w$, and subsequently have available in the disaster state a consumption level of $fx + w$. It is evident that it will be in the farmers' interests to operate on as large a scale as possible, at $x = w/I$. Therefore in the absence of any credit, farmers can feasibly farm the land as long as the return on the crop in the adverse state enables them to survive: that is, as long as

$$\left[1 + \frac{f}{I}\right] w \geq \underline{s}$$

In other words, farming without any credit is feasible only for farmers with a wealth level of at least

$$\underline{w} \equiv \frac{\underline{s}}{1 + \frac{f}{I}}$$

For poorer farmers, the disagreement pay-offs are identical to those of farmers that do not own the land.

For landowning farmers with $w \geq \underline{w}$, the pay-off consequent on absence of credit depends on whether it is in their interests to farm the land rather than abandon it for an alternative occupation. Let $x(w)$ denote min $[I, w/I]$, the maximal scale at which such farmers can cultivate. Then the highest utility they can obtain from cultivation is given by

$$\Pi(w) \equiv \max_e [x(w)R(e) - D(e) + w]$$

Clearly for $w$ sufficiently low this will fall below $\bar{U} + w$, while for $w \geq I$ this exceeds $\bar{U} + w$.[9] Hence there exists $\tilde{w}$ between 0 and $I$ such that for all landowning farmers with wealth levels above $\tilde{w}$, it pays to cultivate even in the absence of any credit. For all poorer farmers, the credit constraint forces them to abandon cultivation.

The disagreement pay-offs under farmer ownership and bilateral monopoly are therefore as follows. The lenders' disagreement pay-off is always zero. The farmers' disagreement pay-off depends on their wealth. If $w \leq \tilde{w}$, then it is $\bar{U} + w$, just the same as when a lender owned the land. But if farmers are wealthier, they can profitably cultivate on the basis of their own resources in the absence of any credit, leading to a higher disagreement pay-off $\Pi(w)$. The set of individually rational pay-offs is thus smaller than the set of feasible pay-offs. This is illustrated in Figure 1. With a wealth above $\tilde{w}$, the disagreement pay-off $D_F$ under farmer ownership lies to the right of the disagreement pay-off $D_L$ under lender ownership. Indeed, if the farmers' wealth exceeds the maximal input required ($I$) then they have no need for credit at all, and the disagreement point coincides with $F^*$, where farmers have all the bargaining power.

A transfer of ownership of the land to farmers will (under most reasonable bargaining solutions) thus allow them to appropriate a larger fraction of the surplus from trade.[10] The extent of increase in the farmers' share is increasing in their wealth level (zero until $\tilde{w}$, and positive thereafter). The contract actually resulting under farmer ownership ($F$ in Figure 1) will thus differ from that under lender ownership ($L$).

The question then arises: do different contracts on the Pareto frontier differ in terms of farmer effort, or efficiency? Or do they merely reflect different distributions of income? To address this question, it helps initially to compare the two polar contracts $L^*$ and $F^*$ where the lender and the farmer respectively have all the bargaining power. The comparison between contracts $L$ and $F$ actually resulting under the two ownership modes will turn out to be qualitatively similar.

The contract $F^*$ where the farmer has all the bargaining power is obtained as the solution to the following problem:

$$\max_{e, c_s, c_f} p(e)\alpha(e) + c_f - D(e)$$

subject to:

$$c_f \geq \underline{s}$$
$$R(e) + w \geq p(e)\alpha(e) + c_f \tag{4}$$

The effort level resulting is described as follows

PROPOSITION 1    *The effort level in the contract where the farmer has all the bargaining power is given by the solution to:*

$$max\ R(e) - D(e)$$

*subject to*

$$R(e) + w \geq \underline{s} + p(e)\alpha(e) \tag{5}$$

The reasoning is straightforward: given the lender's breakeven constraint, and an effort level $e$, an upper bound to the expected value of consumption is given by $R(e) + w$, so an upper bound to the expected utility of the farmer is given by $R(e) - D(e) + w$. This bound can be achieved by setting

$$c_f = R(e) + w - p(e)\alpha(e)$$

and

$$c_s = c_f + \alpha(e)$$

On the other hand, if the constraint is not satisfied, then the effort $e$ is not feasible.

Turn now to the contract $L^*$ where the lender owns the land and has all the bargaining power. This will solve the following problem:

$$\max_{e,\, c_s,\, c_f} R(e) + w - p(e)\alpha(e) - c_f$$

*subject to:*

$$c_f \geq \underline{s}$$
$$p(e)\alpha(e) + c_f - D(e) \geq \bar{U} + w \tag{6}$$

The effort level selected in this contract is described below.

PROPOSITION 2

1.   *Given effort $e$, the contract under landlord monopoly which implements $e$ awards consumption to the tenant as follows:*

$$c_f = \underline{s} + q(e)$$

$$c_s = \underline{s} + q(e) + \alpha(e)$$

   *where*

$$q(e) \equiv \max[0, \bar{U} + D(e) - p(e)\alpha(e) - \underline{s} + w]$$

2.   *The effort level under landlord monopoly* $e_L$ *is determined by solving:*

$$\max_e [R(e) - p(e)\alpha(e) - q(e)]$$

Given effort $e$ which the landlord seeks to induce, the minimum conceivable levels of consumption for the tenant in the two states are $\underline{s}$ and $\underline{s} + \alpha(e)$ respectively, if the participation constraint, is ignored. Such a contract will indeed satisfy the participation constraint if $q(e) = 0$. Otherwise the landlord must pay $q(e)$ additionally in both states to induce voluntary participation. This explains part 1. Therefore $q(e) = 0$ implies that the tenant earns an 'informational rent', the result of a minimum limit on consumption in every state, combined with the need to provide the tenant with the requisite incentive to apply effort. With multiple potential tenants, this corresponds to the case of involuntary unemployment and tenancy 'queues'. This arises when the effort $e$ sought to be induced is 'high'. This is the situation depicted in figure 2, where the participation constraint of the farmer is not binding at the tenancy solution where the landlord has all the bargaining power.

The effective *cost of labour effort* as perceived by the landlord is given by the upper envelope of the two functions

$$\bar{U} + w - \underline{s} + D(e) \qquad \text{and} \qquad p(e)\alpha(e)$$

For small values of effort, the first function dominates, provided $\bar{U} + w - \underline{s}$ is positive. For such effort levels, the tenant obtains no informational rents, and marginal cost of effort from the point of view of the landlord coincides with the tenant's marginal disutility of effort $D'(e)$. For larger effort levels, the tenant earns informational rents, as the required incentive bonus grows sufficiently. Over this range the marginal cost of effort as perceived

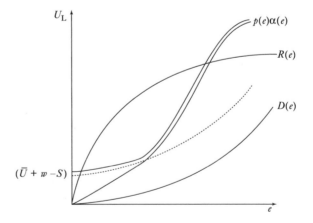

**Figure 2**   [Figure 1.2] Effort cost under tenancy

by the landlord is higher, as it must additionally include the marginal informational rents paid to the tenant.[11]

It is therefore plausible that the effort level selected under landlord monopoly is less than that under farmer monopoly, as confirmed by our first main result:

Theorem 1

1. *For any effort level optimal under landlord monopoly, there exists a (weakly) higher effort level which is optimal under farmer monopoly. Moreover, the effort level under landlord monopoly is strictly lower, as long as it provides a positive surplus to both parties.*
2. *The sum of expected utilities of the lender and the farmer under landlord monopoly is smaller than under farmer monopoly, and strictly smaller as long as landlord monopoly generates a positive surplus for the farmer.*

Proof   Let $e_L$ and $e_F$ denote effort levels optimal under monopoly of the landlord and the farmer respectively. It is readily verified that the monopoly landlord obtains a non-negative expected profit if and only if the monopoly farmer obtains an expected return no less than his alternative $\bar{U} + w$. That is, the two monopoly problems have identical feasible sets. Therefore a switch from $e_F$ to $e_L$ cannot decrease the landlord's surplus when he has monopoly power:

$$R(e_L) - p(e_L)\alpha(e_L) - q(e_L) \geq R(e_F) - p(e_F)\alpha(e_F) - q(e_F)$$

Now suppose that $e_L > e_F$. Noting that

$$p\alpha + q = \max\{p\alpha, \bar{U} + w - \underline{s} + D\}$$

it follows that

$$p(e_L)\alpha(e_L) + q(e_L) - [p(e_F)\alpha(e_F) + q(e_F)] \geq D(e_L) - D(e_F)$$

Hence

$$R(e_L) - D(e_L) \geq R(e_F) - D(e_F)$$

so $e_L$ must be optimal as well for the owner-cultivator.

If the farmer earns positive surplus under landlord monopoly, $q(e_L) = 0$, and

$$\underline{s} + p(e_L)\alpha(e_L) - D(e_L) > \bar{U} + w$$

Hence for a neighbourhood of $e_L$, $q(e) \equiv 0$. So $e_L$ must locally maximize $R(e) - p(e)\alpha(e)$, implying the first-order condition

$$R'(e_L) = D'(e_L) + p(e_L)\alpha'(e_L)$$

This implies $R'(e_L) > D'(e_L)$, and so $R'(e) > D'(e)$ for all $e \leq e_L$. Reasoning in a manner similar to the previous paragraph, it follows that no effort less than $e_L$ can be optimal for the monopoly farmer. Since the landlord obtains a positive surplus at $e_L$, a small increase in effort beyond this is feasible and hence profitable under farmer monopoly.

Under farmer monopoly, the lender earns zero income, while the farmer has an expected utility of

$$R(e_F) - D(e_F) + w$$

When the landlord has monopoly power on the other hand, his expected income is

$$R(e_L) + w - EC$$

while the farmer's expected utility is $EC - D(e_L)$, where $EC$ denotes expected consumption. So the sum of expected utility under farmer monopoly is

$$R(e_F) - D(e_F) + w$$

while that under landlord monopoly is

$$R(e_L) - D(e_L) + w$$

Now apply the argument of 2 above.

The effect of a partial shift of bargaining power in favour of the farmer will be qualitatively similar. Since the set of feasible utilities $\mathcal{U}^*$ is convex, any point on its efficiency frontier can be described as a solution to the maximization of a welfare-weighted sum of utilities over this set: select $c_f$ and $e$ to maximize

$$R(e) + w - c_f - p(e)\alpha(e) + \beta\big[c_f + p(e)\alpha(e) - D(e)\big]$$

subject to $c_f \geq \underline{s}$, where $\beta$ denotes the welfare weight of the farmer relative to the lender. Since the outcome of farmer ownership ($F$ in Figure 1) awards a greater share of the surplus to the farmer than the outcome ($L$ in Figure 1) when he does not own the land, the implicit welfare weight of the farmer will be higher under self-ownership than under tenancy. Since the effort level is selected to maximize

$$R(e) - D(e) + (\beta - 1)[p(e)\alpha(e) - D(e)]$$

in an unconstrained fashion, it immediately follows that the effort level under farmer ownership will be higher.[12]

The underlying explanation for the greater application of labour effort under self-ownership is similar to that conventionally advanced in the literature: that the labour of others is perceived as 'more expensive' than own-labour, owing to incentive reasons. But the conventional explanations of this phenomenon are incomplete, and even misleading in some respects. As explained in section 1, they are based on an implicit notion that owner–cultivators have *no* access to credit or insurance. This overlooks the fundamental symmetry in contractual structures between different ownership modes.

Our theory is based instead on the externality arising from the informational rents accruing to the farmer. To the landlord these rents represent a cost, whilst to the farmer they constitute a benefit. So the farmer desires a higher effort level than does the landlord, and a shift of bargaining power towards the farmer as a result of transfer of ownership causes a higher effort level to be applied. The real cause of the inefficiency of tenancy is a pecuniary externality: the landlord disregards the benefit of higher effort levels accruing to the farmer in the form of higher informational rents. Increasing the bargaining power of the farmer allows greater internalization of these rents.

Turning now to the question of the possible sale of land from the landlord to the tenant, it is obvious that such a sale cannot be mutually advantageous to both parties. This follows from the premise that contracts are complete, so the outcome under either ownership structure cannot be Pareto dominated by the other. Otherwise, if there was scope for a mutually advantageous sale, then both landlord and tenant would be better off following the sale. The same allocation could, however, be achieved by the landlord under tenancy with the design of a tenancy contract that would mimic the effect of the sale. For instance, the landlord could select a composite contract which combined a fixed rent exactly equal to the price of the land, with a supplemental contract which exactly replicated the credit contract arising after the land sale. Since the land sale resulted in a Pareto improvement, this contract would also yield a Pareto improvement over the original tenancy contract, thereby contradicting the premise that the latter was optimally chosen. We therefore formally note:

THEOREM 2 *Starting with a situation where the land is owned by a landlord, a voluntary sale of land to the tenant will never occur.*

Nevertheless, one might wonder how to reconcile this result with that of Theorem 1: if a transfer of ownership increases the welfare of the farmer by more than it reduces the welfare of the landlord, what prevents the former from purchasing the land at a price which compensates the landlord sufficiently? The limited wealth of the farmer plays a crucial role here: the amount that is needed to compensate the landlord is typically likely to greatly exceed the wealth of the tenant. What prevents the farmer from borrowing (either from the landlord directly, or from a third party lender) to finance the land purchase?

To understand the result better, it is worth answering this question directly. Suppose that a mutually advantageous sale were to occur at price $P$. Let the post-sale contract be denoted $(\tilde{c}_f, \tilde{e})$, and the pre-sale contract be $(c_f^L, e_L)$. Since the farmer must be better off:

$$\tilde{c}_f + p(\tilde{e})\alpha(\tilde{e}) - D(\tilde{e}) > c_f^L + p(e_L)\alpha(e_L) - D(e_L)$$

Moreover, the landlord must also benefit:

$$P > R(e_L) + w - c_f^L - p(e_L)\alpha(e_L) \tag{7}$$

But the pre-sale contract $c_f^{\mathrm{L}}, e_{\mathrm{L}}$ was Pareto efficient, so the landlord must have preferred the pre-sale contract to the post-sale contract:

$$R(\tilde{e}) + w - p(\tilde{e})\alpha(\tilde{e}) - \tilde{c}_f \leq R(e_{\mathrm{L}}) + w - p(e_{\mathrm{L}})\alpha(e_{\mathrm{L}})\alpha(e_{\mathrm{L}}) - c_f^{\mathrm{L}}$$

This implies that the lender must fail to break even in the post-sale situation:

$$R(\tilde{e}) + (w - P) - p(\tilde{e})\alpha(\tilde{e}) - \tilde{c}_f \leq R(e_{\mathrm{L}}) + w - p(e_{\mathrm{L}})\alpha(e_{\mathrm{L}}) - c_f^{\mathrm{L}} - P < 0$$

the last inequality following from condition (7). Hence the farmer will be unable to obtain the credit necessary for the purchase.

One way of understanding this result is that the land sale exerts a wealth effect: the farmer's debts grow as a result of the land purchase loan, which exacerbates the moral hazard associated with repayment of the loan. Owing to the 'limited liability' of the farmer, he must be guaranteed at least $\underline{s}$ in the disaster state; whilst in the good state the farmer must repay a larger amount. The debt 'overhang' reduces the farmer's incentive to exert effort on the farm after purchasing it. Anticipating this, lenders assess a default likelihood high enough that they are unwilling to advance the loan.

Alternatively, if the farmer finances the purchase from his own assets, the purchase lowers his wealth subsequent to the purchase. This reduces the collateral available to lenders, with the consequence that he will not be able to obtain the credit necessary to sustain the intended productivity advantages of owner cultivation.

## 4. A Market Setting

We now introduce multiple farmers, plots of land, and lenders-cum-landlords, and explain a number of additional considerations that now bear on the efficiency of tenant or wage labour farms relative to those cultivated by their owners. The main new feature is that the allocation of bargaining power will depend additionally on market structure: the shorter side of the market will tend to obtain a larger share of the surplus.

First note that landless farmers will operate in a different market compared with those that do have land. The former will be seeking tenancy leases which, owing to the usual moral hazard reasons (Braverman and Stiglitz, 1982), will take the form of interlinked tenancy-cum-credit contracts. The suppliers in this market will be landowners who do not plan to cultivate the land themselves. Landowning farmers will operate on the pure credit market on the other hand. The structure of the two markets could be quite different. In contrast to the market for leasing land, the demanders for credit *per se* will include landowning peasants as well as those without any land to farm at all. The suppliers will include all those with money to lend, which will typically include all the landowners that appear in the tenancy market, plus other non-landowning agents of sufficient wealth. Both markets are typically somewhat oligopolistic in nature, with a few large suppliers and numerous small purchasers. There is no *a priori* reason to believe that one market will be characterized by more monopoly power than another. To that extent the conclusions of the earlier section may be reversed, if it is the case that the market for pure credit is characterized by significantly greater monopoly power.

Nevertheless, it is typical of many developing countries, especially in Asia, to have high population densities and large reserves of landless workers. The intrinsic shortage of land in such countries would be expected to confer relatively large degrees of bargaining power to landlords with their tenants. The model developed below confirms this idea: with a sufficiently large number of poor landless workers relative to the land available for tenancy cultivation, the equilibrium contracts are approximated by the landlord monopoly solution described in section 3. In such contexts, therefore, owner-cultivators will have at least as much bargaining power as tenant-cultivators, and often more, so self-ownership will again tend to be the more productive mode.

Consider a village economy with a number of landless farmers or would-be-tenants $T$, and a number of landlords $L$, both of which are given. Technology and preferences are as in the previous section: in particular, a single farmer can cultivate a single plot of land, and landlords are assumed unable or unwilling to farm. For the sake of simplicity, we assume there are no landowning farmers, in order to abstract from the cultivate/lease-out decision. Moreover, no landlord owns more than a single plot.[13] We assume there is no market for land purchases: this can be justified by the arguments in section 3. So we can focus on the outcome of the market for tenancy leases.

We also additionally impose the following two assumptions. First, tenancy is *strictly viable* in the sense that there exists an effort level $e$ such that:

$$R(e) + w - \underline{s} - p(e)\alpha(e) > 0$$
$$\underline{s} + p(e)\alpha(e) - D(e) > \bar{U} + w \tag{8}$$

In other words, it is possible for both landlord and tenant to obtain a positive surplus simultaneously. Second, all potential tenants are homogenous with a common wealth level satisfying

$$w < \underline{s} + p(e_{\mathrm{L}}^{*})\alpha(e_{\mathrm{L}}^{*}) - D(e_{\mathrm{L}}^{*}) - \bar{U} \tag{9}$$

where $e_{\mathrm{L}}^{*}$ denotes an unconstrained maximizer of $R(e) - p(e)\alpha(e)$. This implies that tenants will earn a positive surplus in any Pareto-efficient contract.

The nature of the market for tenancy contracts is assumed to be as follows. The market opens at date $t = 0$, whereby landlords and farmers are matched with one another. We consider the case where there is *surplus labour* in the sense that $T > L$: that is, there are more farmers than plots of land available. Then at $t = 0$, every landlord is matched with a farmer, while a farmer is matched with a landlord with probability $L/T$. Those farmers remaining unmatched must await future dates in the hope of being matched with some landlord, should any landlords decide to remain in the market beyond $t = 0$. Then at $t = 0$, matched pairs bargain over the set of feasible contracts, and we assume that the outcome of this is represented by the Nash bargaining solution over the pay-off set $\mathcal{U}^{*}$, with status quo pay-offs given by the continuation pay-offs expected from $t = 1$ onwards.[14] If a landlord-farmer pair agree on a contract, they leave the market. Otherwise they stay in the market, and the same process repeats itself from $t = 1$ with the agents who remain without a contract. Finally, the cost of delayed agreement is represented by a discount factor $\delta \in (0, 1)$, so an agreement yielding utility $u$ to any agent at the following date is equivalent to an agreement yielding utility $\delta u$ at the current date.

This is essentially the process studied by Osborne and Rubinstein (1990, ch. 6) for a market involving many buyers and sellers of an indivisible good. As in their analysis we assume that the market behaves in an 'anonymous' fashion (that is, agents in the market do not condition their behaviour in a bargaining encounter on their experience in previous encounters, or on the identity of their opponents).

Note that the extent of 'supply-side-shortness' in the market is constant at all dates when it opens, since the number of landlords who leave the market at any date exactly equals the number of farmers who leave. The process continues until there are no landlords left in the market. Each farmer remaining without a contract then proceeds to alternative employment and earns an expected utility of $\bar{U} + w$.

Given the 'anonymity' assumption, the outcome of the continuation game from any date onwards is a function only of the number of farmers and landlords remaining in the market at that date, which effectively becomes the 'state variable'. A (Markov) perfect equilibrium of the market game is thus represented by a set of functions $c^*(B,S), V_L(B,S), V_F(B,S)$, which describe the contract $c^*$ agreed upon by a landlord matched with a tenant, and their expected pay-offs, for any continuation game starting with $B$ 'buyers' or farmers, and $S$ 'sellers' or landlords. Clearly, $B$ is any integer less than or equal to the initial number of farmers $T$, and similarly $S$ is less than or equal to $L$. Moreover, attention can be further restricted to $(B,S)$ pairs satisfying $B - S = T - L$.

Introduce the convention that failure to agree on a contract is defined as agreeing on a null contract, which is denoted by $N$. Then such an equilibrium must satisfy the following conditions.

1. $c^*(B,S) = N$ if it is the case that there exists no contract $c^* \in \mathscr{C}^*$ such that

$$U_L(c^*) \geq \delta V_L(B - S + 1, 1)$$

and

$$U_F(c^*) \geq \delta V_F(B - S + 1, 1)$$

Otherwise $c^*(B,S)$ must be selected from $\mathscr{C}^*$ to maximize the Nash product

$$[U_L(c^*) - \delta V_L(B - S + 1, 1)][U_F(c^*) - \delta V_F(B - S + 1, 1)] \tag{10}$$

2. $V_L(B, S) = \begin{cases} U_L[c^*(B,S)] & \text{if } c^*(B,S) \neq N \\ \delta V_L(B,S) & \text{otherwise} \end{cases}$

3. $V_F(B, S) = \begin{cases} \dfrac{s}{B} U_F[c^*(B,S)] + \left(1 - \dfrac{S}{B}\right)(\bar{U} + w) & \text{if } c^*(B,S) \neq N \\ \delta V_F(B,S) & \text{otherwise} \end{cases}$

The selected contract is therefore the Nash bargaining solution corresponding to status quo pay-offs representing the continuation value of remaining in the market while all other matched pairs enter into an agreement and leave the market at the current date. This presumes that there exists a contract which gives both landlord and farmer at least their continuation pay-offs from the next date onwards; otherwise there can be no agreement. In the event that there is scope for a mutually profitable contract between any given pair, there is a similar scope for all other matched pairs at any date. This is the reason why each pair expects all other pairs to enter into a non-null contract and leave the market at the current date.

Continuation pay-offs for the landlord are defined in an obvious fashion: it is the utility value of the equilibrium contract from the current date, assuming this is non-null; otherwise it is the continuation pay-off from the next date, discounted back to the current date. For the farmer, however, it must incorporate the probability of being selected in a match with a landlord at the current date: if selected it is given by the value of the expected equilibrium contract; otherwise it is the discounted value of continuing in the market from tomorrow. The latter of course equals the utility consequent on not receiving a contract at all, if currently matched partners are all expected to enter into a non-null contract and leave the market at the current date. Otherwise if no currently matched partners are not expected to conclude an agreement, then the market is expected to be in the same position at the next date.

It is easy to see that given our strict viability assumption (8), there cannot be an equilibrium where matched pairs ever fail to agree upon a non-null contract. Otherwise it follows from the expression for continuation pay-offs $V_L(B, S)$ and $V_F(B, S)$ that these pay-offs are equal to zero. Then (8) implies that there does exist a non-null contract which gives both parties a pay-off strictly greater than their status quo payoffs, so the equilibrium contract must be non-null.

The main result of this section is the following.

Theorem 3:

1. *A Markov perfect equilibrium exists.*
2. *Let $\eta > 0$ be given. Then there exists $\delta^* \in (0, 1)$ and integer $K^*$ such that if $\delta \in (\delta^*, 1)$ and the degree of surplus labour $T - L$ exceeds $K^*$, every Markov perfect equilibrium necessarily yields a contract generating utility for each landlord within an $\eta$-neighbourhood of the landlord monopoly solution described in the previous section.*

Proof
(i) Let $\{U_L^*, U_F^*\}$ and $\{U_L^0, U_F^0\}$ denote the utilities associated with the landlord monopoly and farmer monopoly solutions respectively.
Let $eff(\mathcal{U}^*)$ denote the set of Pareto-efficient pay-offs of the set $\mathcal{U}^*$. Finally, define

$$G \equiv \{(u_L, u_F) \in [0, U_L^*] \times [\bar{U} + w, U_F^0] \mid \exists (\bar{u}_L, \bar{u}_F) \in eff(\mathcal{U}^*)$$
$$\text{which Pareto dominates}(u_L, u_F)\}$$

Clearly, $\mathcal{U}^*$ is a subset of $G$, both sets being convex and compact. Given $v \in G$, let $\mathcal{U}_v^*$ denote the set of points of $\mathcal{U}^*$ satisfying $(u_L, u_F) \geq \delta v$, also a convex set.
Define a correspondence $S$ from $G$ to itself with the property that $u \in S(v)$ for $v \in G$ if and only if

$$u_L = u_L^*, u_F = \frac{1}{B - S + 1} u_F^* + (1 - \frac{1}{B - S + 1})(\bar{U} + w)$$

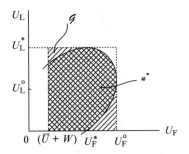

**Figure 3**   [Figure 1.3] Feasible pay-off sets

where $(u_L^*, u_F^*)$ maximizes the Nash product $[u_L - \delta v_L][u_F - \delta v_F]$ over the set $\mathcal{U}_v^*$. This is non-empty-valued. It is also convex-valued: $u_L^*, u_F^*$ are selected to maximize a strictly quasi-concave function over a convex set. So it is defined uniquely, unless it so happens that either $u_L = \delta v_L$ for all $(u_L, u_F) \in \mathcal{U}_v^*$, or $u_F = \delta v_F$ for all such points. In the latter case every point in $\mathcal{U}_v^*$ solves the maximization problem, so this entire set is optimal. Finally, note that

$$\mathcal{U}_v^* \equiv \mathcal{U}^* \cap \mathcal{H} \quad \text{where } \mathcal{H}_v \equiv \{(u_L, u_F) \in \mathbb{R}^2 | (u_L, u_F) \geq \delta . v\}$$

Since the correspondence $\mathcal{H}_v$ is continuous in $v$, it follows that $\mathcal{U}_v^*$ is also continuous. Hence the Maximum Theorem assures that $S(v)$ is upper-semicontinuous in $v$, and by Kakutani's Theorem there exists a fixed point $V^* \in S(V^*)$. Moreover, by construction, there exists $c^* \in \mathcal{C}^*$ which maximizes

$$[U_L(c) - \delta V_{L^*}][U_F(c) - \delta V_F^*]$$

over $C^*$, whilst $V_L^* = U_L(c^*)$ and

$$V_F^* = \frac{1}{B - S + 1} U_F(c^*) + \left(1 - \frac{1}{B - S + 1}\right)(\bar{U} + w)$$

Define

$$c^*(B - S + 1, 1) = c^*(B, S)$$

as the contract $c^*$, and $V_L(B - S + 1, 1)$ and $V_F(B - S + 1, 1)$ equal to $V_L^*$ and $V_F^*$ respectively. Finally, define

$$V_L^*(B, S) = U_L[c^*(B, S)]$$

and

$$V_F(B,S) = \frac{S}{B} U_F[c^*(B,S)] + \left(1 - \frac{S}{B}\right)(U + w)$$

This represents a Markov perfect equilibrium.

(ii) We first claim that there exists integer $K^*$ and a number $k > 0$ such that for $(B - S) > K^*$, every point $U$ on the Pareto-efficient frontier of $\mathcal{U}^*$ satisfies

$$U_F - \delta V_F(\bar{U}_F, B, S) > k$$

for all $\tilde{U}_L, \tilde{U}_F \in \mathcal{U}^*$, and all $\delta \in (0,1)$, where $V_F(\tilde{U}_F, B, S)$ denotes

$$\frac{1}{B - S + 1}\tilde{U}_F + \left[1 - \frac{1}{B - S + 1}\right](\tilde{U} + w)$$

Take $k_1 \in (0, U_F^* - \bar{U} - w)$, so that $U_F > \bar{U} + w + k_1$ for all $u$ in eff $(\mathcal{F})$. Next select $k \in (0, k_1)$, $\theta \in (0, k_1 - k)$ and integer $K^*$ such that

$$\frac{1}{K^* + 1}[U_F^0 - (\bar{U} + w)] < \theta$$

This is possible since $U_F^0 \geq U_F^* > \bar{U} + w$: that is, the tenant obtains positive surplus even when the landlord has all the bargaining power. This implies that

$$|V_F(\tilde{U}_F, B, S) - (\tilde{U} + w)| < \theta$$

whenever $B - S > K^*$, for all $(\tilde{U}_L, \tilde{U}_F) \in \mathcal{U}^*$. It follows that

$$U_F - \delta V_F(\tilde{U}_F, B, S) > U_F - V_F(\tilde{U}_F, B, S) > k_1 - \theta > k$$

thus establishing our claim.

Suppose the result in (ii) is false. Then given $\eta > 0$, we can find a sequence of discount factors $\delta^n \in (0,1)$ $\delta^n \to 1$, and levels of surplus labour $T_n - L_n > K^*$ and a corresponding sequence of equilibrium payoffs $(U_L^n, U_F^n)$ such that $U_L^n < U_L^* - \eta$ for all $n$. Let $(U_L, U_F)$ be a limit point of this sequence, so $U_L \leq U_L^* - \eta$. Then the corresponding sequence of Nash products

$$N^n \equiv \left(U_L^n - \delta^n V_L^n\right)\left(U_F^n - \delta^n V_F^n\right)$$

must be converging to 0, since

$$U_L^n - \delta^n V_L^n = (1 - \delta^n)U_L^n \to 0$$

However, it is feasible for a landlord and tenant to select the landlord monopoly contract which generates the utility pair $(U_L^*, U_F^*)$ and a sequence of Nash products $[U_L^* - \delta^n V_L^n][U_F^* - \delta^n V_F^n]$ which is bounded away from zero, using the fact that

$$\left(U_L^* - \delta^n V_L^n\right) \to U_L^* - U_L \geq \eta$$

and the result of claim 1. This contradicts the hypothesis that the equilibrium contracts maximize the Nash product for large $n$.

The main implication of this result is that farmers in owner-cultivated farms will have at least as much bargaining power with their creditors as will tenant farmers with their landlords, *irrespective of the structure of the market for credit*. Indeed, a sufficient condition for owner-cultivators to obtain a strictly higher share is that their autarky pay-off exceeds that obtained in the landlord monopoly contract. Then our results concerning relative productivity of the two modes of ownership will be as in the case of a bilateral monopoly.

A second implication is that the productivity of tenant farms will be lower, the higher the population pressure on land (as measured by the land : labour ratio). This suggests that the effect of ownership on farm productivity will typically depend on demographic patterns. Precise predictions concerning productivity effects of ownership are rendered difficult because of the difficulty of saying anything about the effect of higher population pressure on the structure of credit markets. But our model is consistent with the productivity differential (and correspondingly the benefits from land redistribution programmes) being higher in overpopulated regions.

## 4.1. Other comparative static properties

We briefly describe a number of other determinants of farm productivity in our model. These could in principle be tested from available data and, if valid, provide useful guidance to policy. In what follows, we shall restrict attention to overpopulated economies where theorem 3 applies to ensure that tenant farms are characterized by the landlord monopoly contract. Moreover, credit markets are also assumed to assign significant monopoly power to lenders, with the effect that owner–cultivators are pressed down to their autarky pay-off levels.

First, consider the effects of varying farmers' wealth levels. For very low wealth levels, there will be no productivity difference between owner-cultivated and tenant farms, as the disagreement pay-offs for both kinds of farmers equals $\bar{U} + w$. There are 'queues' for tenancy contracts among landless farmers, and landlords will attempt to hire the wealthiest farmers first: so 'tenancy ladders' will emerge, for reasons similar to those analysed by Shetty (1988). Within this range, small increases in the farmer's wealth are captured entirely by landlords and lenders (for example, in the form of lower defaults or repayments on past loans), providing such farmers with minimal incentives to augment their wealth and escape a 'poverty trap'. For intermediate wealth levels, the farmers owning their own land will be able to do better than $\bar{U} + w$ by farming the land even in the absence of any credit. They will then enjoy a greater share of the gains from trade compared with tenant farmers, and consequently apply higher levels of effort. They will also derive the full benefit from an increase in their wealth levels, unlike tenant farmers, and so have greater incentives to invest elsewhere to increase their non-farm wealth. Tenancy ladders continue to persist over this range. Finally, as wealth levels grow sufficiently large, the disagreement pay-offs for tenant farmers exceed $\bar{U} + w$, tenancy queues and ladders disappear, and the productivity of tenant farmers grows, eventually arriving at first-best levels. Similarly effort levels of owner–cultivators also grow, eventually arriving at the first-best level. With high enough wealth levels, the productivity gap tends to disappear again, as the Coase Theorem begins to apply. Hence the productivity gap between tenancy and owner-cultivated farms tends to be highest for intermediate wealth levels (figure 4).

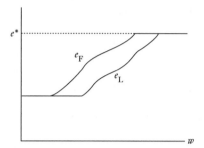

**Figure 4** [Figure 1.4] Effort under tenancy and owner cultivation

Next consider the effect of increasing non-farm opportunities available to the landless, which increase $\bar{U}$. Clearly, owner-cultivated farms are unaffected, as long as the alternative opportunities do not grow so large as to prompt the farmer to abandon cultivation. On the other hand, tenancy farm outcomes will depend on $\bar{U}$. If these alternative opportunities are very unattractive, poor tenant farmers will enjoy a surplus, and increases in their outside options will have no effect at all on productivity in tenant farms. However, when $\bar{U}$ increases sufficiently, tenancy queues and surpluses will disappear, and productivity will consequently increase. This suggests that public employment programmes for the landless may have the beneficial side-effect of increasing productivity on tenant farms, and may even be viewed as a substitute for land redistribution programmes from this viewpoint.

## 5. Risk-Aversion and Dynamics

So far we have assumed farmers to be risk-neutral with respect to consumption variations above the subsistence level. This is clearly unrealistic, especially for low consumption levels. Suppose instead that the farmer has a von Neumann–Morgenstern utility function defined over his consumption and effort level, which is strictly concave. This function can take many different forms. For instance, it could be a function of $c - D(e)$; whence the effort disutility is measured by its monetary equivalent $D(e)$: this is appropriate when the effort level pertains to the purchase and application of certain material inputs, or when the value of the farmer's time can be measured in terms of its opportunity cost in earnings forgone elsewhere. Alternatively, it could take the additively separable form $U(c) - D(e)$, whence $D(e)$ represents the physical or psychic cost of effort.

From an economic standpoint, the main consequence is the introduction of at least two kinds of wealth effects in the farmer's preferences. The first pertains to the demand for 'leisure', defined as the converse of effort. The second is the effect of wealth on the farmer's risk-aversion. The transfer of ownership of land to the farmer and the attendant increase in his bargaining power will induce both kinds of wealth effects. The first wealth effect will tend to lower effort. The second will depend on the precise way that the farmer's risk-aversion varies with his wealth. It is plausible that the farmer become less risk-averse, thereby inducing a contract with stronger incentive properties: this effect (modelled for instance by Bell, 1989) will tend to increase effort. The overall consequence will depend on the precise form of the farmer's preferences.

Both kinds of wealth effects are absent in the case where the utility function takes the form: $-\exp(-[c - D(e)])$, that is, effort costs are monetary and display constant absolute risk-aversion. Then our preceding results concerning productivity comparisons can be shown to be unaffected. In this sense, therefore, our results do not get overturned by the introduction of risk-aversion *per se*. However, the possibility of significant wealth effects can cause our conclusions to be significantly altered. The model should be viewed as providing merely one set of factors pertaining to the effect of ownership on productivity.

We turn now to the issue of dynamics, where the relationship between landlords and tenants or hired workers, or that between owner–cultivators and their creditors, is long-lived. In the tenancy setting, the landlord may be able to ease the incentive constraint by virtue of an ability to use eviction threats as an additional instrument of control. This is particularly true when the tenancy mode results in less effort than owner–cultivation: in such contexts tenants enjoy informational rents, and the prospect of forgoing these in the future can cause the farmer to apply more effort. In particular, the results of Radner (1985) imply that if the relationship between landlord and tenant is long-lived, and both discount the future at a sufficiently low rate, then the first-best outcome can be attained by a landlord, with the application of suitable 'trigger strategy' policy. While such folk theorems pertain to rather extreme situations, they suggest that in a multi-period setting the productivity gap between the tenancy mode and peasant mode may be narrower than is indicated by our preceding analysis. However, if tenants are believed not to be very far-sighted (owing to the high uncertainty of their environment, and their near-subsistence way of life), the ability of the landlord to alleviate the incentive problem via trigger strategy policies will be limited.

Nevertheless, the result concerning the absence of mutually profitable land sales will of course continue to hold for the same reason as in a static setting, if contracts are assumed to be complete. In a multi-period setting a lender of course has access to a larger range of instruments to control the moral hazard of borrowers. This will help ease credit constraints. Nevertheless, at the same time, the landlord will also gain access to the very same range of instruments to control the moral hazard of tenants. The set of feasible contracts is essentially the same under tenancy and owner–cultivation. So while the dynamic structure of debt contracts permit the easing of credit limits for owner–cultivators, the borrowing requirement to finance the land purchase goes up concomitantly, since the price needed to compensate the landlord adequately also goes up.

## 6. Concluding Remarks

### 6.1. Related literature

We first discuss the empirical evidence pertaining to the effects of ownership on productivity in Indian farms. A number of different authors have examined the comparative productivity of owner-cultivated and tenant farms, with mixed results. For instance, Chandra (1974), Rao (1971), Rudra and Chakravarty (1973) and Rudra and Dwivedi (1973) discovered no significant differences. The more recent work of Bell (1977), Sen (1981) and Shaban (1987) does, however, identify a significantly higher productivity on owner-cultivated farms, especially those of small size, after controlling for soil quality and irrigation. Shaban, for instance, controls additionally for family-specific, plot-specific and village-specific effects by utilizing a panel data set. He finds that owned farms apply significantly more inputs per acre, especially those in which the landlords do not share costs, such as family labour and bullock labour. The negative findings of earlier authors are explained by the nature of the data used, which clubbed sharecroppers and fixed rent tenants, and sharecroppers and part owners, besides their failure to control for differences in soil quality, irrigation or degree of mechanization (see also Sen, 1981). Shaban additionally finds the absence of systematic difference in productivity and labour application between owned plots and fixed rent tenancies. This evidence is consistent with our model: that is, fixed rents would be observed as long as the tenant was sufficiently wealthy and, as noted in section 4, productivity differences between owner-cultivated and tenant farms would then disappear.

Consider next the comparison of owner-cultivated farms with varying degrees of reliance on family *vis-à-vis* hired labour. Most authors have identified significant productivity advantages in farms relying primarily on family labour, leading to the well-known inverse relation between farm size and productivity. These differences are insufficiently explained by technological scale diseconomies, and are related primarily to greater application of labour on small family labour farms (Bardhan, 1973; Sen, 1981). The conventional explanation for this is the 'dual economy' hypothesis of Sen (1962, 1964), based on an exogenous gap between market wage rates and the marginal disutility of family labour. It postulates that hired labour is employed to the point where marginal product equals market wages, while family labour is employed to the point where marginal product equals marginal disutility. The empirical evidence on the validity of this hypothesis is mixed. In favour are the facts that productivities rise with farm size, that market wages have significant effects on marginal productivities of hired labour but not of family labour (Bardhan, 1973; Sen, 1981). The negative evidence pertains to the absence of a direct relationship between family labour content and productivity or labour input per acre (Bardhan, 1973; Rudra, 1973a, b). Sen (1981), however, explains this negative result by the nature of the data used, which clubbed owner-cultivated and sharecropped farms amongst those relying primarily on family labour. Within the class of owner-cultivated farms, he obtains a significant positive relationship between family labour content and labour input.

Hence, the positive relationship between family labour content, labour effort and farm productivity appears to be characteristic of owner-cultivated farms. Indeed, Sen (1981, Table 7) finds that the productivity of tenant farms (which does not appear to vary with size) is approximately the same as those of owner-cultivated farms of large size, in turn significantly smaller than owner-cultivated farms of small size. This is exactly consistent with our model: that is, the essential similarity of tenant farms with those relying primarily on hired labour, both of which result in lower effort incentives than a farm cultivated by its owner.

The 'dual economy' hypothesis of an exogenous gap between market wages for hired labour and the shadow cost of family labour is not persuasive, especially as the evidence suggests that family labour does frequently participate in the labour market (Sen, 1981). What prevents family workers from undercutting the going market wage? Some explanation on efficiency wage grounds is perhaps more attractive. Our approach belongs to this genre, whereby involuntary unemployment on the labour market is derived endogenously on the basis of wealth constraints and moral hazard with respect to labour effort. Indeed, our model is consistent with the phenomenon of 'tenancy ladders', whereby landlords give priority to wealthier peasants in awarding leases; see Shetty (1988) for citations of relevant empirical evidence and a similar theoretical explanation.

More generally, our approach draws attention to related imperfections in credit and land markets that seem just as essential as labour market imperfections in understanding the effects of ownership and contracting mode on farm productivity.

We turn now to the evidence concerning the sale of land by landlords to their tenants. The thinness of land markets is part of the folklore of development economics, though the direct evidence concerning this appears to be less systematic than on productivity differentials. Jodha (1981) found in a study of six Indian villages over a three-year period that 14–46 percent of the land was transferred, but sales ranged from only 3 to 23 percent of all transfers. Kumar (1975) presents evidence indicating that the distribution of land ownership in Madras Presidency manifested no trend over a period of almost a hundred years, from 1853–4 to 1946–7, despite substantial inequality. Rosenzweig and Wolpin (1985) studied data for 2900 Indian farm households during the period 1968–71, and found that less than 2 percent of them sold land during the year 1970–1. Moreover, most of these sales appeared to be of the form of distress sales by owner–cultivators. Moll (1988) argues that the thinness of land sales markets is a phenomenon observed in developed countries as well: the percentage of farmland transferred on average each year is 3 percent of the total in the USA, 1–1.5 percent in Britain, 1.5 percent within the white sector in South Africa and 0.5 percent in Ireland and Kenya.

A number of explanations for the absence of significant redistribution of land through the market have been offered. Binswanger and Rosenzweig (1986) and Binswanger, Deininger and Feder (1993) base their explanation on the fact that land has collateral value, over and above its income-earning potential as a productive asset. Mortgaged sales are therefore uncommon, as the buyer cannot compensate the seller for the collateral value on the basis of the future income-stream from the land. However, a transfer of land to a more productive mode ought to result in an increased earning potential, and it is unclear why the collateral value of the land should always exceed this potential. Moreover, this explanation does not preclude the purchase of land by farmers on the basis of their savings.

Heston and Kumar (1983) describe a variety of possible reasons for the thinness of land markets, such as asymmetric information concerning the value of any given piece of land, the value of land as a liquid asset and the desire for portfolio diversification. The extent of asymmetric information concerning land within a close-knit village community is also questionable. Moreover, a tenant farmer experienced in cultivating a plot of land for some time ought to have detailed information regarding its quality. The portfolio diversification argument may have some merit, but requires to be understood better: in particular, is the diversification value necessarily greater for wealthier investors? Alternative explanations may run in terms of tax advantages of investments in land for the wealthy.

Basu (1986) explains the market thinness as a coordination problem manifested as one of many Nash equilibria: owners are reluctant to sell land because others are, implying that buying back land later if worthwhile is not a feasible option. Alternative equilibria are, however, characterized by vigorous land sales and are welfare superior. Rosenzweig and Wolpin (1985) argue that the benefits of learning from past experience in tilling the family land implies that the land is more valuable to family members than to outsiders, so there is no prospect of a profitable sale. This obviously applies to a different phenomenon: why owner–cultivators appear reluctant to sell land belonging to the family to outsiders. It does not apply to the question of why a noncultivating landlord should be reluctant to sell land to a tenant or hired workers. If anything, the benefits of experience should argue in favour of such sales.

Finally, we discuss related theoretical research. A number of recent papers have modelled wealth effects created by credit market imperfections arising endogenously from moral hazard. Aghion and Bolton (1991), Banerjee and Newman (1991, 1993) and Piketty (1992) have studied the implications of these for the dynamics of growth, inequality and occupational choice. In a static setting, Legros and Newman (1994) study the implications of wealth effects on productivity by influencing the choice of organizational form. More productive organizational forms have higher financing requirements, so low wealth levels force selection of less productive forms. Our results concerning the comparative inefficiency of tenancy, however, do not stem from higher capital requirements, but rather from the induced allocation of bargaining power. Consequently, in the Legros–Newman model, the inefficiency resulting from low wealth levels can be removed only by a change in organizational form, induced in turn by changes in wealth distribution or capital market interventions. In our model, a change in organizational form is not necessary: increased wealth or subsidized credit can cause tenancy to turn efficient.

The relationship between informational rents and effort incentives is of course a familiar theme in the principal–agent literature. Nevertheless, the implications for organizational form have not been sufficiently explored, with few exceptions. Shapiro and Stiglitz (1984) identify the superior productivity and welfare levels in labour-managed firms relative to capitalist resulting from the internalization of these rents. Esfahani and Mookherjee (1995) focused on these informational rents as the reason why some profit-maximizing firms select organizational forms with low-powered incentives, and studied the impact of external parameters such as relative factor proportions and product market competition on these choices.

## 6.2. Future directions

The theory sketched here could apply to many other kinds of asset. One example is the ownership of retail outlets or taxis: the theory extends in a straightforward way, since these assets yield uncertain income streams upon application of effort by a single agent. The model then suggests that if the producing agent is wealth-constrained, self-ownership will generate higher productivity than when the asset is leased in. Despite this, the market will not transfer ownership to producing agents, owing to credit constraints.

A more ambitious extension would be to a multiple agent setting: for example, comparing worker-owned cooperatives with capitalist firms which separate ownership and labour. Informational rents of workers subject to incentive problems then suggests one efficiency advantage of cooperatives. If this is sufficient to overcome free-riding and other organizational problems (that is, if there is suitable monitoring of individual contributions, and suitable incentive mechanisms in place), it suggests that cooperative forms may flourish in competition with capitalist firms. This may provide part of the explanation for the prevalence of partnership forms of organization in different contexts where mutual monitoring is relatively costless: accounting and law, start-up companies and credit cooperatives.

Other areas where this approach may be fruitful include vertical integration, and transfer of technology to developing countries by multinational companies. Informational rents can cause the allocation of ownership rights to affect levels of efficiency. The incentive to internalize such rents may provide a strong reason for vertical integration, and for direct foreign investment as a form of technology transfer preferred to technology licensing.

## Notes

1   For an overview of this literature, see Bardhan (1984, 1989), Basu (1990), Binswanger, Deininger and Feder (1993), Otsuka, Chuma and Hayami (1992), Sen (1981) and Singh (1989).
2   This is reviewed in more detail in section 6. For evidence relating to other countries, see Berry and Cline (1979).
3   Indeed, the evidence in Townsend (1994, Table VI) does not reveal an unambiguous pattern across all three villages studied.
4   These two modes differ insofar as the management of cultivation is retained by the landlord rather than delegated to the cultivator. Our model, like most others in the literature (with the exception of Eswaran and Kotwal, 1985), is not rich enough to consider issues of management and delegation. Note that the case of wage labour is not interpreted as employment at a fixed wage rate, but rather allows the payment of wages conditioned on the output of the farm.
5   Section 5 extends the model to a multi-period setting.
6   The effort variable typically represents the amount of labour applied by the tiller and his family and livestock, and is thus difficult to monitor by the landlord or lender. We are assuming for the sake of simplicity that the effort required does not vary with the scale of cultivation.
7   Section 5 describes the consequences of farmer risk-aversion.
8   We assume that the farmer cannot participate in an alternative occupation or in farming another plot as long as the plot in question is farmed at a positive level ($x > 0$), but he can when $x = 0$. This indivisibility plays an inessential role in our analysis: we could alternatively assume that if $x$ fraction of the land is farmed, then the farmer obtains a utility of $x\bar{U}$ from outside activities, without altering any of the essential results.
9   Here we utilize the assumption that $R(e^*) - D(e^*) > \bar{U}$ at the first-best effort level $e^*$.
10  This is clearly true for the Nash bargaining solution, as well as related axiomatic bargaining solutions. As Binmore, Rubinstein and Wolinsky (1986) argue, such bargaining solutions can be rationalized in a noncooperative framework where there is small chance of a breakdown in negotiations, whereupon the disagreement pay-offs are realized. If, on the other hand, the essential friction in bargaining arises from the possibility of delayed agreement, these pay-offs correspond to outside options, which exert an effect on the bargaining outcome only if a player's

pay-off from the latter happens to fall below the option, in which case the player receives a pay-off equal to the option. Nevertheless, even in this context of bargaining, a transfer of ownership to the farmer would have an effect on effort incentives as long as the autarkic solution under owner cultivation gave the farmer higher utility than under tenancy.

11   The derivative of $p(e)\alpha(e)$ equals $D'(e) + p(e)\alpha'(e)$.

12   It will be strictly higher as long as the utility possibility frontier is strictly convex at either $F$ or $L$. Note that $F$ or $L$ may represent randomized contracts, in which case the frontier is linear at these points. However, in such a case, each outcome is a mixture of two pure contracts, one of which involves higher effort, and $F$ involves a greater probability weight on the higher effort contract.

13   This amounts to making the tenancy market 'as competitive as possible'. So our results will be strengthened further when landownership is more concentrated.

14   As Binmore, Rubinstein and Wolinsky (1986) show, this approximates the outcome of the following bargaining process. Suppose that the time period between $t = 0$ and $t = 1$ is divided into a finite but large number of subperiods. In the first subperiod one party makes an offer, which the other either accepts or refuses. If accepted, an offer is implemented. Otherwise the process continues into the following subperiod. With an exogenous probability $q$ the negotiations break down, and there is no agreement; both parties are returned to the population to await being matched with a new partner to bargain with at the following date. If negotiations do not break down in this fashion, then at the next subperiod it is the turn of the party refusing the proposal of the previous subperiod, to make a new proposal, which subsequently the other party must accept or reject. And so the process continues; if at the end of the last subperiod they have failed to agree, then they await a new partner at the following date. If the breakdown probability $q$ at each stage is small, and the number of subperiods is large, then the outcome of bargaining will be to produce this solution.

# References

Aghion, P. and Bolton, P. (1991): "A Trickle Down Theory of Growth and Development with Debt Overhang," mimeo, Paris: DELTA.

Banerjee, A. and Newman, A. (1991): "Risk-bearing and the Theory of Income Distribution," *Review of Economic Studies*, 58, 211–35.

—— (1993): "Occupational Choice and the Process of Development," *Journal of Political Economy*, 101(2), 274–98.

Bardhan, P. (1973): "Size, Productivity and Returns to Scale: An Analysis of Farm-Level Data in Indian Agriculture," *Journal of Political Economy*, 81(6), 1370–86.

—— (1984): *Land, Labor and Rural Poverty*. Delhi: Oxford University Press and New York: Columbia University Press.

—— (ed.) (1989): *The Economic Theory of Agrarian Institutions*. Oxford: Clarendon Press.

Basu, K. (1986): "The Market for Land: An Analysis of Interim Transactions," *Journal of Development Economics*, 20.

—— (1990): *Agrarian Structure and Economic Underdevelopment*. Chur: Harwood.

Bell, C. (1977): "Alternative Theories of Sharecropping: Some Tests Using Evidence from Northeast India," *Journal of Development Studies*, 13(4), 317–46.

—— (1989): "A Comparison of Principal–Agent and Bargaining Solutions: The Case of Tenancy Contracts," in P. Bardhan (ed.), *The Economic Theory of Agrarian Institutions*, Oxford: Clarendon Press.

Berry, A. and Cline, W. (1979): *Agrarian Structure and Productivity in Developing Countries*. Baltimore: Johns Hopkins University Press.

Binmore, K., Rubinstein, A. and Wolinsky, A. (1986): "The Nash Bargaining Solution in Economic Modeling," *Rand Journal of Economics*, 17, 176–88.

Binswanger, H., Deininger, K. and Feder, G. (1993): "Power, Distortions, Revolt and Reform in Agricultural Land Relations," in J. Behrman and T. N. Srinivasan (eds), *Handbook of Development Economics*, vol. III, Amsterdam: North-Holland.

Binswanger, H. and Rosenzweig, M. (1986): "Behavioural and Material Determinants of Production Relations in Agriculture," *Journal of Development Studies*, 22, 503–39.

Braverman, A. and Stiglitz, J. (1982): "Sharecropping and the Interlinking of Agrarian Markets," *American Economic Review*, 72, 289–312.

Chandra, N. (1974): "Farm-Efficiency under Semi-Feudalism: A Critique of Marginalist Theories and Some Marxist Formulations," *Economic and Political Weekly*, 9(32–4). Special Number (August).

Cheung, S. (1969): *The Theory of Share Tenancy*. Chicago: University of Chicago Press.

Esfahani, H. and Mookerjee, D. (1995): "Productivity, Contracting Mode and Development," *Journal of Development Economics*, 46(2), 203–31.

Eswaran, M. and Kotwal, A. (1985): "A Theory of Contractual Structure in Agriculture," *American Economic Review*, 75, 352–67.

Grossman, S. and Hart, O. (1986): "The Costs and Benefits of Ownership: A Theory of Vertical and Lateral Integration," *Journal of Political Economy*, 94, 691–719.

Hart, O. D. and Moore, J. (1990): "Property Rights and the Nature of the Firm," *Journal of Political Economy*, 98, 1119–58.

Heston, A. and Kumar, D. (1983): "The Persistence of Land Fragmentation in Peasant Agriculture: An Analysis of South Asian Cases," *Explorations in Economic History*, 20, 199–220.

Jodha, N. S. (1981): "Agricultural Tenancy: Fresh Evidence from Dryland Areas in India," *Economic and Political Weekly*, 26, December.

Klein, B., Crawford, R. and Alchian, A. (1978): "Vertical Integration, Appropriable Rents and the Competitive Contracting Process," *Journal of Law and Economics*, 21, 297–326.

Kumar, D. (1975): "Landownership and Inequality in Madras Presidency, 1853–54 to 1946–47," *Indian Economic and Social History Review*, 12, 229–61.

Legros, P. and Newman, A. (1994): "Wealth Effects, Distribution and the Theory of Organization," Columbia University, mimeo, revised version.

Marshall, A. (1920): *Principles of Economics*, 8th edn. London: Macmillan.

Moll, P. G. (1988): "Transition to Freehold in the South Africa Reserves," *World Development*, 16, 349–60.

Newbery, D. (1977): "Risk-Sharing, Sharecropping and Uncertain Labour Markets," *Review of Economic Studies*, 44, 585–94.

Osborne, M. and Rubinstein, A. (1990): *Bargaining and Markets*. San Diego: Academic Press.

Otsuka, K., Chuma, H. and Hayami, Y. (1992): "Land and Labor Contracts in Agrarian Economies: Theories and Facts," *Journal of Economic Literature*, 30, 1965–2018.

Piketty, T. (1992): "Imperfect Capital Markets and Persistence of Initial Wealth Inequalities," STICERD discussion paper TE/92/255, London School of Economics.

Radner, R. (1985): "Repeated Principal–Agent Games with Discounting," *Econometrica*, 53, 1173–98.

Rao, C. H. (1971): "Uncertainty, Enterpreneurship and Sharecropping," *Journal of Political Economy*, 51(5), 578–95.

Rosenzweig, M. and Wolpin, K. (1985): "Specific Experience, Household Structure and Intergenerational Transfers," *Quarterly Journal of Economics*, 100, 961–87.

Rudra, A. (1973a): "Direct Estimation of Surplus Labour in Agriculture," *Economic and Political Weekly*, 8(4–6), February.

——(1973b): "Marginalist Explanation for More Intensive Labour Inputs in Smaller Farms," *Economic and Political Weekly*, 8(22), 2 June.

—— and Chakravarty, A. (1973): "Economic Effects of Tenancy: Some Negative Results," *Economic and Political Weekly*, 8(28), 14 July.

—— and Dwivedi, H. (1973): "Economic Effects of Tenancy: Some Further Negative Results," *Economic and Political Weekly*, 8(29), 21 July.

Sen, Abhijit (1981): "Market Failure and Control of Labour Power: Towards an Explanation of Structure and Change in Indian Agriculture," *Cambridge Journal of Economics*, 5, 201–28.

Sen, Amartya. (1962): "An Aspect of Indian Agriculture," *Economic Weekly*, 14, February.

—— (1964): "Size of Holdings and Productivity," *Economic Weekly*, 16, February.

Shaban, R. (1987): "Testing Between Competing Models of Sharecropping," *Journal of Political Economy*, 95, 893–920.

Shapiro, C. and Stiglitz, J. (1984): "Unemployment as a Worker Discipline Device," *American Economic Review*, 74, 433–44.

Shetty, S. (1988): "Limited Liability, Wealth Differences and Tenancy Contracts in Agrarian Economies," *Journal of Development Economics*, 29(1), 1–22.

Singh, N. (1989): "Theories of Sharecropping," in P. Bardhan (ed.), *The Economic Theory of Agrarian Institutions*, Oxford: Clarendon Press.

Stiglitz, J. (1974): "Incentives and Risk-Sharing in Sharecropping," *Review of Economic Studies*, 41, 219–55.

Townsend, R. (1994): "Risk and Insurance in Village India," *Econometrica*, 62(3), 539–92.

Williamson, O. (1975): *Markets and Hierarchies*. New York: The Free Press.

—— (1985): *The Economic Institutions of Capitalism*. New York: The Free Press.

# D: Cooperatives and the Informal Economy

# CHAPTER 14

# Reciprocity without Commitment: Characterization and Performance of Informal Insurance Arrangements

STEPHEN COATE AND MARTIN RAVALLION

Various risk sharing arrangements are common in underdeveloped agrarian economies where households have no formal means of contract enforcement and little access to risk markets. Social insurance is still possible through repeated interaction in an environment with few informational asymmetries. In a simple repeated game model of two self-interested households facing independent income streams, we characterize the best arrangement that can be sustained as a noncooperative equilibrium. We establish precisely how this optimal informal arrangement differs from first best-risk sharing, and identify the conditions under which the divergence between the two is greatest.

## 1. Introduction

Modern insurance arrangements take the form of written and legally binding contracts which stipulate transfer payments contingent on certain events occurring. These arrangements require a government to record and enforce written contracts and a literate population to make such contracts. Thus insurance markets are not found in primitive societies. Nor is insurance based on explicit contracts common in many present day developing countries; illiteracy, cultural intimidation by modern institutions, and problems of asymmetric information can effectively restrict access by the poor even when a formal insurance market does exist.

When explicit and binding contracts are not possible, risk-sharing arrangements will have to be sustainable on an informal basis. This clearly makes them more difficult to implement; if there is only one realization of the risky event, no self-interested person would have an incentive to share realized good fortune, and so will renege on any prior non-binding agreement. However, as first shown by Kimball (1988) and also by Foster (1988),[1] risk sharing among non-altruists may exist in replications of a suitably risky environment without the advantage of binding contracts; current generosity may then be justified by expected future reciprocity. This may not be an unreasonable expectation in a traditional village society, where generations of households remain in relatively close contact, and the need to spread risk is often great.

Indeed, there is considerable evidence of the existence of various forms of informal insurance arrangements in village communities,[2] though they have received rather little attention from economists.[3] Scott (1976) and others have described and discussed at length village level customs of mutual support in traditional societies – the so-called "moral economy". The forms of such behavior which have been observed include gift giving, reciprocal interest free credit, shared meals, communal access to land, sharing bullocks, and work-sharing arrangements. The main risks covered are accidents or illnesses of productive family members or livestock, certain forms of crop damage, such as due to fire or wild animals, and other relatively noncovariate income fluctuations, such as fishing yields. A recurrent feature of these practices is their reciprocity: recipients at one date often become donors at another.

The performance of these informal insurance arrangements has been an issue in the anthropological literature. Popkin (1979) is staunchly critical of the "moral economists" (more of whom were anthropologists than economists) for over-stating the value of indigenous institutions. However, while it is not unusual to find a seemingly romanticized view of these institutions in the literature, it is at least as common to find sobering reservations. For example, Scott (1976, p. 43) writes that: "village redistribution worked unevenly and, even at its best, produced no egalitarian utopia". There is also some evidence to suggest that, even when they do exist, traditional risk-sharing arrangements may well break down, and at particularly bad times for the poor. A number of observers have noticed the collapse of community based insurance during famines; for example, a common Bengali word for describing famine is "durbhiksha" literally meaning that "alms are scarce".[4]

The performance of these institutions also has bearing on longstanding policy concerns. In the absence of informal insurance, incomplete risk markets yield a strong prima facie case for policy intervention (Newbery and Stiglitz, 1981). With the existence of informal insurance possibilities that case is less clear. This can be viewed as an example of a more general point: while there is a case for intervention in one shot games of the Prisoners' Dilemma sort, that case may be significantly weakened if the game is repeated.[5] Indeed, it may even be argued that, without any policy intervention, private voluntary arrangements within the village community will adequately supply insurance against idiosyncratic income shocks.

In this paper we build on the work of Kimball and Foster to further develop a theoretical understanding of the risk-sharing that can be achieved with informal insurance arrangements. We characterize the "best" informal insurance arrangement which can be sustained as a noncooperative equilibrium and compare its properties with those of the arrangement which could, in principle, be achieved with binding contracts. We show precisely how the two differ and try to identify the circumstances under which the divergence between them is likely to be the greatest.

While we use the same basic model as Kimball and Foster, our analysis differs from theirs in focusing on the properties of the optimal informal insurance arrangement and how it differs from the first-best. In Foster's analysis households' actions are restricted to one of two extremes: to pool income fully, or to defect. As we show later, the optimal arrangement will typically involve an intermediate strategy in which, while transfers are made, full income pooling is not achieved. While Kimball does allow for the possibility of less than full income pooling, he limits his analysis to identifying the conditions under which transfers of some form will take place (i.e., a risk-sharing institution will exist) and under which full income pooling will be achieved (i.e., the institution will achieve first-best risk sharing). Thus Kimball is not concerned with the properties of the optimal equilibrium insurance arrangement.

The next section outlines our repeated game model and characterizes those insurance arrangements which are sustainable as subgame perfect equilibria. Section 3 then characterizes the "best" of these implementable arrangements and compares it with first-best risk sharing. Section 4 examines comparative static properties of the optimal insurance arrangement. Section 5 presents parameterized numerical simulations of the optimal arrangement and examines how its performance relative to the first-best varies with the parameter values. Section 6 offers some suggestions for further research, while our conclusions are summarized in section 7.

## 2. A Simple Informal Insurance Game

### 2.1. The basic model

We use the same basic model studied by Kimball (1988). This provides an adequate yet tractable characterization of the sort of environment in which informal insurance may exist. We consider two risk-averse households who face intertemporally variable and independent income streams, so they may have different incomes at any given date. The two households are similar *ex ante*, having the same preferences and the same expected income.

In each period, each household $k = $ A, B receives an income $y^k$ drawn from the set $\{y_1, \ldots, y_n\}$ in which incomes are ranked in ascending order, $y_1 < \cdots < y_n$. The probability that household A receives an income $y_i$ and B an income $y_j$ is denoted $\pi_{ij}$; i.e.

$$\pi_{ij} = \text{Prob}\left\{ \left(y^A, y^B\right) = \left(y_i, y_j\right) \right\}$$

We confine attention to symmetric probabilities whereby, for all $i, j \in \{1, \ldots, n\}$, $\pi_{ij} = \pi_{ji} > 0$. Thus, each income pair is possible and the probability that A gets $y_i$ and B gets $y_j$ equals the probability that A gets $y_j$ and B gets $y_i$.[6] The players have identical preferences defined over own income only and represented by the (per period) utility function $u(y)$. We assume that they are non-satiated and risk averse, i.e., for all $y > 0$, $u'(y) > 0$ and $u''(y) < 0$. In addition, each household has a utility discount rate or "subjective rate of time preference" $r$. As we wish to focus attention on income transfers as a means of insurance, we shall assume that households do not save.

Since both households are risk averse and face uncertain income streams, there are potential gains from state-contingent transfers between them; A agrees to help B out if B is unlucky and, in return, B agrees to help A out when their situations are reversed. In the absence of binding contracts, such arrangements cannot be sustained in one period interactions. No matter what is agreed *ex-ante*, the household who obtains the highest income will always renege. In repeated interactions, however, such transfer arrangements can be sustained.

To make this precise we consider the following repeated noncooperative game. In each period $t$, nature selects an income pair $y(t) = (y^A(t), y^B(t))$. Observing $y(t)$ and knowing the history of the game, each household must choose a transfer to the other household. The game is assumed to be infinitely repeated,[7] and the equilibrium concept we shall employ is the usual one of subgame perfect equilibrium.[8]

Since each individual's life-span is of finite duration our assumption that the game is infinitely repeated needs justification. The idea we have in mind is that, in a traditional village setting, households are likely to be in contact with each other for more than one generation. Thus the current head of the household may decide to help out other households in the expectation that they in turn will be around to help out his/her offspring should they need it. The players can thus be interpreted as dynasties. It may be too strong to postulate that households expect with certainty to be playing the game for the rest of time, but that is more than we need. All that is necessary, is that households believe that there is a positive probability that the game will continue to be played. This probability assessment can be thought of as being reflected in agent's discount rates. The less likely they think that future generations will be playing the game, the higher the discount rate.

## 2.2. Informal insurance arrangements

Our first objective is to characterize the insurance arrangements which can be implemented by the equilibria of this game. An arrangement specifies a net transfer between the two players for each realized income pair. We follow Foster and Kimball in restricting attention to pure insurance arrangements, whereby the transfers at any date depend only on incomes realized at that date. This precludes possible credit features of informal risk-sharing arrangements whereby transfers are more like loans which are paid back at least in part at some later date. We briefly comment on the effects of allowing these in section 6.

Formally then, we define an *informal insurance arrangement* to be an $n \times n$ matrix $\mathbf{\Theta} = (\theta_{ij})$ where the component $\theta_{ij}$ denotes the net transfer from A to B when A gets an income $y_i$ and B gets $y_j$. Feasibility demands that $\theta_{ij} \in [-y_j, y_i]$. Under the arrangement $\mathbf{\Theta}$, A's per period expected utility will be

$$v^A(\mathbf{\Theta}) = \sum_{i=1}^{n} \sum_{j=1}^{n} \pi_{ij} u(y_i - \theta_{ij})$$

and B's expected utility is

$$v^B(\mathbf{\Theta}) = \sum_{i=1}^{n} \sum_{j=1}^{n} \pi_{ij} u(y_j + \theta_{ij})$$

Let $\bar{v}$ denote each household's per period expected utility in the absence of any kind of informal insurance, i.e.,

$$\bar{v} = \sum_{i=1}^{n}\sum_{j=1}^{n} \pi_{ij} u(y_i) = \sum_{i=1}^{n}\sum_{j=1}^{n} \pi_{ij} u(y_j)$$

An arrangement is *implementable* if there exist equilibrium strategies for the players which result in net transfers consistent with it. An arrangement will be implementable if the difference between each household's expected utility under continued participation and the status quo (i.e., zero transfers) is always greater than the gain from current defection. Strategies which follow the arrangement until defection and then punish defections by setting all future transfers equal to zero will implement any such contract. Conversely, since the status quo is the worst possible equilibrium, any implementable arrangement must necessarily satisfy the condition that the difference between each household's expected utility under continued participation and the status quo is always greater than the gain from current defection. Thus an arrangement is implementable if and only if[9]

$$u(y_i) - u(y_i - \theta_{ij}) \leqq \frac{v^A(\mathbf{\Theta}) - \bar{v}}{r} \qquad \text{for all } (i, j) \tag{1}$$

and

$$u(y_j) - u(y_j + \theta_{ij}) \leqq \frac{v^B(\mathbf{\Theta}) - \bar{v}}{r} \qquad \text{for all } (i, j) \tag{2}$$

We refer to these as the *implementability constraints*.[10]

An arrangement is *symmetric* if the net transfer from A to B when $(y^A, y^B) = (y_i, y_j)$ equals the net transfer from B to A when $(y^A, y^B) = (y_j, y_i)$ i.e., if $\theta_{ij} = -\theta_{ji}$.[11] Clearly, if $\mathbf{\Theta}$ is symmetric then $\theta_{ii} = 0$ for all $i$. It follows that a symmetric arrangement is completely characterized by the vector

$$\boldsymbol{\theta} = (\theta_{21}; \theta_{31}, \theta_{32}; \ldots; \theta_{n1}, \ldots, \theta_{nn-1})$$

Thus, if we know the net transfer from A to B for each case where A has a strictly larger income than B, then we know the entire transfer arrangement. Each household's utility can be rewritten in terms of the vector $\boldsymbol{\theta}$. Let

$$v(\boldsymbol{\theta}) = \sum_{i=1}^{n}\left[\sum_{j=1}^{i-1} \pi_{ij}\big(u(y_i - \theta_{ij}) + u(y_j + \theta_{ij})\big) + \pi_{ii} u(y_i)\right]$$

Then it is straightforward to verify that $v^A(\mathbf{\Theta}) = v^B(\mathbf{\Theta}) = v(\boldsymbol{\theta})$. This observation allows us to simplify the implementability constraints. In particular, it is easily verified that a symmetric, non-negative arrangement $\boldsymbol{\theta}$ is implementable if and only if for all $i = 1, \ldots, n$,

$$u(y_i) - u(y_i - \theta_{ij}) \leqq \frac{v(\boldsymbol{\theta}) - \bar{v}}{r} \qquad j = 1, \ldots, i-1 \tag{3}$$

By a non-negative arrangement we simply mean one with the property that the net transfer from A to B is non-negative whenever A has a greater income than B.

## 3. The Performance of Informal Insurance

Our task now is to compare the best possible implementable insurance arrangement with the first-best. Since any implementable arrangement is a possible equilibrium of the game, the reader may wonder why we are focusing solely on the best of the implementable arrangements. The justification is twofold. First, the best arrangement is a natural "focal point" and hence may be more likely to arise than any other implementable arrangement. Second, even if one does not believe this, the best arrangement provides an upper bound on the performance of informal insurance.

Without loss of generality we can confine attention to transfer arrangements which are symmetric and non-negative. The first-best, denoted $\hat{\boldsymbol{\theta}}$, is defined as the set of state-contingent transfers which maximizes average expected utility allowing binding commitments. Formally, it is the solution to the unconstrained problem of maximizing $v(\boldsymbol{\theta})$ with respect to $\boldsymbol{\theta}$. It is straightforward to verify that

$$\hat{\theta}_{ij} = (y_i - y_j)/2, \quad i = 1, \ldots, n, \quad j = 1, \ldots, i-1$$

Thus the first-best involves full income pooling. The best implementable contract, denoted $\boldsymbol{\theta}^*$, is the one which results in the highest average expected utility subject to the implementability constraints, i.e., $\boldsymbol{\theta}$ is the solution to the constrained problem of maximizing $v(\boldsymbol{\theta})$ subject to eqn (3). Recall that we are restricting attention to non-negative and feasible transfer arrangements and hence the choice set is compact and convex. Since the objective function is strictly concave, we can be sure that $\boldsymbol{\theta}^*$ exists and is unique. Our task now is to compare $\boldsymbol{\theta}^*$ and $\hat{\boldsymbol{\theta}}$.

We begin by providing a useful characterization of $\boldsymbol{\theta}^*$. First let $f(y, w)$ denote the function implicitly defined by the equation

$$u(y) - u(y - f) = w$$

Intuitively, $f(y, w)$ can be thought of as the maximal amount of income which can be taken from a household with income $y$ without inducing defection when the cost of defecting (in utility terms) is $w > 0$. Obviously, the larger the cost of defection, the greater is the amount of income which can be taken away. In addition, diminishing marginal utility of income implies that the amount of income which can be taken away without inducing defection gets larger as the household's income increases. Thus $f$ is increasing in both its arguments. The key point to note about the function $f$ is that, given a particular arrangement $\boldsymbol{\theta}$, the maximal amount of income which can be taken from a household with income $y$ without violating implementability will be given by $f(y, [v(\boldsymbol{\theta}) - \bar{v}]/r)$, since it is at this transfer level that the implementability constraint is satisfied with equality.

We now have the following theorem, which underpins all the later results of the paper.

THEOREM    *For all $i = 1, \ldots, n$ and $j = 1, \ldots, i-1$,*

$$\theta_{ij}^* = \min\left\{\hat{\theta}_{ij}, f\left(y_i, \frac{v(\boldsymbol{\theta}^*) - \bar{v}}{r}\right)\right\} \tag{4}$$

PROOF    It will be convenient to use the notation $\boldsymbol{\theta}^*/\theta_{ij}$ to denote the vector $\boldsymbol{\theta}^*$ with $\theta_{ij}^*$ replaced by $\theta_{ij}$. We show first that if

$$f\left(y_i, \frac{v(\boldsymbol{\theta}^*) - \bar{v}}{r}\right) \geqq \hat{\theta}_{ij}$$

then $\theta_{ij}^* = \hat{\theta}_{ij}$. Suppose that, on the contrary, $\theta_{ij}^* \neq \hat{\theta}_{ij}$. Now consider the vector $\boldsymbol{\theta}^*/\hat{\theta}_{ij}$. Since $\partial v/\partial \theta_{ij}$ is negative for all $\theta_{ij} > \hat{\theta}_{ij}$ and positive for all $\theta_{ij} < \hat{\theta}_{ij}$, we know that $v(\boldsymbol{\theta}^*/\hat{\theta}_{ij}) > v(\boldsymbol{\theta}^*)$. In addition, since $f$ is increasing in its second argument it follows that

$$f\left(y_i, \frac{v\left(\boldsymbol{\theta}^*/\hat{\theta}_{ij}\right) - \bar{v}}{r}\right) > f(y_i, [v(\boldsymbol{\theta}^*) - \bar{v}]/r) \geqq \hat{\theta}_{ij}$$

which implies that $\boldsymbol{\theta}^*/\hat{\theta}_{ij}$ is implementable. Since $\boldsymbol{\theta}^*/\hat{\theta}_{ij}$ is implementable and yields a higher level of expected utility, $\boldsymbol{\theta}^*$ cannot be optimal – a contradiction.

We now show that $\theta_{ij}^* = f(y_i, [v(\boldsymbol{\theta}^*) - \bar{v}]/r)$ if $f(y_i, [v(\boldsymbol{\theta}^*) - \bar{v}]/r) < \hat{\theta}_{ij}$. Again, suppose not. Then, by implementability, it must be the case that

$$\theta_{ij}^* < f\left(y_i, \frac{v(\boldsymbol{\theta}^*) - \bar{v}}{r}\right)$$

Now choose $\tilde{\theta}_{ij} \in (\theta_{ij}^*, f(y_i, [v(\boldsymbol{\theta}^*) - \bar{v}]/r))$ and consider the vector $\boldsymbol{\theta}^*/\tilde{\theta}_{ij}$. Since $\partial v/\partial \theta_{ij}$ is positive for all $\theta_{ij} < \hat{\theta}_{ij}$ and $\theta_{ij}^* < \tilde{\theta}_{ij}$ we know that $v(\boldsymbol{\theta}^*/\tilde{\theta}_{ij}) > v(\boldsymbol{\theta}^*)$. Moreover, following the argument given above, it can be shown that $\boldsymbol{\theta}^*/\tilde{\theta}_{ij}$ is implementable. This contradicts the optimality of $\boldsymbol{\theta}^*$.    Q.E.D.

Thus, for any given income pair, the transfer under the best implementable contract either equals the first best or, if this is not implementable, the maximal implementable transfer (i.e., that which equates the gain from current defection from the arrangement with the expected gain from continued participation.)[12] Intuitively this makes good sense. If it were feasible to implement the first-best transfer for a particular income pair, then there is no good reason not to do so. If, on the other hand, this were not feasible, then one would want to get as near to the first-best as possible which would entail setting the transfer at the maximal level.

We can now establish some interesting results concerning the relationship between $\boldsymbol{\theta}^*$ and $\hat{\boldsymbol{\theta}}$. Under the first-best contract, all that determines the size of the net transfer between the households is the difference between their incomes. The level of incomes is irrelevant. This is not the case for the optimal informal arrangement as we show in the following proposition.

PROPOSITION 1    *Let $y_i - y_j = y_g - y_h > 0$ and let $y_i > y_g$. If $\theta_{ij}^* < \hat{\theta}_{ij}$, then*

$$\hat{\theta}_{gh} - \theta_{gh}^* > \hat{\theta}_{ij} - \theta_{ij}^*$$

PROOF   The result follows immediately from the theorem and the fact that the function $f$ is increasing in $y$.   Q.E.D.

Proposition 1 tells us that *if* the informal insurance arrangement diverges from the first-best, this divergence is greatest at dates with low income levels. At low income levels, the marginal utility of income is high and hence the incentives to defect are strong. As a consequence, if the implementability constraint is already binding, then it becomes even tighter at lower income levels. The result is illustrated in figure 1, where $\theta^*(y^A, y^B)$ denotes the informal insurance transfer and $\hat{\theta}(y^A, y^B)$ denotes the first-best.

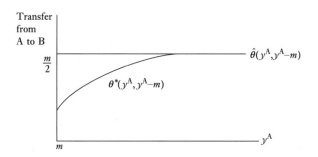

**Figure 1**

Our next experiments involve studying the effects of changes in current (ex-post) income inequality. First suppose we fix household A's income and lower B's income. Under our assumptions, the first-best arrangement has the property that A will always transfer one half of the income difference to B. The following proposition tells us what happens to the optimal informal insurance arrangement as B's income lowers.

PROPOSITION 2   *Let $y_i > y_j > y_h$. Then, if $\theta_{ij}^* < \hat{\theta}_{ij}$, $\theta_{ik}^* = \theta_{ij}^*$.*

PROOF   Since $y_h < y_j$, we have that $\hat{\theta}_{ih} > \hat{\theta}_{ij}$. It follows from the theorem that $\theta_{ih}^* = f(y_i, [v(\boldsymbol{\theta}^*) - \bar{v}]/r)$.   Q.E.D.

Thus, once the implementability constraint bites, there is no scope for additional transfers no matter how low B's income falls. As a consequence, post transfer income inequality will exist and will increase as the income divergence grows. This is illustrated in figure 2.

Finally, let's fix household B's income and increase household A's. Under the first-best contract, household A transfers exactly one half of the difference to household B. What happens under the optimal informal arrangement? The following proposition is established in the appendix.

PROPOSITION 3   *Let $y_i > y_g > y_h$ and suppose that $1/u'(y)$ is concave. If $\boldsymbol{\theta}^* \neq 0$ and $\theta_{gh}^* < \hat{\theta}_{gh}$, then $\hat{\theta}_{ih} - \theta_{ih}^* > \hat{\theta}_{gh} - \theta_{gh}^*$.*

Thus if the utility function satisfies the stated property and if the informal arrangement diverges from the first-best, then this divergence will increase as household A's income increases, holding B's constant. This is illustrated in figure 3.

The condition that $1/u'(y)$ is concave in $y$ is satisfied by a reasonably broad class of utility functions.[13] For example, the constant relative risk aversion utility function $u(y) = y^{1-\rho}/(1-\rho)$ has this property for $\rho \in (0, 1]$. If the utility function does not have this property, however, it is possible that the difference between the first-best and the informal insurance arrangement can close after some point, as illustrated in figure 4. On the one hand, as the income difference grows, the first-best transfer increases which makes implementability more difficult. But, on the other hand, diminishing marginal utility of income implies that the utility cost of a given transfer decreases as income increases.

The preceding three propositions all have the same basic form. Assuming that the optimal informal arrangement diverges from the first-best, they tell us how this divergence behaves. Proposition 1 tells us that it increases as income levels fall; proposition 2 tells us that it increases as B's income falls, holding A's income constant; and proposition 3 gives a condition under which the divergence increases as A's income increases holding B's constant. Note that these results do not tell us that the optimal informal arrangement necessarily diverges from the first-best, even at very low or unequal income pairs. Kimball establishes some results which speak directly to this issue. Assuming that households' utility functions have the constant relative risk aversion form, he finds that unless $\rho$ – the risk aversion parameter – is equal to 1 there will always exist some income pair $(y^A, y^B)$ at

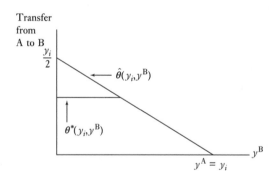

Figure 2

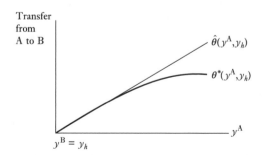

Figure 3

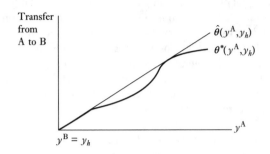

**Figure 4**

which full sharing is not implementable no matter what the gains in expected utility from full risk sharing.[14] As he explains "when $\rho < 1$, diminishing marginal utility is weak enough that a very fortunate farmer enjoys feasting on his hoard so much that he cannot be induced to share it all. On the other hand, when $\rho > 1$, poverty is so painful that when all farmers in the cooperative are doing badly, but one is doing a little better than the others, he cannot be induced to share all of his pitfall pile" (1988, p. 229). For the case $\rho = 1$ he shows that full sharing can be achieved (for all conceivable income pairs) if households are sufficiently patient and if they face sufficiently variability in their incomes.

## 4. Comparative Static Properties

In this section we investigate how the optimal informal insurance arrangement varies with some of the exogenous variables of the model. Specifically, we examine the effects of changes in the households' discount rates and the probability distribution over incomes. Our results should shed light on the circumstances under which the divergences between the optimal informal arrangement and the first-best are greatest.

We began with the discount rate which, it will be recalled, is denoted $r$. Kimball's computations for the constant relative risk aversion case suggest that risk-sharing institutions are less likely to form the more impatient are households. This makes good sense intuitively, since the benefits from being in a risk-sharing arrangement are enjoyed in the future. Thus we would expect the divergence between the first-best transfer and the optimal informal transfer at any income level to increase as the discount rate falls. This is confirmed in the following proposition. The notation $\boldsymbol{\theta}^*(r)$ denotes the optimal implementable contract when the discount rate is $r$.

PROPOSITION 4    Let $r^0 < r^1$ and suppose that $\boldsymbol{\theta}^*(r^1) \neq 0$. Then $\theta_{ij}^*(r^1) \leqq \theta_{ij}^*(r^0)$, with the inequality holding strictly if $\theta_{ij}^*(r^1) < \hat{\theta}_{ij}$.

PROOF    It is clear that $\boldsymbol{\theta}^*(r^1)$ is implementable when the discount rate is $r^0$ and hence that $v(\boldsymbol{\theta}^*(r^0)) \geqq \boldsymbol{\theta}^*(r^1))$. It follows therefore that $[v(\boldsymbol{\theta}^*(r^0)) - \bar{v}]/r^0$ exceeds $[v(\boldsymbol{\theta}^*(r^1)) - \bar{v}]/r^1$. Since $f$ is increasing in its second argument the result now follows from the theorem. Q.E.D.

As was pointed out earlier, the discount rate will reflect households' assessment of the probability of playing the game in the future. Another way of interpreting this result, therefore, is that if households do not expect to be playing the game for long the divergence between the optimal arrangement and the first-best will be large. This suggests that as traditional societies become more mobile, so that future generations are less likely to be in close contact, the moral economy will tend to perform less well. A further important influence on the discount rate is the expected length of time between income draws. If the income draws we are talking about are harvests, this frequency may be annual or biannual. Clearly, more frequent draws correspond to a lower discount rate.

Let us now consider perturbing the probability distribution $\pi = (\pi_{ij})$. One would expect informal insurance to perform poorly if it was unlikely that the households would earn different incomes. For then the potential risk-sharing gains would be small, and there would be less incentive not to defect. Thus one can conjecture that the divergences between the optimal informal arrangement and the first-best will be greater when participants face more covariate income streams. To investigate this possibility we analyze the performance of informal insurance under two probability distributions which differ in the weight they give to divergent incomes. Let $\theta^*(\pi)$ denote the optimal arrangement associated with the probability distribution $\pi$. We now have the following proposition a proof of which can be found in the appendix.

PROPOSITION 5   *Let $\pi^0$ and $\pi^1$ be two probability distributions such that*

(i)   $\sum_{j=1}^{n}(\pi_{ij}^1 - \pi_{ij}^0) = 0$ *and*
(ii)   $(\pi_{ij}^1 < \pi_{ij}^0$ *for all $i \neq j$.*

*If $\theta^*(\pi^1) \neq 0$, then $\theta_{ij}^*(\pi^1) \leq \theta_{ij}^*(\pi^0)$ with the inequality holding strictly if $\theta_{ij}^*(\pi^1) < \hat{\theta}_{ij}$.*

Thus in situations where the optimal arrangement diverges from the first-best, a decrease in the probability of different incomes will increase the divergence.

# 5. Numerical Simulations of Informal Insurance

The results of the previous two sections provide a reasonably complete picture of the qualitative properties of informal insurance. In this section we supplement these results by simulating optimal informal insurance arrangements under alternative assumptions on the relevant parameters. This will allow us to form a clearer picture of the likely quantitative significance of the divergences from the first-best solution in specific circumstances. It will also shed light on the arrangement's analytically ambiguous properties. The parameters focused on are the probability distribution over incomes, the discount rate, and the players' aversion to risk.

The main task is to solve eqn (4) for an explicit utility function and given parameter values. For this purpose we assume a constant relative risk aversion utility function $u(y) = y^{(1-\rho)}/(1-\rho)$. While eqn (4) does not yield an explicit solution for the optimal implementable transfers, it can be solved numerically. Let $\theta^*(t)$ denote the estimated vector of transfers obtained at the $t$th iteration, and set $\boldsymbol{\theta}^*(0) = \hat{\boldsymbol{\theta}}$, being the first-best transfers. Then update these estimates at each iteration using

$$\theta_{ij}^*(t+1) = \min\left\{\hat{\theta}_{ij}, y_i - \left[y_i^{1-\rho} - \frac{(v(\theta^*(t)) - \bar{v})}{r}\right]^{1/(1-\rho)}\right\} \qquad (5)$$

Convergence then implies that (4) is satisfied.[15]

Since our sole aim here is to give a simple illustration, we assume only three possible incomes, $y_1 = 1$, $y_2 = 2$, $y_3 = 3$. The corresponding first-best transfers are then $\hat{\theta}_{21} = 0.5$, $\hat{\theta}_{31} = 1$ and $\hat{\theta}_{32} = 0.5$. Three joint probability distributions are considered ranging from "highly covariate" to "highly noncovariate", where the less covariate distribution is obtained from the more covariate one by transfers of density from diagonal to off-diagonal elements. Specifically the three possible distributions are

   (i)   The "highly covariate" income stream:

$$\pi_{11} = \pi_{33} = 0.2, \pi_{22} = 0.3, \pi_{12} = \pi_{13} = \pi_{23} = 0.05$$

   (ii)   The "moderately covariate" income stream:

$$\pi_{22} = 0.2, \pi_{11} = \pi_{33} = \pi_{12} = \pi_{13} = \pi_{23} = 0.1$$

   (iii)   The "highly non-covariate" income stream:

$$\pi_{11} = \pi_{22} = \pi_{33} = \pi_{12} = \pi_{23} = 0.1, \pi_{13} = 0.15$$

Tables 1, 2, and 3 give the informal transfers implied by a wide range of parameter values for the discount rate and relative risk aversion parameters.[16] Although evidence is scarce (and often conflicting), values for relative risk aversion of around 0.5–1.0 in poor agrarian settings are not implausible.[17] We give results for all values of $\rho$ up to that at which informal insurance achieves first-best risk sharing. Results are given for discount rates of 5%, 15% and 25%; the latter figure may well be quite realistic in underdeveloped rural economies; see Pender and Walker (1989). The tables also give a useful measure of performance relative to the cooperative solution, namely the *proportional gain*, $\gamma$, defined by

$$\gamma = \frac{v(\boldsymbol{\theta}^*) - \bar{v}}{v(\hat{\boldsymbol{\theta}}) - \bar{v}}$$

Tables 1–3 nicely illustrate our previous results. Since $y_2 - y_1 = y_3 - y_2$, our claim that income levels matter can be verified by comparing $\theta_{21}^*$ and $\theta_{32}^*$. As predicted, if $\theta_{32}^*$ is less than the first-best transfer then $\theta_{21}^*$ is always less than $\theta_{32}^*$. Thus lower income levels result in greater divergences from the first-best. Proposition 2 is verified by comparing $\theta_{31}^*$ and $\theta_{32}^*$. If $\theta_{32}^*$ is less than the first-best transfer 0.5, then $\theta_{31}^*$ equals $\theta_{32}^*$ as predicted. Thus the transfer from household A to household B flattens out as B's income falls. Finally, proposition 3 can be verified by comparing $\theta_{21}^*$ and $\theta_{31}^*$. We find, as predicted for utility functions in which $1/u'(y)$ is concave, the divergence from first-best increases as A's income rises for all $\rho$ in this interval. (Indeed, this also happens when the risk aversion

**Table 1** Equilibrium transfers for highly covariate income streams[a, b]

| Discount rate $r$ | Risk aversion $\rho$ | Transfers | | | Proportional gain $\gamma$ |
|---|---|---|---|---|---|
| | | $\theta_{21}^*$ | $\theta_{31}^*$ | $\theta_{32}^*$ | |
| 0.05 | 0.1 | 0 | 0 | 0 | 0 |
| 0.05 | 0.3 | 0 | 0 | 0 | 0 |
| 0.05 | 0.5 | 0.262 | 0.323 | 0.323 | 0.649 |
| 0.05 | 0.7 | 0.500 | 0.687 | 0.500 | 0.942 |
| 0.05 | 0.9 | 0.500 | 0.963 | 0.500 | 0.999 |
| 0.15 | 0.1 | 0 | 0 | 0 | 0 |
| 0.15 | 0.3 | 0 | 0 | 0 | 0 |
| 0.15 | 0.5 | 0 | 0 | 0 | 0 |
| 0.15 | 0.7 | 0 | 0 | 0 | 0 |
| 0.15 | 0.9 | 0 | 0 | 0 | 0 |
| 0.15 | 1.1 | 0.180 | 0.280 | 0.280 | 0.569 |
| 0.15 | 1.3 | 0.299 | 0.500 | 0.500 | 0.819 |
| 0.15 | 1.5 | 0.386 | 0.686 | 0.500 | 0.934 |
| 0.15 | 1.7 | 0.452 | 0.846 | 0.500 | 0.986 |
| 0.15 | 1.9 | 0.500 | 0.982 | 0.500 | 1.00 |
| 0.15 | 2.1 | 0.500 | 1.00 | 0.500 | 1.00 |
| 0.25 | 0.1 | 0 | 0 | 0 | 0 |
| 0.25 | 0.3 | 0 | 0 | 0 | 0 |
| 0.25 | 0.5 | 0 | 0 | 0 | 0 |
| 0.25 | 0.7 | 0 | 0 | 0 | 0 |
| 0.25 | 0.9 | 0 | 0 | 0 | 0 |
| 0.25 | 1.1 | 0 | 0 | 0 | 0 |
| 0.25 | 1.3 | 0.034 | 0.058 | 0.058 | 0.142 |
| 0.25 | 1.5 | 0.149 | 0.271 | 0.271 | 0.544 |
| 0.25 | 1.7 | 0.234 | 0.451 | 0.451 | 0.761 |
| 0.25 | 1.9 | 0.299 | 0.608 | 0.500 | 0.879 |
| 0.25 | 2.1 | 0.353 | 0.750 | 0.500 | 0.946 |
| 0.25 | 2.3 | 0.398 | 0.875 | 0.500 | 0.981 |
| 0.25 | 2.5 | 0.435 | 0.985 | 0.500 | 0.995 |
| 0.25 | 2.7 | 0.500 | 1.00 | 0.500 | 1.00 |

[a] $\pi_{11} = 0.2$, $\pi_{12} = 0.05$, $\pi_{22} = 0.3$, $\pi_{13} = 0.05$, $\pi_{23} = 0.05$, $\pi_{33} = 0.2$
[b] First-best transfers: $\hat{\theta}_{21} = 0.5$, $\hat{\theta}_{31} = 1.0$, $\hat{\theta}_{32} = 0.5$.

coefficient exceeds one.) Similarly, these results illustrate our comparative static results. The performance of informal insurance improves as the discount rate falls and as the income distribution become less covariate.

Note also that higher degrees of risk aversion are found to be associated with a relatively better (or no worse) performance. This is consonant with the results of Kimball who reports that the discount rate above which no risk sharing is possible is increasing in $\rho$. The relationship between $\gamma$ and $\rho$ for $r = 0.10$ and the moderately covariate income stream is depicted in figure 5. (The pattern of concavity beyond some

**Table 2**  Equilibrium transfers for moderately covariate income streams[a]

| Discount rate $r$ | Risk aversion $\rho$ | Transfers | | | Proportional gain $\gamma$ |
|---|---|---|---|---|---|
| | | $\theta_{21}^*$ | $\theta_{31}^*$ | $\theta_{32}^*$ | |
| 0.05 | 0.1 | 0 | 0 | 0 | 0 |
| 0.05 | 0.3 | 0.365 | 0.415 | 0.415 | 0.767 |
| 0.05 | 0.5 | 0.500 | 0.934 | 0.500 | 0.997 |
| 0.05 | 0.7 | 0.500 | 1.00 | 0.500 | 1.00 |
| 0.05 | 0.9 | 0.500 | 1.00 | 0.500 | 1.00 |
| 0.15 | 0.1 | 0 | 0 | 0 | 0 |
| 0.15 | 0.3 | 0 | 0 | 0 | 0 |
| 0.15 | 0.5 | 0 | 0 | 0 | 0 |
| 0.15 | 0.7 | 0.253 | 0.338 | 0.338 | 0.664 |
| 0.15 | 0.9 | 0.424 | 0.628 | 0.500 | 0.916 |
| 0.15 | 1.1 | 0.500 | 0.857 | 0.500 | 0.989 |
| 0.15 | 1.3 | 0.500 | 1.00 | 0.500 | 1.00 |
| 0.25 | 0.1 | 0 | 0 | 0 | 0 |
| 0.25 | 0.3 | 0 | 0 | 0 | 0 |
| 0.25 | 0.5 | 0 | 0 | 0 | 0 |
| 0.25 | 0.7 | 0 | 0 | 0 | 0 |
| 0.25 | 0.9 | 0.123 | 0.177 | 0.177 | 0.398 |
| 0.25 | 1.1 | 0.283 | 0.440 | 0.440 | 0.770 |
| 0.25 | 1.3 | 0.390 | 0.649 | 0.500 | 0.920 |
| 0.25 | 1.5 | 0.469 | 0.827 | 0.500 | 0.983 |
| 0.25 | 1.7 | 0.500 | 1.00 | 0.500 | 1.00 |

[a] $\pi_{11} = \pi_{12} = 0.1$, $\pi_{22} = 0.2$, $\pi_{13} = \pi_{23} = \pi_{33} = 0.1$.

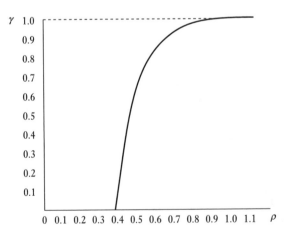

**Figure 5**

Table 3   Equilibrium transfers for highly noncovariate income streams[a]

| Discount rate $r$ | Risk aversion $\rho$ | Transfers | | | Proportional gain $\gamma$ |
|---|---|---|---|---|---|
| | | $\theta_{21}^*$ | $\theta_{31}^*$ | $\theta_{32}^*$ | |
| 0.05 | 0.1 | 0 | 0 | 0 | 0 |
| 0.05 | 0.3 | 0.500 | 0.649 | 0.500 | 0.914 |
| 0.05 | 0.5 | 0.500 | 1.00 | 0.500 | 1.00 |
| 0.05 | 0.7 | 0.500 | 1.00 | 0.500 | 1.00 |
| 0.05 | 0.9 | 0.500 | 1.00 | 0.500 | 1.00 |
| 0.15 | 0.1 | 0 | 0 | 0 | 0 |
| 0.15 | 0.3 | 0 | 0 | 0 | 0 |
| 0.15 | 0.5 | 0.132 | 0.162 | 0.162 | 0.362 |
| 0.15 | 0.7 | 0.426 | 0.570 | 0.500 | 0.872 |
| 0.15 | 0.9 | 0.500 | 0.857 | 0.500 | 0.987 |
| 0.15 | 1.1 | 0.500 | 1.00 | 0.500 | 1.00 |
| 0.25 | 0.1 | 0 | 0 | 0 | 0 |
| 0.25 | 0.3 | 0 | 0 | 0 | 0 |
| 0.25 | 0.5 | 0 | 0 | 0 | 0 |
| 0.25 | 0.7 | 0.059 | 0.078 | 0.078 | 0.186 |
| 0.25 | 0.9 | 0.288 | 0.415 | 0.415 | 0.735 |
| 0.25 | 1.1 | 0.438 | 0.665 | 0.500 | 0.925 |
| 0.25 | 1.3 | 0.500 | 0.866 | 0.500 | 0.989 |
| 0.25 | 1.5 | 0.500 | 1.00 | 0.500 | 1.00 |

[a] $\pi_{11} = \pi_{12} = \pi_{22} = \pi_{23} = \pi_{33} = 0.1$, $\pi_{13} = 0.15$.

critical value is the same for other parameter combinations). Risk sharing only exists for $\rho \geq 0.38$. With increasing risk aversion beyond that point, relative performance improves rapidly, though flattening at high levels of risk aversion.

One striking feature of the results in tables 1–3 is how sharply the performance varies. Even a quite successful risk-sharing arrangement may vanish with certain seemingly modest perturbations to parameter values, such as a small decline in the participants' aversion to risk. Thus Foster's conclusion that family based risk-sharing arrangements are likely to be "highly unstable" (pp. 34–5) appears robust to allowing households to make partial transfers. What causes these sharp variations in performance? The implementability constraints imply that transfers must be reduced below the first-best level. But once transfers have been reduced, there is less incentive to participate and hence the implementability constraints tighten. This necessitates a further reduction in transfers. This process can easily converge to zero transfers. The implication of this variability is that we might expect to find wildly divergent performances of the moral economy in apparently similar communities.

## 6. Suggestions for Further Research

The analysis in this paper could be usefully extended in a number of different ways. First, one could allow households to use non-stationary insurance arrangements; that is, arrangements whose transfers may depend on both current and past income realizations. These are of interest because they allow an element of lending in informal insurance arrangements. A household who has received a transfer may "pay back" the donor household by agreeing to a less favorable transfer arrangement in future periods. This may bring forth a larger transfer from the donor household and hence result in improved risk-sharing. [Platteau and Abraham (1987) have noted the quasi-credit nature of some informal risk-sharing arrangements in practice.] While characterizing the optimal non-stationary insurance arrangement represents a more challenging analytical task, Thomas and Worrall (1988) have analyzed a formally similar problem in wage contract theory and the techniques they have developed should prove helpful.

Another extension would be to relax the assumption that households cannot save. Savings represent another way households can insure against income shocks. It is by no means obvious how the introduction of self-insurance possibilities would affect the nature of informal social insurance. A household's ability to give, or its need for transfers, would depend not only on its income but also on its past savings. Self-insurance may displace social insurance in some circumstances, although there will still (in principle) exist potential gains from informal insurance.

A further extension would be to allow a household's income to depend on its work effort, and in a way which others in the community cannot observe. This would introduce an element of moral hazard into the problem; that is, households may have an incentive to slack off knowing that they will receive an income transfer. This is likely to be more of a problem in urban communities than in village economies where individuals can observe each other fairly closely. An optimal informal insurance arrangement will naturally take into account any such asymmetries in information. This may alter some of our results; for example, as a referee has suggested, the presence of moral hazard may invalidate our finding that the optimal informal arrangement achieves first-best risk sharing for small income differences.

Finally, it might be interesting to relax the assumption that households face identical income distribution. What type of arrangements would arise between a rich and poor household? A referee has suggested that one might expect implementable arrangements to favor the richer household. They may then be "exploitative" in some appropriately defined sense. The logic behind this view is that, because the poorer household has more to gain from insurance, the implementability constraints will be tighter for the richer household. However, it must be remembered that diminishing marginal utility of income will imply that the poorer household has more short-run incentive to deviate.

## 7. Conclusions

Community wide participation in various informal risk-sharing practices is a common feature of traditional rural societies. These practices can be perfectly reasonable and sustainable strategies in the absence of suitable and widely accessible risk markets and legal institutions enabling explicit and enforceable contracts. This does not mean, however, that such arrangements will be particularly good risk-sharing institutions. Even without problems of asymmetric information, the constraint imposed by implementability without commitment will generally reduce performance relative to first-best risk sharing.

This paper has used a simple model to better understand precisely how informal insurance arrangements are likely to diverge from first-best risk sharing. Our analysis suggests that such divergences will be larger in many situations where insurance is badly needed, such as at dates when incomes are generally low, or those at which a few incomes are low, generating high current inequality. It also suggests that these divergences will tend to be greater in societies in which different incomes are less likely and time preference rates are high. Furthermore, our numerical simulations suggest that informal arrangements may be quite sensitive to small changes in initial conditions. An active informal insurance arrangement may vanish entirely with a seemingly small drop in the players' aversion to risk or an increase in their discount rate. Thus our inquiry throws light on the circumstances in which non-market insurance may exist, and how well it will perform.

## APPENDIX

### Proof of proposition 3

Define the function

$$g(y) = (y - y_h)/2 - f\left(y, \frac{v(\theta^*) - \bar{v}}{r}\right)$$

Since $\theta^*_{gh} < \hat{\theta}_{gh}$, the theorem tells us that $\theta^*_{gh} = f(y_g, [v(\theta^*) - \bar{v}]/r)$. In addition, $\hat{\theta}_{gh} = (y_g - y_h)/2$ and hence we have that $g(y_g) = \hat{\theta}_{gh} - \theta^*_{gh} > 0$. Suppose we could show that $g(y_i) > g(y_g)$. Then, since $\hat{\theta}_{ih} = (y_i - y_h)/2$, $\hat{\theta}_{ih} > f(y_i, [v(\theta^*) - v]/r)$ which implies by the theorem that $g(y_i) = \hat{\theta}_{ih} - \theta^*_{ih}$ and hence that $\hat{\theta}_{ih} - \theta^*_{ih} > \hat{\theta}_{gh} - \theta^*_{gh}$, which is the result we want to prove. Thus it suffices to show that $g(y_i) > g(y_g)$. Note first that

$$g''(y) = -f_{11}\left(y, \frac{v(\theta^*) - \bar{v}}{r}\right)$$

It is straightforward to verify that if $1/u'(y)$ is concave, $f_{11} \geq 0$ and hence that $g''(y) \leq 0$. We know that $g(y_g) > 0$. In addition, it is clear that $g(y_h) < 0$. It follows that there must exist some $y^* \in (y_h, y_g)$ such that $g'(y^*) > 0$. But since $g''(y)^0$, this implies that $g'(y) > 0$ for all $y \geq y^*$. It follows that $g(y_i) > g(y_g)$. Q.E.D.

### Proof of proposition 5

In what follows we recognize the dependence of expected utility on $\pi$, by writing $v(\theta, \pi)$. We know by the theorem that, for all $\pi$,

$$\hat{\theta}_{ij}(\pi) = \min\left\{\hat{\theta}_{ij}, f\left(y_i, \frac{v(\theta^*(\pi), \pi) - \bar{v}(\pi)}{r}\right)\right\}$$

Since $f$ is increasing in its second argument it therefore suffices to show that

$$\frac{\nu\big(\boldsymbol{\theta}^*\big(\pi^0\big),\pi^0\big)-\bar{\nu}\big(\pi^0\big)}{r}>\frac{\nu\big(\boldsymbol{\theta}^*\big(\pi^1\big),\pi^1\big)-\bar{\nu}\big(\pi^1\big)}{r}$$

We begin by proving that for any non-zero non-negative vector $\boldsymbol{\theta}\leqq\hat{\boldsymbol{\theta}}$,

$$\nu\big(\boldsymbol{\theta},\pi^0\big)>\nu\big(\boldsymbol{\theta},\pi^1\big)$$

To see this, note that

$$\nu\big(\boldsymbol{\theta},\pi^0\big)-\nu\big(\boldsymbol{\theta},\pi^1\big)=\sum_{i=1}^{n}\left[\sum_{j=1}^{i-1}\big(\pi_{ij}^0-\pi_{ij}^1\big)\big(u(y_i-\theta_{ij})+u(y_i+\theta_{ij})\big)+\big(\pi_{ii}^0-\pi_{ii}^1\big)u(y_i)\right]$$

By condition (i) of the proposition we know that, for all $i=1,\dots,n$,

$$\pi_{ii}^0-\pi_{ii}^1=-\sum_{j\neq i}\big(\pi_{ij}^0-\pi_{ij}^1\big)$$

Thus

$$\nu\big(\boldsymbol{\theta},\pi^0\big)-\nu\big(\boldsymbol{\theta},\pi^1\big)=\sum_{i=1}^{n}\left[\sum_{j=1}^{i-1}\big(\pi_{ij}^0-\pi_{ij}^1\big)\big(u(y_j-\theta_{ij})+u(y_j+\theta_{ij})\big)\right.$$
$$\left.-\sum_{j=1}^{i-1}\big(\pi_{ij}^0-\pi_{ij}^1\big)u(y_i)-\sum_{j=i+1}^{n}\big(\pi_{ij}^0-\pi_{ij}^1\big)u(y_i)\right]$$
$$=\sum_{i=1}^{n}\left[\sum_{j=1}^{i-1}\big(\pi_{ij}^0-\pi_{ij}^1\big)\big(u(y_i-\theta_{ij})+u(y_j+\theta_{ij})-u(y_i)-u(y_j)\big)\right]$$

where the last equality follows by symmetry. Since $\pi_{ij}^0>\pi_{ij}^1$ for all $j=1,\dots,i-1$, and $u(y_i-\theta_{ij})+u(y_j+\theta_{ij})\geqq u(y_i)+u(y_j)$ for all $\theta_{ij}\in[0,\hat{\theta}_{ij}]$ with strict inequality if $\theta_{ij}>0$, the result follows.

From the above result, we know that

$$\nu\big(\boldsymbol{\theta}^*\big(\pi^1\big),\pi^0\big)>\nu\big(\boldsymbol{\theta}^*\big(\pi^1\big),\pi^1\big)$$

Since $\bar{\nu}(\pi^1)=\bar{\nu}(\pi^0)$, this implies that $\boldsymbol{\theta}^*(\pi^1)$ is implementable when the probability distribution is $\pi^0$. Thus

$$\frac{\nu\big(\boldsymbol{\theta}^*\big(\pi^0\big),\hat{\pi}^0\big)-\bar{\nu}\big(\pi^0\big)}{r}\geqq\frac{\nu\big(\boldsymbol{\theta}^*\big(\pi^1\big),\pi^0\big)-\bar{\nu}\big(\pi^0\big)}{r}>\frac{\nu\big(\boldsymbol{\theta}^*\big(\pi^1\big),\pi^1\big)-\bar{\nu}\big(\pi^1\big)}{r}$$

Q.E.D.

## Notes

1 Kimball develops his analysis to assess the scope for farmers' cooperatives as risk-sharing institutions in medieval England. Foster, on the other hand, is concerned with family based risk-sharing arrangements in developing countries.

2 On informal insurance in traditional village societies see Scott (1976), Dirks (1980), Posner (1980), Watts (1983), Caldwell et al. (1986), Platteau and Abraham (1987), Platteau (1988), Ravallion and Dearden (1988), Rosenzweig (1988), Thomas et al. (1989), Townsend (1991), and Ravallion and Shubham (1991). Note that these institutions are not confined to traditional village societies. See, for example the empirical results of Kaufman and Lindauer (1984) (for urban El Salvador), and Ravallion and Dearden's (1988) results (for both urban and rural Java). Transfers between traditional and modern sectors also appear to be common.

3 For example, Newbery's (1989) recent survey, "Agricultural Institutions for Insurance and Stabilization", makes only a brief mention of informal insurance.

4 Declines in patronage and customs of gift giving during famines have been noted by Epstein (1967), Sen (1981), Currey (1981), Greenough (1982), Ravallion (1987), D'Souza (1988), and Drèze and Sen (1989).

5 Sugden (1986), for example, has argued along these lines.

6 This can be interpreted as "*ex-ante* equality"; either player could end up "rich" or "poor" in any period.

7 If the game were of finite duration and the termination date were common knowledge the usual backward induction argument would suggest that the only equilibrium would be zero transfers. If the termination date were uncertain, as seems reasonable in this context, then transfers may still be possible. See Basu (1987) for a discussion of finitely repeated games with uncertain termination.

8 To save notation, we will not define precisely what is meant by a subgame perfect equilibrium. For a definition of this concept, see Friedman (1986). For a general characterization of subgame perfect equilibria in infinitely repeated games with discounting see Abreu (1988).

9 For a formal proof of this assertion see the earlier version of this paper (Coate and Ravallion, 1989).

10 These implementability constaints are similar to those which arise in the labor economics literature on "self-enforcing" wage contracts. See Thomas and Worrall (1988).

11 Note that symmetry of $\Theta$ and $\pi$ implies that the expected value of the transfer is zero. Thus each player has the same expected value of post-transfer income.

12 Our theorem makes precise Kimball's claim that "The optimal arrangement is for grain to be transferred from those who have more than the lowest amount to those who have the least until either (1) the quantities are equalized; or (2) each of the farmers who has more than the lowest amount has contributed as much as the threat of expulsion can force him to contribute" (1988, p. 226).

13 The importance of the concavity or convexity of $1/u'$ arises in a number of other incentive problems [for example, Rogerson (1985)].

14 In terms of our notation, Kimball shows that if $\rho \neq 1$, for all $w > 0$ there exists $(y^A, y^B)$ such that $f(y^A, w) < (y^A - y^B)/2$.

15 A copy of a Fortran program implementing this algorithm is available for use on a PC with the DOS operating system. It is set-up in a user-friendly mode.

16 The convergence criterion is that successive estimates are within 0.1 percent of each other. This was generally achieved within twenty or so iterations.

17 See Binswanger's (1978) experimental results for rural India. Newbery and Stiglitz (1981) discuss this study and other evidence on peasants' risk aversion in poor countries. Kimball discusses evidence for other settings, though estimates vary.

## References

Abreu, D. (1988): "On the Theory of Infinitely Repeated Games with Discounting," *Econometrica*, 56, 383–96.

Basu, K. (1987): "Modelling Finitely-Repeated Games with Uncertain Termination," *Economics Letters*, 23, 147–51.

Binswanger, H. P. (1978): "Attitudes toward Risk: Experimental Measurement Evidence in Rural India," *American Journal of Agricultural Economics*, 395–407.

Caldwell, J. C., Reddy P. H. and Caldwell, P. (1986): "Periodic High Risk as a Cause of Fertility Decline in a Changing Rural Environment: Survival Strategies in the 1980–1983 South Indian Drought," *Economic Development and Cultural Change*, 677–701.

Coate, S. and Ravallion, M. (1989): Reciprocity without Commitment: Characterization and Performance of Informal Risk-sharing Arrangements, discussion paper 96, Development Economics Research Center, University of Warwick, Coventry.

Currey, B. (1981): "The Famine Syndrome: Its Definition for Relief and Rehabilitation in Bangladesh," in J. Robson (ed.), *Famine: Its Causes, Effects and Management*, New York: Gordon and Breach.

Dirks, R. (1980): "Social Responses During Severe Food Shortages and Famine," *Current Anthropology*, 21.

Drèze, J. and Sen, A. (1989): *Hunger and Public Action*. Oxford: Oxford University Press.

D'Souza, F. (1988): "Famine: Social Security and an Analysis of Vulnerability," in G. A. Harrison (ed.), *Famine*, Oxford: Oxford University Press.

Epstein, S. (1967): "Productive Efficiency and Customary Systems of Reward in Rural South India," in R. Firth (ed.), *Themes in economic anthropology*, London: Tavistock.

Foster, A. (1988): Why Things Fall Apart: A Strategic Analysis of Repeated Interaction in Rural Financial Markets, mimeo, Department of Economics, University of California at Berkeley, Berkeley, CA.

Friedman, J. (1986): *Game Theory with Applications to Economics*. Oxford: Oxford University Press.

Greenough, P. R. (1982): *Prosperity and Misery in Modern Bengal: The Famine of 1943–49*. Oxford: Oxford University Press.

Kaufman, D. and Lindauer, D. L. (1984): Income Transfers within Extended Families to meet Basic Needs: The Evidence from El Salvador, working paper 644, World Bank staff, World Bank, Washington, DC.

Kimball, M. (1988): "Farmers' Cooperatives as Behavior Toward Risk," *American Economic Review*, 78, 224–32.

Newbery, D. M. G. (1989): "Agricultural Institutions for Insurance and Stabilization," in P. Bardhan (ed.), *The Economic Theory of Agrarian Institutions*, Oxford: Oxford University Press.

——and Stiglitz, J. E. (1981): *The Theory of Commodity Price Stabilization*. Oxford: Oxford University Press.

Pender, J. L. and Walker, T. (1989): Experimental Measurement of Time Preferences in Rural India, mimeo, Food Research Institute, Stanford University, Stanford, CA.

Platteau, J.-P. (1988): Traditional Systems of Social Security and Hunger Insurance: Some Lessons from the Evidence Pertaining to Third World Village Societies, working paper 15, The Development Economics Research Programme, London School of Economics, London.

——and Abraham, A. (1987): "An Inquiry into Quasi-Credit Contracts: The Role of Reciprocal Credit and Interlinked Deals in Small-Scale Fishing Communities," *Journal of Development Studies*, 23, 461–90.

Popkin, S. L. (1979): *The Rational Peasant, The Political Economy of Rural Society in Vietnam*. Berkeley: University of California Press.

Posner, R. A. (1980): "A Theory of Primitive Society, with Special Reference to Law," *The Journal of Law and Economics*, 23, 1–53.

Ravallion, M. (1987): *Markets and Famines*. Oxford: Oxford University Press.

——and Shubham, C. (1991): Testing Risk-sharing in Three Indian Villages, mimeo, Washington, DC: World Bank.

——and Dearden, L. (1988): "Social Security in a 'Moral Economy': An Empirical Analysis for Java," *The Review of Economics and Statistics*, 70, 36–44.

Rogerson, W. (1985): "Repeated Moral Hazard," *Econometrica*, 53, 69–76.

Rosenzweig, M. (1988): "Risk, Implicit Contracts and the Family in Rural Areas of Low-Income Countries," *The Economic Journal*, 98, 1148–70.

Scott, J. (1976): *The Moral Economy of the Peasant. Rebellion and Subsistence in Southeast Asia*. New Haven, CI: Yale University Press.

Sen, A. (1981): *Poverty and Famines. An Essay on Entitlement and Deprivation*. Oxford: Oxford University Press.

Sugden, R. (1986): *The Economics of Rights, Cooperation and Welfare*. Oxford: Basil Blackwell.

Thomas, J. and Worrall, T. (1988): "Self-Enforcing Wage Contracts," *Review of Economic Studies*, 60, 541–54.

Thomas, R., Brooke, S., Paine, H. B. H. and Brenton, B. O. (1989): "Perspectives on Socio-Economic Causes of and Responses to Food Deprivation," *Food and Nutrition Bulletin*, 11, 41–54.

Townsend, R. M. (1991): Risk and Insurance in Village India, mimeo, Chicago, IL: University of Chicago.

Watts, M. (1983): *Silent Violence, Food, Famine and Peasantry in Northern Nigeria*. Berkeley, CA: University of California Press.

CHAPTER 15

# The Economics of Rotating Savings and Credit Associations

TIMOTHY BESLEY, STEPHEN COATE, AND GLENN LOURY

This paper analyzes the economic role and performance of a type of financial institution which is observed worldwide: rotating savings and credit associations (ROSCAs). Using a model in which individuals save for an indivisible durable consumption good, we study ROSCAs which distribute funds using random allocation and bidding. Each type of ROSCA allows individuals without access to credit markets to improve their welfare, but under a reasonable assumption on preferences, random allocation is preferred when individuals have identical tastes. This conclusion need not hold when individuals are heterogeneous. We also discuss the sustainability of ROSCAs given the possibility of default.

This paper studies rotating savings and credit associations (ROSCAs). These are informal financial institutions which are found all over the world.[1] They are most common in developing countries but are also used by immigrant groups in the United States (see e.g., Ivan Light, 1972; Aubrey W. Bonnett, 1981). Furthermore, many of the U.S. savings and loan associations seem to have started life as ROSCAs (see Edwin Symons and James White, 1984; Richard Grossman, 1992). ROSCAs constitute one of a number of institutions, sharecropping being another example, whose existence is pervasive in developing economies and demands some explanation. Yet while their prevalence and, to some degree, robustness has fascinated anthropologists, they have attracted surprisingly little attention from economists.[2] Our object in this paper and its companion piece (Besley et al., 1992) is therefore to initiate an analysis of their economic role and performance.

The considerable literature on ROSCAs reveals much variation in how they actually work in practice, but two main varieties can be identified. The first, and most prevalent, type allocates its funds randomly. In a *random ROSCA*, members commit to putting a fixed sum of money into a "pot" for each period of the life of the ROSCA.[3] Lots are drawn, and the pot is randomly allocated to one of the members. In the next period, the process repeats itself, except that the previous winner is excluded from the draw for the pot. The process continues, with every past winner excluded, until each member of the ROSCA has received the pot once. At this point, the ROSCA is either disbanded or begins over again.

ROSCAs may also allocate the pot using a bidding procedure. We shall refer to this institution as a *bidding ROSCA*. One individual receives the pot in an earlier period than another by bidding more, in the form of a pledge of higher contributions to the ROSCA, or one-time side payments to the other ROSCA members. Under a bidding ROSCA, individuals may still receive the pot only once – the bidding process merely establishes priority.[4]

We take the view, documented in the extensive informal literature on ROSCAs, that these institutions are primarily used to save up for the purchase of indivisible durable goods.[5] Random ROSCAs are not particularly effective as institutions for buffering against risk, since the probability of obtaining the pot need not be related to one's immediate circumstances. Even bidding ROSCAs, which may allow a member to obtain the pot immediately, only permit individuals to deal with situations that cannot recur, since the pot may be obtained no more than once. Furthermore, since many kinds of risks in LDCs are covariant, individuals will have high valuations at the same instant. ROSCAs do play a greater role in transferring resources to meet life-cycle needs, such as financing a wedding. However, even in this context, they seem more appropriate for dealing with significant, idiosyncratic events, rather than the hump saving required for old age.

Despite its manifest importance, there has been relatively little work in the savings literature on the notion of saving up to buy an indivisible good. Yet, the existence of indivisible goods is a reason for developing institutions which mediate funds. In the absence of access to external funds, individuals must save to finance lumpy expenditures and can gain from trading with one another; the savings of some individuals can finance the purchases of others. This is not true when all goods are divisible, since gradual autarkic accumulation is efficient in the absence of heterogeneity.

ROSCAs provide a means of making joint savings work.[6] They also determine a rule for rationing access to the indivisible good: random allocation in a random ROSCA and bidding in a bidding ROSCA. We use a two-good model with indivisibilities to make precise how a group of individuals without access to credit markets may improve their welfare by forming a random or bidding ROSCA. We demonstrate how these institutions work and examine their impact on savings rates. We also compare random and bidding ROSCAs, focusing on their relative performance in terms of their members' welfare. With homogeneous individuals, randomization is preferred to bidding as a method of allocating funds within ROSCAs under a plausible restriction on preferences. However, with sufficient dispersion in individuals' valuations of the indivisible good, this may not be true.

For ROSCAs to operate successfully it is necessary that individuals keep their commitment to pay into the ROSCA after they have won the pot. This may appear problematic since ROSCA members are often not able to borrow in conventional credit markets precisely because they cannot be presumed to repay loans. ROSCAs circumvent such default problems by exploiting individuals' social connectedness. This is borne out in the anthropological literature, which reveals how the incentive to defect from a ROSCA is curbed by social constraints. ROSCAs are thus typically formed among individuals whose circumstances and characteristics are well known to each other. Defaulters are sanctioned socially as well as being prevented from any further ROSCA participation. Nonetheless, default does sometimes occur, and organizers of ROSCAs must be mindful of this. Thus, we discuss how concerns about default influence the design and performance of ROSCAs.

The remainder of this paper is organized as follows. Section 1 sets up the model. Section 2 describes how ROSCAs work and can improve over autarky. Section 3 provides comparisons of lifetime utilities and other features of the resource allocations under random and bidding ROSCAs. In Section 4, we extend the comparison to allow for the possibility of heterogeneous tastes. Section 5 discusses how considerations of sustainability may influence the design of ROSCAs, and section 6 concludes.

## 1. The Model

We use the simplest model that can capture the essential features of the problem at hand. A group of $n$ individuals would each like to own an indivisible durable consumption good. The group is assumed to have no access to credit markets. Thus they may be villagers in a traditional society or members of an immigrant group, unfamiliar with the banking practices of their new country. Each individual lives for $T$ years, receiving an exogenous flow of income over his lifetime of $y > 0$. We assume, at first, that individuals have identical, intertemporally additive preferences. Each individual's instantaneous utility depends on nondurable consumption, $c$, and on whether or not he enjoys the services of the durable. The durable does not depreciate and can be purchased at a given cost of $B$. Once purchased, it yields a constant flow of services for the remainder of an individual's lifetime. We also assume that the durable's services are not fungible across individuals; one must own it to benefit from its services.

For simplicity, there is no discounting, which precludes any motive for saving or borrowing apart from the desire to acquire the durable. An individual's instantaneous utility with nondurable consumption $c$ is $v(1, c)$ if he owns the durable, and $v(0, c)$ otherwise. We assume that $v(0, \cdot)$ and $v(1, \cdot)$ are increasing, strictly concave, and three times continuously differentiable in their second argument, using $v'(i, c)$, $v''(i, c)$, and so forth to denote differentiation of $v(i, \cdot)$ with respect to $c$, for $i = 0$ or $1$. Given $c$, we define

$$\Delta v(c) \equiv v(1, c) - v(0, c)$$

to be the instantaneous gain in utility from owning the durable, and

$$v(\alpha, c) \equiv \alpha v(1, c) + (1 - \alpha) v(0, c) \qquad \text{for } 0 \leq \alpha \leq 1,$$

as the expected instantaneous utility when $\alpha$ is the probability of owning the durable.

Our results require some further structure on preferences. The first, innocuous, condition is that $\Delta v(c) > 0$ for all $c \geq 0$, which says only that individuals like the durable. We will also assume that $\Delta v'(c) \geq 0$ (i.e., that the marginal utility of nondurable consumption is not decreased by owning the durable). This is critical for much of our analysis and can be interpreted as saying that durable services and nondurable consumption are complements. We regard the assumption as reasonable for many of the uses to which ROSCA funds are put – purchasing a bicycle, a household appliance, or a tin roof for one's house. We will, however, indicate how the assumption affects our analysis as we proceed.

Under *autarky*, individuals save up on their own. Our assumptions imply that it is optimal for each individual to save $B$ at a constant rate $y - c$, over an interval $[0, t]$.[7] Thus, lifetime utility maximization involves each individual choosing $c$ and $t$ to:

$$\text{maximize}\{t \cdot v(0, c) + (T - t) \cdot v(1, y)\} \tag{1}$$

subject to $t(y - c) = B$, and $0 \leq c \leq y$. Let $(t_a, c_a)$ be the solution to (1) and let $W_a$ be the maximal value of lifetime utility.

We exploit a simple way of writing $W_a$. First, substitute for $t$ using the constraint in (1). This yields a one-variable maximization problem involving $c$, and the maximand can be written as

$$T \cdot v(1, y) - B \left[ \frac{v(1, y) - v(0, c)}{y - c} \right]$$

Next, define

$$\mu(\alpha) \equiv \min_{0 \leq c \leq y} \left[ \frac{v(1, y) - v(\alpha, c)}{y - c} \right] \qquad 0 \leq \alpha \leq 1 \tag{2}$$

Setting $\alpha = 0$ in (2), lifetime utility under autarky can be written as

$$W_a = T \cdot v(1, y) - B \cdot \mu(0) \tag{3}$$

Expression (3) has an appealing interpretation, paralleled in our analysis of ROSCAs. The first term represents lifetime utility if the durable were free, while the second term is the minimal utility cost of saving up for the durable. This minimization trades off the benefit of a shorter accumulation period against the benefit of higher consumption during this period. Letting, $c^*(\alpha)$ be the consumption level which solves (2), the optimal autarkic consumption rate, $c_a$, is $c^*(0)$.

Under autarky, no individual has the durable good before date $t_a$, at which time all $n$ individuals receive it. Thus the expected fraction of time that an individual will enjoy the services of the durable during the accumulation period is zero. This explains why autarky is represented by $\alpha = 0$ in (2). Autarky is inefficient; each person saves at rate $y - c_a = B/t_a$ and after an interval of $t_a/n$, there are enough savings to buy a durable which could be given to one of the group members. ROSCAs remedy this inefficiency, with the cost function $\mu(\cdot)$ measuring the extent of welfare improvement.

Before considering ROSCAs, we establish some technical properties of $\mu(\cdot)$ and $c^*(\cdot)$, which prove useful later. The proof of the lemma is in the appendix.

LEMMA    *Under the assumptions on preferences set out above, the minimized cost $\mu(\cdot)$ in (2) is a decreasing, concave function of $\alpha$, and the cost-minimizing consumption rate $c^*(\cdot)$ is an increasing function of $\alpha$. Both are twice continuously differentiable on $[0, 1]$, where they satisfy the identity*

$$\mu(\alpha) \equiv v'(\alpha, c^*(\alpha))$$

*Moreover, if $v'''(i, c) > 0$ for $i = 0$ and $1$, and if $\Delta v''(c) \geq 0$, then $c^*(\cdot)$ is strictly convex.*

## 2. ROSCAs

This section examines how members of a group may improve their welfare by forming either a random or a bidding ROSCA. As well as examining how ROSCAs operate and raise lifetime utilities over autarky, we also consider their effect on savings rates. We begin with random ROSCAs.

## 2.1. Random ROSCAs

Imagine that our $n$-person group forms a random ROSCA which meets at equally spaced dates up to $t_a$ (i.e., $\{t_a/n, 2t_a/n, \ldots, t_a\}$, with contributions of $B/n$ at each meeting). Each time the ROSCA meets, an individual is randomly selected to receive the pot of $B$, allowing him to buy the durable. Each individual continues to save at rate $B/t_a$ over the interval $[0, t_a]$, as under autarky, but can now expect to receive the durable $t_a(n-1)/2n$ sooner. Risk aversion is not an issue here, since from each individual's *ex ante* viewpoint, the random ROSCA does as well as autarky in every state of the world, and strictly better in all but one.[8]

A random ROSCA which lasts until $t_a$ is only one possibility. For example, the group could also have met until $t_a/2$ with contributions of $B/n$ and a durable being bought after each interval of length $t_a/2n$. Given the uniform spacing of meeting dates and the constant contribution rate, the duration of the ROSCA will be inversely proportional to the rate at which the group saves and accumulates the durable.

It seems natural to suppose that the group would agree on a length for the ROSCA which maximizes the (*ex ante* expected) utility of the representative group member.[9] To characterize this length and the implied savings rate, consider a "general" random ROSCA of length $t$, meeting at the dates $\{t/n, 2t/n, \ldots, t\}$, with members contributing $B/n$ at each meeting date. A representative member of the ROSCA views his receipt date for the pot (and hence the durable) as a random variable, $\tilde{\tau}$, distributed uniformly on the set $\{t/n, 2t/n, \ldots, t\}$. Each member saves at rate $B/t$ over the life of the ROSCA, and nondurable consumption is thus $c = y - B/t$ during this period. Given $c$, each member's lifetime utility is the random variable:

$$\tilde{\tau} \cdot v(0, c) + (t - \tilde{\tau}) \cdot v(1, c) + (T - t) \cdot v(1, y)$$

where $t = B/(y - c)$. Lifetime expected utility in this random ROSCA is the expected value of the expression above, and since

$$E(\tilde{\tau}) = \left(\frac{n+1}{2n}\right) t.$$

each member's *ex ante* welfare is

$$W(c) \equiv t\left[\left(\frac{n+1}{2n}\right)v(0, c) + \left(\frac{n-1}{2n}\right)v(1, c)\right] + (T - t)v(1, y) \tag{4}$$

where $t = B/(y - c)$.

The group's problem is now to choose $t$ (or equivalently $c$), to maximize (4). Let $t_r$ denote the optimal length, $c_r$ the associated consumption rate, and $W_r$ the maximal value of expected utility. This problem is similar to that encountered under autarky. Indeed, defining $\bar{\alpha} = (n - 1)/2n$, (4) may be rearranged as follows:

$$W(c) = T \cdot v(1,y) - B\left[\frac{v(1,y) - v(\bar{\alpha}, c)}{y - c}\right]$$

By analogy with the reasoning leading to (3), we obtain

$$W_r = T \cdot v(1,y) - B \cdot \mu(\bar{\alpha}) \tag{5}$$

with $c_r = c^*(\bar{\alpha})$.

The interpretation is the same as that of (3): welfare is the difference between what lifetime utility would be were the durable a free good and the minimal (expected) utility cost of saving up for its purchase. This cost is lower under the random ROSCA than under autarky because each member expects to enjoy the durable's services for a fraction $\bar{\alpha}$ of the time in which he is saving up for the durable. It is now easy to establish the following proposition.

PROPOSITION 1    *By forming a random ROSCA, group members raise their expected lifetime utilities. The optimal random ROSCA involves members saving at a lower rate over a longer interval than under autarky. Nevertheless, if $v'''(i,c) > 0$ for $i = 0$ and $1$, and if $\Delta v''(c) \geq 0$, then individuals expect to receive the durable good sooner in the optimal random ROSCA than under autarky (i.e., $t_r > t_a > (n+1)t_r/2n$).*

PROOF    Equations (5) and (3) imply that

$$W_r - W_a = B[\mu(0) - \mu(\bar{\alpha})]$$

This is positive since, as stated in the lemma, $\mu(\cdot)$ is a decreasing function; so group members' expected utility is higher in the random ROSCA than under autarky. The lemma also established that $c^*(\cdot)$ is increasing. Therefore consumption is greater as well, since

$$c_r = c^*(\bar{\alpha}) > c^*(0) = c_a$$

However, the constraint $t(y - c) = B$ applies under both autarky and the random ROSCA. Hence $t_r > t_a$, and the optimal random ROSCA involves members saving at a lower rate over a longer interval than under autarky.

To prove that the expected receipt date under the optimal random ROSCA is sooner than that under autarky we have to show that

$$t_a > \frac{(n+1)t_r}{2n} = (1 - \bar{\alpha})t_r$$

Since

$$t_a = \frac{B}{y - c^*(0)} \qquad \text{and} \qquad t_r = \frac{B}{y - c^*(\bar{\alpha})}$$

it will suffice to show that

$$y - c^*(\bar{\alpha}) > (1 - \bar{\alpha})[y - c^*(0)]$$

Now, in view of the assumed concavity of $v(1, \cdot)$, inspection of (2) reveals that $y = c^*(1)$. Therefore, we need to show that

$$\bar{\alpha}c^*(1) + (1 - \bar{\alpha})c^*(0) > c^*(\bar{\alpha})$$

This follows from Jensen's inequality and the convexity of $c^*(\cdot)$ established under these hypotheses in the lemma.

Welfare is raised by forming a ROSCA because some financial intermediation reduces everyone's utility cost of saving up. This conclusion is independent of any restrictions we imposed on preferences other than individuals' liking the durable. Showing that nondurable consumption is higher and the accumulation period is longer under the random ROSCA does require the assumption that durable services and nondurable consumption are complements. The result that individuals receive the durable earlier on average under the random ROSCA is less general, requiring the assumptions of positive third derivatives stated in proposition 1.

The ranking of random ROSCAs and autarky does not hold *ex post* since, though individuals have the same prospects *ex ante*, their circumstances differ once the order of receipt has been determined. Using the index $i$ to denote the person who wins the pot at the $i$th meeting, at date $t_r(i/n)$, *ex post* utilities under the random ROSCA are given by

$$u_r^i = t_r\left[\left(\frac{i}{n}\right)v(0, c_r) + \left(1 - \frac{i}{n}\right)v(1, c_r)\right] + (T - t_r)v(1, c_r) \qquad i = 1, \ldots, n \qquad (6)$$

Since his consumption/receipt-date pair $(c_r, t_r)$ is feasible, but not optimal, under autarky, the individual receiving the pot at the final meeting date $(i = n)$ has been made strictly worse off (*ex post*) by joining the random ROSCA.

## 2.2.   Bidding ROSCAs

Suppose now that individuals bid for the right to receive the pot at a certain date (i.e., they form a bidding ROSCA). We assume that ROSCA members determine the order of receipt for the pot when the ROSCA is initially organized at time zero.[10] Since there is no uncertainty, this does not seem unreasonable. By a "bid" we mean a pledge to contribute a certain amount to the ROSCA at a constant rate over its life, in exchange for the right to receive the pot at a certain meeting date. A higher bid would naturally entitle an individual to an earlier receipt date.

Of the many auction protocols that could be imagined, all must result in individuals being indifferent among bid/receipt-date pairs, since individuals have identical preferences and complete information. Moreover, any efficient auction procedure must be structured so that total contributions committed through bids are just adequate to finance acquisition of the durable by the recipient of the pot at each meeting date. This precludes both redundant savings within the ROSCA and the necessity to save outside of the ROSCA.

The two requirements that individuals are indifferent among bid/receipt pairs and that the sum of the contributions equals the cost of the durable completely determine the outcome of the bidding procedure. Thus it is unnecessary to commit to a particular auction protocol. However, to provide a concrete example, fix the duration $t$ of the bidding ROSCA and suppose that a series of $n - 1$ oral, ascending-bid auctions are held at date zero among $n$ group members, determining in sequence who receives the pot at each meeting date except the last, with each winner excluded from participation in subsequent auctions. The last remaining individual has his contribution set so that the sum of all commitments just equals the durable's cost, $B$. It is easy to see, using a backward-induction argument, that every (subgame-perfect) equilibrium of this bidding mechanism leaves all individuals at the same level of lifetime utility. Moreover, by construction, the winning bids (plus the last recipient's contribution) will sum to the cost of the durable. We now show how to characterize these equilibrium bids.

If the bidding ROSCA lasts until time $t$, bidding determines who receives the durable at each of the meeting dates $\{t/n, 2t/n, \ldots, t\}$. Let $b_i$ denote the promised contribution of individual $i$, defined to be the one who wins the pot at time $(i \ / \ n) \ t$. A set of bids $\{b_i\}_{i=1}^{n}$ constitutes an equilibrium if

(i)   no individual could do better by outbidding another for his place in the queue and
(ii)  contributions are sufficient to allow each participant to acquire the durable upon receiving the pot.

If ROSCA member $i$ bids $b_i$, he will have nondurable consumption $c_i = y - (n/t)b_i$ at each moment during the ROSCA's life. Thus, we can characterize the ROSCA in terms of the consumption rates: $\{c_i\}_{i=1}^{n}$. Condition (ii) implies that individual $i$'s equilibrium utility level is

$$t\left[\left(\frac{i}{n}\right) \cdot v(0, c_i) + \left(\frac{n-i}{n}\right) \cdot v(1, c_i)\right] + (T - t) \cdot v(1, y)$$

in a bidding ROSCA of length $t$. Letting $\alpha_i$ equal $(n - i)/n$, condition (i) implies, for all individuals $i$ and some number $x$, that

$$v(\alpha_i, c_i) = x \qquad i = 1, \ldots, n \tag{7}$$

The number $x$ represents the members' common average utility during the life of a bidding ROSCA of length $t$, in a bidding equilibrium.

Now define $\bar{c}$ to be the average nondurable consumption rate of members during the life of the ROSCA [i.e., $\bar{c} \equiv (1/n) \sum_{i=1}^{n} c_i$]. Then condition (ii) is equivalent to

$$t(y - \bar{c}) = B \tag{8}$$

Given the ROSCA's length $t$, the relations (7) and (8) uniquely determine members' nondurable consumption rates and their average utility over the life of the ROSCA, consistent with bidding equilibrium. Equivalently, one could take as given the equilibrium average utility level for the duration of the ROSCA, $x$. Then (7) gives individuals' equilibrium consumption levels, $\{c_i\}_{i=1}^{n}$; and these, via (8), can be used to find the ROSCA's length, $t$.

As in the random ROSCA, it is natural to assume that the length of the bidding ROSCA is chosen to maximize the common utility level of its members. The foregoing discussion and (7) imply that this common welfare is

$$T \cdot v(1,y) - B\left\{\frac{v(1,y) - x}{y - \bar{c}}\right\}$$

Now let $\hat{c}(\alpha, x)$ be the function satisfying $v(\alpha, \hat{c}) \equiv x$, and define

$$\bar{c}(x) \equiv \left(\frac{1}{n}\right) \sum_{i=1}^{n} \hat{c}(\alpha_i, x)$$

Then, when the equilibrium average utility during a bidding ROSCA is $x$, $\hat{c}(\alpha_i, x)$ is individual $i$'s nondurable consumption rate during the ROSCA, and $B/[y - \bar{c}(x)]$ is the ROSCA's length. Denote by $t_b$ and $W_b$, respectively, the duration and common utility level of the optimal bidding ROSCA. Then, using by now familiar arguments, we may write the following;[11]

$$W_b = T \cdot v(1,y) - B \cdot \mu_b \tag{9}$$

where

$$\mu_b \equiv \min_x \left[\frac{v(1,y) - x}{y - \bar{c}(x)}\right] \tag{10}$$

Letting $x^*$ give the minimum in (10), then $t_b = B/[y - \bar{c}(x^*)]$ is the length of the optimal bidding ROSCA.

Lifetime utility expressed in (9) admits the same interpretation noted for autarky and the random ROSCA; it is the difference between lifetime utility if the durable were free and the minimal cost of saving up. The latter, determined in (10), again trades off higher welfare during the ROSCA versus faster acquisition of the durable. We may now establish the following proposition.

PROPOSITION 2    *By forming a bidding ROSCA, group members raise their lifetime utilities relative to autarky. Moreover if $1/v'(0, \cdot)$ is concave, the optimal bidding ROSCA involves group members saving at a lower average rate and over a longer interval than under autarky.*

PROOF    Equations (9) and (3) together imply that $W_b - W_a = B[\mu(0) - \mu_b]$, which is positive if and only if $\mu(0) > \mu_b$. Since $v(\alpha, c)$ increases with both $\alpha$ and $c$, $\hat{c}(\alpha, x)$ decreases with $\alpha$; so,

$$\bar{c}(v(0,c)) = \left(\frac{1}{n}\right) \sum_{i=1}^{n} \hat{c}(\alpha_i, v(0,c))$$

$$< \left(\frac{1}{n}\right) \sum_{i=1}^{n} \hat{c}(0, v(0,c)) = c$$

for $0 \le c \le y$. Therefore $\bar{c}(v(0,c_a)) < c_a$; but then, setting $x = v(0,c_a)$ in (10) and comparing the value of the right-hand side with the minimized value in (2), we see that $\mu(0) > \mu_b$. Thus, by forming a bidding ROSCA, group members raise their lifetime utilities. The proof of the second part of the proposition is given in the appendix.

Again, the welfare dominance of the ROSCA over autarky requires no assumption on preferences other than individuals' liking the durable good. The greater complexity of the bidding ROSCA is reflected in the need to make an assumption on the curvature of the inverse of the marginal utility of income function in order to compare the ROSCA's savings rate to that under autarky. Concavity of this function does not follow from any well-known property of utility functions, though it is satisfied for many cases. For example, for isoelastic utility functions with

$$v(0,c) = \frac{c^{1-\rho}}{1-\rho}$$

$1/v'(0,c)$ is convex if $\rho > 1$ and concave if $\rho < 1$.

Unlike autarky or the random ROSCA, the bidding ROSCA leaves each individual with a different rate of nondurable consumption during the accumulation period. Earlier acquirers of the durable bid a higher contribution to the ROSCA and consume less of the nondurable; $(c_1 < \cdots < c_n)$. Proposition 2 also reveals that the last individual to acquire the durable in a bidding ROSCA must have greater nondurable consumption during accumulation than under autarky $(c_n > c_a)$. These higher contributions of earlier recipients resemble interest payments, and in this sense the bidding ROSCA can be likened to a market.[12]

## 3. Bidding versus Random ROSCAs

While we have already established that either type of ROSCA allows a group to use its savings more effectively than under autarky, they do not yield identical outcomes. We observed above that bidding results in recipients of early pots forgoing consumption. The optimal savings rate may also differ between the two institutions. Comparison of these savings rates and welfare levels is the object of this section. In particular, understanding the latter may yield insight into the circumstances when we would expect to observe one or the other of the ROSCA types in practice. Our main result for a homogeneous group is stated in the following proposition.

PROPOSITION 3    *Group members' expected utility will be higher if they use a random rather than a bidding ROSCA. If the value of the durable is independent of the nondurable consumption rate* *[i.e., $\Delta v'(c) \equiv 0$], and if $1/v'(0, \cdot)$ is a convex function, then the optimal random ROSCA involves members saving at a lower rate over a longer interval than the optimal bidding ROSCA.*

PROOF   From (5) and (9) we see that

$$W_r - W_b = B[\mu_b - \mu(\bar{\alpha})]$$

so we need to show that $\mu_b > \mu(\bar{\alpha})$. The proof is simple. Using (2), the definition of $\hat{c}(\alpha, x)$, and the change of variables $x = v(\bar{\alpha}, c)$, we can write

$$\mu(\bar{\alpha}) = \min_x \left[ \frac{v(1, y) - x}{y - \hat{c}(\bar{\alpha}, x)} \right] \tag{11}$$

Comparing (11) with (10) we conclude: $\mu(\bar{\alpha}) < \mu_b$ if $\hat{c}(\bar{\alpha}, x) < \bar{c}(x)$, for all $x$; but $\hat{c}(\bar{\alpha}, x)$ is $\hat{c}(\cdot, x)$ evaluated at the average of $\alpha_i$ while $\bar{c}(x)$ is the average of the values $\hat{c}(\alpha_i, x)$. Hence, by Jensen's inequality, our conclusion holds if $\hat{c}(\cdot, x)$ is strictly convex. A bit of calculus shows

$$\frac{\partial \hat{c}}{\partial \alpha} = -\frac{\Delta v(\hat{c})}{v(\bar{\alpha}, \hat{c})} < 0$$

A bit more reveals

$$\frac{\partial^2 \hat{c}}{\partial \alpha^2} = \frac{-\partial \hat{c}}{\partial \alpha} \left[ \frac{\Delta v'(\hat{c})}{v'(\bar{\alpha}, \hat{c})} + \frac{d}{dc}\left( \frac{\Delta v(\hat{c})}{v(\bar{\alpha}, \hat{c})} \right) \right]$$

which is positive provided that $\Delta v'(c) \geq 0$. This proves the first claim of the proposition. The proof of the second claim is given in the appendix.

Thus according to proposition 3 our assumptions imply that individuals are better off using a savings association that allocates access to funds by lot. This may explain why randomization is so widely used in practice. Though this finding is at first sight counterintuitive, a natural explanation is available. As will emerge in the next section, however, the assumption of identical preferences is crucial to the result; when individuals' preferences differ, bidding permits them to sort themselves.

The assumption that the durable and nondurable goods are complements is key to proving that random allocation dominates bidding from an *ex ante* viewpoint. To see why, consider two ROSCAs of the same duration. Bidding requires members to have the same average utility over the life of the ROSCA; random allocation requires them to have the same nondurable consumption rates. Each of these requirements constitutes a constraint on the more general scheme which randomly assigns members an order of receipt $i, 1 \leq i \leq n$, and a consumption rate $c_i, 0 \leq c_i \leq y$, but which requires neither equal consumption rates nor equal *ex post* utilities.[13] Were such a scheme designed to maximize *ex ante* expected welfare, it would equate individuals' marginal utilities[14]:

$$v'(\alpha_i, c_i) = v'(\alpha_j, c_j) \qquad 1 \leq i, j \leq n$$

When $\Delta v'(c) \geq 0$, random assignment with equal nondurable consumption more closely approximates this condition than does bidding. In a bidding equilibrium earlier recipients of the pot contribute more to the ROSCA (lower $c_i$) in exchange for greater access to the durable during the ROSCA (higher $\alpha_i$). However, with $\Delta v'(c) \geq 0$, they also have higher marginal utilities than those receiving the pot later. This divergence of marginal utilities is mitigated in the random ROSCA, which sets $c_i = c_r$, for all $i$. Thus, when the two goods are complements, the equal-consumption-rate constraint of random allocation is less inhibiting than is the equal-average-utility constraint of bidding, and the random ROSCA performs better than the bidding ROSCA in this case.[15] This is particularly clear when $\Delta v' \equiv 0$, since equality of consumption rates during the ROSCA implies equality of marginal utilities. However, equality of lifetime utilities constrains consumption so that the marginal utility is higher among those who receive the pot earlier.

Figure 1 illustrates the latter case graphically. We depict lifetime utility possibilities for a two-person group with time horizon $T = 3$ years, and ROSCA length $t = 2$ years. The value of the durable's services, $\Delta v(c) \equiv \xi > 0$, is a constant. Since total annual contributions to the ROSCA must equal the durable's cost, total annual consumption for the individuals equals $2y - B$ during the life of the ROSCA. By considering alternative nondurable consumption levels for the two individuals satisfying this constraint, we trace out two utility possibility frontiers. Which is relevant depends upon who gets the durable first. If individual 1 does, the relevant utility possibility frontier is located to the northwest in the figure, while if individual 2 gets the durable first, the relevant frontier is the one to the southeast. The indivisibility of the durable good causes the overall utility possibility set to be nonconvex.

Because a random Rosca yields equal nondurable consumptions, its utility allocation is either at point A (if individual 1 wins the first pot) or at point B (if individual 2 does). Note that, because $\Delta v' = 0$, the slope of the relevant utility possibility frontier is $-1$ at points A and B; the line containing A and B is tangent to the two frontiers at those points.

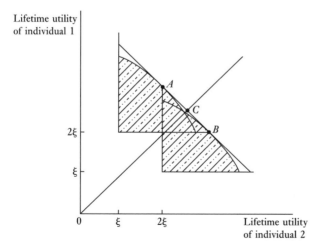

**Figure 1** Lifetime utility possibilities for a two-person group with time horizon $T = 3$ years and ROSCA length $t = 2$ years

*Note:* $\xi \equiv \Delta v(c) > 0$ is a constant

Since these utility allocations have equal probability, each individual's *ex ante* expected utility is at point C. The sum of expected utilities at point C is maximal among all feasible expected utility allocations. A bidding ROSCA, by making utilities equal, produces a utility allocation at the intersection of the two frontiers. The dominance of the random ROSCA is now obvious.[16]

Proposition 3 also compares the savings rates in random and bidding ROSCAs, but it requires that $\Delta v'(c) = 0$ and imposes a restriction on the curvature of $1/v'(0, \cdot)$. No general result appears to be available. Combining propositions 2 and 3, in the case of separable logarithmic utility [i.e., where $v(0, c) = \ln(c)$ and

$$v(1, c) = v(0, c) + \xi, \ \xi > 0]$$

then, since $1/v'(0, c)$ is linear, $t_a < t_b < t_r$. Thus, in this case institutions with higher *ex ante* welfare are also those with lower savings rates and longer accumulation periods.


## 4. ROSCAs with Heterogeneous Individuals

While there is some evidence that ROSCAs are formed among relatively homogeneous groups (see e.g., Thomas Cope and Kurtz, 1980), there is no good reason to suppose that the individuals in any particular group have identical preferences for the durable and, hence, for receipt of the pot. In this section we show how allowing for such differences may reverse the ranking of the bidding and random ROSCAs from an *ex ante* viewpoint. With heterogeneous tastes, bids can be used to order individuals, with those who value the pot more acquiring it sooner. This is true whether or not information about tastes is private. Even if valuations are public information, individuals can use bidding to realize "gains from trade" within the ROSCA, as members who value the pot more exchange greater contributions for earlier access to the pot. When valuations are not commonly known, bidding plays the additional role of inducing individuals to reveal this information. We restrict attention here to the case in which preferences are common knowledge.

We consider the operation of a two-person bidding ROSCA.[17] The preferences of these two individuals are as above, except that individual 1's utility when he has the durable is increased by a constant, with individual 2's utility being reduced by the same constant. Thus, prior to acquiring the durable good, utility for both individuals is $v(0, c)$; after acquiring it, individual 1 has utility

$$v^1(1, c) \equiv v(1, c) + \xi$$

and individual 2 has utility

$$v^2(1, c) \equiv v(1, c) - \xi$$

for $\xi \geq 0$. The parameter $\xi$ measures the difference in the individuals' tastes. Note that $\xi = 0$ is the case of homogeneous individuals considered above and that an increase in $\xi$ yields a mean-preserving spread in the dispersion of the individuals' valuations. The key assumption is that the *difference* in individuals' valuations of the durable is independent of the level of nondurable consumption. Relaxing this would complicate the analysis without adding new insights. As before, $v^i(\alpha, c)$ denotes individual $i$'s expected utility flow at an instant when $\alpha$ is the probability of owning the durable. Hence,

$$v^1(\alpha, c) = v(\alpha, c) + \alpha\xi$$

and

$$v^2(\alpha, c) = v(\alpha, c) - \alpha\xi$$

Consider a bidding ROSCA of length $t$, meeting at dates $t/2$ and $t$. Let $b_i$ be individual $i$'s bid, and let $c_i$ be his nondurable consumption rate during the ROSCA. Then $c_i = y - 2b_i/t$. We will adopt the auction protocol described in subsection 2.2: an oral, ascending-bid auction where the winner gets the first pot and the loser's contribution is set to yield a total payment of $B$ at each meeting date. To understand the outcome of such an auction, note that individual 1 will always exceed the bid $b$, if

$$v^1\left(\tfrac{1}{2}, y - 2\frac{b}{t}\right) > v^1\left(0, y - 2\left[\frac{B-b}{t}\right]\right) \tag{12}$$

The left-hand side of (12) is individual 1's average utility during the ROSCA if he wins with bid $b$, and the right-hand side is his average utility if individual 2 wins with the same bid. As long as (12) holds then, by bidding a little more than $b$, individual 1 raises his welfare if his bid prevails. Since tastes are common knowledge, individual 2 will exceed any bid satisfying (12) knowing that 1 will go higher. In this way, 2 can reduce the size of his own contribution. Thus the outcome of the auction will be that individual 1 wins with a bid for which (12) is an equality.

In bidding equilibrium, therefore, individual 1 will be indifferent between consumption/receipt-date pairs $(c_2, t)$ and $(c_1, t/2)$. Furthermore, consumption rates will satisfy

$$B = \left(\frac{t}{2}\right)(2y - c_1 - c_2)$$

These two conditions uniquely determine the equilibrium consumption (and hence, bids) in a bidding ROSCA of length $t$.[18] We now consider the optimal length for such a ROSCA.

To facilitate comparison with our previous analysis, suppose that the ROSCA is utilitarian, its length being chosen to maximize the average utility of its members. Given length $t$, let $x$ be the average of the members' utility during the ROSCA. In bidding equilibrium

$$x \equiv \left(\tfrac{1}{2}\right)\left[v^1\left(\tfrac{1}{2}, c_1\right) + v^2(0, c_2)\right]$$

Since bidding equilibrium requires $v^1(0, c_2) = v^1(\frac{1}{2}, c_1)$, we conclude that $x = v(0, c_2)$. Using the function $\hat{c}(\alpha, x)$ defined in subsection 2.2 by the identity $v(\alpha, \hat{c}) \equiv x$, write equilibrium consumption rates as

$$c_1 = \hat{c}\left(\frac{1}{2}, x - \frac{\xi}{2}\right) \quad \text{and} \quad c_2 = \hat{c}(0, x)$$

Letting $\bar{c}(x, \xi)$ denote the average equilibrium consumption rate, we have

$$\bar{c}(x, \xi) \equiv \frac{\hat{c}\left(\frac{1}{2}, x - \frac{\xi}{2}\right) + \hat{c}(0, x)}{2}$$

Then the average welfare in bidding equilibrium is

$$\bar{W} \equiv T \cdot v(1, y) - B\left[\frac{v(1, y) - x}{y - \bar{c}(x, \xi)}\right] \tag{13}$$

Denote by $\tilde{W}_b$ the level of average welfare in the optimal bidding ROSCA with heterogeneous preferences. Then (13) implies the following familiar relationship:

$$\tilde{W}_b = T \cdot v(1, y) - B\tilde{\mu}_b \tag{14}$$

where

$$\tilde{\mu}_b \equiv \min_x \left[\frac{v(1, y) - x}{y - \bar{c}(x, \xi)}\right] \tag{15}$$

We can interpret (14) and (15) as before. Mean welfare in the optimal bidding ROSCA is the difference between what it would be if the durable were free and the minimal cost of saving-up. This cost, $\tilde{\mu}_b$, is the value of a minimization problem.

It is revealing to compare the expressions above with the analogous equations (9) and (10) which apply to the homogeneous bidding ROSCA. Mean welfare in the heterogeneous case differs from that in the homogeneous case only because the corresponding average consumption rates, $\bar{c}(x, \xi)$ and $\bar{c}(x)$, differ. In the homogeneous case

$$\bar{c}(x) \equiv \frac{\hat{c}\left(\frac{1}{2}, x\right) + \hat{c}(0, x)}{2}$$

Hence $\bar{c}(x, 0) = \bar{c}(x)$, and so as individuals' tastes become more similar, the outcome with heterogeneity converges to the outcome in the homogeneous bidding ROSCA. Moreover, since $\hat{c}(\alpha, x)$ is increasing in $x$, we know that $\bar{c}(x, \xi)$ is decreasing in $\xi$. So, *a mean-preserving increase in the dispersion of members' valuations of the durable good reduces the mean utility cost of saving up to a bidding ROSCA and, hence, increases the individuals' mean welfare in bidding equilibrium.*

To see why intuitively, let individual 1's valuation of the durable rise and let individual 2's fall by an equal amount, holding fixed nondurable consumption rates. The change in valuations has no impact on mean welfare when both individuals have the durable, and it increases mean welfare when only individual 1 has it. Thus, as long as individual 1 has priority of access, increasing the dispersion of valuations holding consumption fixed raises mean welfare. Allowing consumption rates to move to their equilibrium levels only reinforces this effect.

In a random ROSCA, individuals 1 and 2 consume the nondurable good at the same rate, and both have an even chance of acquiring the durable on either of the same two dates. It follows that the average of the two individuals' expected utilities in a random ROSCA is independent of $\xi$. Setting $\xi = 0$ and using (5), we conclude that average expected utility in the optimal random ROSCA with diverse tastes, denoted $\tilde{W}_r$, is given by:

$$\tilde{W}_r \equiv T \cdot v(1, y) - B \cdot \mu(\tfrac{1}{4}).$$

(Since $n = 2$, $\bar{\alpha} = \tfrac{1}{4}$.) We now have the following proposition.

PROPOSITION 4   *The average of individuals' expected lifetime utilities in the optimal bidding ROSCA exceeds that in the optimal random ROSCA if the dispersion of individuals' valuations is sufficiently large.*

PROOF   The above discussion implies that $\tilde{W}_b > \tilde{W}_r$ if and only if $\tilde{\mu}_b < \mu(\tfrac{1}{4})$. Comparing (15) with (11) we see that $\tilde{\mu}_b < \mu(\tfrac{1}{4})$ if $\tilde{c}(x^*, \xi) < \hat{c}(\tfrac{1}{4}, x^*)$, where $x^*$ gives the minimum in (11) for $\bar{\alpha} = \tfrac{1}{4}$. Writing this out, we have: $\tilde{\mu}_b < \mu(\tfrac{1}{4})$ if

$$\hat{c}\left(\tfrac{1}{2}, x^* - \tfrac{\xi}{2}\right) < 2\hat{c}\left(\tfrac{1}{4}, x^*\right) - \hat{c}(0, x^*).$$

Hence, to conclude that $\tilde{W}_b > \tilde{W}_r$ it suffices to know that

$$x^* - \tfrac{\xi}{2} < v\left(\tfrac{1}{2}, 2\hat{c}\left(\tfrac{1}{4}, x^*\right) - \hat{c}(0, x^*)\right)$$

or

$$\tfrac{\xi}{2} > x^* - v\left(\tfrac{1}{2}, 2\hat{c}\left(\tfrac{1}{4}, x^*\right) - \hat{c}(0, x^*)\right)$$

Thus, bidding dominates for high enough $\xi$, since the left-hand side of the above inequality increases with $\xi$ and the right-hand side is independent of $\xi$. Note that the right-hand side of the inequality is positive since

$$\hat{c}\left(\tfrac{1}{4}, x^*\right) < \tfrac{1}{2}\left\{\hat{c}(0, x^*) + \hat{c}\left(\tfrac{1}{2}, x^*\right)\right\}$$

from the proof of proposition 3. This implies that

$$v\left(\tfrac{1}{2}, 2\hat{c}\left(\tfrac{1}{4}, x^*\right) - \hat{c}(0, x^*)\right) < x^*$$

The reason for the result should be clear. The bidding ROSCA gives the pot to the individual with the highest valuation first, while a random ROSCA does not respect individuals' valuations. If the gain from doing this is large enough, it outweighs that from randomization which we demonstrated in the previous section. Since our welfare criterion is mean expected utility, the interpretation of this result is as follows: given sufficient heterogeneity, individuals choosing "behind the veil of ignorance" (i.e., before they know their tastes) would opt for a bidding ROSCA rather than a random ROSCA.

This analysis of heterogeneity is limited by our assumption that individuals' valuations are commonly known. To relax this assumption would be of interest but would take us far afield from the concerns of the present paper. It is clear, however, that the main insight from the simplest case, that bidding can serve a useful sorting function, will be robust in the face of further analysis.

## 5. The Sustainability of ROSCAs

We premised our analysis on an assumption that the group of potential ROSCA members had no access to external credit markets. This is not unreasonable for most situations where ROSCAs are prevalent, whether among an ethnic group within the United States or in less developed countries. There are various reasons why particular groups may have difficulty in obtaining credit in formal markets. First, immigrant groups or rural villagers may be intimidated by banks, which require their customers to be literate and to be familiar with certain banking practices. Second, groups may be discriminated against, and thus unable to obtain access to credit from regular sources. Third, and perhaps most importantly, banks may perceive the default risk of lending to certain groups to be too high. Default may occur either because borrowers face unreliable income streams, and thus are *unable* to repay, or because they are *unwilling* to repay, with the bank having insufficient sanctions against them to make them do so. Typically, individuals who join ROSCAs tend to lack reliable forms of collateral which can be used to assuage banks' fears of nonrepayment.

Since those who receive the pot early are effectively in debt to the other group members, ROSCAs too would seem vulnerable to problems of nonrepayment, with individuals refusing to honor their membership commitment after winning the pot. However, there are good reasons why ROSCAs do not fall victim to the problem of deliberate default which banks might face. The key to understanding ROSCAs is noting that, unlike markets, they are not anonymous institutions. They use preexisting social connections between individuals to help circumvent problems of imperfect information and enforceability. The rules of ROSCAs reflect concerns of this kind. For example, individuals must be appropriately vetted before being allowed to join.

A typical scenario for a ROSCA is a group of individuals from the same village or, in an urban setting, from the same office.[19] In the United States, as we have noted, ROSCAs are most often formed from among an ethnic group. Thus individuals are likely to have good information about the reliability of their neighbors and co-workers and can enforce sanctions – social and economic – on those who are delinquent without good reason. It seems central to understanding the sustainability of ROSCAs that there be some kind of "social collateral" among a group which can be harnessed in this way.

All this explains very well why ROSCAs tend to avoid large-scale default in practice, and the anthropological literature on ROSCAs is replete with examples to illustrate this point. Summing up these, Ardener (1964 p. 216) observes that "a member may go to great lengths, such as stealing or selling a daughter into prostitution in order to fulfill his obligations to his association; failure to meet obligations can even lead to suicide." Reporting on ROSCAs in Cameroon, a recent *New York Times* article noted that "bankers complain of loan delinquency rates as high as 50%. But [ROSCA] payments are taken so seriously that borrowers faced with delinquency have been known to commit suicide" (Brooke, 1987 p. 30). Perhaps ironically, the inability of ROSCA members to enter credit markets actually strengthens the value of social sanctions, since individuals with bad reputations earned in ROSCAs may expect little other credit-market access.[20]

All of this notwithstanding, it would be misleading to ignore default entirely. Here, we shall examine how such considerations may influence the design and performance of ROSCAs. We do this within our model by supposing that a defaulting individual is subjected to social sanctions inflicted by other group members with an exogenously given utility cost of $K$.[21] This cost might represent the discomfort, loss of face, and other social costs associated with having to confront the other ROSCA members each day or, in the extreme, the costs of finding a new job or place to live. In a more general model, it might also represent the loss from being excluded from ROSCA participation in the future.

Suppose now that individuals choose whether or not to meet their ROSCA obligations. Then a ROSCA will be established only if it satisfies a *sustainability constraint*, ensuring that each individual prefers to maintain his contribution to the ROSCA after he has won the pot. With identical preferences, this constraint takes a very simple form: it holds for every ROSCA member if it holds for the first one to win the pot, the latter having the greatest incentive to default.

Consider a random ROSCA among $n$ identical individuals, as defined in subsection 2.1. If the consumption rate during the ROSCA is $c$, then it lasts until date $t$ and meets at $\{t/n, 2t/n, \cdots, t\}$, where $t = B/(y - c)$. Then, the benefit to the first recipient of defaulting is

$$\left(\frac{n-1}{n}\right) B \left[\frac{v(1, y) - v(1, c)}{y - c}\right]$$

(i.e., the gain from avoiding the $n - 1$ remaining contributions to the ROSCA). The ROSCA is sustainable if this benefit does not exceed the default cost $K$. Letting

$$g(c, \alpha) \equiv \alpha \left[\frac{v(1, y) - v(1, c)}{y - c}\right]$$

and with $\bar{\alpha} = (n - 1)/2n$ as before, the sustainability constraint becomes $g(c, \bar{\alpha}) \leq K/2B$. The analysis of section 2 implicitly assumed $K$ to be large enough for this constraint to be satisfied at the optimal nondurable consumption rate, $c^*(\bar{\alpha})$.

If the constraint were not satisfied, the allocation that we described for the random ROSCA would not be sustainable. Fixing $n$, we can ask how the demands of sustainability would affect the design of the ROSCA. Since utility is concave in $c$, $g(c, \alpha)$ decreases in $c$, for $c \leq y$. Thus, for a given number of members, the sustainability constraint can be accommodated only by increasing $c$ above $c_r$ or, equivalently, increasing $t$ above $t_r$. Thus, deterring default requires increasing the duration of the ROSCA. Holding the duration of the ROSCA fixed, the benefit of default could be reduced by lowering $n$. Fewer meetings implies a shorter period over which the first recipient of the pot might enjoy the benefits of default. Obviously, either of these adjustments will reduce the welfare gain from forming a ROSCA, since the original allocation is being further constrained.[22, 23]

Equation (5) reveals that the expected utility in a random ROSCA of given length increases with $n$. Hence, absent considerations of sustainability, welfare is higher with a larger ROSCA membership. In practice, however, we do not often observe ROSCAs of more than a few score members, and sustainability considerations would seem key to understanding this fact. This is especially so if one considers the determinants of the default cost, $K$. In larger groups it becomes more difficult to keep track of defecting members (the evidence [e.g., Haggblade, 1978] seems to be that larger ROSCAs face bigger default problems). This effect is likely to outweigh the intermediation benefits of a larger membership in groups above a certain size, since the marginal benefit of another member declines with the size of the group, while marginal monitoring and enforcement costs could be expected to increase.

The issues of sustainability are broadly similar for bidding ROSCAs. We should emphasize, however, that, because bidding for priority forces a heavier obligation upon earlier recipients, the incentive issues are more serious. Moreover, there is an interesting complication if individuals differ with respect to their susceptibility to social sanctions and if this difference is private information. Those individuals who care little about such sanctions would have a further incentive to bid in order to get the pot early, knowing that they need not continue paying into the ROSCA after winning the pot. Thus, bidding brings along its own adverse-selection problem.

Our discussion of sustainability has so far focused exclusively on the problem of willingness to continue making payments into the ROSCA, rather than ability to do so. The latter might also be a problem if individuals' incomes are stochastic, since then they might sometimes be unable to contribute. The anthropological literature indicates that on some occasions ROSCAs serve a risk-sharing role, with one or more members paying the contributions of another. Problems of moral hazard and adverse selection seem less likely to pervade such "insurance" schemes than in other contexts, because of the social connectedness of ROSCA members.

## 6. Concluding Remarks

This paper has investigated the economic role and performance of ROSCAs. We have sought their rationale in the fact that some goods are indivisible, a fact which makes autarkic saving inefficient. We have argued here that ROSCAs can be understood as a response by a socially connected group to credit-market exclusion. This seems broadly consistent with what we see in practice. We have made precise how ROSCAs improve over autarky and have compared random and bidding ROSCAs. We found that the indivisibilities which might motivate the existence of ROSCAs can explain why random allocation is so widely used. However, with sufficient dispersion of the valuations of the durable goods, bidding may be preferred as a means of allocating rights to the pot.

Our analysis also discussed the problem of sustainability, and we pointed out some of the constraints that this might impose. In general it may necessitate operating ROSCAs with fewer members and longer durations than would otherwise be desirable. Sustainability seems likely to be more of a problem in bidding than random ROSCAs, since the gains from early default are greater, and individuals with the lowest disutility from social disapproval and sanctions have a stronger incentive to bid in order to obtain the pot early.

The analysis suggests a number of interesting avenues for empirical investigation. While there are many studies of ROSCAs, few have tried to test concrete theoretical hypotheses. Our analysis suggests at least three directions in which this might go. First, there are questions about ROSCA memberships: do the groups appear to be homogeneous, and what social connections between group members circumvent the problem of default? Second, there are questions of ROSCA design – their length, their savings rates, and whether bidding or random allocation is used. On the last issue our model gives predictions in terms of the structure of preferences and the heterogeneity of the group. Third, there are questions of what ROSCA winnings are used for. Our theory predicts their use for the purchase of durable goods.

A number of theoretical issues remain outstanding. This paper has compared the allocations achieved by random and bidding ROSCAs to the autarkic allocation and to each other. It is also interesting to ask how the allocations attained by ROSCAs compare with those that are, in principle, feasible for the group. For example, are ROSCAs efficient? Furthermore, would the group formation of a credit market result in the same allocation as a bidding ROSCA? These and other questions are pursued in our companion paper (Besley et al., 1992). We show there that, in general, ROSCAs do not produce efficient allocations and that bidding ROSCAs are inferior to credit markets. Nonetheless, the element of chance offered by random ROSCAs is still of value. Indeed, we present an example in which an *ex post* efficient market allocation is dominated (under the *ex ante* expected-utility criterion) by a random ROSCA.

APPENDIX

## *Proof of lemma*

It is easy to see that, as long as acquiring the durable good is desirable under autarky, a unique interior solution to (2) exists. The first-order condition for this problem implies

$$v'(\alpha, c^*) = \frac{v(1, y) - v(\alpha, c^*)}{y - c^*} = \mu(\alpha)$$

This is the identity claimed in the lemma. Since $v(\alpha, c)$ is increasing in $\alpha$, $\mu(\cdot)$ must be decreasing. Moreover, since $\mu(\cdot)$ is the value of a minimand linear in the parameter $\alpha$, elementary duality theory implies that $\mu(\cdot)$ is a concave function of $\alpha$. By the envelope theorem,

$$\mu'(\alpha) = -\frac{\Delta v(c^*)}{y - c^*}$$

These relations, the assumed three-times continuous differentiability of the utility function, and the implicit-function theorem establish the extent of differentiability of $\mu(\cdot)$ and $c^*(\cdot)$ asserted in the lemma. Now differentiate $v'(\alpha, c^*) \equiv \mu(\alpha)$ with respect to $\alpha$, and use the envelope result to get

$$\frac{dc^*}{d\alpha} = -\left[v''(\alpha, c^*)\right]^{-1}\left[\Delta v'(c^*) + \frac{\Delta v(c^*)}{y - c^*}\right] > 0$$

given concavity of the utility functions $v(i, \cdot)$, and the assumption that $\Delta v' \geq 0$. Differentiate the identity $v'(\alpha, c^*) \equiv \mu(\alpha)$ twice with respect to $\alpha$ to get

$$\frac{d^2 c^*}{d\alpha^2} = \left[v''(\alpha, c^*)\right]^{-1} \times \left[\mu''(\alpha) - 2\Delta v''(c^*) \cdot \left(\frac{dc^*}{d\alpha}\right) - v'''(\alpha, c^*) \cdot \left(\frac{dc^*}{d\alpha}\right)^2\right] > 0$$

using the assumptions that $\Delta v''(c^*) \geq 0$ and $v'''(i, c^*) > 0$, for $i = 0$ and 1.

### Completion of proof of proposition 2

We need to show that if $1/v'(0, \cdot)$ is concave then $t_b > t_a$. It is sufficient to show that $c_a < \bar{c}(x^*)$ to establish the result. By the lemma, the first-order condition for the minimization in (10), and the fact that $\mu_b < \mu(0)$, we have that

$$v'(0, c_a) = \mu(0) > \mu_b = \left\{\left(\frac{1}{n}\right)\sum_{i=1}^{n}[v'(\alpha_i, \hat{c}(\alpha_i, x^*))]^{-1}\right\}^{-1}$$

However, because $\Delta v'(c) \geq 0$, we have that $v'(\alpha, c) \geq v'(0, c)$. Therefore, using Jensen's inequality and the assumed concavity of $1/v'(0, \cdot)$,

$$v'(0, c_u) > \left\{\left(\frac{1}{n}\right)\sum_{i=1}^{n}\frac{1}{v'(0, \hat{c}(\alpha_i, x^*))}\right\}^{-1} \geq v'(0, \bar{c}(x^*))$$

The result now follows from the fact that $v''(0, c) < 0$

## Completion of proof of proposition 3

We need to show that $\Delta v' \equiv 0$ and $1/v'(0, \cdot)$ convex imply $t_r > t_b$. It suffices to deduce that $c_r > \bar{c}(x^*)$. By the same reasoning as employed in the completion of the proof of proposition 2, the fact that $\mu(\bar{\alpha}) < \mu_b$ (proved in the text) and the assumption that $v'(\alpha, c)$ is independent of $\alpha$, we have

$$v'(\bar{\alpha}, c_r) < \left\{ \left(\frac{1}{n}\right) \sum_{i=1}^{n} [v'(\bar{\alpha}, \hat{c}(\alpha_i, x^*))]^{-1} \right\}^{-1} \leq v'(\bar{\alpha}, \bar{c}(x^*))$$

using Jensen's inequality and the convexity hypothesis. The result follows at once.

### Notes

1  ROSCAs travel under many different names; *chit funds* in India, *susu* in Ghana, *tontines* in Senegal, *njangis* in Cameroon, *cheetu* in Sri Lanka, and *pasanakus* in Bolivia are just a few examples.

2  The classic anthropological studies of ROSCAs are by Clifford Geertz (1962) and Shirley Ardener (1964). The latter paper is particularly recommended as an introduction to the literature; see also Donald V. Kurtz (1973) and Douglass G. Norville and James S. Wehrly (1969). Phillipe Callier (1990) provides an economic interpretation of ROSCAs. For informal economic analyses of ROSCAs in particular countries, see Dale W. Adams and Marie L. Canavesi de Sahonero (1989) on Bolivia, Robert T. Anderson (1966) and S. Radhakrishnan et al. (1975) on India, Girma Begashaw (1978) on Ethiopia, Edgar Fernando (1986) on Sri Lanka, and Adeniyi Osuntogun and Remi Adeyemo (1981) on Nigeria.

3  Some forms of ROSCAs may require members to make in-kind contributions. An example of this form which may be familiar to the reader is that of "barn raisings," which were common among 19th-century frontier farmers in the United States. Consider a group of farmers living in the same region, each of whom wants to build a new barn. On the first Sunday in every month, the group gets together and builds a new barn for one of the farmers selected at random. They reconvene the next month and do the same, continuing until each member in the group has a barn.

4  While bidding and drawing lots seem to be the two most common ways of allocating the pot, it is also sometimes allocated according to need or known criteria, such as age or kinship seniority. The reader is referred to Ardener (1964) for a more detailed discussion.

5  Common examples are bicycles and tin roofs. See Fritz Bouman (1977) and Geertz (1962) for more discussion of the various uses for the pot.

6  This was clearly recognized by Ardener (1964 p. 217). "The most obvious function of these associations is that they assist in small-scale capital formation, or more simply, they create savings. Members could save their contributions themselves at home and accumulate their own funds, but this would withdraw money from circulation: in a rotating credit association capital need never be idle."

7  Note that accumulation for purchase of the durable is not desirable at all for some parameter values. It follows from our analysis of (1) that an individual would choose to save up on his own to purchase the durable only if $T \cdot \Delta v(y)/B$ is sufficiently large. Here we shall consider only such cases where this condition holds.

8  This is also noted by Callier (1990 p. 274). "The creation of a tontine is one of the most obvious Pareto improvements that people who save in order to purchase a bulky asset can create for themselves in a society with fragmented capital markets. . . . The pooling of resources reduces the time of waiting before the purchase for all participants except the one who is last collecting the kitty (who nevertheless does not have to wait more than if he had saved alone)."

9  In Cameroon the typical length of njangis is two years (see James Brooke, 1987). The cundina in Mexico last between one and two years according to Kurtz (1973). These lengths seem to be broadly in line with many other studies of ROSCAs that we have found. The literature reveals considerable variation in the size of ROSCAs. Most seem to range from 10 to 20 members although Osuntogun and Adeyemo (1981) report ROSCAs as large as 100 members in south-western Nigeria.

10  The literature reveals considerable variation in the bidding procedures used in practice. See Ardener (1964) and Fernando (1986) for discussions of particular cases.

11  In this minimization $x$ is restricted to a range defined by the requirement that the consumption levels $c_i = \hat{c}(\alpha_i, x)$ must be no less than zero and no greater than $y, i = 1, \ldots, n$.

12  Our companion paper (Besley et al., 1992) makes the comparison exact.

13  Hybrid ROSCAs of this sort seem not to be observed in practice. This may be due to problems of implementation, since losers in this lottery might prefer to join another ROSCA than to continue in the original one.

14  Otherwise it would be possible to increase *ex ante* expected utility by increasing contributions to the ROSCA by an individual with lower marginal utility and reducing them for an individual with higher marginal utility, keeping total contributions at each meeting just equal to $B$.

15  Conversely, if durable and nondurable consumption are sufficiently strong substitutes, then the equal-average-utility constraint, by forcing $c_i$ and $\alpha_i$ to covary negatively in the group, can produce less inequality of marginal utilities than the equal-consumption-rate constraint. For example, one can easily show that, if

$$r(0, c) = 1 - \exp(-c) \quad \text{and} \quad v(1, c) = v(0, c + \xi)$$

for some $\xi > 0$, then the optimal bidding ROSCA achieves the maximal *ex ante* expected utility among the more general schemes of the sort discussed in the text. Less obvious, but also true, is that this exponential form is necessary for the bidding ROSCA to attain the more general maximum.

16  The failure of bidding to achieve maximal expected utility parallels results obtained in other literatures where indivisibilities are important. See, for example, the model of conscription in Theodore Bergstrom (1986), the location models of James A. Mirrlees (1972) and Richard Arnott and John Riley (1977), and the club membership model of Arye Hillman and Peter Swan (1983).

17  This restriction is for notational simplicity only. The extension to many members is straight-forward.

18  In the natural extension of this analysis to the case of $n$ individuals, equilibrium consumptions will be determined by the equations:

(i)   $v^i(\alpha_i, c_i) = v^i(\alpha_{i+1}, c_{i+1}) \quad i = 1, \ldots, n - 1$

(ii)  $\displaystyle\sum_{i=1}^{n} c_i = n\left[y - \frac{B}{t.}\right]$

19  Adams and Canavesi de Sahonero (1989) conduct a detailed analysis of ROSCAs based in offices in urban Bolivia.

20 This may help to explain why ROSCAs become less important in the process of economic development, however, since as individuals' market opportunities expand, the value of social sanctions declines, and the sustainability of ROSCAs becomes more problematic.

21 It would be theoretically more satisfying to have $K$ determined endogenously, arising from rational behavior by the individuals in some extended version of the model. A natural way of doing this would be to posit a sequence of ROSCAs through time, supposing that failure to perform in the past results in future exclusion from ROSCA participation. Then $K$ would depend positively on the benefit of ROSCA participation relative to autarky, and negatively on individuals' discount rates.

22 Referring to the sustainability constraint, it is also clear that a larger pot also may create problems of sustainability. This is borne out in Stephen Haggblade's (1978) discussions of the njangis in Cameroon. However, he does report that some ROSCAs with $40,000 pots are found there (p. 43). One imagines that the severity of the social sanctions associated with default would also be great in ROSCAs of this magnitude. As we have seen, it is the ratio of default cost to pot size, $K/B$, which matters.

23 This discussion suggests the following reformulation of the ROSCA design problem:

$$\mu^* \equiv \min_{a,c} \left[ \frac{v(1,y) - v(\alpha,c)}{y - c} \right]$$

subject to $g(\alpha,c) \leq K/2B$, where $(\alpha,c)$ must also satisfy $0 \leq c \leq y$, and $\alpha \in \{(n-1)/2n; n = 2,3\cdots\}$. It is easy to show, by writing out the first-order conditions for this constrained minimization, that when the optimal random ROSCA discussed earlier is not sustainable, a solution involves $c > c_r$.

## References

Adams, D. W. and Canavesi de Sahonero, M. L. (1989): "Rotating Savings and Credit Associations in Bolivia," *Savings and Development*, 13 (3), 219–36.

Anderson, R. T. (1966): "Rotating Credit Associations in India," *Economic Development and Cultural Change*, April, 14, 334–9.

Ardener, S. (1964): "The Comparative Study of Rotating Credit Associations," *Journal of the Royal Anthropological Institute of Great Britain and Ireland*, 94 (2), 202–29.

Arnott, R. and Riley, J. (1977): "Asymmetrical Production Possibilities, the Social Gains from Inequality and the Optimum Town," *Scandinavian Journal of Economics*, 79 (3), 301–11.

Begashaw, G. (1978): "The Economic Role of Traditional Savings Institutions in Ethiopia," *Savings and Development*, 2 (4), 249–62.

Bergstrom, T. (1986): "Soldiers of Fortune?" in W. P. Heller, R. M. Starr, and D. A. Starrett (eds), *Equilibrium Analysis: Essays in Honor of Kenneth J. Arrow*, Cambridge: Cambridge University Press, 57–80.

Besley, T. J., Coate, S. and Loury, G. (1992): "On the Allocative Performance of Rotating Savings and Credit Associations," discussion paper 163, Research Program in Development Studies at Princeton University

Bonnett, A. W. (1981): *Institutional Adaptation of West Indian Immigrants to America: An Analysis of Rotating Credit Associations*. Washington, DC: University Press of America.

Bouman, F. J. A., (1977): "Indigenous Savings and Credit Societies in the Third World: A Message," *Savings and Development*, 1 (4), 181–218

Brooke, J. (1987): "Informal Capitalism Grows in Cameroon," *New York Times*, 30 November, 30.

Callier, P. (1990): "Informal Finance: The Rotating Savings and Credit Association – An Interpretation," *Kyklos*, 43 (2), 273–6.

Cope, T. and Kurtz, D. V. (1980): "Default and the Tanda: A Model Regarding Recruitment for Rotating Credit Associations," *Ethnology*, April, 18, 213–31.

Fernando, E. (1986): "Informal Credit and Savings Organizations in Sri Lanka: The Cheetu," *Savings and Development*, 10 (3), 253–63.

Geertz, C. (1962): "The Rotating Credit Association: A Middle Rung in Development," *Economic Development and Cultural Change*, April, 10, 241–63.

Grossman, R. (1992): "Deposit Insurance, Regulation, and Moral Hazard in the Thrift Industry: Evidence from the 1930s," *American Economic Review*, September, 82, 800–22.

Haggblade, S. (1978): "Africanization from Below: The Evolution of Cameroon Savings Societies into Western Style Banks," *Rural Africana*, Fall, 2, 35–55.

Hillman, A. and Swan, P. (1983): "Participation Rules for Pareto Optimal Clubs," *Journal of Public Economics*, February, 20, 55–76.

Kurtz, D. V. (1973): "The Rotating Credit Association: An Adaptation to Poverty," *Human Organization*, Spring, 32, 49–58.

Light, I. (1972): *Ethnic Enterprise in America*. Berkeley: University of California Press.

Mirrlees, J. A. (1972): "The Optimum Town," *Scandinavian Journal of Economics*, March, 74, 115–35.

Norville, D. G. and Wehrly, J. S. (1969): "A Rotating Credit Association in the Dominican Republic," *Caribbean Studies*, April, 9, 45–52.

Osuntogun, A. and Adeyemo, R. (1981): "Mobilization of Rural Savings and Credit Extension in Pre-Cooperative Organizations in South-Western Nigeria," *Savings and Development*, 5 (4), 247–61.

Radhakrishnan, S. et al., (1975) *Chit Funds*. Madras, India: Institute for Financial Management and Research.

Symons, E. and White, J. (1984): *Banking Law*, 2nd edn. St. Paul, MN: West Publishing.

CHAPTER 16

# The Economics of Lending with Joint Liability: Theory and Practice

Maitreesh Ghatak and Timothy W. Guinnane

Institutions that rely on joint liability to facilitate lending to the poor have a long history and are now a common feature of many developing countries. Economists have proposed several theories of joint liability lending that stress various aspects of its informational and enforcement advantages over other forms of lending. This paper analyzes how joint-liability lending promotes screening, monitoring, state verification, and enforcement of repayment. An empirical section draws on case studies to highlight how joint liability works in practice.

> To argue that banking cannot be done with the poor because they do not have
> collateral is the same as arguing that men cannot fly because they do not have
> wings.
>
> *Muhammad Yunus*[1]

## 1. Introduction

Scholars and development practitioners have in recent years devoted considerable attention to specialized lending institutions that use unconventional methods to lend successfully to poor people. Most of these institutions work in developing countries, but some have been transplanted from poor countries to work with poor people in wealthy countries such as the U.S.A. Considerable evidence now shows that in many circumstances, an unconventional lender such as the Grameen Bank can lend to poor people no ordinary commercial lender would want as a customer and do so with a reasonable degree of financial self-sufficiency and repayment rates that are significantly higher than for comparable loans by conventional lending institutions (Hossain, 1988; Morduch, 1999). The literature identifies two distinct but complementary reasons for this success. First, many (but not all) of these lending programs ask borrowers to form a group in which all borrowers are jointly liable for each other's loans. These joint-liability lending institutions (which we abbreviate JLLI, and which are often called more loosely "micro-lenders") have a long history, and although modern institutions such as the Grameen Bank may be the most famous operating today, credit cooperatives using similar methods date back to the mid-nineteenth century. Second, most micro-lenders engage in intensive monitoring of clients, and rely heavily on the promise of repeat loans for borrowers who perform well. We do not address these efforts systematically in this paper, but that is a matter of focus and not meant as a suggestion that such efforts are unimportant.

This paper provides an economic analysis of joint-liability lending, drawing on and extending recent research, and provides concrete illustrations by discussing actual institutions. The burgeoning literature on JLLIs today suggests several reasons why group lending helps an institution such as the Grameen Bank operate successfully. Many writers mention efforts to reduce transactions costs, which can be relatively large for borrowers who take only small loans. Others highlight "peer pressure," "social capital," or similar terms that capture the general idea that people with connections of shared locality or other bonds based on kinship and occupation may be able to support credit contracts that would be impossible with conventional banking practices. More recently economists have applied notions taken from the economics of information and contracts to show how joint liability performs "the apparent miracle of giving solvency to a community composed almost entirely of insolvent individuals."[2] These economic models of JLLIs are efforts to formalize the idea that a well-structured JLLI can deal effectively with the four major problems facing lenders by utilizing the local information and social capital that exist among borrowers.[3] These problems are:

(a)   to ascertain what kind of a risk the potential borrower is (*adverse selection*),
(b)   to make sure she will utilize the loan properly, once made, so that she will be able to repay it (*moral hazard*),
(c)   to learn how her project really did in case she declares her inability to repay (*auditing costs*) and
(d)   to find methods to force the borrower to repay the loan if she is reluctant to do so (*enforcement*).[4]

JLLIs can do better than conventional bankers *in some social contexts* for two distinct reasons. First, members of a community may know more about one another (that is, each other's types, actions, and states, as suggested by points (a)–(c) above) than an outside institution such as a bank. Second, a major source of market failure in credit markets is that a bank cannot apply financial sanctions against poor people who default on a loan, since by definition they are poor. (And in most societies there are restrictions on the application of non-financial sanctions such as violence.) Poor people's neighbors, on the other hand, may be able to impose powerful non-financial sanctions at low cost. An institution that gives poor people the proper incentives to use information on their neighbors and to apply non-financial sanctions to delinquent borrowers can out-perform a conventional bank. Many studies of JLLIs refer in a general way to "information problems" while most economic analyses deliberately focus on one of these four issues.[5]

The literature on micro-finance, like the institutions themselves, is still new. A recent paper by Armendariz de Aghion and Morduch (1998) correctly points out that most studies have focused on the joint-liability aspects of institutions such as the Grameen Bank, and ignored the other program features, such as direct monitoring by the lender, that also promote high repayment rates. Thus far there is little empirical evidence on the relative importance of joint liability as opposed to other program features. Recent work by Wenner (1995) and Wydick (1999) provides preliminary evidence that joint liability works as thought. In their analysis, variables that proxy for social cohesion and better information flow among group members imply improved repayment rates.[6] But these studies are not conclusive because of difficult econometric problems.[7] Moreover, these studies cannot assess the importance of joint liability in comparison to, for example, monitoring by the lending institution. This paper discusses the economics of joint liability lending as a matter of focus, in effect holding constant other features of a particular lender. In addition, we abstract from the problems associated with inducing the lender, a financial intermediary, to monitor borrowers. Conning (1999) shows that these problems pose a constraint to the expansion of microfinance through increased leverage and other means.

There is also the related but distinct question of whether joint-liability lending, or for that matter any type of micro-finance, really helps the poor. As a logical matter the Grameen Bank could function very well in terms of repayment rates but have little impact on poverty. This question is also an area of active research. Pitt and Khandker (1998) find, using data from three programs in rural Bangladesh, that borrowing from group-lending schemes increased consumption of poor households. However, Morduch (1998b) has argued that Pitt and Khandker's result reflects program selection effects rather than the impact of borrowing *per se*. Coleman (1999) studies the question of program impact in northeast Thailand. The quasi-experimental design of his survey allows him to use more straightforward estimation techniques than either Pitt and Khandker or Morduch to econometrically identify the impact of these programs.

Section 2 uses simple economic models to show how joint liability can overcome information and enforcement problems. Section 3 discusses various institutional implementations of joint liability to highlight how it works in practice, and illustrate some of the practical problems that arise in the design of these lending programs. In concluding we offer some remarks on the key policy question facing supporters of JLLIs today. Our discussion stresses the use of simple economic models to understand broadly how joint liability ameliorates information and enforcement problems. Our discussion does not comprehensively review the entire literature in this active area of research.

## 2. Theories of Joint Liability Contracts

In analyzing JLLIs, economists have focused on either the effects of joint liability on the pool and behavior of borrowers, or on the fact that lending to groups as opposed to individuals is a way to reduce transactions costs. While we only discuss the joint-liability aspect of these lending programs, our argument is complementary to the transactions–costs argument Hulme and Mosley (1996a, ch. 2). According to the transactions–costs argument, under many circumstances it is only slightly more expensive to administer a group of *n* loans than to administer a single loan, so group lending enables a reduction in transactions costs per loan.[8] If the projects to be funded are *simple* and *similar* in terms of their characteristics, the time path of their returns, and the geographic location of their activities, then coordinating the lender's dealings with these borrowers by putting them together in a group can save on processing, screening and loan collection costs. Put this way, transaction cost-based theories and joint-liability-based theories can be combined, as we do in subsection 2.3 where we show that the bank can avoid the cost of performing a costly audit every time an individual borrower claims she has low output by inducing her partner to undertake liability for her and audit only when the whole group declares inability to repay.[9]

Joint liability alleviates the four main problems faced by formal credit institutions that lend to poor borrowers who cannot offer much in the way of collateral: adverse selection, moral hazard, costly audits and enforcement. We will illustrate these benefits using a simple model of lending. Our model shows how joint liability affects group formation, induces group members to influence the way other members select their projects, helps the lender avoid costly audits, and encourages borrowers to repay their loans without the lender imposing costly sanctions. In the rest of this section we first outline our model, and then take up each of these problems sequentially and use the model to show how joint liability alleviates the four lending problems.

Throughout we use the following simple set-up: output $Y$ takes two values, high ($Y^H$) and low ($Y^L$) where $Y^H > Y^L \geq 0$. For simplicity we normalize $Y^L$ to zero. Output is high with probability $p \in (0, 1)$. Each project requires 1 unit of capital and the lender needs to be paid back an amount $\rho > 1$ per loan, principal plus interest, on average.[10] Borrowers will borrow only if their payoff exceeds the opportunity cost of their labor, $\bar{u}$. The project returns of different borrowers are assumed to be uncorrelated. We assume that all projects are socially profitable in the sense that the expected return from the project is greater than the opportunity costs of the capital and labor employed in the project

$$p Y^H > \rho + \bar{u} \tag{1}$$

Borrowers have no collateralizable wealth (that is, there is a limited-liability constraint) so the net transfer from the borrowers to the lender has to be non-negative in any state of the world.

Throughout this paper we refer to an outside lender as the "bank." By this we mean an individual or an institution who has the resources to lend to a certain group of borrowers either on an individual basis or to a self-formed group. We also assume limited liability, in the sense that the lender can only seize assets that the borrower has specifically pledged as collateral for a loan. Most JLLIs operate in environments where borrowers do not have physical or financial assets to pledge as collateral, meaning that a lender has no recourse in the case of a defaulting borrower. This limited-liability constraint and the borrowers' lack of wealth rules out most instruments used by conventional lenders to contend with information and enforcement and enforcement problems.[11] If a borrower defaults on a loan and has no physical or financial assets, the lender cannot force the borrower to undertake labor services to repay the debt.

A standard loan contract specifies an interest rate $r$ (this is a *gross* interest rate, namely, principal plus the *net* interest rate) which is the amount the borrower must repay to the bank. This can be interpreted as the *individual liability* of the borrower. We model joint liability in the following way: if a borrower is willing and able to repay her own loan but her partner is unwilling or unable to repay her loan, then the former must pay an additional amount $c$ to the bank. The form of joint liability for defaults in actual group-lending programs often takes the form of denying future credit to all group-members in case of default by a group-member until the loan is repaid. In most cases, intra-group loans are used to ensure timely repayment (Huppi and Feder, 1990). Our static interpretation of joint liability may seem at odds with its institutional implementation. But $c$ can be interpreted as the *net present discounted value* of the cost of sacrificing present consumption in order to pay joint liability for a partner. If these loans from one group member to another are always repaid in the future, in cash or in kind, it may seem that in an intertemporal sense joint liability does not impose a cost on a borrower who has to cover for her partner. That would indeed be true if credit markets were perfect, but given that these borrowers face borrowing constraints to start with (which after all is the reason for introducing group-lending) such sacrifices of present consumption are costly.

## 2.1. Adverse selection

Adverse selection arises when borrowers have characteristics that are unobservable to the lender but affect the probability of being able to repay the loan. A lender can try to deal with this information problem directly, by trying to assess these characteristics, or indirectly by offering loan terms that only good risks will accept. The typical method for separating good risks from bad risks is to ask the borrower to pledge collateral. Risky borrowers are likely to fail more often and lose their collateral. If the bank offers two different contracts, one with high interest rates and low collateral and the other with the opposite, risky borrowers will select the former and safe borrowers the latter. But poor people by definition to do not have assets that make useful collateral, meaning that lenders have no effective way to separate good risks from bad. Group lending deals with adverse selection by drawing on local information networks to achieve the equivalent of gathering direct information on borrowers and using differences in loan terms to separate good from bad borrowers.

Several recent papers have examined the effect of joint-liability on the *selection of groups*; see Armendariz de Aghion and Gollier (1998), Ghatak (1999a, 1999b), Laffont and N'Guessan (1999), Sadoulet (1998), Van Tassel (1999) and Varian (1990). Most of these studies use an adverse-selection framework where borrowers know the characteristics of each other's projects relevant to their creditworthiness, but the bank does not. (From now on, we will refer to these characteristics as a borrower's "type," risky or safe.) While all borrowers prefer to have safe partners (because of lower expected joint liability payments) safe borrowers value safe partners more than risky borrowers because they repay more often, and as a result more likely to realize the gain of having a safe partner. This implies that in equilibrium borrowers end up with partners of the same type. As a consequence the bank can screen borrowers by varying the degree of joint liability. This is because risky borrowers have risky partners, and hence will prefer a contract with less joint liability than will a safe borrower.

The papers by Ghatak (1999a) and Van Tassel (1999) formalize this idea and examine various implications of it; see also Armendariz de Aghion and Gollier (1998), Ghatak (1999b), and Laffont and N'Guessan (1999). Here we illustrate the main idea using a simple model. Assume borrowers are risk-neutral and of two types, safe (a) and risky (b). With a project of type $i$ output takes two values, $Y_i^H$ and 0, and the probability of high output is $p_i, i = a, b$. We assume $p_b < p_a$. If the bank does not know a borrower's type, and if standard screening instruments such as collateral are not available, then the bank has to offer loans to all borrowers at the same nominal interest rate. Under such a contract safe borrowers have to cross-subsidize the risky borrowers because both types of borrowers repay the same amount when they succeed, but safe borrowers succeed more often. The presence of enough risky borrowers can push the equilibrium interest rate high enough to drive the safe borrowers away from the market (as in Akerlof's (1970) lemons model). Alternatively, the presence of safe borrowers subsidizes some undeserving risky projects. If borrowers know each other's types, a joint-liability contract can restore full efficiency. Under a joint-liability credit contract a borrower must repay her loan $r$ whenever her project yields high returns, and in addition, if her partner's project yields low returns, she must pay an extra amount $c > 0$. The expected payoff of a borrower of type $i$ when her partner is type $j$ from a joint-liability contract is:

$$EU_{ij}(r, c) = p_i p_j \left( Y_i^H - r \right) + p_i (1 - p_j) \left( Y_i^H - r - c \right)$$

The net expected gain of a risky borrower from having a safe partner is

$$EU_{ba}(r, c) - EU_{bb}(r, c) = p_b (p_a - p_b) c$$

Similarly, the net expected loss for a safe borrower of having a risky partner is

$$EU_{aa}(r, c) - EU_{ab}(r, c) = p_a (p_a - p_b) c$$

If $c > 0$ the latter expression is larger than the former since $p_a > p_b$. Hence, a risky borrower will not find it profitable to have a safe partner. A borrower of any type prefers a safer partner, but the safer is the borrower herself, the more she values a safe partner. A risky borrower in theory could pay the safe borrower to accept her as a partner, but the expressions above imply that such payments would have to be so large that the risky borrower would not want to make them.[12] As a result, group formation will display positive assortative matching under a joint-liability contract.

Ghatak (1999b) and Van Tassel (1999) show that this assortative matching property allows the bank to screen borrowers "by the company they keep" because risky borrowers are less willing than safe borrowers to accept an increase in the extent of joint liability. If the bank offers two contracts, one with high joint liability and low interest rates and the other with low joint liability and high interest rate, safe borrowers will select the former contract and risky borrowers the latter. Thus the repayment rate and efficiency are higher under joint-liability contracts as compared to conventional individual-liability contracts because the former exploits a useful resource that the latter does not: the information borrowers have about each other.

## 2.2. Moral hazard

Once a borrower has taken a loan, the project's payoff depends in part on the borrower's actions, including levels of labor and other inputs. Ordinarily we would expect the borrower to choose these actions such that the marginal benefit of each action equals its marginal cost. That is not necessarily the case with asymmetric information. In the absence of collateral, the lender and borrower do not have the same objectives because the borrower does not fully internalize the cost of project failure. Moreover, the lender cannot stipulate perfectly how the borrower should run the project, in part because some of the borrower's actions are not costlessly observable.

Theories of peer monitoring are motivated by the fact that group members have an incentive to take remedial action against a partner who mis-uses her loan because of joint liability.[13] With group lending, individual borrowers are made to bear liability for themselves *and* for others in their group, but the savings in the form of better project choice allows the bank to pass on some benefits to the borrowers in the form of reduced interest rates. Thus group lending increases welfare and repayment rates. We illustrate this idea with the following simple model.

Output takes two values. Borrowers are risk neutral, as before. But the borrower's actions determine the probability of success. So output is $Y^H$ with probability $p$ and 0 otherwise. Borrowers choose actions, which can be thought of as a level of effort $p \in [0, 1]$, for they which incur a disutility cost of $\frac{1}{2}\gamma p^2$ (where $\gamma > 0$). The borrower's choice is unobservable to the bank. Notice that social surplus $pY^H - \frac{1}{2}\gamma p^2$ is maximized if $p = p^* = Y^H/\gamma$. Let us assume that

$$Y^H < \gamma \tag{2}$$

so that we have an interior solution. With perfect information the bank could specify that the borrower choose $p = p^*$ and charge an interest rate $r = \rho/p^*$. But if the choice of $p$ is subject to moral hazard then taking the interest rate $r$ as given the borrower chooses $p$ to maximize her private profits:

$$\hat{p}(r) \equiv \arg\max\left\{ p\left(Y^H - r\right) - \frac{1}{2}\gamma p^2 \right\} = \frac{Y^H - r}{\gamma}$$

The interest rate is like a tax on success since it has to be paid only when output is high. Hence, $p^* = \hat{p}(0) > \hat{p}(r)$ and the higher the interest rate the lower is $p$. Substituting $p = (Y^H - r)/\gamma$ in the bank's zero-profit condition $pr = \rho$ we get

$$\gamma p^2 - Y^H p + \rho = 0$$

This is a quadratic equation in $p$ which means there are two values of $p$ consistent with equilibrium. We assume that the equilibrium with the higher value of $p$ is chosen (since the bank is indifferent and the borrower is strictly better off), i.e.,

$$p = \frac{Y^H + \sqrt{(Y^H)^2 - 4\rho\gamma}}{2\gamma}$$

Under joint liability, when the borrower's project fails her partner is liable for the amount $c$. If a borrower's partner chooses an action $p'$ then the payoff function of a borrower who chooses an action $p$ is

$$\max_{\{p\}} pY^H - rp - cp(1 - p') - \frac{1}{2}\gamma p^2$$

Suppose the borrower chooses $p$ to maximize her individual payoff taking the partner's action $p'$ as given. Then her best response function is given by:

$$p = \frac{Y^H - r - c}{\gamma} + \frac{c}{\gamma}p'$$

That is, the safer the partner's project choice, the safer the project choice of a borrower. If a borrower chooses a risky project, this choice reduces the attractiveness of high returns to her partner because of expected joint liability payments. Thus the borrower also chooses a more risky project. If borrowers take decisions about project-choice non-cooperatively then in the symmetric Nash equilibrium,

$$p = p' = \frac{Y^H - r - c}{\gamma - c}$$

The bank's zero-profit condition under joint liability is:

$$rp + cp(1 - p) = \rho$$

Substituting $r$ from this expression into the first-order condition we see that

$$\gamma p^2 - Y^H p + \rho = 0$$

Hence a borrower's equilibrium project choice will be the same as with individual liability: mere joint liability does not alleviate moral hazard in this model. This result follows because a borrower does not take into account her action's effect on her partner's choice of action. This is similar to the fact that if the borrower internalized the effect of the choice of her action on the interest rate under individual liability lending (namely, we incorporated the bank's zero profit condition $pr = \rho$ in the borrower's objective function), she would choose the first-best level of $p$.

If instead borrowers decide on project-choice cooperatively they choose:

$$\tilde{p}(r, c) \equiv \arg \max_{\{p\}} \left\{ pY^H - rp - cp(1 - p) - \tfrac{1}{2}\gamma p^2 \right\} = \frac{Y^H - r - c}{\gamma - 2c}$$

Substituting this expression in the bank's zero-profit condition we get:

$$(\gamma - c)p^2 - Y^H p + \rho = 0$$

This yields (again choosing the higher root),

$$p = \frac{Y^H + \sqrt{(Y^H)^2 - 4\rho(\gamma - c)}}{2(\gamma - c)}$$

Recall that by (2), $\gamma > Y^H$ and since the borrower cannot pay more than what his project yields it must be the case that $c < \gamma$. For $c \in (0, \gamma)$, the numerator of the expression for the equilibrium value of $p$ under joint liability is higher than the corresponding expression under individual liability, while the denominator of the former expression is lower than that of the latter. The equilibrium value of $p$, and hence the repayment rate, is therefore higher under joint-liability lending when borrowers choose $p$ cooperatively compared to individual liability lending.

The above formulation of joint liability assumes that borrowers can contract on $p$ among themselves: i.e., they can observe each other's actions perfectly and costlessly, as well as enforce any agreement regarding their levels.[14] However, if monitoring is costly, then borrowers must be given incentives to monitor. Suppose that if a borrower chooses a level of monitoring $a$, then with probability $a$ she can observe the true action chosen by her partner, and with probability $1 - a$ she receives a completely uninformative signal. If the action undertaken by her partner is different from that agreed on, then she can impose a non-monetary punishment of $S$ (standing for social sanctions). The cost of monitoring is given by the increasing and convex function $M(a)$. Let $p^D(r, c)$ denote the individual best response of a borrower given that her partner chooses $p = \tilde{p}(r, c)$. Then

$$p^D(r, c) = \frac{Y^H - r - c}{\gamma} + \frac{c}{\gamma}\tilde{p}(r, c) = (1 - \frac{c}{\gamma})\tilde{p}(r, c) < \tilde{p}(r, c)$$

Now the incentive compatibility constraint of a borrower to choose $\tilde{p}$ and not deviate to $p^D$ given that her partner chooses a level of monitoring $a$ and the agreed upon project choice $\tilde{p}$ is given by:

$$\tilde{p}(Y^H - r) - \tilde{p}(1 - \tilde{p})c - \tfrac{1}{2}\gamma\tilde{p}^2 \geq p^D(Y^H - r) - p^D(1 - \tilde{p})c - \tfrac{1}{2}\gamma p^2 - aS$$

Since monitoring is costly, the minimal level of monitoring consistent with the above constraint will be chosen. This implies that the constraint will be satisfied with equality in equilibrium. Let the corresponding level of $a$ be denoted by $\tilde{a}(r, c)$. One must ensure that a borrower has the incentive to undertake the requisite level of monitoring to ensure her partner chooses $p = \tilde{p}$. That is,

$$\tilde{p}(Y^H - r) - \tilde{p}(1 - \tilde{p})c - \tfrac{1}{2}\gamma\tilde{p}^2 - M(\tilde{a}) \geq \tilde{p}(Y^H - r) - \tilde{p}(1 - p^D)c - \tfrac{1}{2}\gamma\tilde{p}^2$$

or,

$$\tilde{p}(\tilde{p} - p^D)c \geq M(\tilde{a})$$

So long as social sanctions are effective enough (i.e., $S$ is large) or monitoring costs are low enough (i.e., $M(\tilde{a})$ is small) joint liability lending will improve repayment rates through peer monitoring even when monitoring is costly.

## 2.3. Costly state verification

Formal lenders sometimes cannot lend to poor borrowers because such lenders cannot easily verify whether borrowers who say they cannot repay are indeed unable to do so. We are assuming that all parties are risk-neutral, which implies that the ideal contract is one in which the borrower pays a fixed fee (such as an interest rate) regardless of what happens. But because of the borrower's limited wealth there may be situations where the borrower cannot pay very much, for example when her project fails. For the bank to accept partial repayment is like charging a lower interest rate to the borrower, and if the bank applies this lower fee to all states of the world it cannot break even. At the same time, any other option introduces some degree of state contingency in the contract. Since states are costly to verify, a state-contingent contract creates an incentive for the borrower to report those states of the world where her repayment obligations are the least, irrespective of the true state. To solve the twin problems of false reporting and costs of state verification the optimal contract takes the following simple form: so long as the borrower is willing to pay a fixed fee the bank does not audit, but if she reports that she is unable to pay this fee the bank audits her and takes away all her returns. This is a standard debt contract.[15] With this kind of contract, if the borrower claims her output was too low to repay, the bank audits her and takes all her output (Townsend, 1979). But if the costs of auditing borrowers are too high there may be no contract which allows the bank to break even on loans. This problem is especially likely for the kind of borrowers served by JLLIs.

Here we propose a simple model to show that joint-liability contracts reduce expected audit costs and improve efficiency.[16] The intuition is that if group members face a lower cost of verifying each other's output (say, because they live close to each other's work-place), then the bank can avoid the cost of performing its own audit every time a borrower claims she has low output by inducing her partner to undertake liability for her. The partner has the incentive to audit a borrower since she is partly liable for her repayment. Only when the whole group announces its inability to repay will the bank have to incur auditing costs. Assume that all projects are identical and the only departure from the first-best is costly output verification: the outside lender has to pay $\gamma > 0$ to verify the return of each individual project. There are no problems of moral hazard, adverse selection or enforcement of contracts. The financial contract specifies three numbers: the transfer from the borrower to the bank when the project succeeds $(r)$, and the probabilities of an audit, $(\gamma_H$ and $\lambda_L)$ when output is high and low. As before, everyone is risk-neutral and there is a limited liability constraint. Formally, the optimal contract then solves:

$$\max p\left(Y^H - r\right) - \bar{u}$$

subject to the following two constraints:

$$Y^H - r \geq \max\left\{0, (1 - \lambda_L)Y^H\right\}\rho \leq p(r - \lambda_H\gamma) + (1 - p)(-\lambda_L\gamma)$$

The first constraint is a "truth-telling" constraint which says that given the contract the borrower will have an incentive to repay the loan when output is high rather than announce that output is low and risk an audit (with probability $\lambda_L$) in which she could lose all the output to the bank. The second constraint says the bank should break even on the loan under the contract.

Since there are no risk-sharing issues, the optimal contract has a very simple structure: it minimizes auditing costs by auditing with positive probability $\lambda > 0$ when the borrower claims output is low and the bank takes all output. Otherwise the borrower pays an interest $r$ in which case there are no audits.[17] From the two constraints we get:

$$r = \lambda Y^H$$

$$\lambda = \frac{\rho}{p Y^H - (1-p)\gamma}$$

Notice that to ensure $\lambda \leq 1$ we need:

$$p Y^H - (1-p)\gamma \geq \rho \qquad (3)$$

This condition means that the expected return from the project less the expected costs of auditing has to be at least as large as the opportunity cost of capital. This condition also ensures that

$$p Y^H - (1-p)\gamma > 0$$

and hence $\lambda \geq 0$. Finally, substituting in the borrower's payoff, we see that an optimal contract exists if

$$p\left(Y^H - r\right) - \bar{u} \geq 0 \qquad (4)$$

That is, the borrower's expected return net of interest payments has to be as large as the opportunity cost of her labor.

Assume that the borrowers can write side-contracts with each other costlessly and that there is no cost for a borrower to observer her partner's project returns. This means that all members make the same announcement about the state of the world. There are two relevant truth-telling constraints. The first one is similar to the previous case which ensures that a borrower has incentives to make truthful announcements when output is high. The second one says that if a borrowers own project yields high returns and her partner's project yields low returns, she has the incentive to report this state truthfully and repay her own loan as well as joint liability for her partner. Clearly, only the second truth-telling constraint,

$$Y^H - 2r \geq \max\{0, (1-\lambda)Y^H\}$$

will bind. The bank's zero-profit condition is now:

$$p^2 r + p(1-p)2r - \lambda(1-p)^2\gamma = \rho$$

Solving the truth-telling and the zero-profit constraints we get:

$$r = \lambda \frac{Y^H}{2}$$

$$\lambda = \frac{\rho}{\{pY^H - (1-p)\gamma\} - \frac{1}{2}p\{pY^H - 2(1-p)\gamma\}}$$

As

$$pY^H - (1-p)\gamma > pY^H - 2(1-p)\gamma > \frac{1}{2}p[pY^H - 2(1-p)\gamma]$$

the equilibrium rate of interest will be lower under joint liability. So long as

$$[pY^H - (1-p)\gamma] - \frac{1}{2}p[pY^H - 2(1-p)\gamma] = (1 - \frac{p}{2})[pY^H - (1-p)\gamma] + \frac{p}{2}(1-p)\gamma \geq \rho$$

$\lambda \leq 1.$[18] Audits take place less often under joint liability, so expected audit costs are lower and so is the equilibrium interest rate. Hence social surplus is always higher under joint-liability contracts. Even if banks would not lend to borrowers under individual-liability contracts due to high audit costs (which happens if (4) is not satisfied), a joint-liability contract might make lending possible.

## 2.4. Enforcement

The final problem, enforcement, arises not from informational asymmetries but from the lender's limited ability to apply sanctions against a delinquent borrower. Even if the borrower's project succeeds so that she is able to repay she may still refuse to repay if the legal system does not work very well and if the poverty of the borrower restricts the amount of effective sanctions. Besley and Coate (1995) address the question of how joint-liability contracts affect the willingness to repay. They show that group lending has two opposing effects on repayment rates. The advantage of groups is that they allow a member whose project yields very high returns to pay off the loan of a partner whose project does very badly. The disadvantage is that a moderately successful borrower may default on her own repayment because of the burden of having to repay her partner's loan. However if social ties among members are sufficiently strong, the net effect is positive because by defaulting willfully a borrower incurs sanctions from both the bank and the community. With sufficient social capital a borrowing group enforces repayment better than would take place with individual liability.

Consider the following simple model that illustrates this point. We now assume borrowers are risk-averse.[19] Suppose the only departure from the first-best stems the fact that borrowers can default intentionally even when they are capable of repaying. The punishment a bank can impose on a delinquent borrowers is limited and consists entirely of never lending to her again. If a borrower's project yields output $Y \geq r$ so that she is able to repay, she will repay only if the benefit of defaulting, the interest cost, is less than the (discounted) *net* benefit of continued access to credit, $B$:

$$u(Y) - u(Y - r) \leq \bar{B}$$

The term $\bar{B}$ reflects the present value of the net benefit to the borrower from having continued access to loans from the bank. As is well known, infinitely repeated games have many possible equilibria. For simplicity we are restricting attention to stationary equilibria of the supergame between the borrower and the lender where cooperation is achieved by trigger strategies, namely, both parties revert to the worst subgame perfect equilibrium of the supergame if one of the parties misbehave. In the current context, if the borrower defaults once, the bank never lends to the borrower again, and the borrower never repays if she receives a loan again. We are also assuming that the bank does not pre-commit to future interest rates and hence the benefit from future access to loans viewed from the current period is independent of the interest rate $r$. Even if $\bar{B}$ depends on $r$ (it is expected to be decreasing in $r$) the above argument goes through: for a given $r$ there will be some critical $Y(r)$ such that borrowers will repay if $Y \geq Y(r)$.[20]

Let $Y(r)$ be the income level that satisfies this condition with strict equality. If there is diminishing marginal utility of income, then for a given $r$, the borrower will repay only if $Y \geq Y(r)$. If the returns are not very high, repayment is costly because the marginal utility of income is high. Under a joint-liability contract, all group members are considered to be in default unless every loan is repaid and in the event of a default no one gets a loan in the future. A borrower will choose to repay even if her partner defaults (given that she is able to repay, i.e., $Y \geq 2r$) if:

$$u(Y) - u(Y - 2r) \leq \bar{B}$$

If $Y > Y(2r)$, she will default on both her own and partner's liability. Note further that $Y(2r) > Y(r)$: since paying off both her own and her partner's debts is more onerous than paying off just her own loan, only when income is very high would borrowers want to repay under this contract. Assume for simplicity $Y(r) > 2r$ and that if both members have an income $Y > Y(r)$ then they repay under joint liability.[21] There are two distinct cases.

- One group member is *unable* or *unwilling* to repay (i.e., has an income realization $Y \leq Y(r)$) and the other member is *willing* to repay both her own and her partner's obligation (i.e. has income $Y \geq Y(2r)$). In this case joint liability is beneficial compared to individual-liability lending.
- One member is unable or unwilling to repay her own debt (i.e., $Y < Y(r)$) and her partner is willing to repay her own debt but not both of their debts (i.e., $Y(r) < Y < Y(2r)$). Now individual liability is better than joint liability.

Depending on which of these cases is more likely to occur (which depends on the probability distribution of output), default may be more or less common with joint liability. However, social sanctions alter the effect of joint liability. Suppose a default by one borrower that hurts the other group-member (because she is cut off from loans in the future) elicits some punishment from the community ("social sanctions"). These social sanctions alter the repayment condition under joint liability. Social sanctions reduce the attractiveness of the payoff stream in the case when one party defaults intentionally $(r < Y < Y(r))$ and the other party was willing to repay her own loan but not her partner's $(Y(r) < Y < Y(2r))$. In this case, repayment would definitely be higher under joint-liability contracts.

If *repayment decisions* are taken cooperatively repayment behavior under joint liability is identical to repayment behavior with individual liability. To see this, let the income realization of the two members in a given group be $Y_1$ and $Y_2$. If the group maximizes joint welfare, members will always share *net* income (i.e., net of repayment) so as to equate marginal utilities of consumption. In that case the crucial variable in the determination of repayment decisions is not individual income, as in the non-cooperative formulation above, but total (or average) income. Accordingly, borrowers will be voluntarily jointly liable for each other's loans regardless of whether the formal terms are joint or individual liability.[22]

Recent work by Diagne (1998) and Armendariz de Aghion (1999) has considered several extensions of the role of joint liability in mitigating the problem of strategic default. Diagne (1998) proposes a peer-pressure model in which borrowers are incompletely informed about their partner's willingness to apply or to tolerate social sanctions. He shows that peer pressure works only because of a potential defaulter's intolerance of passive social sanctions. Armendariz de Aghion (1999) develops a model of strategic default where a borrower's partner(s) can verify her true project return (and impose sanctions if she defaults strategically) at some cost and allows for project returns of group members to be correlated. She examines the issue of optimal design of group lending programs in terms of optimal group size and monitoring structures.

## 3. Institutional Implementations of Joint Liability

In the previous section we used a model of lending to show how joint liability can work in theory. This section uses the history and institutional structure of some joint-liability lending programs to illustrate how joint liability works in practice. We emphasize practical problems that arise in its implementation because a central issue in joint-liability lending today is how to transplant the Grameen Bank and other successful JLLIs to other countries.[23] We begin our discussion with two important institutions that have successfully used joint liability: Germany's historical credit cooperatives and the Grameen Bank today. Between them these two institutions provide a basic outline of the various ways joint liability lending can work. We then turn to discussion of how joint liability has worked in lending programs today.

Ideally we would like a fine-grained analysis of the factors that contribute to the success or failure of joint-liability lending schemes. One can imagine a regression, where the observations are information on the experience of various JLLIs, the dependent variable a measure of program performance, and the right-hand side variables describe aspects of the social and economic environment, borrower characteristics, and program design. Unfortunately this approach is not possible given the current state of the literature; as we noted in the introduction, the empirical literature does not even yield a clear answer on how important joint-liability is in comparison to the other instruments used by most micro-lenders. The discussion here is intended to illustrate the theoretical discussion of the previous section, and not as any concerted effort to assess the role of joint liability in any particular institution.

## 3.1.  Two examples of successful joint-liability lending

Credit cooperatives were first introduced in Germany during the 1850s. By World War I there were about 19,000 such cooperatives and together they had issued some 8 percent of all German banking liabilities. The German credit cooperatives had parallels and imitators in several European countries in the nineteenth century, and in some sense are forerunners of lending schemes that rely on joint liability.[24] We stress the rural cooperatives because they most nearly resembled contemporary institutions in their goals and clientele. Rural cooperatives tended to make long-term loans (often 10 years or more) and financed those loans from local deposits. Most loans were secured by a co-signer. The co-signer did not have to be a member of the cooperatives but was held responsible for any loan the borrower did not repay. To apply for a loan a potential borrower presented himself at the monthly meeting of the management committee and explained the size and terms of the loan he wanted, the purpose for which he intended the loan, and his security.[25] Loans were used for many different purposes, including fertilizer, tools and machinery, and livestock for agriculturists, raw materials for artisans, and stock for shopkeepers. Co-operatives as a matter of policy avoided consumption loans.

The German cooperatives made loans of varying sizes and terms, depending on their location and competition with other lenders. But their claim to fame was their ability to make and obtain repayment on very small loans from people who had no assets acceptable to a commercial lender. To take one specific example, in April of 1908 two brothers, both laborers, applied to a credit cooperative in the Prussian Rheinland for loans of 100 Marks each. The loans were granted at 5 percent interest, which is only slightly more than an established business would have paid its bank for a much larger loan. The only security the brothers offered the cooperative was each other as co-signers on the promissory note.[26]

Most credit cooperatives today and in the past are variations on this basic theme. An important feature of the credit cooperatives is that, especially in rural institutions, all of these people lived in a small area, interacted regularly, and had many other ties, both economic (such as employer/employee) and extra-economic (such as kinship or member-ship in the same social groups). Members in urban credit cooperatives had less tight connections to another, as they could live in different parts of a city and did not necessarily know one another. These weaker member ties probably explain the fact that urban credit cooperatives more nearly resembled commercial lenders in their policies.

Our second example is the most famous group-lending organization today, Bangladesh's Grameen Bank. The Grameen Bank has been imitated in several other countries so the impact of this form of lending goes far beyond Bangladesh. In Bangladesh the Bank currently lends to about two million people, most of whom are rural, landless women. The Bank operates in 36,000 villages, or about half of all villages in the country. Grameen Bank borrowers organize themselves into self-selected groups of five people (men and women are in different groups, as dictated by social norms in Bangladesh). All group members must be from the same village. After the formation of the group, members receive training from Bank employees and begin weekly meetings. From the outset each member makes small, weekly savings deposits. Several weeks after the group is formed two members receive a loan. If the initial borrowers make their required weekly payments and if the group otherwise adheres to the rules of the Grameen Bank, two more members receive loans, and so on. Loans are small and must be repaid in weekly installments over a period of one year. If any member of a group defaults, all members are ineligible for Grameen Bank credit in the future (Khandker, Khalily and Khan, 1995).

The borrowing groups are combined into larger entities called Centers. Among other responsibilities these Centers manage two important funds. The first, the Group Fund, is comprised of the compulsory savings deposits already noted, a 5 percent fee charged on all loans at initiation, and any fines the center chooses to levy on borrowers who violate Grameen rules. Each center manages its own Group fund and can use it for loans to cover emergency consumption needs, including the funeral and wedding obligations that have often been a cause of recourse to money lenders. A second fund, called the Emergency Fund, comes from compulsory surcharges on borrower interest. The Emergency Fund is used to provide insurance coverage for events such as natural disaster or a borrower's death or default. These two funds provide Grameen Bank borrowers a margin of safety against the default of a borrower in their group, since in many cases either the Group Fund or the Emergency Fund can be used to make good the loss. These funds are the only financial connection between groups within a Center. That is, an individual in one five-person group stands to lose from the misbehavior of someone in another five-person group only through potential losses to the Group or Emergency Funds. Typically Grameen loans are for small-scale enterprises that require working capital. Examples include grocery shops, tea stalls, sewing machines, and agricultural livestock.

Both the credit cooperatives and the Grameen Bank illustrate the basic joint liability framework modeled above. Borrowers self-select into groups in which all members are liable for all other members' loans. All borrowers accept the threat that if their group does not fully repay its loans, then all members are cut off from future credit from this lender. Underlying the entire group notion is the idea that these individuals, because of shared location and other ties, know a great deal about one another, can observe each other's day-to-day business activities and the outcome of those activities, and have ways of pressuring each other to repay loans. But there are important differences between the credit co-operative structure and that of the Grameen Bank. In the cooperative there are two different layers of the group. For loans with co-signers the first layer consists essentially of one borrower and his co-signer. The second layer consists of the cooperative member-ship as a whole, who are liable for the cooperative's debts.[27] Notice that within each "group" the members have the incentives noted above, although to different degrees. For the first group the co-signer bears all financial responsibility for the borrower's loan. In the second, much larger group, the failure of any one loan threatens the cooperative's long-term growth and health, and possibly its ability to pay dividends (if it has the policy of doing so). In the Grameen Bank, on the other hand, there is only the one borrowing group. Bank staff combine several borrowing groups into a "Center" for meetings, training sessions, etc., but groups within a Center bear no financial responsibility for the loans of other groups.

There are two other important differences between the two institutions. One is the source of loan funds. Some German cooperatives borrowed substantial shares of their loan funds from external financial institutions, but most relied on local funds, a combination of the cooperative's assets (built up from member capital contributions as well as retained earnings), member deposits, and deposits of those who were not members. The Grameen Bank and other institutions, on the other hand, obtain most of their lending funds from external institutions. A second difference turns on the longevity of the lending group. In the cooperatives the first level (borrower and co-signer) exists only for the life of a loan, while the second level, the cooperative membership, is a corporate body that exists independent of any loan. A borrowing group in the Grameen Bank, on the other hand, exists only for the purposes of the loan in question, and while it may be reconstituted for a later loan there is no institutional reason why the members cannot just select other partners (Tohtong, 1988, p. 5).

Accounts of both the cooperatives and the Grameen Bank illustrate concretely the ways they used their structure to achieve screening, monitoring, auditing, and enforcement. A few examples will suffice. German cooperatives screened both their members (not all were admitted) and loans (members could be denied loans). To take an example, the Limbach cooperative (Saarland) denied membership to two individuals in 1913, although it did not say why.[28] Cooperatives also ejected members who did not adhere to the rules.[29] These institutions also denied loans to some applicants. The cooperative in Diestedde (Münster-land) denied a fairly small loan to a skilled artisan in 1888.[30] Cooperatives would also approve a loan but demand different co-signers or other security. The cooperative in Leer (Münsterland), for example, agreed to make a loan in March of 1909, but required the borrower to find another co-signer.[31] Auditing of borrowers who could not repay their loans took several forms. Cooperatives sometimes granted a borrower an extension (reflecting the cooperative's ability to see that an extension would allow the borrower to repay the loan in full). For example, in 1892 and 1893 the Leer cooperative granted short (three to six-month) extensions to several borrowers. In one case the reason for the extension is stated; both the borrower and his son have been ill, and in addition, potato prices had been high. Potatoes were an important consumption good, and the cooperative was using its knowledge of the relevant state of the world to alter loan terms.[32] Finally, enforcement of repayment sometimes worked through the legal system, but more often relied on social sanctions of the type discussed above. Co-signers were also required to repay loans for borrower who defaulted. One co-signer in Diestedde was put in this position in 1889.[33] Members who defaulted on loans could be thrown out of the cooperative. Throwing someone out of the cooperative for failure to repay was rare but it did happen. The Oberdrees (Rheinbach) cooperative took this step with a member, for example.[34]

The many accounts of the Grameen Bank suggest similar processes that correspond to our models of screening, monitoring, auditing, and enforcement. Two words of caution with these accounts probably apply to other situations as well. First, Todd (1996b), although impressed with the Grameen Bank's accomplishments, notes on the basis of her fieldwork in Bangladesh that in some cases there are important gaps between what the Bank thinks happens on the ground and what really happens on the ground. She notes, for example, that many loan applications deliberately mis-state the loan's purpose, obviating the Bank's statistics on loan uses. This practice occurs because borrowers either want to use the loan for a forbidden purpose or because the Bank official on location wants to ensure the loan's approval and so puts down an uncontroversial purpose (pp. 23–5). Todd's observation is not at variance with our modeling; as she notes, "The members all know who is doing what with their loans" even if the Bank management does not. Second, although most studies are careful to document the full range of activities the Grameen Bank uses to obtain its high repayment rates, the joint-liability lending groups often receive pride of place. As we have noted more generally, there is not as yet clear evidence on how much of the Grameen Bank's success, or that of similar institutions, reflects the effect of joint liability alone.[35]

## 3.2. Problems with joint liability: Group formation and size

The empirical literature on JLLIs devotes considerable attention to the issue of group size. On *a priori* grounds group size can have two countervailing effects in joint-liability lending. If project returns are uncorrelated, an increase in group size improves the effectiveness of joint liability because it increases the number of states of the world in which the group as a whole can repay its members' loans. On the other hand, joint liability works better than other financial contracts because group members have superior information on one another and can impose non-financial sanctions on one another.[36] These advantages are most likely diluted in larger groups. With large groups there may also be free riding in the provision of some activities which have the character of public goods, such as monitoring and auditing. These considerations would tend to imply small optimal group sizes. Experience has shown that in very large groups, coordination difficulties and free-rider problems in organizational matters overwhelm the informational and enforcement benefits of a group.

In the German cooperatives the first level of groups has two members and the second a much larger number. Most rural cooperatives had somewhere between 75 and 250 members at the turn of the twentieth century. In the Grameen Bank the group size is set at five persons, a figure arrived at through a process of trial and error. Mosley and Dahal (1985, p. 202), for example, note in the context of a Nepalese program that there is evidence that in lending groups larger than twenty persons, mutual trust is more meager. Owusu and Tetteh (1982, pp. 80–1) report that the Ghanian program they studied had groups ranging in size from 10 up to 100 persons. Not surprisingly, "the very large groups present serious problems of loan supervision and collection." Even twenty persons is a very large group by the standards of most programs in existence today. Devereux and Fishe (1993, p. 108) draw on evidence from the Dominican Republic to argue that small groups are essential to joint liability schemes. The Group Funds of the Grameen Bank are a wise effort to achieve the insurance benefits of pooled risk without robbing the groups of their power to screen, monitoring, and so forth.

Practitioners have devoted considerable attention to the way in which groups are formed. As we showed in section 2.1, screening is an important function of group formation, and several studies suggest the importance of practical measures in screening. For example, Wenner (1995, pp. 270–2) shows that FINCA groups that directly screened members according to their local reputations, or that had adopted a written internal constitution, experienced significantly fewer problems with loan delinquency.[37] Wenner interprets the written constitution as a screening device; individuals selected in or out of groups with written codes, depending on their seriousness about adhering to the expectations of the group. Kevane (1996, p. 26) notes some extreme examples of ill-formed groups in the Credit with Education lending program in Burkina Faso.[38] Groups seem to have been formed by program officials. Some groups included individuals who had never met one another, and there was confusion over just who bore liability for bad loans.

Another issue raised by joint liability lending is the degree to which group members know each other and interact on a regular basis. Case studies of JLLIs today suggest a variety of experiences. One study of BancoSol, for example, suggests that some of its lending groups are reconstituted forms of older groups that existed as ROSCAs (Rotating Savings and Credit Associations) prior to the formation of BancoSol.[39] ROSCAs are informal credit associations which are an important source of credit in many developing countries. In a typical ROSCA each member agrees to pay periodically a small sum into a common pool and gets to draw one large sum in rotation to purchase some indivisible good (Besley, Coate, and Loury, 1993). The survival of a ROSCA depends on ensuring payments from all members particularly once a member has his turn. Hence they tend to form among groups that are socially cohesive as well as are rationed in the credit market. While both group lending and ROSCAs are group-based informal credit institutions that exploit the information and enforcement advantages of close-knit social networks to overcome credit market failures, they are very different in the source of funds as well as the nature and the (state-contingent) distribution of liability among members. Kovsted and Lyk-Jensen (1999) analyze the efficiency of various types of ROSCAs when the information about a member's return from investing his draw is private and Handa and Kirton (1999) provide an empirical analysis of the organizational design of ROSCAs in Jamaica. Thus the success of BancoSol groups that had earlier been ROSCAs is no surprise. On the other hand, one third of the BancoSol groups surveyed in this study did not meet at all except for chance encounters unrelated to membership in BancoSol (Mosley, 1996, p. 15). One U.S. effort to replicate the Grameen Bank recognizes the special difficulty of forming a group in a U.S. urban area, and has adapted to those circumstances rather than obviate the point of a group. Chicago's Full Circle Fund has adopted most aspects of the Grameen Bank's system. Balkin (1993, pp. 241–2) notes that it takes six to eight months for groups to form in the Fund, and explains it by noting that "In a setting where potential members, generally, do not initially know each other...it does seem it would take considerable time for people to perceive just how honest and trustworthy others would be in a linked lending system..." Some lenders such as the Grameen Bank require that groups participate in a host of activities not strictly related to the credit operation. In Grameen, for example, groups meet regularly to pledge adherence to Grameen's 16 decisions and to receive training. These activities are in part a reflection of Grameen's sense of a larger development, but they also help to strengthen group solidarity and thus enhance Grameen's ability to lend to the poor.[40]

One practice used in Kenya's Jehudi scheme illustrates both the problems in larger groups and a subtle feature of a cooperative's dual group levels.[41] The small borrowing group, the *watano*, is formed by its members. As in the Grameen Bank, these *watanos* are grouped into larger associations called KIWAs.[42] In the Grameen Bank and most imitators, however, the larger group does not have any liability role. In Kenya all members of a KIWA are liable for all loans to everyone in the KIWA, even people associated with a different *watano*. Thus borrowers under this scheme are liable for loans to someone they had no role in choosing for their liability group. According to Mutua (1994, p. 275), the scheme started following Grameen principles, with each *watano* responsible for its own loans, but the original policy "contributed to a lack of cohesion among KIWA members."

Mutua refers to the new system with approval, noting that at the outset there had been some *watanos* where all clients defaulted, leaving the Juhudi with no mechanism for recovering the loan. Buckley (1996a, p. 310) notes that some participants in the current Jehudi scheme expressed reservations about this arrangement, even though with the group funds defaults in any one *watano* are unlikely to cause significant financial losses for borrowers. This unwise aspect of the Jehudi program is to our knowledge unique among Grameen-style lenders. The subtle difference between this arrangement and a credit cooperative is important: in a cooperative, members and loans are screened by elected managers, so no member is guaranteeing loans for someone else without some voice in the matter. In the Kenyan program the *lending officials* formed the KIWAs.

Another problem that arises with JLLIs is that the institution keeps the group but abandons the joint liability that makes the group valuable. Buckley (1996b) offers an account that documents this problem: abandonment of joint liability in the Smallholder Agricultural Credit Administration (SACA) in Malawi. SACA at first lent to individuals formed into groups that undertake joint liability for all loans in a group. These "farmers'" clubs had at least ten members and thus were somewhat larger than those in Grameen and similar lenders, but the operating principle is the same. Buckley notes (1996b, p. 349) that these clubs had operated effectively at first. But then in April of 1992 SACA adopted a policy of allowing any individual who had repaid his or her *own* loan access to further credit, even if one or more borrowers in his group was in default. The World Bank opposed this change in policy, Buckley notes, and it is easy to see why: the new policy effectively ended joint liability for loans. Repayment rates have plummeted, although a drought that caused severe shortfalls in maize yields must bear some of the responsibility as well.

### 3.3. Problems with joint liability: Social ties

A major obstacle to joint liability as a lending mechanism arises when social ties among possible borrowers are too weak to support feelings of group solidarity. This is a significant problem in efforts to transplant Grameen-style arrangements to wealthier countries. Mondal and Tune (1993, pp. 224–5) discuss the problems of transplanting joint liability from Bangladesh to rural Arkansas. The Good Faith Fund, formed in 1988, has adopted most aspects of Grameen practice. But as the authors note, significant social and cultural differences mean that joint liability does not work in Arkansas precisely as it does in Bangladesh. Rural Arkansas has much lower population density, meaning that group members are likely to know less about one another, and unlike Bangladesh, within small areas Arkansas has significant racial and religious heterogeneity, a further burden to group formation and solidarity. Wydick (1999, Table 4) shows for a Guatemalan lending program that groups in which members' business are close together have higher repayment rates, underscoring the role of population density in making joint liability work. But the most important problem for groups in Arkansas may turn on the idea of groups themselves; "...people in Bangladesh derive more of their identity from membership in groups such as the family than do Americans, who very much express individualism" (p. 225). Conlin (1999) discusses a variety of innovations used among micro-lending programs in Canada and the United States. A common theme is a need to rely less on social ties among borrowers than is the case in, for example, Bangladesh. Sometimes the lending scheme can be adapted to take advantage of features of the local environment that will enhance repayment rates. This kind of adaptation has taken place in Malaysia's AIM program. AIM seeks to identify the program with Islamic moral principles, including the spiritual obligation to repay loans. "Islam is thus used as an additional factor to ensure commitment to AIM and fosters high rates of repayment" (Hulme, 1990, p. 294).

Joint liability also may not work if the individuals involved are unwilling, for whatever reason, to put pressure on delinquent borrowers and to sanction those who default. The failed experience of German-style credit cooperatives in Ireland in the nineteenth century provides a case in point. Other cooperatives (such as creameries) had been successful in Ireland, and in 1894 Irish cooperators introduced credit cooperatives modeled very closely on rural German cooperatives. The Irish institutions were with only a few exceptions unsuccessful, as even the Irish leadership acknowledged. The reasons for this failure are doubtless complex, as Guinnane (1994) stresses. Some observers argued that the basic norms of rural society in Ireland worked against the entire basis of the cooperative's functioning:

> It is difficult in a country with no business traditions, and where the natural kindliness of the people renders them easy-going with regard to mutual obligations, to make them realize the necessity of adhering resolutely to the rules, so that no mistaken kindness to unthrifty borrowers should be allowed to endanger the interests of the Society [cooperative] and of other members (IAOS, 1902, p. 13).

Suggestions for reforming the Irish cooperatives show that this problem was lethal. Timothy O'Herlihy, the former secretary of a cooperative, advocated increasing the area covered by each Irish cooperative on the grounds that a borrower's neighbors would be unwilling to force him to repay. O'Herlihy saw the need for outsiders who could bear the blame for seemingly harsh decisions (Great Britain, 1914, Q3971–6). This recommendation amounts to throwing away all the information local people have on one another. This problem is not limited to Ireland, of course. Several studies refer to discomfort over the need to penalize those who do not repay their loans. Kevane (1996, p. 25) reports that in one program in Burkina Faso, "Women seemed uncomfortable with the idea that persons who failed to repay should be charged a penalty."

The Irish case illustrates an important point that is second nature to economists but may be lost in the enthusiasm for JLLIs: the mechanism will not work everywhere. The models we outlined in section 2, like most economic models, presume that a set of parameter values are satisfied. For example, both group lending and individual lending is aided by dynamic incentives, but only to the extent borrowers care about future credit availability and view the lender as preferable to alternatives. More generally, group lending derives its effectiveness from the social ties among potential group members. If those ties are weak, or if they imply an unwillingness to sanction one another (as in the Irish example) the mechanism will not work.

The literature on group lending shies away from discussing the possible negative implications of peer pressure and other aspects of joint liability. One exception is Montgomery, Bhattacharya, and Hulme (1996, pp. 154–5), who noted examples of BRAC group members taking aggressive action against defaulters.[43] In some instances action took the form of seizing the individual's assets, such as livestock or household goods. They note other examples of action that amounts to violence: for example, one group of BRAC borrowers tore down a woman's house because she had not repaid her loan. There are two implications of these aspects of joint liability. First, to create the effects we describe in section 2, there has to be pressure of this type (or at least the credible threat of pressure, which amounts to the same thing in many circumstances). Second, aggressive action such as tearing down a woman's house may rupture other, more important social ties. In evaluating the impact of group lending schemes, practitioners must bear in mind the implicit risk to those ties. Montgomery, Bhattacharya, and Hulme (1996, p. 154–5) note that the leadership of both TRDEP and BRAC are aware of these risks.[44]

## 3.4. Problems with joint liability: Dynamic incentives

Our model of enforcement through joint liability schemes relies on the dynamic incentives inherent in the lender's threat to cut off from future loans all members of any group that defaults. For this threat to be meaningful borrowers must be in a position where this is a serious possibility, and the lender must be willing and able to make this threat real for those who default. Most JLLIs today are either NGOs or private institutions, and for good reason: for political reasons, governments have a difficult time carrying out on threats to impose sanctions on poor borrowers who do not repay their loans. This was part of the cause for the problems in Irish credit cooperatives discussed above. Unlike their German counterparts, the Irish credit cooperatives garnered few deposits. Most of what they lent was a loan to the cooperative from the government. Given the political situation in Ireland at the end of the nineteenth century it was not realistic to think that the government would sue poor Irish farmers to recover these monies, making the liability of cooperative members meaningless. The only real threat the government had was to not renew its loans to the cooperatives, which in fact happened, but only after several years of obvious problems in the cooperatives. A similar problem arose in the MMF in Malawi. Borrowers are aware that this is a government program, which made at least some think that they would not be held to strict standards of repayment. Some of the problems in this case might reflect more basic "misunderstandings concerning the difference between grants and loans" (Buckley, 1996b, p. 389). A variant on this problem arose in the SACA program in Malawi.[45] In 1991–92 many SACA borrowing clubs were unable to repay their loans because a drought had devastated maize production in several parts of the country. The government (which effectively ran SACA) announced a policy whereby any borrower who could not repay his loan because of the drought would be granted a repayment moratorium. Just how such borrowers were to be distinguished from others is unclear, and this announcement by itself might harm discipline among borrowers. But once announced, rumor spread to the effect that all loans had been granted an extension. "Once this belief became ingrained it was difficult to change, especially in an election year" and repayment rates plummeted to about 21 percent (Buckley, 1996b, p. 350–1).

Sometimes the JLLI, for whatever reason, adopts policies that undermine dynamic incentives. For example, if a program's rules stipulate that a particular loan will be the last loan, regardless of how the borrower behaves with it, then the lender forsakes all benefit from dynamic incentives. Mosley and Dahal's study of a program in Nepal reports examples where some borrowers refuse to make their payments, even when able to do so. Withholding payments "seems to be particularly common among farmers who are taking out what they believe will be their last loan" from the program.[46] This Nepalese program is not unique in this regard; Bangladesh's TRDEP, for example, limits any single person to four loans in total. Neither Grameen nor the other Bangladeshi lender (BRAC) has a policy like this (Montgomery, Bhattacharya, and Hulme, 1996, p. 107–10). This aspect of dynamic incentives has the paradoxical implication that joint liability schemes are undermined if the lender tries to establish rules whereby borrowers cannot treat the lender as a permanent source of credit. Buckley (1996b, pp. 359–60) notes disapprovingly that in the Malawi SACA scheme the vast majority of borrowers had received several loans from the program. He is right to worry that this feature of the program makes it difficult to extend assistance to new borrowers, but potential access to repeat loans is crucial to enforcing repayment. A related problem arises when a lender is so weak that borrowers suspect it might not exist in the future to provide loans. Westley and Shaffer (1996) study loan deliquency rates among 55 Latin American credit unions in the early 1990s. They find that credit unions with a low rate of return on assets in the previous year had higher delinquency rates, and attribute this result to borrower suspicion that the credit union may soon go out of business and thus be unavailable for future loans.

In other cases, competition among JLLIs leads them to undermine repayment incentives for *each other*'s borrowers. Malawi, for example, has two different programs, SACA and a newer attempt to replicate the Grameen Bank called the Mudzi Fund. Buckley (1996b, pp. 387–8) found that many borrowers who were participants in the Mudzi Fund had been dropped from earlier participation in the SACA program for not repaying a loan. To the extent these two program continue to exist side-by-side, they run a real danger of undermining one another. The threat to exclude a defaulter from one program is less effective if individuals can simply move to another. This situation seems likely to become more common with time, as several countries now have similar programs that operate in the same geographic area. In Bangladesh, for example the Grameen Bank, BRAC, and TRDEP increasingly operate in the same areas. Those who advocate increased competition as a mechanism for improving credit delivery to poor people must bear in mind that such competition could well undermine the very basis of joint-liability lending schemes.[47]

Attempts to replicate the Grameen Bank in the United States illustrate a perverse aspect of the success of joint liability lending in developing countries. The dynamic incentives depend heavily on the alternative sources of credit being very expensive or non-existent. The Grameen Bank works in part because alternative credit sources in rural Bangladesh are either very expensive or non-existent. One problem for Irish credit cooperatives was that alternative credit sources were not bad enough to make the end of cooperative credit a powerful threat. Similarly, access to credit in countries such as the United States is not impossible, even for poor people, and poses a challenge to joint-liability lending in wealthy countries. This line of argument also implies that the Grameen Bank may undermine itself: if it can improve conditions for the rural poor, it may also improve access to alternative forms of credit.

Dynamic incentives are important and perhaps under-appreciated aspect of successful institutions such as the Grameen Bank. But to some extent these incentives do not, we should be clear, require group lending at all.[48] The Grameen Bank and other lenders sometimes condition future loans not on lending-group behavior but on individual behavior. The repayment incentives we discuss are stronger with group lending, for the reasons shown above, but the possibility of future credit will under some circumstances improve borrower incentives with individual lending. Similarly, the efforts of some micro-lenders to construct buildings and other visible signs of permanence are to some extent innovations that signal to borrowers that the institution will exist in the future and thus encourage borrowers to adopt a longer planning horizon. The brick-and-mortar institution building has a stronger incentive effect with group lending, but works with individual lending, as well.

## 4. Conclusions

This paper outlines the economic logic of joint-liability lending using a simple model that illustrates the way joint liability can mitigate some problems that arise in lending to poor people. The central issue in such credit markets is two-fold: the lender does not know much about the borrower (asymmetric information), and effective, commonly-used con-tractual arrangements for contending with asymmetric information do not work because the borrowers are too poor for the lender to use financial sanctions to achieve repayment of loans. We show that joint liability can achieve better screening to contend with adverse selection, encourages peer monitoring to reduce moral hazard, gives group members incentives to enforce the repayment of loans, and reduces the lender's audit costs for cases where some group members claim not to be able to repay.

Our empirical discussion has focused on problems of institutional implementation. The focus has been to tie the theory to actual practice and not to provide recommendations to practitioners. Given the underdeveloped state of the empirical literature, we do not claim that joint-liability lending is the most important feature of successful micro-lenders such as the Grameen Bank. There is clear evidence that joint-liability improves repayment, but these institutions use other instruments as well, and no study yet tries to apportion the reasons for success. We have also avoided the entire issue of sustainability. Whether the Grameen Bank and similar joint liability programs will ever be completely self-sustaining is not clear, as Morduch (1999) argues. Conning's (1999) analysis suggests that sustain-ability could indeed be difficult to achieve in many circumstances. Efforts to replicate the Grameen Bank and other successful JLLIs face difficult problems of adapting the system to local conditions without destroying the incentives that make joint liability work. We cited examples of apparently slight modifications of the rules that robbed group lending of the joint-liability aspect that accounts for the high repayment rates. The case studies we located only rarely mention the potential social costs of joint liability. These schemes draw on close ties among members to achieve the benefits we noted. When things go wrong, such as when an entire group is denied future loans, bitterness and recrimination among group members may have far-reaching consequences for village life. This risk is inherent in the system and needs to be viewed as a potential cost.

### Notes

1  Yunus is the founder of the Grameen Bank. The quotation is the epigraph to Wahid (1993).
2  Plunkett (1904), quoted in Guinnane (1994). Horace Plunkett was a pioneer in the credit-cooperative movement in Ireland at the turn of the twentieth century.

3   The four information and enforcement problems we stress are general and lie at the heart of all theories of financial intermediation. The recent textbook by Freixas and Rochet (1997) provides a clear and comprehensive introduction to the theory of financial intermediation in general.

4   By "auditing costs" in this paper we mean the costs of state verification (Townsend, 1979) where the relevant state is the return from the borrower's project.

5   Morduch (1998a) provides an excellent review of microfinance that is complementary to the aims of this paper. In particular, he considers two issues we do not consider, impact analysis and financial sustainability of these programs. See Rashid and Townsend (1994) for a general equilibrium approach to the issue of targeting credit to the poor. For general discussions of credit markets in underdeveloped countries see Hoff and Stiglitz (1990) or chapter 14 of Ray's recent textbook (Ray, 1998).

6   See sections 3.2 and 3.3.

7   See Morduch (1998b) for a discussion of the econometric problems of evaluating the impact of these programs. The main issues are endogenous program placement and self-selection into programs.

8   Schaefer-Kehnert (1982, p. 10) notes that in an early lending scheme in Malawi, repayment rates for individual loans was about the same as for group loans. But the former required much greater effort to collect.

9   The complementarity of the two approaches is recognized in some policy-oriented studies. See, for example, Fischer (1995, pp. 14–15).

10   We will assume that the lender earns zero economic profits, either by design (because it is a not-for-profit organization) or through the forces of economic competition.

11   Our limited-liability assumption also rules out physical punishment, slavery, or bonded labor as instruments for supporting credit contracts.

12   Since we are assuming that borrowers have no assets, such transfers are implausible if interpreted in purely financial terms. What we have in mind is that borrowers within a group might make transfers to each other in forms which are not feasible with an outsider (e.g., free labor services).

13   Armendariz de Aghion (1999), Banerjee, Besley and Guinnane (1994), Conning (1996), Madajewicz (1998), Stiglitz (1990) and Varian (1990) explore various aspects the theory of peer monitoring in joint liability lending.

14   This is the assumption, for example, of Stiglitz's (1990) formulation of peer monitoring.

15   Auditing in our discussion means the lender investigating the borrower's condition to see how much wealth is available to seize in lieu of loan repayment.

16   Prescott (1997) makes a related argument based on the delegated-monitoring model of Diamond (1996).

17   See Mookherjee and Png (1989) for a general treatment of the problem.

18   If this condition is not satisfied, then $\lambda = 1$ under joint liability. Then the relevant condition for the interest rate to be lower under joint liability becomes

$$\frac{Y^H}{2} < \frac{\rho Y^H}{p Y^H - (1-p)\gamma}$$

or

$$2\rho \geq p Y^H - (1-p)\gamma$$

19   The original insight of the Besley-Coate model is that in the absence of strong social sanctions there is a tradeoff between repayment under joint liability and individual liability. This tradeoff does not depend on whether borrowers are risk averse. We assume borrowers are risk averse to make their point in a much simpler model.

20    In this case $Y(r)$ is a solution of $u(Y) - u(Y - r) = \bar{B}(r)$. A referee noted that default is often motivated by a borrower's desire to take advantage of an investment opportunity that requires more than $Y - r$, that may not arise in the future, that leads to a higher payoff stream and for which the lender is not willing to lend. These considerations can be incorporated in the current formulation if one interprets

$$f(Y,r) \equiv u(Y) - u(Y - r)$$

not as the difference in *one period* utility from defaulting and repaying but the difference in the income streams from taking advantage of an investment opportunity that a capital of $Y$ permits versus one that a capital of $Y - r$ permits. So long as $f(Y,r)$ is increasing in $Y$ and decreasing in $r$ our conclusions go through.

21    That is, we are assuming there are no coordination problems between the borrowers. See Besley and Coate (1995).

22    In particular, the group will not repay any loan, repay one loan, or repay both loans according as

$$u(\frac{Y_1 + Y_1}{2}) - u(\frac{Y_1 + Y_1 - r}{2}) > \bar{B}$$

$$u(\frac{Y_1 + Y_1}{2}) - u(\frac{Y_1 + Y_1 - r}{2}) \leq \bar{B} < u(\frac{Y_1 + Y_1}{2}) - u(\frac{Y_1 + Y_1 - 2r}{2})$$

or

$$u(\frac{Y_1 + Y_1}{2}) - u(\frac{Y_1 + Y_1 - 2r}{2}) \leq \bar{B}$$

23    Adams and von Pischke (1992) is the classic paper on this subject. Most studies at least mention the issue. Studies that emphasize the transplantation of the Grameen Bank include the contributions to Getubig et al. (1993), Hulme (1990, 1991), the contributions to Todd (1996a) and several of the articles collected in Wahid (1993). Edgcomb et al. (1996) summarize micro-lending efforts in the United States.

24    Several studies draw more or less serious parallels to the German credit cooperative movement. See, for example, Schaefer-Kehnert (1982, p. 15) or Huppi and Feder (1990, p. 189).

25    Huppi and Feder (1990, p. 189) note that in many present-day credit cooperatives, the amount any member can borrow is tied to his or her capital contributions. This was not the norm in the nineteenth-century German institutions.

26    Loan approval in the *Protokollbuch für den Vorstand, Oberdreeser Darlehnskassen-vereine.* An agricultural laborer in this region would earn 15–20 Marks per week in the early twentieth century.

27    Each member's exposure depends, of course, on how liability in the cooperative is arranged.

28    The cooperative records were public and often do not state a specific reason for an action that might have been troubling to those in a small village. The cooperative records used here are discussed more fully in Guinnane (1997a). The German material discussed here is part of a book manuscript in progress. Guinnane thanks the managements of the several extant *Raiffeisenbanken* for access to this material. The incidents alluded to in the text are reported in *Protokollbuch für den Vorstand*, Limbach-Dorfer Spar- und Darlehnskassen-verein, November 2, 1913, and December 26, 1913.

29    For example, a member in Diestedde (Münsterland) was ejected in 1887 because he never paid his capital share. *Protokollbuch für den Vorstand*, Diestedde-Sünnighausen Spar- und Darlehnskassen-verein, June 21, 1887.

30    *Protokollbuch für den Vorstand*, Diestedde-Sünnighausen Spar- und Darlehnskassen-verein, June 30, 1888.

31  *Protokollbuch für den Vorstand*, Leer Spar- und Darlehnskassen-verein, October 3, 1909.
32  *Protokollbuch für den Vorstand*, Leer Spar- und Darlehnskassen-verein, various entries dated 1892 and 1893. The specific case is June 3, 1892.
33  *Protokollbuch für den Vorstand*, Diestedde-Sünnighausen Spar- und Darlehnskassen-verein, March 29, 1889.
34  *Protokollbuch für den Vorstand*, Oberdreeser Spar- und Darlehnskassen-verein, March 19, 1909.
35  Armendariz de Aghion and Morduch (1998) stress other program elements such as direct monitoring, weekly meetings with borrowers, and non-financial threats.
36  In addition, if member A repays member B's loan today, member B typically repays A's loan some time in the future.
37  FINCA (Fundacíon Integral Campesina) is a Costa Rican micro-lender.
38  Credit with Education is a joint effort of Freedom from Hunger, an NGO, and Réseau des Caisses Populaires.
39  BancoSol is a very successful lending program in Bolivia. While relying on groups of five to seven borrowers, in imitation of the Grameen Bank, BancoSol differs considerably in that it is willing to lend to people who are more prosperous than the target group served by the Grameen Bank.
40  In the development practitioner's literature there is a recognition that "minimalist" lenders, those that have no non-credit activities, are sacrificing a mechanism for strengthening groups.
41  The Jehudi Kiberia credit scheme is run by the Kenyan Rural Enterprise Program, a donor-funded NGO. The Jehudi program has been in effect since 1990. Most aspects of the small groups (*watano*) imitate Grameen practice (Buckley, 1996a).
42  KIWA is an acronym for *Kikundi Cha Wanabiashara*, "group of entrepreneurs."
43  BRAC (Bangladesh Rural Advancement Committee) is an NGO formed in the early 1970s. Originally it emphasized the health sector, but has since, through its Rural Development Programme, become an important provider of credit for the poor.
44  TRDEP (Thana Resource Development and Employment Programme) is a project overseen by the Ministry of Youth and Sports in the government of Bangladesh. The credit project began in 1972 and was originally funded by the World Bank.
45  SACA (Smallholder Agricultural Credit Administration) is a continuation of a program started in the 1960s, and is run by the Minister of Agriculture. SACA lends to farmers with up to 10 hectares of land, in contrast to the MMF, which only lends to individuals with less than 1 hectare of land or the equivalent in assets.
46  Mosley and Dahal (1985, p. 202).
47  Salloum (1995, p. 97) is one such advocate of competition. He is of course correct that competition among lenders that do not rely on these dynamic incentives ordinarily improves the welfare of borrowers.
48  We thank a referee for this observation.

## References

Adams, D. W. and von Pischke, J. D. (1992): "Microenterprise Credit Programs: *Déjà Vu*," *World Development*, 20 (10), 463–70.
Akerlof, G. (1970): "The Market for Lemons: Quality Uncertainty and the Market Mechanism," *Quarterly Journal of Economics*, 84 (3), 488–500.
Armendariz de Aghion, B. (1999): "On the Design of a Credit Agreement with Peer Monitoring," *Journal of Development Economics*, 60 (1), 79–104.
——and Gollier, C. (1998): "Peer Group Formation in an Adverse Selection Model," working paper, University College, London.
——and Morduch, J. (1998): "Microfinance Beyond Group Lending," working paper, University College, London.

Balkin, S. (1993): "A Grameen Bank Replication: The Full Circle Fund of the Women's Self-Employment Project of Chicago," in A. N. M. Wahid (ed.), *The Grameen Bank: Poverty Relief in Bangladesh*, San Francisco: Westview Press.

Banerjee, A., Besley, T. and Guinnane, T. (1994): "Thy Neighbor's Keeper: The Design of a Credit Cooperative with Theory and a Test," *Quarterly Journal of Economics*, 109 (2), 491–515.

Besley, T. (1995): "Nonmarket Institutions for Credit and Risk Sharing in Low-Income Countries," *Journal of Economic Perspectives*, 9 (3), 115–27.

——and Coate, S. (1995): "Group Lending, Repayment Incentives and Social Collateral," *Journal of Development Economics*, 46 (1), 1–18.

——, —— and Loury, G. (1993): "The Economics of Rotating Savings and Credit Associations," *American Economic Review*, 83 (4), 792–810.

——and Jain, S. (1994): "Collusion and the Design of Credit Cooperatives," working paper, LSE.

Buckley, G. (1996a): "Financing the Jua Kali Sector in Kenya: The KREP Juhdi scheme and Kenya Industrial Estates Informal Sector Programme," in Hulme and Mosley (1996b).

——(1996b): "Rural and Agricultural Credit in Malawi: A study of the Malawi Mudzi Fund and the Smallholder Agricultural Credit Administration," in Hulme and Mosley (1996b).

Coleman, B. (1999): "The Impact of Group Lending in Northeast Thailand," *Journal of Development Economics*, 60 (1), 105–41.

Coleman, J. (1990): *Foundations of Social Theory*. Cambridge, MA: Harvard University Press.

Conlin, M. (1999): "Peer Group Micro-lending Programs in Canada and the United States," *Journal of Development Economics*, 60 (1), 249–69.

Conning, J. (1996): "Group Lending, Moral Hazard and the Creation of Social Collateral," IRIS working paper 165, University of Maryland at College Park.

——(1999): "Outreach, Sustainability and Leverage in Monitored and Peer-Monitored Lending," *Journal of Development Economics*, 60 (1), 51–77.

Devereux, J. and Fishe, R. P. H. (1993): "An Economic Analysis of Group Lending Programs in Developing Countries," *The Developing Economies*, 39 (1), 102–21.

Diagne, A. (1998): "Default Incentives, Peer Pressure, and Equilibrium Outcomes in Group-based Lending Programs," working paper, IFPRI.

Diamond, D. (1996): "Financial Intermediation and Delegated Monitoring," *Review of Economic Studies*, 51, 393–414.

Edgcomb, E., Klein, J., and Clark, P. (1996): *The Practice of Microenterprise in the U.S.: Strategies, Costs, and Effectiveness*. Washington: The Aspen Institute.

Fischer, B. (1995): "The Basic Problem in Financing Small Businesses," in E. A. Brugger and S. Rajapatirana (eds), *New Perspectives on Financing Small Business in Developing Countries*, San Francisco: Institute for Contemporary Studies.

Freixas, X. and Rochet, J.-C. (1997): *Microeconomics of Banking*. Cambridge, Mass: MIT Press.

Getubig, I. P., Johari, M. Y., and Kuga Thas, A. M. (eds), (1993). *Overcoming Poverty through Credit: The Asian Experience in Replicating the Grameen Bank Approach*. Kuala Lumpur: Asian and Pacific Development Centre.

Ghatak, M. (1999a): "Group Lending, Local Information, and Peer Selection," *Journal of Development Economics*, 60 (1), 27–50.

——(1999b): "Screening by the Company You Keep: Joint Liability Loans and the Peer Selection Effect," working paper, University of Chicago.

Great Britain (1914): "Report of the Departmental Committee on Agricultural Credit in Ireland," House of Commons sessional papers, vol. 13.

Guinnane, T. W. (1994): "A Failed Institutional Transplant: Raiffeisen's Credit Cooperatives in Ireland, 1894–1914," *Explorations in Economic History*, 31(1), 38–61.

——(1997a): "Cooperatives as Information Machines: German Agricultural Credit Cooperatives," working paper, Yale University.

——(1997b): "Regional Organizations in the German Cooperative System, 1880–1914," *Ricerche Economiche*, 51 (3), 251–74.

Handa, S. and Kirton, C. (1999): "The Economics of Rotating Savings and Credit Associations: Evidence from the Jamaican 'Partner'," *Journal of Development Economics*, 60 (1), 173–94.

Hoff, K. and Stiglitz, J. (1990): "Imperfect Information and Rural Credit Markets – Puzzles and Policy Perspectives," *The World Bank Economic Review*, 4 (3), 235–50.

Hossain, M. (1988): *Credit for Alleviation of Rural Poverty: The Grameen Bank in Bangladesh*, research report 65, IFPRI, February.

Hulme, D. (1990): "Can the Grameen Bank be Replicated? Recent Experiments in Malaysia, Malawi and Sri Lanka," *Development Policy Review*, 8, 287–300.

——(1991): "The Malawi Mundi Fund: Daughter of Grameen," *Journal of International Development*, 3 (4), 427–31.

——and Mosley, P. (eds) (1996a): *Finance Against Poverty*, vol. 1. London: Routledge.

——and——(eds) (1996b): *Finance Against Poverty*, vol. 2. London: Routledge.

Huppi, M. and Feder, G. (1990): "The Role of Groups and Credit Cooperatives in Rural Lending," *The World Bank Research Observer*, 5 (2), 187–204.

IAOS (1902): *Annual Report of the Irish Agricultural Organization Society, Limited*. Dublin.

Johnson, S. and Rogaly, B. (1997): *Microfinance and Poverty Reduction*. Oxford: Oxfam.

Kevane, M. (1996): "Qualitative Impact Study of 'Credit with Education' in Burkina Faso," research paper 3, Freedom from Hunger.

Khandker, S., Khalily, B. and Khan, Z. (1995): "Grameen Bank: Performance and Sustainability," discussion paper 306, World Bank.

Kovsted, J. and Lyk-Jensen, P. (1999): "Rotating Savings and Credit Associations: The Choice Between Random and Bidding Allocation of Funds," *Journal of Development Economics*, 60 (1), 143–72.

Laffont, J.-J. and N'Guessan, T. (1999): "Collusion and Group Lending with Adverse Selection," working paper, IDEI, Toulouse.

Madajewicz, M. (1998): "Capital for the Poor: The Effect of Wealth on the Optimal Loan Contract," working paper, Stockholm School of Economics.

Mondal, W. I. and Tune, R. A. (1993): "Replicating the Grameen Bank in the North America: The Good Faith Fund Experience," in A. N. M. Walid (ed.), *The Grameen Bank: Poverty Relief in Bangladesh*, San Francisco: Westview Press.

Montgomery, R., Bhattacharya, D. and Hulme, D. (1996): "Credit for the Poor in Bangladesh: the BRAC Rural Development Programme and the Government Thana Resource Development and Employment Programme," in Hulme and Mosley (1996b).

Mookherjee, D. and Png, I. (1989): "Optimal Auditing, Insurance, and Redistribution," *Quarterly Journal of Economics*, 104 (2), 399–415.

Moore, J. (1992): "Implementation, Contracts and Renegotiation in Environments with Complete Information," in J.-J. Laffont (ed.), *Advances in Economic Theory*, vol. 1, Cambridge University Press.

Morduch, J. (1998a): "The Microfinance Promise," working paper, Princeton University.

——(1998b): "Does Microfinance Really Help the Poor? New Evidence from Flagship Programs in Bangladesh," working paper, Princeton University.

——(1999): "The Role of Subsidies in Microfinance: Evidence from the Grameen Bank," *Journal of Development Economics*, 60 (1), 229–48.

Mosley, P. (1996): "Metamorphosis from NGO to Commercial Bank: The Case of BancoSol in Bolivia," in Hulme and Mosley (1996b).

——and Dahal, R. P. (1985): "Lending to the Poorest: Early Lessons from the Small Farmers' Development Programme, Nepal," *Development Policy Review*, 3, 193–207.

Mutua, A. K. (1994): "The Juhudi Credit Scheme: From a Traditional Integrated Method to a Financial Systems Approach," in M. Otero and E. Rhyne (eds), *The New World of Microenterprise Finance: Building Healthy Financial Institutions for the Poor*, West Hartford, CT: Kumarian Press.

Owusu, K. O. and Tetteh, W. (1982): "An Experiment in Agricultural Credit: The Small Farmer Group Lending Programme in Ghana (1969–1980)," *Savings and Development*, 1 (6), 67–83.

Patten, R. H. and Rosengard, J. K. (1991): *Progress with Profits: The Development of Rural Banking in Indonesia*. San Francisco: ICS Press.

Pitt, M. and Khandker, S. (1998): "The Impact of Group-based Credit Programs on Poor Households in Bangladesh: Does the Gender of Participants Matter?" *Journal of Political Economy*, 106 (5), 958–96.

Plunkett, H. (1904): *Ireland in the New Century*. Reprinted 1970, Dublin: Kenniktat Press.

Prescott, E. S. (1997): "Group Lending and Financial Intermediation: An Example," *Federal Reserve Bank of Richmond Economic Quarterly*, 83 (4), 23–48.

Rashid, M. and Townsend, R. (1994): "Targeting Credit and Insurance: Efficiency, Mechanism Design, and Program Evaluation," ESP discussion paper 47, the World Bank.

Ray, D. (1998): *Development Economics*. Princeton: Princeton University Press.

Sadoulet, L. (1998): "Non-Monotone Matching in Group Lending: A Missing Insurance Market Story," mineo, ECARE and Princeton University.

Salloum, D. (1995): "The Business of Lending to the Smallest of the Small Enterprises," in E. A. Brugger and S. Rajapatirana (eds), *New Perspectives on Financing Small Business in Developing Countries*, San Francisco: Institute for Contemporary Studies.

Schaefer-Kehnert, W. (1982): "Success with Group Lending in Malawi," *Development Digest*, 1, 10–15.

Stiglitz, J. (1990): "Peer Monitoring and Credit Markets," *World Bank Economic Review*, 4 (3): 351–66.

Todd, H. (ed.) (1996a): *Cloning Grameen Bank: Replicating a Poverty Reduction Model in India, Nepal and Vietnam*. London: IT Publications.

—— (1996b): *Women at the Center: Grameen Bank Borrowers after One Decade*. Boulder: Westview Press.

Tohtong, C. (1988): "Joint-Liability Groups for Small-Farmer Credit: The BAAC Experience in Thailand," *Rural Development in Practice*, 1, 4–7.

Townsend, R. (1979): "Optimal Contracts and Competitive Markets with Costly State Verification," *Journal of Economic Theory*, 21 (2), 265–93.

Van Tassel, E. (1999): "Group Lending under Asymmetric Information," *Journal of Development Economics*, 60 (1), 3–25.

Varian, H. (1990): "Monitoring Agents With Other Agents," *Journal of Institutional and Theoretical Economics*, 146 (1), 153–74.

Wahid, A. N. M. (1993): *The Grameen Bank: Poverty Relief in Bangladesh*. San Francisco: Westview Press.

Wenner, M. (1995): "Group Credit: A Means to Improve Information Transfer and Loan Repayment Performance," *Journal of Development Studies*, 32 (2), 263–81.

Westley, G. D. and Shaffer, S. (1996): "Credit Union Policies and Performance in Latin America," presented at the 1996 Annual Meeting of the Latin American and Caribbean Economics Association.

Winkler, H. (1933): "Die Landwirtschaftlichen Kreditgenossenschaften und die Grundstze Raiffeisens," *Jahrbücher für Nationalkonomie und Statistik*, Band 138, III Folge, Erste Hefte, 59–76.

Wydick, B. (1999): "Can Social Cohesion be Harnessed to Repair Market Failures? Evidence from Group Lending in Guatemala," *Economic Journal*, 109, 463–75.

Yunus, M. (1994): *Grameen Bank As I See It*. Grameen Bank, Dhaka.

CHAPTER 17

# Learning by Doing and Learning from Others: Human Capital and Technical Change in Agriculture

Andrew D. Foster and Mark R. Rosenzweig

Household-level panel data from a nationally representative sample of rural Indian households describing the adoption and profitability of high-yielding seed varieties (HYVs) associated with the Green Revolution are used to test the implications of a model incorporating learning by doing and learning spillovers. The estimates indicate that (i) imperfect knowledge about the management of the new seeds was a significant barrier to adoption; (ii) this barrier diminished as farmer experience with the new technologies increased; (iii) own experience and neighbors' experience with HYVs significantly increased HYV profitability; and (iv) farmers do not fully incorporate the village returns to learning in making adoption decisions.

## 1. Introduction

That individuals learn from their peers, neighbors, or friends is an important public policy assumption that underpins, for example, public subsides of schooling and has been hypothesized to be a significant source of economic growth (Romer, 1986; Lucas, 1993). Quantitative evidence on the importance of learning externalities, however, is not extensive. While there are studies reporting associations between the behaviors of individuals and their neighbors, these studies may be wholly spurious in that they may be driven by common unobservables (Case, 1991; Evans, Oates, and Schwab, 1992), or they may reflect, if real, peer influences that do not entail learning. The principal feature that distinguishes external effects due to learning from those due to mere mimicking or social pressure is that an individual's productivity, not just his or her behavior, is affected by his or her neighbor's behavior.

Just as the most appropriate test of learning by doing requires the measurement of changes in productivity, or the rewards to productivity, that accrue from experience (see, e.g., Bahk and Gort, 1993), the identification of learning from neighbors also requires information on productivity or its rewards in addition to measures of neighbors' characteristics or behavior relevant to productivity growth. It is not sufficient, however, to find that an individual's productivity is affected by a neighbor's behavior to confirm the existence of learning from neighbors. It is possible, for example, that social pressure – by which neighbors collectively induce an individual to behave in some way – can improve that individual's productivity without any learning on the part of the individual. To test for knowledge spillovers and learning externalities requires a more precise specification of the learning mechanisms and of the production technology.

In this paper, we incorporate learning by doing and learning from others in a modified target-input model of new technology (Wilson, 1975; Jovanovic and Nyarko, 1994). We use the model to establish and carry out tests for individual and external learning effects based on panel data describing farmer behavior and profitability at the onset of the "Green Revolution" period in India. This time period, when new agricultural technologies were first imported into India, is particularly useful for examination of hypotheses concerning learning: while prior to the introduction of new seeds farmers had been using essentially the same technology for decades, new opportunities for greater productivity arose at least in some areas of the country for the first time.

The modeling approach we take, which emphasizes the problem of deciphering the optimal management of a new technology, contrasts with the recent work by Besley and Case (1993, 1994) on learning spillovers in agriculture. In their model, estimated using data from one village in India, the technology adoption problem is one in which the profitability of adoption is uncertain and exogenous; farmers thus learn from experience about true profitability. In target-input models, what is unknown and stochastic is the best use of inputs under the new technology. There are two reasons we adopt this alternative approach. First, optimal input use appears empirically to be central to farmers' concerns in environments subject to technological change, and there appears to be some suggestive but direct evidence of learning about the best use of inputs from others. Table 1 reports the results from questions posed to farmers in Green Revolution areas, taken from three surveys carried out in two countries, on farmers' sources of information on fertilizer input use (two surveys) and on agricultural practices, the latter for farmers using new seed varieties. In the Indian surveys, it is interesting to note that the only questions on information pertained to input use; there were none on the profitability of seeds. In all these surveys, neighbors appear to be important sources of information about input use, as important as formal public information dissemination sources.[1]

A second reason we adopt the target-input model is that, in contrast to models with uncertain but exogenous profits, the profitability of any new technology grows over time as knowledge accumulates. It is thus possible to test directly for learning externalities in terms of productivity, rather than by inference from farmer adoption behavior. Moreover, while it is not necessary to assume away the additional exogenous stochastic elements to new-technology profitability that are emphasized in Besley and Case's framework in estimating the consequences for profitability of learning about optimal practices, doing so provides testable implications for farmer adoption behavior that are otherwise difficult

**Table 1**  Information sources of farmers in three surveys

|  | India | | Philippines: Bukidnon: Most important source of information about cropping practices[‡] |
|---|---|---|---|
| Source | ARIS: Source of information about fertilizer use[*] | REDS: Source of information about fertilizer use[†] |  |
| Friends and neighbors | 30.4 | 42.5 | 41.6 |
| Government agency | 51.4 | 62.9 | ... |
| Local extension agent | ... | 35.0 | 0 |
| Demonstration projects | 3.2 | ... | 50.0 |

[*] Percentage reporting source among 17 mutually exclusive categories.
[†] Percentage reporting source among seven nonexclusive categories.
[‡] Percentage reporting source among eight mutually exclusive categories.

*Source:* For India: ARIS: NCAER Additional Rural Income Survey, 1970–71 (national); farmers, population-weighted counts. REDS: NCAER Rural Economic Development Survey, 1981–82 (national); 186 villages with HYV use. For the Philippines: IFPRI Bukidnon Survey, 1986; 12 corn farmers using HYV seeds.

to derive. In particular, we are able to derive tests of whether neighbor and own-experience are perfect substitutes and whether there is efficient learning.

In section 2, we set out the basic model, deriving implications for the effects of own and neighbors' experience with new technologies on profitability and on the scale of the new technology used. In section 3 the data are described and the estimation procedures discussed. Section 4 presents the estimates of the profit functions and adoption decision rules. Evidence is first presented on the existence of spurious correlation of neighbor behavior and individual profitability in the cross section, which is evidently eliminated using the estimation procedures employed subsequently. The profit function estimates show that new-technology profitability increases significantly with increases in both own and neighbor new-technology experience in ways consistent with the learning model: the returns to experience of both types diminish rapidly over time and at the same pace. The estimates of the adoption decision equations also are consistent with learning from neighbors, but they reject a model in which the learning externalities are completely internalized. Section 5 presents dynamic simulations based on the estimates and calibrated from the data that show the effects of differences in farm wealth (scale) of farmers and their neighbors on the pace and magnitude of new-technology adoption and on profits. These simulations show that the estimates predict the well-known adoption S–curve that has characterized new-technology adoption in agricultural environments (Feder, Just, and Zilberman, 1985) and that, as a result of learning spillovers and nonexclusion, a poor farmer with richer neighbors will benefit more from the introduction of new varieties than a poor farmer with similarly poor neighbors. Section 6 contains concluding remarks.

## 2. Theory

To establish a framework providing empirically implementable tests of the presence of learning from others in terms of both productivity and behavior, we use a modified version of the target-input model, which has been used to study information acquisition and its effects on the productivity of innovations (see, e.g., Wilson, 1975; Jovanovic and Nyarko, 1994). The basic features of this model are that

(i)   individuals deciding on input decisions each year know the technology of production up to a random "target" for input use that has both a systematic and an idiosyncratic component,

(ii)  payoffs are decreasing in the square of the distance between actual input use and the target, and

(iii) *ex post*, each individual can observe what the target had been in each year and thus draw inferences about the systematic component of the target.

This model is particularly suitable for the study of Indian agriculture at the onset of the Green Revolution, when the newly available technology was in the form of high-yielding variety (HYV) rice and wheat seeds. A well-known feature of HYVs is that yields are sensitive to modern inputs such as chemical fertilizer and pesticides as well as traditional inputs such as water. Both over- and underuse of these inputs can reduce yields, with the optimal level of use being influenced by region- and year-specific variables such as the quality of the soil, temperature, and the level of rainfall and groundwater.[2] Because there is regional variation in optimal input use, countrywide guidelines may have limited value compared with local experience in raising yields. Finally, traditional varieties are generally less sensitive to the use of these inputs, and because farmers have substantial experience with these varieties, additional experience with these crops is unlikely to affect yields.

We modify the basic model to make it more applicable to the Indian agricultural context. In particular, not only does the model incorporate the possibility of learning from the experience of neighboring farmers, but

(i)   the scale of operation is endogenous and importantly influences the precision of new information;

(ii)  farmers can use two technologies, traditional and new, simultaneously; and

(iii) farmers can engage in strategic behavior.[3]

To measure scale and to capture variation in the suitability of land to HYVs, we divide up the farmer's land into parcels of arbitrary size (e.g., acres, hectares, and decimals).[4] The production technology and information restrictions are as follows: optimal or target-input use on each parcel of land $i$ planted using the new seeds by farmer $j$ in each period $t$, $\tilde{\theta}_{ijt}$ is given by

$$\tilde{\theta}_{ijt} = \theta^* + u_{ijt} \tag{1}$$

where $\theta^*$ is the mean optimal use and $u_{ijt}$ is an independently and identically distributed (i.i.d.) normal random variable with variance $\sigma_u^2$. We consider below the implications of contemporaneous spatial correlations in the target shocks. Farmers are assumed to know $\sigma_u^2$ and have priors over $\theta^*$ that are $N(\hat{\theta}_{jo}, \sigma_{\theta jo}^2)$. Yield per parcel using traditional varieties is $\eta_a$, but yield per parcel using HYVs varies according to the suitability of land to HYVs and to input use. The (per parcel) yield from HYV seeds on the $i$th most HYV-suitable parcel for a farmer with $A_j$ total parcels of land is given by

$$\eta_a + \eta_h - \eta_{ha}\frac{i}{A_j} - (\theta_{ijt} - \tilde{\theta}_{ijt})^2 \tag{2}$$

where $\theta_{ijt}$ denotes actual input use and $\eta_{ha}$ reflects the loss associated with using less suitable land as more HYVs are used.

## 2.1. Learning and profit growth

It is easy to show that under the assumptions of the model, expected profits at time $t$ are a function of the farmer's posterior distribution for $\theta_j^*$ at time $t$:

$$\pi_{jt} = \left(\eta_h - \eta_{ha}\frac{H_{jt}}{2A_j} - \sigma_{\theta jt}^2 - \sigma_u^2\right)H_{jt} + \eta_a A_j + \mu_j + \epsilon_{pjt} \tag{3}$$

where $E_t(\epsilon_{pjt}) = 0$, $\mu_j$ captures variation among farmers in the overall productivity of their land, and $\sigma_{\theta jt}^2$ represents the variance of farmer $j$'s posterior distribution over $\theta_j^*$ at time $t$.[5]

At the end of the harvest, the set of true or *ex post* optimal input levels, $\tilde{\theta}_{ijt}$, for each of the farmer's parcels in that year becomes known.[6] The farmer can use this information to update his priors with regard to the expected optimal input use, $\theta^*$. When the shocks are independent across space, the variance associated with this signal is $\sigma_u^2/H_{jt}$. Thus the precision of the signal, $H_{jt}/\sigma_u^2$, increases proportionately with the number of parcels on which the farmer plants new-technology seeds. If the parcel-specific $\tilde{\theta}_{ijt}$ on land planted with the new-technology seeds by the farmer's neighbors are also revealed to the farmer, then the signal precision in that year for the farmer will also depend on the amount of the neighbor's HYV area. However, to allow for the possibility that information from neighboring farmers is more noisy than that from own cultivated area, we assume that for each parcel of neighbors' land cultivated with the new seeds, what is revealed is $\tilde{\theta}_{ijt} + \xi_{ijt}$, where the variance of neighbors' noise, $\sigma_\xi^2$, is also known.[7]

Given the stationarity in the distribution of the $\tilde{\theta}_{ijt}$, the time of information is irrelevant.[8] Assuming that farmer $j$ has $n$ neighbors, we may therefore use Bayesian updating to write

$$\sigma_{\theta jt}^2 = \frac{1}{\rho + \rho_o S_{jt} + \rho_v \bar{S}_{-jt}} \tag{4}$$

where $\rho = 1/\sigma_{\theta 0}^2$ is the precision of the farmer's initial priors, $\rho_o = 1/\sigma_u^2$ is the precision of the information obtained from each parcel planted by $j$ on his own farm, $S_{jt}$ is the cumulative number of parcels planted by farmer $j$ up to time $t$, and $\rho_v = n/(\sigma_u^2 + \sigma_k^2)$ is the precision of the information obtained from an increase in $\bar{S}_{-jt}$, the average of the cumulative experience of neighboring farmers.

There are three important restrictions on the profit effects of experience implied by this learning technology. First, increases in the cumulative number of the parcels planted in

HYVs by farmer $j$ up to time $t$ and in the cumulative HYV parcels of $j$'s neighbors raise the profitability of $j$'s high-yielding varieties at time $t$. To see this, substitute (4) into the profit equation (3). This yields a conditional (on HYV use) profit function

$$\pi_{jt} = \pi(H_{jt}, S_{jt}, \bar{S}_{-jt}, A_j, \mu_j, \epsilon_{pij})$$

such that

$$\frac{\partial \pi_{jt}}{\partial S_{jt}} = \frac{\rho_o}{\left(\rho + \rho_o S_{jt} + \rho_v \bar{S}_{-jt}\right)^2} H_{jt} \tag{5}$$

and

$$\frac{\partial \pi_{jt}}{\partial \bar{S}_{jt}} = \frac{\rho_v}{\left(\rho + \rho_o S_{jt} + \rho_v \bar{S}_{-jt}\right)^2} H_{jt} \tag{6}$$

Second, as seen from (5) and (6), the ratio of the profitability effects of cumulative experience – measured in HYV area – of farmer $j$ and of his neighbors on farmer $j$'s HYV profitability is a time-invariant constant, $\rho_v / \rho_o$. Finally, with nonzero use of HYVs, the returns per hectare to both own and neighbors' experience diminish over time and at the same rate:

$$\frac{\dfrac{\partial \left( \pi_{jt+1} / H_{jt+1} \right)}{\partial S_{jt+1}}}{\dfrac{\partial \left( \pi_{jt} / H_{jt} \right)}{\partial S_{jt}}} = \frac{\dfrac{\partial \left( \pi_{jt+1} / H_{jt+1} \right)}{\partial \bar{S}_{-jt+1}}}{\dfrac{\partial \left( \pi_{jt} / H_{jt} \right)}{\partial \bar{S}_{-jt}}} = \frac{\left( \rho + \rho_o S_{jt} + \rho_v \bar{S}_{-jt} \right)^2}{\left( \rho + \rho_o S_{jt+1} + \rho_v \bar{S}_{-jt+1} \right)^2} < 1 \tag{7}$$

So far, we have assumed that the information is perfectly correlated within parcels and perfectly uncorrelated across parcels, so that the precision of the information is proportional to the number of parcels. Similar implications of Bayesian learning arise even if there is a village-level shock to the optimal target in each year. If the year-specific common shock variance is $\sigma_v^2$, the variance of farmer $j$'s posterior distribution at time $t$ is then

$$\sigma_{\theta jt}^2 = \frac{1}{\rho + \displaystyle\sum_{x=1}^{t} \frac{1}{\left[ 1 / \left( \rho_o H_{jx} + \rho_v \bar{H}_{-jx} \right) \right] + \sigma_v^2}} \tag{8}$$

which reduces to equation (4) when $\sigma_v^2 = 0$. We show in appendix A that the predictions of positive and declining experience effects and the constancy of the ratio of own and neighbor experience effects are identical to those arising in the i.i.d. case, but in this case in terms of the year-specific marginal additions to experience rather than cumulative experience.

These implications of the learning-by-doing model with neighbor effects can be tested through estimation of the profit function conditional on HYV use. Estimates of this function provide direct evidence of learning in addition to establishing whether and by how much individuals learn from their neighbors' experience, $\rho_v$.[9] Note that if the only source of uncertainty were imperfect knowledge about the profitability of HYVs as in Besley and Case (1994), learning would not affect the growth of profits conditional on HYV use. However, in that case, shocks to profitability influence the adoption decision. This has implications for the appropriate method for estimating the profit function, as discussed below.

## 2.2. Learning and technology adoption

In addition to affecting the structure of the profit function, the existence of learning by doing and learning from neighbors' experience with respect to input use also has implications for adoption, that is, the choice of the scale of $H_{jt}$. In particular, if each farmer wishes to maximize expected discounted profits, with $\delta$ the discount factor, then the (unconditional) problem faced by farmer $j$ at time $t$ is

$$V_{tj} = \max_{H_{jx}} E_t \sum_{x=t}^{T} \delta^{s-t} \pi \left( H_{jx}, S_{jx}, \mathbf{S}_{-jx}, A_j, \mu_j, \epsilon_{pjx} \right) \tag{9}$$

where $\mathbf{S}_{-jt}$ is the vector of experience for other farmers in $j$'s village, and therefore we may write

$$V_{jt} = \max_{H_j} E_t \left[ \left( \eta_h - \eta_{ha} \frac{H_j}{2A_j} - \sigma_u^2 - \frac{1}{\rho + \rho_o S_{jt} + \rho_v \bar{S}_{-jt}} \right) H_j + \eta_a A_j + \mu_j + \epsilon_{pjt} \right]$$
$$+ \delta V_{jt+1} \tag{10}$$

As is evident in equations (9) and (10), the decisions made by each farmer depend on the past planting decisions of neighboring farmers and his expectations about planting decisions in the future. Therefore, those neighbor characteristics that predict their future planting decisions will enter into the decision rules of every farmer. For example, a farmer whose neighbors have characteristics that make it likely that they will experiment with HYVs may tend to curtail his own experimentation. The reason is that he can realize a higher short-term return from planting the traditional variety and then shifting to the HYV when there is sufficient experience from his neighbors to make adoption directly profitable.

To capture the influence of neighbor characteristics on farmer adoption and to obtain more precise insights into how adoption is affected by learning, it is necessary to characterize strategic behavior. In particular, we make use of the solution concept of a *Markov perfect equilibrium*.[10] This solution concept implies that choices of farmer $j$ as well as his neighbors at time $t$ depend only on the experience and asset variables and that, conditional on these variables, choices of $H_{jt}$ and $\mathbf{H}_{-jt}$ constitute a Nash equilibrium in each period.

The following first-order condition characterizes the internal solution choice of the number of parcels $H_{jt}$ planted with the new seeds at time $t$ by farmer $j$, conditional on the time $t$ choices of his neighbors and the state variables (farm size and own and neighbors' experiences):

$$\eta_h - \eta_{ha}\frac{H_{jt}}{A_j} - \sigma_u^2 - \frac{1}{\rho + \rho_o S_{jt} + \rho_v \bar{S}_{-jt}} = \frac{\partial \pi_{jt}}{\partial H_{jt}} = -\delta\frac{\partial V_{t+1}}{\partial S_{jt}} \qquad (11)$$

Expression (11) indicates that the marginal contribution to profits of the last parcel planted with HYV seeds in any period $t$ is optimally negative. Farmers will always use more than the within-period profit-maximizing amount of the new technology because of the future profit gains that accrue as a result of learning by doing.

Formal solution of this problem requires backward induction from the final period $T$. Analytic solutions for the HYV decision rule cannot easily be derived for $t < T$. However, given a value function at time $t + 1$ and the restrictions imposed by Markov perfection, equation (11) for a farmer and his $n$ neighbors can be solved to obtain decision rules of the form

$$H_{jt} = h_t\left(S_{jt}, \mathbf{S}_{-jt}, A_j, A_{-j}\right) \qquad (12)$$

Insight into the nature of decisions made prior to period $T$ may be gained through the examination of partial derivatives of the HYV decision rules at time $T - 1$ with respect to the state variables evaluated at the symmetric equilibrium (e.g., $A_j = A$, $S_{jt} = S_t$, $H_{jt} = H_t$). The expressions, which are complex, are contained in appendix B. However, the effects of neighbors' assets on a farmer's adoption decisions permit discrimination among three models of learning:

(i)   if there is no learning from neighbors ($\rho_v = 0$), there are no effects of neighbors' assets on any farmer's adoption decision;

(ii)  if a social planner decides on the planting decisions for all farmers or learning externalities are otherwise internalized, the effect of neighbors' average assets on the amount of area planted to HYV by any farmer with $n$ neighbors should be $n$ times the effect of his own assets and both effects should be positive; and

(iii) if, as is assumed in the model, information externalities are not internalized, the effects of neighbors' assets that predict future plantings of HYV on a farmer's adoption of HYV can be negative, although the own effects must remain positive.

The negative effect of neighbors' characteristics on adoption will depend on whether the returns to experience are increasing or decreasing. Consider a village made up of two farmers. An increase in a farmer's assets increases adoption in period $T$ and thus increases the returns to experience in that period. Thus given the amount of HYV planted by farmer A, an increase in the assets of his neighbor, B, will increase B's HYV area in period $T - 1$. An increase in HYV use by B in period $T - 1$ increases the precision of information available to A in period $T$. How this increase in precision for the behavior of farmer A affects the adoption decision depends on the sign of $\partial^2 V_{jT}/\partial S_{jT}^2$, that is, on whether the returns to experience for him in period $T$ are increasing or decreasing in experience.[11] If they are increasing (decreasing), then this increased precision will increase (decrease) the

HYV planted by A in $T - 1$. Thus if B's assets increase and there are decreasing returns to experience, A is given an increased incentive to free-ride on his neighbor's learning by decreasing his own learning. This incentive results in a negative effect of B's wealth on HYV use by A. By contrast, a positive effect of B's wealth will result if there are increasing returns to experience.

The model also yields implications for the relative magnitudes of the own and neighbors' experience effects that are testable. First, if own and neighbors' experience contain the same amount of information $(\rho_v = n\rho_o)$, then a further restriction on behavior is implied:

$$\frac{\partial H_{jT-1}}{\partial \bar{S}_{-jT-1}} = \frac{\rho_v}{\rho_o}\frac{\partial H_{jT-1}}{\partial S_{jT-1}} = \frac{1}{n}\frac{\partial H_{jT-1}}{\partial S_{jT-1}} \tag{13}$$

That is, the relative effect of neighbors' and own experience on the amount of HYV chosen in each period is constant across all periods and is identical to their relative contribution to profits, as in (5) and (6). If information is transmitted imperfectly $(\sigma_k^2 > 0)$, then the relative magnitudes of the effects depend again on whether the value function in period $T$ exhibits increasing or decreasing returns to experience. In particular, if the returns to experience are decreasing, then

$$\frac{\partial H_{jT-1}}{\partial \bar{S}_{-jT-1}} < \frac{\rho_v}{\rho_o}\frac{\partial H_{jT-1}}{\partial S_{jT-1}} \tag{14}$$

with the inequality reversed if the returns to experience are increasing. The reason that own and neighbors' experience can have different effects in the decision rule than they have in the profit function is that the value function for farmer $j$ depends on the precision of his own information as well as the precision of his neighbors' information, whereas the profit function depends only on the precision of his own information. In the presence of imperfect information, experience by $j$ will increase the precision of $j$'s information more than it will increase the precision of his neighbors' information, whereas an increase in neighbors' experience will have the opposite effect. If information is transmitted perfectly, then these two measures of precision coincide and thus equation (13) holds.

## 3. Data and Empirical Implementation

### 3.1. Data

The data that we use come from a panel data set from India, the National Council of Applied Economic Research (NCAER) Additional Rural Incomes Survey (ARIS), which describes rural households from a national probability survey begun in the crop year 1968–9, soon after the onset of the Indian Green Revolution when new HYV seeds first became available. The panel data set provides longitudinal information for 4,118 households pertaining to the crop years 1968–9, 1969–70, and 1970–1 on the area planted with the new high-yielding seed varieties (for wheat and rice), schooling, farm profits, and asset stocks and additions. An important feature of these data is that the 250 villages in which the households reside are identified. It is thus possible to construct village-level aggregates, based on sampling weights, that are representative of village inhabitants and have sufficient variation to test hypotheses about the influence of neighbors' characteristics and behavior. Both the extensive coverage and the longitudinal feature of the data set, as discussed below, are important for identifying cross-household learning effects.

Approximately two-thirds of the households interviewed in 1970–1, those in which the household head had remained the same up through 1981, were resurveyed by NCAER in 1981–2 (the Rural Economic and Demography Survey). While the data from this more recent panel round do not provide information on the use of HYV seeds or, more relevant to that period, on the vintages of the seeds used, information is provided on the assets inherited by the household heads prior to the 1968 round of the survey. This information will be used to construct instruments, as described below, for use with the earlier panel data set.

The ARIS data show that farmers' adoption of HYVs was rapid and occurred at an accelerated rate over the initial 3-year period: among farmers in villages in which at least one farmer cultivated with HYV seeds by 1970, only 19 percent were using HYV seeds in 1968, 29 percent had used the new seeds by 1969, and 42 percent had used them by 1970.[12] Among the farmers using HYV seeds in the 1970–1 crop year, HYV acreage had also increased at an accelerated pace, rising from only 4 percent of their cultivated acreage in the 1968–9 crop year and 3 percent of their acreage in the crop year 1969–70 to over 20 percent of their acreage in 1970–1.[13]

## 3.2. Specification of the profit function

The specification of the conditional profit function is obtained by substituting (4) into (3). We also incorporate the possibility that a farmer's schooling may also improve productivity of the new technologies, in accord with the hypothesis of Schultz (1975) that schooling is particularly useful in decoding information in a situation of "disequilibrium":

$$\pi_{jt} = \left( \eta_h - \sigma_u^2 - \eta_{ha} \frac{H_{jt}}{2A_j} - \frac{1}{\rho + \rho_o S_{jt} + \rho_v \bar{S}_{-jt}} + \eta_{he} E_j \right) H_{jt} + \eta_a A_{jt} + \mu_j + \epsilon_{pjt} \quad (15)$$

where $\epsilon_{pjt}$ is the stochastic shock reflecting among other things, the differences between the realized optimal $\tilde{\theta}_{ijt}$ and actual input choices $\theta_{ijt}$.[14]

We use two different approaches to estimate equation (15). First, we estimate a linear approximation to the HYV profitability term in (15) and use this approximation to test the broad implications of the model. Then we take the exact specification of the profit function in the model entirely seriously in order to obtain structural estimates of the parameters. The linear approximation may be written as

$$\pi_{jt} \approx \left( \eta_h' + \beta_{ot} S_{jt} + \beta_{vt} \bar{S}_{-jt} + \eta_{he} E_j \right) H_{jt} + \eta_a' A_{jt} + \mu_j + \epsilon_{pjt} \quad (16)$$

where $\eta_h'$ and $\eta_{ao}'$ are coefficients on $H_{it}$ and $A_{it}$, respectively, and, to first order,

$$\beta_{ot} = \frac{\rho_o}{\rho + (\rho_o + \rho_v) S_t}$$

and

$$\beta_{vt} = \frac{\rho_v}{\rho + (\rho_o + \rho_v)S_t}$$

for some $S_t$ that is representative of average experience at time $t$. The information coefficients, $\beta_{ot}$ and $\beta_{vt}$, for own and village experience, respectively, embody the implications of the model; they thus should fall over time because experience is cumulative and, from (5) and (6), the ratio

$$\frac{\beta_{ot}}{\beta_{ot+1}} = \frac{\beta_{vt}}{\beta_{vt+1}} = \lambda_{pt} \tag{17}$$

is a time-specific constant, $\lambda_{pt}$.

We have specified the profit function (2), and its representation (15), to include a fixed effect $\mu_j$. Because there is no asset accumulation in the model, the fixed effect does not influence the HYV decision net of assets. With assets endogenous, investment decisions and HYV choices are influenced by the unmeasured fixed effect, and equation (16) cannot be estimated using ordinary least squares (OLS) applied to cross-sectional data. For example, farmers who are persistently more profitable because they live in areas with better land will tend to accumulate more assets inclusive of land. This gives them a greater incentive to gain experience with HYVs since the returns to HYVs are increasing in land (eqn (15)) and will thus affect their and their neighbors' HYV use (eqn (12)). This will lead to a positive and spurious relationship between own profits and own and neighbors' prior HYV use.

We can exploit the panel characteristic of the data both to discern whether there are spurious relationships and to correct them. Differencing (16) over two points in time yields

$$\begin{aligned}
\Delta\pi_{jt} \approx {}& \eta_h'\Delta H_{jt} + \beta_{ot+1}S_{jt+1}H_{jt+1} + \beta_{vt+1}\bar{S}_{-jt+1}H_{jt+1} \\
& - \beta_{ot}S_{it}H_{it} - \beta_{vt}\bar{S}_{-jt}H_{jt} + \eta_{he}E_j\Delta H_{jt} + \eta_a'\Delta A_{jt} + \Delta\epsilon_{pjt}
\end{aligned} \tag{18}$$

which removes the fixed effect. Note that there are now four coefficients associated with the experience variables in the differenced form of (16) because the model implies that both the experience coefficients and the variables vary over time. In particular, the experience coefficients, which reflect the profitability of additional experience, diminish whereas experience increases over time.

In the context of the model, OLS estimation of (18) would yield unbiased coefficients, since the compound error terms associated with the differences in the period-specific discrepancies between the choices of $\theta$ and their realizations $\tilde{\theta}_{ijt}$ cannot be correlated with any of the right-hand-side variables, given the independence of input-target shocks across time: $H_{jt}$ is chosen prior to any knowledge about the $\tilde{\theta}_{ijt}$. It is possible, however, that the differenced profit shocks ($\Delta\epsilon_{pjt}$) may be correlated with the differenced HYV area measures. First, if some component of the shock is known prior to planting, then there will be a contemporaneous correlation between profit shocks and planting decisions.

Second, lagged profit shocks may affect contemporaneous HYV use. For example, if the returns to HYV, net of the optimal input and observed weather shocks, are uncertain, as in Besley and Case (1993, 1994), lagged profit shocks affect profit expectations and therefore contemporaneous adoption.[15] This problem may be addressed using instrumental variables applied to (18): instrumental variables fixed effects. Given the removal of the fixed effect, the inheritance data may serve as instruments, and if all the shocks are independently distributed over time, decisions made before the resolution of the $\epsilon_{pjt}$ such as $\Delta A_{jt-1}$ and $H_{jt-1}$ may serve as instruments as well.[16]

In addition to using standard instrumental variables fixed-effects methods to estimate equation (16), we implement a constrained fixed-effects approach that imposes and tests the equality of coefficient ratios for the experience variables (eqn (17)). Finally, nonlinear instrumental variables fixed-effects methods are used to directly estimate the structural parameters of equation (15) by differencing over time and then using a standard nonlinear instrumental variables procedure.

### 3.3. HYV cultivation

Estimation of the HYV decision rule proceeds in essentially the same way as that for the linear approximation to the profit function. In particular, the analogue to equation (18) is thus

$$
\begin{aligned}
\Delta H_{jt} \approx\ & \alpha_{ot+1}S_{jt+1} + \alpha_{vt+1}\bar{S}_{-jt+1} - \alpha_{ot}S_{jt} - \alpha_{vt}\bar{S}_{-jt} \\
& + \gamma_t\Delta t + \gamma_{ao}\Delta A_{jt} + \gamma_{av}\Delta\bar{A}_{-jt} + \Delta\epsilon_{hjt}
\end{aligned}
\tag{19}
$$

which includes information on village average HYV experience and asset changes in addition to own experience and asset changes. Because the HYV decision rule is likely to have a time-specific component (e.g., given learning, HYV decisions will depend on the horizon over which the farmer is discounting), a linear time trend belongs in the linear level equation, and thus $\Delta t$ appears in (19). Note that because we have not actually solved out for the decision rule, we cannot obtain measures of structural parameters using the decision rule estimates as in the case of the profit function. However, as noted, the magnitudes and signs of the estimated coefficients can be used to distinguish whether there is autarchy (neighbors' experience should not influence adoption, so that the $\alpha_v = 0$), whether own and neighbors' experience are equivalent (the relative effects of own and neighbors' experience are the same over time and as in the profit function), and whether there is strategic behavior in the form of free-rider effects (neighbors' assets decrease own use so that $\gamma_{av} < 0$).

## 4. Results

### 4.1. Profit function estimates and spurious village effects

To obtain the estimates of the conditional profit function (15), we differenced the last two rounds of the three rounds of data for all farmers cultivating with HYV seeds in both of those rounds and applied instrumental variables estimation.[17] The own HYV experience variables include lagged cumulative HYV use by year for each farmer, measured in hectares, based on information from the first two rounds of the survey. The neighbor HYV experience variables include the lagged, round-specific cumulative sum of hectares cultivated under HYV averaged (using sample weights) over all sampled farmers in each village, whether or not they used HYV in any period, excluding the respondent farmer.[18] We use as measures of the potential scale of operation, $A_{jt}$, variables that would be expected to augment the intensity of cultivation. They include the values of farm equipment, farm animals, and farm irrigation assets, which varied across rounds. Land owned and schooling did not change between rounds for any farmers and thus do not appear in the differenced equation.

As a specification test and a check on the ability of the differencing and instrumental estimation procedures to eliminate (and not cause) any spurious correlation of village (minus respondent) and individual variables, we first estimated the profit function for farmers *not* planting HYV seeds, using only the third-round cross-sectional data. For such farmers, the prior HYV acreage and experience of their neighbors using HYV seeds should be irrelevant to profitablity, on the basis of traditional cultivation, whatever the true model underlying the transfer of knowledge of new technologies. If, however, high-profit areas are also areas in which farmers tend (not) to adopt HYV seeds, then it is possible to find a purely spurious positive (negative) correlation between past HYV use among village neighbor farmers and the profitability of non-HYV-using farmers. Column 1 of table 2 reports the cross-sectional estimates of the profit function based on the sample of traditional-technology farmers. The positive and (marginally) significant coefficient for the village-level HYV experience variable suggests the importance of area-specific unobservables: farmers who are not using HYV seeds apparently benefit from having neighbors with HYV experience. And, indeed, consistent with the proposition that this result is completely spurious, use of the fixed-effects procedure eliminates the association between the village-level variable and farmer-specific profits: in column 2, estimates of the differenced profit function (fixed effects) are presented, on the same sample of farmers, but they exclude any who had cultivated with HYV seeds in the second year. With the fixed effect removed, the relationship between neighbor HYV experience and the profitability of traditional seeds is no longer positive nor significant. Finally, columns 3 and 4 report estimates using the fixed-effects instrumental variables procedure based on the same sample as in column 1, column 4 including as well the prior-period experience variable suggested by the model. The use of instruments, while affecting the coefficients on the asset variables, does not substantially affect the estimated coefficient for the village experience variable estimated using fixed effects alone.

The results in table 2 suggest that, on the basis of the fixed-effects instrumental variables estimates, there is no positive relationship between the profits of traditional farmers and the experience of their neighbors with the new-technology seeds. If there is learning from neighbors, such experience should be relevant, however, for farmers using the new seeds. The HYV-conditional profit estimates (eqn (15)) for the sample of farmers using HYV seeds are presented in table 3. In the estimates in column 1, which assume that there are no village-level effects of experience, there is evidence of learning by doing: both the $\beta_{ot}$ and $\beta_{ot-1}$ coefficients, which reflect the effect of the farmer's own experience with HYVs on the current return to HYV cultivation, are positive and statistically significant. Moreover, as predicted by the model, the returns to experience diminish over time. The average area

Table 2    Cross-sectional and panel estimates of profit function for farmers not using HYVs

|  | OLS (N = 1,536) | Fixed Effects (N = 1,277) | Instrumental variables fixed effects (N = 1,277) | |
| --- | --- | --- | --- | --- |
|  | (1) | (2) | (3) | (4) |
| Village experience | .137 | −.187 | −.246 | −.240 |
|  | (1.84) | (.654) | (.804) | (.784) |
| Initial period village experience |  |  |  | .166 (.514) |
| Equipment | .085 | .597 | 2.94 | 2.90 |
|  | (1.29) | (2.11) | (2.90) | (2.85) |
| Irrigation assets | .162 | .050 | .425 | .440 |
|  | (7.68) | (.691) | (2.00) | (2.06) |
| Animals | .657 | −.377 | −1.74 | −1.76 |
|  | (17.9) | (2.30) | (4.16) | (4.20) |
| Primary schooling ($\times 10^2$) | 1.77 | . . . | . . . | . . . |
|  | (2.01) |  |  |  |
| Irrigated land | .018 | . . . | . . . | . . . |
|  | (7.01) |  |  |  |
| Unirrigated land | .032 | . . . | . . . | . . . |
|  | (9.34) |  |  |  |
| House | .026 | . . . | . . . | . . . |
|  | (3.41) |  |  |  |

All variables are treated as endogenous for instrumental variables, fixed-effect estimates. Instruments include inherited assets, lagged asset flows, lagged profits, lagged village HYV use, and weighted averages of these variables by village. Absolute asymptotic $t$-ratios derived from Huber standard errors are in parentheses.

under HYV cultivation for an HYV-using farmer in the second period was 0.12 hectare; the coefficient for own experience in period 2 ($\beta_{ot-1}$) of .754 thus implies that a doubling of experience (from 0.1 to 0.2 hectare) in that period would result in a 905-rupee or 21 percent increase in mean profits. The coefficient for period 3 is substantially smaller as predicted by the model; however, the fact that by the third year the average cumulative area already cultivated under HYV was 0.12 hectare and average HYV area cultivated in the third year was 0.43 hectare implies that a doubling of HYV experience in the third period would increase profits by approximately the same magnitude (938 rupees or 22 percent).

The estimates from the specification allowing for both own and village-level experience effects are reported in column 2 of table 3. The estimated effects on HYV profitability from increases in the experience of the village farmers, when own experience and the fixed effect are controlled for, are consistent with the hypothesis of learning from others: like the own experience effects, they are positive and significant and diminish over time. The own estimates suggest that a doubling of own experience in each of these periods results in a 39 percent and 36 percent increase in profits, respectively. It is interesting that the village experience effects on HYV profitability are similar in magnitude to the own effects, with the ratio of the two coefficients (and thus an indirect estimate of $\rho_v/\rho_o$) being 1.2 and 1.8 for periods 2 and 3, respectively. Thus either households make use of information from only a

**Table 3** Determinants of farm profits from HYV use ($N = 450$)

| HYV effects | Linear approximation | | Constrained instrumental variables fixed effects | Structural estimates: Nonlinear instrumental variables fixed effects |
| --- | --- | --- | --- | --- |
| | Instrumental variables fixed effects | | | |
| | (1) | (2) | (3) | (4) |
| $\beta_{ot}(\times 10^5)$ | .170 | .293 | .187 | ... |
| | (2.13) | (2.54) | (1.88) | |
| $\beta_{ot-1}(\times 10^5)$ | .754 | 1.05 | ... | ... |
| | (2.47) | (2.18) | | |
| $\beta_{vt}(\times 10^5)$ | ... | .349 | .341 | ... |
| | | (2.16) | (2.63) | |
| $\beta_{vt-1}(\times 10^5)$ | ... | 1.93 | ... | ... |
| | | (2.64) | | |
| $\lambda_{pt}$ | ... | ... | 4.33 | ... |
| | | | (10.6) | |
| $\rho_o(\times 10^{-3})$ | ... | ... | ... | 1.29 |
| | | | | (3.31) |
| $\rho_v(\times 10^{-3})$ | ... | ... | ... | 3.46 |
| | | | | (1.33) |
| $\rho(\times 10^{-3})$ | ... | ... | ... | .298 |
| | | | | (6.23) |
| $\eta_{ha}(\times 10^4)$ | ... | ... | ... | −.290 |
| | | | | (3.24) |
| $\eta_h - \sigma_u^2(\times 10^4)$ | ... | ... | ... | .139 |
| | | | | (.77) |
| $\eta_h'(\times 10^4)$ | −.206 | −.545 | −.344 | ... |
| | (1.17) | (2.50) | (1.73) | |
| $\eta_{he}(\times 10^4)$ | .276 | .434 | .298 | .610 |
| | (1.22) | (1.91) | (1.34) | (3.54) |
| Farm equipment | 2.25 | 2.64 | 2.55 | 1.67 |
| | (2.98) | (2.59) | (2.68) | (2.73) |
| Farm animals | .641 | .813 | .543 | .189 |
| | (.57) | (.68) | (.49) | (.207) |
| Irrigation assets | −1.06 | −1.17 | −.693 | −1.40 |
| | (2.39) | (2.41) | (1.39) | (3.35) |

HYV use is measured in hectares and asset values in rupees. All variables except education and Indian Agricultural Development Program (IADP) are treated as endogenous. Instruments include inherited assets, lagged asset flows, lagged profits, lagged village HYV use, and weighted averages of these variables by village. Absolute asymptotic $t$-ratios derived from Huber standard errors are in parentheses.

couple of neighbors ($n$ is small) or if the experience of many neighbors is used by a farmer, the value of experience on others' farms is considerably less than the value of own experience.

Inclusion of the neighbor experience variables increased the size of the estimated effect of own experience in both periods 2 and 3 compared with the estimates in column 1. This suggests that, net of individual (and therefore village) fixed effects, own and village experience are negatively correlated. This result is consistent with the notion that certain characteristics may have opposite effects on own and neighbors' usage, a result that will be readily apparent below.

An important implication of the learning model is that, although the relative contributions to new-technology profitability of own and neighbors' experience may differ in each period, the diminution in the profitability of HYVs from additional experience should be the same for own and neighbors' experience. A test of this hypothesis (which is nonlinear in the estimated coefficients) was carried out and not rejected ($p = .11$). To obtain a more precise estimate of the decline in the returns to experience, we thus estimated a third model that imposes this constraint. The nonlinear constrained estimates are presented in column 3. They provide a direct estimate of the $\lambda_{pt}$ ratio in (17) for both own and neighbors' experience across the second and third years. The point estimate is 4.33, suggesting that the effects of experience with the new technology on the profitability of the new technology fell rapidly over time as more experience was acquired.

The other coefficients for the first three models are broadly similar across specifications; we focus attention on the statistically and theoretically preferred estimates in column 3. The coefficients measuring the profitability of HYV seeds relative to traditional seeds, although they are not precisely measured in the third specification, suggest that such seeds were not profitable for a totally inexperienced farmer with no experienced neighbors. The point estimate of $\eta_h'$, which measures the relative profitability of HYVs for an uneducated person with no experience, suggests that for each additional 0.1 hectare of HYVs planted in the first period there would be a loss in profits of 344 rupees (14 percent of average profits for uneducated farmers in that period). The positive value of $\eta_{he}$ indicates that inexperienced educated farmers would lose considerably less: only 46 rupees.

The other model coefficients appear to be reasonable. The effects of equipment and animals on profitability are positive, with the former being strongly significant. The negative (but insignificant in the preferred specification) effect of irrigation assets is surprising, but it is worth noting that the average of the asset coefficients, which measures the average effect of an additional rupee of asset stocks on annual profits, is .80, which is significantly different from zero ($p = .03$).

Given that the linear models yield conclusions that are broadly consistent with the specific structure of the profit function that was assumed in section I, we used nonlinear instrumental variables fixed effects to estimate the exact specification of the profit function (15). The structural estimates of the precision of the farmers' priors on input use in the initial new-technology period, $\rho$, the precision of the information obtained from an additional acre of own and neighbors' cultivation of HYVs, $\rho_o$ and $\rho_v$, and the effect on profits from using less suitable land, $\eta_{ha}$, are presented in column 4 of table 3. The estimates, as expected, indicate that own experience, neighbors' experience, and better initial priors increase the precision of knowledge about the appropriate choice of the target input $\theta$ and thus increase profitability. The estimate of $\rho_o$ indicates that each additional hectare of own experience results in an increase in precision of .00129. The ratio

$\rho_v/\rho_0 = 2.7$ measures the relative precision of information from own and neighbors' experience, which is only slightly larger than the figure obtained from the linear approximation estimates, although in this case the village-level effect is not precisely measured. Similarly, the ratio $\rho/\rho_o = .23$ measures the precision of the farmers' initial priors relative to the precision of each hectare planted and suggests that the precision of the priors held by the farmers prior to any experience with the new seeds was equivalent to what could be gained by planting 0.23 hectare of HYV. This is less than the average amount of information gained from own and neighbors' experience in the first year (0.37 hectare).[19]

## 4.2. Determinants of HYV use

The fixed-effects, instrumental variables estimates of the HYV conditional profit function indicate that there is both learning by doing and learning from what others do. Estimates of the HYV decision rule (12) indicate whether own and neighbors' experience and predicted experience influence HYV adoption in a way that is consistent with the learning model. These estimates are presented in table 4. The estimates in column 1, based on a specification in which village-level experience effects are excluded, indicate that, consistent with the model and with the fixed effect controlled for, farmers having more prior experience with HYV seeds tend to use more of the new seeds in the current period. The point estimates, which are statistically significant, suggest that in year 2, an increase in prior experience from 0.1 hectare of HYV cultivation to 0.2 would have resulted in a 0.08-hectare (68.5 percent) increase in HYV use in that period. The effect in year 3 is larger, with the same increase in experience resulting in a 0.098-hectare increase, although the higher average HYV use in that period means that the percentage increase would be smaller (22.6 percent). The fact that the experience effect on the use of HYV does not fall over time, even though the contemporaneous profitability effects of experience diminish over time, is not surprising: in contrast to the case of the HYV-conditional profit function, the model does not yield clear predictions about how experience effects on adoption will change over time. Experience effects on adoption may increase over time, for example, if the effects of experience on the cost of learning (i.e., the cost of planting more HYV than would be dictated by equating the marginal profitability of HYV and traditional crops) dominate those arising from the diminishing returns to experience given adoption.

The inclusion of the neighbor experience and asset variables, reported in column 2 of table 4, results in a reduction in the coefficients on own experience, although these effects are still positive and significant. Although neither village-level experience coefficient is precisely measured, both effects are positive, as expected. It is interesting that the set of own and neighbor experience coefficients is consistent with the hypothesis that neighbors' and own acres are equally valuable in augmenting information (13), since the change over time in the effects of each type of experience is the same statistically ($p = .165$). This constraint is imposed, for efficiency, in the final specification, the estimates from which are reported in column 3. In this specification, the coefficients on the own and village-level experience variables are both significantly different from zero. For the HYV decision rule, the estimated ratio of period 2 to period 3 effects, $\lambda_{ht}$, is $.78 < 1$, indicating that the effect of an additional hectare of experience was greater in the third period than in the second period.[20]

An additional implication of the equivalence of own and neighbors' experience is that, as indicated in equation (13), the ratio of the coefficients of own to village average

**Table 4** Determinants of HYV use ($N = 2,716$)

| | Instrumental variables fixed effects | | Constrained instrumental variables fixed effects |
|---|---|---|---|
| | (1) | (2) | (3) |
| $\alpha_{ot}$ | .975 | .791 | .600 |
| | (4.48) | (3.16) | (2.54) |
| $\alpha_{ot-1}$ | .810 | .691 | ... |
| | (2.60) | (2.39) | |
| $\alpha_{vt}$ | ... | .715 | 1.04 |
| | | (1.60) | (1.70) |
| $\alpha_{vt-1}$ | ... | .450 | ... |
| | | (.66) | |
| $\lambda_{ht}$ | ... | ... | .780 |
| | | | (4.38) |
| Farm equipment: own ($\times 10^{-4}$) | 4.26 | 3.11 | 2.90 |
| | (2.05) | (2.08) | (2.08) |
| Farm animals: own ($\times 10^{-4}$) | 1.81 | .687 | .695 |
| | (4.57) | (2.58) | (2.53) |
| Irrigation assets: own ($\times 10^{-4}$) | .0681 | .235 | .240 |
| | (.88) | (1.73) | (1.68) |
| Farm equipment: neighbor ($\times 10^{-4}$) | ... | −.0878 | −.0194 |
| | | (.34) | (.06) |
| Farm animals: neighbor ($\times 10^{-4}$) | ... | −.995 | −.948 |
| | | (2.08) | (1.85) |
| Irrigation assets: neighbor ($\times 10^{-4}$) | ... | −2.12 | −2.07 |
| | | (3.58) | (3.38) |
| Trend ($\times 10^{-2}$) | 3.85 | 4.04 | 4.07 |
| | (2.54) | (2.65) | (2.53) |

HYV use is measured in hectares and asset values in rupees. All variables except education, IADP, and trend are treated as endogenous. Instruments include inherited assets, lagged asset flows, lagged profits, lagged village HYV use, and weighted averages of these variables by village. Absolute asymptotic $t$-ratios derived from Huber standard errors are in parentheses.

experience ($\alpha_{ot}/\alpha_{vt}$) should be the same as the ratio of the own and village experience ($\beta_{ot}/\beta_{vt}$) coefficients obtained from the profit function. The estimated ratios are remarkably close: The $\beta$ ratio computed from the linearized profit function estimates (table 3, col. 3) is 1.8, and the ratio of the experience ($\alpha$) coefficients, from column 3 of table 4, is 1.7.[21]

The estimates of the effects of own and neighbors' assets on HYV use also are supportive of the learning-from-others model and suggest that learning externalities are not internalized by the village. In particular, each of the own-asset effects is positive and each of the neighbors' asset effects is negative. With the exception of the own asset effect of irrigation and the neighbors' asset effect of equipment, the estimated coefficients are also significantly different from zero at the 5 percent level or better. When the average coefficients for own assets are used, an increase of 1,000 rupees in the stock of assets owned by a farmer yields a 0.13-hectare increase in HYV adoption. By contrast, an increase of 1,000 rupees in the average stock of assets owned by neighbors results in a

0.10-hectare *decrease* in HYV adoption. While the model does not rule out the possibility that an increase in own and neighbors' assets increases adoption (i.e., there are increasing returns to experience), these estimates are clearly inconsistent with a model in which there is coordinated decision making on the part of the village: under such circumstances, own and village assets should have the same effect on adoption.[22]

## 5. Simulations Based on Estimated Parameters and Calibration

The HYV decision rule and profit equation estimates can be combined with additional information to describe the dynamics of profit growth and new-technology adoption implicit in the learning model. They can also be used to assess the consequences for technology adoption of changes in the distribution of assets. In particular, they permit an assessment of whether the estimated parameters yield an S-curve for adoption and whether the existence of learning from others matters for the temporal patterns and profitability of new-technology adoption.

Although the estimates in tables 3 and 4 provide most of the information necessary to carry out dynamic simulations, some additional information is needed. First, it is necessary to make some assumption about how the level of assets owned by households accumulates over time. This was done by fixing the savings rate, based on detailed savings data available in 1971, at .204, the ratio of net savings to profits among cultivator households. Similarly, gross cropped area (1.9) is based on its 1971 value.

Second, because fixed-effects methods were used to estimate the profit functions and HYV decision rules, no estimates are available for the constants. They were therefore calibrated along with the initial stock of assets by selecting values that matched, given the parameter estimates from tables 3 and 4 and the assumed savings rate and land area, in the third year of the simulation, actual average values of the levels of assets, profits, and HYV use among cultivators in the HYV-using villages in 1971.[23] The constants selected were as follows: the constants in the profit and HYV equations were computed to be 1,428 and −.166, respectively, and the initial stock of assets was found to be 1,561 rupees.[24]

One final problem for simulation arises from the implication of the model that the effects of experience are not necessarily constant over time, and we estimate parameters pertaining to only two periods. Diminishing returns to experience in profitability is an implication of the model and was confirmed by the profit function estimates. However, that we directly estimated the structure of the profit function implies that the relationship between experience and profitability can be computed at any point in time. This is clearly not the case for the decision rule in which the complex nature of the problem precludes direct estimation of the structural parameters. The coefficients for the adoption equation are thus specific to the second and third years of adoption experience. In order to predict adoption in the fourth or fifth year of the program, therefore, some plausible rule must be used to select the appropriate coefficients.[25]

Fortunately, in contrast to the linear estimates of the profit function, it does not appear that the experience coefficient in the adoption decision equation in the relevant period is changing very much. The estimate of $\lambda_{ht}$ of .78 reported in table 4 for years 2 and 3 is not significantly different from one at conventional levels ($p = .21$). Assuming that this relationship continues after the second and third years, one can compute experience coefficients for subsequent years by dividing by this estimated ratio. Thus, for the purposes of the simulation, we assumed that $\alpha_{ot} = \alpha_{o0}/\lambda^t$ and $\alpha_{vt} = \alpha_{v0}/\lambda^t$ for the own and village effects of information, respectively, on HYV use in period $t$.[26] We also imposed the constraints that HYV acreage should not fall below zero and should not exceed the point at which land is sufficiently unsuited to HYV that, even under perfect information about $\theta^*$, the traditional varieties would be more profitable at the margin than high-yielding varieties.[27]

The importance of learning and learning spillover effects for the profitability of HYVs is illustrated in figure 1, which, for different rates of experimentation, plots the growth in HYV profits per hectare relative to traditional-variety profitability on land that is well suited to new varieties. The dotted line shows profit growth when a constant amount of HYV (0.1 hectare per period) is grown in each period. This shows the diminishing returns to learning in terms of profitability per hectare. In particular, during the initial period when farmers have no experience with the new varieties, profits per hectare are actually negative (−829 rupees). The first 0.1 hectare of experience raises the profitability 1,014 rupees so that HYVs yield positive profits in the second period, although profitability is less than that of traditional varieties (1,136 rupees). The increment to profitability for the second period is only 543 rupees, however. Between the fifth and sixth periods, profits increase by only 168 rupees, although by this point HYVs yield higher profits than traditional varieties do.

By contrast, when the rate of planting changes optimally with experience, given the estimated adoption rates of the model, profitability increases dramatically between the third and fourth years. Even if only the profitability effects of own experience are

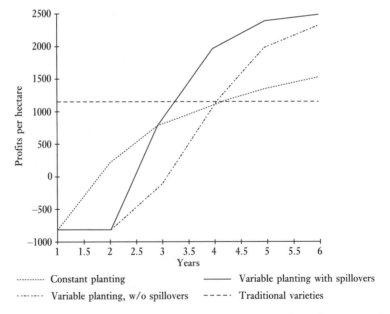

**Figure 1**  Predicted effects of learning profitability per hectare under various assumptions about adoption and learning

considered,[28] profits increase by 667 rupees between periods 2 and 3 and by 1,185 rupees between periods 3 and 4. Profitability increases even more rapidly when both own and neighbors' experience effects are allowed to affect learning: HYVs become more profitable than traditional varieties almost a year earlier than they do when only own experience affects learning.

To assess the relative importance of own and neighbor learning effects on the temporal patterns of adoption, simulations were performed for farmers and their neighbors differentiated by their initial asset stocks.[29] The simulation results for adoption are presented in figure 2 for four cases: poor farmers with poor and rich neighbors and rich farmers with poor and rich neighbors. A "poor" farmer (neighbor) is assumed to have an initial asset stock 200 rupees (13 percent) less than the average calibrated value (1,561 rupees), and a "rich" farmer or neighbor is assumed to have an inital asset stock 200 rupees above the calibrated average value. There are a number of striking features of the adoption plots. First, they all follow closely the S-curve that is generally thought to characterize adoption. In this case, the adoption trajectories reflect the accumulation of experience and the absence of declines in the effects of experience on adoption. Consider, for example, the adoption curve of a poor farmer with poor neighbors. In the first period, he plants no HYVs, and in the second period, there is a small increase to 0.036 hectare. Over the next two periods, the amount planted to HYVs increases by 0.137 and 0.441 hectares, respectively. By the fifth period, all land suitable to the cultivation of HYVs is planted to these varieties and there is no subsequent increase in adoption.

The simulations also indicate that the rate of adoption is importantly influenced by the production wealth (operation scale) of a farmer and his neighbors. In particular, when the

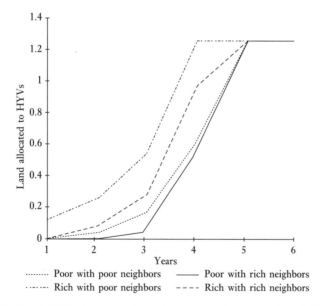

**Figure 2**   Predicted HYV adoption under various assumptions about the initial assets held by a farmer and his neighbors

wealth of a farmer's neighbors is held constant, a difference of 400 rupees (29 percent) in a farmer's initial asset stock results in a more than threefold increase in adoption by the third year. Consistent with the finding that wealthier farmers adopt more rapidly and that learning externalities are not internalized in the village, the simulations also indicate that poor farmers with wealthy neighbors are slower to adopt than those with poor neighbors. In particular, the simulations suggest that a farmer whose average neighbor has an initial asset stock of 1,761 rupees does not adopt at all until the third year, although he catches up quite rapidly after that. This catch-up reflects the fact that a farmer who is able to initially rely on his neighbors to undertake experimentation when it is costly (because little experience has been accumulated) will be subsequently wealthier on average than a farmer who has to rely on his own experimentation.

The simulation results indicate that overall gains to profits associated with the adoption of high-yielding varieties, which depend on both profitability per hectare and the amount of the crop that is adopted, are modest, given the evident initial losses that must be sustained in order to benefit from the new technologies. The simulations in figures 1 and 2 indicate that a poor farmer with poor neighbors experiences cumulative profits over an 8-year period following the introduction of the new varieties that are only 7.4 percent higher than those he would have earned staying with traditional varieties. If the poor farmer has wealthier neighbors so that own experimentation can be reduced, however, the relative increase in profits from adopting the new varieties rises to 9.6 percent. The effects are comparable for the better-off farmers.

## 6. Conclusions

In this paper we have used a model that incorporates learning by doing and learning spillovers to derive implications for the adoption and profitability of new technologies. Household-level panel data from a nationally representative sample of rural India have then been used to test the main implications of the model as well as to assess the magnitudes of learning spillovers, the extent to which potential learning externalities are internalized, and the implications of these effects for the level and distribution of benefits associated with new technologies.

The primary conclusions of the paper are as follows. First, the estimates indicate that imperfect knowledge about how to use new varieties is a significant barrier to the adoption of these varieties. The fact that own and neighbors' experience influence profitability net of the adoption of HYVs in addition to affecting the rates of adoption suggests that experience effects operate, at least in part, by augmenting the ability of farmers to make appropriate decisions about input use for the new technologies. The rapid decline over time in the effects of experience on profitability indicates, however, that the importance of this barrier substantially diminishes in the first few years of use as experience increases.

Second, we find evidence of learning spillovers. We find that farmers with experienced neighbors are significantly more profitable than those with inexperienced neighbors and, consistent with this result, that the former are likely to devote more of their land to the new technologies. The magnitudes of the effects indicate that a given increase in average experience by a farmer's neighbors increases profitability by almost twice as much as the same increase in own experience. The fact that the effects of own and neighbors' experience on profitability decrease at the same rate between adjacent periods, as predicted by the model, provides further support for the notion that village experience, as with own experience, operates through its effect on knowledge about the correct management of the new varieties.

Third, the estimates indicate that the spillover effects associated with learning from others are small but not unimportant. In terms of adoption, the estimates indicate that a 29 percent increase in own initial assets advances the rate of adoption by about a year and that this results in a somewhat smaller reduction in the rate of adoption on the part of neighbors, who curtail their own costly experimentation. The effect of neighbors' experimentation on the profitability of HYVs is also significant, resulting in a decrease by about a year in the time at which the profitability of HYVs exceeds that of traditional varieties. The overall effects indicate that total profits over an 8-year period following the introduction of HYVs are two percentage points higher when one has neighbors with 29 percent higher initial assets.

The finding that, net of own and neighbors' experience, own and neighbors' assets have opposite effects on adoption indicates that farmers tend to free-ride on the learning of others. Given that optimal learning requires that the marginal profitability of HYVs relative to the traditional crop be negative, a farmer can reduce his losses in a given period if he can rely on his neighbors to gain the relevant experience and then increase his use of the new technology as it becomes more profitable. These results suggest that information on the management of HYVs within the village is not excludable: if information gained by one farmer could be kept from other farmers, then a market for information could arise that compensated farmers for experimentation that benefited other farmers.[30] The results also indicate that there is not sufficient coordination of HYV adoption within the village to generate levels of learning that are socially efficient. Thus these results provide some support for public efforts to increase adoption through subsidies to early adopters.

## APPENDIX A: EFFECTS OF EXPERIENCE ON HYV PROFITS WITH VILLAGE-LEVEL SHOCKS

Let

$$f(z) = \frac{1}{(1/z) + \sigma_v^2} \tag{A1}$$

so that the posterior variance presented in equation (8) is

$$\sigma_{\theta jt}^2 = \frac{1}{\rho + \sum_{x=1}^{t} f(\rho_o H_{xt} + \rho_v \bar{H}_{xt})} \tag{A2}$$

It follows that

$$\frac{\partial \pi_{jt}}{\partial H_{jt-1}} = -\rho_o \sigma_{\theta jt}^4 f'(\rho_o H_{jt-1} + \rho_v \bar{H}_{-jt-1}) H_{jt} \tag{A3}$$

and

$$\frac{\partial \pi_{jt}}{\partial \bar{H}_{-jt-1}} = -\rho_v \sigma_{\theta jt}^4 f' \left( \rho_o H_{jt-1} + \rho_v \bar{H}_{-jt-1} \right) H_{jt} \tag{A4}$$

Note that $f'(z) < 0$ and $f''(z) < 0$. Thus (A3) and (A4) are both positive, and their ratio is $\rho_o/\rho_v$. Assuming $H_{jt+1} \geq H_{jt} \geq H_{jt-1} > 0$ for all $j$ and thus $\sigma_{\theta jt+1} < \sigma_{\theta jt}$ implies

$$\frac{\partial (\pi_{jt}/H_{jt})}{\partial H_{jt-1}} > \frac{\partial (\pi_{jt+1}/H_{jt+1})}{\partial H_{jt}}$$

Thus the own and neighbor experience effects have a constant ratio for all $t$, and the effects diminish over time as in the case of i.i.d. shocks.

## APPENDIX B: COMPARATIVE STATICS FOR THE HYV DECISION RULE IN PERIOD $T - 1$

In order to construct comparative statics for period $T - 1$, we first solve the problem as of period $T$. At that point, since there are no returns to additional learning and thus there is an interior solution, each farmer sets the differential profitability of HYV to zero, giving

$$H_{jT} = \frac{A}{\eta_{ha}} \left( \eta_h - \sigma_u^2 - \frac{1}{R_{jT}} \right)$$

and

$$V_{jT} = \frac{1}{2} \frac{A_j}{\eta_{ha}} \left( \eta_h - \sigma_u - \frac{1}{R_{jT}} \right)^2 + \eta_a A_j$$

where the precision of information for $j$ at time $t$ is denoted by

$$R_{jt} = \rho + \rho_o S_{jt} + \rho_v \bar{S}_{-jT}$$

Also, let

$$V_{SS} = \frac{\partial^2 V_T}{\partial^2 S_T} = \frac{\rho_o^2}{R_T^3} \frac{A_j}{\eta_{ha}} \left[ -2(\eta_h - \sigma_u^2) + \frac{3}{R_T} \right]$$

and

$$V_{SA} = \frac{\partial V_{jT}}{\partial S_{jT} \partial A_j} = \frac{1}{\eta_{ha}} \left( \eta_h - \sigma_u^2 - \frac{1}{R_T} \right) \frac{1}{R_T^2}$$

Differentiating the value function at time $T - 1$ for farmer $j$ and each of his $n$ neighbors with respect to their respective HYV use in period $T - 1$ yields $n + 1$ first-order conditions that must jointly hold. Define matrices $\mathbf{M}_H$, where

$$\mathbf{M}_H[j,j^*] = \frac{\partial^2 V_{jT-1}}{\partial H_{jT-1}\partial H_{j^*T-1}}$$

$\mathbf{M}_S$, where

$$\mathbf{M}_S[j,j^*] = \frac{\partial^2 V_{jT-1}}{\partial H_{jT-1}\partial S_{j^*T-1}}$$

and $\mathbf{M}_A$, where

$$\mathbf{M}_A[j,j^*] = \frac{\partial^2 V_{jT-1}}{\partial H_{jT-1}\partial A_{j^*}}$$

for all $j$ and $j^*$ over the range $[1, n + 1]$. Inverting $-\mathbf{M}_H$ and multiplying by $\mathbf{M}_S$ and $\mathbf{M}_A$ yields expressions for the effects of own assets and experience on HYV adoption in period $T - 1$ as well as the effects of the assets and experience of an arbitrary neighbor. Multiplying the latter by the number of neighbors yields expressions for the effects of an increase in average assets and experience on adoption. Thus we have

$$\frac{\partial H_{jT-1}}{\partial S_{jT-1}} = \frac{1}{D}\left(\frac{\rho_o}{R_{T-1}^2} + \delta V_{SS}\right)\left[\frac{\eta_{ha}}{A} - \delta V_{SS}\left(1 + \frac{\rho_v}{\rho_o}\right)\left(1 - \frac{\rho_v}{n\rho_o}\right)\right] \tag{B1}$$

$$\frac{\partial H_{jT-1}}{\partial \bar{S}_{-jT-1}} = \frac{1}{D}\left(\frac{\rho_o}{R_{T-1}^2} + \delta V_{SS}\right)\frac{\eta_{ha}}{A}\frac{\rho_v}{\rho_o} \tag{B2}$$

$$\frac{\partial H_{jT-1}}{\partial A_j} = \frac{1}{D}\left(\eta_{ha}\frac{H_{T-1}}{A^2} + \delta V_{SA}\right)\left[\frac{\eta_{HA}}{A} - \delta V_{SS}\left(1 + \frac{n-1}{n}\frac{\rho_v}{\rho_o}\right)\right] \tag{B3}$$

and

$$\frac{\partial H_{jT-1}}{\partial \bar{A}_{-j}} = \frac{1}{D}\left(\eta_{ha}\frac{H_{T-1}}{A^2} + \delta V_{SA}\right)\frac{\rho_v}{\rho_o}\delta V_{SS} \tag{B4}$$

where

$$D = \left[\frac{\eta_{ha}}{A} - \delta V_{SS}\left(1 - \frac{\rho_v}{n\rho_o}\right)\right]\left[\frac{\eta_{ha}}{A} - \delta V_{SS}\left(1 + \frac{\rho_v}{\rho_o}\right)\right] \tag{B5}$$

We assume that interior solutions obtain in each period and restrict attention to equilibria that are stable. Second-order conditions imply that $(\eta_{ha}/A) - \delta V_{SS} > 0$, and thus since neighbors' experience is no more efficient than own experience, $\rho_v/n\rho_o \leq 1$,

$$\frac{\eta_{ha}}{A} - \delta V_{SS}\left(1 - \frac{\rho_v}{\rho_o n}\right) > 0$$

Local stability of the equilibrium in period $T - 1$ requires $D > 0$, and thus it may be shown that

$$\frac{\eta_{ha}}{A} - \delta V_{SS}\left(1 + \frac{\rho_v}{\rho_o}\right) > 0,$$

$$\frac{\eta_{ha}}{A} - \delta V_{SS}\left(1 - \frac{n-1}{n}\frac{\rho_v}{\rho_o}\right) > 0$$

and

$$\frac{\eta_{ha}}{A} - \delta V_{SS}\left(1 - \frac{\rho_v}{\rho_o}\right)\left(1 + \frac{\rho_v}{\rho_o}\right) > 0$$

Also, $V_{SA} > 0$. These conditions are sufficient to establish that own and neighbor effects of experience on adoption as well as the own effect of assets on adoption are positive. The sign of the effect of neighbors' assets on experience is determined by the sign of $V_{SS}$: if there are increasing returns to experience ($V_{SS} > 0$), then an increase in neighbors' assets will increase adoption; whereas the opposite occurs if there are decreasing returns to experience ($V_{SS} < 0$). As is evident from the expression for $V_{SS}$, the former effect is likely to be present if experience is low and the latter is likely if experience is high.

The ratio of neighbors' to own experience effects may be written as

$$\frac{\dfrac{\partial H_{jT-1}}{\partial \bar{S}_{-jT-1}}}{\dfrac{\partial H_{jT-1}}{\partial S_{jT-1}}} = \frac{\rho_v}{\rho_o}\left[\frac{1}{1 - \frac{A}{\eta_{ha}}\delta V_{SS}\left(1 - \frac{\rho_v}{n\rho_o}\right)\left(1 + \frac{\rho_v}{\rho_o}\right)}\right] \tag{B6}$$

In the special case in which information from neighbors is equivalent to own information, $\rho_v = n\rho_o$, the estimated ratio of neighbors' to own experience effect is $\rho_v/\rho_o = n$. A similar result obtains if $V_{SS} = 0$. On the other hand, if neighbors' information is imperfect as assumed and $V_{SS} < 0$ ($V_{SS} > 0$), the resulting ratio should be less than (greater than) $\rho_v/\rho_o$.

## Notes

1 These answers do not indicate the importance of the information for either profitability or behavior.

2 Indeed, experimental plot data describing seed yields for wheat in Uttar Pradesh, India, presented in Bliss and Stern (1982) suggest that the relationship between fertilizer use and output per acre conforms closely to a quadratic for both traditional and high-yielding varieties. These data also show that HYV output is considerably more sensitive than traditional output to fertilizer use and that optimal fertilizer use for HYV exceeds that for traditional seeds.

3 Jovanovic and Nyarko (1994) consider a menu of technologies, but this generalization is not relevant to the setting we study.

4 We introduce variation in the suitability of land to the adoption of HYVs in order to ensure an interior solution for the HYV decision rules.

5 It may be shown that

$$\epsilon_{pjt} = -\sum_{i=1}^{H_{jt}} \left( \hat{\theta}_{jt} - \theta^* - u_{ijt} \right)^2 + H_{jt} \left( \sigma^2_{\theta jt} + \sigma^2_u \right)$$

Note also that for notational convenience we use a continuous approximation to write the quadratic HYV term as $\eta_{ha} H_{jt}^2 / 2A_j$ rather than $\eta_{ha}(H_{jt} + 1)H_{jt}/2A_j$. With a suitably small choice for area units, the error associated with this approximation falls to zero.

We have assumed for simplicity that the input is costless. If the input price were $p$, then the *ex ante* optimal $\theta = \theta_{jt} - (p/2)$ and profits would include additional terms in $\theta_{jt}$. The exclusion of $p$ has no consequences for the implications derived from the profit function relations in (3), but would complicate the decision rules for $H$. The reason is that an individual with a history of shocks signaling low expected target use will anticipate a higher return to HYVs than an otherwise identical individual whose experience suggests high target use. Although incorporating this effect would substantially complicate the theory, because $\theta_{jt}$ follows a random walk, it would have only minor implications for the empirical implementation given our use of fixed-effects methods.

6 Note that the information generated by a parcel sown to HYVs is independent of the input decision. This implies that there is no return to input experimentation, i.e., conscious variation across plots in a given year in input use. This assumption simplifies the input decision, which depends only on current expected profits and the information structure.

7 Note that since each neighboring farmer's choice of the *ex ante* optimal input reflects that farmer's history of target realizations, these actual neighbor inputs are sufficient statistics to farmer $j$ for his neighbor's prior experience and could be used instead of the full history.

8 We exclude the possibility that farmers tend to forget experience over time.

9 Note that the value of $\rho_v$ depends on both the number of neighbors and the relative precision of information obtained from their experience; however, one cannot distinguish a situation of many neighbors with imprecise information from one of few neighbors with precise information using estimates of the profit function.

10 See Fudenberg and Tirole (1991). The key feature of a Markov perfect equilibrium is that choices can depend only on past behaviors to the extent that these behaviors influence the potential payoffs or choice sets of the players. Thus the only variables summarizing the history of play that influence the value function at time $t$ are $S_{jt}$ and $S_{-jt}$ because past HYV use affects payoffs only through its effects on the subjective distribution of $\theta^*$ for each farmer. Note that this solution concept effectively rules out the use of multiperiod penalties that could in principle be used to support efficient HYV decision making from the perspective of the community. Besley and Case (1994) also use this solution concept.

11  It may be shown that

$$\frac{\partial^2 V_T}{\partial S_{jT}^2} = \frac{A_j}{\eta_{ah}} \left[ 2\frac{\rho_o^2}{(\rho + \rho_o S_{jT} + \rho_v \bar{S}_{-jT})^3} - \eta_h - \sigma_u^2 \right]$$

Note that for small (large) $S_{jT}$ the returns to experience are increasing (decreasing) in experience. Although greater experience decreases the returns to future experience given the choice of HYV area, it also increases the return to planting HYVs in that period, which in turn raises the returns to experience.

12  In these villages, 80 percent of the cultivators were growing either wheat or rice.

13  The 1968–9 crop year was marked by extremely poor weather. This evidently had an effect on the following year's planting decisions. The possibility of prior weather shocks influencing HYV choice, although not explicitly modeled, is taken into account by the estimation procedure we use, as described below.

14  Note that eqn (15) and the linear approximation derived from it (eqn (16)) assume i.i.d. shocks. Incorporation of village-level common shocks (eqn (8)) would require that separate coefficients in the linear approximation appear on each of the components of $S_{jt}$, i.e., $H_{ji}, \ldots, H_{jt-1}$. In principle, this result might be used to distinguish the two models. However, with only three years of HYV data and thus only two years over which experience effects can be estimated, the two models cannot be distinguished using linear methods. The reason is that the differenced linear approximation given village-level shocks that is analogous to eqn (16) has essentially the same specification; i.e., it includes cumulative own and neighbors' experience for each of the previous two years and yields the same predictions with regard to the ratios of these coefficients.

15  In addition, the existence of borrowing constraints creates a correlation between contemporaneous HYV decisions and past input and weather shocks. Moreover, if capital accumulation is allowed and is also credit-constrained, then $A_{jt+1}$ and $\Delta \in_{pjt}$ will also be correlated.

16  We exclude the use of $H_{jt}$ as an instrument because some component of the profit shock (e.g., the timing of the monsoon) may be known at the time $H_{jt}$ is chosen.

17  All these farmers grew wheat or rice in the 1970–1 crop year, for which we have crop data. Of these farmers, 70 percent grew wheat, with almost half of the wheat-growing farmers also growing rice. The data do not provide crop-specific profit and input information.

18  As a result of differences in agroclimatic conditions, there was substantial variability across India in the suitability of HYVs during the initial stages of the Green Revolution. Because our model implies that HYVs will be used only when, under optimal use, they are more profitable than traditional varieties, we limit our analysis to villages in which at least one household used HYVs in the third year of the study (1970–1). Thus 101 of the 250 villages are included in our analyses. Village-level variables reflect the characteristics of all cultivating households, whether or not they use HYVs.

19  The other estimated profit function parameters are well behaved: the coefficient on the parameter estimate that captures the diminishing suitability to HYV adoption of land, $\eta_{ha}$, is negative and significant, as expected, and that for the level coefficient, $\eta_h - \sigma_u^2$, is positive.

20  While, as noted, the model does not yield strong predictions about the magnitude of $\lambda_{ht}$, some insight into the implications of this figure may be gained by noting that if adoption were proportional to experience ($\lambda_{ht} = 1$ and no constant term), then HYV acreage would exhibit exponential growth. The fact that this coefficient increases over time suggests that growth will be more than exponential in the initial stages of adoption.

21  As discussed in the appendix, however, the fact that this ratio is somewhat less than that observed for profits is also consistent with a model with imperfect information in which there are diminishing returns to experience. In either case, the similarity of these results provides

good support for the central premise of the model: that own and village experience affect HYVs *only* through their effect on current and future profitability. If, e.g., adoption decisions were driven by rules of thumb or peer group effects, then one might expect a much greater effect of village relative to own experience on adoption than on profitability.

22 This interpretation of the results assumes that the social planner can reallocate variable assets across land in the same village. In a more restricted model, the planner would allow these assets to be used only on the land owned by the farmer in question. Under these circumstances, own and neighbors' assets may have different effects on the level of HYV acreage by differentially affecting gross cropped area for the different farmers. The effect of an increase in own and neighbors' assets on the *share* of gross cropped area allocated to HYVs should nonetheless be the same for all farmers in the same village. Thus HYV decision rules using the share of area devoted to HYVs as the left-hand-side variable were also estimated. The hypothesis of equal own and neighbor effects was also rejected under this specification ($p = .011$), with the own and neighbors' asset effects having opposite signs for each asset.

23 Because the HYVs first became available in the 1968–9 crop year, the figures in 1971 reflect the third year of experience. In addition to providing a systematic way of selecting these constants, calibration using the data is important because the linear approximations of the decision rule may yield inaccurate predictions if they are used to extrapolate well beyond the range of the data used for estimation. Figures for 1971 were used rather than, e.g., for 1968 because information on asset *stocks* was available only in 1971 and because, since this was the final period of the data, the use of the 1971 data minimizes the extent of extrapolation used in computing HYV usage for subsequent years.

24 This figure reflects only variable assets. Assets that are fixed over time enter, in effect, through the constant in the profit equation.

25 Coefficients on experience for the first year are also not available in table 4, but this presents no problem because experience with HYVs is taken to be zero in that period.

26 An alternate approach is to use the fact that $\lambda_{ht}$ is not significantly different from one to assert that the effects of experience on adoption remain constant. This change has little effect on the results presented below, and thus we present the simulations only for $\lambda_{ht} = .78$.

27 This latter figure is determined by $A(\eta_h - \sigma_u^2 + \eta_{he}ed)/\eta_{ha}$, where $ed$ is the proportion with primary schooling and $A$ is gross cultivated area.

28 These simulations refer to an uneducated farmer with an initial asset stock of 1,561 rupees.

29 The simulations are carried out under the assumption that the farmer has no primary schooling, as is the case for the majority of farmers. Simulations assuming that the farmer has primary schooling yield broadly similar results, the main difference being that the initial profits associated with adoption on the most suitable acreage are positive in that case.

30 The resulting market would not, in general, field efficient outcomes because, in the context of our model, information on HYV use is nonrival as well as nonexcludable. See Romer (1990) for a discussion of this distinction.

## References

Bahk, B.-H. and Gort, M. (1993): "Decomposing Learning by Doing in New Plants," *Journal of Political Economy*, 101, August, 561–83.

Besley, T. and Case, A. C. (1993): "Modeling Technology Adoption in Developing Countries," *American Economic Review Papers and Proceedings*, 83, May, 396–402.

——(1994): "Diffusion as a Learning Process: Evidence from HYV Cotton," manuscript, Princeton, N. J.: Princeton Univ. Dept. Econ.

Bliss, C. J., and Stern, N. H. (1982): *Palanpur: The Economy of an Indian Village*. New York: Oxford University Press.

Case, A. C. (1991): "Spatial Patterns in Household Demand," *Econometrica*, 59, July, 953–65.

Evans, W. N., Oates, W. E. and Schwab, R. (1992): "Measuring Peer Group Effects: A Study of Teenage Behavior," *Journal of Political Economy*, 100, October, 966–91.

Feder, G, Just, R. E. and Zilberman, D. (1985): "Adoption of Agricultural Innovations in Developing Countries: A Survey," *Economic Development and Cultural Change*, 33, January, 255–98.

Fudenberg, D. and Tirole, J. (1991): *Game Theory*. Cambridge, Mass.: MIT Press.

Jovanovic, B. and Nyarko, Y. (1994): "The Bayesian Foundation of Learning by Doing," manuscript, New York: New York Univ., Dept. of Econ.

Lucas, R. E., Jr. (1993): "Making a Miracle," *Econometrica*, 61, March, 251–72.

Romer, P. M. (1986): "Increasing Returns and Long-Run Growth," *Journal of Political Economy*, 94, October, 1002–37.

——(1990): "Are Nonconvexities Important for Understanding Growth?" *American Economic Review Papers and Proceedings*, 80, May, 97–103.

Schultz, T. W. (1975): "The Value of the Ability to Deal with Disequilibria," *Journal of Economic Literature*, 13, September, 827–46.

Wilson, R. B. (1975): "Informational Economies of Scale," *Bell Journal of Economic and Management Science*, 6, Spring, 184–95.

# Index